NOT LIKE US

Also by Richard Pells

Radical Visions and American Dreams:
Culture and Social Thought in the Depression Years

The Liberal Mind in a Conservative Age:
American Intellectuals in the 1940s and 1950s

NOT

LIKE

US

*How Europeans Have
Loved, Hated, and Transformed
American Culture
Since World War II*

RICHARD PELLS

BASIC BOOKS
A Member of Perseus Books, L.L.C.

Published by Basic Books,
A Division of HarperCollins Publishers, Inc.

Designed by Elliott Beard

Library of Congress Cataloging-in-Publication Data
Pells, Richard H.
    Not like us : How Europeans have loved, hated, and transformed
American culture since World War II / by Richard Pells. — 1st ed.
        p. cm.
    Includes bibliographical references and index.
    ISBN 0-465-00164-5 (cloth)
    ISBN 0-465-00163-7 (paper)
    1. Europe—Relations—United States. 2. United States—Rela-
tions—Europe. 3. Europe—Civilization—American influences.
4. Popular culture—Europe. 5. Europe—Intellectual life—20th century. I. Title.
D1065.U5P388 1997
303.48'27304—DC20   96-38183
                                                           CIP

98 99 00 01 02   RRD 10 9 8 7 6 5 4 3 2 1

For Molly

Contents

———————CHAPTER FOUR———————

American Studies in Europe

94

———————CHAPTER FIVE———————

Transatlantic Misunderstandings:
American Views of Europe

134

———————CHAPTER SIX———————

Transatlantic Misunderstandings:
European Views of America

152

Preface

Early on a frigid morning in January 1979, I arrived in Amsterdam. For years, I had fantasized about living in a foreign culture. Now I was in Europe for the first time in my life, on the brink of an adventure in a strange land with strange customs, knowing no one, unable to speak the language, not sure what I was supposed to do or how I would be expected to behave.

I had departed Austin—a place filled with friends and familiar sights, my home for nearly a decade—the previous afternoon and had flown all night from Houston. I disembarked at Schiphol, an airport noted for its modernity and efficiency but not for any qualities that might be described as exotically Dutch. My instructions were to take an airport bus to the KLM terminal on the Museumplein, and then a taxi to the Fulbright Commission office on Reguliersgracht. At first, gazing out the window of the taxi at the bright yellow trams and the bridges spanning the quaint canals, I felt that I was indeed no longer in America, a country where streetcars were abolished ages ago and any surviving canals would have been considered an obstacle to urban progress. But then, as we sped past the gabled houses of seventeenth-century Amsterdam, the taxi driver switched on the radio, and I heard the voice of . . . Willie Nelson. I had just traveled ten hours and thousands of miles, crossing an ocean and landing on a different continent, only to discover that I had not left America or even Austin behind.

At that moment, I was looking at one culture while listening to another. The juxtaposition of Europe's sights and America's sounds came to symbolize for me the way that each culture collided with and depended on the other. It suggested as well the mutual infatuation and frustration that has marked the relationship between the two continents for centuries. The sense of conflict and entanglement—the ambivalence that shaped the personal, political, and cultural confrontations between Europeans and Americans—was what I encountered regularly in Amsterdam. These contradictory feelings became the inspiration for and a central theme of this book.

But I did not yet know that this was a book I wanted to write. That epiphany came several years later while I was living and teaching in Copenhagen. In the fall of 1983 I was invited to give a lecture in Czechoslovakia, at the University of Brno. After my pontifications on the "Americanness" of American culture, delivered to a group of bewildered students languishing (no doubt) behind the Iron Curtain, the rector of the university asked me to sign a guest book. He showed me as well the first postwar guest book, before the darkness descended upon his country. The year was 1947. The first name on the first page was F. O. Matthiessen, one of the giants of the American Studies movement in the United States and the author of *American Renaissance*, a classic interpretation of the works of Emerson, Thoreau, Hawthorne, Melville, and Whitman.

I knew that Matthiessen had lectured in Czechoslovakia because in 1948 he published a book about his experiences there. He called it *From the Heart of Europe*, but the book got him into a lot of political trouble in the heart of America because he sympathized entirely too much with the goals of the Czech Communists. And 1948—when the Soviets blockaded Berlin and completed their Stalinization of Eastern Europe—was definitely the wrong year for an American writer to tell his fellow citizens that they should be more tolerant of their Communist enemies.

Peering at Matthiessen's signature, however, I realized that I was part of a tradition, another American lecturer bringing enlightenment to the benighted Europeans, espousing the virtues of the United States to an audience ready to acknowledge that intellectual leadership had long since passed from the Old World to the New. I wondered how and why that tradition began. What was Matthiessen doing in Brno? What was I doing in Brno?

The answer, I thought, lay in the alliance between American culture and Washington's foreign policy, an alliance that began on the eve of World War II and then flourished during the Cold War. The U.S.

government regarded culture as an important weapon in the contest with the Soviet Union. It was thus in America's strategic interest to establish the Fulbright program, open "America Houses" in West Germany, finance the Salzburg Seminar and the Congress for Cultural Freedom, and send professors to Europe to lecture on American history and literature. Those of us who later found ourselves teaching and speaking at conferences in Europe were never told what to say, but we were serving (whether we wished to or not) as representatives of the United States in the eyes of our government.

This was a point driven home to me by the American ambassador to Denmark. The ambassador had asked me if he could attend one of my classes at the University of Copenhagen, just to see what the students were like. On the way to the classroom, he seemed befuddled about who arranged for me to come to Copenhagen. Had I been hired by the university? By some private foundation? By the Danish government? I informed him that I was in Copenhagen on a Fulbright grant. "Oh," he exclaimed: "*We* hired you."

Apparently, the ambassador believed that he and his supervisors back in Washington had hired me to persuade the Danes to become more like Americans. This mission, though, did not originate with the Cold War.

For nearly four centuries, the inhabitants of America presumed that they were a chosen people, a model society, and that everyone else either wanted to come to the new Eden or construct a replica of it in their own lands. Since most foreigners were unable to flee to America, they could at least follow America's example from afar. And Americans would aid them in their quest. By the twentieth century, well before the titanic confrontation between Washington and Moscow, American corporate and advertising executives, as well as the heads of the Hollywood studios, were selling not only their products but also America's culture and values, the secrets of its success, to the rest of the world.

The government came late to this enterprise. But when officials in Washington tried to "reeducate" the Germans, or offered Europeans the Marshall Plan, or helped Hollywood reclaim its European markets, or defended the ideals of free trade in the face of Europe's cultural protectionism, they were acting on a set of assumptions rooted in America's Puritan and Jeffersonian past, and in its more entrepreneurial present. If—with assistance from America—people elsewhere were given the same democratic freedoms and the same economic skills, if they modernized along American lines, if they purchased American consumer goods and learned English well enough to enjoy America's mass culture, then they would surely turn into "Americans" themselves.

Yet what if people abroad do not want to be just like us? What if they adopt our methods, buy our products, watch our movies and television shows, listen to our music, eat our fast food, and visit our theme parks, but refuse to embrace our way of life? What if they insist on remaining "foreign," un-American, even anti-American?

Europeans have been exposed more than anyone else to the full force of America's economic, political, and cultural power in the twentieth century. Western Europeans, in particular, have been the primary targets of Washington's attention since 1945. Nevertheless, the longer I lived and traveled in Europe, the more I recognized that the American government's role in expanding America's cultural influence overseas was only a small part of the story. In addition, I became increasingly convinced that America's culture—whether transmitted by Washington or by Hollywood—had not significantly altered the values or behavioral patterns of most people in Western Europe.

So, by the end of the Cold War in 1989, I had grown more interested in Europe's response to the totality of American culture, not just to those elements that Washington elected to advertise. I still intended to write about America's desire to transport its culture to Europe. But I also wanted to analyze the reactions of Europe's politicians, intellectuals, journalists, and filmmakers to American culture. I wanted as well to understand the attitudes of ordinary Europeans, as reflected in their replies to questionnaires and opinion polls, and in the American products and forms of entertainment they accepted or spurned.

My book, therefore, deals as much with Europe as it does with America. I argue throughout that the "Americanization" of Europe is a myth. A powerful and enduring myth, often cherished by the Europeans themselves because they can use it to explain how their societies have changed in ways they don't like, but a myth nonetheless.

It is true that in the Cold War years Britain, Scandinavia, and the countries of Western Europe surrendered much of their political and economic independence to the United States. It is also true that the U.S. government, along with America's corporations and the American media, exported their ideas and their merchandise to postwar Europe on a much greater scale than in the nineteenth or early twentieth centuries.

Still, despite the flood of American products, the undeniable impact of America's mass culture, and Washington's efforts to make Europeans more appreciative of American foreign policy, Western Europe did not become a miniature version of the United States. Nor were Europeans passive victims of America's "cultural imperialism." Instead, the people of Western Europe adapted American culture to their own needs, tastes, and traditions, ultimately "Europeanizing" whatever they received from the United States. Through a process of resistance and modification, each country in Western Europe was able to preserve its cultural distinctiveness no matter how strong were the temptations to imitate America.

Furthermore, the relationship between Europe and the United States in the last half of the twentieth century has not been as one-sided as European politicians and intellectuals have usually charged. Americans are as affected by European products and fashions as Europeans are influenced by American technology and mass entertainment. The result is a complex interaction between different and increasingly heterogeneous cultures and societies.

So heterogeneous, in fact, that to talk about "America" or "Europe" as if either were a unified whole is mostly a matter of verbal convenience. I am conscious of the enormous differences among the countries and cultures of Europe. Indeed, I have concentrated on Western Europe—especially on Britain, France, Germany, Italy, the Netherlands, and Norway—because America's cultural presence in Eastern Europe was severely limited during the Cold War. I am equally mindful of how culturally diversified the United States has always been. Yet I believe it is possible to generalize about the cultural dissimilarities between "America" and "Europe." Certainly, the Europeans have never hesitated to do so. As a Dutch friend once said to me, "we know what we mean when we refer to America's culture—your culture—because we live with it every day."

Americans live with it too. And not always happily. When they travel abroad, hoping to experience the idiosyncratic charms of other countries, they are often horrified by the extent to which foreign lands seem—superficially—Americanized. The new hotels and office buildings gleam just as they do at home; the shops sell Nikes and Levi's; the movie marquees publicize the latest Arnold Schwarzenegger epic; a Burger King is just around the corner.

But for many Americans, the effects of America's mass culture and its global economy are even more unsettling within the United States.

Americans are as ambivalent about what it means to be modern, computerized, and technologically sophisticated—attributes synonymous with the American way of life—as are Europeans. The fear of losing one's unique cultural heritage as one becomes an affluent consumer of America's goods and services, movies, and mass circulation magazines is as strong in the United States as it is in Europe.

Hispanic and Asian American parents, worried about the attractions of a homogeneous American culture, want their children to remain bilingual and remember the traditions of the old country while they strive to enter the white middle class. Native Americans try to hold on to their sacred customs and ceremonies even while they run casinos on tribal lands. African Americans are torn between their allegiance to the neighborhood—with its indigenous culture, its history, and its collective aspirations—and their yearning to escape its dangers and decay. Jews are uncomfortable with intermarriage despite their assimilation into American society. People in Charleston or Savannah or Austin welcome economic development as long as they do not have to jettison their small-town amenities and become "another Houston."

For Americans and Europeans alike, the problem is how to live in two different worlds—one global, the other local or regional—while reaping the benefits of both. Because the Europeans have withstood the barrage of America's products and culture, because they have been able to preserve to some extent their national and ethnic identities while participating fully in the modern global economy, they might now be in a position to teach the Americans a more valuable lesson than the Americans ever taught them.

Perhaps, then, my analysis of the European encounter with America's culture during the twentieth century may say more to Americans than it does about Europe. Yet as an American who has come to think of Amsterdam as his "home" outside the United States, but who discovered in Copenhagen (along with the Danes) the addictive joys of watching *Dallas*, I know how confusing it can be to live in two distinct but intermingled cultures at the same time. So I have tried in this book to maintain a dual sensibility—to convey what it has been like for Europeans to live uneasily and often reluctantly with America's culture, while explaining why that culture has captivated millions of people not only in Europe but all over the world.

When the taxi deposited me at the Fulbright Commission in Amsterdam on that January morning in 1979, Minke Krings was waiting outside to take me in hand. Her official responsibility had been to arrange for my housing, which turned out to be in a flat without a stove and with a bathroom several yards down an unheated hall. This is how I discovered that the Dutch (or many of them) lived rather differently from suburban Americans. But Minke also became my first friend in Europe, helping me to unravel the Continent's mysteries, offering her advice and wisdom whenever I asked, roles she has played in my life ever since.

Many other Europeans over the years have been instrumental in teaching me about their countries and cultures. Three were especially significant as I worked on this book. Renate Semler of the America House in Berlin set up innumerable speaking engagements for me, both in her own city and in eastern Germany. More important, she allowed me a glimpse of what her life had been like from her childhood in the shadows of World War II, through the turbulence of West Berlin in the 1960s, to the contemporary reemergence of the city as one of the great cultural capitals of Europe. And she did so while ignoring (I like to think) my periodic outbursts of anxiety and frustration. Christopher Wilkins, for many years the person at the U.S. embassy in London every itinerant American lecturer depended upon for scheduling and long-distance hand-holding, displayed inordinate patience while sending me on excursions, sometimes on airlines of dubious distinction, from Belgium to Bulgaria. Without his assistance, I could not have had the professional or personal encounters that enabled me to learn and ultimately write about Europe. Rob Kroes, director of the America Institute at the University of Amsterdam, invited me to lecture at conferences at precisely those moments when I was trying to refine my ideas. He too had the forbearance to listen and the willingness to encourage me, without letting on that he knew far more about the subject than I did.

In the United States, several people have been just as supportive. When I was wrestling in the early stages of the project with how to approach the material, Shannon Davies helped me understand the prewar experiences of American scientists in Europe and the centrality of the European migration to America in the 1930s. More than that, she made me feel that I could and should write this book. In Washington, Bill Bate and Judy Siegel endured my brief and not particularly memorable incarnation as a government servant (I was in 1985–86 the grandly titled but underemployed "Resident Scholar in American Studies" with the United States Information Agency).

Later, they both read portions of the manuscript, corrected my mistakes, pointed me in the right directions, and probably hoped their names would not be mentioned in these acknowledgments. Susan Glenn also read several chapters, asked me hard questions I had preferred not to consider, and spent long hours on the telephone exchanging therapeutic remedies for whatever ailed either of us. Above all, she was an intimate and invaluable friend on those many occasions when I needed her.

I have been fortunate to receive institutional and editorial support, again when I most needed it. Nearly all Fulbright grantees talk about how much the award changed their lives. It certainly changed mine. I would not have conceived of this book without the two Fulbright lectureships I had at the universities of Amsterdam and Copenhagen. I am equally grateful to USIA for giving me the opportunity to see how the agency operated, and to the Woodrow Wilson International Center for Scholars, the Guggenheim Foundation, and the University of Texas for the fellowships and financial aid that permitted me to embark on the research and gave me time to think and to write. Responding (I hope cheerfully) to my perennial requests for their testimonials, David Oshinsky, Stephen Whitfield, Allen Matusow, and William Chafe wrote more letters of recommendation on my behalf than they could have ever envisioned when they first became my friends and colleagues. For this, they have my lasting gratitude. Steve Fraser demonstrated his interest and editorial expertise from the moment I first talked to him about the project, while Paul Golob proved to be a shrewd and skillful editor who knew how to make a book better than it might otherwise have been.

Finally, Molly Dougherty read every word, told me what she liked and disliked, persuaded me to alter my prose (which I sometimes did grudgingly though I knew she was always right), and made me cherish her extraordinary mixture of courage and curiosity. She has shared my travels and my life, while challenging me to reexamine my assumptions—intellectual and emotional—every step of the way. This book, then, is hers too.

NOT LIKE US

ONE

Cultural Relations Before 1945

During the first half of the twentieth century, according to the conventional wisdom, the United States was a minor and fitful participant in the planet's crises, a force to be reckoned with only because of its economic dynamism. Europe, though considerably weakened as a consequence of World War I, was still the center of the Western world, politically and culturally. America remained on the periphery, affected by but relatively detached from Europe's problems and preoccupations.

World War II changed all that. The war transformed America into a global power. It also dramatically altered the relationship between the United States and Europe. Until America entered the war, the ties between the two continents seemed looser, the contacts more intermittent, than they were to be after 1945. Americans and Europeans appeared to inhabit their own separate worlds, however much they shared a common cultural heritage. Then, in the postwar years, the United States became intimately involved in European affairs, overseeing Western Europe's economic recovery and its political destiny.

But viewed from another angle, World War II did not represent such a sharp departure from the past. If anything, the war deepened the bonds and accentuated the controversies that had existed between the United States and Europe long before 1945. The issues over which Americans and Europeans argued after the war—whether America should be a model for Europe, the impact on Europe of American products and investments, the influence of Hollywood and other manifestations of America's mass culture, the need for Europeans to resist the "Americanization" of their societies—were all very much a part of the transatlantic dialogue in the nineteenth and early twentieth centuries.

In truth, there was never a moment when the Old World and the New were not politically and culturally intertwined, or at odds over what each meant to the other. From the instant the first British settlers landed in Massachusetts and Virginia, Americans began telling their story proudly and loudly to the Europeans they had left behind. And Europe listened with a mixture of awe and bemusement, fascination and envy, empathy and exasperation. No American longings for disentanglement and isolation, no European feelings of unease and distrust, prevented people on both continents from indulging in a persistent and not altogether healthy obsession with one another.

Yet much of the conversation between the United States and Europe, before and after 1945, has been characterized more by an exchange of metaphors than by a sharing of information. For many Europeans, "America" was and is a symbol; a receptacle for fears and fantasies; a state of mind, rather than a real country. Americans, for their part, have regarded "Europe" as equally fictional. Both continents have indulged in the language of melodrama to portray the "other."

This flight to the realm of imagination has made it enormously difficult for Americans and Europeans to understand one another. But the resort to hyperbole, to the search for portents and hidden meanings, to interpretations more suitable for dreams and nightmares, also explains why the cultural and political connections between the United States and Europe have been so intense and so intriguing for so long.

The New World and the Old

The idea of a "new" world, located somewhere beyond the boundaries and horizons of the known world, had inspired European explorers for centuries. The legend turned into reality when they stumbled upon the continent they named America. But the concept of a new world quickly became, for Americans and for Europeans, a means of distinguishing between two entirely different civilizations. The dichotomy between new and old had not just geographic but normative significance: It pointed to a disparate set of values and attributes; it emphasized antagonistic ideals and patterns of behavior; it helped the people of each continent define their separate identities by using the other as a foil, a negative image, a lesson in what to avoid.

From the beginning, it was natural for Americans, as people who had escaped the political, religious, or economic constraints of Europe, to think of themselves and their environment as unique. The rhetoric of the earliest Puritan sermons portrayed America as a new promised land, a City Upon a Hill, a chance to start over and do it better, a model community for the rest of the world to emulate. By the late eighteenth century, at the time of the Revolution and the writing of the Constitution, the language had become secularized but it conveyed the same message: America would be different, exceptional, a place of infinite opportunity and possibility for all who settled there. A vast untapped and unspoiled continent beckoned. Americans were embarked on a special errand into the wilderness.

For eighteenth-century colonists and nineteenth-century immigrants, such notions led inevitably to an assertion of superiority. But the claim that America was more admirable and more virtuous rested on a series of contrasts that allegedly differentiated the United States from Europe. The polarities were simple yet compelling. America embodied innocence, youthfulness, vigor, confidence, optimism, freedom, and (once the wilderness was conquered) prosperity and modernity. Europe represented deviousness, cynicism, corruption, decadence, fatigue, poverty, social and ideological conflict, war.[1] This type of discourse—self-congratulatory, heavily moralistic, serene in its conviction that America was good and Europe was evil—had grown familiar by the early nineteenth century and remained central to America's image of itself as a real and symbolic alternative to Europe through much of the twentieth century.

But these beliefs concealed a sense of fear. If many Europeans were susceptible to certain strains of anti-Americanism during the years of the Cold War, Americans in the late eighteenth and the nineteenth centuries were equally worried about an outbreak on their own continent of the "European" disease. America might not achieve its visionary aspirations if it were to lapse into European patterns of living and thinking. To prevent this from happening, Europe in all its manifestations had to be repudiated. Thus, the founding fathers, particularly

Thomas Jefferson and James Madison, warned against the erection of large European-style cities with their physical congestion, frustrated mobs, and social dislocations. Similarly, they deplored the factionalizing effects of European politics, with their tendency to set class against class, and they tried to create constitutional mechanisms that would neutralize the power of contending groups and restrain ideological strife. Their admonitions were repeated throughout the nineteenth century, even as America became more industrialized, more urbanized, and more vulnerable to wars and social disturbances within its own borders. Indeed, the more the United States began to resemble Europe, the more the Jeffersonian maxims were invoked. Yet the hope persisted that if Americans avoided a repetition of Europe's political and cultural experience, they could live free of the depravity, the historic intrigues, and the periodic upheavals of the Old World.

On the other side of the ocean, the New World-Old World duality was frequently reversed. From Europe's perspective, America appeared irredeemably materialistic, avaricious, frantic, violent, crude, without spirit or soul—in vivid contrast to the mature, tolerant, sophisticated, socially conscious, and responsible European civilization that was adept at creating and preserving the amenities of human life (no inkling here of Nazism, Stalinism, and two world wars, all lurking in the future). Most of these stereotypes were formed in the early nineteenth century and endured well into the twentieth. The impressions of American childishness and vulgarity were reinforced by the reports of nineteenth-century European travelers and journalists. They described a land populated by savages, none of them conspicuously noble. Greed ruled. Machines dominated every human activity. Slavery was barbaric, but conditions in northern factories were no better. The West was immune to law and refinement. Everywhere, people were culturally illiterate, indifferent to the very existence of music, painting, and literature. For French observers in particular (Alexis de Tocqueville aside), Americans lacked the sort of cultivation and taste so characteristic of France—a judgment that would shape French attitudes toward America throughout the twentieth century.[2]

The European view of a dangerous, uncivilized, even barbaric America revealed fears similar to those the Americans had of Europe. Just as Americans dreaded the creeping "Europeanization" of their own country, so European writers held up "America" as a somber warning of the fate that could befall Europe if it succumbed to the American example. The idea that each continent might be a moral and symbolic menace to the other was hard to relinquish; it retained a permanent grip on the imagination of intellectuals and ordinary people, both in Europe and in the United States.

For Immigrant Americans, Europe was at least a place they could remember, if only to measure how much their lives had changed in the New World. But for those Europeans who remained behind, America served as a myth, an abstraction to be used for any number of often-conflicting purposes. Untroubled by the need to test their theories against the realities of American life, they invented a land overflowing with their own mixed emotions. The European image of America was never fixed. Depending on who was speaking, America could be either fascinating or appalling, a repository of hope or horror.[3]

In the nineteenth century, as after 1945, the contradictory appraisals of America usually corresponded to class. In the eyes of European aristocrats and wealthy members of the bourgeoisie, America was a nightmare threatening to obliterate all respect for tradition, culture, privilege, and social position. Frightened by the legacies of the American and French revolutions, suspicious of democratic appeals to freedom and equality, the European elite saw in the New World mostly radicalism and anarchy.[4]

But the apprehensions of British, French, and German conservatives were always counterbalanced by the magnetic attraction America exerted on Europe's lower classes and reform-minded intellectuals. For European workers, craftsmen, peasants, liberal and socialist activists—most of whom were prospective immigrants to the United States—America seemed not only a new Eden but a promise of redemption for the common folk. In this view, the United States was a gigantic political and economic laboratory in which the libertarian and egalitarian ideals of the eighteenth-century revolutions could be tested, modified, improved, and implemented.[5] Here, for people who experienced daily the poverty and oppressiveness of the Polish ghetto, the Italian village, or the Irish farm, the chance for advancement appeared real and visible. Letters from friends and relatives who had already settled in America confirmed this sense of mobility and expansiveness. The references to the steady increases in one's income, the chronicle of the move from the first tenement to a better neighborhood, and the pride in the vaulting aspirations of one's children were all unmistakable signs that in America the horizons looked broader, economically and psychologically. The encrusted institutions of Europe need not be overthrown; they could simply be abandoned in the journey across the ocean. The success of the democratic experiment depended not on rebellion but on flight.

Sympathy for America among the poor and the less affluent middle class sometimes ascended to the level of worship and wish fulfillment. It was difficult for the European masses to resist the fable that in America the streets were paved with gold, and that the newcomers could rise from rags to respectability if not to riches. To a considerable extent, these tales represented a moral and social rejection of the European status quo.

Yet by the late nineteenth century, Europe was itself changing, as were the attitudes of Europe's political and economic leaders toward the United States. Especially in Germany, where trade with America became increasingly important, businessmen began to admire American technology and industrial efficiency. German politicians saw in America's overseas policies an analog to their own imperial ambitions. The growing presence of American power, the emergence in the early twentieth century of Theodore Roosevelt (whose disdain for pacifism and faith in the destiny of strong nations sounded so familiar to contemporary German ears), encouraged a reevaluation of the United States among the elites not only of Germany but also of Britain and France.[6]

Despite the variations in Europe's portrait of the United States, and however much the European image of America differed from America's view of itself, there was one matter on which everyone appeared to agree. Culturally, America was a province, its literature a pale replica of Britain's, its regional art overshadowed by the achievements of the French modernists, its music and philosophy hardly a serious challenge to Germany's reign.[7] No one shared these perceptions more than America's own intellectuals and cultural arbiters. From the nineteenth century on, publishers and museum directors traveled to Europe to buy up the latest masterpieces. Meanwhile, American novelists, poets, artists, musicians and composers, scientists, and social critics assumed that their works were inferior to those of their counterparts in Europe—that one had to go to London or Paris or Rome or Berlin or Vienna to learn how to write or paint and even to think. Some stayed permanently: Henry James, T. S. Eliot, Ezra Pound, Gertrude Stein. Others became temporary expatriates, absorbing as much as they could of Europe's art and ideas. But through the 1920s, the feeling that American culture was shallow, derivative, second rate, lacking in social texture and intellectual complexity, would not subside no matter how many Hawthornes, Melvilles, Twains, Faulkners, or Hemingways the nation produced.

During the nineteenth century, given their lack of substantive knowledge about each other, Americans and Europeans found it equally easy to maintain the mythic distinctions between the New World and the Old. At the dawn of the twentieth century, however, Americans and Europeans began to encounter one another more directly and in greater numbers. If their language and mental constructions remained largely the same, the nature of their relationship was about to radically change.

THE AMERICAN IMPACT ON EUROPE IN THE EARLY TWENTIETH CENTURY

In 1901, the British journalist William Stead published a book called *The Americanization of the World*. Whatever the author's intent, the title sounded ominous, and it was to reverberate throughout the twentieth century. In fact, the term *Americanization* originated in Britain in the 1830s, and it had spread across the rest of Europe by the 1850s. Initially, the word referred to America's mechanical inventions and technological ingenuity, phenomena that both intrigued and repelled Europe's statesmen and intellectuals. But once the United States had matured into a major industrial and military power at the beginning of the twentieth century, Europeans started to pay attention to America's influence and fear its economic and cultural intrusiveness.[8]

No event better demonstrated America's arrival as a significant force in European affairs than World War I. "The United States for the first time became an important element in my thought," the Norwegian Sigmund Skard recalled. Skard, who became one of the principal architects of the American Studies movement in Europe after 1945, was originally attracted to the United States by the charisma and visionary internationalism of Woodrow Wilson. Skard also remembered the war as a time when "there was a general feeling of fellowship between democratic Europe and democratic America." In his eyes, the war against imperial Germany reminded the British, the French, and the Italians of their common political heritage with the United States. It also taught the European allies that America could no longer be ignored.[9]

The spectacle of democratic solidarity, which Skard found so inspiring, may not have materialized spontaneously. In April 1917, one week after the United States entered the war, President Wilson authorized the creation of the Committee on Public Information, installing his former campaign aide and editor of the *Rocky Mountain*

News, George Creel, as its director. The committee's primary mission (and the source of its subsequent notoriety) was to sell the war to the American people—not a simple task in view of the divisions in public opinion and the vocal opposition of many politicians and intellectuals. But Creel's efforts were aimed at an international audience as well. Employing most of the techniques that came to be identified with twentieth-century propaganda, Creel enlisted advertising executives, filmmakers, newspapermen, playwrights, and anyone else with the skills and experience to publicize the Wilsonian dream of a world made safe for democracy. Creel and his colleagues designed posters, put together exhibits, and issued pamphlets describing the American way of life to unenlightened foreigners. His agents dropped leaflets behind enemy lines. The committee opened reading rooms overseas to acquaint people with American books and magazines, and offered them free courses in the English language to facilitate their conversion to American values. It brought foreign journalists to the United States to increase their understanding of America's objectives in the war. Creel's film division made documentaries and organized tours of Hollywood stars to familiarize other nations with American products and ideals. Finally, the committee made sure that Wilson's speeches and photographs were distributed everywhere. With all these devices, Creel hoped to portray the United States as a prosperous and democratic society that was worthy of emulation throughout the world.

Abroad, Creel's tactics might well have helped strengthen the sense of shared purpose among the Allies, at least until the goals of democracy and peace without victory crumbled at Versailles. At home, he was mistrusted and attacked. Disturbed by the manipulative and propagandistic aspects of Creel's crusade, Congress abolished his committee in 1919.[10] Nevertheless, Creel's endeavors were not entirely forgotten; they served as a precedent for the government's more exuberant embrace of political and cultural propaganda during and after World War II.

The majority of Europeans, however, were dazzled less by America's democratic virtues than by its natural resources and industrial efficiency. The economic superiority of the United States was clearly on display in the mechanized equipment, organization, and energy of the 2-million-man army it quickly raised and dispatched to France. Compared to countries exhausted by four years of military carnage, America seemed innovative, adaptable, and immensely powerful. The admiration of the Europeans was tempered with some irritation and jealousy, especially on the part of the French who resented (as they would for the rest of the century) their excessive political and economic dependence on the "Anglo-Saxons." The British too were anxious about America's potential economic preeminence. Germans, on the other hand, attributed their defeat to material rather than military prowess, and thus were more eager to imitate American economic techniques.[11] Yet the lesson of the war was unmistakable: The United States no longer languished as an appendage to Europe, backward and marginal. America was now at the center, a symbol of modernity and an exemplar of success.

In many ways, America's impact on Europe following World War I was a precursor of what happened, on a much larger scale, after 1945. The United States had emerged by the 1920s as a formidable, though not yet dominant, influence in European life. But it was during this decade that America embarked on policies that eventually led to its economic and cultural supremacy. And the ambivalent reactions of European politicians, businessmen, and intellectuals anticipated the greater confusion of their successors about how to understand and cope with the "Americanization" of their continent in the second half of the twentieth century.

Economically, Europeans had been feeling the presence of the United States even before the 1920s. In the late nineteenth century, American companies began to sell more of their industrial products to Europe, in contrast to the earlier years of the century when the United States depended primarily on agricultural exports. This shift was due to a growing reliance on machines, assembly lines, and mass production. American companies were thus able to produce high-quality goods more cheaply and offer them at lower prices than could most of their European competitors who were still largely craft oriented. As a result, by the early twentieth century, American-made telephones, typewriters, sewing machines, cash registers, elevators, cameras, phonographs, toothpaste, and packaged foods became popular items in the European marketplace.[12]

Exports were not the only or the most important form of American economic penetration. During the first two decades of the twentieth century, American corporations purchased factories, established subsidiaries, and expanded their investments in selected European countries. The names of American companies—Singer, International Harvester, General Electric, Westinghouse, H. J. Heinz, American Tobacco, Carnation Milk—were increasingly recognizable to Europeans. With investments and the creation of branch plants came the potential for managerial control, a tendency that Europe's political and economic leaders noticed and disliked.[13]

Building on these prewar foundations, American businesses intensified their activities in the 1920s. Now Europe experienced a much broader economic invasion. American investments soared, climbing steadily in value from nearly $700 million in 1919 to $1.3 billion in 1929. American corporations paid special attention to newer, technologically advanced, and profitable industries that manufactured products like electrical equipment, farm machinery, and automobiles. More American companies entered into local partnerships and set up factories in European cities: Ford, Monsanto Chemical, and Kodak in Britain; General Motors, General Electric, and Du Pont in Britain and Germany; International Business Machines and International Telephone and Telegraph throughout the Continent. These enterprises required lawyers, financial experts, and marketing specialists, whom the home offices in the United States were pleased to provide. American retail chains like Woolworth's and Montgomery Ward opened European outlets, featuring low prices and a cornucopia of merchandise. Advertising agencies (particularly the J. Walter Thompson Company) introduced Europe to American-style packaging and sales techniques. Given the rising tide of American investment and the abundance of American products pouring into Europe, it was not surprising that French automobile manufacturers fell behind their American counterparts in the production and sale of small cars for the European market, or that New York supplanted London as the world's leading financier. Nor was it strange that Europe's businessmen and politicians started to wonder if their countries might soon become economic colonies of the United States.[14]

The fear of colonization was heightened by the sight of more and more Americans traveling through or taking up residence in London, Paris, Rome, and Berlin. Europeans had always been accustomed to a small number of Americans in their midst. During the nineteenth century, perhaps as many as thirty thousand mostly affluent Americans annually undertook the grand tour of European palaces, cathedrals, art galleries, and historical monuments. By the 1920s, an average of a quarter of a million American tourists, businessmen, and expatriates flocked to Europe each year. Many of them were attracted more by the dollar's strength in relation to European currencies than by the artifacts of Old World culture.

The scale of tourism in this period was tiny compared to the mass of Americans who swarmed into Europe after World War II. But as early as the 1920s, Americans were making their presence known to their European hosts. Tourists and temporary residents affected local economies both by how much they spent and by their appetite for American products. In addition, they reproduced the kinds of institutions with which they were familiar at home. American-run churches, schools, hospitals and medical clinics, newspapers, university alumni associations, clubs, and sporting events flourished wherever Americans congregated. Europeans, especially Parisians, reacted to American tourists in the 1920s with much the same hostility that their successors displayed after 1945. From the European perspective, American tourists were loud, arrogant, materialistic, and provincial.[15] Still, these Americans—and the culture they brought with them—were difficult to avoid or ignore.

The combined effect of exports, investments, and tourism drove many European intellectuals to consider with a greater sense of urgency the meaning of *Americanism* or *Americanization* (the terms were often used interchangeably). By the 1920s, even more than in the nineteenth century, the United States had come to stand in a vague and symbolic way for modernity, and for a "future" that seemed inescapable. In language that was frequently apocalyptic, European writers described America as (in Sigmund Skard's words) "an indicator of direction," an exemplification of economic and cultural trends certain to happen everywhere, and an unwelcome harbinger of Europe's own destiny. More specifically, the United States had become synonymous with efficiency, advanced technology and industrial dynamism, the worship of machines and assembly lines, "streamlined" and standardized products, commercialism, mass consumption, and the emergence of a mass society. German artists and playwrights, in particular, were fascinated by a country they knew mostly from movies, magazines, and photographs. For them, America represented the triumph of "Fordismus," a savage but riveting and sometimes contradictory mixture of skyscrapers, slums, urban violence, organized crime, smoke-belching factories, Puritanism, sexual licentiousness, and raw human energy unmatched in the Old World. Above all, to Europeans (like the young British student D. W. Brogan, who had experienced the wartime devastation of France, the rise of Fascism in Italy, and the rampant postwar unemployment of his native Glasgow), America seemed indecently optimistic, a country that believed itself to be "immune from most human ills" and "to have conquered most human problems."[16]

Here again was a thoroughly imaginary America, a land somehow exempt from the burdens of history and human suffering, where the future had already arrived in the form of unbridled industrial power—a land filled with omens and prophecies of Europe's inexorable fate. Yet despite the warnings of European intellectuals, the actual economic and social impact of the United States in the 1920s was fairly limited. Ordinary Europeans might buy American products and encounter an increasing number of American tourists, but they did not live like Americans nor did they adopt "American" values. Much of the time, they experienced America vicariously. The degree of their exposure to the American universe depended largely on what they could read, see, and hear. For them, the most important commodity the United States exported to Europe was its popular culture.

As in the case of its economy, America's cultural influence preceded the 1920s. In the late nineteenth century, various types of popular entertainment had sprung up on both sides of the Atlantic. These included cheap novels, tabloid newspapers, circuses, amusement parks, and world's fairs. Their appeal was hardly elitist, and they were usually scorned by intellectuals (although Henry Adams was famously transfixed by the mystery of the dynamo at the Paris Exposition in 1900). The unique American contribution to nineteenth-century popular culture was the Wild West show. Combining history and spectacle, this extravaganza introduced Europeans to a simplified rendition of America's founding myth.

Europe's fascination with the American West had been growing throughout the century. The European tendency to romanticize the wilderness, to see in the violent and lawless frontier the key to an understanding of the American psyche, was fueled by the translations of James Fenimore Cooper's novels (which established Cooper as the most widely read American author in Europe during these years); by European fictional portraits of America's western saga like those of the German novelist Karl May, who sold 30 million copies of his books between 1875 and 1912; and by the paintings of the German American artist Alfred Bierstadt, whose monumental depictions of western landscapes and Indian lore were enormously popular when they were exhibited in London, Paris, Brussels, and Berlin.[17]

But no one captured the imagination of European audiences as spectacularly as William F. Cody, the legendary Buffalo Bill. Cody's Wild West show was a nineteenth-century version of the struggle between civilization and savagery that Hollywood would later perfect. Relying on sophisticated forms of publicity, from posters to newspaper and magazine advertisements, Cody's cast of aging scouts, cowboys, Indians, and trick-shot artists performed before enthusiastic crowds in England, France, Spain, Italy, Germany, and Austria-Hungary between 1887 and 1906. The show certainly exploited Europe's fantasy about a land of open spaces inhabited by primitive but self-reliant individualists. Yet it also reinforced the European respect for law and social order since, according to the immutable formula of the drama, the West was always won and evil was always conquered.[18] The person who held these disparate emotions together was Buffalo Bill himself, a man of considerable theatricality who recognized that, given a choice, modern audiences would invariably prefer entertainment to authenticity. Buffalo Bill's charismatic demeanor and his intuitions about the predilections of his fans made him America's first international "star" of the twentieth century.

Until the 1920s, however, most people's contact with popular culture was episodic. A world's fair was not an annual event. Wild West shows toured infrequently. One had to wait for the circus to come to town. Because of the cold and dismal winters in northern Europe, amusement parks like Copenhagen's Tivoli Gardens stayed open only in the summer (a custom the late twentieth century creators of Euro Disney airily discounted). But by World War I, new forms of communication had been invented or refined, making popular culture a far more pervasive presence in the daily lives of Americans and Europeans. And as the country most adept at employing and controlling these instruments, the United States emerged as a significant force in the diffusion of mass entertainment.

Radios and phonographs facilitated the spread of American popular culture. One reason for America's leadership in developing and marketing these technologies was the close link between corporate needs and government policy. Washington believed that America's commercial and cultural goals were virtually indistinguishable. In this view, the country's continuing ability to export its products depended on greater knowledge overseas about the virtues of American life, precisely the sort of information the entertainment industry could provide. It would therefore serve the national interest if the government offered its support to businesses that were involved in the field of communications. Moreover, Washington wanted to undercut the traditional British monopoly over worldwide cable lines by persuading American corporations to construct their own independent cable and communications networks. Promising technical assistance from the navy, the government urged cooperation among companies such as General Electric, Western Electric, American

Telegraph and Telephone, and Westinghouse, all of whom could jointly strengthen America's position in international communications. In 1919, this collaboration resulted in the birth of the Radio Corporation of America, a leviathan that came to dominate global broadcasting for the next half century.[19]

Among the beneficiaries of the new techniques in communications and entertainment was American popular music, particularly jazz. During the 1920s, Europeans were introduced to jazz through phonograph records, radio broadcasts, and live performances. The primary port of entry was Paris, where black musicians, in flight from America's segregated cities, acquired a following in nightclubs, cabarets, and concert halls. Paris was also the point of departure for tours across the Continent. By the early 1930s, audiences in Britain, the Netherlands, Belgium, Italy, Switzerland, and Scandinavia had heard of or listened to Louis Armstrong or Duke Ellington, not to mention many other less celebrated bands. American jazz especially attracted European intellectuals and self-proclaimed members of the avant-garde, for whom it seemed to symbolize America's devotion to experimentation, improvisation, and all things new and modern. The identification of jazz with rebellion and personal freedom was notably strong in Germany, which may explain why it provoked the fury of the Nazis in the 1930s. Even so, jazz continued to be cherished in underground clubs by a minority of young urban Germans, disenchanted with but unable to find any political ways of protesting against Adolf Hitler's regime.[20] In the meantime, European musicians began to copy American jazz bands, a testimonial to the growing power of America's popular culture in every area.

Yet of all the forms of mass entertainment that flourished in the 1920s, none was as captivating as the movies. Here, America exerted its greatest influence. It was in this decade that cinema became synonymous with Hollywood. The United States dominated every facet of popular filmmaking, and with it the power to "Americanize" the imaginations, if not the behavior, of audiences throughout the world.

Hollywood's ascendancy was not preordained. On the contrary, before World War I both the French and Italian movie industries regularly surpassed the United States in film exports. France was also ahead of America in manufacturing new equipment and developing new cinematic techniques.[21] After the war, most American and European film critics and intellectuals regarded Hollywood's efforts as infinitely inferior to the work of the German expressionists or the revolutionary Soviet directors. They might praise Charlie Chaplin or Buster

Keaton as film artists (at the same time reminding readers that comedy was about all one could expect from a fundamentally frivolous country, and that in any case Chaplin was really British). Few other American filmmakers in the 1920s could gain admittance to a European pantheon that included Sergei Eisenstein, F. W. Murnau, G. W. Papst, Fritz Lang, and Carl Dreyer.

Nevertheless, the war destroyed the ability of the European cinema to compete economically with Hollywood. British, French, and Italian productions were suspended or curtailed during the conflict, and the need to invest in economic reconstruction in the early 1920s meant that little money was left over in Europe for large-scale moviemaking. The United States, unscathed by the war, was the only country that had the resources to expand its film operations. As a result, Hollywood soon emerged as the leader in the production and distribution of movies to a worldwide audience, a distinction the European studios were never able again to challenge.[22]

The postwar decline of the European film industry was not the only reason for Hollywood's supremacy. The existence of a large domestic audience in the United States enabled American studios to recover the costs of production and make a substantial profit on a movie before they ever turned to the international market. Then, they charged lower rental fees overseas and undersold their European rivals. In addition, through the devices of block booking, the imposition of tariffs on imported foreign films, and other discriminatory practices, Hollywood effectively protected its home market against the encroachment of European moviemakers. The studios also adopted the assembly line techniques successful in other major American industries, signing their employees to long-term contracts, standardizing their product, creating "brand names" through the star system, and exercising firm control over their distribution networks. Meanwhile, related businesses shared in Hollywood's affluence. Kodak manufactured 75 percent of all the film used in the world. Western Electric produced most of the sound equipment that became so important for the "talkies" at the end of the decade. American companies owned half the most fashionable movie houses abroad, including three-quarters of all the theaters in France; not surprisingly, most of their screen time was devoted to American films.[23] All these elements combined to ensure that Hollywood and its subsidiaries would remain prosperous and powerful.

Still, commercial factors were just a partial explanation for the international strength of the American film industry. Many members of the audience, both in the United States and in Europe, believed that

Hollywood simply made better movies. The stories seemed more absorbing than those of European filmmakers, the "look" was more luxurious, and the stars were more magnetic. But whether the roots of Hollywood's domination were economic or stylistic, there was no doubt that American movies were immensely popular, particularly in Europe. By the mid-1920s, approximately 95 percent of the films shown in Britain, 85 percent in the Netherlands, 70 percent in France, 65 percent in Italy, and 60 percent in Germany were American.[24] These figures remained nearly the same for the remainder of the decade.

For many European intellectuals, and ultimately their governments, this preference for American movies was alarming. On one level, they worried that the health of the European film industry would continue to deteriorate, given the overwhelming popularity of Hollywood's creations. It was becoming increasingly difficult for European studios to raise money, develop and retain local talent, and produce films of high quality. These constraints, in turn, made it that much harder for them to attract audiences and compete with American films.[25] Thus, Hollywood represented a real threat, economically, to the very existence of the European cinema.

An even larger issue involved Hollywood's role as the primary instrument of Americanization. Through movies, it was argued, people became familiar with American products, lifestyles, patterns of behavior, and values. The opulence of the average Hollywood film made Europeans want to drive American cars, eat American foods, smoke American cigarettes, and wear American clothes. Even worse, according to some intellectuals, Europeans were losing respect for their native cultures and traditions. The seductive appeal of American movies was especially troubling to French writers, who suspected that Paris might not survive as a center of fashion, cuisine, or ideas. The fear that Hollywood somehow endangered the standards, customs, and tastes of the Old World might have been exaggerated, but it was by no means limited to France. Across the Continent, members of the political and cultural elite agreed that the national "identity" of each country was being undermined by American films, that governments were no longer exercising much influence over how their citizens spent their leisure time, and that this trend had to be resisted or all Europe would soon be engulfed by American habits and states of mind.[26]

The belief that Hollywood's power needed to be restrained arose for the first time in the 1920s, though it would reemerge on many occasions in the following decades. But the initial efforts of various countries in Europe to defend their national cultures by reducing the influence of American films is instructive, both for the methods used and why they failed.

Beginning in the mid-1920s, several European governments decided to limit the import, and thereby the impact, of American movies. From 1925 to 1927, Germany, Britain, France, and Italy all imposed quotas either on the absolute number of Hollywood productions that could be brought in, or on the amount of screen time exhibitors were permitted for showing American films. These regulations were designed both to exert some leverage over the domestic film market, and to open up more theaters to local moviemakers.[27]

The most striking consequence of the quota system was its inability to achieve any of its objectives. American studios overcame the new laws by investing in or directly financing inexpensive, poorly made German and British movies, called "quota quickies." These movies fulfilled the requirements for more "local" productions, but they were often so uninspired and feeble that audiences avoided them while retaining their affection for American films. The French government, seeking other alternatives, attempted to force American theaters to import French movies in exchange for American exports to France. This action resulted in a Hollywood boycott of the French film industry. In 1928, the studios announced their refusal to send any more American films to French distributors, or to allow French movies to be shown in the theaters the studios owned in the United States. The French government promptly relaxed its restrictions on American films, though this was of little help to French moviemakers: In 1929, only nineteen French films were exhibited in the United States.[28]

Eventually, the quota system collapsed. But the idea that the influence of American popular culture could be subjected to a set of numerical limitations lived on. European governments would try to enact quotas again, in the late 1940s and the early 1990s—though their efforts would be equally futile.

For a brief moment, at the end of the 1920s, some European critics and moviemakers imagined that sound might accomplish what quotas had not. Silent films, after all, transcended language barriers and could be universally understood. But the first American sound films distributed overseas were marred by inadequate subtitles, execrable dubbing, and inept synchronization between the movement of the actors' mouths and the words they spoke. It was therefore assumed that European audiences would at last turn to their own domestic productions, with performances in a language they could comprehend.

In fact, Hollywood's dominance was barely affected by the coming of sound. If anything, the heightened cost of producing a sound film forced Hollywood to rely even more heavily on the international, and especially the European, market to ensure its profits. And, as sound technology and equipment improved, subtitles and dubbing became more sophisticated and more acceptable to foreign audiences. In some cases, Hollywood simply made two versions of a film, one in English for American and British audiences, the other in French or German for audiences on the Continent.[29]

Meanwhile, sound increased the American film industry's need for talent both on and off the screen. In response, Hollywood (having always looked to Europe for artistic expertise) accelerated its import of European filmmakers, though not their films. Offering high salaries and assisted by the rise of fascism in Germany and central Europe, American studios welcomed a generation of British and continental directors, cameramen, editors, set and costume designers, and performers. Giants of the European cinema like Fritz Lang, Alfred Hitchcock, Greta Garbo, and Marlene Dietrich were transplanted to the United States, further crippling Europe's ability to compete with Hollywood. Movies had become at once truly international and distinctively American. Under these circumstances, it was appropriate that the role of Scarlett O'Hara, the quintessential Southern heroine of *Gone with the Wind*, should have gone to a virtually unknown British actress, Vivien Leigh. And that *Casablanca*, the ultimate movie tribute to exiles and refugees, featured a cast which was (except for Humphrey Bogart and Dooley Wilson) composed entirely of European expatriates.

Hollywood was thus able to hold on to its European market in the 1930s. American films occupied 80 percent of the screen time in Britain and 60 percent in the Netherlands. Many young Italian moviegoers were attracted to American films—especially Westerns, with their laconic heroes and elementary moral rules—because these movies offered some relief from Benito Mussolini's pomposity and grandiloquent rhetoric. Roger Asselineau, who later became a leading French critic of American literature, was struck in his youth by the ubiquity of American movies in France. On the pretext of learning English, he recalled, "I saw as many American pictures as I could, and there were quite a few to be seen in Paris in the middle and late thirties: *The Informer*, *Duck Soup* (which was my first introduction to American wisecracks), *Modern Times*, *Mr. Deeds Goes to Town* (which I saw several times), *Green Pastures*, *Dead End*, *You Can't Take It with*

You, Snow White and the Seven Dwarfs."[30] Asselineau's enthusiasm for American films—from comedies to Frank Capra melodramas to Disneyesque fantasies—was shared by millions of Europeans during the depression years.

A number of governments in the 1930s tried once again to protect their national cinemas through artificial restrictions on imports, subsidies, and harsh financial decrees, all in an effort to persuade audiences that domestic productions were worth seeing and supporting. But only the totalitarian regimes in Nazi Germany and the Soviet Union finally succeeded in curbing Hollywood's power, mostly by investing large amounts of money to build up their own film industries while censoring or prohibiting American exports. After 1939, the Nazis banned American movies in every country they overran.[31] In resisting America's cultural influence, conquest was clearly superior to quotas. This was not a model, however, that most countries in Europe would be eager to emulate in the postwar years.

Before the outbreak of World War II, Hollywood had come to represent in the minds of many prominent European intellectuals everything they dreaded and despised about American mass culture. To these intellectuals, their governments' inability in the 1920s and 1930s to diminish the popularity of American films was an instance of Europe's greater failure to preserve its economic and cultural distinctiveness. But the question of how the European democracies could combat Americanization without resorting to the solutions of a Joseph Stalin or a Hitler remained unresolved.

No one effectively answered this question because, as in the nineteenth century, what was really at stake was not policy but symbolism. The conflict between Europe and America was seen once more as allegorical, two opposing civilizations and value systems—one with a reverence for tradition and the human spirit, the other modern and profane—both contesting for supremacy. Framing the issues in this way, European intellectuals found it easier to indulge in portentous generalizations about the dissimilarities between the two continents than to examine empirically how each had diverged from yet continued to mirror the other.

Still, this propensity to generalize, and to inflate subtle differences into moral categories, had a serious purpose. A number of writers thought it was imperative for them to identify and repudiate the special characteristics of American life in order to salvage what was left of Europe's declining power and prestige. Among those who undertook this mission in the late 1920s and early 1930s were the French authors

André Siegfried in *The United States Today* (1927) and Georges Duhamel in *America the Menace: Scenes from the Life of the Future* (1931), and the Dutch essayist Menno ter Braak in "Why I Reject 'America'" (1928). Their works were widely read and their judgments often quoted. They all focused on the kinds of problems that seemed endemic to the United States: urbanization, the grip of finance capitalism, the monotony of the assembly lines, racial strife, the omnipresence of advertising and the mass media.

Although writers like Siegfried and Duhamel had actually traveled to the United States, their impressions of America and those of their readers were frequently lifted from the novels and essays of Americans themselves. It was fashionable in the 1920s, as it would be again in the 1950s and 1960s, for Europeans to reaffirm their prejudices about the United States by relying on the works of America's most disenchanted and acerbic authors. In Britain, for example, the American writers who received the greatest praise in the 1920s were Upton Sinclair, Jack London, Theodore Dreiser, H. L. Mencken, and Sinclair Lewis. In France, the list was similar, augmented by Sherwood Anderson and John Dos Passos. Often, passages or characters from their books were used selectively to illustrate the inhumanity of mass production, the claustrophobia of the American small town, or the mediocrity of the middle class. No novel was more influential than *Babbitt* in exposing the banality of the classic American male; the name became part of the European vocabulary, a handy code word for American blandness and conformity.[32] It was therefore fitting that in 1930 Sinclair Lewis should be the first American novelist awarded the Nobel Prize for literature. Although Lewis graciously accepted the honor on behalf of his generation of American writers, he had probably been chosen by the Swedish academy as much for his indictments of American society as for his inherent skills as a novelist.

Whether they spent time in the United States or simply depended on images gathered from American books (and from those mindless but mesmerizing Hollywood films), European intellectuals were obsessed with certain "typical" American deformities. In placid Norway, Sigmund Skard was horrified by the violence and racism of the Ku Klux Klan, and by the "shameless corruption" of the American legal system as revealed in its persecution of Sacco and Vanzetti. In Holland, Menno ter Braak feared that America's popular entertainment, vulgar and excessively commercialized, would if allowed to infiltrate Europe destroy all respect for art and literature. In Britain,

D. W. Brogan recalled, everyone agreed that American culture was "shallow, naively optimistic, barren, without ideas—as all the best American authors pointed out."[33]

Most of all, in the view of Siegfried, Duhamel, and other writers, Americans were automatons, chained to machines and assembly lines at work, and hypnotized (like Babbitt) by gadgets and material possessions at play. They wore identical clothes, purchased identical products, and held identical opinions.[34] From this perspective, America seemed the archetype of a modern mass society, one that was relentlessly hostile to all signs of eccentricity, with no appreciation for the person who did not fit in or for the benefits to be derived from maintaining social and class distinctions. In sum, America by the 1920s and 1930s had become (and not just for Aldous Huxley) the Old World's nightmarish vision of a "brave new world."

America was also the embodiment of everything Europe was not. Throughout these years, European intellectuals, like their predecessors in the nineteenth century, insisted that the United States and Europe stood for antithetical ideals. If America was industrialized, France was pastoral; if Americans were conformists, the British were individualists; if American social life was rootless and unstable, German society was harmonious and communal. In the New World, products were standardized and uniform; in the Old World, the craftsman remained supreme. The contrasts could not have been purer, or more flattering to Europe. Unfortunately, the more invasive America became, the harder it was for Europe to remain "European." And so the cultural and economic defense of "Europe" automatically entailed a rejection of every trait associated with "America."[35]

Of course, Europe could hardly be considered a unified entity. This was, after all, an *interwar* era. Thus, the definition of what was uniquely European often changed to suit the needs of particular countries. Intellectuals in small nations like the Netherlands, feeling more vulnerable to American influences, usually identified with Europe as a whole in the hope of strengthening their own cultural fortifications. British and French writers, more confident of their countries' cultural resources, frequently spoke of Europe as if it were a collection of national virtues, most notably the regard for individual idiosyncrasies so evident in Britain and France. The German version of Europe, especially after the rise of fascism, tended to glorify the collective spirit of the people.[36]

But whichever Europe writers invoked, the message was clear. America must be resisted or Europe—any form of Europe—would eventually vanish. This was not so much a strategy as a premonition, and one that sounded more than a little paranoid. At the moment these warnings were delivered, the United States remained a distant force, its culture not yet global, its economy not yet dominant, the weight of its political and military power still to be felt. The European effort to deal with the consequences of Americanization may have been premature; it was in any case superseded by the far graver crises of depression and war. But the problem reemerged after 1945 with greater intensity, and it demanded a more complex response from European intellectuals and their governments than either had furnished in the years between the wars.

AMERICAN FOUNDATIONS AND EUROPEAN REFUGEES

For all the talk of America and Europe as adversarial civilizations, more artists, writers, and professors were moving back and forth across the Atlantic in the 1920s and 1930s than ever before. Most of this interchange was privately organized and financed, with little or no governmental supervision. The people involved were scholars, scientists, painters, musicians, novelists, and students. Few seemed to be in any position to affect the economic or political destinies of their respective countries. But ultimately, they had as much to do with the shift of power from Europe to the United States as did Hollywood or the major American corporations.

Such a shift might not have happened at all had it not been for the guidance and resources supplied by America's philanthropic foundations. Between the two world wars, the Rockefeller and Guggenheim Foundations, the Carnegie Endowment for International Peace, the American Council of Learned Societies, and the Commonwealth Fund dispensed fellowships for Americans to study abroad, sponsored conferences and international journals, funded libraries and visiting lectureships, and recruited European scholars and scientists to university positions in the United States. In an informal yet systematic fashion, the foundations functioned as the channel through which Americans were able not only to learn about but to domesticate the latest European ideas. Constructing a network of personal and professional relationships among intellectuals and academics on both sides of the ocean (which turned out for many of the Europeans in the 1930s to mean the difference between life and death), the foundations helped to close the cultural gap between the continents.

Of all these, the Rockefeller Foundation was the most encyclopedic in its cultural pursuits, and the most influential in heightening America's visibility overseas. From its inception in 1914, the foundation financed programs in medicine and public health, particularly in China. During the 1920s, it broadened its efforts, offering fellowships for American faculty and graduate students to study in Europe, and helping to launch the Social Science Research Council, which funded many European projects in the natural and social sciences. Often, the foundation made grants for specific purposes. It gave $2 million to Oxford for the renovation of the Bodleian Library. Similarly, the foundation gave money to the Niels Bohr Institute at the University of Copenhagen for work in theoretical physics (thereby forging a bond of increasing importance to the United States by the eve of World War II); to the universities of Kiel, Heidelberg, Rotterdam, and Stockholm and the London School of Economics for the study of the modern economy; and to the University of Munich and the University of Berlin for programs in psychiatry and anthropology, respectively. By 1934, the foundation had allocated nearly $18 million for the social sciences and $15 million for academic exchanges.[37] These expenditures enabled the United States to play a significant role in European intellectual life for the first time, while simultaneously exposing young American scholars to the theories of their more eminent European counterparts.

The day when the Rockefeller and other foundations could function as private ad hoc agencies, indulging their own cultural interests without having to worry about political or social upheavals, soon came to an end. By the 1930s, American philanthropists could no longer devote themselves to the lofty task of uplifting minds. They turned now to the grim business of saving thousands of people from the realities of terror and extermination.

No single person was more responsible for transforming the role of the foundations and the cultural balance of power between Europe and the United States than Adolf Hitler. In the spring of 1933, three months after he became chancellor of a new Reich, Hitler launched a massive purge of German intellectual life. Libraries were "cleansed," books were torched, and professors (many of them physicists, mathematicians, chemists, economists, and sociologists) were fired. In October of the same year, psychoanalysis was anathematized as a "Jewish science," and its expositors were prohibited from practicing therapy or holding academic positions. In 1937, following a Nazi-inspired exhibition in Munich of "degenerate" (i.e., modern) art, a large number of

Jewish museum curators, art dealers and historians, architects, and painters were deported. The devastation inflicted on German culture was enormous. Approximately twelve thousand scholars and intellectuals had been discarded by the end of the decade. In the universities, 39 percent of all faculty members were dismissed; among social scientists, the figure rose to 47 percent. In time, 60 percent of those who lost their jobs left Germany.[38]

The flight from Germany was only the beginning. As Nazi armies marched into Austria and Czechoslovakia in 1938, the number of refugee intellectuals climbed. With Germany's conquest of Poland in 1939 and its invasion of western Europe in 1940, an entire generation of endangered writers and scholars sought to escape the Continent.

During the mid-1930s and certainly before the war broke out, many émigrés hoped that Nazism might be a temporary phenomenon and that with its collapse, they would be able to return to their homelands. Since they were only in the early stages of their migration, they did not want to think of their exile as permanent. So a substantial number initially elected to stay in Europe, resettling in nearby countries, particularly Britain, Holland, France, Switzerland, and Czechoslovakia. Unfortunately, funds were limited and there were never enough university positions either in Britain or on the Continent to absorb the majority of the refugees.[39] As the years passed and the war approached, they had to consider another, more distant, sanctuary.

Although the United States eventually admitted the largest proportion of refugees, it seemed at first too provincial and far away, too preoccupied with its own domestic problems, and too inhospitable to the classical culture of Europe. Yet America, the traditional land of immigrants, came to be an ideal destination for intellectuals who were already uprooted and in transition. Before they even reached America, most of them had psychologically deserted Europe. As Jews or Marxists or both, they were regarded by many of their countrymen as outsiders; as writers and artists, they felt marginalized and alienated; as people of high education, they were cosmopolitan but cut off from their native societies.[40] They were ready, consciously or not, to move on.

Moreover, the conditions for their journey to the United States had been prepared in the 1920s. Intellectual life, especially in the sciences, had become internationalized, not least because of the fellowships, exchanges, conferences, and journals paid for by the American foundations. With their help, American artists and writers learned about modernism in Paris and Berlin; American scholars and students deepened their knowledge at European research institutes; Europeans visited one another to share the newest techniques and ideas, and accepted invitations to teach in the United States. Young American physicists like J. Robert Oppenheimer, I. I. Rabi, and Linus Pauling found it essential to continue their studies in Europe, while Enrico Fermi and Niels Bohr lectured, respectively, at the University of Michigan and the California Institute of Technology. Language barriers were rarely a problem, since international journals had made everyone familiar with the mathematics and symbols of the new physics. Similarly, American psychologists undertook the obligatory pilgrimage to Germany and to Sigmund Freud's Vienna, bringing back to their colleagues the most recent methodologies and theoretical insights.

A major result of this interaction was the improvement of teaching and research, and the establishment of a European-style academic community within American universities. Disciplines such as nuclear physics, experimental psychology, and psychoanalysis were already developing rapidly in the United States before the arrival of the European émigrés. So, at the moment the exodus began, the intellectual environment in America was highly favorable for the reception of the newcomers. American scholars had the structures in place, an awareness of the future needs of their own departments, and close contacts with their European counterparts. The Americans wanted the further inspiration and guidance the Europeans would provide, and were in a position to welcome and utilize the refugees as no other country could.[41]

In effect, the rise of Nazism reversed the migration of American expatriates to Europe. From 1933 on, European novelists, artists, intellectuals, musicians, and scientists fled to America, where they discovered that the New World now provided shelter and sustenance for the culture of the Old. Over seven thousand and five hundred came, two-thirds of them from Germany and Austria, and the rest from central and eastern Europe, Italy, and France. The great majority were Jewish.[42] Although the number may appear small, they included the most creative and productive members of the European intelligentsia.

The roster of émigrés to America—even a partial one—was extraordinary. Among the natural scientists, there were Albert Einstein, Enrico Fermi, Edward Teller, Leo Szilard, Hans Bethe, and Victor Weisskopf. Among the political and social scientists were Erik Erikson, Hannah Arendt, Leo Strauss, Erich Fromm, Max Horkheimer, Paul Lazarsfeld, and Theodor Adorno. The anthropologists Claude

Lévi-Strauss and Bronislaw Malinowski came, along with the psychologists Karen Horney and Bruno Bettelheim. So too did the philosophers Herbert Marcuse and Rudolf Carnap, and the theologian Paul Tillich. The most well-known refugee novelists and playwrights were Thomas Mann, Erich Maria Remarque, Vladimir Nabakov, and Bertolt Brecht. Yet their reputation was no greater than the musicians and composers: Igor Stravinsky, Béla Bartók, Arnold Schoenberg, Paul Hindemith, Darius Milhaud, Kurt Weill, Arturo Toscanini, Bruno Walter, Otto Klemperer, George Szell, Erich Leinsdorf, Dmitri Mitropoulos, Rudolf Serkin, and Gregor Piatigorsky. The art critic Erwin Panofsky arrived, in addition to architects and designers like Walter Gropius, Ludwig Mies van der Rohe, and Marcel Breuer. The painters and sculptors who fled to America were particularly notable: Marc Chagall, Wassily Kandinsky, Piet Mondrian, Marcel Duchamp, Fernand Léger, Lyonel Feininger, George Grosz, Max Ernst, André Breton, Jacques Lipchitz, Yves Tanguy, Salvador Dali, and Joan Miró. If one also added the names of the émigrés to Hollywood, the list would represent for Europe a hemorrhage of talent and intellect from which the Continent never recovered.

Clearly, the most important group in terms of their impact on America's national security were the nuclear physicists. The majority relocated at universities with strong physics departments, recruited by American colleagues who knew their work. Surrounded by sophisticated equipment and the expertise of American engineers, and given the freedom to improvise, the Europeans began to test their theories and refine their experiments.[43] At the close of the 1930s and with the onset of World War II, they and their ideas became increasingly indispensable to the American government. And so they graduated from academic classrooms and laboratories to the secrecy of the Manhattan Project and Los Alamos, there to ensure their fame forever with the creation of the atomic bomb.

For the less exalted refugees to flourish in America, some more systematic procedure to receive and place them had to be devised. The primary responsibility for this task fell, once again, to the foundations. In May 1933, at the beginning of the Diaspora, a group of university executives, scientists, and officials of the Rockefeller Foundation formed the Emergency Committee in Aid of Displaced German (later Foreign) Scholars. The committee was to act as an employment agency, seeking to induce universities constrained by the depression to hire the refugees. With money obtained largely from Jewish philanthropies, the committee promised to pay half the annual academic salary of an émigré, up to $2,000, for the first two years. The remainder would come from other private sources, which usually meant the Rockefeller Foundation. Under this arrangement, universities could add distinguished, even Nobel prize-winning, scholars to their faculty free of charge.[44]

For its part, the Rockefeller Foundation was following its tradition, originated in the 1920s, of supporting European scholars. Several of the refugees, especially in the natural and social sciences, had received assistance from the foundation in earlier years. After a decade in the business of cultural exchange, the foundation had better contacts, wider experience, and more effective personnel (including staff members at a permanent office in Paris) than any of the other rescue agencies. It was no surprise, then, that the Rockefeller Foundation became the primary financier of the intellectual migration to the United States, providing over 50 percent of the funds (or $1.4 million) to pay for the costs of 303 émigrés, a contribution that no other organization surpassed.[45]

For physicists and other natural scientists, whose qualifications were readily evident and whose skills were in demand, the process of relocation was relatively smooth. It was more difficult, at least initially, to place social scientists, literary critics, art historians, and museum curators in decent jobs. Despite the reverence American scholars felt for the pre-Hitler German educational system, and despite as well the financial incentives offered by the Emergency Committee and the Rockefeller Foundation, many universities hesitated before employing a host of Germans and central Europeans who might eventually overcome their gratitude for being given a class to teach and start inquiring about tenure. In addition, the American academic world was not itself immune to anti-Semitism. Quotas limiting the admission of Jewish students, and restrictions—if not outright prohibitions—on the hiring of Jewish professors, were commonplace at most of the elite universities in the United States. Hence, the Emergency Committee and the Rockefeller Foundation decided to assist only senior scholars with impeccable reputations who would not be competing for positions or for promotion with younger American academics just beginning their careers. They also tried to disburse the émigrés throughout the country in order to minimize whatever resentments and hostility the native-born faculty might feel toward an influx of foreigners and Jews.[46]

Nevertheless, certain institutions—usually those that had been recently created or were sympathetic to intellectual experimentation—

became known for their willingness to hire the refugees. From its inception in the early 1930s, the Institute for Advanced Study at Princeton offered asylum to prominent Europeans. Its first appointment, in 1932, was Albert Einstein. Individual members of the Frankfurt Institute for Social Research (more often called the Frankfurt School) migrated to Geneva and Paris before reuniting at Columbia. New York City itself had a multiplicity of museums, galleries, and libraries; a large Jewish population; and a number of wealthy German Jewish families (the Guggenheims, the Warburgs, the Schiffs, the Rosenwalds, the Seligmans, and the Lewisohns) who had long supported the arts and were now subsidizing the rescue and relocation of the refugees. Consequently, the city became a new home for many émigré art historians, critics, and dealers, the majority of whom were Jewish victims of the Nazi expulsions. The Institute of Fine Arts at New York University was an especially important center for the refugees, offering Erwin Panofsky, for example, his first American position before he moved on to Princeton's institute. Other universities that were hospitable to the immigrants included Black Mountain College in North Carolina and Roosevelt University in Chicago.[47]

But the most reliable haven for refugee intellectuals was the New School for Social Research in New York City. The New School had been created in 1918 by liberal academics affiliated with the *New Republic* (John Dewey, Charles Beard, Thorstein Veblen, James Harvey Robinson) who wanted to stimulate critical research in economics and social theory, and make teaching more relevant to the problems of daily life. Alvin Johnson, the New School's director, shared his colleagues' desire for a university that was both intellectually innovative and politically engaged. During the 1920s, he had become familiar with the work and personalities of many European scholars when he served as coeditor of the *Encyclopedia of the Social Sciences*, another project funded by the Rockefeller Foundation and the Carnegie Endowment. Johnson saw the refugee crisis as an opportunity for the New School to integrate the ideas of European social scientists with the needs of American reform. Toward that end, he opened a "University in Exile" at the New School in October 1933. Staffed mostly by German social scientists who were also social democrats, the University in Exile represented the prototype of the activist European intellectual community Johnson hoped to reconstruct in the United States. Here, the refugees could carry on their work under conditions similar to those they remembered in Weimar Germany, while also being able for the first time to communicate with American academics. Ultimately, with a $540,000 grant from the Rockefeller Foundation, the greatest amount of money it gave to any university, Johnson recruited 178 émigré scholars to his faculty.[48] The New School thus became a shelter for the largest concentration of European immigrant intellectuals in America.

Yet for all the efforts of the Emergency Committee, the various foundations, individual philanthropists, and the universities, the problems of resettling the Europeans intensified, especially when the number of potential émigrés escalated after the outbreak of World War II in September 1939 and the German conquest of France in June 1940. Britain and the United States became the only safe countries left for those scholars who had taken refuge earlier in France, Denmark, or the Netherlands and were now trying frantically to get out of Europe.

The situation in America was bleak. By the end of the 1930s, the Emergency Committee had depleted its funds, and the academic job market for refugees—always limited—had virtually evaporated. Worse, at a time when more European intellectuals than ever before were begging for permission to enter the United States, the Department of State made it harder for them to emigrate. Unsympathetic to people it assumed were Jews, Marxists, and security risks, the State Department deliberately delayed issuing visas to Europeans trapped in Vichy France, Spain, and Portugal.[49]

Despite these impediments, both the Rockefeller Foundation and the New School believed that the latest crisis represented yet another opportunity to bring the best of European culture to the United States. The foundation had enough money to accelerate its rescue operations, and the political expertise to convince Washington that it should selectively relax its immigration policies to admit those émigrés who would be useful if and when America joined the war. Meanwhile, the New School acted as the employer of last resort for the refugees.[50]

Whereas the majority of the New School's appointees in the 1930s had been German or central European, the most significant group among the new arrivals in the early 1940s were Belgian and French. Men like Jacques Maritain and Claude Lévi-Strauss differed from their predecessors not only in nationality, but also in their attitudes toward America. The earlier wave of emigrants eventually came to accept the United States as their permanent home. The French, committed politically to Charles de Gaulle and the Gaullist wing of the resistance movement, and yearning to reconstruct their country after the war, viewed their residence in America as temporary. In February

1942, they constituted themselves as the École Libre des Hautes Études, an independent French university in exile within the New School. They taught their courses in French, defended the virtues of French culture, functioned as de Gaulle's emissaries to Washington and to the American people, and urged the United States to withdraw its support for Vichy and endorse the Free French instead. Once the Allied armies liberated Paris in August 1944, almost all of them repatriated to France.[51]

But notwithstanding their insistence on maintaining their autonomy, the French like other émigrés—discovered that they had become part of a truly international community of scholars, intellectuals, and scientists, now gathered in America to contribute to the war effort either through the government's intelligence and communications agencies or in the race to build the atom bomb. Their language skills and their knowledge of European history and culture made them ideal consultants to the military, the Office of Strategic Services, the Office of War Information, the Rand Corporation, and eventually (in the case of Herbert Marcuse) the same State Department that had been so suspicious of the immigrant intellectuals. Evidently, "leftist" opinions, whether held by refugees in Washington or J. Robert Oppenheimer at Los Alamos, were irrelevant—at least for the duration of the war. Many of the New School's faculty, for example, were socialists, but they were also authorities on German affairs. Therefore, the government wanted their analysis of Germany's economic and military capacities, their special insights into Nazi politics and Hitler's mind, and their advice on how to deal with the German people after the war. Émigré art historians, otherwise apolitical, helped draw up lists of Italian monuments, churches, and classical buildings for Allied bombers to avoid. The French émigrés (Maritain, Lévi-Strauss, Denis de Rougemont, André Breton) tended to be more conservative but they were especially useful in broadcasting messages and information on the Voice of America to occupied France.[52]

In the end, it was the government that enabled the refugees to complete their journey from outcasts in Europe to important and influential members of American society. The bond between the émigré scholars and Washington would strengthen in the years of the Cold War, as intellectuals (both foreign born and native) shifted their focus from Nazi Germany to the Soviet Union.

Beyond the immediate pressures of the war, the experiences of the Europeans in the United States during the 1930s and 1940s were a dramatic illustration of how much the intellectual vitality of the Old

World had been preserved and transformed in the New. In large measure, the philanthropic foundations were responsible not just for the rescue of individual European scholars and scientists, but for the general migration of European culture and civilization to America. It remained only for the government to take advantage of what the private sector—the foundations and the universities as well as the corporations and Hollywood—had already achieved.

THE ORIGINS OF AMERICA'S CULTURAL DIPLOMACY

Washington's willingness to employ the refugee intellectuals, or indeed intellectuals of any kind, in the pursuit of its military and diplomatic objectives was not unprecedented. But neither was it customary. From the American Revolution through the Civil War, Benjamin Franklin, Thomas Jefferson, John Adams and his descendants, had all represented the United States abroad. Yet they were conspicuous exceptions in a country where, by the late nineteenth and early twentieth centuries, people of culture and intellect rarely entered the world of domestic commerce or politics, much less the labyrinth of foreign policy. There was a vast distance, as Henry Adams never tired of pointing out, between being a public figure, living in or serving the White House (as his great-grandfather, grandfather, and father had done), and observing the conduct of power from a secluded home on Lafayette Square.

So the notion of enlisting the talents of intellectuals occurred infrequently to government officials. The idea of using American culture as a whole for the purposes of diplomacy—despite or because of the experience with George Creel's World War I Committee on Public Information—was even more unimaginable. Examples of how culture might be made an instrument of foreign policy did exist overseas, but until the 1930s Washington remained oblivious.

France, predictably, was the first country to utilize its culture for transnational goals. After its defeat in the Franco-Prusssian War of 1870–71, the French government sought to repair the nation's shattered prestige by teaching the French language and literature in the colonies and elsewhere, creating the Alliance Française for this purpose in 1883. Presumably, as foreigners grew more familiar with the French intellectual tradition, they would come to sympathize with French economic and political policies. The projection of French culture abroad thus became a significant component of French diplomacy.[53]

Italy and Germany were also concerned with their international images, as well as with the loyalties of millions of their emigrants now living in foreign lands. They too emphasized language instruction as a way of maintaining and extending their political influence overseas. The Italian government, following the model of France, founded the Dante Alighieri Society in 1889. Germany relied on a variety of private organizations in the early twentieth century before it formed the Goethe Institute in 1932.[54] The selection of Goethe as a symbol, like the Italian government's use of Dante, was designed to remind people everywhere of Germany's many contributions to Western art and literature. Still, Goethe was an inauspicious choice of names for a country about to entrust its cultural inheritance to Hitler and Joseph Goebbels.

These initial experiments with cultural diplomacy were incurably elitist. The focus on language and literature was likely to be effective only with a relatively educated clientele, one already predisposed to value a nation's culture. The French understood this better than anyone else, since theirs was the language spoken internationally by decision makers and opinion shapers. But for almost every major European government at the beginning of the twentieth century, the official uses of culture were clear: They were to help promote a nation's interests among people who inhabited the foreign ministries, the universities, and the boards of trade.

By the 1920s, however, the growth of overseas investments, the emergence of mass movements and ideologies, and the appearance of new forms of international communication made culture and foreign policy no longer the special province of intellectuals, career politicians, aristocratic families, and professional diplomats.[55] Now governments had to employ every device at their disposal to appeal to a broad, heterogeneous audience whose emotions and allegiances could fluctuate with each new message or passing impression.

Advertising, automobile races, aviation speed and endurance contests, international athletic events, short-wave radio broadcasts, the movies—all these could be used to reinforce a nation's reputation and stature. Radio was particularly important in explaining national policy to people in other countries, and European governments quickly launched overseas and foreign-language broadcasting services: the Soviet Union in 1926, the Netherlands in 1927, France in 1931, and Britain in 1932.[56]

No country deployed its media more spectacularly than Germany in the 1930s. From the moment Hitler assumed power, every facet of the "new" German culture was conscripted to serve the doctrines and objectives of the Nazi regime. Newspapers and magazines, schools and churches, student exchanges and German-language clubs, international radio broadcasts and the movies, torch-light parades, and the 1936 Olympics, all were weapons in the arsenal of Nazi propaganda.[57] Perhaps the most notorious, and the most skillful, example of how the media could be used to glorify the current national myth was Leni Riefenstahl's *Triumph of the Will,* a documentary film that transformed the Nuremberg rallies into a mythic spectacle—a visual hymn to Aryan purity, the collective spirit of the German people, and the demonic passions of the Führer.

The ability of Nazi propaganda to mobilize the German populace at home astonished other governments. The Nazis' efforts to attract foreign audiences, especially those of German ancestry, were even more ominous. Responding to the growing threat of German (and Italian) influence overseas, the British government set up the British Council in 1934, an institution devoted to the more traditional techniques of teaching language and literature through libraries and cultural centers in major foreign cities. By the late 1930s, the British Broadcasting Corporation's Empire Service had expanded its foreign-language operations to cope with the competition from German, Italian, Soviet, and Japanese radio networks.[58]

For most of this time, Washington refrained from officially sponsored cultural activities, leaving intellectual and educational exchanges to the foundations and the dissemination of American values to Hollywood. But by the middle of the 1930s, the Roosevelt administration concluded that America's security depended on its ability to speak to and win the support of people in other countries. Cultural and educational programs were indispensable to this task. Yet the nation's traditional reliance on private efforts like those of the foundations seemed no longer sufficient. If the United States hoped to compete in a world where culture was increasingly connected to foreign policy and governments were intimately involved in reshaping and projecting their national images, then Washington would have to adopt some of the same strategies.

What induced the Roosevelt administration to pursue a more activist cultural policy was its alarm at the spread of German and Italian influence in Latin America. There were large numbers of immigrants from both countries living in Argentina, Brazil, and Chile, many of whom were sympathetic to the fascist regimes in their homelands. In addition, public and university libraries throughout Latin America were well stocked with German and Italian books, newspapers, and magazines.[59] In contrast, America's cultural presence—apart from its movies—was relatively small, a set of circumstances with dangerous political implications. In response, Washington launched a series of educational and cultural programs designed to promote Latin America's loyalty to the United States. For the first time since the demise of the Creel Committee in 1919, the American government was experimenting again with cultural diplomacy.

The initial, halting steps were taken in 1936 at the Inter-American Conference for the Maintenance of Peace, held in Buenos Aires. There, the American delegation agreed to a government-sponsored exchange of professors, graduate students, and secondary school teachers between the United States and the Latin American nations. This was followed in 1938 by the formation of a Division of Cultural Relations within the Department of State. The division's primary purpose was to supervise America's cultural and educational exchange programs in Latin America, and to open and operate libraries, American schools, and cultural centers in the capital cities. Although Washington promised that the exchanges would be reciprocal, they were from the outset one-sided. Latin American students and professors traveled to the United States, while America in turn sent its books and art exhibitions to Latin America, and offered English-language instruction as well as classes in American history and literature in its cultural centers.[60] Still, the programs in Latin America marked the beginning of America's permanent commitment to the use of culture as an element in its international relations.

With the Japanese attack on Pearl Harbor, the United States entered the global conflict prepared, economically and militarily, to fight a total war. This commitment included the mobilization of America's cultural and media resources beyond anything contemplated during World War I. In February 1942, two months after Pearl Harbor, the federal government inaugurated a short-wave radio service called the Voice of America to reach and guide the unseen, unheard people of occupied Europe. The VOA quickly became America's most important means of projecting its messages overseas because its signals could be picked up almost everywhere. Its impact was supplemented by the Armed Forces Radio Network whose programs, though intended for American soldiers, also appealed to civilian populations.[61] In June, the Roosevelt administration went further, creating the Office of War Information. The OWI's mission, grandly conceived, was to coordinate all of America's efforts to define for audiences at home and abroad the nation's wartime policies and its vision of the postwar world.

For the most part, the OWI engaged in a variety of activities that were now typical of modern cultural diplomacy. Working closely with Madison Avenue, Hollywood, the major publishing houses, and the radio networks, the OWI opened information offices and libraries in the unconquered or subsequently liberated countries of Europe; distributed magazines and inexpensive paperback copies of American books, both in English and in translation; printed excerpts of Roosevelt's speeches and digests of important newspaper articles and radio broadcasts; issued news releases and reproduced press photographs; kept in close contact with foreign newspaper editors and invited scores of exiled European journalists and political leaders to the United States; arranged for art exhibitions and the showing of documentary films; and conducted public relations campaigns with a blizzard of posters and pamphlets. The OWI was especially active in Britain, dispatching American intellectuals, scholars, and government officials to lecture at universities and secondary schools, before women's clubs and trade unions, over the BBC—in sum, to any audience deemed insufficiently knowledgeable about the United States. All these efforts, in whatever country they occurred, were designed to reacquaint Europeans (particularly those who had been cut off from the news by the Nazi occupation) with the latest accomplishments in American science, literature, the arts, and social reform.[62]

The OWI also assisted the military and the Office of Strategic Services in carrying out "psychological" warfare. After the Allied invasions of Italy and France, OWI personnel dropped 3 billion leaflets and set up loudspeakers encouraging German and Italian soldiers to surrender. In addition, the OWI commandeered movie theaters and radio stations, took over European newspapers, and operated mobile units close to the front lines, all in an effort to weaken enemy morale and hasten the end of the war. It was, of course, the Allied armies, rather than American propaganda, that ultimately defeated Germany. But the OWI gained considerable credit for its contribution to the climactic military campaigns.[63]

Toward the end of the war, both the OWI and the VOA turned their attention to the task of creating a more favorable impression of the United States in Europe. The OWI began to publish its own booklets and magazines, while the VOA put on programs designed to educate Europeans about America's wealth and productivity, about its democratic impulses, above all about its power to shape the destiny of the postwar world. The picture the agencies painted was meant to be attractive and reassuring. Its purpose was to help Europeans better understand and appreciate America's values and institutions so that they might more easily accept America's benevolent rule.[64] These were themes that would be repeatedly emphasized in the postwar era.

Yet whatever successes the OWI enjoyed, its ability to survive World War II was always in doubt. By the summer of 1945, no one in the government could decide what role (if any) an agency like the OWI should have in peacetime. At this point, it seemed easier to put off any serious consideration of the nature and purposes of government-sponsored cultural programs until some new crisis arose. In August, President Truman abolished the OWI as an independent entity and transferred its few remaining functions, along with a diminished VOA, to the Department of State. There they resided—unloved, unwelcome, with no clear marching orders—until they were rejuvenated by the Cold War.[65]

But the idea that America's cultural ties with Europe should depend in part on government support did not entirely vanish. Neither did the notion that Europe ought to be remade in America's image. In the years after 1945, Europeans became the chief targets of Washington's renewed and more bombastic cultural diplomacy. The Europeans also found themselves trying more desperately than in the prewar era to resist or revise America's plans for their future.

TWO

American Culture and the Cold War

The Reshaping of Western Europe

By the end of World War I, the United States had established itself as a significant presence in world affairs, a nation whose economy and popular culture affected the attitudes and consumption patterns of millions of people overseas. Yet throughout the 1920s and 1930s, America shared the international stage with Europe. The most important political and military decisions were still made in London, Paris, and Berlin. Until the rise of Nazism, the most advanced scientific theories were still being debated chiefly in European universities and research institutes, while the most provocative innovations in literature and the arts still originated in the cafés, salons, garrets, and studios of Europe's great cities. In its transactions with Europe, the United States was no longer a junior partner, but neither did it dominate the relationship. During the interwar years, Americans and Europeans seemed wary but respectful of one another, as one might expect from two evenly matched competitors in the global arena.

By the close of World War II, any sense of equality between the United States and Europe had vanished. America stood alone as the world's mightiest nation. Its armies were triumphant. Its cities had escaped bombardment. Its civilian population had been neither uprooted nor terrorized. Its economy had recovered from the depression and was once again strong. Its standard of living was unsurpassed. Its technological superiority was unquestioned, and its mastery of atomic weaponry was—at least for the time being—unchallenged. In 1945, the United States had reached the summit of its power and prestige.

The contrasts with Europe could not have been more glaring. Americans, dreaming of new houses in the suburbs, stared uncomprehendingly at newsreels showing once-lively, near-mythical European cities now suffocating in garbage and rubble. American factories, returning to the manufacture of consumer goods after four years of war production, were beginning to flood the marketplace with automobiles, refrigerators, clothes, an infinite variety of soaps and toothpastes and breakfast cereals, the first television sets—in short, all the necessities of a modern consumer society. At the same moment, the specter of hunger and starvation haunted the European winters. The United States was exploding with energy and optimism: The future would surely be America's to shape and define. Europe, on the other hand, was wrecked, exhausted, finished as an international force—its influence and glory, its claim to represent the best in human civilization, all obliterated by the war and the gas chambers. Europe's very survival now depended on America's economic resources, political leadership, and military protection. Americans would decide on their own what the major issues were and how they should be resolved. In return for America's liberation of (Western) Europe, and its promise of assistance and guidance in the postwar era, the United States asked of Europeans only that they be grateful and properly deferential. Given the stark discrepancy between an exuberant America and a ravaged Europe, it was little wonder that Americans might regard themselves as the chosen people of the twentieth century, even though the Europeans often thought of the Americans as creatures from another planet.

Americans certainly inhabited a different world; whether it was Jerusalem or Mars hardly mattered. The United States could as easily be seen as a reincarnation of Rome. But if Americans were the newest Caesars, they arrived on the European continent both as conquerors and as custodians. Having subdued the vandals of the 1930s and preparing to fend off the territorial appetites of the barbarians in the

Soviet Union, Americans presented themselves to Europe as the guardians of democracy on the one hand and of Western civilization on the other. The dual image was not unpersuasive. By 1945, the United States had become the center not just of commerce and power, but also of art and ideas. Washington had replaced London and Berlin as the overseer of Western politics, and New York had replaced Paris as the home of Western culture.

The migration of European scholars, artists, and scientists to the United States contributed to America's intellectual preeminence at the end of the war. But the transformation of the United States from a cultural colony to a cultural colossus was more directly a product of America's political, economic, and military supremacy in 1945. American culture and American power were inextricably connected. Just as Europeans now had to pay close attention to America's domestic political disputes and diplomatic goals, so too did they need to familiarize themselves with America's literature, painting, science, social thought, and academic life. Where uncultivated Americans once traveled to Europe in search of enlightenment, Europeans in the 1940s and 1950s came to the United States to study America's past and learn from America's present. Here, in universities abundantly equipped with libraries and laboratories, they could absorb the unrivaled wisdom of American professors. They could listen to the opinions of American intellectuals; read the works and try to imitate the techniques of American novelists and poets; find out about the most recent developments in American art and architecture; and experience, if only temporarily, the exhilaration of living in the heartland of modernism. Europe—previously urbane and sophisticated—had become hopelessly provincial. America, in turn, was the embodiment of the cosmopolitan ideal.

Because the United States was now the leader and principal defender of Western civilization, it soon found itself inescapably engaged in a Cold War with the Soviet Union, a war waged as much for cultural influence as for political, economic, and military domination. Europe, physically and politically divided, with tensions mounting daily in Berlin, a continent that had been a breeding ground for crises and an eternal killing field, was pivotal to the outcome of the contest.

Ironically, the Cold War gave the Europeans, particularly the Western Europeans, some room to maneuver. They might be economically and politically dependent on the United States, but since they were also being courted by the Soviet Union, their loyalties could not be taken for granted. What Western Europe's governing classes did, what the intel-lectual leaders and the ordinary people of Europe thought, how much or how little they understood and appreciated America, whether they grasped the moral distinctions between the United States and the Soviet Union, whether they were willing to choose sides or would try instead to maintain their emotional and ideological neutrality—these were questions of the greatest magnitude for the White House and the State Department. It was clear that in the battle for the allegiance of Western Europe, the United States would have to commit not only its armies and its wealth, but all its cultural assets as well. Thus, the marriage of Amer-ican culture and American diplomacy, first proposed with some mis-givings during World War II, was ardently consummated in the early years of the Cold War.

THE REFORMATION OF GERMANY

For many Western Europeans during and after World War II, Amer-ica's foreign policy and its culture were personified by the American army. The ubiquitous GI was often the first American most people in Britain, France, Italy, or Germany had ever met, the first American whose behavior they were able to observe at close range. The encounter was not necessarily pleasant. American soldiers—tossing chewing gum and chocolates to the natives, trading stockings and cigarettes for women's favors, threatening to flatten pedestrians as they roared through town in their Jeeps and luxuriously upholstered cars, noisily in-vading the neighborhood pubs, bulging with dollars to squander on the black market—aroused among their European hosts a mixture of feel-ings, from fascination to exasperation to envy.' As they swaggered down the street, brimming with health and confidence, looking larger than life and certainly more robust than the local population, the sol-diers seemed the embodiments of a vulgar, flamboyant, mythological America.

In no country did the presence of the army more strongly reinforce the notion of how a typical American acted than in Germany. To Ger-mans living in the American zone, the soldiers seemed more insou-ciant, more relaxed and informal, and more antiauthoritarian than any occupying force ever seen on the Continent. This was an army imbued with a civilian mentality. Its conduct contrasted sharply with the obedience displayed by Hitler's legions or the robotic demeanor of the Soviet army in the Eastern zone. But the most striking attribute of the American army was its wealth. While Germans, as well as the British and Italians, struggled to survive on little food and less heat, the Americans—with no worries about the provenance of their next meal or the costs of electricity and gasoline—appeared to take their affluence for granted.[a] The American army, of course, was made up largely of people with vivid memories of their own impoverishment during the depression years. Yet this fact mattered little to the many Europeans for whom scarcity and destitution were now the norms of daily life.

American troops brought to Europe and especially to Germany not only their canned goods and cash but also their language, their attitudes, and their popular culture. Even if one did not come into direct contact with a GI (and fraternization between American soldiers and German civilians was at first discouraged), it was possible to learn a great deal about the United States simply by listening to the Armed Forces Radio Network. Although the programs on the AFN were aimed at military personnel, local inhabitants comprised 90 percent of the audience after the war. Through the medium of the AFN, Germans in the Western zones and in Berlin could hear American jazz, the latest songs and dance music, news and information about movies and politics, and a distinctive form of "American" English.[3]

Whether the Germans resented or admired the prosperity and culture of the average American soldier, the primary role of the army was to try to make the former Third Reich into a replica of the United States. And in this endeavor, there was no doubt, at least from the American point of view, that the Germans had been reduced to the status of colonials awaiting the commands of the mother country across the ocean, as transmitted to her proconsuls in Berlin.

Of all the cultural missions undertaken in Europe by the American government after World War II, none was larger or more ambitious than the effort to create within its own zone of occupation an entirely new Germany in the years between 1945 and 1949. The moment could not have seemed more propitious. Germany was prostrate and in need of every conceivable form of assistance; the American army was in complete control of a docile population; Washington could presumably accomplish whatever it wanted. Here was an incomparable opportunity for political reform, social engineering, and cultural rejuvenation—all of which would serve the interests both of America's democratic ideals and of its postwar foreign policy.

Yet despite America's power and Germany's helplessness, the United States was unable to achieve its grand design. Instead, America's experience in West Germany in the late 1940s and early 1950s became a case study of how a country that was determined to defend its national traditions and local customs in the face of enormous outside pressure could adapt to, modify, and resist the political and cultural policies of the United States. This mixture of acquiescence and defiance would characterize the general West European response to American influence for the rest of the century.

America's far-reaching plans for the renovation of Germany were stymied from the beginning both by the formidable political and economic problems of postwar German life, and by the capacity of the Germans themselves to deflect and frustrate the American agenda. The clash between American intentions and German realities was initially dramatized in the attempt to eliminate Nazi party members and sympathizers from all public institutions. At the conclusion of the Potsdam conference in July 1945, the four occupying powers (Britain, France, the Soviet Union, and the United States) officially resolved to de-Nazify Germany, though they upheld their right to use any strategy they wished in their own zones. In 1945 and 1946, American military authorities, on instructions from the White House and the State Department, pursued a strict policy designed to purge, prosecute, and punish ex-Nazis. Civil servants, policemen, lawyers and judges, physicians, university faculty, and secondary school teachers all were subject to dismissal if not to imprisonment. In Bavaria alone, 50 percent of the secondary school administrators and teachers had been fired by 1946.[4]

Most Germans in the American zone, however, regarded de-Nazification not as a form of permanent ostracism, but as an initial step on the road to rehabilitation and redemption. Their views were not irrelevant since the Americans found themselves having to rely increasingly on Germans to carry out the de-Nazification policies, and to make sure public institutions continued to function in some minimal fashion. The army, it turned out, could not govern—much less distinguish between the guilty and the innocent—without German cooperation. The military and its civilian advisers had neither the resources nor the personnel to hunt down Nazis, manage the political and economic affairs of the zone, and launch a social revolution, all at the same time. To perform their assigned tasks, the Americans needed the technical and administrative skills that only the Germans were able to provide.[5]

Moreover, as the conflict between the United States and the Soviet Union began to take precedence over prolonged investigations of people's murky political pasts, the legacy of Nazism seemed less troubling to the Americans than did the dangers of Communism. American policymakers, interested now in West Germany as a potential ally in the Cold War, aborted the de-Nazification crusade before it accomplished its mission.[6] By 1948, the natives had mostly reclaimed their positions in the town halls, the judiciary, the hospitals, and the classrooms. In effect, the Germans achieved their own absolution with the benediction of their American vicars in Berlin.

To convert the Germans in the American zone from beggars to partners, the United States had to help rebuild the economic and cultural infrastructure. This was no small undertaking. At the end of World War II, Germany was in shambles. The extent of the physical destruction was massive. Nothing worked. There was barely enough food or shelter. Coal supplies were nearly exhausted. Schools were closed. There were shortages of every item, from clothing to utensils to textbooks. As late as 1947, starvation remained a real threat, and the majority of people spent their time and energy trying to survive from day to day.

Eventually, conditions improved. Public transportation resumed. Secondary schools, universities, and libraries quickly reopened. Supplies of paper miraculously reappeared for the printing of newspapers and books. New, if cheap and temporary, housing sprang up.[7] The rebirth and relative normalization of life in the American zone was made possible by a combination of financial aid from Washington, military supervision from Berlin, and the ingenuity of the local German population.

But American leaders were concerned with more than Germany's institutional and physical recovery. As the Cold War grew more tense in the late 1940s, the United States sought to teach the Germans in its zone how to become good democrats and, by implication, good Americans.[8] Democratic values and practices became synonymous with the American way of life. By paying close attention, the Germans could recast themselves in the American image. Or so the Americans, in their naiveté about the malleability of other cultures, believed.

No institution could implant the principles of democracy more effectively than the schools. If the Germans were to reenter Western civilization and, not incidentally, learn to appreciate America's goals in the Cold War, they would have to be reeducated. Hence, the U.S. government and the military commanders in Berlin set out to reform the entire German educational system.[9] Their failure to do so represented a classic instance of how easy it was for the United States to overestimate its own power, while discounting the complexities and durability of Germany's educational and cultural traditions.

To oversee this project, the army called in a platoon of professional educators, expert in such matters as school administration, classroom management, and pedagogy. They were led by Herman Wells, the president of Indiana University who became the chief educational and cultural adviser to General Lucius Clay, the Military Governor of the American zone; Alonzo Grace, previously a commissioner of education in Connecticut; and Richard Alexander, dean of the Teachers College at Columbia.

These were the type of people who believed that education was more than a formal exercise devoted only to the dissemination of knowledge. For them, schools were the key institutions in the creation of a democratic sensibility. But they assumed, as one might have predicted of specialists in educational structures and techniques, that any change in the German system had to begin with the way schools were organized and how students were taught. Thus, they concentrated on issues like teacher training, curriculum reform, and textbook revisions, as if improving educational methods and materials would produce not only better students but a transformation in the political values and behavior of the entire society.[10]

The educational consultants also shared with the army and the decision makers in Washington an abiding faith in the applicability of the American model. Mistrustful of any educational apparatus unlike the one they knew at home, they regarded the German way of doing things as "flawed" and unsatisfactory. To set matters right, German administrators ought to copy American procedures while teachers, both in secondary schools and in universities, needed to imitate the style and practices of their counterparts in the United States. Even the design of the new German schools should replicate the architecture of an American high school or college campus. In the eyes of one native observer, "the American program of reeducation was basically an attempt to graft the ideals of a Midwestern town on German conditions."[11]

From the American perspective, the principal defect of the German educational structure, dating from the pre-Hitler years, was its elitism. The Americans aimed their heaviest criticism at the German custom (practiced everywhere in Europe) of consigning students at a young age to two separate educational tracks—one for the intellectually gifted or economically blessed, who would go on to universities and then to leadership positions in politics or business, and the other for those who were considered fit only for vocational training and who were therefore destined to occupy the lesser rungs of the social ladder.

The remedy prescribed by the democrats from across the ocean was the American-style "comprehensive" school, one in which children from the lower classes would have equal opportunities for educational advancement, and where all students would learn the same subjects and absorb common values. At the university level, the Americans—in the spirit of John Dewey—recommended an end to authoritarian instruction, less classical training, and more courses in social studies to promote good citizenship and prepare students for the practical demands of daily life. They also emphasized the importance of extracurricular activities: student government, college newspapers, discussion groups, anything that would encourage a greater sense of democratic participation.[12] These panaceas, they hoped, would eliminate the economic inequities, class divisions, and hierarchical attitudes that were originally spawned in the schools but eventually infected the whole social order.

Nowhere in these recommendations was there any acknowledgment that, in practice, American education might itself be neither democratic nor egalitarian. The Americans rarely mentioned that students in the United States were usually segregated by wealth, class, race, and intellect—that those attending private schools had educational and economic advantages not always available to their counterparts in the public schools, that many students in public high schools were "tracked" into vocational curricula, and that African Americans received few of the educational benefits reserved for whites.

In any case, most of the German educational administrators, secondary school teachers, and university professors in the American zone were not eager to adopt the proposals of their mentors from the United States. Whether or not they had been tainted by the Nazi experience, they were often too old and inflexible to contemplate sweeping reforms. They fought instead to reestablish the aristocratic institutions and standards that had existed long before the Third Reich. They were extremely skillful in figuring out ways to delay and resist what they regarded as the imposition of a foreign educational scheme that had no roots in the German past. In their efforts, they were supported by a public increasingly resentful of ideas and initiatives identified exclusively with the United States.

The hostility to any structural change in the school system was greatest in Bavaria—the most conservative region, with the deepest feelings of cultural nationalism, in the American zone. Bavaria's intransigence, and its success in preserving the classical gymnasium and other features of the authoritarian system, served as an example to traditionalists elsewhere in the zone. Opposition on the part of educators as well as ordinary people grew exponentially, the vanquished refusing to accede to the dictates of the victor. By 1949, as the military government came to an end, the effort to reconstruct Germany's educational system along American lines collapsed. Thereafter, German officials regained full control over their educational system.[13]

One reason why the United States did not prevail in its efforts to democratize German education was that the Americans were using undemocratic tactics. It was inherently contradictory to preach the benefits of democracy while relying on the ultimate authority and enforcement powers of the army. It was equally paradoxical to expect embryonic democrats in Germany to take orders from outsiders, even if the directives came from well-meaning Americans. What Washington and the military command in Berlin sometimes forgot was the old-fashioned American notion that to achieve their objectives, leaders have to obtain the consent and cooperation of the governed.[14]

A larger reason for the failure of educational reform was the American tendency to minimize, if not ignore, the significance of local circumstances. Americans seemed habitually bewildered by cultural traditions different from their own. Sometimes this perplexity concealed a touch of arrogance, as when the army and its civilian experts thought they could radically alter—despite predictable objections from parents and politicians—an institution so basic to a society as its schools. In Germany and in the rest of Western Europe, Americans too often overlooked the need to pursue programs that fit the values and corresponded to the desires of a particular nation, and that preferably coincided with the active involvement of the indigenous population.

There was one episode in the late 1940s when American policy in Germany adhered to these precepts, when Americans acted purely as advisers rather than as autocrats. In the creation of the Free University of Berlin—the most innovative educational experiment in postwar Germany—the United States was a sponsor and participant, but the primary inspiration came from the Germans themselves.

The Free University was an outgrowth of the division of Berlin and the escalating conflict between the United States and the Soviet Union. Just as the city of Berlin had emerged by 1948 as a principal battleground of the Cold War, so the struggle to establish a new, democratic university in Berlin reflected the larger issues over which the Cold War was being fought.

At the end of World War II, Berlin was partitioned like all of Germany into four zones of occupation. The Russian sector included the historic center of prewar Berlin, where the government buildings that had not been entirely destroyed, the cathedrals and museums, and Berlin University (renamed Humboldt University in 1949) were all located. The Soviets were thus in charge of some of the most famous monuments and real estate in Europe: the Brandenburg Gate, the once-majestic boulevard called Unter den Linden, and Alexanderplatz. Their control over Berlin's eastern precincts also meant that they could determine the future of Germany's premier university.

In 1946, the Soviets began their own efforts at educational reform. The Russian version of "democratization" involved the elimination of all private schools (considered incubators of elitist and conservative values); a revised admissions policy for the university aimed at widening the social composition of the student body by giving preference to children from working-class, peasant, and antifascist families; the installation of Communist Party members as university administrators; and obligatory courses in Marxism to convert the students into partisans of the new socialist order arising in the Eastern zone. Given the power of the Soviet authorities, buttressed by the police and the Red Army, there were few opportunities to mount a conservative counterattack of the sort that had obstructed educational change in West Germany.[15]

By 1947 and 1948, the battle over the fate of postwar Europe was becoming more ominous. With America's announcement of the Truman Doctrine (pledging economic and political aid to "friendly" countries like Greece and Turkey threatened by Communist subversion and guerrilla insurgencies), the inception of the Marshall Plan, the impending merger of the Western zones of Germany into a single republic, the Communist coup in February 1948 against the social democratic government in Czechoslovakia, and the imposition of Stalinist regimes in all of Eastern Europe, Berlin became the flash point of the Cold War. The Russians consequently tightened their control over the students and faculty at Humboldt University.[16]

Soon, a resistance movement erupted among the students. It was led by those who were affiliated with the social democratic or more conservative political parties in the Western zones, and who were not thrilled to see the resurrection of totalitarianism in Berlin. The insurgents were opposed to admissions procedures that seemed to favor Communist sympathizers rather than simply the offspring of the working class, and hence that enabled the Communists to dominate the student organizations. They also criticized the growing number of Party members who were being appointed to the faculty and the Marxist indoctrination that saturated the classrooms and the entire curriculum. The price of opposition could be high. Some of the disaffected students were arrested in 1947 and subsequently vanished. When the leaders of the movement were expelled from Humboldt in April 1948, the dispute exploded into petition drives, mass demonstrations, and the demand for an alternative and authentically democratic university. Recognizing the need for powerful adult allies, the dissidents sought and won support from the media, West German businessmen and academics, and all the political parties in the Western sectors of Berlin.[17]

Up to this point, the concepts and initiatives had been exclusively German. Yet the leaders of the student insurrection understood from the start that a new university could be established only with the help of at least one of the occupying powers in the West.

The most likely candidate was the United States. The Americans alone appeared willing to offer not only general encouragement but concrete assistance. They were already interested in reviving cultural activities and institutions of higher learning in their sector. They had buildings (some of them occupied by research institutes formerly under Humboldt's jurisdiction) at their disposal in the Dahlem district of West Berlin. They possessed the financial resources necessary to underwrite the venture. Above all, they had the motivation to create a "free" university in a city that the Russians began to blockade in June 1948 and whose survival now depended on Allied airlifts of food and every other requirement of daily life.

Thus, the students, together with West German politicians, the cultural advisers to the American army, and members of the military high command, all plunged into secret and frenzied negotiations, mindful that they were plotting a miniature revolution in the midst of the most serious international crisis since the end of World War II. Their discussions culminated in Lucius Clay's decision to approve the establishment of a second university in Berlin, one without the ideological repression characteristic of Humboldt.[18]

The Free University, which opened in December 1948, was meant to be a model for the rest of West Germany. Its democratic structure, the participation of students in the selection of faculty and the administration of the university, the communal spirit that attended its birth— these were clearly different qualities than those associated with the universities in the Western zones, which were still wedded to the hierarchical and authoritarian ideals of the pre-Hitler years.[19]

More significantly, the Free University owed its existence to the energy and imagination of the Berliners. The Americans provided money, advice, the physical plant, equipment, and military protection—indispensable contributions, no doubt, but auxiliary support for an idea that was essentially German. From the outset, it was important to the Americans and Germans alike that the United States not impose its own agenda on the Free University, that the university not be seen as an American creation.[20] If the university was to succeed, it would have to preserve its autonomy and its identity as a distinctively *German* institution.

In the following decades, the United States maintained a close and special relationship with the Free University. Although two-thirds of the funding for the university came from the city government in West Berlin and the Federal Republic in Bonn, the American government and the Ford Foundation provided grants to subsidize the construction of medical clinics, libraries, and an Institute for American Studies. In the eyes of the Americans, the university was both a product and a symbol of the Cold War. Its pugnacious anti-Communism (inherent in its origins), its commitment to democratic values, and its ability to flourish in beleaguered Berlin made it seem a perfect antidote to the totalitarian disease in the East.[21]

Nevertheless, the students at the Free University launched a new kind of rebellion in the 1960s, reasserting their political independence by attacking America's role in Vietnam and calling for even more radical reforms in the curriculum and administrative structure. These upheavals dismayed the institution's American benefactors. But the turmoil was a reminder that the Free University had its roots not only in the Cold War, but in the politics and culture of Berlin. This was, in sum, a university the Americans could assist but never control.

America's willingness in 1948 to play a subordinate role in the formation of the Free University was indicative of the changes that were about to occur in the overall relationship between West Germany and the United States. Within the space of the next seven years, the West Germans ceased to be a defeated and divided people. Instead, they rejoined Western Europe, participated in its economic recovery, and became its first line of defense against the Soviet Union. In 1949, the separate British, French, and American zones of occupation were abolished, and a new Federal Republic emerged. West Germany remained for a time under the supervision of high commissions established by each of the three former occupying powers. This arrangement meant, in Washington's case, that administrative authority for West Germany was transferred from the army to the Department of State, which could now conduct America's educational and cultural activities throughout the Federal Republic. The era of the high commissions was transitional, ending in 1954 with the Federal Republic's metamorphosis into a sovereign state exercising full control over its own political, economic, and cultural affairs. In 1955, West Germany joined the North Atlantic Treaty Organization and was now a respected ally in the Cold War.[22]

As a result of these developments, the United States in the early 1950s shifted its cultural stance toward West Germany. "Reeducation" gave way to "reorientation"; teaching the West Germans the benefits of democracy seemed less urgent than making sure they appreciated the virtues of America. The new campaign, while still encouraging the West Germans to accept the United States as their political and cultural model, was to be less heavy-handed and more indirect. No longer would there be military decrees. The State Department approached the Germans as partners, susceptible to discreet persuasion, prepared (if their sensitivities were taken into account) to collaborate in their own transformation.[23]

Among the instruments on which the State Department relied were its twenty-seven cultural centers, called America Houses, which were located in all the major cities of the Federal Republic as well as in West Berlin. First opened after the war in the American zone, the centers by 1950 were attracting 1 million West Germans per month to conferences, lectures by visiting American writers and academics, art and photographic exhibitions, concerts, and films. The State Department supplemented the activities of the America Houses by sponsoring performances of *Oklahoma, Porgy and Bess,* the Boston Symphony Orchestra, and the Juilliard String Quartet—all designed to show the Germans that the United States had its own authentic musical tradition as well as a reverence for European classical music.[24]

Although the State Department and the America Houses provided entertainment along with instruction, their objectives were serious. They wanted to familiarize West Germans with life in America, strengthen the cultural and political bonds between the Federal Republic and the United States, and convince their audiences that both countries had a mutual interest in opposing Communism and Soviet expansion.

Washington was equally intent on transplanting America's style of journalism as well as its content to West Germany. In the late 1940s, the military government reintroduced German publishers, editors, reporters, and columnists to the advantages of a free press and economic competition. The effort was remarkably successful. By the 1950s, the postwar generation of West German journalists not only endorsed the policies of the Atlantic Alliance, but did so in the pages of newspapers and magazines that looked exactly like their American prototypes (the most celebrated imitation being *Der Spiegel,* which faithfully copied the format and layout of *Time).*[25] At least in this area, the Federal Republic had become thoroughly "Americanized."

Yet other programs aimed at affecting German attitudes had more mixed results. Officials in Washington believed that the best way to enhance the image of the United States among the West Germans was by bringing to America people who were already in or had the potential to hold leadership positions in the Federal Republic. While in the United States, these persons could meet with their professional counterparts, travel across the country, and see for themselves what Americans were really like. Then they would return to Germany and share their presumably favorable impressions with their friends and colleagues, thereby expanding the radius of America's influence. Between 1948 and 1954, eleven thousand West Germans visited the United States, their trips paid for by the State Department or private foundations. For the most part, they were actual or future members of the West German elite: politicians, jurists, police officials, academicians, businessmen, trade unionists, journalists, religious and cultural leaders, and students in secondary schools and universities who seemed destined for success.[26]

According to surveys conducted by the State Department in the mid-1950s, the majority came away with a high regard for America's economy and its democratic institutions. They were particularly struck by the ability of the American people to fulfill their civic responsibilities while retaining their devotion to personal freedom, a combination not noticeable in the German past. The West Germans sounded most pro-American when they praised America's foreign policy in the Cold War. It is not surprising that those from West Berlin were especially grateful for America's military support. But almost all the visitors understood how much the alliance with the United States benefited the Federal Republic.[27]

Despite their admiration for America's economic and military power, and their positive descriptions of how democracy functioned in the United States, the West German visitors did not necessarily want their homeland to become another America. Indeed, they were unusually critical of certain aspects of American life. This skepticism was most evident among the university students who seemed, according to the State Department's surveys, much less ready than their elders to embrace America's values. A number of students complained that the United States had not lived up either to its ideals or to their expectations. In their view, America was afflicted with materialism and racial injustice; its people were more interested in technology and machines than in human relationships; its educational system was fundamentally anti-intellectual and had no respect (as did Germany) for cultural achievements or high standards.[28]

These were precisely the sorts of accusations often heard from European intellectuals before and after World War II. Yet the reactions of the students had ominous implications for the future. In the 1950s, the Federal Republic was the country in Europe most dominated by and most dependent on America. If the United States did not entirely appeal to West German youths, then what reservations about America might be lurking in the minds of young people in the rest of Europe?

American leaders, preoccupied with the threat of the Soviet Union, did not wish to entertain such questions. During the 1940s and 1950s, members of the Truman and Eisenhower administrations, and officials in the State Department assumed that the United States could be a paradigm not only for West Germany but for all of Western Europe. Resistance to American influence among German educators, and displays of independence or hostility among German students, were not welcome at the White House or in Foggy Bottom. Expressions of thanks and an eagerness to be Americanized—these were what America's leaders anticipated at the end of World War II. So they were perplexed by the occasional recalcitrance of the West Germans who did not always appreciate America's advice. They were even less prepared to understand how other Western Europeans might neither trust nor be grateful for America's postwar largess.

EUROPE'S RESPONSE TO THE MARSHALL PLAN

The attempt to rebuild West Germany according to American specifications, and to secure its allegiance in the struggle with the Soviet Union, was not just an experiment designed for one country. It was part of a much grander strategy that embraced what America's leaders increasingly called the Atlantic Community. At stake was nothing less than the physical reconstruction and economic future of Western

Europe, and the solidification of its political and military alliance with the United States. For such a far-reaching strategy to succeed, most officials in Washington believed, the Western Europeans (as in the case of the West Germans) would have to accept America's guidance in their internal affairs.

In June 1947, at Harvard, in one of the most famous commencement speeches ever given, Secretary of State George Marshall announced America's willingness to help finance Europe's postwar economic recovery. Detailed ideas about how the funds would be used were to come from the Europeans themselves—both Western and Eastern, until the Soviet Union refused to allow its satellites to participate. The European governments were invited to submit proposals for assistance, almost as if they were applying for a foundation grant. Yet though there was considerable emphasis on how much the Europeans were taking the initiative to solve their own problems, it was clear that the American role would be more than merely supportive.[29] Control of the money, and with it the power to supervise the politics and the economy of Western Europe, remained in Washington.

After nearly a year of intense discussions among government officials, foreign policy experts, and economists on both sides of the Atlantic, Congress enacted the Marshall Plan in the spring of 1948. The Department of State, supplemented by the Departments of Agriculture and Commerce, together with a new agency called the Economic Cooperation Administration (ECA), were to have overall responsibility for carrying out the program. The Marshall Plan lasted from 1948 to 1952. By mid-1951, it had allocated $12 billion in various forms of aid to Western Europe.[30]

The economic revival of Western Europe was the most important, but not the only, purpose of the Marshall Plan. The Truman administration also viewed the plan as a crucial weapon in its battle to contain the expansionist impulses of the Soviet Union. It was on this basis that the plan was sold to a reluctant Congress and to the American people, neither of whom had displayed much enthusiasm until now for massive foreign aid programs. But American policymakers had long since concluded that Communism prospered in the midst of poverty, social dislocation, and political instability. Thus, they argued that the Marshall Plan could reduce the influence of local Communist Parties (particularly where they were strong, as in France and Italy) by raising Western Europe's standard of living, thereby enhancing the popularity of centrist politicians.[31]

The Marshall Plan's effectiveness in combating Communism was not left to chance. Nations who received assistance under the plan were expected to provide information on the fluctuating strength of the Communist Parties within their borders. In France and Italy, American officials feared that the Communists might win enough votes in the national elections of 1948 to become part of the ruling coalitions in both countries. Hence, the United States poured money into the campaigns of the more conservative parties, much of it secretly disbursed by the newly created Central Intelligence Agency. One million dollars alone went to the Christian Democrats and Socialists in Italy. The United States also reactivated its techniques of psychological warfare. In France, American propagandists tried to sway the media and the labor unions. In Italy, the United States appealed to workers and the lower middle class by broadcasting messages over the Voice of America from Hollywood stars like Frank Sinatra and Gary Cooper, and by sending letters and cables from Italian Americans warning of the dangers of Communism. These interventions succeeded in electing the Christian Democrats in Italy and in holding down the Communist vote in France. But it was little wonder that polls taken in Britain and France during the late 1940s showed that people believed the United States was meddling in the domestic politics of Western Europe.[32]

The promotion of economic recovery and anti-Communism were the most well-known objectives of the Marshall Plan. Yet the plan also had a cultural component, which was less publicized but no less significant. In one of the largest propaganda crusades mounted during the entire postwar era, the State Department and the ECA sought not just the resurrection of capitalism in Western Europe, but the adoption of economic practices that were quintessentially American. ECA administrators dispensed advice as well as aid, offering Europeans the American model along with American money. Through documentary films, radio programs, posters, pamphlets, photographic exhibits, cartoon strips, and mobile puppet shows, they advertised the United States as a land of free enterprise, free unions, free trade, and free spending—a land that Europe could emulate if it accepted the key American principles of economic efficiency, high wages, and unlimited productivity. According to the Americans, the structure of Europe's governments had to be streamlined, businessmen and workers had to stop waging a class war, and citizens had to begin thinking of themselves primarily as consumers. In effect, the Marshall Planners functioned as evangelists on behalf of the American way. Their mission was to make Western Europe resemble the United States. They assumed that the Western Europeans were incipient Americans who, if given the proper tools and instructions, would turn out to be (in line with the Marshall Plan's implicit promise) "just like us." [33]

The ECA was attempting to do throughout Western Europe what the army and the State Department had tried to accomplish in West Germany. As with the Germans, the Western Europeans had to be shown how to operate a modern economy. Their bad habits, historically ingrained, could be eradicated through "exchange" programs, which were invariably one-sided since American experts journeyed to Europe to teach while European businessmen, farmers, labor leaders, and mid-level technicians came to the United States to learn. The task of the Americans was to unravel the mysteries of industrial organization for the unenlightened Europeans, to familiarize the visitors with the latest developments in their specialties, to explain (as one European apprentice put it) "how things were done [in America], and why." [34] In time, it was hoped, these exchanges would produce a new and elite class of managers in Europe, trained and nurtured in or by the United States, and ready to utilize their skills to create an American-style economy in their own countries.

One-quarter of all the Europeans who traveled to the United States under the auspices of the Marshall Plan came from France. Like the trainees from other countries, the French were impressed by America's postwar affluence—the high standard of living enjoyed by American workers in contrast to the miseries of the French proletariat, and the abundance of cars, refrigerators, and television sets, all hard to find and even harder to pay for in France. The French were told that America's prosperity was the result of labor's productivity, and that American production techniques were the answer to European scarcity.

Yet the American emphasis on cooperation between union leaders and industrialists was not easily transferable to France, where workers and businessmen were paralyzed by ideological antipathy and mutual distrust. Nor were the French or other Europeans convinced that they could employ American managerial practices in the administration of their own factories and farms. [35] In the end, the Marshall Plan trainees did learn how things worked in America, but not how American methods might work in Europe.

If the Europeans did not seem enthralled by America's tutelage, they were even less charmed by its benevolence. Americans were often shocked and angered by the European reaction to the Marshall

Plan—especially by the willingness of Western European governments to accept America's economic aid and military protection while suspecting America's motives. "Americans," the Italian journalist Luigi Barzini observed, "expected gratitude, good will and friendship as their reward." Having liberated Western Europe and saved it from Communism, Americans found it unimaginable that anyone would question their sincerity, their altruism, or their "disinterestedness." André Visson, a European-born American citizen whose writings in the late 1940s were shaped by his transatlantic heritage, echoed Barzini: "There could be . . . no evidence more convincing of our good intentions, of our determination to play our part in international affairs, of our political maturity, . . . of our devotion to the great principle of American humanitarianism, than the Marshall Plan."[36]

Europeans clearly felt otherwise. Many believed that the United States was motivated more by self-interest than by generosity. The French, in particular, were skeptical about philanthropic endeavors of any sort. According to a 1947 Gallup poll conducted in France after the announcement of the Marshall Plan, 47 percent of the respondents thought Washington wanted to improve Europe's standard of living so that it could reopen markets for American products and create new opportunities for American investment. Throughout Western Europe, left-wing political parties viewed the plan as an instrument to prop up conservative regimes and establish client-states, thus turning the Continent into a potential battlefield in some future war. Across the political spectrum, Europeans assumed that the United States intended for them to become not only loyal allies in the conflict with the Soviet Union, but also faithful consumers of American merchandise and American culture. Given the notion that the United States was hiding its true impulses under the cloak of compassion, Europeans might well seem "ungrateful" in the eyes of their American benefactors.[37]

The misgivings about the Marshall Plan were especially pronounced among the middle and upper classes of Western Europe, who (as Visson noted) felt "humiliated and indignant at the thought that they may now be reduced to accepting American charity." These were proud people who were embarrassed, in Barzini's words, "by the gifts and by the manner with which they are given." They resented, said a British conservative politician, "the sense of being under an obligation to the United States."[38] Like many other Western Europeans, they disliked their role as supplicants and saw no reason to feel indebted to the

United States. On the contrary, they believed Western Europe deserved American assistance as compensation for its cooperation in the Cold War.

Yet Europeans of all classes and political persuasions were being more than a little disingenuous in their complaints about the Marshall Plan. Granted, the United States did not offer its aid without conditions. The Americans undoubtedly wanted to export their values to Western Europe. But the governments of Western Europe were as keen as Washington to rebuild and modernize their economies, and they were just as anxious to exclude the Communists from power. Consequently, they accepted America's advice and its leadership, even while they grumbled about its arrogance. And notwithstanding Washington's ultimate control over the purse strings, the Europeans determined for the most part how America's money would be spent. Moreover, despite the passion with which European intellectuals denounced America's inhumane industrial practices and its elevation of machines over artisanship, both before and after the war, American attitudes toward business and labor were not incompatible with those of Europe. Economic efficiency and the need for increased productivity were hardly alien concepts in countries like Germany and the Netherlands, which may explain why 85 percent of the Dutch people welcomed the Marshall Plan in 1948.[39] In sum, the political and economic interests of the United States and Western Europe were in harmony more often than they collided.

The Marshall Plan was not the sole cause of Western Europe's recovery, though it did contribute substantially to the "economic miracle" experienced by most of America's allies in the 1950s. More important, as Raymond Aron—one of the few French intellectuals sympathetic to the United States—pointed out, the plan "accelerated a historically significant trend—the spread in Europe of American products, customs, and ideas." Yet, he added, "even without the Marshall Plan, this would certainly have occurred."[40]

Still, the European fear of American economic and cultural domination was real. During the contest with the Soviets, the United States needed Western Europe, so the Europeans could exert some influence over American policies. Nevertheless, no matter how skillfully they moderated or sometimes evaded America's directives, the Europeans remained dependent on American power. Western Europe's fate was tied to America's—a theme American leaders repeatedly sounded as they mobilized the rest of their cultural resources to fight the Cold War.

THE BIRTH OF THE FULBRIGHT
PROGRAM

On matters as momentous as the reeducation of West Germany and the economic reconstruction of Western Europe, Washington was not at all reluctant to use every cultural tool at its disposal, from the mass media to exchange programs, to demonstrate the merits of America's political and economic system. Yet in areas of less immediate political importance, the government was initially more hesitant to reengage in the types of global cultural and informational activities it had sanctioned during World War II.

As the Cold War expanded in the late 1940s and early 1950s, however, President Truman and his State Department realized that the United States needed to develop programs and techniques to counter Communist propaganda in Europe. Washington had to provide more accurate information about American institutions and social life, as well as explain America's motives to a continent filled with people who appeared not to hear or believe what the United States was saying or stood for.[41]

It was in this context that the American government launched its first, and ultimately its most celebrated, academic exchange program. Of all the cultural enterprises undertaken by Washington in the second half of the twentieth century, none seemed more pristine and less corrupted by politics than the Fulbright program. For thousands of graduate students and professors, foreign and American, being awarded a Fulbright scholarship became as prestigious an accomplishment as winning a Rockefeller or a Guggenheim grant. Indeed, most recipients thought of a Fulbright grant as indistinguishable from the fellowships offered by private foundations. Few people in or out of the academic world understood or cared about the relationship between the Fulbright program and the U.S. government.

Nevertheless, for all its success in maintaining its intellectual and scholarly integrity, the Fulbright program was a product of the Cold War. As the program evolved in the late 1940s, its political and financial support from Congress, its administrative framework, and its underlying objectives were tied, however tenuously, to the demands of foreign policy.

The idea that Washington should underwrite an academic exchange program might not have arisen at all, much less gained momentum, were it not for the special political and economic circumstances of 1945 and 1946. The prewar educational and cultural exchanges sponsored by the foundations, especially those between the United States and Europe, had been shut down during World War II. The scarcity of hard currency in many countries at the war's end made it difficult for foreign governments to resume cultural activities of any kind. One conspicuous exception was the Soviet Union which, despite the devastation to its economy, began to set up exchange programs and "friendship societies" with its satellites in Eastern Europe, inviting students to study in Soviet universities where they might learn the finer points of Marxism and Stalinism.[42] This was a development that did not go unnoticed by American policymakers.

The conditions were therefore favorable for a postwar exchange program conducted by the American government. But the inspiration for such a venture came from a man whose passion for international and multicultural education coincided with his appreciation of how to seize the political moment. Before his election first to Congress and then to the Senate in 1944, J. William Fulbright had spent most of his life in the academic world. His faith in the value of educational exchange was kindled by his own experience as a Rhodes scholar at Oxford, where he studied for three years, followed by an additional year on the Continent. Later, he became a law professor and president of the University of Arkansas. During his time in Europe, Fulbright saw the way that myths, stereotypes, and sheer ignorance could lead to an international conflagration. He concluded that conflicts between nations could be diminished and managed more effectively if politicians and citizens had greater knowledge of cultures and societies different from their own. This belief became the underlying rationale for the exchange program he proposed to Congress in September 1945— a program that bore his imprint and his name, and for which he served as the moral and intellectual custodian from its passage in August 1946 until the end of his life.

Officially, the program's purposes were entirely educational. The language of the original and subsequent legislation emphasized the "promotion of international good will through the exchange of students in the fields of education, culture, and science." By such means, the exchanges might "increase mutual understanding between the people of the United States and the people of other countries." Fulbright insisted throughout his career that none of these objectives would be "quickly realized" or could be "measurable in immediate tangible returns." The exchanges, he argued, had nothing to do with political persuasion, propaganda, or image building. Fulbright specifically rejected any suggestion that they might be seen as "weapons or instruments with which to do combat." Instead, his program would be devoted solely to the "cultivation of ideas," and to a long-range, never-ending effort to "acquaint Americans with the world as it is and to acquaint students and scholars from many lands with America as it is." If one raised the question of national interest, Fulbright had an answer: Americans would themselves be enriched by their exposure to other cultures, other political systems, and other social and economic arrangements.[43]

Yet despite its lofty rhetoric, the Fulbright program was not immune to the pressures of diplomacy. The fact that the exchanges were sponsored by Washington, and that formal agreements with foreign ministries had to be negotiated by the State Department, guaranteed a high degree of government control. This in turn enhanced the possibility that the program's administrators might pursue a different agenda from the one the senator envisioned.

The structure of the Fulbright program, for example, was entangled from the beginning in the tentacles of the State Department—a circumstance inconsistent with the idea that cultural and educational exchanges should operate free from governmental intrusions. To shield the exchanges from political influences, both at home and abroad, the program's founders had hoped to rely on private agencies, along with a semiautonomous administrative board. These entities were to draw heavily on the expertise of college faculties so that the program might seem more an instrument of the universities than of the American government. Grants were to be awarded exclusively on the basis of academic merit, and the mission of promoting an international interchange of students and scholars was not to be compromised.

A Board of Foreign Scholarships, a group of distinguished professional educators appointed by the president, was set up to supervise the program and protect its independence. The Institute of International Education was given the task of evaluating the credentials of American and foreign graduate students, while a Council for the International Exchange of Scholars screened the applications of American university professors. Binational commissions, composed of American and foreign academics and businesspeople, were also created in most of the countries where Fulbright agreements had been signed. The commissions were to help select the students who would go to the United States, provide final approval for American Fulbright scholars nominated by Washington, and take care of housing and university affiliations for the U.S. grantees once they arrived overseas.[44]

These institutions were supposed to insulate the Fulbright program from outside interference. But their ability to act as a buffer was circumscribed by their dependence on the U.S. Congress for funding and the State Department for personnel. The members of the Board of Foreign Scholarships were, after all, political appointees whose views and values normally coincided with those of the president who chose them. Meanwhile, most of the board's staff work and the actual administration of the exchanges were handled by State Department employees. Overseas, the binational commissions were usually chaired by American foreign service officers, and the American representatives on the commissions were picked by the U.S. ambassadors. The involvement of the American embassies in the decisions of the commissions, combined with the fact that Washington at the outset supplied the bulk of the money for the exchanges, ensured that the program's activities abroad would reflect America's priorities and interests.[45]

Those priorities were demonstrated most clearly by the emphasis on Western Europe in the late 1940s and 1950s. Although the State Department concluded its first Fulbright agreement with China in 1947, followed shortly by contracts with Burma and the Philippines, exchanges with Europe dominated the program from its inception. Belgium, England, France, Greece, Italy, Luxembourg, the Netherlands, and Norway all had programs in place or about to begin by the end of the 1940s. Exchanges expanded in the 1950s to include Austria, Denmark, Finland, Spain, Sweden, and West Germany. Notwithstanding the global ambitions of the program, the majority of American grantees during the 1950s elected to go to Europe, while more Fulbright students and scholars came to the United States from Europe (especially from Britain, France, and West Germany) than from any other part of the world.[46] These trends were a reflection of Western Europe's political and economic importance to American policymakers, so much so that the Fulbright program became a sort of cultural Marshall Plan helping to revive and defend the intellectual vitality of America's closest allies.

The relationship of the Fulbright program to the Cold War in Europe was underscored in 1948 when Congress provided a more comprehensive framework for America's cultural diplomacy. Throughout 1946 and 1947, senators and representatives traveled to Europe to assess the state of America's postwar reputation. They came back appalled by how little Europeans knew about the United States, how much the "average person" saw America "primarily through the eyes of Hollywood," how readily people accepted Communist propaganda, how widespread were the misconceptions and prejudices even of intellectuals and government leaders when they discussed American culture and social life. Disturbed by the general ignorance of the Europeans and afraid that the United States was losing the loyalties of its friends because of its ineffective response to the lies of the Communists, the returning senators and representatives were convinced that America had to counter the Soviets' ideological offensive by mounting a more purposeful campaign to improve America's image in Europe.[47]

This resolve led to the passage in January 1948 of the Smith-Mundt Act, a sweeping law that authorized the government for the first time in the postwar era to use all its educational, information, and propaganda resources in the cultural and psychological confrontation with the Soviet Union. Under its provisions, the United States would employ magazines, films, embassy libraries, government-sponsored lectures, and the Voice of America to combat Communist misrepresentations and distortions, and engage in a public relations effort to gain foreign support for America's foreign policy. The State Department now set out to communicate the "true story" of America's ideals and motives and, more specifically, to "sell" the United States to the Europeans.[48]

In this undertaking, even the Fulbright program became a reluctant participant. Although it remained a reciprocal arrangement between the United States and other countries, whereby students, teachers, and researchers were supposed to move back and forth expanding their awareness of how different people lived and thought, the program was also regarded by Congress and the State Department as a means of increasing worldwide appreciation for America's values and institutions. Presumably, foreigners would learn about the history and culture of the United States by studying in American universities, while American students and professors could exemplify to their overseas hosts the richness of America's traditions and the nobility of her ideals.

Fulbright fellows were not oblivious to the ways in which the program might be used to serve American needs. An Italian student suspected that despite the emphasis on joint planning between countries and the sharing of insights among people from different cultures, the exchanges were mostly designed to teach foreigners like himself about the "superiority of American-style democracy." Similarly, an American grantee worried that he and his cohorts would be expected "simply to [publicize] the scholarly, cultural and scientific achievements of the U.S. to those less fortunate than ourselves."[49]

These fears were exaggerated but not entirely unwarranted. From its earliest years, the Fulbright program was involved in more than student exchanges. American professors were sent to lecture in European universities on the history, politics, and literature of the United States. By the 1950s, a growing number of grants were given to American and foreign physicians, engineers, specialists in agriculture and marketing, civil servants, public health officials, social welfare workers, librarians, artists, and journalists. The purpose of these grants, as well as the more conventional academic awards, was to promote America's interests among the political, economic, and intellectual elites in Europe and elsewhere. Senator Fulbright himself later conceded that his was "not a general education program for all needy people but a program designed to influence political matters through the intelligent leadership of the important countries." Like the exchanges conducted under the Marshall Plan and with West Germany in the late 1940s and early 1950s, the Fulbright program tried to identify potential opinion molders and policymakers overseas whose "minds might be shaped at U.S. universities" (in the words of one British observer) before they went home to take up important positions in government, business, or the media.[50]

The aims of the Fulbright program, and of America's other cultural activities, were further clarified and enlarged in 1961 with the passage of the Fulbright-Hays Act.[51] But the conflicts between the goals of mutual understanding and the requirements of American foreign policy persisted. If anything, as the pressures of the Cold War increased in the early 1950s, America's cultural programs became more one-sided, more deliberately propagandistic, and more intimately linked to the defense of the nation's security. At this juncture, education gave way to exhortation, and American culture (despite Senator Fulbright's admonishments) became merely another weapon in the crusade against Communism.

THREE

Truth, Propaganda, and Cultural Combat

The Contest with the Soviet Union

Although the Cold War lasted for over half a century, no period seemed more perilous than the years 1947 to 1953. In 1947 and 1948, the Soviet Union consolidated its control over Eastern Europe. In 1949, after twenty years of civil war, the Communists triumphed in China. In the same year, the Soviet Union successfully exploded its first atom bomb, ending America's monopoly on nuclear weapons. In June 1950, war broke out in Korea, continuing for three years and costing fifty-five thousand American lives.

For its part, the United States set out in 1947 to block Soviet ambitions in Europe, particularly by strengthening the economies and military defenses of Western Europe. This policy was implemented over the next two years through the Marshall Plan, the Truman Doctrine, and the creation of the North Atlantic Treaty Organization. In 1949 and 1950, the Truman administration decided not only to commit American troops to Korea, but to accelerate the arms race through the construction of a hydrogen bomb.

64

These were also the years in which the cultural war between the United States and the Soviet Union was waged with the greatest ferocity, each side seeking to win over the uncommitted. In this effort, the Soviets were initially more adept, or at least more theatrical, than the Americans. Exploiting the worldwide fear of nuclear incineration, Moscow embarked on a highly publicized "peace" crusade, complete with international conferences, global petitions calling on all governments to renounce the use of atomic weapons, and the awarding of "Stalin prizes" to politicians, intellectuals, and clergymen who advanced the cause of disarmament. The centerpiece of the Communist campaign was the Stockholm peace appeal, designed especially to attract those in Western Europe who dreaded the possibility of another war on their continent and who opposed the American-inspired formation of NATO. In France alone, the Communists gathered 15 million signatures for the Stockholm appeal in the early 1950s.[1] More generally, the Soviet Union expanded its exchange programs, organized lecture series, issued books and pamphlets, utilized films and radio broadcasts, all in an attempt to gain the active or tacit support of artists, writers, professors, students, entertainers, labor leaders, and ordinary citizens throughout Western Europe.

The Soviet propaganda offensive bolstered the conviction of American policymakers that the Cold War was as much about ideas as about tanks and aircraft carriers. In April 1950, addressing the American Society of Newspaper Editors, President Truman described the Cold War as a "struggle, above all else, for the minds of men." At the moment, Truman warned, the Communists were winning the battle for those minds by subjecting the United States to a "constant stream of slander and vilification." But the American people would eventually prevail if they made themselves "heard round the world in a great campaign of truth."[2]

As carried out, the campaign of truth involved a barrage of radio broadcasts over the Voice of America to Eastern Europe and a torrent of books, magazines, press releases, documentary films and newsreels, posters, and handbills meant for audiences in Western Europe. The principal American objectives were to convince the Eastern Europeans to resist whenever possible their Soviet rulers, and to make Western Europeans feel a greater sense of solidarity with the people and policies of the United States. Yet the campaign was often as strident in its anti-Communism as were the anti-American polemics of the Soviets.[3] Credibility, honored in the abstract, usually yielded in practice to high-pressure salesmanship.

With American soldiers protecting Western Europe and dying in Korea, the ideal of international understanding and mutual enlightenment receded before the demands of national security and unilateral indoctrination. Thus in 1951, the Board of Foreign Scholarships reformulated the purposes of the Fulbright program, explicitly delineating the program's obligations in the Cold War. Now the exchanges were to make clear to foreign grantees America's "moral, spiritual and material strength"; emphasize the need for a common defense of the free world; and support the diplomatic goals of the United States. In keeping with these aims, the BFS criticized some of the binational commissions for focusing too heavily on the needs of their own countries rather than taking into account America's concerns, a complaint that revealed how much the members of the BFS regarded the commissions as overseas representatives of the U.S. government, not as autonomous bodies. As if to underline their true role, the BFS urged the commissions and other cooperating American agencies to concentrate on the "achievement of immediate and short-range results," and specifically to develop their plans and select their grantees "in terms of the needs and objectives of United States policy in the current world crisis."[4]

In effect, the BFS had converted the Fulbright program—for the time being—into a preeminently political instrument. The willingness of the BFS to violate the program's original intentions was an understandable and probably unavoidable reaction to the national anxiety about the survival of democracy in an increasingly totalitarian world. Nonetheless, the metamorphosis of the Fulbright program reflected the extent to which American culture as a whole had become thoroughly enmeshed in the Cold War.

THE CONGRESS FOR CULTURAL FREEDOM

For many Western Europeans, the Soviet "peace" conferences and petition drives, and America's "campaign of truth," were equally unwelcome. Having barely survived the fascist dogmas of the 1930s, Europeans in the postwar years were terrified by the prospect of a new ideological crusade, this time pitting the world's two nuclear titans against each other. But just as in the 1930s, there seemed little that any bystander could do to halt or avoid being swept up in the clash of slogans and the buildup of armaments.

Members of the intelligentsia were especially sensitive to Europe's postwar impotence, not least because they had once benefited from Europe's prewar stature and strength. Images of faded power and waning creativity—a recognition of their own as well as Europe's decline—were pervasive in the rhetoric of the intellectuals. "From the sixteenth century onward," Bertrand Russell recalled in 1951, "Europe . . . dominated the world, from a cultural no less than a military point of view. Now that domination is lost; the inheritance is divided between Russia and America." At the beginning of the twentieth century, the Swiss philosopher Denis de Rougemont similarly remembered, "Europe still reigned over our planet. . . . Today it stands dethroned by history in favour of two non-European colossi." The British novelist Malcolm Bradbury, looking back in 1980 on the mood of the early 1950s, attributed Europe's (or more specifically Britain's) sorrows to an agent more celestial than fate or history: "It appeared . . . that God, whom in the wartime years one had taken to be Anglophile, bourgeois and anti-Fascist, was dividing His favours unkindly, and granting the universe to the two new Superpowers, who would fight for the coming world between them." Whatever the cause of Europe's misfortune, it seemed clear to Wyndham Lewis, commenting in 1948 on the British fall from grace, that the United States and the Soviet Union would henceforth "exercise almost complete control over our national life."[5] According to these and many other writers, Europe was now a trapped and helpless pawn, no longer in charge of its own destiny or able to prevent another war on its soil.

In the laments of the intellectuals, one could detect a large measure of self-pity and a pervasive sense of victimization. But there was also a feeling of anger at being pressured by both Moscow and Washington to choose sides. A significant number of Western Europeans, perceiving no moral or political distinctions between the Soviets and the Americans, did not want to marry either suitor. They hoped instead to remain neutral, free from the influence and the threats of the superpowers.[6] The urge to withhold their allegiance was motivated not by indecision but by a yearning for independence, a desire for the power and autonomy that Europe had enjoyed before the United States and the Soviet Union partitioned the Continent.

Neutralist sentiment was particularly strong in France during the late 1940s and 1950s. Some of this was fantasy, as if the French could unilaterally withdraw from the Cold War and declare a separate peace for themselves. The influential newspaper *Le Monde* continually praised the merits of nonalignment between the East and West, calling on the French government to pull back from NATO, refuse Washington's demands for a pro-American anti-Communist foreign policy, and negotiate agreements with the Kremlin that served the interests both of France and of Europe. These ideas constituted what many French intellectuals called a "third way"—a means of maintaining a diplomatic balance and acting as a mediator between the United States and the Soviet Union, and of creating a mixed economy at home that would be different from the models of American capitalism or Soviet Communism. Some intellectuals and politicians dreamed as well of a united Europe, subservient neither to America nor to Russia, a Europe capable of exerting its own authority in global matters.[7]

Such visions were not unique to the intellectual or political elites. Polls throughout the 1950s showed that a majority of the French people hungered for a strategy of neutrality and disengagement—a reservoir of popular support that enabled Charles de Gaulle to pursue his own independent foreign policy in the 1960s. But during the early Cold War years, there was really no diplomatic ground midway between the Atlantic and the Urals for France to occupy. Nevertheless, the French—whether on the Left or the Right—wanted to distance themselves from both superpowers so they could reclaim, if only symbolically, their cherished notion of France's unique cultural identity and special role in world affairs.[8]

It was the intelligentsia of Western Europe, more than any other group, whose refusal to distinguish between the United States and the Soviet Union most mystified and exasperated American policymakers. Edward Barrett, the assistant secretary of state for public affairs who was in charge of the campaign of truth, acknowledged Washington's bewilderment: "We are stunned to find ourselves . . . persistently criticized by the intellectual elite of other nations. We are baffled when we find affluent, well-educated non-Communists in France or Sweden . . . groping publicly for a middle course." U.S. officials felt that, of all people, Europe's intellectuals should realize how much their own survival was at stake in the conflict between freedom and totalitarianism, between the American reverence for civil liberties and the Stalinist repression of dissent. Instead, as Barrett complained, the Europeans focused on America's materialism and its lack of high culture, its "movie queens" and "gangsters" rather than its "universities, libraries, museums, and symphony orchestras."[9]

Intellectuals in Western Europe were obviously misinformed (so the Americans thought) but, unlike writers in the United States, they were also influential—especially in France, where their ideas had shaped public policy and swayed popular opinion for over a century. Hence, the United States could lose the Cold War if it failed to explain its diplomacy to the European intellectuals or rectify their dismal assessments of its culture.

In this effort, the role of the American intellectual community was crucial. "We look in vain," sighed one French writer who sympathized with the United States, "for clarification of the larger issues in the European Press by American men of letters."[10] By the late 1940s, a number of prominent American intellectuals (Sidney Hook, Arthur Schlesinger, James Burnham, Irving Kristol, Reinhold Niebuhr) were eager to undertake just such a mission. Having flirted with Communist movements and ideas in the 1930s, they now urged Washington to make use of their experience and expertise, and their contacts with the European intelligentsia. They wanted the government to give them the resources to refute the propaganda of the Soviets, diminish the European passion for neutrality, and demonstrate America's commitment to political freedom and cultural excellence. Like the officers in the State Department and the members of the Fulbright Board of Foreign Scholarships, they too believed that the Cold War was as much a form of cultural combat as a political and military contest.

The U.S. government recognized the importance of the intellectual class, both at home and abroad. The Fulbright program, as well as the exchanges with West Germany and Western Europe under the auspices of the Marshall Plan, were all designed to improve America's image in the eyes of Europe's intellectual leaders. But exchange programs, by themselves, might be too indirect and too ineffective in counteracting the Communist "peace" campaign, or in mobilizing European writers who were friendly to the United States.

Indeed, there were intellectuals in Europe with whom Washington could work. These writers were sufficiently left wing that they could not be ignored by their fellow intellectuals, yet they rejected both Communism and neutralism. In France, for example, Raymond Aron dismissed as delusional the quest for a third way between the American and Soviet camps. Europeans had to choose, he argued, and "for an anti-Stalinist there is no escape from the acceptance of American leadership." If France wanted to reassert its political and cultural independence, it could do so "only within the framework of an Atlantic Community in which, inevitably, the United States must hold first rank." From Britain, Bertrand Russell insisted that Europe's freedom was "only capable of being maintained by cooperation with America."[11]

It was "Atlanticists" such as Aron and Russell—writers who were not uncritical of America but who consented to its political, military, and economic protection in the early years of the Cold War—that the State Department began to cultivate.

Initially, the Communist-inspired "peace" conferences provided the most opportune occasions for the U.S. government to utilize the talents of its own intellectuals, and to form alliances with European writers who were inclined to defend American interests. In March 1949, a Cultural and Scientific Conference for World Peace met in New York at the Waldorf-Astoria hotel. The conference was officially organized by a committee of artists and writers who had campaigned for Henry Wallace in the presidential election of 1948. The sponsors and participants included some of the most illustrious names in American and European culture: Albert Einstein, Charlie Chaplin, Leonard Bernstein, Aaron Copland, Lillian Hellman, Norman Mailer, Arthur Miller, Thomas Mann, and Dmitri Shostakovich. The Communists, however, controlled the conference's agenda and its list of speakers. A small but vociferous group of anti-Stalinist American writers and activists—Sidney Hook, Dwight Macdonald, Mary McCarthy, Robert Lowell, and Norman Thomas—tried to disrupt the meeting, issued press releases describing themselves as "Americans for Intellectual Freedom," and generally denounced the entire affair as a Communist charade. The State Department offered encouragement (though with more discretion than the Communists displayed), persuading Norman Cousins, the editor of the *Saturday Review of Literature*, to deliver a speech at the conference attacking totalitarianism.

A month later, the Communists staged a Congress of World Partisans of Peace in Paris. Sidney Hook, always present to protest such gatherings, helped arrange an alternative rally called the International Day Against Dictatorship and War, an event supported surreptitiously by the State Department and the American embassy in Paris. Whether or not these ad hoc interventions impressed the larger intellectual community in New York or Paris, they convinced anti-Stalinists on both sides of the Atlantic as well as key members of the American government that a more permanent organization of writers was required to challenge the Communists' command of the ideological battlefield.[12]

Thus in June 1950, with bulletins from Korea swirling through their ranks, 118 intellectuals from twenty countries convened in Berlin—the symbolic capital of the Cold War—to launch the Congress for Cultural Freedom. The overwhelming majority came from the United States and Western Europe. Their names and reputations were as glittering as any of those the Communists had attracted to their conclaves. Sidney Hook, Arthur Schlesinger, James T. Farrell, and James Burnham represented America. From Britain came the historian Hugh Trevor-Roper and the philosopher A. J. Ayer; from Italy, the novelist Ignazio Silone; from France, the novelist Jules Romains; from Hungary, the novelist, political theorist, and long-time anti-Communist Arthur Koestler; from Switzerland, Denis de Rougemont; from Austria, the historian Franz Borkenau; and from Germany, Ernst Reuter, the mayor of West Berlin. Many equally prominent personages sent messages and statements endorsing or agreeing to act as sponsors of the congress: Eleanor Roosevelt, Reinhold Niebuhr, John Dos Passos, Upton Sinclair, Ralph Bunche, Walter Reuther, Raymond Aron, and André Gide. Five of the West's best-known philosophers—John Dewey, Bertrand Russell, Karl Jaspers, Benedetto Croce, and Jacques Maritain—served as honorary presidents.

Most of the congress's participants and supporters had personally witnessed, suffered from, and fought against twentieth-century totalitarianism in both its fascist and Stalinist incarnations. Some were refugees from Nazi Germany (Koestler, Borkenau) or Mussolini's Italy (Silone), and had been political prisoners in Spain during the Spanish civil war (Koestler, Silone) or had joined the Free French movement after the German conquest of Paris (Aron, Romains). Many were former Communists and disenchanted Marxists, now fervently hostile to the Soviet Union (Hook, Burnham, Farrell, Koestler, Silone, Borkenau, Reuter). But almost all regarded themselves as still somewhere on the Left, committed either to a diluted version of democratic socialism or to the liberal welfare state. As left-wing anti-Communists, they assumed they had the appropriate credentials to check the spread of neutralism among workers, politicians, and other intellectuals in Europe.[13] They hoped to translate their cultural prestige into a political organization as effective in its opposition to the Soviet Union as were the Communist "peace" conferences in criticizing NATO and the foreign policy of the United States.

The Congress for Cultural Freedom later became infamous for having been one of the numerous cultural enterprises secretly subsidized by the Central Intelligence Agency during the height of the Cold War. This disclosure, appearing first in the *New York Times* in 1966 and then in *Ramparts* magazine in 1967, ignited a scandal among intellectuals both in Europe and the United States, their indignation further fueled by the U.S. government's war in Vietnam. But in the 1950s, such an alliance did not seem so outrageous or incomprehensible. On the contrary, the congress intellectuals saw themselves as indispensable in the struggle against Communism, a perception of their importance shared by the CIA. The intellectuals and the spies, after all, were on the same side; each was an "asset" for the other.

Three people were most responsible for the congenial relationship between the congress and the CIA. Melvin Lasky—a veteran anti-Stalinist and editor of *Der Monat*, the cultural journal sponsored by the U.S. military government in Berlin—organized and persuaded the CIA to underwrite the first meeting of the congress. Eventually, Lasky became an editor of *Encounter*, the congress's magazine in Britain. In this capacity, he maintained his clandestine connections with the CIA, perhaps not as an agent but certainly as a conduit for CIA money and advice.

Michael Josselson, the congress's executive director, had engaged in psychological warfare with the Office of Strategic Services (the predecessor of the CIA) during World War II, and reemerged as a State Department foreign service officer stationed in Berlin. By 1950, when the congress was inaugurated, Josselson had already joined the CIA, though he functioned less as an undercover operative than as a dedicated anti-Communist apparatchik.[14]

Lasky and Josselson recognized that their fledgling organization needed a substantial and dependable endowment, which they did not think they could get from the State Department (whose open patronage might be unsuitable for an "independent" and international association of intellectuals), or from the U.S. Congress (suspicious of left-wing activities in the age of McCarthyism), or from private sources (although the Ford Foundation contributed $7 million from 1957 through the early 1960s).[15] The CIA, happily, had few restraints on its coffers and no reservations about financing intellectuals, however dubious their political pasts.

The third member of the triumvirate, therefore, and the one who secured permanent CIA support for the congress, was Thomas Braden. An officer in the CIA's International Organizations Division, Braden had considerable experience navigating between government bureaucracies and the world of artists and intellectuals. After graduating from the wartime OSS, he had taught English at Dartmouth and served as executive secretary of the Museum of Modern Art before he entered the CIA. Braden felt comfortable with left-wing writers and ideas (in the 1980s, he assumed a new role as the designated "liberal" bickering with Robert Novak and Pat Buchanan on CNN's *Crossfire*).

Braden concluded (as he recalled in an unapologetic article in 1967) that since the Soviets were sponsoring conferences and subsidizing propaganda, so too should the United States—largely by creating overseas cultural organizations of its own, or "penetrating" and bankrolling those that already existed. Braden and his CIA colleagues realized that the best way to rebut the Soviets and win the allegiance of European intellectuals was not to employ flag-waving reactionaries but to use leftist intellectuals because, as self-proclaimed dissenters and free-thinkers, these were the most credible foes of Communism. They need not subscribe to "every aspect of official American policy" as long as they agreed on "cold-war fundamentals." The participants in the congress were exactly the type of intellectuals Braden and the CIA had in mind. Still, the CIA had to "disguise the extent of American inter-est" or Europe's intellectuals might balk at working with the congress, and its apparent independence would be jeopardized. Consequently, the true provenance of the funding was camouflaged, with money funneled through fake foundations whose only purpose was to give legitimacy to the CIA's cultural ventures.[16]

From the perspective of the 1950s, little appeared to be wrong with this arrangement. American and European scholars and intellectuals already received grants from the government-financed Fulbright pro-gram, much of the money aimed at increasing knowledge abroad about American history and literature and at generating support for American foreign policy. The difference, of course, was that the CIA's involvement with the congress was deliberately concealed, though some of the members suspected but chose not to inquire too closely about where the cash was coming from. Yet if everyone had known, how many would have rejected the CIA's assistance?

In truth, most of the intellectuals who were affiliated with the con-gress did not regard the CIA as a sinister influence in the world. Besides, their anti-Communist convictions originated long before Washington's secret agents began to spend money on the cultural Cold War. The CIA purchased neither the minds of the intellectuals nor their souls, though it ultimately caused them embarrassment in the 1960s once the identity of their benefactor was revealed. But during the 1950s, the American and European writers who belonged to the congress believed they were engaged in a project that was politically necessary, morally ennobling, and entirely theirs to superintend. They had no qualms and some sense of power when their ideas and activi-ties happened to coincide with the needs of the U.S. government.

So, having acquired an adequate war chest, the Congress for Cultural

Freedom kept busy throughout its first decade. It opened offices in thirty-five countries, though Lasky and Josselson concentrated their attention on France and Italy where Communist influence was the strongest. The congress published magazines, held innumerable conferences and seminars, exposed the persecution of writers in the Soviet Union and Eastern Europe, and tried to convince neutralist intellectuals that their true home was in the Atlantic Community.[17]

At least one of the congress's undertakings was spectacular. In May 1952, the congress sponsored a month-long festival in Paris for artists, musicians, novelists, and poets. The purpose of the festival was to demonstrate the vitality of Western European and American culture—a culture that was modernist but not decadent, as the Communists persistently charged. Orchestras and chamber-music groups from Vienna, Berlin, London, New York, and Boston (whose appearance was paid for by the CIA) performed one hundred symphonies, concertos, operas, and ballets. Some of the musical selections had political implications. These included works by Sergei Prokofiev and Dmitri Shostakovich currently banned in the Soviet Union, and by Virgil Thomson, Igor Stravinsky, and Arnold Schoenberg—composers who were either born in or had emigrated to the United States, where classical music now flourished. The festival also presented an exhibition of 150 modern paintings and sculptures, many of them from France, and a debate about twentieth-century literature featuring William Faulkner, Katherine Anne Porter, Allen Tate, James T. Farrell, W. H. Auden, and André Malraux—all writers whose political views the congress esteemed.[18]

The congress linked the defense of modernist culture with the politics of anti-Communism more explicitly in its magazines. The London-based *Encounter*, launched in 1953 with a subsidy from the CIA and edited initially by Irving Kristol and Stephen Spender with a brief assist from Dwight Macdonald, was the congress's most influential journal. Combining literary and social criticism with support for the Atlantic Alliance, *Encounter* welcomed articles by American, British, and Western European intellectuals, most of whom were associated with the congress. By 1958, it enjoyed a circulation of sixteen thousand—the largest audience for any monthly journal of opinion printed in the English language.[19]

The congress's other magazines in Europe followed *Encounter*'s formula, but had less success attracting readers. *Preuves*, published in Paris, where many intellectuals were still entranced by the Soviet Union, attained a circulation of only three thousand in the 1950s. Its regular contributors were familiar to devotees of the Congress: Bertrand Russell, Raymond Aron, Arthur Koestler, Franz Borkenau, Denis de Rougemont, Sidney Hook, Daniel Bell, and Leslie Fiedler. Its political positions—antineutralist, Atlanticist, pro-NATO, sympathetic with U.S. foreign policy but occasionally critical of America's domestic life, committed to documenting the iniquities of Stalinism—were predictable and, by the end of the decade, increasingly routine. In Italy, Ignazio Silone and Nicola Chiaromonte edited *Tempo Presente* with a similar roster of writers augmented by Soviet dissidents like Boris Pasternak and Andrei Sinyavsky. *Forum*, published in Vienna, had the most distinctive role, serving as a channel for aid to intellectuals and students fleeing from Hungary after their failed uprising against Soviet domination in 1956.[20]

Despite its magazines, festivals, and symposiums, the Congress for Cultural Freedom did not have as much impact in Europe as it desired. Its members often seemed too partisan, too predisposed to reflect the outlook of Washington rather than the concerns of an independent intelligentsia. By the 1960s, the congress was afflicted with ideological ennui. Searching for a mission and an identity after the memories of Stalin had begun to fade, the congress sought to rejuvenate itself by establishing ties with heretical intellectuals in Eastern Europe and the Soviet Union. The congress was particularly effective in Poland, finding publishers in the West for works prohibited by the Communist authorities, providing stipends for writers to travel abroad, and sending books and magazines to people who were cut off from the latest cultural trends.

Yet the congress's moment had passed. A new generation of Western Europeans was less interested in hearing about the perils of Communism than in protesting American imperialism. The demise of the congress was imminent even before its dependence on CIA funding was revealed, although the news was certainly lethal. The congress officially disbanded in 1967. Efforts to create a successor, financed by the Ford Foundation, foundered in the 1970s.[21]

Essentially, the Congress for Cultural Freedom was a creature of the Cold War. In its early years, it helped fashion a consensus among many American and Western European intellectuals about the need to combat Soviet propaganda. But when the political orthodoxies of the 1950s crumbled in the 1960s, when the congress's own intellectuals could not agree on issues like the Vietnam War (with Bertrand Russell, a former honorary president, now presiding over an international "tribunal" of writers and activists bent on convicting the United States of "war crimes"), the congress became obsolete. It had neither an incentive nor the imagination to adapt to a world that was no longer listening.

Modernism and McCarthyism

For those like Melvin Lasky and Michael Josselson who sought financial support in the 1950s for America's cultural activities abroad, the CIA had one distinct advantage: It could fund "controversial"—even "radical"—writers and artists without having to bother about security clearances or congressional approval. The CIA's latitude in cultural affairs was especially important in a era when loyalty oaths, investigations, and blacklists had become a regular feature of America's domestic political life. Indeed, there were occasions during the postwar years when the United States seemed a nation composed not of enlightened defenders of freedom but of dim-witted Babbitts who, like their Stalinist counterparts, were intolerant of any form of intellectual debate or artistic and literary experimentation.

It was ironic that McCarthyism should blossom in the United States at precisely the moment when the country was trying to present itself to the world as the home both of civil liberties and high culture. This paradox was additionally striking because America could legitimately argue that it had become, for the first time in its history, the focal point of modern painting and fiction, the place to which foreign artists and novelists now looked for inspiration, ideas, and techniques. Yet such a development, in the hands of conservative politicians, could be made to appear dangerous, subversive, "un-American." Between 1946 and the mid-1950s, these notions nearly paralyzed the government's cultural exchange programs in Europe and elsewhere.

The conservative hostility to modernism was best exemplified in the congressional attacks on abstract expressionism—America's most original contribution to Western art. The abstract expressionist movement arose in New York in the final years of the depression, partly as a revolt against the prevailing esthetic and political conventions of the 1930s. The "social" artists of the 1930s had been realistic and didactic, populist in their commitments and sensibilities, interested in traditional "American" as opposed to "European" themes, and concerned with pictorially dramatizing the issues of the depression in a manner that viewers could understand. The abstract expressionists, in contrast, were nonrepresentational, apolitical, and introspective; indifferent to the plight of the masses; inaccessible to the uninitiated; "international" in their orientation; and self-consciously avant-garde.[22] Though many of them had once participated in the left-wing movements of the depression years, their radicalism was now stylistic rather than ideological.

The abstract expressionists rejected the fashions of the 1930s in other ways. Where the realists had drawn sustenance from regional history and folklore, the expressionists turned away from what they considered the provincialism of the past in order to embrace the cosmopolitanism of the future. In this, they were influenced by the presence in America of Europe's émigrés—artists like Marc Chagall, Piet Mondrian, Marcel Duchamp, André Breton, Jacques Lipchitz, Joan Miró, Wassily Kandinsky, Lyonel Feininger, Salvador Dali, Max Ernst, Max Beckmann, Josef Albers, and Hans Hofmann, all of whom were central figures in the evolution of European modernism, and who acted as mentors and role models for the Americans. In addition, where the depression-era artists had been put to work by the WPA decorating public buildings, the abstract expressionists relied on the private art market, which was itself dominated by refugee art dealers and gallery owners who capitalized on America's postwar affluence, its fascination with anything new and innovative, and the tendency of the well-to-do to treat modern art primarily as an investment.[23]

By 1945, the penchant for social protest, in painting as well as in politics, had virtually disappeared, supplanted by domestic prosperity and an awareness that the locus of power had shifted to the United States. All the elements were in place for the triumph of abstract expressionism and with it, the emergence of America as the preeminent force in modern art. New York, not Paris, was now the epicenter of modernism. Jackson Pollock, Willem de Kooning, and Robert Motherwell—having learned from but no longer subservient to the European exiles—were ascending to the status of culture heroes. Their personalities were publicized in the media; their work was explicated and championed by critics like Clement Greenberg and Harold Rosenberg; museum directors scrambled to acquire their latest paintings; their role as leaders of a new generation of American artists was proclaimed by the cognoscenti and confirmed by the escalating prices of their paintings.[24]

Yet the importance of the abstract expressionists derived not just from their artistic skills or their success in the marketplace. To intellectuals in New York and some government officials in Washington, the expressionists demonstrated to Europeans (particularly to Parisians) that America had a sophisticated culture to match its economic and military might.

Moreover, the abstract expressionists could serve as an advertisement for American values in the Cold War. While Soviet artists, bowing to the dictates of the Kremlin, continued to employ the clichés of "socialist realism," America's modernists were iconoclastic and unfettered by ideology. They were free to "express" their individuality, their subconscious emotions and private visions, without having to answer to cultural commissars. They were "action" painters (as Harold Rosenberg insisted); their work was improvisational and spontaneous, like America itself. And to make the point unmistakably clear, modernism (so its defenders claimed) could flourish only in a society that was open, democratic, and capitalist, a society that believed in nonconformity and competition as catalysts to artistic and economic achievement. Thus, in the eyes of anti-Stalinists in the intelligentsia and liberals in the State Department, abstract expressionism should be welcomed as an essential ingredient in America's cultural diplomacy, another way of contrasting the vibrancy of life in the United States with the monotony of totalitarianism.[25]

This was not, however, a view shared by congressional conservatives, or by traditionalists in the art world whose influence had steadily declined. Although they were not eager to return to the agit-prop art of the 1930s, neither were they persuaded that abstract expressionism reflected typically "American" ideals. In a country populated by practical people who respected hard and serious work, where even the WPA demanded that its murals have a social or illustrative function, modern art seemed purposeless and self-indulgent, a series of pranks by eccentric painters who covered their canvasses with drips and blotches any schoolchild could duplicate. Worse, in their deliberate obscurity, their disdain for the tastes of the middle class, and their cultivation of elite intellectuals and wealthy collectors, the abstract expressionists were hardly representative of the democratic ethos.[26]

The most ardent critic of abstract expressionism was George Dondero, a Republican congressmen from Michigan. Throughout the late 1940s, Dondero led a crusade against modern art, fusing conservative rhetoric with moralistic denunciations in a style later perfected by Senator Jesse Helms. Far from accepting the idea that the modernists were of use to America in the Cold War, Dondero in his more hysterical moments accused them of participating, perhaps unconsciously, in a Communist conspiracy to undermine the nation's treasured norms and beliefs. At the very least, they were in his eyes too abstract (and hence unwilling to portray American life in a favorable, or even a comprehensible, light) and too contaminated by their past associations with Soviet front groups. Consequently, on both esthetic and political grounds, they should be barred from all government-financed cultural exchanges.[27]

It did not occur to Dondero and his allies that their arguments against abstract expressionism were identical to those of the Soviets, who also wanted an art the "people" could easily grasp, with recognizable and uplifting scenes that advanced the national myth. Yet for congressional right-wingers as well as Communist functionaries, the exemplary modern artist resembled Norman Rockwell, not Jackson Pollock.

During much of this period, the conservatives were able to block the government's efforts to show the work of modern American artists to audiences overseas. In 1947, the House Un-American Activities Committee charged that half the artists in a State Department exhibition of contemporary paintings circulating through Europe and Latin America had once sympathized with the Communist Party. The State Department promptly terminated the exhibition. As a token of its repentance, the Department promised not to spend any more of the taxpayers' money on avant-garde art, and to mount no exhibits without prior congressional certification that the artists were patriotic Americans. In the 1950s, the newly formed U.S. Information Agency (USIA) refused to send abroad the work of any artists with Communist or politically questionable backgrounds, especially those who had declined to testify before congressional committees investigating their past affiliations and beliefs—a policy that led to the cancellation of a worldwide exhibition of one hundred twentieth-century American paintings in 1956. At the same time, the State Department called off an international tour of Arturo Toscanini's NBC Symphony of the Air, succumbing to allegations that four of the orchestra's 101 members harbored pro-Communist attitudes.[28]

Many people who were concerned with cultural exchange realized that the conservatives' antipathy to modern art was injurious to America's reputation abroad. It undercut the government's efforts to convince foreigners that the United States was not a cultural backwater. In this instance, however, private institutions—particularly the Museum of Modern Art—functioned as surrogates for the State Department and USIA. MOMA promoted contemporary American painting and sculpture at a time when the government could not, and it did so without having to submit to political inquisitions or conceal its involvement, as did the CIA. Thus in 1953, MOMA purchased a pavilion at the Venice Biennial Exposition for a display of American art, the only nongovernmental patron at an event devoted to trumpeting the cultural accomplishments of all the participating countries. MOMA also provided funding for exhibitions of current American painting shown throughout Europe in 1956 and 1958.[29] MOMA's international activism enabled the United States to maintain its identity as the bellwether of modernism despite the objections of reactionary congressmen.

Abstract expressionists were not the only targets of conservative suspicion. In 1953, after the Republicans had regained the presidency and majority control of the Senate and House of Representatives, almost all the government's cultural and information programs came under political scrutiny. On this occasion, the job of detecting subversive influences in modern American culture fell to the most authoritative anti-Communist in the land: Joseph McCarthy, chair of the Senate Committee on Government Operations and master of his own Subcommittee on Investigations, a forum for whomever and whatever he wished to probe.

In February, McCarthy conducted hearings on the Voice of America, inquiring into the loyalties of its chief administrators and staff, and criticizing its broadcasts for being insufficiently zealous in attacking the Soviet Union. Thereafter, as Edward Barrett observed, the VOA's announcers competed with one another "to sound so stridently anti-Communist that the Senator couldn't charge them with 'softness.'"[30]

McCarthy seemed even more distrustful of American literature, as exemplified by the books on the shelves of U.S. embassy libraries. When the libraries were opened in the late 1930s and during World War II, they were meant to offer foreigners a balanced perspective on American life, a goal reaffirmed in the Smith-Mundt Act of 1948. No authors were to be excluded merely on the basis of their political affiliations. What mattered was how well the content of their books or articles increased the understanding of America's institutions and culture. Yet by the late 1940s, in reaction to the Cold War, the libraries were already becoming more propagandistic, with books and magazines chosen for their effectiveness in delivering a pro-American anti-Communist message.[31]

This growing orthodoxy did not satisfy McCarthy. Claiming that the libraries still possessed thirty thousand "Communist" books, he dispatched two aides—Roy Cohn and G. David Schine—to investigate. In April 1953, Cohn and Schine swept through the libraries in Paris, Bonn, Frankfurt, Munich, Vienna, Belgrade, Athens, Rome, and London. They managed to locate eighteen volumes written by people alleged to be Communist and seventy-eight by authors who had refused to cooperate with the House Un-American Activities Committee. Cohn and Schine seemed particularly disturbed to find works by notorious radicals like Mark Twain and Theodore Dreiser.[32] Not surprisingly, the European press ridiculed their "discoveries" and their expertise as literary critics. But their trip had intensified the pressure on the libraries and the Eisenhower administration. (Cohn and Schine resurfaced a year later as supporting players in the Army-McCarthy hearings—with Cohn, having failed to extricate Schine from the draft, trying next to intimidate the military into giving Schine a commission and an assignment to McCarthy's staff so that together they could all continue their search for Communists.)

The State Department was already cleansing its libraries of objectionable books. From February through April 1953, the Department issued a series of directives, one signed by Secretary of State John Foster Dulles, prohibiting the use of materials written by "controversial persons, Communists, fellow-travelers," witnesses who took the Fifth Amendment before congressional committees, and anyone else considered too left-wing or too critical of America's values and purposes.[33]

These edicts resulted in the removal of three hundred titles from the overseas libraries. In their frenzy, embassy officials burned eleven of the books, apparently oblivious to how much this act reminded Europeans of the Nazi bonfires twenty years before.

The banned authors included some predictable offenders like Henry Wallace, once vice president of the United States but too tolerant of Communists during his campaign for the presidency in 1948; Howard Fast, at the time the Communist Party's favorite novelist; W. E. B. DuBois, indicted by the Justice Department in 1951 for failing to register as an "agent" of the Soviet Union, though eventually acquitted; Lillian Hellman and Dashiell Hammett, both with long-time Communist connections who declined to name names before investigative bodies; and Norman Mailer and Arthur Miller, each a supporter of the Cutural and Scientific Conference for World Peace in 1949. Less explicable was the presence on the list of some of the leading American novelists, poets, historians, and philosophers of the twentieth century. Among these were John Dewey and Reinhold Niebuhr (notwithstanding their endorsements of the Congress for Cultural Freedom), Lewis Mumford, Charles Beard (whose ostensible sin was having exposed in 1913 the economic motivations of the Founding Fathers), Sherwood Anderson, John Dos Passos (now a conservative but whose depression-era trilogy, *U.S.A.*, presented a portrait of America so negative that it might give foreign readers the wrong impression), Erskine Caldwell, and Ernest Hemingway (the Nazis too had thought his novels dangerous and tossed them on the flames in 1933). Composers and architects were not spared, no matter how famous. George Gershwin (despite having died in 1937), Aaron Copland, Virgil Thomson, Leonard Bernstein (another compulsive signer of petitions and contributor to leftist organizations), and Frank Lloyd Wright were all blacklisted. Not everyone was a member of the cultural elite: Also forbidden were the collected works of Mickey Spillane.[34]

The draconian policies of the State Department resulted in damaging publicity around the world. By July 1953, prodded by Dulles and President Eisenhower, the State Department softened its position. It now allowed embassies to take into account the usefulness of a book in advancing the democratic cause, regardless of the author's political commitments. Unorthodox works, at least those "expressing honest differences of opinion," once more became acceptable; no longer would they be condemned as un-American. But in practice, the libraries continued to proscribe books by suspected Communists and uncooperative witnesses, and to prefer those that echoed the views of administration officials.[35]

Except for the McCarthyites, few people in or out of Washington believed that censorship, book burnings, and tirades against modern art were the best ways to wage the cultural Cold War. It should have been possible to defend freedom without resembling the totalitarian enemy. But if the government was not going to rely indefinitely on proxies like the CIA, the Ford Foundation, and the Museum of Modern Art to export American culture, it would need to invent a new agency—one with the resources and ability to convince Europeans and others that the United States was indeed distinguishable from the Soviet Union.

USIA IN THE 1950S

If 1953 was the year of McCarthy's assault on the embassy libraries and the Voice of America, it was also, paradoxically, the year that Stalin died (in March) and the war in Korea ended (in July). There were signs as well that the tactics employed by the campaign of truth were beginning to embarrass America's career diplomats. Increasingly, foreign service officers in the State Department and at posts overseas complained that America's cultural programs sounded too shrill, too evangelical, too single-minded in warning foreigners about the evils of Communism and the menace of the Soviet Union.[36] Per haps, they suggested, Washington needed to speak in a calmer, more confident voice, an approach that would be more effective with audi-ences abroad.

These criticisms arose in part because the United States was no longer competing solely with the Russians for the sympathies of listen-ers in Europe and elsewhere. By the 1950s, Britain, France, Italy, and West Germany were all promoting their own cultures, and doing so in ways that differed from the efforts of the American government. The United States (befitting a nation devoted to pragmatism and comfort-able with its political past, but still uncertain about its artistic or liter-ary accomplishments) tended to advertise its business triumphs, its labor-management cooperation, its technological supremacy, and its democratic heritage. The European countries—often ashamed of the behavior of their prewar governments, and suffering in the immediate postwar years from economic chaos and social dislocation—empha-sized their art, literature, language, and philosophy. Their primary objective was to retrieve their stature, not to defeat Communism.

This did not mean that their cultural programs had no political or economic implications. The British Council, for example, was set up as an autonomous agency to operate Britain's overseas libraries and cul-tural centers; organize film and art exhibitions; conduct academic exchanges; arrange tours for writers, scholars, musicians, and theater companies; and advance the teaching of English—a project that sig-nificantly accelerated the spread of British and American popular cul-ture throughout the world. But these endeavors also served the needs of the Foreign Office, which was trying to increase British exports and encourage foreign investments. Similarly, France extolled its language and literature in order to neutralize the political and linguistic influ-ence of the Anglo-Americans, boost its economy, and restore its inter-national prestige after the humiliation of having been occupied by the Germans. The Italians hoped that postwar tourists, rediscovering Italy's museums, might forget Mussolini. The West German govern-ment had an equally compelling reason for stressing music, philoso-phy, and literary events like the Frankfurt book fair. Bonn longed to remind everyone that Germany had given the world not only Nazism and genocide, but also Bach, Beethoven, Brahms, and Goethe.[37]

The desire to keep up with the Europeans and to adopt a more moderate tone in its public diplomacy led the Eisenhower administration to create the United States Information Agency in August 1953. Under its mandate from President Eisenhower, USIA was supposed to be factual and objective in its descriptions of life in the United States. Yet the agency was also expected to follow the guidelines of the State Department in explaining and interpreting the news, and in showing how America's values coincided with the aspirations of other people for political freedom and economic progress. The State Department retained control over educational exchanges like the Fulbright program and continued to sponsor overseas appearances by writers and performing artists. USIA was to administer the embassy libraries, cultural centers, and America Houses as well as supervise book translations, exhibits, and English-language courses. Theoretically, there was supposed to be a division of labor, with the State Department responsible for people and USIA responsible for things.[38] But whatever the bureaucratic distinctions, the cultural activities of USIA and those of the State Department were necessarily intertwined.

From its inception, USIA was a schizophrenic agency. It acted as a clearinghouse for culture as well as a ministry of information and propaganda. It was authorized both to tell the truth about the United States and to make foreigners more appreciative of America's domestic institutions and global ambitions. In setting up the agency, the Eisenhower administration reinforced and institutionalized the symbiotic relationship between American culture and American foreign policy, a relationship that was itself dependent on the Cold War.

Yet as the 1950s wore on, the rivalry between the Soviets and the Americans became less ideological, the issues less clear-cut. Nikita Khrushchev, the new Kremlin leader, officially repudiated Stalin's tactics in 1956, though this did not prevent him from dispatching the Red Army to suppress the Hungarian revolution in the same year. The West, unwilling to help Hungary, stopped talking about the liberation of Eastern Europe. Instead, both sides started talking to each other at summit conferences. The pleasantries of "peaceful coexistence" replaced the confrontational language of the late 1940s and early 1950s. Relentless propaganda was no longer in fashion; the Cold War would now be fought with greater subtlety.

Under these new ground rules, demonstrations of cultural superiority became increasingly important. Moscow set out to prove that the Communist countries were more civilized and more advanced than a capitalist America concerned only with piling up profits and material possessions. Russian tanks might be rumbling through the streets of

Budapest, but Russian ballet companies, symphony orchestras, and circuses traveled through the cities of Western Europe. International sporting events could show which social system was ahead at any given moment, with the Olympics as the principal venue for keeping score. But even the accumulation of gold medals won by Soviet and Eastern European athletes could not match the achievements of Communist science, as dramatized by the announcement in 1957 that the Russians had launched the first unmanned satellite into space. In the race that mattered most to the Americans and the Russians, the United States was clearly behind.

The State Department and USIA responded with their own cultural extravaganzas. During the late 1950s and early 1960s, they flooded Europe with concerts by orchestras from Boston, New York, and Cleveland, and by soloists like Isaac Stern, Rudolf Serkin, and Marian Anderson. The government also offered examples of American dance from the New York City Ballet; plays by Eugene O'Neill, Thornton Wilder, and Tennessee Williams; art exhibitions (though not of the disagreeable abstract expressionists); photographic collections like Edward Steichen's *Family of Man,* a multicultural homage to the common experiences of people throughout the world; tours of baseball teams; and performances of Broadway musicals, including *My Fair Lady*. Presumably, Europeans would be persuaded at last that America was as rich in culture as it was in consumer goods.[39]

Initially, jazz had been excluded from the government's repertoire despite its distinctively American roots, perhaps because it lacked the cachet of European classical music. After 1955, however, the State Department sent Benny Goodman, Louis Armstrong, Dizzy Gillespie, Dave Brubeck, and other jazz musicians to Europe for a series of extraordinarily successful concerts. The public relations value of jazz and later of rock and roll was amplified by Willis Conover's *Music U.S.A.,* the Voice of America's most popular program with an estimated 30 million listeners, many of them in Eastern Europe and the Soviet Union. Jazz was also featured on RIAS (the army's Radio in the American Sector, located since 1946 in West Berlin, with its broadcasts beamed primarily to East Germany), and on Radio Free Europe (inaugurated in Munich in 1950, staffed largely by émigrés from and directed at audiences in Eastern Europe, and secretly funded by the CIA).

The impact of these stations was immense, one Austrian recalled, not because of their politics but because of their music. Without the money to buy records, he and his friends depended on American-sponsored radio for their "daily fix" of jazz and rock and roll—the cultural exports that, more than any others, made the United States seem unique and appealing. The Communist regimes in Eastern Europe did not have "the least inkling of what was really going on," particularly with their young people. If they had known, "they would have jammed the music, not the news."[40]

However subversive jazz or rock and roll might be, contacts between people on either side of the Iron Curtain were virtually nonexistent. But in a season of dialogue, this situation too began to change. In 1958, for the first time since the dawn of the Cold War, the United States and the Soviet Union entered into a government-sanctioned cultural relationship, agreeing to exchange books, magazines, and films; radio and television programs; students and professors; scientists and intellectuals; performing artists; and delegations of farmers and industrialists. Such exchanges offered the Americans access, albeit limited, to the Soviet elite as well as to ordinary citizens.[41]

The exchange also provided an occasion for USIA to stage one of the most heavily publicized examples of political theater in the 1950s. As part of the agreement, the Soviets mounted a cultural exhibition in New York in 1959. USIA designed a similar exhibit in Moscow, complete with displays of American painting and photography, fashion shows, an IBM computer, a geodesic dome, and free samples of Pepsi-Cola. The basic intent of the U.S. effort was to show how well the average American family lived. This was accomplished by erecting a model of what USIA called a "typical" American home, a suburban-style ranch house filled with the artifacts of a consumer society, including the latest kitchen appliances and a color television set. It was in this "kitchen" that Richard Nixon "debated" Nikita Khrushchev.[42] News photos of their encounter were distributed throughout the world. Momentarily, the Cold War seemed to have dissolved into a quarrel about which country produced better washing machines.

Three million Russians eventually visited the exhibit. The administrators of USIA had good reason to feel triumphant. Yet at the close of the decade, few Americans were even aware that the agency existed. The specialists in public diplomacy had not yet achieved, in their own country, a public identity.

EDWARD R. MURROW AND JFK

Despite the impact of the VOA's music broadcasts and USIA's Moscow exhibition, the United States had been primarily interested since 1945 in influencing the leaders of Western Europe. The exchanges organized by the Fulbright program and the Marshall Plan, the activities of the America Houses and the Congress for Cultural Freedom, the libraries and book translations, the art exhibits and lecture tours, the appearances of symphony orchestras and ballet troupes, were all designed to create sympathetic constituencies among the European elite. Washington's principal target was not the young or the masses, but people in the chancelleries, the media, the business and professional communities, and the academic world. The ideal recipient of a Fulbright fellowship or a USIA travel grant was a future president or prime minister—someone like Margaret Thatcher, Helmut Schmidt, Willi Brandt, or Valéry Giscard d'Estaing, all of whom came to the United States under the U.S. government's auspices in the 1950s and early 1960s.

Yet popular opinion could not be ignored, particularly when foreigners were critical of America's image or unimpressed by American accomplishments. Two polls conducted by USIA in 1960 revealed that for all of Washington's information and cultural efforts over the previous fifteen years, neutralist sentiment was still high in Western Europe. If anything, America's prestige seemed to be declining. Eighty-one percent of the respondents to the polls in Britain, 74 percent in France, and 53 percent in West Germany thought that the Soviet Union's advantage in the space race signaled the end of America's postwar supremacy in science and technology. Many also believed that the Soviets were catching up economically with the United States.[43]

The results of these polls indicated, at the least, that America's cultural diplomacy had been ineffective. One problem was that both the State Department and USIA too often cultivated those Europeans who already agreed with America's values and policies, rather than seeking out people who were considered "anti-American" or were simply unknown to the press and cultural attachés. Another problem, endemic to any bureaucracy, was the reluctance of officials in the field to question the wisdom of their superiors in the home office. Hence, the embassies tended to send reports back to Washington proclaiming that every concert, every speaker, and every exchange program had been a smashing success, a testimonial to the brilliance of whatever initiative was presently in vogue.

But USIA confronted a special problem at home. Throughout the 1950s, neither Eisenhower nor Dulles regarded USIA as an pivotal agency in the conduct of foreign policy. USIA's directors did not have the sort of close personal relationship with Eisenhower that George

Creel had once enjoyed with Woodrow Wilson.[44] The indifference of the president and the secretary of state contributed to USIA's invisibility and sense of drift.

John F. Kennedy was more concerned with international attitudes than Eisenhower had been, and he campaigned in 1960 partly on the issue of America's deteriorating image overseas. Thus, he saw some value in USIA's polls and in the potential of the agency to affect foreign perceptions of the United States. Kennedy seemed ready to make better use of USIA if he could find someone sufficiently prominent to serve as its director. The person he found was Edward R. Murrow.

Next to Adlai Stevenson (who agreed to be U.S. ambassador to the United Nations), Murrow was the new administration's most famous appointee. At CBS, he had virtually invented broadcast journalism. As the archetype of the daring and improvisational foreign correspondent, Murrow brought an intimacy and an urgency to his reports on the Czechoslovak crisis in 1938, the German air attacks on British cities in 1940, and the gigantic battles of World War II. After the war, Murrow became the most authoritative voice in radio and television news. He embellished his reputation with a series of provocative documentaries on *See It Now* and *CBS Reports,* particularly his half-hour dissection of Joseph McCarthy in 1954 and his exposé of migrant labor camps in *Harvest of Shame* in 1960.

Nevertheless, by the close of the 1950s, Murrow no longer felt appreciated at CBS. His somber style, perfectly suited to the mood of World War II and the early Cold War years, now seemed out of place, a bit too oppressive for an audience that was weary of crises and hungry for comic relief. Murrow had always appeared ill at ease on camera. When he interviewed celebrities on *Person to Person,* his strained attempts at informality were painful to watch, his smile barely distinguishable from a grimace. At the end of his broadcasts, when he told his viewers "good night, and good luck," he sounded as if he thought they would need some luck just to get through the night. Meanwhile, over at NBC, a new star had emerged who was very different from Murrow. David Brinkley never took anything too seriously, least of all politics. Brinkley seemed to relish the world's absurdities, so much so that he sometimes had trouble delivering the news without dissolving into laughter. By the beginning of the 1960s, contemporary audiences evidently preferred Brinkley, with his wry detachment, rather than the legendary Murrow, who looked increasingly like a man haunted by demons.

Murrow's long career at CBS might be ending, but his credibility and stature as a journalist remained unchallenged. These were precisely the attributes that Kennedy hoped to transfer to USIA. In addition, Murrow brought glamour to an agency that was unaccustomed to recognition or respect.[45] Throughout his three-year tenure, from 1961 through 1963, Murrow personified USIA; he was the symbol with whom everyone could identify. Agency personnel no longer had to explain what they did; it was enough to say "I work for Ed Murrow."

In return, Kennedy offered Murrow access to power, a seat at the table where decisions were made, a role in the formulation of policy that past USIA directors never had. As head of an agency that was supposed to know what foreigners were thinking, Murrow could become Kennedy's chief adviser on the psychological and propagandistic consequences of America's diplomatic strategies. He would therefore be an active participant in meetings of the National Security Council, providing his expertise where it counted. Moreover, Murrow's principal deputies had their own links to the White House. Thomas Sorensen, a veteran of USIA, was the brother of Ted Sorensen, Kennedy's leading speech writer. Donald Wilson, a former correspondent for *Life* and *Time* magazines, had worked on Kennedy's 1960 presidential campaign and was friendly with Robert Kennedy. So USIA no longer seemed a peripheral agency, merely explaining American foreign policy to the world. Now it was at (or near) the center of government, with Murrow a valued member of Kennedy's team.[46]

These illusions did not last long. In April 1961, three months after his inauguration, Kennedy approved the CIA's plan to instigate a rebellion against Fidel Castro's regime in Cuba by landing a band of anti-Communist guerrillas at the Bay of Pigs. Kennedy did so without consulting Murrow or USIA even though the invasion's success depended on the willingness of the Cuban people to join the guerrillas in overthrowing Castro. Before he launched the operation, the president presumably needed to know how the majority of Cubans felt about their government, as well as how foreigners might react to the invasion—information USIA could well have provided.[47] But no one asked for the agency's input, and the anticipated uprising never occurred.

This was not the only occasion when Murrow was ignored. Many members of the Kennedy administration—notably Vice President Lyndon Johnson, Secretary of State Dean Rusk, Peace Corps director Sargent Shriver, and Adlai Stevenson—were still skeptical about USIA's usefulness. They regarded the "propagandists" as intruders who were only in the way at moments of crisis, when the big and often secret decisions had to be made. Over time, these views prevailed, notwith-standing Kennedy's promise that Murrow would be an important player in the administration.[48] Murrow found himself increasingly excluded from the inner sanctum. He became an ornament of the New Frontier, a person of immense prestige but little power.

Murrow himself seemed ambivalent about his role in the government. He had come to Washington from the world of journalism, but he was now required to act as a public relations man. It was never easy for Murrow to reconcile his training as a reporter with the responsibilities of a spokesman. In the same speech, he could insist that as head of USIA he would "operate on the basis of truth," and then acknowledge that he had to "emphasize those aspects of American life . . . which are of greatest significance in furthering [America's] foreign policy objectives."[49] This was the sort of contradictory pronouncement that bedeviled America's cultural diplomacy throughout the postwar years.

The journalistic credentials of the Voice of America, for example, were increasingly suspect once USIA took over its operation in 1953. The VOA suffered continually from unfavorable comparisons to the British Broadcasting Corporation. Although the BBC was funded by the British government and often served as an advertisement for British culture, it was not obliged to defend the decisions of the Foreign Office or help fight the Cold War, in part because Britain left this latter chore to the United States. Consequently, audiences tended to think of the BBC as an independent entity, broadcasting accurate and trustworthy information about world affairs.[50] In contrast, the VOA's close ties to and reliance on the "guidance" of the State Department and USIA made it seem less believable, more of a megaphone for official policy.

Murrow tried to improve the reputation of the VOA by stressing the need for veracity and objectivity in its news programs. As a journalist, he sympathized with the notion that the VOA should function not just as the voice of the current administration but as a reflection of America's diversity, a channel for the expression of multiple points of view. Ideally, he wanted the VOA to be autonomous, like the BBC, free to say whatever it wished without some bureaucrat censoring its scripts. But as a government official, Murrow recognized that he was primarily an advocate, and that the VOA in its capacity as a state-sponsored radio station had to persuade foreign audiences rather than simply deliver the news. Hence, he was caught between his commitment to telling the truth and his job as a propagandist. (In 1965, John Chancellor left *NBC News* to become head of the Voice of America.

Like Murrow, Chancellor found that his journalistic sensibilities were in conflict with what seemed to be the excessive interference of the State Department and USIA. By 1967, he had grown weary of having to defend the VOA's integrity and returned to NBC.)[51]

The most poignant illustration of Murrow's divided loyalties occurred in 1961 when the BBC arranged to show *Harvest of Shame*. This documentary was one of Murrow's proudest achievements at CBS. Yet he now tried to persuade the BBC to cancel the broadcast on the grounds that it would harm America's image abroad, an effort that ultimately failed.[52]

Eventually, Murrow resolved his dilemma. By 1963, his final year at USIA, Murrow considered himself exclusively a servant of the president, a publicist for (if not a participant in) the political programs of the Kennedy administration. It was not a happy resolution. In the last months of his life, ill with cancer, Murrow frequently talked about resuming his career as a newsman. But he no longer had the time or the energy to start over. In January 1964, Murrow resigned. A few months later, he was dead.

Murrow was revered by the people who worked for USIA. He had made them feel important, even if their skills as information specialists were not universally admired by the best and the brightest in the Kennedy administration. Yet for all his magnetism and his fame, Murrow seemed the most troubled, and perhaps the most melancholy, director the agency was ever likely to have.

CHARLES FRANKEL AND LBJ

Because of Murrow's background as a journalist, USIA had focused most of its attention in the early 1960s on news and information, rather than on cultural projects. Kennedy himself underscored the differences between political advocacy and sending writers or performing artists abroad by creating a new position in the State Department in 1961, the assistant secretary of state for educational and cultural affairs. In theory, the assistant secretary had responsibilities in the area of culture equivalent to those of USIA's director in the field of information and propaganda. But whoever ran CU (the State Department's acronym for the new cultural bureau), ended up sharing USIA's frustration at not being heard or taken seriously by the White House.

In 1965, Lyndon Johnson chose Charles Frankel, a professor of philosophy at Columbia, to be the State Department's cultural czar.

Frankel had recently completed *The Neglected Aspect of Foreign Affairs,* a highly critical study of America's cultural diplomacy. He concluded that the "premises of official policy were largely wrong and the government's mode of operation [was] outlandish." Given these sentiments, Frankel did not expect the appointment. Furthermore, he knew that culture had been of only marginal concern to the career diplomats in the State Department. Nevertheless, he accepted the post in the hope that cultural programs might "move to the foreground of foreign policy" now that the country had a president who was making education the cornerstone of his Great Society.[53]

Like Murrow, Frankel wanted to play a central role in the government. Like Murrow, he would be disappointed. But Murrow was not a revolutionary, eager to transform the structure and purposes of USIA. Frankel, the State Department's in-house intellectual, offered a set of proposals that would have fundamentally changed the mission of America's postwar exchange programs, as well as how and by whom the programs were administered. At bottom, Frankel wished to separate culture from foreign policy. Such an idea threatened the jobs of numerous bureaucrats both in USIA and the State Department. It also challenged the axiom that the Cold War was in large part a cultural struggle between the United States and the Soviet Union.

Frankel began with the proposition that Washington was too patronizing in its cultural relationships with other nations. "The emphasis," he observed, "was usually on what we were doing for others, or to them. We were assisting them, enlightening them, correcting their erroneous views of us, helping them to learn to like us." It would be better if the United States seemed less superior and if its exchange programs were not so political, without the government so conspicuously involved.[54]

Frankel was not simply recommending cosmetic reforms. Echoing Senator Fulbright, Frankel believed in the dictionary definition of exchange. It should be a reciprocal interaction in which Americans no longer traveled abroad only as lecturers and role models, but also as students of other cultures and societies, using conferences as occasions to explore problems of mutual interest. Essentially, Frankel's ideal was "not the 'Americanization' but the internationalization of scholarship and education."[55]

In Frankel's opinion, neither USIA nor the State Department were set up to realize this vision. USIA's "most important objectives" were antithetical to the values of culture and education, he argued. The agency's "main reason for being [was] political and propagandistic"; it did not "provide the atmosphere or resources desirable for long-range" cultural enterprises. But the State Department offered no better environment for the cultivation of scholarship and the arts because its officers were normally preoccupied with short-term tactical considerations in the midst of some international crisis.[56]

Frankel's solution was to remove all America's overseas cultural activities from the "orbit" of the State Department and USIA, as well as from the CIA. This action would permit the diplomats, the information specialists, and the intelligence agents to concentrate on their primary tasks, without the bother of having to deal with obstreperous artists, professors, and intellectuals. In place of the government, Frankel urged the "creation of a semi-autonomous foundation for educational and cultural exchange" whose financial support could come from both the private and public sectors and whose staff would be drawn from universities, museums, publishing houses, and philanthropic foundations. Examples already existed of what he had in mind: the British Council, the National Science Foundation, the National Endowment for the Humanities, and the Smithsonian Institution.[57]

Frankel's ideas were clearly those of an academic. Unfortunately, professors and their ideas were becoming increasingly unwelcome in the closing years of the Johnson administration. Frankel arrived at CU just as the American involvement in the Vietnam War was escalating, and the cities and campuses were beginning to explode. Vietnam and the upheavals at home distracted everyone, from Johnson to Dean Rusk to Frankel himself. "The war," Frankel recorded in his diary in 1966, "is on my mind almost every minute I'm not at my desk." Under the circumstances, and given his growing opposition to the war, Frankel felt he could accomplish nothing. "I had simply come to the end of the path."[58] In December 1967, he resigned.

Frankel may have departed, but he had offered a thoughtful critique of how Washington conducted its cultural business with other countries. And he had suggested a plausible alternative to the government's supervision of educational and intellectual exchanges. Yet during the worst years of the Cold War, it was impossible to separate America's culture from its diplomacy. Until the 1970s, the government remained the driving force behind America's efforts to export its values to Europe, and to the rest of the world.

FOUR

American Studies in Europe

When Charles Frankel criticized the government's exchange programs for being too concerned with indoctrinating foreigners in the virtues of the American way, rather than with discovering what other societies might have to offer, he was questioning a central assumption behind America's cultural diplomacy in the second half of the twentieth century. Most government officials believed that the more people knew about the United States, the more they would come to admire its political and economic values, and its foreign policy. Unilateral instruction was therefore necessary, especially in the years of the Cold War. Reciprocity and mutual understanding, however worthy as educational goals, would have to wait.

Almost all the government's cultural efforts throughout the postwar era were aimed at introducing foreigners, and particularly Europeans, to a civilized and sophisticated America. Yet the America Houses and embassy libraries, the art exhibitions and jazz concerts, the touring ballet companies and symphony orchestras, could not erase the deeply ingrained notion, reinforced by Hollywood, that the United States was a land of enormous wealth, with modern appliances and efficient plumbing, but without an authentic culture or a respect for tradition.

To overcome these stereotypes, Europeans would need to learn more about America's history and literature. This would not be a simple task, given the chronic resistance of European academics to the inclusion of American subjects in their classrooms and textbooks. Nevertheless, after World War II, the U.S. government embarked on a major campaign to incorporate the study of the United States into the curricula of European universities and secondary schools, and to help create chairs and institutes in American history and literature. American Studies became an essential component of Washington's cultural diplomacy, its importance enhanced by the recognition that this was one of the most effective ways to reach and influence a generation of students who would eventually acquire powerful positions in the government, the media, and the universities, passing on to the next generation their knowledge of and appreciation for the United States.

Over time, the American Studies movement in Europe accomplished many of the objectives visualized by its sponsors across the Atlantic. But it did not result in a transplantation of American values. Instead, European scholars used American Studies for their own purposes, reinterpreting American history and literature in terms that were relevant to European problems. In the end, American Studies became a lens through which Europeans could more clearly see and understand themselves, which was not what Washington originally intended when it set out to teach the Old World about the United States.

PREWAR ANTECEDENTS

In 1948, Harold Laski—the historian, political scientist, and leading theoretician of the British Labour Party—published *The American Democracy,* a mammoth work designed to make the United States "intelligible to Europeans." Toward the end of the book, Laski reflected on Europe's "absurd and willful ignorance of American institutions and culture" in the nineteenth and early twentieth centuries. "American literature was little read," he observed, while "few people, the scholars included, knew much of American history. . . . There was [no] serious effort to teach American history in the universities, let alone the schools."[1]

Laski's lament was echoed by others who remembered how little attention the United States received from European academics or intellectuals in the first decades of the twentieth century. "America played a very small role in the education of those [of us] who grew up in

Germany between 1910 and 1930," one journalist recollected. "We were taught almost nothing about its history" or "about the role it was beginning to assume with World War I." Similarly, Sigmund Skard—one of the principal advocates in the 1940s and 1950s of American Studies in Europe—confessed in his autobiography that his knowledge of America's history and literature had once been nonexistent. At the University of Oslo, where he was a student in the 1920s, "America was still largely ignored." At best, American history was treated as a "peripheral field in world history." The situation was the same in literature. Skard could not recall "having read even Hemingway that early, nor his other contemporaries. . . . Nor did I read the modern American poets at the time." Indeed, "not a single American writer was among my models."[2]

Until the beginning of the twentieth century, professorial indifference to America was common throughout Europe. In Britain, conservative dons at Oxford and Cambridge usually spoke of the United States with condescension. In their view, American history was dull, American intellectual life was insignificant, and American literature was merely an inferior by-product of British literature. These dismissive opinions were shared by Dutch, Norwegian, and Danish academics, who looked to both Britain and Germany for cultural guidance. French professors, preoccupied with the glories of their own civilization, were equally inattentive to developments in the United States. Authoritarian educators and politicians in Germany, Austria, and Spain seemed either incurious about or hostile toward America's democratic institutions. Even in countries like Italy, Greece, Poland, Sweden, and Ireland, where immigration to the United States was of considerable importance, few scholars displayed any inclination to find out more about the land to which so many of their people had migrated.[3]

This disinterest was exacerbated by the absence in European libraries of American novels, political tracts, newspapers, magazines, and government documents, materials that might have facilitated scholarly research. Consequently, most of the information about America in the nineteenth century came from travel books, many of which were filled with sweeping and often supercilious generalizations about American politics and social life that served only to harden the prejudices of European readers. In Frances Trollope's *Domestic Manners of the Americans* (1832) and Charles Dickens's *American Notes* (1842), the New World seemed a thoroughly unpleasant place, inhabited by people who were avaricious and uncouth, frantically pursuing (in Dickens's famous words) the "almighty dollar." Alexis de Tocqueville's *Democracy in America* (1835) was a far more perceptive and sympathetic depiction of life in the United States. But Tocqueville wanted primarily to warn his fellow-Europeans about the perils of the democratic experiment which, he feared, would lead either to anarchy or mass conformity. In *The American Commonwealth* (1888), James Bryce tried to evaluate the United States on its own terms, rather than as a verification of Europe's superiority. Still, his book was a lonely exception to the critical portraits of America that usually told Europeans what they wanted to hear.[4]

Meanwhile, European academics were content to focus on topics closer to home. Literature, philosophy, music, the arts—these were the specialties of Britain, France, Germany, and Central Europe. History was what had happened in classical Greece and Rome; in the medieval world; or, at most, in the Renaissance. America was entirely too new and too modern to have a past worthy of investigation.[5] And it was too distant, geographically and culturally, to be noticed or taken seriously.

There were sporadic signs in the early years of the twentieth century, and certainly after World War I, that the scholarly neglect of America might be coming to an end. The emergence of the United States as an economic and military power meant that Europe was no longer alone at the center of the universe. America's decisive intervention in the war, the presence of American troops in France, the way in which Woodrow Wilson and his entourage dominated the peace conference at Versailles, the impact of American products and movies in the 1920s, all these made it necessary for Europeans to know more about the United States.

Much of this attention took the form of a new interest in and respect for American literature. Despite their general disdain for American novelists and poets, European (and especially French) critics had long been fascinated with James Fenimore Cooper and Edgar Allen Poe. Now translations of Mark Twain, Bret Harte, Edward Arlington Robinson, and Jack London appeared, while the works of expatriates like T. S. Eliot, Ezra Pound, and the young Ernest Hemingway raised the possibility that at least a few American writers were worthy of inclusion in the modernist pantheon. Two milestones indicated that, in the eyes of some Europeans, American poetry and fiction had come of age: the publication of D. H. Lawrence's *Studies in Classic American Literature* in 1923 and the awarding of the Nobel Prize for literature in 1930 to Sinclair Lewis.

Significantly, Lawrence was not an academician. Nor was his passion for American writing shared by the professoriate. Inside the universities, the acceptance of America as a subject of scholarly inquiry was more halting and less cordial. Still, a number of prominent figures in the European academic world began to publish books and offer courses on the United States.

The great Dutch historian Johan Huizinga, normally absorbed with medieval and early modern Europe, paused briefly to comment on America's literature and civilization in two books. *Man and the Masses in America* (1918) had its origins in a course on American history Huizinga taught at the University of Leiden during World War I, while *Life and Thought in America: Stray Remarks* (1926) was a collection of notes and observations from his one visit to the United States. Huizinga's assessment, like Tocqueville's, was decidedly ambivalent. On the one hand, Huizinga was charmed by the exuberant optimism of the Americans and their childlike faith in the benefits that an industrial economy could infinitely bestow. On the other hand, he disliked America's glorification of efficiency, its hunger for instant results, its love affair with machines, and its satisfaction with the superficial and the mass-produced. Along with other European intellectuals in the 1920s, Huizinga saw America as the embodiment of modernity, which only made him treasure the quieter, less acquisitive ambience of his native Holland.[6]

For Huizinga, the United States was an object lesson on what could go wrong if Europeans followed the American example. Other scholars saw America not so much as a symbol but as a country whose history and development needed to be explained. At the University of Oslo, in the years before and after World War I, Halvdan Koht became the first Norwegian to write and teach extensively about America. His approach was more favorable than Huizinga's, emphasizing America's idealism, its commitment to social reform, and the broadening of its democratic heritage as a consequence of its remarkable economic growth. Koht's influence was considerable, particularly on Sigmund Skard who married Koht's daughter in 1933, thus laying the foundations for Skard's personal and intellectual involvement with the United States during and after World War II.[7]

Between the wars, French academics also became more active in scrutinizing the United States. Universities in Paris, Lyons, Lille, and Bordeaux established positions in American literature and history, beginning with a professorship at the Sorbonne, held from 1919 to 1941 by Charles Cestre, who was primarily responsible for launching the study of the United States in France. André Siegfried and Bernard Fay, the first French scholar to earn a doctorate in American history, taught courses regularly on America at other Parisian universities during the 1920s and 1930s. At the same time, French libraries slowly enlarged their meager holdings in American source materials, aided by American foundations like the Carnegie Endowment and the presence of the American Library in Paris, which opened in 1918.[8]

The Germans too devoted more attention to American subjects, which reflected both their expanding commercial ties to the United States at the dawn of the twentieth century and their defeat at the hands of the American army in 1918. As early as 1906, a bilateral exchange of scholars began, with German universities offering visiting posts to American academics, who were called Roosevelt Professors in honor of Theodore Roosevelt. One of these professors, John Burgess, a historian at Columbia, helped organize an American Institute in Berlin in 1910, complete with a library that housed one of the largest collections of Americana on the Continent. During the 1920s, interest in American culture intensified among German academics, artists, and intellectuals, though they were alternately captivated and repelled by what they heard and read about life in the United States. Even under the Nazis, teaching and research on the United States continued to flourish, at least for a while and in a heavily censored form. The number of courses on America steadily increased. In 1936, the University of Berlin established itself as the premier institution in Germany for American Studies by creating a professorship in American literature and cultural history. A year later, the government announced new regulations for examinations taken by secondary school teachers, requiring them to know as much about American as British literature. Nevertheless, the analyses and appraisals of American civilization had to conform to Nazi dogma, usually by pointing out the decadence of America's multiracial society.[9]

It was in Britain, however, that the magnitude and the limits of Europe's investment in American Studies were best exemplified. The academic links between Britain and the United States had been forged at the beginning of the twentieth century with the inauguration of the Rhodes scholarships in 1902, enabling Americans to do post-graduate work at Oxford. In return, the Commonwealth Fund, set up by the Harkness family in the United States in 1918, permitted British university graduates to study in the United States, starting in 1925. The Rhodes and Commonwealth awards were meant mainly for students. The teaching of American history in Britain awaited the creation in

1922 of the Harmsworth Chair at Oxford, intended for visiting American scholars, the first of whom was Samuel Eliot Morison. A few years later, in 1930, the Harkness family endowed a Commonwealth Professorship in American history at the University of London, designated as a permanent appointment for a British Americanist.[10] Both these positions were supposed to educate British students in the complexities of the American past, and make research on American topics more respectable in the British academic world.

During the 1930s, the development of American Studies in Britain depended largely on the largess of foundations in the United States. In addition to the Commonwealth Fund, which sent 361 British students to America between 1925 and 1939, the Carnegie Endowment paid for the trips of British historians to the annual conventions of the American Historical Association and gave small amounts of money to British universities for the purchase of books on the United States. The ability to travel to and around America was particularly important for Herbert Nicholas. Nicholas attended Yale from 1935 to 1937 as a Commonwealth Fund Fellow intending to become a historian of seventeenth-century England. But he found himself increasingly entranced by American literature and colonial history, as well as with the sheer size and diversity of America itself.[11] The experience prepared him for his eventual transformation into an Americanist after World War II.

Despite all of these efforts, American Studies remained weak in Britain throughout the interwar years. Universities were reluctant to make room in their curricula for courses on the United States, students' interest was negligible, materials for teaching and research were inadequate, and neither Oxford nor the University of London seemed willing to do much more than provide an institutional shelter for two otherwise marginal chairs in American history. Nor did the British and American governments see any reason why they should support educational initiatives to enlighten British students or the British public about the United States.[12]

The outbreak of World War II forced policymakers in London and Washington to revise their estimation of the importance of American Studies. Nearly everyone in Franklin Roosevelt's administration and in Winston Churchill's War Cabinet recognized that a close relationship between the two countries was now more imperative than at any time in the past. From the British standpoint, a political and military alliance with the United States was essential, first for survival and then for victory. Hence, it was desirable to strengthen Britain's cultural ties with America. For their part, American officials believed that the British people needed to gain a better understanding of the social and political traditions of the United States, not only to cement the wartime partnership, but to prepare the local population for the 3 million U.S. soldiers and civilians who would soon be swarming into Britain. Educating the British about America's history and literature could help illuminate the common democratic heritage and shared destiny of the Anglo-Americans.

The war was thus a catalyst for the growth of American Studies, encouraged by both the British and American governments. In 1941, the American ambassador to Britain, John Winant, and the British minister of information, Duff Cooper, urged teachers in elementary and secondary schools to devote more time in their classrooms to American topics. To assist the teachers, the British Board of Education asked Allan Nevins, then occupying the Harmsworth chair and one of the leading authorities on the Civil War and the Gilded Age, to write a forty-thousand-word survey of American history for use in secondary schools. The board also arranged for teachers to attend week-long training seminars in American history. Meanwhile, Cambridge, which had not joined Oxford and the University of London in creating a position in American Studies during the 1920s, hurried to catch up, demonstrating its appreciation for the variety of life in the United States by inviting Henry Steele Commager, one of America's most eminent academic historians, and J. Frank Dobie, a specialist in Texas humor and folklore, to lecture on American history. In 1944, Cambridge went further, establishing the Pitt Professorship in American History and Institutions, to be held by visiting American scholars. Throughout the war years, British libraries received grants from the Rockefeller Foundation to expand their American collections. In addition, the Office of War Information supplied British audiences, in and out of school, with books, newspapers, films, and lectures by American intellectuals like Alfred Kazin—still youthful but already well known for his panoramic interpretation of modern American literature in *On Native Grounds,* who undertook a speaking tour for the OWI and the British Council in 1945.[13]

Nevertheless, the British government's enthusiasm for American Studies was inspired by the wartime emergency, not by some deeply rooted determination to improve the quality of teaching and research on the United States. By 1945, as the war neared its end, with American troops having left England for Paris and Berlin, Whitehall's interest in American history and literature subsided.[14] If professors in

Britain and Western Europe were going to devote more of their scholarly time to the United States in the future, the incentive for them to do so would have to come from Washington and from America's private foundations. They would also have to acknowledge, on their own and however reluctantly, that the history and culture of the world's newest superpower could no longer be belittled or ignored.

THE POSTWAR SETTING

Twenty years after the end of World War II, American Studies had developed into a growth industry in Europe. The reason for this was hardly mysterious to Norman Podhoretz, editor of *Commentary* and a member in good standing of the New York Jewish intelligentsia at a time when the world beyond Manhattan still looked like a Saul Steinberg cartoon. "Does Finland have a great literature?" Podhoretz asked in his 1967 autobiography *Making It*. "Does Afghanistan? Does Ecuador? Who knows or cares? But give Finland enough power and enough wealth, and there would soon be a Finnish department in every university in the world—just as, in the 1950s, departments of American Studies were suddenly being established in colleges where, only a few years earlier, it had scarcely occurred to anyone that there was anything American *to* study."[15]

The situation had indeed changed, as many European academics were forced to concede. Harry Allen, a British historian who became an Americanist soon after 1945, recalled in the 1970s the connection, so clear to his own generation, between the American Studies movement and American power. "It was . . . no accident," he observed, "that the rapid rise of American studies in Europe coincided with [the] international ascendancy of the United States in the years after World War II." A younger British scholar, noting the postwar expansion of American subjects in British universities and secondary schools, and the emergence of a "more respectful attitude toward American history" among his peers, saw these trends as having originated at precisely the moment "when the U.S. was asserting its role in the world." The importance of America, Sigmund Skard pointed out, was "obvious to everybody" in the European academic community, so much so that the historic "discrepancy between the position of the United States in the world and its place in syllabuses and curricula" seemed increasingly "intolerable."[16]

Despite the general European awareness of America's postwar preeminence, the motivations for studying the United States differed from country to country. For many officials in the British government, teaching students about American history and literature was one way of strengthening the Atlantic Alliance in the midst of the Cold War, and of solidifying Britain's "special relationship" with the United States. The French too were anxious to know more about the United States, if only to bolster their resistance to America's cultural influence. In smaller nations like the Netherlands, Denmark, and Greece, the impact of the Marshall Plan and the creation of the North Atlantic Treaty Organization made scholars and students less Eurocentric; a greater knowledge of American society and politics was now obligatory.[17]

No people seemed more eager to learn about the United States than the West Germans. Much of their curiosity was genuine, but it was also a matter of necessity, the Americans having arrived as conquerors and masters of West Germany's fate. The United States, as one German Americanist remarked, "was the overwhelming entity with which everyone had to be acquainted, if you were intellectually enterprising at all." The Germans may have wished to please the new authorities by displaying a scholarly interest in America, but they were equally keen to forget the war and get on with their lives. American Studies offered a path to the future for professors, teachers, and young intellectuals, as Alfred Kazin discovered when he taught a course on "American civilization" in Cologne in 1952. Half the city was still in ruins, but for Kazin's students "the war was over. The war was not to be mentioned. Not a word was said by my students about the war. They were busy getting ahead on the magic road of *Amerikanistik*."[18]

The popularity of American Studies in postwar Europe did not depend simply on the recognition that the United States was a mighty country whose culture and institutions ought to be better understood. After a century of skepticism, European academics might still not have accepted American history and literature as areas suitable for teaching and research without the active intervention of the American government and a massive infusion of American money.

Washington's willingness to support the American Studies movement in Europe was inspired by the onset of the Cold War. Later on, the idea that the United States promoted American Studies in order to advance its political agenda made some European Americanists uncomfortable, as if there may have been few indigenous or purely intellectual reasons for them to take up the field. Looking back on the early postwar years from the perspective of the 1980s, the British literary critic Denis Donoghue worried that the European participation in the spread of American Studies sprang from a "network of sentiments and purposes partly our own ... but at least equally the concern of diplomats and officers of the State Department. An entirely reputable academic interest has been furthered—sponsored, indeed—by other motives," particularly those of American foreign policy. Yet in the late 1940s, these impulses did not seem suspicious. On the contrary, a number of European academics and intellectuals were quite prepared to embrace American Studies as an instrument of American diplomacy. In 1948, Stephen Spender, describing the "battle for the mind of Europe" in the *New York Times Magazine,* urged the United States to help Europe's students "understand the best in American civilization, and the American conception of freedom." Similarly, Max Beloff, a lecturer in American history at Oxford, suggested in 1949 that, in view of the Communists' current efforts to denigrate the United States throughout Western Europe, materials on U.S. history and literature could be used "for the better projection of America abroad."[19]

American policymakers agreed. From 1945 until the early 1970s, they offered European scholars and students a variety of resources and inducements aimed at making it easier for them to become specialists in American history and literature. The State Department (working mostly through the Fulbright program) and the U.S. Information Agency, together with the Rockefeller and Ford Foundations, supplied the Europeans with textbooks and course outlines, organized summer seminars for secondary school teachers, funded conferences on every aspect of American civilization, subsidized the publication of professional journals, sent American professors to lecture in European universities, provided travel allowances and fellowships for Europeans to study in the United States, endowed chairs and institutes, arranged for the translation of American novels and scholarly works, and paid for the upgrading and cataloguing of American holdings in European libraries.[20]

For much of this time, American aid was indispensable since the majority of European academics could not afford to visit the United States on research trips, buy American books, improve their library collections, or underwrite American Studies programs on their own. But what the U.S. government and the foundations most wanted to do was make sure that American history and literature would be taught on a permanent basis in Europe. To accomplish this goal, they would have to recruit and train a cadre of Americanists in Britain and on the Continent. And in the view of their American patrons, the Europeans would need not only books and travel grants, but mentors and intellectual role models—emissaries from the United States who could introduce them to the latest analyses and interpretations, recommend them for fellowships, and launch them on their new careers.

The American Guest Professors

Whatever its roots in the early years of the twentieth century, the American Studies movement in Europe would not have blossomed in the postwar era without the assistance and the example of a powerful American Studies movement in the United States. After 1945, European scholars began to pay serious attention, often for the first time, to the ideas of their American counterparts. The influence of the Americans rested, in part, on the perception that they possessed some special understanding of a culture that had previously been disparaged as exotic and second rate, but was now an object of intense concern.

In the United States, the attraction to American Studies had arisen in the 1930s, mainly among a small group of faculty members in the English and History departments of the country's elite universities. The architects of the movement were young and ambitious. They were also dissatisfied with what seemed to them the excessively narrow approach to the American past fostered by the traditional academic "fields." They proposed instead to be "interdisciplinary," to cross departmental boundaries, to invent a new way of writing about America that would combine the insights and techniques of intellectual history, literary criticism, political theory, and sociology.

They were affected as well by the various forms of cultural nationalism that became increasingly prevalent in the United States during the late 1930s and the war years—the references in the popular press to the "American Dream," the rhetorical celebrations of the "American Way of Life," and the assertion of America's democratic superiority over a Europe infested with swaggering dictators. These notions were reinforced by the work of cultural anthropologists like Margaret Mead and Ruth Benedict, who argued that societies should be seen as more than a collection of institutions, that they could be best comprehended through their unifying myths, traditions, and patterns of conduct. Such concepts suggested that America was not just a conventional nation-state but a distinctive civilization, one with a "national character" that could be discovered and defined. It was therefore necessary to explain what was "American" about America, to embark on a quest for what the historian Perry Miller and others called the "meaning of America."

There was always an evangelical tone to their enterprise, a sense that they were not merely scholars but also missionaries to the world beyond the borders of the United States. In his introduction to a collection of essays about colonial and early nineteenth-century America, Perry Miller recalled his youthful "epiphany" while watching an apparently inexhaustible supply of American oil drums being unloaded in Africa. At that moment, struck by the absolute "uniqueness of the American experience," Miller felt a "pressing necessity for expounding my America to the twentieth century."[21]

Miller's America, and the America of his colleagues, was never cohesive. On the contrary, the nation they portrayed was surprisingly diverse. Their methods were eclectic, weaving together a variety of texts and sources: Puritan sermons, the political rhetoric of the Jacksonians, the novels of the nineteenth century, the mythology and symbolism enclosed in hundreds of legends and folktales, the letters and reminiscences of immigrants, painting and architecture, clothing and furniture, hand tools and industrial machinery. Their books described a country made up of people who were persistently ambivalent about everything—the wilderness, cities, wealth, power, technology, religion, science, eastern refinements, and westward expansion.

Nevertheless, their ultimate purpose was to uncover the idiosyncratic features of the "American mind." They sought to identify the special political and cultural traditions that had so far shielded the nation from the cataclysms of the twentieth century. The titles of their books were illustrative of this search for the quintessential America: Perry Miller's two-volume *The New England Mind* (1939 and 1953), F. O. Matthiessen's *American Renaissance* (1941), Richard Hofstadter's *The American Political Tradition* (1948), Henry Nash Smith's *Virgin Land: The American West as Symbol and Myth* (1950), Daniel Boorstin's *The Genius of American Politics* (1953), David Potter's *People of Plenty: Economic Abundance and the American Character* (1954), Louis Hartz's *The Liberal Tradition in America* (1955), John William Ward's *Andrew Jackson: Symbol for an Age* (1955), R. W. B. Lewis's *The American Adam* (1955), Richard Chase's *The American Novel and Its Tradition* (1957), Leslie Fiedler's *Love and Death in the American Novel* (1960), Leo Marx's *The Machine in the Garden* (1964).

The period from the end of the 1930s to the mid-1960s was the golden age of American Studies in the United States. During these years, a remarkable group of scholars wrote about the nation's social and cultural history with an eloquence and a comprehensiveness that their successors never attained, and perhaps never craved. A later generation of academics, products of the social and cultural ruptures of the 1960s, would never talk in such holistic terms about the "American Experience" or the "national character," never think they could depict the "mind" of New England, much less the "mind" of America. They would instantly ask: Whose mind, whose experience, whose novels, whose tradition? The historians and literary critics of the 1940s and 1950s may have differed among themselves about what aspects of the past to emphasize, and they may have concentrated as much on the tensions as on the unifying themes in American culture. But they did assume that the nation had developed in ways that were "typically" American. By the 1970s and 1980s, it was no longer fashionable in academic circles to write about America as a community of shared beliefs and values. The new scholarship focused on fragments of the "American Experience," on local particularities, on "micro-history"—and, most of all, on the implacable repercussions of race, class, gender, and ethnicity.

Yet in the postwar years, it was precisely the willingness of historians and literary critics in the United States to generalize, to try to unravel the mystery and meaning of America, that impressed their European audiences. Moreover, European readers were accustomed to broad interpretations of America's literature and social life, having grown up on Tocqueville, Bryce, Huizinga, and Lawrence. Now the Americanists from across the ocean were providing the grand theories and sweeping metaphors. When they descended upon Europe in the 1940s and 1950s, they seemed to be bringing enlightenment to the Old World as once the Old World had enlightened the New.

One of the places where they had their greatest impact was at the Salzburg Seminar. As a mechanism for transmitting America's culture to postwar Europe, the seminar was unusual because the U.S. government played no role in its creation. Instead, the seminar was the brainchild of three Harvard students: Richard Campbell, an undergraduate; Scott Elledge, an instructor in the English Department; and Clemens Heller, a Ph.D. candidate in history who was also an Austrian refugee. In the course of raising money for food shipments to Europe during the winter of 1946, they began to worry not only about alleviating the Continent's physical distress but about how to restore its intellectual life after the years of Nazi domination. There should be some way, they felt, for European students to reestablish contact with one another and at the same time learn more about the United States—

the country that would most affect their lives for the foreseeable future. A seminar in American Studies, staffed by professors from the United States and attended by students from all over Europe, seemed the perfect device for achieving these objectives.

By February 1947, Campbell, Elledge, and Heller had decided to organize such a seminar. They chose Austria as the locale, partly because of Heller's connections to the country, but also because it lay in the heart of Europe, accessible to students from both the West and the East. Within Austria, Salzburg appeared to have special advantages as the site for an American Studies seminar since it was the headquarters of the U.S. Army. Indeed, Salzburg was filled with so many "American signs and cars" that it looked to Alfred Kazin like "an American shopping center." Heller was able to persuade the widow of Max Reinhardt, the legendary German-Jewish theater director and Hollywood producer, to rent to the seminar the Schloss Leopoldskron, an eighteenth-century rococo country house on the outskirts of Salzburg that Reinhardt acquired in 1918 and had used for cultural events in the 1920s. Soon Campbell, Elledge, and Heller obtained permission from the State and War Departments to hold the seminar in Salzburg, collected $23,000 in private donations to underwrite its costs, put together a small library, recruited a faculty, and arranged with educational and university organizations in Europe to select a student body.[22]

The first seminar met in July and August 1947. Ninety-eight students, teachers, artists, writers, journalists, labor leaders, and junior government officials from eighteen countries, including several in Eastern Europe, gathered at the Schloss. Most of their eleven instructors were celebrities in the American academic and intellectual world. Alfred Kazin and F. O. Matthiessen (whom Kazin called the "star" of the seminar) lectured on nineteenth- and twentieth-century American literature; Wassily Leontief and Walt Rostow gave courses on the American economy; Margaret Mead taught anthropology. Students at the second seminar in 1948 heard Randall Jarrell on recent American poetry, Henry Nash Smith on the American West, and Talcott Parsons on the structure of American society.[23]

The eminence of the faculty at the Salzburg Seminar, and their status as authority figures, reflected the altered cultural relationship between the United States and Europe after World War II. In the past, Americans had gone to Europe to study, to learn as much as they could from the savants of the Old World. F. O. Matthiessen's predecessors, he recalled, had been either "passionate pilgrims" like Henry James or "innocents abroad" like Mark Twain. Matthiessen himself was once a neophyte, first traveling to Europe as a Rhodes scholar in 1924. Now, as Alfred Kazin observed, the Americans came to Europe as "teachers," while the Europeans had become the "earnest students and dutiful inquirers." At the seminar, "the European students watched the American lecturers with awe. They were the audience, and we in Europe were the main event, absorbed in ourselves, in the rich, overplentiful runaway society whose every last detail we discussed with such hypnotized relevance to ourselves. In this still war-torn year of 1947, the Europeans could not help [but be] aware that they were simply out of it. We *were* the main event. We were America."[24]

Kazin and his colleagues were also America's chief interpreters. One of the main goals of the Salzburg Seminar, as conceived by its founders, was the re-creation of a European intellectual community. But from its inception, the seminar was an instrument both for educating an elite group of European students about America, and for introducing them to the ideas and research techniques of American Studies as it was practiced in the United States. After listening to lectures on American history, literature, politics, economics, and law, the students would presumably return home as newly minted experts on American institutions and policies. Given the political and economic ramifications of the Salzburg Seminar, it soon received funding from a variety of sources, not all of them interested solely in cultural exchange. The Rockefeller and Ford Foundations and the Commonwealth Fund supported the seminar over the next several decades. But so too did a number of major American and European corporations, as well as the U.S. government.[25]

The Salzburg Seminar was just one of the vehicles for the export of American Studies to postwar Europe. The Fulbright program was equally committed to promoting American history and literature in European universities. Although Senator Fulbright had originally meant to subsidize only *student* exchanges, the State Department and the Board of Foreign Scholarships understood from the beginning the benefits of sending senior American scholars to teach and lecture abroad. In addition to making America comprehensible to foreigners, the guest professors could assist in the development of American Studies curricula and, by their very presence, heighten the prestige of their host institutions. These considerations were not lost on European educators who also preferred to have big names addressing large classes (at no cost to their own, frequently impoverished, universities), rather than graduate students squirreled away in libraries doing research on obscure topics for their doctoral dissertations.[26]

Consequently, from the late 1940s through the mid-1960s, some of the best-known historians and literary critics in the United States journeyed to Europe, either on Fulbrights or as visiting chair-holders, to spread the word about America's culture and civilization. When the first Salzburg Seminar ended in August 1947, F. O. Matthiessen moved on to Charles University in Prague, where he taught American literature. Matthiessen was proud to be "the first American ever to be a regular visiting professor at a Czech university," though after the Communist coup in 1948 he would be the last American visitor for a very long time. David Potter occupied the Harmsworth chair at Oxford in 1948, as did C. Vann Woodward in 1954–55. Perry Miller was a Fulbright lecturer at the University of Leiden in 1949–50. Wassily Leontief lectured in Britain in 1951 and in West Germany in 1961 on a Fulbright grant. Daniel Boorstin was a Fulbright lecturer in Rome in 1950–51 and a visiting professor at the Sorbonne in 1962–63. Alfred Kazin, a visiting professor at the universities of Nice and Cologne and a Fulbright lecturer in Britain, Sweden, and Norway in 1951–52, remembered "lapping up the good life in Europe while paying for it with 'instruction' in Melville, James, Dickinson, and Emerson." Leslie Fiedler, originally trained as a medievalist, received a Fulbright grant for two years, from 1952 to 1954, to lecture in Italy. In Rome, he discovered that he was "expected as an American to talk only about American literature—no questions asked and no protests possible." By the time his fellowship ended, Fiedler had taught not only in Rome but in Bologna and Venice; some of his students later held the first chairs in American literature in Italy. Edmund Wilson was on the faculty of the Salzburg Seminar in 1954. Leo Marx lectured on a Fulbright in Britain in 1956 and in France in 1965. Henry Steele Commager was a Fulbright professor in France in 1957–58. Richard Hofstadter was the Pitt Professor at Cambridge for the 1958–59 academic year.[27]

The long-term mission of all these American visitors was to train a new generation of European Americanists who might go on to establish American Studies programs in their own universities and secondary schools. Once the guest professors had departed, the job of teaching American history or literature would fall to the Europeans. At least this was the expectation. In some instances, however, university administrators in Europe used the existence of visiting chairs and Fulbright lectureships as an excuse not to create permanent positions in American Studies for their own nationals.[28] Notwithstanding the efforts of the American government, the private foundations, and the

Salzburg Seminar, the majority of European academics still seemed reluctant in the 1940s and 1950s to embrace American Studies. In the end, the struggle for its acceptance would have to be waged not by visitors from the United States, but by a small band of European converts, against the resistance of their colleagues, and against all the old snobberies that—despite America's political and economic preeminence—showed no signs of fading easily away.

THE EUROPEAN AMERICANISTS: THE FIRST GENERATION

They thought of themselves as pioneers. Their successors called them the "founding fathers." A few, like D. W. Brogan in England and Mario Praz in Italy, were already well known for their books and essays on American history and literature. But others—Sigmund Skard in Norway; Harry Allen, Herbert Nicholas, Frank Thistlethwaite, and Marcus Cunliffe in Britain; Arie N. J. den Hollander in the Netherlands; Roger Asselineau in France; Max Silberschmidt in Switzerland—were either just starting out or had not yet achieved recognition outside their own countries.

Most of them were at once iconoclastic and entrepreneurial; they saw American Studies both as a new and exciting field, and as a launching pad for their careers. To some extent, they were advocates for America. In their books and newspaper articles, in their public lectures, and in their classrooms, they tried to puncture the prevailing clichés about the United States. Their task, as they conceived it, was to offer an honest but sympathetic portrait of a country the majority of their fellow citizens had difficulty comprehending.

They benefited as well from America's stature in the postwar world. "As students of the United States," Harry Allen acknowledged, "we . . . acquire some reflected strength from the . . . stark fact of American power." At times, they seemed too closely allied with America, too ready to defend its policies and its culture. How objective could they be, their audiences might have wondered, when they were so dependent on American money to finance their fellowships, research trips, institutes, conferences, journals, and libraries? But they were not merely opportunistic, nor was it America alone that ultimately interested them. As Sigmund Skard pointed out, the United States had come to embody certain "general tendencies" in the twentieth century, trends that one could now observe in Western Europe. Thus, for Skard and the other

Americanists of his generation, the desire to study the United States was not "a sign of cultural submissiveness"; rather, it was "essential to the understanding of ourselves."[29]

Skard was the patriarch and chief proponent of the American Studies movement, not only in Norway but throughout Western Europe. In many respects, his was a classic story of the European scholar who became—partly by accident, but mostly by taking advantage of the historical circumstances in which he found himself—a specialist on the United States. He was the prototype; in one way or another, everyone in the first generation shared his experiences, and his uncertainty about what it meant to be an Americanist in postwar Europe.

"Hitler made Americanists of us all," Harry Allen recalled. This was unquestionably true for Skard, who had devoted himself exclusively to European subjects before World War II. When the Germans invaded Norway in April 1940, Skard fled to Sweden. Because his father-in-law, Halvdan Koht, was working with the Norwegian government-in-exile in London, Skard could not return to occupied Norway. Hence, he and his family decided to head for America. They made their way through Siberia to Japan, crossed the Pacific Ocean and the Panama Canal, and reached New York on December 7, 1940, exactly a year before the Japanese bombed Pearl Harbor. This was Skard's first encounter with the United States, and he had at the time no thought of becoming an expert in or a champion of American Studies.[30] Yet that is precisely what happened. Over the next several years, he ceased to be simply a refugee and became instead a student of America's culture and politics.

Aided by Koht's contacts in Washington and by the employment services of the Emergency Committee in Aid of Displaced Foreign Scholars, Skard got a temporary job at the Library of Congress. The appointment enabled him to travel and lecture throughout the country, and to meet American academics and foundation executives. In 1943, he joined the Office of War Information. Broadcasting over the Voice of America, he explained the United States—its political institutions, its social characteristics, its cultural life, and its war aims—to his homeland, acquiring skills that would be useful for a prospective Americanist. Along the way, Skard began to feel "personally attached to America," or at least to that part of America represented by Franklin Roosevelt and the New Deal. He immersed himself in American books and newspapers, listened to American radio programs, went to American movies, talked to Americans about public events, and "came to look at the world from an American angle."[31]

Skard realized that after the war Norway and all the other countries of Western Europe would be bound to the United States. Given his own prior ignorance about American history and literature, he understood how little the average Norwegian knew about the United States, how tenacious were the "old stereotypes," how necessary it was—in view of America's capacity to determine the fate of postwar Europe—to replace the myths with factual information. Thus, Skard urged that Norwegian students and scholars be brought to the United States once the war was over, and he arranged with the Rockefeller Foundation to have American books, unobtainable during the German occupation, donated to the library of the University of Oslo.[32]

Most of all, Skard wanted to make sure that the University of Oslo would offer courses about the United States on a regular basis, which it had not done before the war. His wishes were granted when the Norwegian government, eager to strengthen its relationship with Washington, created a professorship in the "literary history" of America at the university in 1946, the first position in Scandinavia with a mandate to focus mainly on the United States. The post was designed for Skard himself. But Skard realized that a "serious" program in American Studies "could not get under way . . . without substantial financial support from American sources." He also reckoned that the U.S. government and the Rockefeller Foundation (with which he was in constant touch) would provide him with greater economic assistance if a separate American Institute, with its own research facilities, were established. In 1948, Skard became the director of just such an institute, giving American Studies a permanent home in the Norwegian academic world.[33]

Meanwhile, Skard returned to the United States in 1946, on a grant from the Rockefeller Foundation, to prepare himself for his new role as an Americanist. He studied America's literature more systematically and sought guidance from some of the leading practitioners of American Studies in the United States—especially Robert Spiller, Kenneth Murdock, F. O. Matthiessen, and Perry Miller. With the help again of the Rockefeller Foundation, he purchased books, magazines, maps, and phonograph records for his institute's library. Back in Oslo, Skard continued to profit from his ties to the United States. He became a "point of contact, more or less official, with individuals and institutions, private and governmental, on both sides of the ocean." He worked closely with the American embassy in Norway, entertained visiting American professors (with the bills paid by the Fulbright program), imported Murdock and Spiller in 1949 and 1950 to lecture and help teach his seminars, and received a Fulbright professor of American literature at the institute every year from 1957 to 1969.[34]

Despite his dependence on the U.S. government and the Rockefeller Foundation, Skard remained ambivalent about America. One of the advantages, he later remarked, of all the travel grants and other forms of support given to European Americanists was that they could "go to America and see for themselves," basing their judgments not on books but on "personal observation." Skard did not always like what he saw. In his notes about his experiences in wartime and postwar America, and in his book *American Problems* (1949), Skard—sounding much like Johan Huizinga—contrasted the simple intimacies of Norwegian life with the dehumanizing effects of capitalism and mass culture in the United States. The defects of American life were all too obvious: "ruthless automatism," "social callousness and economic exploitation," "racial inequality," the rise of McCarthyism. Yet Skard still found America fascinating; it had (as Norway did not) a "vitality and vigor," an "openness of mind," a "lack of hampering tradition," and a "willingness to start afresh" that accounted for the general prosperity and "well-being" of its population. Skard's mixed feelings about America led him, for a time, to hope that Norway would not have to choose between the Soviet Union and the United States in the Cold War. But after the Communist coup in Czechoslovakia in 1948, he rejected neutralism and accepted instead the "absolute necessity of Norway's alignment with the United States within the framework of NATO." For all its faults, the United States had become in Skard's eyes "the most realistic hope for the future of my most cherished values."[35]

Thereafter, Skard settled into his "frontier" role, opening up the "virgin field" of American Studies in Norway and throughout Western Europe. Like his mentors in the United States, he too wanted to explore the "Americanness" of his materials, and to convince his audiences that America had a "distinctive" civilization. But he was more of an organizer and promoter than an original thinker. Thus, his greatest contribution came in 1958, when he published his two-volume masterpiece, *American Studies in Europe,* a work partly funded by the Rockefeller Foundation and distributed by USIA. Skard's ostensible purpose in writing the book was to circulate information about the current state of American Studies among his colleagues in the rest of Europe.[36] Yet the book turned into a history of Europe's cultural engagement with America, from the eighteenth century to the postwar years. In this sense, it mirrored Skard's own professional and intellectual transformation. At the time of its publication, he had with some difficulty suppressed his doubts about the United States, though they would surface again in the 1960s. For the moment, he was an enthusiastic spokesman not only for American Studies but for America itself.

Not everyone in the first generation had to completely re-tool. Mario Praz, originally a specialist in British literature, began writing about American novelists and playwrights as early as the 1920s. His essays on Nathaniel Hawthorne, Edgar Allan Poe, Theodore Dreiser, Sinclair Lewis, Thornton Wilder, Eugene O'Neill, John Dos Passos, William Faulkner, and Ernest Hemingway, almost all of them published before World War II, had a enormous impact on the Italian Americanists of the 1950s. Similarly, Arie den Hollander had traveled to the United States in the early 1930s, on a Rockefeller Foundation fellowship, to conduct research for his dissertation on poor rural whites in the American South. He was therefore an obvious choice to fill a chair in "Americanistics," created in 1947 at the University of Amsterdam, and to become head of the university's new American Institute.[37]

But Roger Asselineau's experience was more typical. Though he had fantasized before the war about going to America, mostly to perfect his English, Asselineau knew almost nothing about the country except what he had gleaned from Hollywood's movies. He finally arrived in 1945, courtesy of a fellowship from the American Field Service, and proceeded to Harvard where he "absorbed American literature by osmosis" from the triumvirate of Murdock, Miller, and Matthiessen. Like Skard, Asselineau also traveled, getting his first real exposure to America from the windows of a Greyhound bus. When he returned to France, even after he was appointed in 1960 to a chair in American Studies at the Sorbonne, Asselineau considered himself a "generalist rather than a true specialist," and one who had to "find his way all by himself" in an academic community still suspicious of American subjects.[38]

Skard and den Hollander shared Asselineau's sense of isolation; in their own countries, they had students but no peers with whom they could jointly explore the field. The situation was different in Britain. A considerable number of young British academics were attracted to American Studies in the postwar years. Many felt "personally caught up" in America's "struggles and aspirations" either because they had been stationed in Washington or New York during the war (like Herbert Nicholas), or because they had "driven in American vehicles and fired American guns" while fighting in Normandy, Holland, and the

Ardennes in 1944 and 1945 (like Marcus Cunliffe). They were grateful for America's "vast and omnipresent" role in defeating the Germans, and they did not question its aims in the Cold War.[39] After 1945, they had other reasons to be appreciative. The American government was eager to recruit them, offering fellowships from the Commonwealth Fund or the Fulbright program so they could study in the United States, and giving money to British universities for the creation of positions in American Studies that they might fill when they returned.

The British Americanists enjoyed additional advantages unavailable elsewhere in Europe. They wrote, of course, in English, which made it easier for them to have their essays and books accepted by American journals and publishing houses, giving them a better chance to catch the attention of American scholars. Moreover, British libraries had a greater supply of research materials on the United States, especially in colonial and diplomatic history. So, British Americanists could write about Massachusetts or Virginia in the seventeenth and eighteenth centuries, or the American Revolution, or American foreign policy without having to finance an expedition to the archives in the United States. Above all, as Sigmund Skard noted with just a little envy, it was generally assumed that "the British should be able to understand the Americans better" than anyone else because they were more closely tied, historically and culturally, to the United States. Thus, the British might have some special insights about America not granted to their European colleagues. They could speak more authoritatively as "Atlanticists," emphasizing (in the case of Harry Allen, Herbert Nicholas, and Frank Thistlethwaite) the singular Anglo-American heritage, and the "special relationship"—present and past—between the United States and Britain.[40]

Nevertheless, the attitudes of the first generation of British Americanists were not all that dissimilar to those of their counterparts in Scandinavia or on the Continent. The British Americanists also regarded themselves as missionaries on behalf of American Studies, preaching to a congregation of traditionalist academics who did not always welcome the new religion. They too believed they were "breaking new ground," as Marcus Cunliffe put it, literally discovering or inventing a new discipline previously unknown or scorned in Britain.[41]

They tended as well to think of themselves as rebels, outsiders, people from the proverbial provinces, having only the most tenuous connections to the British economic and professorial establishment. They were definitely not the offspring of the privileged or the powerful. Their roots were in Scotland (D. W. Brogan) or Wales (Herbert Nicholas) or the north of England (Marcus Cunliffe). A number of them were Jews (Harold Laski, Max Beloff, Lewis Namier). Their backgrounds were not disgraceful, just vaguely unfashionable. "I came from . . . that strange hinterland just above the working but not quite safely into the middle classes," Malcolm Bradbury, a member of the next generation, reported. Though he was not exactly an angry young man or the hero of *Room at the Top,* Bradbury described himself as a "Hoggartian first-generation scholarship boy at grammar school who then continued his class-ascent by becoming a first-generation, but red-brick, university student." Given their origins, it was not surprising that, while studying in America, they might have "felt liberated" (as Cunliffe did) "from the intricate discriminations of the mother country." America offered an escape from what Bradbury called the "constraining, class-oriented, provincial embrace" of Britain. It was equally natural that they should see American Studies as a means of further advancement, a way to break into the closed and conservative world of British academia.[42]

Essentially, they viewed the United States as a land receptive to ethnic differences and social eccentricities, a land tolerant of people like themselves. This belief made them, if not fervently pro-American, at least evenhanded in their assessments of the country's weaknesses and strengths. Like Skard, they noticed America's shortcomings. But they had learned, said Harry Allen, "to approve of the society and very much to like the people."[43]

Yet what the British Americanists had most in common with their partners both in Europe and in the United States was a propensity to generalize about America's uniqueness. In books like D. W. Brogan's *The American Character* (published in 1944 and revised in 1956), Geoffrey Gorer's *The American People* (1948), Harold Laski's *The American Democracy* (1948), and Marcus Cunliffe's *The Literature of the United States* (1954), they sought to distinguish America's culture, political system, and social values from those of Europe. Brogan, for example, wanted to know what ideas were "peculiarly American," how the United States had reshaped Europe's institutions and customs, and which elements in America's civilization could be transported back to Europe. This was not simply a matter of comparing the New World with the Old. As Cunliffe admitted, "we were predisposed to agree that the United States was different from, and in important respects better than Europe: exceptional, and exceptionally good."[44] During the

1940s and 1950s, few historians or literary critics in the United States would have dissented.

Brogan and Cunliffe, Skard and den Hollander, Allen and Asselineau—all the members of the first generation were right to consider themselves pioneers, even if they were following a trail already blazed by their American guides. The real difficulties came after the initial exploration, when the founding fathers and their children settled down to the prosaic task of consolidation, of converting American Studies from an adventure into an institution, with all the rituals and procedures of a conventional academic discipline. It was clear that American Studies, with the assistance of the United States, had been planted in Europe. Whether it could flourish and expand, no one yet knew.

AMERICAN STUDIES IN THE 1950S

From the mid-1940s until the early 1960s, the number of European scholars and students who were willing to pursue a career in American history or literature remained small. In the universities of many countries, American Studies was still regarded as a marginal field, or as a form of propaganda paid for by Washington. Those who did become Americanists had to struggle for respect, and for more chairs and institutes—which, in fact, they could not have attained without continuous help from the United States.

One way the European Americanists acquired some legitimacy in the eyes of their academic colleagues was to make American Studies less of a calling and more of a profession. Starting in the 1950s, often with the encouragement and financial support of USIA, the Fulbright program, and the local American embassies, the European Americanists set up national and continent-wide organizations to coordinate their activities, hold conferences, and publish journals.

In 1952, the British Fulbright commission funded an American Studies conference at Cambridge, attended by the leading British Americanists as well as by Henry Steele Commager, Allan Nevins, Alfred Kazin, and Merle Curti from the United States. More conferences were arranged over the next three years, with subsidies from the Fulbright Board of Foreign Scholarships, the Rockefeller Foundation, and the U.S. embassy in London. At the last of these conferences, in 1955, a British Association for American Studies was created. In 1956, the BAAS began issuing a *Bulletin*, edited by Marcus Cunliffe, which evolved by 1967 into the *Journal of American Studies*, the best-known periodical in Europe for essays and book reviews on American history and literature.[45]

Meanwhile, in 1953, at the instigation of the American embassy in Bonn, a similar German association was formed. In 1954, the Salzburg Seminar provided the setting for the establishment of the European Association for American Studies, which brought together Americanists from throughout Western Europe. From the outset, USIA underwrote the association's biennial conferences. Over the next two decades, national and regional organizations proliferated. A Nordic association, embracing Americanists in Norway, Sweden, Denmark, and Finland, was launched in 1959. A French association was founded with assistance from USIA in 1967; it began publishing a journal, the *Revue Française d'Etudes Américaines,* in 1976. In 1969, the Belgian-Luxembourg association was created, followed by American Studies associations in Italy in 1973, Austria in 1974, and the Netherlands in 1977.[46] The existence of these organizations, with their meetings, executive committees, and publications, helped to raise the morale and the status of the European Americanists, and gave them a sense of collective purpose.

As the American Studies movement became more businesslike, the self-image of its practitioners changed. Those who entered the field during these years did not appear to have the evangelical impulses of their predecessors. They thought of themselves as specialists rather than generalists, preferring to write well-researched monographs rather than impressionistic surveys of American history or literature aimed at the general public. Mainly, they were interested in addressing topics of professional concern to other academics.[47]

The trend toward professionalization was evident in West Germany. The Germans who taught American history in the early postwar years were "amateurs" and "autodidacts," in the words of Willi Paul Adams, one of their successors. They had not been formally trained, nor could they afford to travel to the United States. Mostly, they "had to think about eating, keeping warm, finding books, and borrowing a typewriter."[48] For them, America was an exemplification of the good life, not a country with real problems and a complicated history.

Adams was a member of the second generation of German Americanists—a generation that grew up under more favorable circumstances, learned English, visited the United States, and took advantage of "the chance to really specialize in American history." Adams himself was a teenager during the West German "economic miracle" of the 1950s and spent a year in the United States as a high school exchange student, where he first developed an interest in American history and literature. Thereafter, he studied in West Berlin, at the Free University's American Institute, concentrating on the constitutional history of the late colonial and early national eras.[49] Adams went on to become one of Germany's foremost historians of the United States, holding professorships first at the University of Frankfurt and then at the Free University. But he never claimed that he was a missionary, or that he wished to be considered anything other than a serious scholar.

Perhaps it was inevitable, with the passage of time, that the European Americanists should want to become professional academics, rather than participants in a crusade. The same tendencies could be observed by the 1970s and 1980s among those who supplanted the originators of the American Studies movement in the United States. On both continents, the impulse to specialize resulted in a generation of scholars who were obsessed with methodology, whose works had a narrower focus, and who showed little interest in writing for a non-academic audience.

Still, in most of Western Europe, the study of American history—as opposed to American literature—had not progressed very far. The situation in France was not unusual. Many French intellectuals were fascinated with American novels and films in the years after World War II, but few scholars displayed a comparable curiosity about American history. For those who followed the precepts of the journal *Annales*, the United States did not have a past lengthy enough to merit a study of its anthropology and ecology. One could not take a "long view" about a country with such a short history, a country that had not evolved over centuries but instead appeared suddenly, a country without a collective memory because its people had nothing to remember. Besides, whatever there was to say about America, Tocqueville had already said. In any case, France had plenty of history, the right kind of history, for anyone who wished to be a historian.[50]

A more formidable obstacle to the development of American history in Europe was the dearth of materials on the United States in libraries outside Britain. To many European academics, the prospect of uprooting themselves and their families, and trying to raise the money for innumerable research trips to the United States were excellent reasons not to go into American history at all. Those Europeans who did take up American history tended, like the British Americanists, to work in areas in which primary sources were readily available at home—analyzing the bilateral relations between their own countries and the United States, or specializing in intellectual history where most of the "documents" were books and essays that could be read without crossing the Atlantic.[51]

The indifference of Europe's academics to America's history suggested that the version of American Studies practiced in the United States could not be easily exported. In the United States, the effort to interpret the past from an interdisciplinary perspective was what distinguished American Studies programs from the work done in traditional history or English departments. In Europe, American Studies courses and curricula were rarely interdisciplinary during the 1950s. Only in Britain and at the University of Amsterdam's American Institute did scholars try to combine history, literature, politics, and sociology. Elsewhere, European academics—long accustomed to behaving like feudal lords—were fiercely protective of their own departmental prerogatives. They loathed any newfangled experiment, particularly one imported from America, that encroached on their domain or jeopardized their control over chairs and junior appointments. Moreover, their students—seeking credentials that were marketable—did not themselves have any interdisciplinary aspirations; no job in a university or secondary school required such exotic skills.[52]

A knowledge of the English language, on the other hand, was exceedingly useful. From 1945 on, learning and teaching English became a priority in every country on the Continent, France conspicuously excepted. By the 1950s, English was rapidly replacing French and German as the favored foreign language of the educated classes, and of the young whatever their social origins. In West Germany, Austria, Italy, the Netherlands, Norway, and Sweden, English instruction was often compulsory in primary and secondary schools. But the accent and pronunciation of teachers and students alike were unmistakably British. Much of this preference for the Queen's English had to do with Britain's geographic proximity to continental Europe, the overseas broadcasts of the BBC, the language programs of the British Council, and the tendency of many Western Europeans (again excluding the French) to idolize British culture. To overcome this unfortunate predilection, the Fulbright program and USIA began to promote and subsidize the teaching of "American" English, which was also a means of spreading information about America's culture.[53]

One of the most effective ways of familiarizing students in universities and secondary schools with the American vernacular was by having them read American writers. Those who could teach both language and literature were therefore eminently employable. Indeed, a considerable number of Americanists in the 1950s started out as instructors of English before they moved into the field of American literature. As a result, American Studies in Europe meant, more often than not, the study of American fiction and poetry.

Specialists in literature were at an advantage everywhere on the Continent. In countries or at universities with no independent American institutes, American Studies programs and courses were usually sheltered in English departments, where students had some proficiency in the English language. Whenever university administrators created new positions in American Studies, they normally hired people with literary training, rather than historians or political scientists.

Given these incentives, it was understandable that the majority of the Americanists in France, the Netherlands, Belgium, West Germany, Austria, Italy, and Spain should have concentrated on American literature. The leading Italian Americanists, for example, included Agostino Lombardo, who began editing *Studi Americani,* a largely literary magazine, in 1955; Glauco Cambon, who translated William Faulkner's *Absalom, Absalom!;* Sergio Perosa, an expert on F. Scott Fitzgerald; and Biancamaria Tedeschini Lalli, who wrote on Thoreau and Emily Dickinson. Some of the Western European Americanists were influenced by the "new criticism" of the 1950s, with its emphasis on a close textual analysis of novels and poems—a formalistic approach to literature that made it unnecessary for them to know a lot about American history or social life, or to do research in the United States.[54]

This preference for literature was even stronger in Eastern Europe. After 1948, the Communist regimes tightly controlled what was taught in university classrooms. Yugoslavia was the lonely exception: There, translations of American novels were plentiful, students and teachers could attend the Salzburg Seminar, and USIA was able to function with relative freedom. Otherwise, the U.S. government had little access to scholars in Eastern Europe during the 1950s. The libraries of U.S. embassies were closed, educational exchanges were not allowed, and no American Studies movement of any sort existed. Nevertheless, the Communists did permit courses on American literature, as long as professors paid attention only to authors approved by the authorities. The esthetic criterion was exclusively Stalinist. The reading lists were dominated by social "realists"—Walt Whitman, Mark Twain, Jack London, Upton Sinclair, Theodore Dreiser, Sinclair Lewis, John Steinbeck, Howard Fast—writers whose works supposedly illustrated the exploitation, injustice, inequality, and decadence that afflicted the American people under capitalism. Despite these biases, officials in Washington and Americanists in Eastern Europe seemed happy to confine themselves to projects involving literature, on the theory that it was less provocative to talk about novels than to discuss U.S. politics or the benefits of the free market.[55]

During the Cold War, then, there were limits to how much Washington could accomplish in promoting American Studies in Eastern Europe. In Western Europe, on the other hand, the actions of the U.S. government could seem intrusive. At times, Americanists in the West had misgivings about their dependence on U.S. money and advice. It was more than a little embarrassing that the Fulbright program or USIA frequently organized their conferences, provided them with travel grants, supplied their libraries with books, subsidized their journals and professional associations, endowed their chairs, and arranged for American professors to visit their classes and institutes.

The problem was not that the European Americanists were in danger of becoming propagandists for the United States. Rather, as Marcus Cunliffe observed, "American Studies was as yet a frail plant, artificial to the degree that it required irrigation." If U.S. aid "dried up," American Studies programs "would not disappear," but their "development would ... be stunted and retarded." Cunliffe understated the importance of America's help; without it, there would have been no American Studies movement in Europe at all. Still, Americanists in Britain and elsewhere felt the same sort of ambivalence toward their benefactors as did other Western Europeans during the years of the Marshall Plan. There was, Sigmund Skard admitted, "a great need for American assistance," yet there was also "resentment at having to accept it."[56] The question for Western European Americanists, as for ordinary Europeans, was whether they could extricate themselves from the American orbit, and set out on their own independent course.

EXPANSION AND CONTRACTION: FROM THE 1960s TO THE 1980s

There was a certain coziness about the American Studies movement during the 1940s and 1950s, as if it were a small, intimate club, whose members all knew one another and had banded together for mutual encouragement and support. This sense of comradeship began to dissipate in the 1960s and 1970s. European universities underwent a radical transformation, and so too did American Studies. These were the boom years for academics, whatever their field, and Americanists shared in the bounty. No longer feeling beleaguered, they grew in numbers and importance. Along the way, they altered the meaning and purposes of American Studies, so much so that by the 1980s it bore only the slightest resemblance to what its founders—both in Europe and the United States—envisioned in the 1940s.

The economic revival of Western Europe during the 1950s and early 1960s made it possible for governments to start investing in higher education, partly as a way of sustaining the postwar prosperity. In most countries, the sums spent on universities steadily increased throughout the 1960s and 1970s. This educational expansion had two conspicuous results: the creation of a substantial number of new universities, all of which needed faculty, and a major increase in the student population. By 1985, 60 percent of all the universities in Western Europe had been operating only since 1950, and most of these had opened for business between 1965 and 1975. Meanwhile, the percentage of college-age men and women attending universities doubled from a mere 7 percent in the 1960s to 15 percent in the 1980s; then soared to between 30 and 50 percent, depending on the country, by the mid-1990s.[57]

For those who entered American Studies in this period, the construction of universities and the explosive enrollment figures translated into jobs. The European Association for American Studies estimated that at least two thousand Americanists were employed in Britain and on the Continent by the 1980s. Not all of these Americanists were Europeans; a number of Americans took permanent positions in European universities during the 1970s, a reflection of the depressed academic job market in the United States and the opportunities available in Europe. But the majority of the new posts were held by natives. "American Studies was well on the way toward becoming a truly European endeavor," declared Rob Kroes, the director of the American Institute at the University of Amsterdam since 1976. "A new crop of European scholars" like Kroes himself "stood ready to take over from the Americans" who had once been so ubiquitous as guest professors, swiftly filling the chairs in American literature and history that "sprang up all across Europe."[58]

The vitality of American Studies was particularly noticeable in Britain. By the beginning of the 1980s, nearly every university in Britain had a historian of the United States on its faculty. The need for

British students to take courses on American history was no longer in dispute. Students who wished to become Americanists did not have to go to the United States on Fulbright or Commonwealth Fund fellowships to absorb the wisdom of the American masters, as earlier generations had done. They could stay home and be trained by British Americanists who were now confident of their ability to write about the United States with the same skill and archival sophistication as their American counterparts, and who thought of themselves not as outcasts or rebels but as academic insiders.[59]

Although the proliferation of new positions in American Studies was most evident in Britain, similar trends existed elsewhere in Western Europe. In the Netherlands, from the mid-1960s until the early 1980s, chairs in American literature were established at the universities of Leiden, Utrecht, Groningen, and Nijmegen. In France and Italy, escalating enrollments and the demand for more courses in modern subjects meant that, for the first time, scholars could go into the field of American history in the expectation that they would easily find jobs. In Norway, Sigmund Skard retired from the University of Oslo in 1973, his mission accomplished. By then, as a result of the increase in students, America's literature and its history were taught regularly at all the Norwegian universities.[60]

West German universities also grew rapidly in the 1960s and 1970s, as did the number of chairs and lectureships in American Studies. But nowhere in Europe did American Studies prosper more than at the Free University of Berlin. Little attention had been paid to the university's American Institute until November 1963. At that point, it changed its name to the John F. Kennedy Institute in honor of the murdered president whose visit to West Berlin the previous June, when he declared himself a symbolic Berliner, was one of the most dramatic episodes in the city's recent history. Thereafter, with support from Washington and the Ford Foundation, the Kennedy Institute improved its facilities, added new faculty, and built up its library. No other institution tried to be as interdisciplinary, eventually creating professorships in eight different areas—American culture, literature, linguistics, history, political science, sociology, economics, and geography. And no other library amassed as large a collection of American books, magazines, newspapers, government documents, and research materials, nearly four hundred thousand volumes in all. By the 1980s, the Kennedy Institute had developed into the leading center for American Studies, not just in Germany, but on the European continent.[61]

Yet at the very moment when courses in American history and literature were finally winning acceptance in universities throughout Western Europe, a new generation of Americanists and their students became much more critical of the United States. American Studies programs were by no means immune to the political and cultural upheavals of the late 1960s and early 1970s. At the Kennedy Institute, for example, senior faculty members—most of them pro-American and anti-Communist—found themselves battling with Marxist-oriented students and teaching assistants over reading lists, the content of courses, and who should be appointed to all those chairs. U.S. officials could do little more than express their horror at the "radicalization" of an institute they had considered an American outpost behind the iron curtain. Similarly, students in France and Britain demanded that more attention be paid to the history and subculture of groups customarily excluded from the standard American Studies curriculum: women, blue-collar workers, African Americans, Hispanic Americans, Native Americans, leftists (old and new)—anyone whom their professors had not been thinking of when they generalized about the "American Experience" or the "national character" of the American people.[62]

Much of this curiosity about and sympathy for the American underclass was stimulated by the emergence of a counterculture and the opposition to the Vietnam War, movements that captured the allegiance of students and young scholars on both sides of the Atlantic. Not everyone who became an academic in the 1970s occupied university buildings in the 1960s or marched in the streets of Berkeley or Boston, Paris or West Berlin. But Americanists in Europe, like their colleagues in the United States, were influenced by the intercontinental spirit of protest, and by a generational disaffection with existing institutions, conventional politics, and mainstream culture. They shared as well a dissatisfaction with traditional approaches to history and literary criticism, and they felt the same attraction to those theories and methodologies that promised to shift the focus away from "elite" intellectuals and decision makers to the everyday lives of the "inarticulate." So it was predictable that European Americanists in the 1970s would replicate, at least to some extent, the work of the "new" social historians and postmodernist literary critics in the United States—many of whom were in turn disciples of such European gurus as Antonio Gramsci, Jacques Derrida, and Michel Foucault. These impulses resulted in an interpretation of America's past and present that sounded less reverential and more cantankerous.

Nevertheless, the European Americanists of the 1970s were engaged in the same sort of exploration that had inspired the pioneers of the 1940s and 1950s. They were as eager as Sigmund Skard or Marcus Cunliffe to discover the "meaning of America," only now they had a different notion of where to look. Those who specialized in American literature, whether in France, West Germany, Italy, Holland, or Greece, were no longer interested in the legendary writers of the nineteenth century. Why search for the essence of America in the novels of Herman Melville when one could employ Toni Morrison as a more percipient guide? Who was better at illuminating the darker realms of the American psyche, Nathaniel Hawthorne or Sylvia Plath? Why have students read Ralph Waldo Emerson when they could be taught to decode Joyce Carol Oates, Leslie Marmon Silko, and Maxine Hong Kingston? The canon was obsolete, or rather the canon was contemporary, ethnic, and feminist.[63]

Historians were equally revisionist. Earlier British scholars had worried and written about their country's "special relationship" with America as a whole. Their successors in the 1970s and 1980s were less appreciative of the Anglo-American alliance, and concentrated instead on that portion of America represented by minority groups and the working class. In France, the post-1960s professoriate was similarly unimpressed with the idea of a harmonious America made up of people who had the same values and bourgeois fantasies. Marianne Debouzy was a literary critic who believed that "class, ideology, and politics were . . . central to the making of culture and literature." After accepting a position in 1969 at the new and experimental University of Paris-VIII in Vincennes, she transformed herself into a social historian intent on challenging the "altogether false image," prevalent among French and European intellectuals, that American workers had "no tradition of militancy." Her perspective, shared by her radicalized colleagues in West Germany and Italy, was shaped by the work of U.S. social and labor historians like Herbert Gutman and David Montgomery, who were themselves influenced by the two most prominent neo-Marxist scholars in Britain: E. P. Thompson and Eric Hobsbawm.[64]

In effect, the urge to reexamine the American past, and the fascination with the cultural and social experiences of workers, African Americans, Native Americans, and women was a transatlantic phenomenon. For historians in both Europe and the United States, the real America could now be found in union halls and working-class saloons, in the camps of migrant laborers, in the ghettos and barrios, on the reservations, and among women who rebelled against the cult of domesticity.

Notwithstanding their empathy for those at the bottom or on the outside, academics in the 1960s and 1970s led a relatively privileged life. Endowments and government subsidies rose; grants and fellowships were easy to get; new positions appeared all the time. Then suddenly, the era of expansion and affluence vanished, first in the United States in the late 1970s and then in Western Europe in the 1980s. This too was a transatlantic phenomenon, and one that brought even more (though far less welcome) changes to the world of academe.

Most of the countries in Western Europe suffered through a recession at some point in the 1980s. Under such circumstances, the smorgasbord of social services provided by European governments since the end of World War II now seemed too extravagant, particularly when tax rates had reached their upper limits and national treasuries were depleted. Political leaders—social democrats as well as conservatives—began to call for a reduction in government spending; more privatization; and a reassessment, if not a gradual dismantling, of the welfare state.

All these developments affected higher education. Even though student enrollments continued to mount, universities in Western Europe faced the same financial restrictions, hiring freezes, and elimination of positions that American universities had been confronting since the 1970s. More students, less funding, and fewer teachers led to overcrowded classrooms, decaying buildings and facilities, and a spreading sense of gloom, made worse by the fact that graduates could no longer expect to find jobs in universities or secondary schools. Consequently, there was little reason for students to specialize in, or for administrators and government officials to keep on supporting, "nonessential" subjects like American Studies. It seemed wiser to invest in programs that were more European oriented and more vocational—an eminently practical policy in a period of economic retrenchment.

The tribulations of academic life were especially severe in Britain. The impact of the recession was bad enough. But in the view of many scholars, Margaret Thatcher's efforts to reduce government funding for universities and her obvious disdain for the professorial class were principally responsible for the decline of British higher education in the 1980s. Whatever the cause, chairs and lectureships in American Studies evaporated, and new appointments for those just beginning their careers were virtually nonexistent. A number of senior faculty members retired early or departed for the United States (like Marcus

Cunliffe, who left Sussex in 1980 to accept a chair at George Washington University). Their positions often remained vacant for years or were simply abolished.[65]

In other countries, the situation was not much better. With governments and ministries of education in the Netherlands, France, West Germany, and Italy cutting their budgets and requiring academics to be more efficient in the use of their diminished resources, grants for travel and research declined, jobs disappeared, and the prospects for young Americanists became exceedingly grim.[66]

After the end of the Cold War, however, interest in American Studies steadily revived in Western Europe and rapidly expanded in Eastern Europe, in part because the United States was now the only superpower left in the world.[67] More important, despite the hard times of the 1980s, the leaders of the movement had begun to analyze America's development from a distinctively European point of view. The question was whether Americanists in the United States, accustomed to lecturing rather than listening to their European colleagues, would now want to hear what the Europeans had to say.

THE EUROPEANIZATION OF AMERICAN STUDIES

After decades of treating the European Americanists as apprentices, in need of constant counseling and supervision, it was hard for government officials and scholars in the United States to acknowledge that the Europeans no longer required their services. The Americans continued to regard themselves as indispensable because the Europeans still relied on USIA to bankroll many of their conferences, and to provide guest speakers and visiting professors.

Meanwhile, American academics seemed barely aware of what the Europeans, apart from the British, had written about the United States. The European most often quoted by American scholars was Tocqueville. References to the works of modern European Americanists might occasionally turn up in footnotes, but not as a body of ideas or interpretations with which American authors felt they must deal. The notion persisted that the really significant books on American history and literature were produced exclusively in the United States.

The spread of English had a great deal to do with this perception of American superiority. American scholars, along with their counterparts in Britain, could expect their publications to be read by academics throughout the world. Americanists in France, Germany, Italy, Holland, or Scandinavia could expect their books and articles to be read only by scholars in their own countries. If they wanted historians and literary critics in the United States to notice their work, they had two choices. They might try to write in English, a difficult task for those who could understand but not necessarily compose in what was, after all, a foreign language. Or they could arrange to have their work translated, usually with the help of a foundation, since American publishing houses were reluctant to put up their own money for translations of scholarly books whose sales would likely be minuscule.[68]

For many Americanists on the Continent, neither option resolved the dilemma of who they should be writing for. Willi Paul Adams found himself addressing three different audiences simultaneously: "the German-reading general public, the German guild of professional historians, and American professional colleagues." The first two audiences demanded that he publish in German, but the Americans would have ignored his work unless it appeared in English. Which, then, was his primary constituency? Maurizio Vaudagna, an Italian Americanist, confronted the same question. Vaudagna discovered that publishing in English was "not always appreciated in Italian academic circles or prized in the distribution of financial or institutional resources." Hence, he could either seek the approval of Americanists in the United States, or write primarily for the "Italian scholarly community" and "the non-English-speaking" citizenry.[69] Most Americanists on the Continent tried to maintain a dual allegiance, honoring the language and culture of their native lands while attempting to participate as equals in a movement that was monolingual and American centered.

For the British Americanists, language was not a problem. What they worried about was a lack of originality. Repeatedly, the British complained that their own works, and those of their partners in the rest of Europe, were not "seminal" or "innovative." Where, Marcus Cunliffe asked in 1971, "are the modern Tocquevilles? Has the movement in Europe produced any interpretations of American civilization which reveal a . . . non-American freshness" of outlook? His answer, gloomily delivered, was no. "In practically every branch of American Studies," Cunliffe declared, "the organizing ideas, the bold interpretations, the controversy have been introduced by Americans. European contributions have tended to function within the context of received ideas." No matter what theories the European Americanists put forward, they were "likely to find that [their] transatlantic colleagues have been there first." Cunliffe concluded that the Europeans were "doomed to scholarly provincialism. . . What Harvard or Chicago or Berkeley thinks today, in American Studies, is what Oxford or Berlin or Paris thinks tomorrow." Twenty years later, matters had not much improved. According to Tony Badger, a British historian of the United States, the European Americanists were still following too faithfully the "historiographical guidelines . . . laid down in the United States."[70]

To Badger, it was ironic that in their desire to be considered professionals and to "achieve credibility" in the eyes of their American mentors, Americanists in Britain and Europe might have surrendered the chance to utilize their special insight as foreigners to reevaluate America's history and literature. Yet the need for what Cunliffe called a "non-American" version of American Studies had always been clear. As early as 1958, at the end of his survey of American Studies in Europe, Sigmund Skard urged the Europeans "to establish their . . . own methods and standards, learning from each other as much as from the Americans." In 1980, Malcolm Bradbury stressed "the importance of evolving a European approach to American Studies."[71] But what would such an approach look like? And how much could it lead not only to a new understanding of the American past, but to a better understanding of the European present?

One way for Americanists in Europe to become more inventive was to examine American culture from a comparative perspective, a technique normally neglected by their colleagues in the United States who tended to be fairly parochial when they wrote about America. The United States was not the same country when seen from outside its borders.[72] The Europeans were certainly outsiders. As such, their angle of vision, their concerns, the themes and issues they emphasized, all these might well be different, less derivative, and authentically new.

Indeed, as Maurizio Vaudagna discerned, what the Americanists "imported from the United States . . . ended up as something quite different in the course of [its] transfer to European soil." Writing and teaching about America, especially an America that had become such a "visible presence" abroad, was a way of responding to and coping with the "cultural and public needs" of contemporary Europe.[73] Thus, the Europeans could use their training as American Studies specialists to illuminate the complexities of social life in Britain and on the Continent. In this way, American Studies would mutate into a form of European Studies.

Many European Americanists recognized the pertinence of their work to conditions in their own societies. Tiziano Bonazzi, an Italian historian of the United States, suggested that "the impulse to write American history came ... from inside Italian culture, from the hunger for a history that was relevant to the Italian political debate." Marianne Debouzy was similarly motivated. "American history often became an indirect route to tackling present French problems," she conceded. "Interest in Indians was a detour" to explore the issues of "colonialism and imperialism." Analyses of the American labor movement might shed light on the policies of French unions and the attitudes of French workers. Or if one was a British historian, as Michael Heale noted, one could analyze the "failure of labor to emerge as a powerful and radical political force in the U.S." in order to explain the growing conservatism of the British working class. Then there was the plight of the guest workers in every country in Europe. Willi Paul Adams "began to study the situation of German immigrants in American society" because Germany itself was now the destination for a multitude of immigrants, almost all of them unwelcome. Adams thought it would be "useful to remind Germans of their own experience as migrants."[74]

The issue that attracted the greatest attention, however, was the impact of America on Europe. The United States should be treated as a "cultural phenomenon within Europe," Rob Kroes argued. This was precisely what many European Americanists began to do. And they understood what was at stake. "The interest moving [European] students and ... scholars as well to look at the United States," Maurizio Vaudagna observed, "has often to do with music, film, the media, consumerism. In summary, it has to do with the 'Americanization' of our countries."[75] American Studies specialists became increasingly preoccupied with how Europeans received, opposed, and reconfigured American culture to suit their own tastes, how they might be able to "Europeanize" what the United States exported.

Starting in 1979, Rob Kroes edited or inspired a series of volumes, under the general heading *European Contributions to American Studies,* in which the essayists focused as much on Europe's encounter with and reaction to America, as on America itself. The titles of many of the volumes made clear that the United States was being viewed through a European prism: "Image and Impact: American Influences in the Netherlands since 1945," "Anti-Americanism in Europe," "The American West: As Seen by Europeans and Americans," "Within the U.S. Orbit: Small National Cultures vis-à-vis the United States," "Cultural

Transmissions and Receptions: American Mass Culture in Europe," "Hollywood in Europe: Experiences of a Cultural Hegemony."

Works like these revealed the Europeans' ambition to transform and domesticate a set of ideas and techniques that American scholars had originally used to gain a better understanding of the history and culture of the United States. The Europeans were not engaged just in an act of revisionism, nor was this merely a methodological squabble among professors. American Studies had always been more than an academic enterprise. It was from the outset an effort to identify the idiosyncratic and superior qualities of American life. It had also been utilized by the American government to win affection and support for the United States overseas. So from Washington's vantage point, the European Americanists seemed ungrateful, even insubordinate, when they converted American Studies into a movement that questioned, and thereby enabled people to resist, America's influence. But as with other facets of American culture, the United States could not in the end determine what American Studies should be, or how it might be used, after it crossed the ocean.

FIVE

Transatlantic Misunderstandings: American Views of Europe

Until World War II, the majority of Americans (including the children of the immigrants) had little direct contact with Europe, and most Europeans had never met an American. During the first half of the twentieth century, few Europeans visited the United States. Those who did make the journey usually arrived not as champions of an older civilization, but as immigrants or as refugees from fascism, under pressure to jettison their European heritage and adapt to the United States as quickly as possible. In contrast, the Americans who turned up in Europe were not expected to assimilate at all. They came instead as glamorous and exotic emissaries from a strange new world. But which of these representatives, from a European's perspective, best personified America? Buffalo Bill or Woodrow Wilson? A movie star commandeering the most opulent suite in a luxury hotel, or an obscure expatriate poet sipping pernod at a Parisian café? The well-heeled tourist gaping at castles and cathedrals, or the manager of a branch office hoping soon to be summoned home? These vastly different types only confused Europeans about the realities of American life.

If Europeans in America were supposed to forget where they came from, while Americans in Europe rarely fraternized with the natives, it was no wonder that people on both continents had so many misconceptions about one another. It was precisely this lack of substantive knowledge, this reliance on fleeting impressions and images from the movies, that Washington sought to remedy by setting up exchange programs, disseminating information about American culture and politics through the State Department and the U.S. Information Agency, and encouraging European universities and secondary schools to add courses in American Studies to their curricula.

Yet despite the millions of Americans who flocked to Europe after World War II, and the growing number of European writers, intellectuals, and students who traveled to the United States, misunderstandings continued to multiply. Occasionally, the opportunity to live in and learn about a different society helped to shatter some of the stereotypes that Americans had of Europe, and that Europeans had of America. More often, the traveler's prejudices were merely reaffirmed. To the European observer, America's sumptuous supermarkets and sleek new washing machines could not compensate for its culture of poverty, violence, and greed. To the postwar American sightseer, Paris might have been inspiring if only the plumbing were not so deplorable. Out of these transatlantic explorations came a series of travelogues, meditations, and amateur attempts at cultural anthropology, most of them distinguished by an inability to appreciate any country other than one's own. Or to accept another society on its own terms.

It was probably natural for Americans to judge Europe according to criteria that existed only in the United States. And for Europeans to apply to America a set of assumptions more useful in comprehending Britain or France, Germany or Italy. Nevertheless, the era of intercontinental travel and cultural exchange frequently led not to mutual understanding but mutual suspicion, not to greater sophistication but greater provincialism.

TOURISTS AND TEMPORARY RESIDENTS

Nobody seemed more provincial, or more proud of their parochialism, than the Americans living in or wandering around postwar Europe.

Perhaps they felt they had earned the right to scorn those who had once treated them with disdain. For three-and-a-half centuries, from the seventeenth to the mid-twentieth, Americans had been told that Europe stood for high culture and haute cuisine, for the best in painting and architecture, for the finest achievements in human civilization. Now the Americans descended upon Europe as liberators, military commanders and GIs attached to NATO, State Department officers and Marshall Plan administrators, business executives, professors, students, and tourists, many bringing with them a certain measure of arrogance and condescension toward a continent devastated and demoralized by the war.

The Americans were everywhere, and everywhere they went in Western Europe they created tiny replicas of the United States. Herbert Kubly, a Fulbright professor in Italy during the early 1950s, was struck by the American ghetto in Rome. On the Via Veneto, "kiosks were papered with American newspapers and magazines; posters advertised American movies"; the street itself had been turned into an "American Rome"—a "rich, free-spending community of expensive hotels, American cocktail bars, . . . gasoline stations, and, at its foot, the American Embassy."[1]

These enclaves permitted Americans to segregate themselves both from Europe's present and its past. Many observers complained that America's soldiers knew nothing of European history or culture and were unwilling to learn. Instead, the GIs kept to their military compounds, happy to patronize the PX and the pinball machines. American diplomats and government officials seemed equally incurious about European literature or art. They had crossed the Atlantic to help Europe recover from the war and strengthen its defenses against Communism, not to become experts on Picasso or Proust. American businessmen and women hoped to open up the European market; in their off-hours, they socialized only with other Americans, frequenting restaurants where the waiters spoke English. They and their children, noted Edward McCreary in his book on the "Americanization" of postwar Europe, were "shielded from cultural jolts of any kind"; they returned to America "virtually untouched" by their experiences abroad.[2]

As another commentator pointed out, the Americans found it hard to adapt to Europe because their only frame of reference was the sort of life they had led in the United States: "They were not prepared to measure a civilization by the quality of the paintings on the walls" or "by the selection of the custom-bound books on the shelves. . . . They judged [European] homes by the kitchens and bathrooms and were shocked to find them so outdated." Mostly, Herbert Kubly asserted, they spent their days and nights "longing for Texas or Pennsylvania."[3] There were many Americans living temporarily in Europe, but only a few had really left the United States.

This tendency to avoid any prolonged exposure to European culture, and to be startled by the obsolescence of Europe's facilities, was particularly true of the tourists. Starting in the 1950s, the number of Americans visiting Europe rapidly escalated, especially after jet airplanes began to be used on commercial transatlantic flights in 1958. For middle-class American vacationers who had neither the money nor the time for sybaritic ocean voyages, jets made a trip to Europe feasible and affordable. Mass-produced package tours further reduced the costs and anxieties of traveling in a foreign land. The choice of hotels, the lunch stops at restaurants with English-language menus, escorted shopping excursions, sightseeing from the cocoon of air-conditioned buses with explanations provided and schedules maintained by indispensable if not always knowledgeable guides, all these were carefully prearranged, sequestering the tourists from the local population and from the bother of having to make their own independent decisions, converting travel itself into a series of staged events memorialized by souvenirs, postcards, and photo opportunities.

Still, for all the European anecdotes about vulgar, corpulent Americans in their garish Bermuda shorts, draped with cameras, sprinting from one country to another, demanding instant service and cautioning each other not to the drink the water, tourism had become more democratic. It was no longer, as in the nineteenth century or the 1920s, a privilege reserved for the idle rich or the aspiring novelist hoping to be the next Hemingway. Now almost anyone in the middle class could have a European adventure—one that, for all its contrivances, did offer a glimpse of a different way of life. By the end of the 1950s, eight hundred thousand Americans journeyed to Europe each year, most of them heading for France, Britain, Italy, Germany, and Switzerland. By the 1970s, the annual influx of American tourists had reached 4 million.[4]

Many Europeans, not just the surly waiters in Paris, were ambivalent about this new American invasion. On the one hand, the majority of countries in Western Europe needed the tourists' dollars to ease their balance-of-payment problems during the 1950s and to help keep their economies prosperous thereafter. On the other hand, the natives resented having to restructure their societies to accommodate the visiting Americans.

Up to a point, tourism visibly contributed to the Americanization of Western Europe. The tourists insisted on all the comforts of home. They wanted, and the Europeans tried hard to give them, modernized American-style hotels with elevators, room service, thick mattresses, Kleenex boxes, television sets, and a plentiful supply of hangers in the closet. The Americans also required hamburgers washed down with Coca-Cola; grocery stores stocked with gum, Hershey bars, and Fritos; and popcorn (not espresso) at the movie theaters.[5] Even the disciples of Arthur Frommer, who believed they could enjoy Europe on five dollars a day, expected American standards of cleanliness and efficiency at their rustic bed and breakfasts. So Europe's hoteliers and shopkeepers, its restaurant owners and gas-station attendants, made the necessary adjustments to suit their American customers.

Yet notwithstanding the Pizza Huts and Holiday Inns that soon proliferated in the cities of Europe, the tax-free stores with their posters of Marilyn Monroe and James Dean, and the American magazines on the newsstands, the Western Europeans never completely surrendered to the tastes of the tourists. This was evident whenever one heard American travelers grumble about the paper-thin towels and slivers of soap in their hotel rooms, and the difficulties of obtaining ice water in restaurants or a proper martini at a bar. For all its museums and monuments, the tourists invariably concluded, Europe was no match for the United States when it came to the essential amenities of daily life.

The Europeans could never understand the American fixation with showers and toilets. Or how these could become a test of whose civilization was superior. But Edmund Wilson, though hardly a typical American, sounded very much like a typical tourist in explaining why the New World was preferable to the Old. "I have not the least doubt," he declared after a trip to Europe in 1954, "that I have derived a good deal more benefit of the civilizing as well as of the inspirational kind from the admirable American bathroom than I have from the cathedrals of Europe." The cathedrals certainly added "stature to human strivings," Wilson conceded, but the bathroom (provided it was "well-equipped") also served as a sanctuary for "uplifting thoughts, creative and expansive visions." Moreover, he mused, it "shelters the spirit, it tranquilizes and reassures, in surroundings of a celestial whiteness. . . . Here, too, you may sing, recite, refresh yourself with brief readings, just as you do in church." The fact that one could perform these rituals alone, without a priest or the presence of a congregation, was for Wilson a distinct advantage. Having completed the morning ablutions, one could emerge "fortified" and "serene," ready to "face the world."[6]

Could it be true that sitting on the pot might be more exhilarating, and more ennobling, than trudging through Chartres or Notre Dame? Such a notion must have seemed bizarre to those Europeans not yet fully Americanized. But then, in the eyes of their European hosts, the American tourists were rather peculiar guests, affable if a little overwhelmed, often petulant when confronted with anything unfamiliar, plebeian in their attitudes toward art and food, yet always well scrubbed. And, since they were also well upholstered with cash, their whims were to be indulged during the day, even as the Europeans returned each night to their own neighborhoods, their own pubs, their own flats, and their own lives.

The Americanization of Europe, at least of the tourists' Europe, was a superficial phenomenon. The real question for visiting Americans was whether it was possible to discard, if only momentarily, their many preconceptions and try to appreciate Europe's culture and history.

American Writers in Postwar Europe

Despite the belief, shared by people on both sides of the Atlantic, that the United States had emerged from World War II as the new center of Western culture, Europe was still a magnet for American writers and intellectuals. Many continued to think of Europe, even a Europe pulverized by the war, as more artistic, more refined, more aware of the depths and pinnacles of human experience than a blandly optimistic and therefore innocent America. This was the wise and urbane Europe that had attracted expatriate Americans throughout the nineteenth and early twentieth centuries, and it retained its allure for writers during the late 1940s and 1950s. Literary colonies reappeared. Gore Vidal, Tennessee Williams, Truman Capote, Ralph Ellison, and Mary McCarthy all lived in Italy for various lengths of time. Paris became Richard Wright's permanent home in 1946, as well as an intermittent refuge for James Baldwin. From 1948 to 1950, Saul Bellow resided in Paris on a Guggenheim fellowship.

This was also the Europe, a symbolic Europe, that drew hundreds of visiting professors and lecturers who came not just to explain America to their audiences but to explore the Old World, to absorb its culture, and to learn whatever it might still have to teach. During the winter of 1949–50, William Phillips—the coeditor of *Partisan Review*—traveled to Europe for the first time, under the auspices of the Rockefeller Foundation. Although he was received as a celebrity, meeting with the leading members of the British, French, and Italian intelligentsia, and with American diplomats, Phillips "felt like the mythologized American primitive abroad, lost in the sophisticated intellectual jungles of Europe." Similarly, Leslie Fiedler arrived in Italy as a Fulbright professor in 1952, uncertain whether he had undertaken a "pilgrimage to the shrines" of Western culture or a "descent into Hell." Either way, the Americans remained students even in their role as tutors. James Baldwin understood the dual nature of the American intellectual's encounter with postwar Europe, recognizing that the Americans and the Europeans were engaged in a reciprocal transaction: "Europe has what we do not have yet, a sense of the mysterious and inexorable limits of life, a sense, in a word, of tragedy. And we have what they sorely need: a new sense of life's possibilities."[7]

In passages like Baldwin's, one could hear the voice of Henry James. For many American writers, Europe remained a haven for intellectual pursuits, as well as a place of intrigue, sensuality, and decadence—a place about which they were forever ambivalent.

The Americans were frequently appalled by the mood of postwar Europe. "Depraved" and "macabre" were two of Edmund Wilson's favorite adjectives in describing the European state of mind. Wilson particularly loathed Britain, with its class divisions and entrenched cultural hierarchies, as exemplified by the "cliques and snobberies" rampant among the dons at Oxford. Not to be outdone, Saul Bellow called the Paris of the late 1940s "one of the grimmest cities in the world." A feeling, left over from the wartime occupation, of "disgrace and resentment darkened the famous facades," contributing to the general "oppressiveness" of the Parisian air. When Bellow revisited Paris in the 1980s, he was unimpressed by its economic recovery and offended by its embrace of modernity. The French had become addicted to technology and consumerism, he groused; they were passionately in love with "sinks, refrigerators, and microwave ovens." The old Paris, however gloomy, had vanished. The "family bistros that once served delicious, inexpensive lunches" and the "dusty . . . shops in which you might lose yourself for a few hours" had given way to an "unattractive, overpriced, overdecorated newness." Worse, in Bellow's eyes, Paris was now the home not of young avant-garde artists, but of aspiring terrorists.[8]

For most American writers, a sojourn in Europe only magnified the contrasts with the United States. They often revived all the stereotypes traditionally used to describe the differences between the two civilizations. Where Europe was aristocratic in its culture and politics, with those in the upper classes demanding deference from their social inferiors, America was impeccably democratic and egalitarian. Where America was an open and mobile society, opportunities in Europe for social advancement were constricted. Where Americans believed in progress and the future, Europeans were tired, corrupt, slow to change, and wedded to the past. "We have always had something to build, to win," Wilson observed of his fellow Americans, while the Europeans "have too much to look back on."[9]

Yet as Wilson acknowledged, Europe possessed certain attributes unknown in America: "attractively built cities, good and quiet manners, appetizing food, respect for the arts." William Phillips discovered in England a "cohesive culture" and a "genuine literary establishment," both sadly absent in the United States. Saul Bellow envied the Europeans' ability to "enjoy intellectual pleasures as though they were sensual pleasures," a capacity that the majority of Americans, including American intellectuals, conspicuously lacked. So despite his distaste for much of Parisian life, Bellow admitted that the city had affected him deeply. "For the soul of a civilized . . . man," he declared, "Paris was one of the permanent settings, a theater . . . where the greatest problems of existence might be represented." To Bellow and other American writers, Paris was the ultimate Jamesian city, a city of paradoxes: "human, warm, noble, beautiful," but also "morbid, cynical, and treacherous."[10]

These contradictions made not only Paris but all of Europe seem as enticing and disturbing for America's postwar intellectuals as it had been for their illustrious predecessors. In this sense, those who lived or traveled in Europe during the 1950s still managed to sound like innocents abroad.

MARY MCCARTHY'S ITALY

A few writers tried to discuss European culture without lapsing into platitudes about innocence and experience, none more successfully than Mary McCarthy. In two remarkable books, *Venice Observed* (1956) and *The Stones of Florence* (1959), McCarthy entered intellectually and emotionally into the art and political life of Renaissance Italy.

Each was in part a travel book, in part a guide to Italian painting and architecture, and in part a history of two very different cities. Neither work seemed as if it were written by someone who was just passing through. McCarthy approached her subject not with the tourist's glance but with the eye of an expert, a person drenched in the details, who had read everything, walked every street, seen every church and museum. Her books were the products of the years she had spent in Italy, and they reflected her personal, almost intimate feelings about the country's people and its former glories.

Yet McCarthy was sensitive to the contemporary implications of her analysis. She constantly shifted her time frame, giving her readers a kaleidoscopic view of the present and the past, comparing her own impressions of modern Florence and Venice with a description of what the cities were like in their golden age. Moreover, her books had a metaphorical quality about them, as though she were writing not just about Italy's civilization, but about America's as well. For all her efforts to penetrate the mysteries and meanings of Italian art, to understand the impulses behind the paintings and sculpture, the bell towers and piazzas, she could not help using a language and a set of images more suitable for a portrait of the United States. McCarthy may have scrutinized the Renaissance and modern Italian society with the eye of an expert, but she also saw them both through the eyes of an American.

Of the two books, *The Stones of Florence* was more abstract. McCarthy seemed to be keeping her distance from a city whose values she respected but disliked. Renaissance Florence emerged from her pages as a "manly town," a stern and austere place hostile to ostentatious consumption or display, where few concessions were made to "the pleasure principle." The absence of a feminine sensibility was ominous to McCarthy; she found the architecture of Florence functional and utilitarian, with no "blandishments, no furbelows—almost no Gothic lace or baroque swirls." The buildings had the "spare look of a regiment drawn up in drill order," no space set aside for "games of make-believe." McCarthy admitted that Florentine painting had its playful, lyrical moments, its fantasies of Venus in springtime. And there was, after all, Leonardo's mysterious Mona Lisa, surrounded by a surreal landscape, her smile both enigmatic and magical. But in McCarthy's view, the masculine spirit was dominant. The city's heroes were bachelors, monks, prophets, hermits, and soldiers; its paintings were mostly "virile"; many of its most celebrated artists were homosexual. This was a city where Giotto and Michelangelo, not Botticelli, reigned.[11]

The Florentines, according to McCarthy, were a rational people, devoted to the idea (if not the practice) of good government, justice, and equity. Their statues and buildings were designed to convey a political message, a lesson in civic virtue for a citizenry who yearned for a republic that never existed in fact. The Florentines were also believers in science, in mastering nature, in discovering and surveying the world around them—hence their experiments with spatial depth and the use of linear perspective on their canvasses. "In Leonardo," McCarthy declared, "all the genius of the Florentine people"—their gift for engineering and map-making as well as for painting and architecture—"seemed to concentrate."[12]

Yet despite their love of order and proportion, they could at times surrender to superstition and demagoguery, to fits of "arson and image-breaking." Machiavelli was a quintessential Florentine, McCarthy pointed out, harboring visions of an "ideal city washed in the pure light of reason," but so too was Savonarola.[13] Here the connections between Renaissance Florence and modern America began to surface. The United States, like Florence, was for the most part a society that shunned extremes and absolutes. Nevertheless, America occasionally produced its own zealots and book burners who were bent on purifying the realm, as in the case of Joseph McCarthy. It was difficult for someone writing in the 1950s not to notice the similarities between the Florentine and the American brand of fanaticism.

Mary McCarthy's emphasis on other Florentine traits made the city seem even more "American." The people of Florence, as she depicted them, embodied the Puritan and capitalist ethics. They were energetic; innovative; self-reliant; thrifty; competitive; determined to excel; and, above all, commercial minded, just like the Americans. Florence sometimes seemed to her a frontier town, one that could have easily been transplanted to the American West, a town inhabited by pioneers who had no interest in the past, only in what they could make of the future.[14]

By the 1950s, the future had arrived. And it was unmistakably urban. Given the traffic (on any street corner, one could watch the "whole history of Western locomotion . . . being recapitulated"), the congestion, and the noise (a din that was "truly infernal, demonic"), Florence had all the frenzy but few of the charms of New York. Sightseeing in contemporary Florence, McCarthy warned, was nearly impossible: "Driving in a car, you are in danger of killing; walking or standing, of being killed." Yet for all its hazards and discomforts, Florence was alive. It was a railway junction and a center of manufacturing;

a city where everyone was "on the move, buying, selling"; a city that did not cater to or care about the needs of tourists. Florence had no ruins or a "reverence for antiquity" like Rome, nor had it become a "shrine" like Ravenna or an amusement park like Venice. McCarthy admired the Florentine bustle, the sounds of work still being done. Florence might no longer be the city of Leonardo, but it was the city of Gucci and Ferragamo—artists in their own right.[15]

McCarthy was put off by the blunt masculine mentality of Renaissance Florence, and by the abstract idealism that could be used as a weapon of terror in the hands of the grand inquisitors. But the modern city—with its businesslike pragmatism, the sounds of the craftsmen at their anvils and sewing machines, the clatter of trucks and motorcycles making their deliveries, the workmen carrying furniture, and the jackhammers tearing up the streets—reminded her of home.

Venice was another matter. It was difficult for McCarthy or anyone else to offer a new insight about Venice because "nothing can be said here . . . that has not be said before." Besides, all the clichés were true. The Piazza San Marco did look like an "open-air drawing room," and St. Mark's at night did resemble a "painted stage flat," as every tourist since Napoleon had remarked.[16]

One way McCarthy dealt with this problem was to write not only about Venetian art, but about her landlady. In *The Stones of Florence,* there were no memorable personalities; the people of Florence seemed abstract, like the city itself. They appeared from time to time in the book only to illustrate a point McCarthy was making. In *Venice Observed,* McCarthy allowed individuals to speak for themselves, in their own eccentric voices, as characters in a novel might do. And so they lingered in the reader's mind, more than her descriptions of the Titians and Tintorettos crowding the walls of the city's museums.

Still, McCarthy's characters were playing roles, performing for the tourists, who had been the Venetians' only visible source of income since the collapse of their other industries in the eighteenth century. Where McCarthy's Florentines were practical and analytical, her Venetians—starting with her landlady—were devious and theatrical. Florence nurtured intellectuals and theoreticians; Venice turned its people into connoisseurs and clowns. Rationality was neither an esthetic ideal in Venice nor did it ring the cash register. Everyone, from children to priests to the gondoliers, was a tour guide, ready (for a fee) to show the visitor the sights. Venice itself, unlike busy Florence, was a picture postcard, a city of "views," a place devoted not to reality but to simulation, an Italian Disneyland complete with a Grand Canal.

McCarthy relished the Venetians' bag of tricks, the "false vistas" and architectural deceptions, the makeup and masks, the sensation of being at a circus or a carnival in which everything was counterfeit but fabulous."[17] McCarthy had begun her career as a drama critic; in Venice, she was once more reviewing a play.

But it was an American, as much as a Venetian, play. In McCarthy's opinion, the Renaissance Venetians, far more than their Florentine counterparts, had reduced life to a business transaction, converting their palaces into warehouses and making money off the Crusades. Stubbornly secular, they ignored the Inquisition and sheltered the Jews (again for a price, though it was with the Jews that they were most often compared). The Venetians had specialized in printing rather than writing books, the better to profit from their sale. Their artists had painted not for the pope but for a new leisure class. They had created a political system designed to check the power of the doge; his "oath on taking office," McCarthy noted, "was simply a list of things he promised not to do," which especially meant not interfering with commerce and trade.[18] These were values familiar to any American. The merchants of Venice seemed distant cousins of Willy Loman.

There was certainly a paradox here, both for Venice and for America. How, McCarthy asked, could "a commercial people who lived solely for gain . . . create a city of fantasy, lovely as a dream or a fairytale?" Her answer was reminiscent of F. Scott Fitzgerald. She pointed to the connection between money and beauty, riches and love, or the longing for love. Fairy tales, she remembered, were about finding a pot of gold at the end of the rainbow. They summoned up images of "the miller's daughter spinning gold all night long, thanks to Rumpelstiltskin, the cave of Ali Baba stored with stolen gold and silver, the underground garden in which Aladdin found jewels growing on trees." But the search for hidden treasures was not an end in itself, not really inspired by a passion for possessions. The goods the Venetians bought and sold—gems, silk, spices, bolts of cloth—aroused in McCarthy a "sense of pure wonder."[19] Which was what Fitzgerald imagined the Dutch sailors felt when they first glimpsed the "fresh, green breast of the new world."

Venice's wealth was transitory, and it had been used to finance illusions. Nonetheless, McCarthy insisted that "a wholly materialist city is nothing but a dream incarnate." Elsewhere, she had argued that Americans were among the least materialistic people on earth, that their "dream of the conquest of poverty" was less economically than spiritually motivated, with wealth as an instrument to achieve an "ideal state of freedom."[20] Naive perhaps, a bit absurd, like Gatsby's dream of recovering Daisy Buchanan or Willy Loman's dream of being well liked, but not ignoble. This was why McCarthy could delight in the ethereal quality of Venice, why she could write so eloquently of its romanticism and its haunting, doomed grace.

In the end, there was not much difference between the Venetian and the American Dream. Where other writers stressed the contrasts between Europe and the United States, McCarthy perceived the similarities. Thus, the fate of Venice became for her a cautionary tale, as well as a fairy tale, a tale that had as much to do with America's future as Venice's past. McCarthy preferred Venice to Florence because she recognized that the Venetian temperament was profoundly American. But then, Venice was open to many interpretations; it was a hall of mirrors reflecting whatever the beholder wanted to see. In *Venice Observed,* the beholder peered into the canals and saw her own image, and that of her country, reflected back.

STUDENTS, PROFESSORS, AND THE REDISCOVERY OF AMERICA

The main reason tourists, soldiers, diplomats, business people, and writers had such trouble understanding Europe was that they rarely came into sustained contact with the Europeans themselves. The tour bus and the military base, the embassy and the branch office, the carefully orchestrated meeting with selected luminaries from the local literary establishment, all these were forms of insulation and invitations to solipsism. Mary McCarthy was hardly the only American in Europe who found herself looking into the mirror, rather than out the window.

For the thousands of students and professors who came to Europe from the 1940s on to learn or to teach, isolation was neither possible nor desirable. They encountered Europeans all the time—in university classrooms, on buses and at the market, in pubs and cafés. If the student or the guest professor were lucky, they might be asked to dinner or a birthday party at some European's home. If they were very lucky, a friendship—perhaps even a love affair—might ensue.

Yet the relationship would always be complicated. One had the disorienting sense of being alone in the company of others. The American was forever having to defend the United States—its history, its culture, its strange social customs, the actions of the government. Since most of those with whom one had any dealings spoke English, it was easy to assume that everybody attached the same meanings to the same words and, therefore, that the American visitor was being understood. Only later did it become apparent that a common language did not facilitate communication or comprehension. Then one began to realize that living in Europe was really an occasion for introspection, an opportunity not only to explore another country and another culture but to rediscover America.

Europeans might wail about the "Americanization" of their societies, but to a professor or student who had just arrived from the United States and was trying to set up housekeeping, nothing seemed familiar. You had to learn how the banks and the post office worked; how to open the windows or turn on the heat; how to take a shower without a shower curtain (and without turning the bathroom into a lake); where to buy the slugs that operated the washing machines and dryers; how to make do with a refrigerator a fourth the size of the one at home. You especially had to remember to bring your own bags to the grocery store, and to sack your purchases quickly before someone else's bottles came hurtling down the chute.

Gradually, you acclimated. You kept your fork in your left hand after you carved your food. If you were a woman, you stopped shaving your legs. When you were able to remain nonchalant as you contemplated the astronomical bill for your dry cleaning, you knew you were no longer a greenhorn. Now you smirked when some hapless tourist could not figure out how to insert a *strippenkaart* into the ticket-punching machine on the tram; you had a monthlong pass, with your picture on it, like all the other natives.

The one institution that seemed recognizable was the university. All universities, whether in Europe or the United States, were identically equipped. They all had secretaries who were willing to help with the Xerox machine, supply closets bursting with stationery and paper clips, and classrooms filled with eager students waiting on the first day of the semester to look over the syllabus and sit through the introductory lecture.

But the similarities between universities in America and in Europe were deceptive. Almost everything about the European university turned out to be different. Indeed, the "university," in the American sense of a meticulously landscaped campus with lawns, dormitories, libraries, and a student union, did not exist in Europe. Outside Britain, most universities were simply a collection of separate buildings scattered throughout a city. They were not the sort of places where people lingered; after class, everyone disappeared. The guest professor or the exchange student, accustomed to the convivial atmosphere of an American university, was often bewildered by the impersonality of the European "institute." It was necessary to learn a new etiquette. One did not simply drop in to a colleague's office to gossip or continue a conversation with a fellow student in the halls, particularly when the next class might be several kilometers away. One made an appointment, sometimes weeks in advance, to meet and to talk—a formality that the gregarious American, valuing spontaneity, never quite fathomed.

The European university was not a social center, nor was it an interval between adolescence and adulthood. The concept of the "undergraduate," taking courses in the "liberal arts" while deciding what he or she wanted to do in life, was peculiar to the United States. Many American professors found their European students more widely read and better prepared than the average undergraduate in the United States. The Europeans had received an undergraduate education in secondary school. When they reached the university, they were on the same level as American graduate students, and they were seeking professional training for their future careers.

In such a setting, the professor was not the students' friend or surrogate parent but an authority figure, often remote and imperious. American lecturers, coming from a country that regarded academics as either dotty or dangerous, were initially surprised by the high status and prestige of their European counterparts. It did not take long, however, before the American determined that being treated like the other Herr Professors, privileged and properly respected by the lower orders, was rather pleasant and probably justified.

Nevertheless, it was hard to feel magisterial when no one came to your classes. The educational system on the Continent gave priority to papers and oral examinations based on independent work spread out over several years. Courses did not count; there were no tests or grades at the end of the term. Thus, students had little incentive to read the assignments, listen to the lectures, participate in the discussions, or show up for office hours. Attendance steadily dwindled, and the guest professor was normally not around long enough to direct theses or serve as a student's patron. Americans frequently lamented that they did not have enough to do, that their specialties were not in demand. The European professor, hurrying off to a faculty meeting or home to write a book review for the local newspaper, could only shrug.

Yet the greatest disappointment for the visiting professor or student was that they rarely got to know their colleagues. The American, after all, was a transient, someone who could be a valuable professional contact but not potentially an intimate friend. Moreover, while the European might speak English adequately, having to spend an evening conversing entirely in a foreign language was exhausting. As a result, the Americans—particularly those who came with families—ended up spending most of their time with other Americans in similar circumstances, all the while wondering whether they were missing out on the "European experience."[21]

Even when an American and a European did become close, the relationship was often strained because of the European's hostility toward the United States. Many American students and professors were surprised by the vehement anti-Americanism they encountered in Europe, not only in the 1960s when opposition to the Vietnam War was widespread, but also in the 1950s and 1980s when the domestic and foreign policies of Western Europe and the United States seemed more in harmony. Whichever the decade, the visitor became a convenient symbol and target, as if he or she—as a representative American—was responsible for the sins of Washington and Hollywood.

It was difficult to know how to respond. If one agreed with the critiques of America, as Leslie Fiedler discovered, then one was seen as exceptional, "the 'Good American' of the anti-American Europeans," equivalent to "the 'Good Jew' of the anti-Semite . . . not really a Jew or an American, not really the unmodifiable legendary figure of contempt." Or if one was African American like James Baldwin and hence an obvious casualty of America's racism, then one could expect to be "pitied as a victim."[22]

Alternatively, you could reply to criticism by presenting a more benign interpretation of some American horror. If, for example, a European student in a class on McCarthyism asked why American artists and writers did not leave the country, as many German intellectuals had fled Nazism in the 1930s, you minimized the effects of the witch-hunts and blacklists (which you would never do with American students). McCarthy, you pointed out, was no Hitler; no one was sent to a concentration camp, and civil liberties were preserved. In effect, you took positions the very opposite of those you held in the United States.

Many American professors and students found themselves cast in a new role in Europe. Leslie Fiedler considered himself a "dissenter" at home. In Italy he became an apologist for America, a patriot forced to proclaim the "virtues of his society" on every occasion. Norman

Podhoretz was a student at Cambridge from 1950 to 1953; he too felt compelled to correct the British misconceptions about the United States. "Time after time," Podhoretz recalled, "one would find oneself protesting, 'No, it isn't really like that in America, you've got it all wrong,' and then ... to one's own astonishment one would hear oneself offering a spirited defense of this or that aspect of American life which one had never felt the slightest inclination to defend while at home."[23]

However they reacted to the diatribes of their European hosts, the visiting Americans started to feel nostalgic for the United States. One eventually grew weary of Europe's charms, which too often meant having to slog through Arctic winds from the butcher's shop to the vegetable store to the fruit stand to the quaint little bakery (where you bought the lovely fresh bread unsullied by preservatives that was certain to be hard as a brick by the next morning). One yearned for the glossy American supermarket with its half dozen types of lettuce, its infinite selection of potato chips, and its aisles that by now you imagined to be as wide as an interstate highway. The picturesque canals and seventeenth-century houses were no longer as captivating as the stories about American politicians and celebrities in the *International Herald Tribune* or in the European editions of *Time* and *Newsweek*. "After days, weeks, months of genuflection in cathedrals and galleries and museums and chateaux," Norman Podhoretz remembered, he and his fellow American students began to "vie with one another in expertise in the culture that was really in our bones, dredging up the lyrics of long-forgotten popular songs, advertising slogans, and movie plots that neither Michelangelo nor Chartres could ever drive from our minds."[24]

It was possible, of course, that this renewed appreciation of America might lead to equally unrealistic projections. Where the American had once romanticized Europe, he or she was now idealizing the United States. James Baldwin observed this phenomenon among the American students in Paris during the 1950s. At first, he noticed, they were "enamored" with the "legend of Paris." But in reality they had "no love for French tradition," or for the French language, or for the monuments and palaces. Nor did they have any special "admiration, or sympathy" for the French people. Once the "brief period of enchantment" was over, the students became homesick for America, a land still "crude" but also *"simple,* and *vital,"* above all a "place where questions are not asked."[25]

Yet it was precisely because the Europeans asked questions that

American professors and students were able to reevaluate those characteristics of life in the United States which they had previously taken for granted. The visitors were challenged to think about America from an entirely different perspective. Baldwin, despite his long residence in France and his efforts to associate himself with the anticolonial struggles of African Intellectuals, concluded that he had no cultural ties to Europe or to Africa, that his identity and his problems were as inescapably American as those of "any Texas G.I." Podhoretz had a similar epiphany. "It was," he acknowledged, "the American in myself I stumbled upon while trying to discover Europe." Others spoke of their "cultural reawakening," their heightened understanding of America, their greater awareness of its strengths and deficiencies.[26]

The necessity of having always to explain the United States to the Europeans could be irritating, though it was also invigorating. Yet at the end of one's stay in Europe, the cross-cultural conversation was not what mattered. The real benefits of the American's European adventure were intensely personal. Along the way, you learned much about Europe and even more about America. But mostly, in Amsterdam or Copenhagen, Paris or Venice, you learned something important about yourself: both how much and how little you could adapt to a culture that, for all its attractions and similar preoccupations, was fundamentally different from your own.

SIX

Transatlantic Misunderstandings: European Views of America

Europeans—especially those living in small nations like Denmark, the Netherlands, Portugal, or Switzerland—frequently ask American visitors what people in the United States think of their country. The visitor usually tries to respond politely, inventing some opinion Americans might have of the country in question if they had any idea where it was. The honest answer would be that, unless a European country was recently in the news because of an earthquake or a terrorist bombing, most Americans have no opinion of it at all; a Norway or an Austria never enters their minds.

Even in the case of Britain, France, Germany, or Italy, Americans are vague about such details as the history, politics, and contemporary economic problems of Washington's major allies. Winston Churchill, Charles de Gaulle, and Konrad Adenauer were recognizable figures in the postwar years, as was Margaret Thatcher in the 1980s. But what policies these leaders pursued (apart from de Gaulle's penchant for infuriating the United States) did not often penetrate the American consciousness. For many Americans, the larger European countries existed mainly as tourist stops or as a series of establishing shots in Hollywood movies. For all they knew, the boulevards of Paris and the banks of the Seine were props for Gene Kelly's dance routines; the Berlin Wall was where you could expect to find Richard Burton declining to come in from the cold.

The United States, however, was very much on the minds of Europeans. They could not afford to be ignorant of who America's president was or how his decisions affected Europe. It was imperative that Europeans know something about America's economy, its society, and its culture. Sources of information were plentiful. European newspapers and television stations posted reporters in New York, Washington, and Los Angeles; European writers traveled to America and recorded their impressions in books and magazine articles; European "experts" on the United States emerged, ready to analyze the latest trends in American politics and social life.

Yet ordinary Europeans, as well as the pundits on whom they relied, seemed to have as many misconceptions about the United States as American tourists, policymakers, and intellectuals had of Europe. Just as American perceptions of Europe were conditioned by a set of images inherited from the nineteenth and early twentieth centuries, Europeans looked at the United States through a haze of antiquated but still influential metaphors and stereotypes. If anything, the impact on Europe of America's postwar culture, as well as its military and economic power, reinforced the Europeans' tendency to resort to symbolic and sometimes apocalyptic language when interpreting the United States.[1]

The Europeans who visited America after 1945 often sounded like Charles Dickens or Johan Huizinga, or like Edmund Wilson in Europe. There was the same temptation to evaluate the "foreign" culture on the basis of what one was used to at home, and to conclude that one's own country was infinitely better. A British Commonwealth Fund Fellow, making his first trip to the United States in the early 1950s, admitted that for several months after his arrival he "did not question the validity of [his] subconscious acceptance of Britain as the model for comparison." He therefore "found much to criticize" in America. Even if one found much to admire, it was easier to understand the political system and the social customs of the United States by employing a vocabulary and set of standards imported from Europe, regardless of whether these had anything to do with the actual situation in America. The real difficulty, for Europeans in America as for Americans in Europe, was to accept the idea that another culture could be different without being defective, that the United States like Europe had its own mores and traditions, its own unique characteristics that ought to be appreciated rather than anathematized.[2]

Nevertheless, it had always been important, psychologically and culturally, for Europeans and Americans to translate their differences into a form of disparagement. Each needed the other for self-definition. Everyone needed someone else, preferably someone demonstrably inferior, in order to feel special. How could you know what was distinctively British or French without describing what was peculiarly German or Italian or Danish or Dutch? And how could you identify what was "European" without defining what was "American"? Thus the obsession with "models," negative and positive: France or Britain as the embodiments of history and civilization, uplifting or blood soaked, depending on one's perspective; or America as the harbinger of the future whether the rest of the world liked it or not. All of these mental constructs were ways for people and nations to decide what to embrace and what to escape (if they could). In the second half of the twentieth century, America became the yardstick with which Europeans measured both their economic progress and the preservation of their idiosyncratic social and cultural institutions.[3]

The measurements varied according to how the citizens and leaders of a particular European country viewed their relationship with the United States. The British, for example, were prone to think of Americans as their natural if still inexperienced successors on the world stage, the well-meaning but bumbling "cousins" who mucked up George Smiley's operations in the novels of John le Carré, with a State Department in need of constant coaching from the wiser heads in Whitehall. The West Germans were more eager to emulate the Americans, largely as a means of shedding their Nazi past. Many people in Ireland, Italy, and Poland continued to see the United States as a mythic land, a place one could dream about going to even when such a journey was impossible. The tales of American abundance were bolstered by the letters of immigrants who remained in close touch with their relatives and friends back home, sending money and photographs, returning on visits, maintaining more faithfully than other ethnic groups the emotional connections between the old country and the New World.[4]

The Franco-American relationship was the most problematic. The disputes between the two nations and the misinterpretation of motives may have been exacerbated by the small number of French émigrés to the United States, and by the consequent lack of accurate information available to people in both countries about life in the other. But even when American tourists flooded into France after World War II, and French politicians and writers traveled often to the United States, the controversies did not subside. Greater familiarity did not lead to mutual affection or respect. America's leaders tended to regard their French counterparts as uncooperative, frustrating, and slightly irrational, perpetually whining that France's desires and prerogatives were not being taken seriously.[5] For their part, French intellectuals and government officials regarded the United States as a menace to Western (that is, French) culture—a land of skyscrapers, deserts, and Disneyland where maniacs like Joseph McCarthy could thrive. America was in this view the antithesis of France.

Within a European country, peoples' opinions about the United States were frequently linked to their party affiliations and the positions they took on domestic issues. A British Tory or a Christian Democrat in West Germany was far more likely than a socialist or Communist in France or Italy to identify with and support America's economic (though not its cultural) policies. Indeed, the popularity of Marxism from the 1940s to the 1970s, particularly among Western European intellectuals, led to indictments of America's institutions in terms that were more relevant to conditions in nineteenth-century Britain or France. The influence of Marxism also accounted for much of the anti-American sentiment that so disturbed American visitors. On the other hand, when Marxist recipes for social change lost their appeal in the 1980s and 1990s, even the European Left began to praise the virtues of the market economy as it operated in the United States.[6]

Yet European attitudes toward America were not shaped simply by misinformation and misunderstandings. There were real conflicts between the United States and its Western European allies, involving the most basic conceptions of national interest. The disintegration of the colonial empires, the Suez crisis, the French war in Indochina and the American war in Vietnam, the West German attempts at rapprochement with the Soviet Union and Eastern Europe, the arms race, and the installation of more nuclear weapons on European soil, all these were occasions for substantive disagreements over policy.[7] Whatever the psychological roots of the European reaction to America, however allegorical the language in which the arguments were framed, the differences between the two continents were profound and not easily eradicated by diplomatic communiqués or cultural exchanges.

THE ANTI-AMERICANS

To hear officials in the State Department or the U.S. Information Agency tell it, Western Europe was a hotbed of "anti-Americanism" from the 1940s through the 1980s. They did not mean that some Europeans criticized the United States from time to time for one reason or another. Instead, they believed there were large numbers of people who seemed to despise everything associated with America. In this sense, anti-Americanism was an ideology, providing all-purpose explanations for the wickedness of the United States. It was also a set of powerful emotions, bordering on fanaticism, that could be triggered at any moment regardless of the specific issue.

Calling an unfavorable statement anti-American was a convenient way for America's leaders to dismiss both the foreign critic and the criticism. But such a response tended to trivialize attitudes that were extremely complex. Besides, anti-Americanism may have had little to do with America. The shrill attacks on the United States were a means of reasserting a European identity in the face of America's overwhelming economic, military, and cultural presence in Britain and on the Continent. To be anti-American was for many Europeans a matter of honor and a cry for recognition.

The signs of hostility to the United States were certainly ubiquitous in postwar Europe. In the 1950s, according to Herbert Kubly, the streets of Rome and Milan "were littered with anti-American posters," discarded after the latest demonstration against U.S. policy. Nearly every day someone told Kubly that he, along with America's soldiers, diplomats, and business executives, should all go home, leaving Italy to the Italians. Perry Miller, lecturing in the Netherlands in 1949, found anti-Americanism "so deeply embedded" in the minds of Dutch professors that it did not have to be "explicitly uttered," much less thoughtfully examined.[8]

Yet throughout the years of the Cold War, there were European writers who sympathized with the United States. In 1953, Luigi Barzini published *Americans Are Alone in the World,* a witty and knowledgeable assessment of American life. The book became a best-seller in Barzini's native Italy. Barzini had no ideological agenda. But he did appreciate America's accomplishments. "The United States," he wrote, "has created the greatest organization for the production and distribution of goods in history. No people has enjoyed better health and kept the old folks alive so long. . . . The machinery of government is in the hands of reasonably honest men. . . . There are more schools, universities, . . . welfare organizations, orchestras, dramatic societies, garden clubs, hospitals, clinics and libraries . . . than in all the rest of the globe." Consequently, it was "America's job to provide leadership, to maintain peace, to facilitate economic exchanges, to further prosperity."[9] No USIA pamphlet could have presented the case for America more eloquently.

Raymond Aron was less effusive in his descriptions of the United States. He was also less popular in his own country, largely because his qualified support of American foreign policy did not conform to the neutralist, Gaullist, or pro-Soviet sentiments that were prevalent from the 1950s to the 1970s among the majority of French intellectuals. A disciple of Tocqueville rather than Marx, and a sponsor of the Congress for Cultural Freedom, Aron saw the Cold War as a struggle between democracy, however flawed, and totalitarianism—not (as did many French leftists) between Soviet-style progress and American-style reaction. As a result, he dedicated himself to exposing the mendacity and the delusions of the French Communists and their fellow travelers; not for nothing did William Phillips call Aron the "Sidney Hook of France." Aron endorsed the Marshall Plan, the formation of NATO, and the American interventions in Korea and Vietnam, positions which made him a pariah in the circles that admired the geopolitical wisdom of Jean-Paul Sartre and Simone de Beauvoir. Yet because of his pugnacious anti-Communism, Aron became a hero in the eyes of American intellectuals and government officials. He first visited the United States in 1950 but returned frequently over the next twenty years, participating in high-level conferences in Washington and at the major universities.[10] Aron came to be regarded as a "good" European at a time when such types were hard to find outside the chancelleries of America's allies.

Most Europeans, however, were ambivalent about the United States. On the one hand, they respected America's wealth and military strength, and were grateful for its role in liberating Western Europe. In addition, they recognized the need for American dollars to help stimulate Europe's postwar economic recovery, and they accepted the United States as the leader of the Western alliance. On the other hand, they distrusted America's motives, feared its interference in their domestic affairs, and envied its preeminence, all of which caused them to exaggerate its deficiencies. Much of the time, their feelings ranged widely from awe to disdain, attraction to repulsion.[11] The United States was occasionally seen as a savior, but more often as a necessary evil.

In their books and essays, European writers alternately praised and condemned America, sometimes offering contradictory opinions in a single sentence. From the 1960s to the 1980s, the British historian J. H. Plumb lectured extensively in the United States on American and European topics. He was a member of the advisory board of *American Heritage;* a regular contributor to the *New York Times Book Review,* the *Saturday Review of Literature,* and the *New York Review of Books;* and a friend of some of America's most prominent intellectuals: Daniel Patrick Moynihan, Richard Hofstadter, Lionel Trilling, Daniel Bell, Arthur Schlesinger Jr., and Irving Kristol. Plumb freely acknowledged his love affair with America, but his "passion" for the country "was entangled with anger, anxiety and at times even flashes of hate." Jean Baudrillard, the French sociologist, philosopher, and prophet of postmodernism, was equally fascinated and appalled by the United States. In *America,* a collection of hyperbolic ruminations based on his journey across the continent in 1986, Baudrillard announced that "America is powerful and original; America is violent and abominable. We should not seek to deny either of these aspects, nor reconcile them."[12] All one could do, apparently, was to revel in the opposing impulses America inspired.

People in Europe had mixed emotions about the United States for many reasons. Among the most important was the contrast between America's vitality and Europe's postwar malaise. Germany was defeated and divided; Italy had given up its pretensions of grandeur; Britain, France, Holland, and Belgium had lost or were losing their empires. Europe as a whole no longer had global ambitions. America had assumed the role and the importance that Europe previously enjoyed.

To realize that your country did not matter as much as it had was distressing. It was even more galling to have to entrust your fate to a land that had not shared your suffering during World War II, that was robust and supremely confident, that had never experienced (or at least never admitted) failure. "It was unjust," declared D. W. Brogan, normally an admirer of the United States, "that America should be so rich; it was infuriating that she should be so powerful, so indispensable." It was above all embarrassing, Luigi Barzini observed, that the "once proud nations" of Europe now had to "beg for their living, survival and safety."[13]

Despite what they heard from the State Department, most Europeans did not believe they were America's full-fledged and highly esteemed allies. Instead, they felt like subordinates, a condition that bred resentment, especially in Britain and France. Britain's prime ministers hoped that their "special relationship" with Washington might help preserve British prestige and influence in the world. But the Eisenhower administration's opposition to the British-French-Israeli invasion of Egypt in the Suez crisis of 1956, and the American threats to undercut the British pound if London did not withdraw, made it clear that Britain could not pursue an independent foreign policy without first consulting the White House. Thereafter, Britain seemed at best America's junior partner, to be kept informed of U.S. military decisions, as in the case of the Cuban missile crisis in 1962, or to have its airstrips conscripted for America's bombing raids on Libya in 1986. It was no wonder that many people in Britain complained that their country had become America's fifty-first state.[14]

France was similarly humiliated over Suez, as well as by Eisenhower's refusal in 1954 to use American air power to relieve the pressure on the French garrison surrounded by North Vietnamese troops at Dien Bien Phu. The French, far more than the British, disliked their dependence on U.S. economic aid and their diminished stature as just another member of NATO shielded by the American nuclear umbrella. Nor were they thrilled by America's alleged favoritism toward a resurgent West Germany. During the late 1940s and 1950s, many intellectuals and politicians charged that the Americans were ignoring the needs of France, and that French history and culture were insufficiently appreciated in Washington, a situation Charles de Gaulle proposed to rectify when he returned to power in 1958.[15]

From the 1940s until the mid-1960s, West Germany was the most reliably pro-American country in Europe. Yet even here, the stationing of thousands of U.S. soldiers was a constant reminder of the Federal Republic's subservience to Washington.[16] With the emergence of a new generation whose antiwar and environmentalist views strongly affected West German political life from the late 1960s on, the U.S. military bases began to be seen not as a minor irritant but as an outpost of American imperialism.

The Western Europeans had legitimate grievances about the way Washington treated them, particularly since, as Barzini pointed out, the United States did little to help them "forget their weakness and their dependent status." Malcolm Bradbury detected a "certain American satisfaction" in the impotence of the Europeans.[17] Nevertheless, Europe's anti-Americanism was rooted not only in a sense of powerlessness but also in a conflict over roles and symbols.

The European attitudes toward the United States were reminiscent of the cultural dramas of the ancient world—with Western Europe playing the part of the Greeks, defending their classical civilization against the newest Roman conquerors, the mighty but still primitive American newcomers to imperial dominance. In the 1940s and 1950s, a number of writers invoked this image to explain Europe's decline and to justify its ingrained feelings of superiority. In *The Coming Caesars* (1957), the French historian Amaury de Riencourt described the "American expert, adviser, army officer, proconsul, diplomat, and businessman" as the "Roman of our times." The United States, André Visson agreed, had a duty to "maintain order," just as the Romans once did. But even though Europe might have been reduced to a mere province, compelled to follow where the Americans led, the Europeans refused to concede that the United States had become the cultural capital of the Western world. And so they were free to scorn America, much as the Greeks had condescended to Rome.[18]

In the eyes of many Europeans, the loss of autonomy did not have to result in a surrender of cultural sovereignty, or mean that Europe needed to abandon its special cultural mission. On the contrary, the Europeans, like the ancient Greeks, believed they could compensate for their diminished political clout by recalling their long history of artistic and literary supremacy, and by proclaiming themselves still to be the guardians of high culture. The "Athenian complex," as Visson labeled it, the tendency to identify one's country with the ideals of Western civilization, was especially noticeable in France, though it affected other countries in Europe as well. For all its money, machines, and atomic bombs, the argument ran, the United States did not possess the cultural heritage and sophistication that was uniquely and eternally European. Thus, while the Europeans could not elude America's raw power, they could resist its vulgarity and thereby uphold the French, British, Dutch, Norwegian, or Italian way of life.[19]

The analogy with Athens was particularly appealing to Europe's intellectual and political elite. In fact, upper-class Europeans were more apt to be anti-American, on cultural grounds, than were those on the lower rungs of the social and economic ladder. In Britain, France, and West Germany, polls taken in the 1950s showed that blue-collar workers, farmers, and operators of small businesses had a more favorable impression of the United States than did people in government or the professions. Europe's ordinary folk thought of America as a land of high wages and upward mobility, a country where the majority lived well (certainly better than the average European).[20] Those in flight from Europe's postwar poverty seemed undisturbed by America's mass culture and its addiction to consumerism since they too flocked to Hollywood movies and yearned to buy cars, refrigerators, and television sets. While they supported politicians who indulged in nationalistic rhetoric, as in the case of Charles de Gaulle in France, they did so in the hope of improving their own economic situations, not to protect their nation's culture from American contamination.

Still, cultural anti-Americanism was not confined to the privileged or the politically conservative classes. The Communist parties in Western Europe—especially in Britain, France, and Italy—were adept at exploiting anti-American sentiments from the 1940s through the 1960s by posing as cultural nationalists. The Communists benefited as well from their participation in the wartime resistance movements, the role of the Red Army in defeating Hitler's legions, and the hostility of Western European leftists both to American-style capitalism and the Cold War. But the Communists' denunciations of America's cultural invasion—whether it took the form of movies, books, comic strips, or Coca-Cola—and their vociferous defense of the British theater and French painting won them many converts among the European intelligentsia. In Italy and France, writers, artists, and academics relied on Communist theoreticians to define the issues and set the agenda for public debate. Jean-Paul Sartre and Simone de Beauvoir became loyal, and predictable, fellow travelers—supporting the Soviet "peace" campaigns of the 1950s, charging that McCarthyism and the persecution of Julius and Ethel Rosenberg were indications of America's collective insanity, making a pilgrimage to Castro's Cuba in 1960, and serving on Bertrand Russell's International War Crimes Tribunal in 1967 (which found America guilty of terrorism and genocide in Vietnam).[21] During these years, evidently, an intellectual could be a Communist, an opponent of American imperialism, and a custodian of Europe's traditional culture and values, all at the same time.

Even after the luster of Communism and Gaullist nationalism faded in the 1970s and 1980s, anti-Americanism continued to flourish in Western Europe. Now, however, America seemed more like Nero's Rome than Julius Caesar's. The European press was filled with stories of America's political scandals and corruption, its urban violence, its extremes of wealth and destitution.[22] The United States was still a country to be feared, particularly if you were a tourist worried about being robbed or murdered, but it no longer had to be respected.

By the 1990s, many Europeans may have forgotten just why they were anti-American, but the original or specific causes seemed unimportant. What mattered throughout the last half of the twentieth century was their disenchantment with the United States, their anger at having been so thoroughly disappointed, their tendency (as Leslie Fiedler observed) not to hate America's failings but to "hate us for those failings, taking our faults for our essence."[23]

To some extent, the Europeans were retaliating for America's ceaseless expressions of moral superiority, which began with the Puritans and became almost insufferable in the years after World War II.[24] The United States, after all, was a country that could proclaim itself the home of freedom, tolerance, and peaceful problem solving, yet exterminate the Indians, ostracize the African Americans, and pulverize the Vietnamese—actions that persuaded the Europeans that they were no more barbarous than the Americans. This was cold comfort, but no doubt it made people in Western Europe less reverential toward the United States.

It was also easier to criticize a country whose shortcomings were painfully familiar. The United States was a member of the Western family, embroiled in what was essentially a family quarrel. In most families, one member is usually assigned the role of scapegoat. America was a perfect choice because it cared what the rest of the family thought (unlike the Soviet Union, whose culture and values seemed radically different from those of Western Europe, and whose behavior could not be affected or altered by disapproving parents and siblings in London or Paris).[25] The United States, in contrast, could be conveniently blamed for everything that had gone wrong in modern Europe. If the countries of Western Europe were economically dependent after World War II, their dependence was due to the policies of Washington and Wall Street. If American films and television programs proved to be more popular with European audiences than did the local product, this was not because the Americans made what the Europeans wanted to see; instead, the European market was being manipulated by Hollywood's monopolistic practices. If European children seemed indifferent to the customs of their parents, that too was America's fault.

As with all scapegoats, the United States was castigated for the very traits the Europeans disliked in themselves. Some writers argued that anti-Americanism resembled anti-Semitism, with the United States as yet another alien force, manipulating the destiny of Europe, concerned only with commerce and moneymaking, using its power to hasten all the unwelcome changes identified with modernity.[26] But the Jews could be defined as the "others," the ultimate outsiders who would never be fully assimilated. The Americans were too recognizable to be dismissed as foreign intruders. Their material aspirations, for instance, were not readily distinguishable from those of the Western Europeans. The United States was both a temptation and a threat because it represented what Europe could all too easily become—might even wish to become, though such an ambition was rarely admitted. Rather than confront their own distasteful impulses, the Europeans could project their anxieties about who they were and what they wanted onto the Americans. Anti-Americanism was thus a form of denial, a way for Europeans to publicly repudiate the United States while secretly adopting its culture and values.

Given the psychological needs of the Europeans, as well as the transatlantic disputes over economic and foreign policy, the anti-Americans seemed unshakable in their hostility to the United States. Only direct exposure to life in America could modify perceptions and compel a reexamination of prejudices. In the years after 1945, a growing number of European intellectuals set out to discover America for themselves, an exploration that yielded new insights though it did not often change minds.

New York to Los Angeles: Impressions of a Continent

Some came as exchange students or guest lecturers; others, as famous authors on an inspection tour of postwar America. They were a different breed from the prewar immigrants and refugees who had fled to the United States hoping to remake their lives and careers, and who therefore needed to grasp the nuances of their new environment. Their successors had neither the time nor the disposition for subtleties. They were interested in the big picture. A "fact" picked up in conversation, a glance at the passing scenery, a predilection for the weird or extravagant features of American life, a quote from a "representative" citizen confirming what the observer already thought, all gave rise to superficial generalizations about the United States. Then, their expedition or sabbatical ended, the visitors returned to Europe, certain that their travels had revealed the essential America.

Simone de Beauvoir's four-month journey through the United States in 1947 was a classic example of this phenomenon. When she arrived in Manhattan, de Beauvoir was greeted by the New York intellectuals as if she were a movie star. In the immediate postwar years, they were fascinated by the French existentialists, and here was a leading specimen, the embodiment of Parisian brilliance and charm, qualities not in abundant supply at *Partisan Review*.

The encounter was a disaster. Everyone felt patronized—and infantile. As William Barrett complained, de Beauvoir acted like a "schoolmarm or governess who has to explain matters to the benighted children," arrogantly lecturing her hosts on the "true nature of America and Americans." For her part, de Beauvoir was exasperated by the "condescending tone" the Americans displayed toward France, whose behavior they compared to that of an "undisciplined child."

The real problem for the American intellectuals was that de Beauvoir's opinions seemed (in the words of William Phillips) "pro-Soviet and anti-American," making her sound like just another "simpleminded fellow-traveler" rather than a "renowned European thinker." Moreover, her views in the eyes of the Americans were preconceived, intransigent, and wrong—which meant that she refused to listen to or agree with their interpretations of American society. Instead de Beauvoir believed, inexplicably, that the United States in the late 1940s was becoming more conservative and more hysterical about the Cold War, that American women were insufficiently independent, that admission to elite universities was based primarily on wealth and class background, and that the country was infested with psychoanalysts. She rejected the notion that her "suggestions were those of a Soviet agent," and accused her interlocutors of being apologists for "American imperialism." Clearly, there had not been a meeting of minds.

De Beauvoir's record of her experience, *America Day By Day,* was published in French in 1948 and in English in 1952. Its reception in the United States was not kind. "Her book is consistently misinformed in small matters as well as large," declared Mary McCarthy.[27] But unfortunately for the Americans, the book expressed many of the ideas about the United States that other European visitors also had.

Almost every writer was transfixed by America's opulence. Wherever de Beauvoir went, she scented the "smell of money." "I looked in wonder," Luigi Barzini confessed, "at the proud abundance of everything, at the shop windows, at the well-dressed people, . . . at the long queues of shining cars on the roads." The contrast with the shortages and rationing of goods in postwar Europe was striking. Given the austerity of British life in the 1950s, America seemed to Malcolm Bradbury "a paradise of consumer splendors." During his first trip to America in 1945, J. H. Plumb spent hours in an "A. & P. supermarket just watching . . . people" hauling away "carloads of food." Rom Landau, a Moroccan living in Britain who was invited to lecture at various

American universities in 1953, remembered the "little, inconspicuous" signs of an affluent, even profligate, society: the hotel chambermaids who replaced any cake of soap that showed the slightest indication of having been used; the restaurants that discarded their leftover milk, butter, meat, and bread at closing time; the Chinese laundryman who told Landau to buy new socks rather than have his old ones darned, unless he wished to be mistaken for a pauper.[28]

For decades, New York was the American city Europeans most wanted to see. In countless magazine and newspaper photographs and in hundreds of films, they had gazed at its silhouette, the legendary skyscrapers symbolizing for them America's wealth and power. In the late 1940s and early 1950s, New York still seemed a city of glamour and romance, the city Leonard Bernstein evoked in *On the Town*. At that point, neither Bernstein nor anyone else conceived of New York as a dismal, gang-infested setting for *West Side Story*.

In its postwar incarnation, New York was the realization of a European fantasy, the "great city of my dreams" for J. H. Plumb, a place filled with "magic" even for the otherwise skeptical Simone de Beauvoir. Repeatedly, the European visitors cited New York's beauty, its energy and vitality. They were also enthralled with its modernity. When Cyril Connolly, the editor of the British cultural journal *Horizon,* traveled to the United States in 1946, his first and most memorable stop was New York, "the supreme metropolis of the present." To Plumb, New York was the only city in the world that "looks truly of the twentieth century." De Beauvoir was more visionary; New York, she announced, "belongs to the future."[29]

On the other side of the continent stood another mythical city, another exemplification of the future, but one that was decidedly more sinister. To a European, New York was familiarly urban; one could walk its streets and battle its crowds as one might do in London, Paris, or Berlin. But where could one find a reminder of Europe in Los Angeles, or in the whole of California? Lacking a context, the Europeans resorted to imagery borrowed, appropriately, from the media. In describing this fabled locale, they often sounded as if they were composing movie blurbs or selling real estate. De Beauvoir was initially thrilled to be in the "land of the gold-rush, the pioneers and cowboys." Marcus Cunliffe, who came to the United States in 1949 as a Commonwealth Fund Fellow, proclaimed California a radiant "Avalon" for millions of migrants, the "last repository of the American Dream." To Luigi Barzini, California had become for America what America was for Europe: "a clean new world, where everything is easy and possible, where the embarrassing traditions and the errors of the past are forgotten, the empty slate on which to start writing anew."[30]

Yet once the realities of life in Los Angeles intruded, the Europeans adopted a prose style more reminiscent of Nathaniel West. After a few days, de Beauvoir admitted that the city "bewildered" her, and the "traffic was frightening." Another Commonwealth Fund Fellow regarded the inhabitants of Los Angeles, in their greed and "callousness," as typically American. Christopher Isherwood, contributing to *Horizon*'s special issue in 1947 on the subject of America, thought the sin of the Angelenos was not avarice but sloth, "Out there, in the eternal lazy morning of the Pacific," he mused, "days slip away into months, months into years; . . . one might pass a lifetime . . . between two yawns, lying bronzed and naked on the sand." For Barzini, as for Nathaniel West, Los Angeles was the end of the rainbow where people rather than pots of gold were buried, sometimes while they were still alive. "You look at the old men in their canvas baseball caps and sunglasses," Barzini wrote, "the old women with the fancy trousers and the greenish false teeth, the poor people who don't know what to do with themselves, who have everything money can buy and industry, science and advertising can provide—new machines, new diets, new medicines, new religions, wonderful movies, the best climate in the world—and [you] wonder whether they would be more or less miserable dead."[31]

Many Europeans reluctantly concluded that New York, however scintillating, was less a microcosm of America than southern California, however macabre. Los Angeles seemed the archetypal American city. As such, it epitomized America's utter rejection of European civilization.

When Jean-Paul Sartre took a six-week tour of the United States in 1945 as a guest of the Office of War Information, he was mystified by the absence of "*quartiers*" not only in Los Angeles but in every other city he saw. He missed the sense of enclosure, the twisting footpaths, the intimacy of neighborhood life, the cluster of houses and shops that were characteristic of European cities and towns. "The American street is a . . . highway," Sartre decided. With few curves or oblique angles, stretching for miles, it presented an unobstructed view of "mountains or fields or the sea," a glimpse of "infinity" somewhere beyond the horizon. Forty years later, Jean Baudrillard made the same point, noting that the "only tissue of the [American] city is that of the freeways," a peculiar form of social bonding since their purpose was to keep people perpetually "on the move." Both Sartre and Simone de Beauvoir conceded that the sheer size of American cities discouraged walking. Cars were indispensable. In a "drive-in" culture, Baudrillard insisted, any pedestrian was likely to be seen as a "threat to public order."[32]

The cities, despite their sprawl, despite even their spectacular vistas, were only an introduction to the gigantic American continent. Once Europeans ventured into the countryside, they were usually stunned by the vastness of the interior. They found it difficult to adjust to the dimensions of America, to the open and empty space, to the regional diversity and extreme variations of climate. America demanded an entirely different sense of scale and proportion, a recognition that one might travel hundreds of miles without leaving a state, much less the country. For some, this was a terrifying idea. The "enormity of the continent," Marcus Cunliffe observed, "can strike dismay" in the foreigner. "At night," admitted Luigi Barzini, "America was especially frightening, when you no longer saw the faces of people but looked at the immense landscapes." Moreover, the visitor had to contend with the potential savagery of those landscapes. This was a nation, D. W. Brogan warned his readers in *The American Character,* of floods, earthquakes, devastating hurricanes, sudden frosts, debilitating heat waves, and droughts. It was "no accident" he added, that the "great American fairy tale, *The Wizard of Oz,* begins with a tornado and a storm cellar."[33]

Still, one's exposure to nature, especially in the West, could be exhilarating. More important, as a Swiss traveler in the early 1950s pointed out, only in the West was an "understanding of America . . . possible." In the East, America still seemed an extension of Europe. Out west, the European finally left the Old World behind and started to judge America by entirely new criteria.[34]

No writer was more eager to jettison Europe and plunge into the American wilderness than Jean Baudrillard. If the wilderness by the 1980s was no longer as pristine as it had been in the age of Natty Bumppo, this did not bother Baudrillard. His West was "fictional" anyway, along with America itself. Other writers were interested in the physical details of America life—like Simone de Beauvoir, who was mesmerized by the decor of hotel bars and the "shameless profusion of goods" in the drugstores. But the material world, with its social and political institutions, was too tedious for Baudrillard. He "went in search of *astral* America," the America of the deserts and interstate highways, of road signs and theme parks, of speed and freedom and soaring skies (unspoiled by the "little fleecy" European clouds that reminded him of Europe's "fleecy thoughts"). Compared to America, Europe was heavy, slow, small-minded, earthbound, claustrophobic. In the deserts of the American West, according to Baudrillard, one felt insignificant yet unchained. One could luxuriate in the "extreme distances" and the "radical absence of [European-style] culture."[35] Or at least one could fantasize about a West, based on thousands of movie metaphors, in which freedom depended on riding or driving alone through the wide open spaces, into the twilight and the fadeout.

In truth, Baudrillard did not want to know where reality ended and the movies began. He adored what he called the "hyperreality" of America, the illusions of reality offered by Las Vegas and Disneyland, the idea that Monument Valley could be both a geological formation and a "tracking shot" in one of John Ford's cavalry epics. Where Simone de Beauvoir derided the West as a tourist trap and Las Vegas as a "triumph of artifice," Baudrillard believed that the images in the movies and on television, in advertising and on billboards, constituted the "authentic" America. "The whole way of life" in America, he argued, was "cinematic." Sounding like Mary McCarthy describing Venice, Baudrillard asserted that "everything" in the United States was "real and pragmatic, and yet it is all the stuff of dreams too." Thus, in their simulations of reality, the movies and Disneyland captured America's essence.[36]

Mary McCarthy, however, had taken the time to study the particulars of Venetian art and history. Baudrillard, hurtling across astral America, could offer only a few breathless impressions. But his reactions were characteristic of the many European intellectuals who saw America primarily as a symbol, which they could either idolize or reject. Even for those who stayed longer, America seemed endlessly surreal. Nevertheless, their task was to set aside the symbolism, and make America intelligible to the readers back home.

THE OPEN SOCIETY

One way to explain the Americans was to emphasize how greatly their expectations differed from those of the Europeans. America's culture, its political practices, and its social structure may have originated in Europe, but to the majority of European visitors the United States was still an exotic land, where the natives had strange habits and beliefs. To unravel the mysteries of America, one had to be part anthropologist and part sleuth, alert to the meanings hidden in what people said and how they behaved.

The investigation was never dispassionate. The Europeans wanted not only to decode but to judge America, sometimes admiringly but more often critically. Ultimately, the contrasts between the United States and Europe served as a reminder that America failed to measure up, that its way of life was inferior. The Europeans could thus justify their anti-Americanism by demonstrating that what America stood for was un-European.

Unlimited space, for example, was not just a physical attribute of the American continent; it was for most European writers a key to the American psyche. Here the disparities between the United States and Europe were obvious. In small countries like Britain, Switzerland, or Italy, those who lived there noted, spatial restrictions led to "social conservatism and political prudence," and to a sense of "limited possibilities." In America, Harold Laski asserted, the horizons were infinite and so too were the opportunities. There were few obstacles to economic or social ascent. In Laski's view, "the element of spaciousness in American life" resulted in a dynamism that was the opposite of Europe's inbred "rigidity."[37]

The dissimilar attitudes toward space were underscored by the antithetical ways in which Americans and Europeans thought about the concept of the frontier. In Europe, a frontier meant a boundary, a barrier, a line of demarcation, the border where you showed your passport. In America, the frontier suggested unobstructed movement and constant expansion, a fascination not only with open space but (by the time of John F. Kennedy's "New Frontier") outer space.[38]

These differences extended to the actual use of space in people's daily lives. Americans in Europe frequently complained about feeling confined. The wife of an American Fulbright professor in Germany during the 1980s thought that the Germans were not at all Americanized because of the "boundaries" they cherished—the fences separating one house from another, the "doors to rooms" that were always "kept closed," the "lines drawn, and distinctions made." Conversely, Jean Baudrillard drew all sorts of cultural conclusions by comparing the conduct of a French and American family on a California beach. "The American child roams far and wide," he observed; "the French one hovers around its parents" who themselves remained encamped on their "little sandy domain." The Americans, Baudrillard argued, seemed more at ease on the beach because they were accustomed to "lots of space." They felt free to spread out and move around. They did not have to worry about their "manners" or pay attention to the "social niceties," as did the Europeans who came from a world of crowded cities and cramped flats. Hence, the American definition of freedom was "spatial and mobile," not "static" as in the case of Europe.[39]

Baudrillard was not the only European intellectual who noticed the connections in America between space, freedom, and mobility. Many visitors were impressed with how readily Americans moved from one place to another, how prevalent their assumption that they could improve their luck by changing their address or embarking on a new career. To Europeans who normally went to school, married, and spent their adult years living in the same house and working at the same job, all within a few miles from where they were born, America appeared to be a nation of nomads. Everything seemed temporary and unsettled. The cities, particularly Los Angeles, had an air of impermanence as neighborhoods vanished to make room for new office buildings. Family ties were tenuous. Once past adolescence, children invariably left home, relocating in another part of the country.[40] To stay put was a sign of failure.

Some writers found this rootlessness appealing because it reinforced America's democratic ethos. In a "fluid society" where anyone could "climb to the apex of the social pyramid" and blue-collar workers regarded themselves as potential capitalists, Harold Laski, Amaury de Riencourt, Rom Landau, and J. H. Plumb all agreed, there was none of the "snobbery" or obvious class divisions that existed in Europe. Simone de Beauvoir was equally pleased that the "rich American" had no sense of "grandeur" and that "salesmen, employees, waiters and porters [were] never servile." For the French sociologist Michel Crozier, who taught and did research at various American universities and think tanks from the 1940s on, the absence of bureaucratic formalities in the United States was refreshing compared to the "stifling" hierarchical structure of academic life in France.[41]

Geoffrey Gorer, a cultural anthropologist who had studied with Margaret Mead, Ruth Benedict, and John Dollard during the 1930s, returned to the United States in the late 1940s for further work on the American family. In *The American People* (1948), he used his training to explain why Americans were rarely deferential to authority figures, whether political, professorial, or parental. Just as the colonists had rebelled against paternalistic Britain, and the second-generation immigrants had escaped the patriarchal culture of Europe, Gorer contended, so all American children were taught first to reject and then to surpass their fathers. The result was a permissive, freewheeling, antiauthoritarian society, egalitarian in its human relationships if not in its distribution of wealth. Even those who held power retained the common touch. "Democratically obscene in their language," wrote Gorer, greeting subordinates in their "shirt sleeves and with their feet on the desk," on a first name basis with everyone they met, America's political leaders were careful to act like "plain citizens," especially at election time.[42]

Indeed, the reserved Europeans were disconcerted by the affability of the Americans, by their casual demeanor and their willingness to throw open their homes to virtual strangers. In Harold Laski's opinion, the Americans' swift and indiscriminate hospitality "embarrassed" Europeans, who were used to being intimate only with close friends and family members. The Americans revealed too much too soon about themselves; they seemed unaware of the pleasures of privacy or of secrecy. While Europeans thought of their houses as castles or sanctuaries, surrounded by gates, hedges, or high walls, Rom Landau and Geoffrey Gorer submitted, the Americans lived behind picture windows, their domestic arrangements "exposed to the gaze of every passer-by," implying that they had nothing to hide from the outside world. The Americans also lacked the European talent for artful seductions and deceptions, Jean Baudrillard declared.[43] Instead, they assumed that any difficulty could be overcome with a genial smile.

For a number of European writers, America's aversion to guile and intrigue was a reflection of its indifference to history. Ever since the nineteenth century, Europeans had been fond of claiming that they were sensitive to historical complexities while the Americans had no respect for the past. Despite the postwar efforts of the State Department and the U.S. Information Agency to teach American Studies overseas, many Europeans continued to doubt that the United States had any traditions worthy of remembrance or veneration. According to Amaury de Riencourt, America had been miraculously emancipated from the "shackles of history," and "from the memory of past loves and hatreds"—a curious statement in view of the legacy of the Civil War. There was no need in America for a "founding truth," argued Jean Baudrillard, as if the Declaration of Independence had never been written. Simone de Beauvoir believed the average American could not grasp "the idea of a living past, integrated with the present." Even Harold Laski, who in *The American Democracy* provided a seven hundred-page history of the United States, insisted that Americans rarely looked backward because they were certain their golden age lay in the future.[44]

In the eyes of the European analysts, this obliviousness to history accounted for the optimism of the Americans, for their faith in progress, their compulsion to experiment and innovate, and their conviction that every problem had a solution. The Europeans were consistently impressed with the vigor and zestfulness of the American people, their enthusiasm (in de Beauvoir's words) for the "fresh conquest," traits that sharply contrasted with the "dreary caution of the [European] *petit bourgeois*." Hence, it did not astonish Bertrand Russell or Geoffrey Gorer that corporate executives in the United States were more adventurous and more willing to take risks than were their pessimistic counterparts in Western Europe, who preferred old-fashioned but predictable ways of doing business. Similarly, American consumers seemed uninterested in the durability of an item, nor did they sentimentalize craftsmanship. Instead, they assumed that any new product was always better than the one it replaced. But to Luigi Barzini, there was a special poignancy to this confident, if antihistorical, state of mind. "When things are not as they should be," he warned, "when injustice prevails, when failure crowns your efforts, when, in spite of all hopes, man shows himself as he has always been, Americans are . . . surprised and maddened—more so than any other people . . . because they are [so] defenseless" and so ignorant of the lessons of the past.[45]

How accurate were these descriptions of America? Was it really true that Americans were excessively friendly, naively exuberant, and unburdened by the misfortunes of history? Was the United States as "open" and "mobile" a society as the visiting Europeans assumed? In trying to differentiate America from Europe, the European intellectuals had presented an assessment that was mostly flattering to the United States. But the Europeans were not as enchanted with the freedom and expansiveness of American life as they sometimes sounded. Nor did they think that every American they encountered had a sunny disposition and limitless aspirations. Rather, what emerged from their travelogues was a country far gloomier and more disturbing than even they had originally anticipated.

THE UNDERSIDE OF AMERICA

The chief purpose of Washington's postwar exchange programs was to implant in foreign visitors a greater appreciation for America's values and institutions. Yet the chance to travel around the country and meet the people did not necessarily make the visitors more favorably disposed toward America. On the contrary, the experience often confirmed their worst fears about the United States. European writers, in particular, usually found what they were looking for: a reason to reject America because it failed to live up to its own or to Europe's ideals.

In this, they were aided immeasurably by the Americans' own appetite for self-criticism. Europeans were amazed by the media's relentless exposure of America's problems, and by the eagerness of ordinary citizens to complain about the incompetence of the government. One need not depend on foreign sources for revelations about the deficiencies of the United States, a visiting Spanish professor noted at the end of the 1950s; the Americans "tell everything about themselves and even insist on the disagreeable aspects of their country, which others would conceal: statistics on crime, reports on juvenile delinquency, full accounts of any immoral act whatever." The obsessiveness with which the United States disclosed its shortcomings prompted Marcus Cunliffe to declare that there was "no anti-Americanism as eloquent as that of the native American."[46]

Among the natives, those who seemed most authoritative to the Europeans were America's novelists, poets, and intellectuals. Since the 1920s, the European image of the United States had been shaped by satirists like Sinclair Lewis and H. L. Mencken, or by critical portraits of American society in the novels of Theodore Dreiser and John Dos Passos. It was fitting, therefore, that Simone de Beauvoir dedicated *America Day By Day* to Richard Wright, and that she relied for her understanding of southern rural poverty on the works of John Steinbeck, Erskine Caldwell, and James Agee.[47]

By the 1950s and 1960s, Europeans' conceptions of the United States were heavily influenced by the language and theories of C. Wright Mills, John Kenneth Galbraith, Vance Packard, David Riesman, and William Whyte.[48] These writers reinforced the Europeans' suspicion that there was a huge discrepancy between the American Dream and the realities of postwar American life. According to America's leading intellectuals, widespread prosperity had not alleviated the psychological discontents of the middle class, the possibilities of social advancement were rapidly diminishing, and democratic decision making was giving way to a centralization of power.

European commentators incorporated these ideas into their own indictments of contemporary America. In *The Unfinished Society* (1960), Herbert von Borch—a correspondent for *Die Welt* stationed in

Washington—drew on the ideas of Mills, Galbraith, and Whyte to explain to his West German readers why America had ceased to be a land of opportunity. The United States, von Borch asserted, was ruled by a Millsian power elite; its economic structure was marked by a Galbraithian conflict between private abundance and the inadequacy of public services; and individuals, as Whyte had pointed out, were now "ensnared" in a maze of organizations. Similarly, in *The American Invasion* (1962), the British writer Francis Williams—composing most of his book while a visiting professor at Berkeley—argued that the social order in the United States was far from open and that mobility was largely a myth. Instead, America was becoming more like Europe—increasingly rigid and "stratified," a nation composed not of aspiring entrepreneurs but of employees and bureaucrats who wanted nothing more than a "safe job with a pension."[49]

The charge that Americans were conservative and complacent was a staple of American social criticism in the 1950s. Yet in describing the perils of mass production, advertising, and rampant consumerism, European writers cited not only the warnings of Vance Packard but also the older caveats of André Siegfried and Georges Duhamel. Their jeremiads against the evils of standardization, first enunciated in the 1920s and early 1930s, were reprised and embellished in the postwar years.

Everything in America looked and sounded alike, the Europeans claimed. Automobiles, trucks, airplanes, advertising, television, movies—all these had "flattened out regional differences," D. W. Brogan lamented, replacing "rural folkways" with the homogeneous culture of the cities and the suburbs. As a result, one never knew where in the country one had landed. The streets, the office buildings, and the supermarkets in the cities seemed identical. Simone de Beauvoir, traveling from one midwestern town to another, felt as if she never left Cleveland. If you entered an American home, Geoffrey Gorer mused, the furnishings were predictable; it was "rare to come across a house with decorations distinctive enough to be remembered." Inside those houses, Marcus Cunliffe recalled, one invariably heard the "same Hit-Parade tunes" on the radio or phonograph and saw the "same best-sellers" displayed on the coffee table. For Americans, uniformity was synonymous with perfection, Rom Landau concluded: "Not only does the average American take no exception to having a car, bathroom or TV set exactly like everyone else's, but he actually insists on not having it otherwise. . . . The ideal is that a given item should be indistinguishable from others of the same kind."[50]

Standardized products led, of course, to standardized minds. The Europeans hardly needed David Riesman to tell them that Americans were other directed. Well before the publication of *The Lonely Crowd* in 1950, Simone de Beauvoir suggested that Americans looked outside themselves, to the people around them, for their "models [of] conduct." Consequently, Amaury de Riencourt argued, the "psychological pressure of conformity" was "overwhelming." America's famed egalitarianism struck J. E. Morpurgo, a British writer who had attended the College of William and Mary, as suffocating: "The right to be as good as your neighbor had become a necessity to be the same as your neighbor." In the United States, agreed Francis Williams, one had to "do the same things, play the same games, . . . serve the same drinks, think the same thoughts, join the same voluntary organizations, accept the same civic responsibilities, be sociable in the same sort of way."[51]

Under these circumstances, Morpurgo and others believed, "heterodoxy was . . . an un-American activity." Anyone who expressed an unconventional opinion or engaged in "unusual" forms of behavior was shunned. Political dissenters in the era of Joseph McCarthy were harassed. The mores of the group prevailed over the instincts of the individual. A craving for solitude was considered the mark of a misfit. To de Riencourt, America was developing a "type of society" that resembled an "ant heap."[52]

What especially frightened European intellectuals about the United States, an apprehension they shared with American writers like Riesman and Whyte, was the tendency of individuals to internalize the values of the larger society. Americans found "loneliness intolerable," Geoffrey Gorer proclaimed. Individuals yearned for the affection and approval of their peers, associating success and self-esteem with being well liked and "well adjusted." In response, those who controlled the corporations and the government made sure they appeared benevolent and solicitous, observed Jean-Paul Sartre. They offered constant advice on the radio, on billboards, and in newspapers and magazines; they persuaded and manipulated, rather than threatened; their authority depended not on the secret police but on public opinion. This informal consensus, these covert but no less intrusive customs and codes, depended on the individual's "quasi-spontaneous adherence," Jean Baudrillard submitted. And so the power of the people at the top was more insidious and more difficult to resist. "To live sanely" in America, said Christopher Isherwood, one must learn to ignore "the unceasing hypnotic suggestions" of the media, "those demon voices which are forever whispering in your ear what you should desire, what you should fear, what you should want and eat and drink and enjoy, what you should think and do and be. They have planned a life for you . . . which it would be easy, fatally easy, to accept."[53]

If it was hard to escape the ant heap, it was equally hard to love your fellow ants. Americans, it turned out, might wish to fit in but not to be intimate. In the view of Simone de Beauvoir, Rom Landau, and Raymond Aron, Americans did not know how to create "enduring" relationships. Their legendary friendliness was "superficial," fleeting, impersonal, contrived, not at all like the "painstaking exploration of another's personality" that occurred so often in European cafés. Even the American smile was a mask, remarked Jean Baudrillard, "a bit like the Cheshire Cat's grin," continuing to "float on faces long after all emotion has disappeared." Americans smiled to demonstrate their candor, regardless of whether they had anything to say. They smiled because they were expected to smile. They might have no authentic "identity," Baudrillard suspected, "but they do have wonderful teeth."[54]

Here was the ultimate paradox. For all their hunger to conform, the Americans were unable to achieve a sense of community. And this failure was, for the Europeans, the unfortunate consequence of the very tendencies in American life that they had earlier portrayed as virtues.

Was America a mobile society? Yes, but mobility contributed to "the loneliness and isolation Americans dread so much" (Geoffrey Gorer). Did the American concept of freedom depend on the existence of unlimited space? Yes, but the assumption of an endlessly expanding frontier implied that there was enough space for everyone, making social bonds and communal obligations unnecessary. So people in American cities "pass in the street without looking at one another, which may seem a mark of discretion and civility, but which is also a sign of indifference" (Jean Baudrillard). Did Americans believe in working hard, rather than relying on a paternalistic government? Yes, but they were perpetually anxious and insecure, seeking comfort from drugs, alcohol, psychiatrists, and faith healers (D. W. Brogan, Jacques Maritain, Herbert von Borch, Cyril Connolly). They did not know how to relax, how to enjoy their leisure time, how to stop trying to succeed and instead appreciate the value of idleness (Gorer, Baudrillard, Maritain, Amaury de Riencourt, Harold Laski). Were Americans antiauthoritarian? Yes, though their frontier mentality, combined with the glorification of gunplay in the movies, resulted in a disrespect for the law and acts of random violence committed by demented individuals with no connections to the state and no attachment to an ideology—as was normally the case when Europeans maimed or murdered one another (Gorer, Baudrillard, von Borch).[55]

Above all, despite their optimism about the future, and their belief that with sufficient energy and ingenuity all problems could be solved, the Americans overlooked the persistence of evil in human history. They did not have, like the Europeans, a tragic sensibility. This was an argument especially popular with French intellectuals from Jean-Paul Sartre, Simone de Beauvoir, and Raymond Aron in the 1940s and 1950s to Michel Crozier and Jean Baudrillard in the 1970s and 1980s. People in the United States were hopelessly utopian and pitifully innocent, they all insisted. You could tell this, added Geoffrey Gorer and Luigi Barzini, by the Americans' desperate efforts to look forever young, and by their refusal to talk or think about death.[56] The allegation that Americans habitually evaded reality gave European intellectuals another justification for feeling smug and disdainful.

For all its faults, the United States was indisputably a place where ordinary people lived well. Yet even America's affluence was subject to European criticism. If anything, when Europeans confronted the high standard of living enjoyed by the middle class, their deepest reservations about America became apparent.

COMMERCE AND CULTURE

Since the nineteenth century, it had been almost obligatory for European travelers to compare America's excessive materialism with Europe's ancient respect for art, music, literature, and philosophy. During the 1940s and 1950s, before the economies of Western Europe had completely rebounded from World War II, when the contrasts between America's prosperity and Europe's penury were especially glaring, European writers seemed even more eager to ridicule the American preoccupation with wealth, largely as a way of defending the nonmaterialistic advantages of their own civilization.

Their judgments were unequivocal and severe. "In no other country," Harold Laski declared, did the "pursuit of money-making" assume such importance or "wear a more virtuous air." Money was "the sole object" for most Americans, Simone de Beauvoir asserted. The acquisition of wealth had become "the measure of every human accomplishment," reducing all "other values . . . to this one denominator." If an American's sense of achievement depended so heavily on a display of money and possessions, this was because of the pernicious effects of the Protestant Ethic. In the United States, wrote Jean-Paul Sartre, money was a sign that the individual enjoyed "divine protection." The accumulation of worldly goods was not only a way to demonstrate one's social status, Laski and Geoffrey Gorer pointed out, but an "outward and visible [indication] of an inward and spiritual grace." The "man of wealth" believed himself to be a "chosen vessel of the Lord."[57]

Some intellectuals did concede that the typical European could be just as avaricious as the average American, that Europeans were just more decorous and less conspicuous in their quest for material satisfaction.[58] It might also have occurred to the European commentators that if people in the United States were truly descendants of Cotton Mather, then their materialism had a spiritual dimension, a moral purpose unknown to the French farmer or the British shopkeeper or the German burgher who cared little for theological rationalizations but only wanted what the Americans had.

Yet for many European writers, America far more than Europe was a "business civilization" (in Marcus Cunliffe's words). No other American, according to Cunliffe and Harold Laski, had greater prestige or was more influential with politicians and the common folk than the prosperous corporate executive.[59] Such reverence for commercial success made Americans both eminently practical and suspicious of anything that reeked of "culture."

In the view of the Europeans, America's materialism coincided with and reinforced its anti-intellectualism. They were positive that Americans distrusted, even feared, ideas. "No American," proclaimed Luigi Barzini without qualification, "ever talks in abstract terms." When Americans encountered an idea, especially one advanced by a European, they would respond with "facts, statistics, or lived experience," wrote Jean Baudrillard, "thereby divesting [the idea] of all conceptual value." It came as no surprise to the Europeans that pragmatism was the only philosophy Americans had ever produced, a perfect philosophy for an uncontemplative society concerned with immediate results rather than with the leisurely pleasures of reading and reflection.[60]

To those who were familiar with America's history, like Laski, the need to master the wilderness and extract its natural resources, to construct great cities and develop a modern industrial nation, had required a practical, problem-solving cast of mind. Consequently,

Americans preferred the "man of action" to the theorist, the person who "rejected absolutes in favor of concrete solutions that worked in the particular instance." The classic American hero was the inventor, the engineer, the technological wizard, not the artist or academic: Henry Ford or Thomas Edison, not Henry James or Henry Adams.[61]

Perhaps the European refugee scholars felt the greatest discomfort in a society predisposed to think empirically. Regarding themselves as intellectuals and as generalists, accustomed to more speculative forms of research, they were often unwilling to specialize, to become mere experts and technicians—the fate, they imagined, of their American colleagues.[62]

No one was more adamant about retaining his European intellectuality than Theodor Adorno. A charter member of the Frankfurt School, Adorno arrived in the United States in 1938 and joined the Princeton Radio Research Project under the direction of Paul Lazarsfeld. After three unhappy years in which he never adjusted to the American demand for statistical samples and public-opinion polling, Adorno left for California in 1941. During the 1940s, he continued to insist that as a European-style social scientist his primary responsibility was to "*interpret* phenomena—not to ascertain, sift, and classify facts and make them available as information." Accordingly, he avoided quantification whenever possible. In *The Authoritarian Personality* (1950), a collaborative study of the psychological roots of fascism that drew on the talents of American scholars and European émigrés, Adorno contributed the theoretical essays. Always ill at ease with the commercial pressures on American culture and the refusal of American academics to relate their data to any larger concerns, Adorno returned to Germany in 1949 and remained there permanently after 1953.[63]

Adorno's experience in the United States was not typical of all European refugees or exchange professors. Moreover, the emphasis on empiricism in the social sciences and in literary criticism would eventually fade. By the 1970s and 1980s, much of American scholarly writing had become thoroughly Europeanized, resulting in a prose style that was abstract and often unintelligible, but theoretically sound.

In the 1940s and 1950s, however, many European visitors agreed with Adorno (and with William Whyte's *The Organization Man*) that American scholarship was too utilitarian, and that the curriculum in American universities was too vocational. Repeatedly, they complained about the proliferation of courses in accounting, marketing, and advertising—courses designed in Herbert von Borch's opinion to turn out "the socially adjusted young executive, psychologically equipped for leadership and group relations, in tune with society, scientifically trained in the techniques of industrial management, distribution, sales and publicity." This concern for life after school, the Europeans argued, led teachers from kindergarten on to instill in their pupils the importance of being popular and getting along with others, of teamwork rather than personal ingenuity, of making contacts that could be useful in adulthood. By the time they reached college, American undergraduates had been coddled, not challenged. Youthful conformists, taught to repress their idiosyncrasies, they were more interested in finding suitable mates than in learning how to think. No wonder European guest professors came to the same conclusion as American Fulbright professors teaching in Europe: Students in the United States were intellectually immature and knew less about literature, philosophy, and science than their counterparts in European universities.[64]

Pity, then, the eccentric graduate who wanted to be an artist or a writer. Many Europeans persisted in the belief—inherited from the nineteenth and early twentieth centuries—that America was a cultural desert from which the intellectual could only flee. "There is no place in the States where the creative life ... can be pursued," announced the British writer Wyndham Lewis with the usual European certitude about these matters that permitted no rebuttal. The artist, a Spanish visitor claimed, "is always an exile" in America, "lost in a strange land of Philistines." For Simone de Beauvoir, the difficulty confronting America's intellectuals was more specific. There were no cafés or salons where writers could gather, she lamented, no *Deux Magots* or *Le Flore* to provide the proper ambience for conversations about the literary life and world affairs. American intellectuals were condemned to "solitude."[65] No one, it appeared, had ever taken her to the Carnegie Delicatessen.

Given these cheerless conditions, writers in the United States evidently had two choices. Either they could treat their talent as a commodity and churn out best-sellers, hoping to catch the eye and the purse strings of a Hollywood producer (Cyril Connolly, J. E. Morpurgo). Or in the Kennedy years, they might serve as advisers and speechwriters, aspiring political insiders (Herbert von Borch). What they could not do was be like the Europeans. They could not, Simone de Beauvoir and Jacques Maritain pointed out, become the conscience of the society, inspire the public to action, or combine the roles of artist and revolutionary.[66] Jean-Paul Sartre was the model of the European intellectual. All the Americans could offer as an alternative were Herman Wouk and Walt Rostow.

The absence of an authentic intellectual community in the United States meant that America could have no high culture comparable to the one that had flourished for centuries in Europe. Notwithstanding the ascendancy of abstract expressionism and the international influence of America's postwar novelists, most European writers were convinced that Americans lacked the refinement to appreciate or to support symphony orchestras, ballet companies, the theater, avant-garde poetry and fiction.

It was hard for the majority of European intellectuals to see how traditional forms of culture could thrive in a country whose people were so mobile and so impatient with anything that did not promise tangible improvements in the standard of living. Americans might be adept at managing a modern economy. But when it came to creating great works of art or unraveling the mysteries of the atom, they lacked the vision, the genius, the originality of the Europeans. The best the Americans could hope to do was apply the ideas of their mentors across the Atlantic.[67]

The Europeans never sounded more confident about their continuing cultural superiority than when they turned to the field of "serious" music. American composers like Aaron Copland, Virgil Thomson, and George Gershwin were dismissed as mere popularizers, transposing the modernist experiments of an Igor Stravinsky or an Arnold Schoenberg into melodies that American audiences could whistle or hum. Similarly, American conductors, soloists, and symphony orchestras were criticized because they offered a display of technical virtuosity rather than a new interpretation of a work—which was what one could expect from a country that elevated means over ends.[68]

Europe's condescension toward America's culture and intellect had a lengthy history. But in the postwar years, this snobbishness also reflected the fear among European intellectuals that Americans were following their own tastes, that Europe's version of culture was no longer preeminent.[69] It was bad enough that the United States had surpassed Europe in economic and military strength. It was even more vexing that Europe's cultural standards and influence were now being ignored. The Europeans could continue to play the role of Athenians, hoping to civilize the American Caesars. But the task would not be easy if the Americans refused to accept their cultural subservience, and insisted instead that they be the judge of what was creative in the arts and intellectual life throughout the world.

POLITICS AND DIPLOMACY,
AMERICAN-STYLE

At times, European visitors to the United States were less critical of than bewildered by America. They tended to magnify the differences between the two continents because so few American behavioral patterns seemed to correspond with those they were familiar with at home. But their shock at how little America had in common with Europe was also disingenuous; it enabled them to ignore or deny the ways in which Western Europeans after 1945 were increasingly copying American practices.

Nothing was more mystifying to a European observer than the American attitude toward politics. Here was a system that rewarded a politician's charm and charisma, that depended on the packaging of a candidate's personality, that converted a political campaign into a theatrical extravaganza. Never mind that Charles de Gaulle or Margaret Thatcher turned themselves into icons just like Dwight Eisenhower, or that they were as skilled at performing as Ronald Reagan. And never mind that lesser European politicians by the 1970s and 1980s were adopting the tactics of their American peers—dispensing with outmoded ideologies and advertising their competence, all the while calibrating their appeals for the television cameras. These developments could be overlooked and the anomalies of the American system exaggerated.

So, for example, Simone de Beauvoir concluded in the late 1940s that "there is no political life in America." Forty years later, in the midst of the Reagan ascendancy, Michel Crozier assured his readers that "no 'Conservative Revolution' is possible because Americans are . . . uninterested in politics of any kind." What they and other commentators meant was that Europe's brand of "politics," especially in its socialist incarnation, had no resonance in the United States. Voters did not think in terms of class, or rather, they all aspired to be middle class. The Democrats and Republicans muted their disagreements (if, in fact, they ever disagreed about anything) and took refuge in bipartisan coalitions. The labor movement, declining to become a Labor Party, acted like just another pressure group—negotiating, compromising, working within the capitalist system, accepting the prerogatives of management. Of course, the British Labour Party and the Social Democrats in Western Europe followed these strategies too. Nonetheless, a European intellectual still addicted to the language of Marxism could readily assume that the American people—surfeited with consumer goods and tranquilized by mass culture—were indifferent to social issues, that they were more interested in their private lives than in matters of public concern.[70]

If America's domestic politics were incomprehensible, its foreign policy sometimes seemed hazardous to other people's health. The United States presented itself to the world as an omniscient practitioner of diplomacy, adhering to a set of ideals that all nations should emulate. Such hubris, from a European perspective, was reason enough to question America's global hegemony, and to try to instill in the impetuous Americans the sort of wisdom only the Old World possessed.

It was never easy for people in Europe to accept the idea that Americans had all the answers to the world's problems. But during the nineteenth and early twentieth centuries, America's assertion that it was no ordinary nation-state, that its institutions and singular landscape had produced a morally superior society, could be ignored. After World War II, the United States had the power and prestige to persuade, if not to compel, other countries to follow its example.

Missionaries, exuding self-righteousness, with a high regard for their own virtue, are always annoying. The Americans, attempting to convert the heathens—whether in Asia, the Middle East, or Europe—were no exceptions. Europeans, who until 1945 had thought of themselves as the protectors of Western civilization, were especially irritated by America's usurpation of their traditional function. They disliked even more the implication that they too were in need of America's salvation.

Consequently, a number of European writers objected to the notion that the "American way of life" was vastly preferable, and should be adopted as soon as possible by everyone else. The Americans assumed that all foreigners secretly wished to be midwestern Rotarians, Luigi Barzini and Francis Williams grumbled. If people in other countries fell short of this goal, a British Commonwealth Fund Fellow suggested, they were considered incompetent because they had "not yet remodeled [their] institutions on the American pattern." Americans tended to judge other countries by how closely they resembled the United States, argued Geoffrey Gorer—by how faithfully foreigners imitated America's political practices and installed in their homes such "signs of . . . Americanism" as "proper plumbing" and modern kitchens.[71]

This was not simply a case of American presumptuousness. As many commentators pointed out, the Americans seemed unaware that there were other avenues to the good life. It was difficult for Americans, wrote Gorer, "to concede the desirability of forms of organization other than those they [were] used to, or to take into account values, preferences, or prejudices which they have not encountered inside the United States." Thus, Americans were often baffled when foreigners perversely choose to remain foreign.[72]

Moreover, in their drive to impose their standards on other cultures, the Americans were apparently misreading their own history. The Europeans frequently complained that America's past had little relevance to the experience of societies elsewhere on the earth. The United States developed under "exceptional circumstances," Raymond Aron declared. Americans had been fortunate in their exemption from the world's conflicts and catastrophes. But this meant that America's institutions and values were not "transplantable to other continents." Aron counseled his American audiences to keep in mind the "non-universal nature of their own spiritual and historic roots" and to refrain from posing as instructors or exemplars for the rest of humanity.[73]

Aron was not being entirely impartial when he denied the universality of the American experience. The French, after all, had long believed that their own culture was infinitely exportable, and that the history of France had worldwide significance. Both the Americans and the French saw themselves as model societies, each with a mission to transport the ideals of their respective revolutions to the far corners of the planet. The Americans spoke in the name of "democracy" and the French defended "civilization," but their global ambitions were similarly grandiose.[74]

By the postwar years, however, France and America were no longer well-matched rivals, economically or militarily. The French continued to compete with the United States in the cultural arena. The Americans, preoccupied with the Soviet threat, appeared not to notice that they were also in a contest with France for the world's affection. No doubt this obliviousness was infuriating to French intellectuals and politicians. Yet the French—and other Western Europeans—could do little more than evaluate America's performance on the international stage, and offer advice on how better to play the role of world leader.

In the judgment of their European reviewers, even those who identified with the goals of U.S. foreign policy during the Cold War, the Americans could never quite get it right. No matter what Washington did abroad, the French or the British would have done it differently and more effectively.

The Europeans seemed impossible to please because their criticisms of American diplomacy were contradictory. At times, they worried that the United States was too confident about its ability to shape the postwar world, too certain (until Vietnam) that its wealth, military might, and technological skills could accomplish any task the nation undertook. On other occasions, especially during Jimmy Carter's presidency, the Europeans complained that American policymakers were weak, indecisive, erratic, and unreliable.

Alternatively, when John Foster Dulles was secretary of state in the Eisenhower administration, the chief American sin appeared to be an extravagant faith in moral pronouncements, and in diplomatic abstractions like treaties, covenants, official resolutions, and global alliances—an odd predilection for a country the Europeans had otherwise berated for being too pragmatic. Yet even when they believed they were acting on principle, the Americans—with their characteristic impatience and hunger for quick results—were prone to underestimate the complexities of a particular region, usually one composed of Europe's former colonies that only the ex-imperialists in London, Paris, Brussels, or The Hague could properly understand.[75]

The Europeans were consistent, though, in their claim that their American allies were hopelessly inexperienced and immature. American leaders often behaved like "children in world politics," remarked D. W. Brogan. They lacked the finesse to handle dangerous situations. Their naiveté was terrifying, given their arsenal of nuclear weapons. What they needed was Europe's parental guidance. The Europeans proposed to correct America's mistakes and teach its policymakers how to operate in a world of permanent tensions and anxieties, where a nation's military and economic strength might not matter and issues were never completely resolved. To be an adult in foreign affairs meant, from the European point of view, an acceptance of international arrangements based on the balance of power and national self-interest, as well as a shrewd assessment of when to intervene and when to step aside.[76] Given these precepts, American diplomacy would never come of age until someone with a European sensibility, a practitioner of *Realpolitik,* maybe a disciple of Metternich and Bismarck—someone like Henry Kissinger—ascended to power.

In the meantime, the Europeans remained caustic in their appraisal of America's conduct overseas. Perhaps no book reflected the European attitude toward the United States more provocatively than Graham Greene's *The Quiet American*. When the novel was published in 1955, it enraged many intellectuals and government officials in the

United States.[77] As far as his American readers were concerned, Greene had committed the worst crimes of the 1950s: He was a "neutralist," incurably "anti-American," and probably pro-Communist. These accusations revealed less about Greene's politics than about how sensitive Americans could be to the charge that they did not always know what they were doing abroad, and that their efforts to "Americanize" others might end in disaster for themselves and for those they wished to convert.

The place, appropriately as it turned out, where Greene chose to consider the consequences of America's missionary zeal was Vietnam. But this was Vietnam before the massive intervention of American soldiers and nation builders. The French are still the colonial masters of Indochina at the time the novel begins. They are at war with the Vietminh, and do not yet envision the prospect of humiliation at Dien Bien Phu.

The novel is populated by a gallery of sophisticated and cynical characters who seem left over from the cast of *Casablanca:* journalists who pride themselves on their realism; French police inspectors who like to philosophize about human nature; enchanting but enigmatic women; Vietnamese with shady pasts, forged papers, and multiple identities. Greene's Rick is Thomas Fowler, a jaded British newspaperman who has "no politics" and refuses to take sides, who merely wants to report the war without becoming "involved," the personification of neutrality who sticks his neck out for no one.[78]

Into this jungle of intrigue strides Alden Pyle, an American idealist in the realm of the disenchanted. He is therefore genuinely dangerous. Like Robert Cohn in *The Sun Also Rises,* Pyle behaves like a perpetual undergraduate, a schoolboy who gets all his ideas out of books. Young, naive, earnest, a walking compendium of European clichés about American innocence, Pyle does not comprehend the subtleties and deceptions that all the other world-weary adults in the novel take for granted. He is a true believer, a principled fanatic on behalf of democracy, in search of a local messiah who will save the Vietnamese from both the French and the Communists.[79]

Pyle's impulses are admirable, even noble. He wants only the best for the Vietnamese people, and imagines (as presumably all Americans do) that he alone can alleviate their suffering and bring another New Deal to the Mekong Delta. But he succeeds only in blowing up hundreds of civilians—foreshadowing the well-intentioned American bombardments of the 1960s.

"I never knew a man," says Fowler in the novel's famous epitaph for

Pyle, "who had better motives for all the trouble he caused." The Vietnamese—and the Europeans—need to be protected from Pyle's (and, by extension, America's) benevolence. "God save us . . . from the innocent and the good," Fowler pleads, and he proceeds to do so by arranging to have Pyle killed. Ironically, Fowler has at last taken sides. He is no longer detached from the struggles of the postwar world, though his form of engagement is not exactly what American policymakers had in mind when they denounced those Western Europeans who longed to remain neutral in the Cold War.[80]

Graham Greene's portrait of one American's misadventures in Vietnam was prophetic. Yet in the golden age of American power, Greene's "European" pessimism sounded cranky. The American Caesars had tasted neither defeat nor disillusion. So it was convenient for them to dismiss *The Quiet American* as just another expression of Europe's petulance at the decline of its own stature. For the moment, the Alden Pyles could continue to think that the world might be reconstructed according to America's blueprint. And the place that seemed most receptive to American ideas, values, products, and culture was Europe itself.

SEVEN

The Americanization of Europe's Economic and Social Life

The criticisms leveled at the United States by European intellectuals would probably have been sufficient to convince most people in Western Europe of the need to restrain America's influence. But the impact on their countries of American industry, advertising, and consumerism was even more alarming. During the 1950s and 1960s, America dominated the economies of Britain and the Continent as never before. One did not have to travel to the United States to examine the "American" way of doing things. American tastes and attitudes had come to Europe, and their effects were inescapable.

The deluge of American products in the postwar years revived the Western Europeans' fear that their societies were becoming too "Americanized." The memories of the liberation and the Marshall Plan, and the desire for economic development and a rising standard of living, were gradually supplanted by a dismay at the proliferation of sugar-saturated soft drinks and fast-food emporiums.

Since the beginning of the twentieth century, the word *Americaniza-*

tion had summoned up a sense of danger—a feeling that the United States was imposing its economic and cultural will, either unconsciously or with sinister intent, on Europe. Now the American threat to Europe's identity and institutions appeared overpowering. The question was whether the countries of Western Europe could retain their unique characteristics while enjoying the advantages of a modern, American-style economy. And whether their citizens could transform themselves into American-style consumers without surrendering their older attachments to small businesses, family farms, and neighborhood markets. In the early years of the postwar era, the prospects of resisting "America" and remaining "European" did not seem promising.

THE ECONOMIC INVASION

Despite the suspicions of some Europeans, the Marshall Plan was not designed solely to make Western Europe susceptible once again to U.S. economic penetration. Still, the plan did help to stimulate Western Europe's economic recovery, thereby providing a favorable setting for the renewed export of American capital and merchandise. As Western Europe grew stronger and more prosperous, it became more attractive to American corporations and investors. This meant that European companies found themselves increasingly dependent on absentee managers and policies formulated by executives across the Atlantic.

The economic revival of Western Europe began in earnest in 1953. Productivity and employment rates rose steadily throughout the rest of the decade and into the 1960s. The return of prosperity inspired a baby boom, which led in turn to a soaring demand for goods and services. In 1957, the Common Market was inaugurated, further fueling the expansion within individual countries and accelerating Western Europe's economic integration.[1]

American industrialists and advertisers were eager to take advantage of Western Europe's "economic miracle." They also wanted to circumvent any efforts by the Common Market to limit imports from the United States. In their eyes, the postwar recovery opened up new opportunities for investment, for the purchase of European firms and the creation of American subsidiaries, and for the sale of American products, all of these on a scale much greater than what U.S. businesses had achieved in the 1920s.

In 1950, American investments in Western Europe were still

relatively small, amounting to $2 billion, slightly higher than the levels of 1929. By 1967, in Britain alone, the value of U.S. investments had climbed to $6 billion. In the 1960s, Britain became the most important destination outside Canada for the transfer of American capital. Meanwhile in West Germany, American investments totaled $3.5 billion, and in France and Italy, nearly $2 billion. In addition, between 1958 and 1963, 1,000 American companies set up operations or formed subsidiaries in Britain. The figures elsewhere were nearly as striking: 600 U.S firms established branches in France, 300 in Belgium, and 250 in the Netherlands.[2]

As was the case in the 1920s, American money after World War II flowed into the most technologically advanced industries, as well as into those sectors of the European economy that were likely to experience the greatest growth through the remainder of the century. These included electronics and semiconductors, telecommunications, precision instruments, chemicals and synthetics, office machinery, air conditioners, and prescription drugs. American firms also exported a host of consumer products: automobiles, kitchen appliances, vacuum cleaners, washing machines and dryers, radio and television sets, cameras and film, cosmetics, detergents, breakfast cereals, canned goods, frozen foods, and cake mixes. As a result, the profits of American corporations and their subsidiaries far exceeded those of their local competitors.[3]

Most European governments did not object to these activities. On the contrary, they encouraged American investments through tax breaks and subsidies, even though this policy intensified the pressure on their own industries and led, as it had in the 1920s, to an increase in American control over output and decision making. More important, American companies brought to Western Europe not only their cash and their products, but also their ideas about how to manage plants and offices, their theories on dealing with unions, their techniques for enlarging consumer demand, and their methods of packaging and marketing any item the Europeans might wish to buy.[4]

Yet there was always an undercurrent of unease in Western Europe. To welcome American consultants, investors, and corporate managers in the interest of creating more jobs and raising productivity was one thing. To be forced to embrace American values was quite another. During the 1950s and 1960s, the Europeans debated among themselves the best ways to utilize the wealth and know-how of the United States while avoiding the dreaded consequences of Americanization.

EUROPEAN REACTIONS TO THE AMERICAN CHALLENGE

Any credible response to America's economic influence depended first on an understanding of how and why Western Europe might be imperiled by the actions of American corporations. For a number of writers and political leaders, America's industrial and agricultural superiority constituted a threat not only to Europe's autonomy but to its way of life. Hence, the Europeans had to figure out what structural changes they needed to make in order to compete effectively with the United States. But they also had to decide what traditions they wanted to conserve.

Whether the United States was behaving imperialistically, as the European Left frequently charged, or was simply benefiting from its greater wealth and natural resources, misgivings about America's economic dominance were evident in Britain, in Scandinavia, and on the Continent. The French seemed more apprehensive than anyone else. To intellectuals and government officials in Paris, the issue was both economic and cultural. American business practices were seen as a menace to French manufacturers, as well as to French folkways. Because the French presumed that they spoke for Western civilization, they had no qualms about portraying their own situation as a paradigm for all of Europe.

It was therefore appropriate that the most portentous assessment of Europe's economic predicament should come from France. In 1967, Jean-Jacques Servan-Schreiber—the founder and editor of the weekly news magazine *L'Express*—published *The American Challenge,* which quickly became a best-seller in France. The book was also widely read throughout Western Europe, especially by the people Servan-Schreiber most wanted to reach: politicians, economists, bankers, university administrators, and business executives.

The book's success resulted in part from Servan-Schreiber's ability to articulate the deepest fears of many Western Europeans. His message was easily grasped because it was delivered in a series of sound bites, both gloomy and glib. American investments did not just involve the export of capital, he argued. They amounted to a *"seizure of power"* over the "European economy." If the most important business decisions continued to be made in the home offices of American corporations, Servan-Schreiber predicted, Europe would be reduced to a "satellite" populated by underlings filling out forms and carrying out orders. Yet even this was not the worst that could happen. Since the

United States currently had a "monopoly on technological innovation," Europe was in danger of being "forever . . . confined to second
place," condemned to a position of permanent "inferiority" in the
"race for economic progress." The Europeans might grow rich serving
as America's overseas agents and subcontractors. But they would be
"overtaken . . . for the first time in [their] history by a more advanced
civilization." The United States, Servan-Schreiber warned, would
"stand alone in its futuristic world."[5]

Given these dire prophecies, what could the Europeans do to elude
their fate? One possibility was to jettison the familiar economic arrangements that had existed since the nineteenth century and begin to copy
the Americans.

It was easy enough to recognize the disadvantages of holding on to
older forms of economic behavior. Servan-Schreiber and other critics
argued that most European businesses had for too long been family
run, usually by owners who tended to celebrate the virtues of skilled
craftsmanship over mass production. The old guard also preferred a
benevolent paternalism to unbridled competition. For its beneficiaries,
this system may have seemed idyllic, but in fact it was inflexible. It
encouraged authoritarian decision making, economic inefficiency,
and a rigid devotion to the status quo.

Now, according to the reformers, Europe's corporate chieftains
needed to delegate power to specialists and middle managers, as their
American counterparts had been doing since the early twentieth century. In addition, the Europeans had to pay more attention to long-
range planning, the design and packaging of products, and market
research on consumer preferences, rather than rely on custom and
intuition. Instead of resisting change, European executives were
advised to expand their plants and work more closely with government trade ministers as well as with engineers, research scientists, and
experts on commerce in the universities. Above all, they should commit themselves to economic growth.[6] These were the reasons for
America's economic success, Servan-Schreiber believed, and Europe
would be left behind if it did not follow the American example. By the
1960s, French and other European industrialists had accepted this thesis, and were trying to modernize their operations in accordance with
American principles of organization and management.

Such efforts might make France and Europe more productive and
technologically sophisticated. But modernization caused difficulties of
its own. Servan-Schreiber and those who agreed with him were focusing primarily on the economic contest between Western Europe and

the United States. They were not particularly interested in the question of what might be lost once France and the rest of Europe adopted American methods. Other Europeans, though, worried about precisely this issue.

From the late nineteenth century on, many Europeans (not all of them Marxists) had regarded American capitalism as ruthless, brutal, impersonal, and inhumane.[7] How then could they embrace a model that not only appeared monstrous in its own right, but that promised to obliterate all those features of European life they cherished? What would happen to the local artisans, the corner grocery stores, the comfort of dealing with the same merchants every day after the gigantic factories, the supermarkets, and the shopping malls came to town? Did these transformations not demand a renunciation of European-ness itself?

The central problem for the Western Europeans was how to live in two worlds at the same time—the American world of mass production, modern technology and communications, and unrestrained consumerism, and the European world whose culture and values seemed almost preindustrial. For some, the answer was to adapt to the American future while preserving as much as possible Europe's heritage and independence.[8]

The European leader who struggled hardest in the 1960s to translate these conflicting impulses into a coherent political and economic strategy was Charles de Gaulle. Although American politicians and journalists could never decide whether de Gaulle was deranged or merely mischievous, his policies sprang from the conviction that French and European interests were fundamentally different from those of the United States. In the midst of the Cold War, with all the talk of an Atlantic Community acting in concert to repel the expansion of Soviet power in Europe, American officials found de Gaulle's emphasis on the divergences between the United States and Western Europe bewildering. But from de Gaulle's perspective, the notion that Europe should have exclusive sovereignty over its affairs made perfect sense, however much this might undermine the goals of America's postwar diplomacy.

De Gaulle was undoubtedly influenced by the historic antagonism of French intellectuals to American culture and power. He shared their view, prevalent since the 1920s, that the United States was a country addicted to machines, moneymaking, and mass consumption, a country with no traditions and no passion for philosophy or the arts. Yet de Gaulle's disagreements with American foreign policy were inspired less by ancient animosities than by the belief that France and Western Europe had become by the 1960s too dependent on America's wealth and military protection.

These perceptions drove de Gaulle to rebel against Washington's stewardship over the Western alliance. He proposed that Europe, with France in the lead, pursue its own economic and diplomatic objectives. Toward this end, de Gaulle forced NATO to remove its headquarters from France in 1966. He also shut down America's military bases in France and refused to allow French troops to participate in NATO's war games. As an alternative to a unified defense force overseen by the Pentagon, de Gaulle wanted France to have a separate nuclear arsenal not subject to the allied chain of command. In addition, he attempted to restrict American investments in France and insisted that U.S. subsidiaries be managed by local personnel, policies aimed at permitting the French to regain control over their economy.

Since the majority of commentators in the United States could think of no rational explanation for de Gaulle's behavior, they concluded that he was congenitally anti-American. But de Gaulle was more concerned with arresting the decline of France and Europe than with assailing America. Each of his actions was designed to strengthen Europe so it could mediate between the United States and the Soviet Union. Presumably, as the authority of the superpowers eroded, Europe would once again matter in the international arena.[9]

Initially, de Gaulle's tactics were popular in France because they promised to restore French pride and give Western Europe some measure of freedom from American supervision. Nevertheless, his policies did not end Europe's reliance on America's nuclear umbrella, nor did they stop American corporations from taking over European companies. Because France was alone in trying to limit U.S. investments during the 1960s, American businesses simply diverted their dollars and resources to Britain, Holland, Belgium, West Germany, and Italy. France's neighbors benefited from the export of American technology, as well as from the creation of new jobs. Meanwhile, the French continued to buy American products—many of which were manufactured by American subsidiaries in the countries next door. Consequently, the French government decided in 1966 to relax its restraints on American investments, though it still hoped to keep French industries out of American hands.[10]

Servan-Schreiber attacked de Gaulle for being too nationalistic, but their positions were not all that dissimilar. Both wanted a more unified and independent Europe that would be as economically innovative and as technologically ingenious as the United States. Yet this implied that the Europeans would have to construct a replica of the American economy, with large-scale multinational enterprises committed to mass production and mass consumption, as the only way of curtailing America's power.[11] It was hard to see how the countries of Western Europe could salvage their traditions or their distinctiveness at the same moment they were converting themselves into diminutive versions of the United States. At the end of the 1960s, the issue of whether Europe could modernize on its own terms, using its own methods, remained unresolved.

MASS CONSUMPTION AND THE NEW MIDDLE CLASS

In 1960, after a visit to Stockholm, James Baldwin reported that he had heard a lot of people "bitterly complaining about the 'Americanization'" of Sweden. He was puzzled. The only American artifacts he had come across were "juke boxes grinding out the inevitable rock-and-roll tunes"; a "few jazz joints" that failed to remind him of "anything in the States"; and the ubiquitous poster (more like an "effigy") of "the late James Dean" on a motorcycle, accompanied by a "masochistic girl friend," both of them glaring at the camera, giving their best rendition of a 1950s juvenile delinquent, lips curled in a mandatory snarl.[12]

As Baldwin suggested, the symptoms of Americanization were frequently inconsequential. But the concerns about America's imprint on Europe, while overstated, were not imaginary. By the 1960s, it would have been difficult for anyone not to notice the immense popularity of American movies and music. Nor could one have ignored the European infatuation with American fashions, tastes, and lifestyles.

Yet in these realms, the influence of the United States was more psychological than economic. When Swedes, Germans, or Italians spoke of being "Americanized," they were referring to the changes taking place not just in the corporate world but in their own households, in the relationships between husbands and wives, and between parents and children. Here, the American presence was measured less by investments or exports than by the modification of attitudes, expectations, and patterns of conduct. At bottom, imitating the Americans involved more than the purchase of a refrigerator and a new car, or (if one was young) a pair of blue jeans and a black leather jacket. It meant thinking of oneself as a perpetual consumer, soon to arrive in or already a member of the affluent middle class.

Americans were the first people to experience the pleasures of consumerism because U.S. manufacturers had introduced and refined the techniques of mass production in the late nineteenth and early twentieth centuries, and because by the 1920s America had a larger population with a higher per capita income than any of the other industrialized countries in the West. But if the United States was the prototype of a modern consumer society, the model along with the merchandise could be easily transported to Europe, as they both were after World War II. No matter how many Marxist intellectuals or aristocratic conservatives sneered at the materialism of the Americans, the commoners in Britain and on the Continent turned out to be as acquisitive as their cousins across the ocean. Everywhere in Western Europe, people who suffered through the war (including the critics themselves) now craved the creature comforts that had become synonymous with the American way of life.[13]

The emergence of consumerism in postwar Europe coincided with a substantial growth in personal and disposable income. In France, for example, wages rose more rapidly than the cost of living during the 1950s, leading to a sharp increase in purchasing power. Consumption was additionally stimulated by an expansion of credit and by people's willingness to go into debt to buy what they wanted. Similar developments occurred in Britain, Italy, and especially West Germany. As a result, Western Europeans began to spend less of their money on basic necessities like food, clothing, and shelter, and proportionally more on such "luxuries" as new furniture, electrical appliances, crystal and china, high-fidelity phonographs and records, television sets, and leisure wear—most of these made in America.[14]

No item was in greater demand or more quickly procured than an automobile. To own a car, preferably a glossy American car, the kind one could barely maneuver through Europe's cramped and congested streets, brought instant status.[15] But even the smaller European cars enabled families to take longer holidays, shop outside their immediate neighborhoods, and move away from the city centers where rents were expensive and facilities were often dilapidated. Soon, more superhighways and cloverleaves were constructed, radically altering the landscape and making the majority of Western Europeans as mobile and as speed crazed as the average American.

The most significant consequence of consumerism was the muting of class divisions, not only in Scandinavia with its social democratic ethos or on the Continent but even, to some extent, in class-obsessed Britain. Much of this change was stylistic, rather than ideological; one might buy a washing machine without deserting the Labour Party. Nevertheless, a growing number of blue-collar workers could afford to purchase the same products, drive the same cars, and wear the same clothes as those in the middle class.[16] It was this trend, more than any other, that made Western Europe a radically different place in the 1960s and 1970s than it had been before the war.

Thus, in France, nearly half the population still lived on the land in 1945, and class-conscious peasants, workers, and petit-bourgeois shop-keepers thought of themselves as the soul of the nation. Four decades later, France more closely resembled the United States, at least demo-graphically. Less than 5 percent of the French population were farm-ers and fewer than a third of the labor force was composed of indus-trial workers. Most people held white-collar positions in business, the government, the professions, or the service sector of the economy. The other, more unfortunate, similarity with America was the appearance of a seemingly permanent underclass: immigrants from Africa and the Middle East or refugees from civil wars closer to France, warehoused in high-rise slums on the outskirts of the cities, unemployed or toiling at low-wage dead-end jobs, their children aimlessly riding the Métro and organizing themselves into gangs, surrounded by a culture of vio-lence and drugs, feared and despised by the prosperous and the privi-leged.[17] These new forms of ethnic and economic stratification were hardly unique to France and America. In every country in Western Europe by the 1980s, the lines between the middle class and the poor had become more visible and more intractable.

For the majority of Western Europeans, however, affluence had become the norm. It was also an avenue to a better, more enjoyable life. In Europe, as in the United States, the principal sign of social and economic ascent was the move to a more spacious flat or to a free-standing house in a cheerier part of the city—or even to some new res-idential development in an outlying area striving hard to look like an American suburb.

In the twentieth century, the ideal of home ownership became an es-sential component of the American Dream. American zoning commis-sioners—true believers in "free enterprise" and pressured by bankers, building contractors, and real estate speculators—were perfectly will-ing to let the countryside be transformed into an endless series of subdivisions. As an additional stimulus to the housing market, Con-gress allowed home owners to deduct the interest on their mortgage payments from their taxable income. Given this tax incentive and an expanding supply of moderately priced homes for sale, ordinary Americans grew accustomed to the notion of living in single-family houses. In contrast, Europeans—faced with limited amounts of usable land, particularly in small countries like Holland, and the high costs of residential construction compounded by government restrictions on what could be built—thought of themselves mainly as renters and apartment dwellers.[18]

Yet as early as the 1950s, there were indications that Western Europeans too were eager to become home owners and suburbanites. In Britain, "new towns" sprang up, complete with detached houses, tiny but immaculate front lawns, backyard gardens, and fences, all of these touches reminding one critic of the set for an Andy Hardy movie. By the 1980s, tract houses and long commutes were becoming commonplace throughout Western Europe.[19] Although most Europeans still lived in cities, the suburban experience—with its supermarkets, shopping centers, and mammoth parking lots—was no longer an exclusively American phenomenon.

Wherever one's residence, in the prosperous postwar era one could always make home improvements. More was involved here than redecoration. By remodeling the living room, modernizing the bathroom, or installing an "American-style" kitchen, Europeans were seeking relief from the time-consuming and often exhausting chores of the prewar world, a world in which broken fixtures were repaired and dinner was cooked without the aid of power drills and food blenders. For women in particular, the new machines and appliances were emancipating.[20] But the entire family was affected. Increasingly, wives could work outside the home. Husbands, with reluctance, might have to give up their role as primary breadwinners and authority figures. Children could be raised less traditionally and more permissively, an excellent if unintentional preparation for the generational upheavals of the 1960s and 1970s. In the meantime, everyone could devote more of his or her waking hours to recreation and mass entertainment.

All of these trends were unsettling. And all of them seemed very "American." The paradox of Americanization was that it promised to liberate as well as to alienate people from the past. At the same time, it offered a future filled with both greater abundance and more anxieties. This paradox explained why many Western Europeans, though eager to join the middle class and participate in the consumer revolution, were deeply ambivalent about the long-term effects of America on their societies and on their private lives.

THE WAR AGAINST COCA-COLA

Before McDonald's and Euro Disney, there was Coca-Cola. No export served as a more potent symbol of the American way of life than Coke. And no product was more controversial or provoked as much resistance, at least during the early stages of its arrival in Europe. A legion of intellectuals, Communists, wine makers, and beer brewers strode into battle, each group proclaiming itself the protector of Europe's taste buds and culinary traditions. Yet for all the overblown rhetoric about America's "coca-colonization" of Europe, the struggle ended as quickly as it began. Nonetheless, the episode was important because it called forth a mixture of feelings about old customs and new habits. It also raised questions about modern marketing, and about how or whether local industries could survive in the age of the multinationals.

Until the 1920s, Coke was a drink known mainly to Americans and Canadians. The Coca-Cola company had not tried in any serious way to expand its sales overseas. But by the 1930s, Coke was being increasingly exported to Latin America, Europe, and Asia. Much like McDonald's later on, the home office in Atlanta strictly controlled the ingredients—in this case the "secret" recipe—and handled international advertising, while assigning bottling franchises to foreigners who put up their own money for manufacturing plants, delivery trucks, and employees. This was a profitable arrangement both for the company and for the local operators, although the latter had to take most of the financial risks.

It was World War II, however, that transformed Coca-Cola into a truly international beverage and a global American icon. Wherever American soldiers landed, Coke came ashore too. With the encouragement of the Roosevelt administration and the military authorities who thought that the easy availability of a five-cent ice-cold Coke would boost the morale of the troops, bottling plants were established just behind the front lines, first in North Africa, then in France, and ultimately in Berlin. Consequently, the identification of Coca-Cola with America's presence and power became stronger than ever.

At the end of the war, the company was in an excellent position to enlarge its operations throughout the world. In Europe, Coke opened bottling plants in Holland, Belgium, Luxembourg, Switzerland, and Italy between 1947 and 1949. West Germany had ninety-six plants by 1954, making it the most important market for the sale and distribution of Coca-Cola outside the United States.[21]

Not everyone was thrilled with this latest American invasion.

Among those especially horrified were American visitors to Europe, who had hoped to escape the barbaric effects of their country's mass culture by going abroad. F. O. Matthiessen, for example, could not understand why the European students he taught at the Salzburg Seminar now preferred Coke to beer. "I felt that I was witnessing a monstrous moment of decay in the civilizing tastes of the palate," he sighed.[22]

Others had more practical complaints. In Denmark, Belgium, and Switzerland, the producers of rival beverages argued that the growing popularity of Coca-Cola jeopardized their industries and livelihoods. The opposition was fiercest in France. After Coke built a plant in Marseilles in 1949, the owners of wineries, the manufacturers of fruit juices and mineral water, and the Communist Party joined together to demand that the government ban the drink altogether. They denounced Coca-Cola not only because it endangered French agriculture, but also because its caffeine was presumed to be unusually addictive (unlike coffee) and its sugar content could rot children's teeth. Coca-Cola was therefore accused of undermining the nation's health, and probably its moral standards as well.[23] Given the vehemence of these allegations, it was clear that Coke had come to epitomize both the economic and cultural imperialism of the United States.

Yet the rebellion against Coke was doomed from the outset, in France and elsewhere in Western Europe. The company's executives, working through the State Department, successfully pressured the French and other governments to keep their markets open.[24] Besides, as Matthiessen had noticed, people in Europe liked the stuff. Still, the acceptance of Coca-Cola did not mean that Europeans were becoming more "Americanized" or that they had abandoned beer and wine. Coke, after all, was a soft drink, not a foreign ideology. One could swallow it without giving up one's cultural loyalties or sense of national identity. Nor did the local brewers and vintners perish in the face of Coke's global appeal. In the end, they learned to coexist with Coke, and eventually became international exporters themselves.

If some Western Europeans in the late 1940s regarded Coca-Cola as yet another American intrusion, many Eastern Europeans in the 1990s greeted it as the apotheosis of American capitalism. Until the collapse of the Communist regimes, Pepsi-Cola dominated the soft-drink market throughout the Soviet bloc, owing to an agreement between the company's chairman and Nikita Khrushchev negotiated during Richard Nixon's visit to Moscow in 1959. Because Pepsi had to rely on state-run bottling companies, as the agreement stipulated, it experienced continual problems with deliveries and quality control. Consequently, Pepsi could never disentangle its image from the backwardness and inefficiency of the Eastern European and Soviet system as a whole.

Coke, on the other hand, was equated with the West, with America, with everything contemporary and up-to-date. So, after 1989, it had a distinct psychological advantage over Pepsi in the competition for the Eastern European and Russian markets. The Coca-Cola company formed alliances with private retailers and kiosk owners, and exported its own techniques for bottling, advertising, and distribution. In a country like Romania, it promoted the values of investment and entrepreneurship, offered training in management and salesmanship, and brought some measure of technological sophistication to a land otherwise noted for its economic decrepitude. As a result, by the mid-1990s Coke was outselling Pepsi by better than two to one from Poland to Albania, as well as in several republics of the former Soviet Union.[25] In this part of the world, far from being perceived as an imperious multinational corporation, the Coca-Cola company had come to stand for economic progress and rejuvenation.

The different reactions to Coca-Cola in Western and Eastern Europe were illustrative of a larger conflict over how much change a particular region could tolerate. And how much of the past should be discarded. Eastern Europeans, understandably, did not regret the dismantling of their postwar institutions, nor were they particularly suspicious of America's influence, whether in the form of cosmetics or Coke. But among those Western Europeans still nostalgic for the culture of the nineteenth and early twentieth centuries, the response to Coke and therefore to America was more complicated because both represented something new, perhaps unwanted but enormously seductive and ultimately unavoidable.

THE MENACE OF MODERNITY

Coca-Cola and consumerism might have been novelties in postwar Europe, but the idea that America embodied the future was as old as the first settlements in seventeenth-century Massachusetts and Virginia. Certainly, at the dawn of the twentieth century, a growing number of European intellectuals were troubled by the prospect that their own countries would soon look like the United States. After World War II, when Wyndham Lewis wrote that "we can read our . . . future" in the American present, or when Raymond Aron declared that America's "technical civilization" was a blueprint for the "common destiny of all peoples," they were merely restating what many Europeans had long suspected.[26]

Yet there was always a difference between visualizing Europe's future by looking at the United States, and blaming America for what Europe became. European writers and political leaders often found it convenient to depict America's economic and cultural policies as the cause of whatever they disliked in their own societies. They were less willing to admit that the transformations taking place in Europe were part of a trend prevalent in every industrialized nation. The mass production of consumer goods and the standardization of tastes promoted through advertising and the media may have blossomed more luxuriantly in the United States than anywhere else, but they were hardly indigenous to America.[27] When Europeans complained that "America's" economic and social influence was excessive, that the United States was exporting its values as well as its products, they were really expressing their discomfort with developments attributable less to America than to the modernization of daily life in the West.

For the most part, the debate over Americanization was an argument about the meaning and consequences of modernity. Modern societies, on either side of the Atlantic, shared certain characteristics: a welfare state superimposed on a market economy, a shift from blue-collar to white-collar occupations as manufacturing jobs vanished to Asia and Latin America, greater social mobility, more two-income families with fewer children, people living longer and demanding better and lengthier medical care, a decline in the political and cultural importance of villages and small towns, a diminished sense of community, a blizzard of information and speedier forms of communication, rapid changes in fashions and lifestyles, a swifter tempo at work and play.[28]

For some Europeans, particularly those who had grown up in the prewar years, none of these features seemed like improvements. Just the opposite. In their view, to be modern was to be American, and to be American was to delight in the destruction of all the rustic simplicities and familial bliss that had supposedly been central to the European past. This was a mythic past, of course, an idealization of earlier times full of fantasy and folktales. But the feelings of loss were real. Modernity threatened to "devour . . . what I appreciate most in our own old civilization," lamented Sigmund Skard in 1978. So in the face of America, in the face of the new and the modern, Skard stubbornly reasserted his "Nordic and Norwegian" identity.[29]

He was not alone. One way to resist America, and to withstand the pressures that accompanied life in the late twentieth century, was to insist on the preservation of one's national culture. British culture, French culture, Nordic culture—it scarcely mattered. Any of these might serve as an antidote to Americanization, and as a brake on the pace of change.

Yet it was in the realm of culture, far more than in economics, that the effects of Americanization were most apparent. At a moment when intellectuals like Skard and politicians like de Gaulle were reemphasizing the importance of national traditions, America's culture—especially America's mass culture—threatened to weaken a Norwegian or a French person's sense of identification not only with their own countries but with the whole of Europe.

EIGHT

Mass Culture: The American Transmission

From the outset of the twentieth century, European intellectuals and political leaders defined "Americanization" in a variety of ways. They described it as the export of American products and values, as an investment strategy designed to penetrate and control the economies of other countries, as an effort to educate foreigners in the superiority of American institutions and the virtues of American diplomacy, and as a form of modernization. But sooner or later, any discussion of America's influence turned into a debate, or more often a complaint, about the spread of American culture.

When Europeans contemplated the "culture" of the United States, they were not thinking about America's postwar leadership in science, literature, painting, or architecture, as officers at the State Department and the U.S. Information Agency would have preferred. For Europeans in the 1940s and 1950s, even more than for their predecessors in the 1920s, American culture meant movies, jazz, rock and roll, newspapers, mass-circulation magazines, advertising, comic strips, and ultimately television. This was a culture created not for the patricians but for the common folk. And it was a culture whose sounds, images, and subliminal messages had become so powerful and so beguiling by midcentury as to nearly drown out the competing voices in other lands.

What struck Europeans as new about American mass culture in the decades after World War II was not its presence—they had been going to American movies and hearing American music since the 1920s—but its pervasiveness. Throughout Western Europe, America's culture had become dominant, capturing (in the words of one Italian observer) the "collective imagination" of those who grew up in the postwar years. "Our cartoons were Donald Duck, Little Orphan Annie, Dick Tracy, and Superman," a Danish literary critic recalled. "Our favorite boys' games were cowboys and Indians, and the movies were westerns or Walt Disney productions. . . . The first records we bought were in English. . . . During our teen years we idolized James Dean and Marilyn Monroe, [and we] listened to Elvis Presley, Brenda Lee, and Jerry Lee Lewis. . . . Our food was Kentucky Fried chicken, burgers, fries, and Cokes, and our clothes were T-shirts, sweatshirts, and jeans. TV was full of *Bonanza* and *Laredo,* and our language became full of what seemed necessary words: 'groovy,' 'crazy,' 'cool,' and 'heavy.'" Indeed, as another Italian pointed out, American mass culture did not even feel like an import, so deeply imbedded were its conventions and formulas in the consciousness and daily experience of young Europeans.[1]

The ascendancy of American mass culture did not happen by accident. But neither was it the result of a conspiracy by Hollywood, the television networks, and the American government. To explain how figures as disparate as Madonna and Mickey Mouse, J. R. Ewing and Woody Allen, became international icons, one has to understand both the economics of the American entertainment industry and why that industry was so successful at making precisely the movies and television programs audiences everywhere wanted to see.

THE EXPORT OF NEWS AND ENTERTAINMENT

For any nation wishing to project its culture and its political ideas throughout the world, the ability to communicate in a language the citizens of other countries comprehend is crucial. That was the reason the Foreign Ministry in Paris always emphasized the teaching of French overseas. Nevertheless, the French gradually lost the battle for linguistic, and therefore cultural, supremacy to their eternal adversaries: the Anglo-Americans.

This did not mean, as many American tourists seemed to assume, that if you bellowed at a foreign waiter or salesperson in English, he or she would eventually understand what you were trying to say. Still, by the last decade of the twentieth century, 1 billion people on the planet did speak some recognizable form of English. In fact, people who had learned English as a foreign language outnumbered those who were native speakers. More important, English had become the international idiom for science, medicine, air travel and space exploration, business, diplomacy, and mass culture—a language used not only by the professional class in every country, but increasingly by ordinary citizens as well.[2]

The spread of English was a reflection, first, of Britain's commercial strength and imperial expansion in the nineteenth and early twentieth centuries, and then of America's emergence as a superpower after World War II. Yet the diffusion of English was not dependent solely on the economic and military power of Britain or the United States. English was also a language eminently suited to the demands of mass culture and the mass media. More than other languages, English tends to have shorter words and a simpler grammar, and its sentences are often less abstract and more succinct. These qualities were especially useful if one was composing headlines and newspaper stories, captions or cartoons, song lyrics or advertising copy, movie subtitles, or the terse dialogue favored by film directors and television producers.[3]

The global preeminence of English meant that both Britain and the United States were able to disseminate their culture and their influence more easily than could France or Germany, Russia or Japan. But Britain not only exported its own culture; it also imported America's. Because the British were the primary recipients of American culture, they frequently acted as intermediaries—absorbing, modifying, and retransmitting American news and popular music to English speakers in Scandinavia and on the European continent, at least until the arrival of CNN and MTV. In countries like the Netherlands and Italy, much of what passed in the 1950s for "American" rock and roll was really a British mutation. The role of cultural broker, however, was not confined to London-based journalists, rock musicians, and record companies. By the 1960s, West German television was equally instrumental in filtering and reinterpreting America's popular culture for East Germany, Austria, Czechoslovakia, Hungary, and Poland.[4]

Though Britain and West Germany were important conduits for

American culture, the United States did not have to rely on foreign messengers to communicate with other nations. Even before it was possible to broadcast directly and instantaneously over international satellites and cable television networks, the American media succeeded in reaching a global audience.

The United States was in an especially advantageous position because it had developed and refined the techniques of mass communications before anyone else. Just as American industrialists had been pioneers in the use of mass production and in the creation of a consumer society, so too did American publishers early in the twentieth century determine the format of the modern newspaper with its mixture of stories, syndicated columns, photographs, comic strips, and advertisements. By the 1920s, they had also launched weekly news magazines, offering readers a brisk insider's view of politics, economics, science, sports, the theater, books, and show business. Similarly, Hollywood producers in the second decade of the twentieth century resolved that a feature-length film should tell a story and typically last two hours, a principle ultimately accepted by moviemakers in the rest of the world. In the 1950s, television became America's premier medium for news and entertainment at a time when TV programming in other countries had hardly begun and most people were still listening to the radio. As a result of their head start in all these areas, American media executives could influence the nature and shape of mass communications not only within the United States but also overseas.[5]

The power and primacy of the American media were particularly evident among the world's journalists. No other country's newspapers or magazines attracted as many foreign readers or were as widely imitated—a tribute as much to the style as to the content of American journalism. In Europe, as elsewhere, the journalistic models were American, especially after 1945. This was not simply a matter of the European press subscribing to the news services of the leading American newspapers. Rather, European publishers, editors, correspondents, and commentators were swayed by how the news was presented in the United States and what was considered worthy of coverage.

The American conception of the news was exemplified in the dispatches and wire photos distributed through the Associated Press and United Press International; in the stories printed in the *New York Times,* the *Washington Post,* the *Los Angeles Times,* the *International Herald Tribune, Time,* and *Newsweek*; and in the nightly newscasts on CBS, ABC, NBC, and CNN. In contrast to the old-fashioned, ideologically tinged, often ponderous articles appearing in European newspapers and magazines, and the relative absence of eye-catching graphics and computer wizardry on European television, American news stories were aimed at a modern audience with a short attention span, an audience that wanted to be amused as well as informed. Consequently, American journalists blended objective reporting with gossip and punditry, grisly pictures of wars and earthquakes with restaurant reviews and investment advice.

Given the pyrotechnic style and visual theatrics of this form of journalism, it was not surprising that European readers and viewers in the postwar era might prefer their news delivered in the American way. By the 1970s, the European edition of *Time* outsold both *The Economist* and *L'Express*.[6] The popularity of the daily tabloids in Britain, the growing concentration on sex and scandals even in "serious" newspapers on the Continent, and the tendency of European newscasters to copy the sonorous delivery of a Walter Cronkite or incorporate into their programs material supplied by CNN were all testimonials to America's journalistic impact.

The widespread knowledge of English, combined with America's technological and stylistic ingenuity in the field of mass communications, were significant factors in facilitating the export of American culture to Europe and to other parts of the world. Yet these were not the only or even the most compelling reasons for the worldwide allure of American news and entertainment. The principal explanations for the globalization of American mass culture were economic and demographic.

It was clear from the 1920s on that Hollywood's studios benefited from a huge domestic market, a market far larger than any of their foreign competitors. Because there were so many Americans who could purchase movie tickets, the studios usually expected to retrieve their production costs and turn a profit solely within the borders of the United States. This enabled them to finance big-budget extravaganzas and to spend more money on stars, sets, script revisions, special effects, location shooting, and publicity—the very ingredients that attracted international audiences, as well as those at home, to Hollywood movies.[7] American publishing houses and television producers similarly profited from the sheer number of people in the United States who could buy books or boost the ratings of a TV show. While overseas sales of movies, videos, television programs, and books became increasingly important after World War II, the American media could always count on the home market for a substantial proportion of its earnings.

But the size of the American audience mattered less than its composition. The heterogeneity of America's population—its ethnic, racial, class, and regional diversity—forced the media to experiment with messages, images, and story lines that had a broad multicultural appeal, an appeal that turned out to be equally potent for multiethnic audiences abroad. Once American moviemakers, newspaper and magazine publishers, and television producers learned how to speak to a variety of groups and classes inside the United States, they had little trouble captivating people from different nations and backgrounds overseas. In sum, the domestic market was a laboratory for and a microcosm of the world market. On the other hand, the Europeans, operating for the most part in countries with homogeneous populations, had no incentive to communicate with a multicultural audience and were thus ill equipped to compete in the international arena.[8]

Those involved in the American media became extremely skilled at creating products that transcended internal social divisions, national borders, and language barriers. It was not that the dramatization of universal themes—romance, solitude, mystery, tragedy, humor, violence, and redemption—existed only in Hollywood movies. These preoccupations were just as evident, and often more explicitly treated, in European films. Instead, what made American movies and television programs distinctive and internationally popular were their riveting plots, their visual expressiveness, and their often eccentric but spellbinding stars.

European audiences frequently complained that the films made in their own countries were too languid, with too many characters talking interminably about abstract ideas.[9] American movies seemed less verbal and more cinematic. They were driven by their narratives, by action and spectacle that required no dubbing or subtitles, and by actors who did not need to use words to convey their deepest emotions. The most famous American performers were either laconic (Gary Cooper, John Wayne, Humphrey Bogart, Henry Fonda, Paul Newman, Jack Nicholson, Clint Eastwood, Kevin Costner) or inarticulate (Montgomery Clift, Marlon Brando, James Dean, Marilyn Monroe, Warren Beatty, Sylvester Stallone, Robert De Niro). Even those actors and actresses who were noted for their verbal agility—James Cagney, Cary Grant, Bette Davis, Katharine Hepburn—communicated as eloquently through their body language, their eyes, and the timber of their voices as by what they actually said on screen.

How else could Woody Allen be appreciated abroad? Not because foreign audiences understood the vernacular of a New York Jewish neurotic obsessed with love, death, salvation, and whether in the here-after you could find a restaurant that stayed open late. It helped, of course, if you got the jokes. But Allen's melancholy face, his obsti-nately unfashionable eyeglasses, the drab sweater or corduroy jacket that never seemed to change from one film to the next—these were as iconographic as Chaplin's cane or Groucho's mustache or Brando's torn T-shirt—all emblems of an attitude toward the universe that made language nearly superfluous.

Yet the presence of such symbols and visual cues did not, by itself, make a movie or a television program interesting or worth seeing. The attitude of producers, directors, writers, and actors toward the audi-ence was much more important. All too often, European filmmakers seemed patronizing, as if they thought their job was to educate and elevate the masses, to introduce them to "art" and high culture. Holly-wood, by comparison, was adamantly antielitist. The studios recog-nized that high-minded or well-meaning films could be both preten-tious and soporific. The greatest American directors, from Orson Welles and John Ford to Robert Altman and Martin Scorsese, realized that their movies had to engage the audience before they could be chal-lenging or enlightening. "The audience has a right when they sit down to be entertained," Woody Allen declared. "No matter how intelligent your message is, no matter how smart or wonderful [or] progressive your ideas are, if they are not entertaining, then they should not be in a movie." Sydney Pollack put it more bluntly: "My primary obligation as a film-maker . . . is not to bore the pants off of you."[10]

To many critics both in the United States and in Europe, this urge to entertain sprang from the need to sell a product, rather than create a work of art. In their opinion, the emphasis on entertainment was a sign of the commercialization of American culture, another example of how every art form had been "commodified" in a country devoted more than any other to the capitalist ethos. The European response was to insulate films and television programs as much as possible from the pressures of the marketplace. Until late in the twentieth century, European governments controlled the programming on radio and television, offered subsidies to their national film industries, and tried to limit cultural imports from America. In effect, the state guaranteed that a certain portion of screen and broadcasting time would be set aside for local productions. Supposedly, these protectionist policies ensured that European audiences would not be engulfed and their tastes polluted by the trash emanating from Hollywood and the American television networks.

If, however, you knew your television program would automatically be broadcast or your movie would be shown, why worry about whether anyone was watching? Why bother with such trivia as stories, characters, and performances when you could concentrate on being esthetically avant-garde? Unfortunately, the cultural strategies of the European governments often led not to artistic experimentation or social improvement but to greater self-indulgence on the part of writers and directors.

In the United States, moviemakers and television producers had to pay attention to the audience because if they did not, their films would quickly disappear from the theaters and their shows would be canceled within weeks. The hunger for a hit and the fear of commercial failure gave American films and television programs, as well as newspapers and magazines, their vitality, their emotional connection with viewers and readers, and their immense global popularity. Not infrequently, the effort to enthrall an audience also resulted in works that were original and provocative. In fact, the market had always served as a stimulant for art: Shakespeare cared as much as Walt Disney about box-office receipts. Despite the assertions (and the snobbery) of European and American media theorists, there was no inherent contradiction between commerce and culture. If anything, the relationship was symbiotic—a point that the European cultural ministries, unable to halt the decline of their film industries through the use of quotas and subsidies, might have done well to consider.

In the end, the reasons for the success of American mass culture were linguistic, technological, economic, demographic, *and* artistic. As a consequence, foreigners found it increasingly difficult to challenge America's supremacy in the global entertainment market. No matter how proficient the Western Europeans or the Japanese were in selling their automobiles or computers throughout the world, they could not compete with the United States when it came to the export of news, movies, videos, music, and television programs. The sale of American audiovisual products to Europe alone totaled $3.7 billion in 1992, while in the same year Europe sold just $288 million worth of its cultural wares to the United States. Mass culture had become America's second most lucrative export, exceeded only by the output of the aerospace industry.[11] Eighty percent of all the movies and television programs anyone, anywhere might see were either made in the United States or were financed by American studios and production companies.

Still, America's mastery of news and entertainment was not inevitable. During the postwar years, European governments struggled to preserve the independence first of their film industries and then of their television programming. The fight, though ultimately futile, was not only about mass culture. It involved as well the question of whether Europeans could, or even wished to, resist what many believed was the most insidious form of "Americanization."

HOLLYWOOD, WASHINGTON, AND POSTWAR EUROPE

Whenever Europeans pondered the effects of America's mass culture on their own societies, they focused primarily on the power and impact of American movies. For most of the twentieth century, those Europeans who wanted to limit America's cultural influence regarded Hollywood as their principal enemy. From their perspective, the studios—with the collaboration of the U.S. government—were bent on monopolizing the European film market, thereby destroying not just the local competition but all traces of Europe's distinctive identity. The Americans replied that they were interested only in free trade and consumer choice, in keeping markets open so that European audiences could decide for themselves what movies they preferred. The positions of Hollywood and its European adversaries often seemed irreconcilable. So the cinema became a battleground in a cultural war between Europe and the United States, a war that had begun in the 1920s and resumed with greater ferocity in the 1940s.

In this conflict, Hollywood enjoyed a number of advantages at the end of World War II. The film industries in many European countries were badly damaged by the war, much as they had been during World War I. Production had declined, equipment had deteriorated, and facilities had been commandeered for the war effort. In addition, the prospects for a rapid revival of European filmmaking did not look bright, given the overriding demands of postwar reconstruction. Meanwhile, because the Nazis had prohibited American movies from being shown in occupied Europe, Hollywood had a large stockpile of unseen films ready to be shipped to European theaters and to eager European audiences in 1945.[12]

The studios looked on the European market not only as a potential gold mine, but also as a partial solution to their growing problems at home. During the 1920s and 1930s, Hollywood had not been overly concerned with foreign revenues or with making movies that would appeal to international audiences, since domestic ticket sales were normally sufficient to cover expenses and assure a profit.[13] By the late 1940s and early 1950s, the studios were no longer so complacent.

In 1948, the Supreme Court forced the studios to sell the theaters they owned in the United States and to end the practice of block booking. Thus, the studios lost control over the exhibition of their films; in the future, they could not count on a steady flow of domestic receipts as they had in the past. At the same moment, television—free entertainment one could savor in the comfort of one's living room—started to draw people away from the movie theaters. To make matters worse, the costs of making a movie sharply escalated because of inflation; higher salaries for stars, directors, and technicians; the tendency to shoot more pictures on location; and the production of wide-screen extravaganzas—Hollywood's way of competing, albeit ineffectively, with television in the 1950s. For all these reasons, it became increasingly difficult for the studios to depend on the home market alone. Now, foreign sales—particularly exports to Europe—often determined a film's success or failure, at least according to Hollywood's balance sheets.[14]

To penetrate and profit from the European market on a permanent basis, the studios needed to make sure that there were no artificial restrictions on the showing of their films, no import quotas or high tax rates imposed by European governments to reduce their earnings abroad. For help in achieving these objectives, Hollywood turned to Washington.

There was nothing new about the partnership between the movie industry and the government. Since the early twentieth century, officials in the State and Commerce Departments had recognized that films, along with radio programs, records, newspapers, and magazines, could be a splendid advertisement for the American way of life—and not incidentally for American cars, cigarettes, clothes, kitchen appliances, and hundreds of other products on sale overseas. For their part, Hollywood lobbyists always identified the industry's needs with the national interest. Rarely did they mention that assistance with a foreign government or special exemptions from the antitrust laws might also enhance the studios' profit margins.[15] Hence, Washington and Hollywood each benefited from what was essentially a marriage of convenience.

Until World War II, the motives for cooperation had been largely economic. During the war years, however, the Roosevelt administration began to emphasize the political and propagandistic importance of American movies. The Office of War Information arranged to have Hollywood, like Coca-Cola, accompany the troops into battle—not only by sending stars to entertain the soldiers but also by dispatching forty films, all illustrating some positive feature of American life, to the liberated areas behind the front lines. This strategy was useful both to the government and to the studios: People in countries like Italy and France might be persuaded to identify with America's postwar aims, while European audiences were once again exposed to American films.[16]

By the late 1940s, the State Department had come to view Hollywood as a valuable ideological ally. In the midst of the Cold War, American movies—provided they were the right sort of movies—could serve as another weapon in promoting democratic ideals and weakening the appeal of Communism in Western Europe.[17]

As a reward for Hollywood's participation in the anti-Communist crusade, the government was willing to aid the studios in their postwar efforts to reenter the European market. In 1918, Congress had passed the Webb-Pomerene Act, allowing companies that normally competed at home to form a cartel for the purposes of exporting their products overseas. Under the auspices of this legislation, the major studios joined together to organize the Motion Picture Export Association in 1945. Preaching the virtues of free trade and calling at every opportunity for the unfettered circulation of culture and ideas, the MPEA (backed by the State Department) negotiated with or simply pressured European governments to remove all their impediments to the import and exhibition of American films.[18]

Yet regaining the European market was not the only problem. Faced with a severe shortage of hard currency in the late 1940s and early 1950s, and the need to spend what little money there was on food, housing, and economic recovery, Britain and most of the countries on the Continent refused to let the studios as well as the publishers of American books and magazines convert their profits into dollars that could be transported back to the United States. Consequently, Congress enacted the Informational Media Guarantee Program in 1948, promising that the government would repay Hollywood and other exporters of American culture in dollars for the amounts they had earned in nonconvertible currencies abroad. The studios received $16 million between 1948 and 1966 as a result of this arrangement.[19]

In exchange for its help, Washington wanted Hollywood to export movies that reflected favorably on the United States. Fewer gangsters, less violence, more positive depictions of the American people, perhaps a dozen versions of *The Best Years of Our Lives*—this would have pleased the propagandists worried about America's image abroad.

Occasionally, the studios complied. The MPEA agreed to withdraw *The Grapes of Wrath* from France so as not to reinforce the Communists' allegation that American farmers were living in extreme rural poverty (although French viewers seemed to have learned from the film that in America even the sharecroppers owned cars).[20] More often the studios ignored the government's wishes. Some of Hollywood's most memorable films from the mid-1940s to the early 1960s—*Double Indemnity, The Big Sleep, Sunset Boulevard, All About Eve, High Noon, On the Waterfront, Rebel Without a Cause, East of Eden, Psycho, The Hustler, Splendor in the Grass*—presented a far more disturbing portrait of life in the United States than a movie supposedly as "negative" as *The Grapes of Wrath*.

Whatever the tensions between the studios and the State Department, their postwar alliance appeared ominous to many intellectuals and political leaders in Europe. In the 1920s and 1930s, British, French, German, and Italian movie producers had difficulty competing with Hollywood because they lacked a vast domestic market of the kind that existed in the United States. Now, the Europeans feared, if American studios gained unlimited access to audiences in Britain and on the Continent, even the strongest of the prewar film industries might never rebound from World War II. This was not just an economic issue, nor did it affect only moviemakers. A national cinema was considered essential since it could help citizens appreciate the culture, mores, language, and traditions of the country in which they lived. Hence, some form of protection was required, some way of ensuring that European film companies would not perish under the avalanche of American movies.[21]

As they had in the 1920s, most European governments in the 1940s resorted to quotas. At times, foreign ministries sought to restrict the number of American movies that could be imported. In other instances, they specified how many days or weeks during the year must be devoted to the showing of locally made films.[22] Neither type of quota, however, could induce audiences to patronize domestic productions or prevent them from flocking to American movies.

In the effort to resuscitate European filmmaking, West Germany was a special case. The prewar German studios, both in the 1920s and under the Nazis, had been artistically innovative and economically resourceful. World War II left Germany and its film industry in ruins. It also left the British, French, and American armies in control of the radio stations, printing presses, newspapers and magazines, and what remained of the sound stages and movie equipment in western Germany.

Believing they had the power to determine the future of the West German media, the military authorities in the American zone set out to restore the political and economic independence of the German cinema so that it could exemplify the values of democracy and free enterprise. But the generals in Berlin underestimated Hollywood's influence in Washington. By 1950, the MPEA had persuaded the State Department that American movies—with their celebration of freedom and affluence—could more effectively reeducate the Germans and convert them into dependable anti-Communists in the Cold War than could films made by West German studios. Here again, Hollywood managed to translate its economic ambitions into a language that coincided with Washington's political and ideological interests. As a result, neither Washington nor the new West German government in Bonn erected barriers to the importation of American films.[23] Until the 1960s, West Germany was Hollywood's ideal overseas market, one that the American studios could dominate without having to bother with quotas or grouchy intellectuals muttering about cultural imperialism.

The situation was different in France. The French considered themselves to be pioneers in the development of the cinema, a claim reinforced by a band of brilliant prewar directors (Jean Renoir, René Clair, Jean Vigo, Jacques Feyder, Julien Duvivier, and Marcel Carné) whose work was known and respected throughout the world. In the 1930s, French studios turned out an average of 120 movies a year, featuring an assortment of genres and stars—the most famous of whom was Jean Gabin. During the war, film production in France declined less than it did in the rest of occupied Europe. If anything, the German ban on American movies meant that the French could regain control over their domestic market as they had not been able to do since World War I. Thus, the French film industry seemed relatively healthy as it entered the postwar era. Indeed, French studios released ninety-six movies in 1946.[24]

This resurgence ended abruptly. Like every other country in Western Europe, France needed American assistance to finance its economic recovery. But America's aid came with conditions, principally an insistence on open markets for American products. The Truman administration made it clear, for example, that any country receiving money under the Marshall Plan should also be willing to accept an unlimited supply of American movies. Since the Europeans were in no position to refuse America's help, there was little they could do to protect their own film industries or restrict imports from Hollywood.[25]

The French discovered that they were not immune to American pressure in May 1946. In that month, negotiations between Léon Blum, the former prime minister of France, and Secretary of State James Byrnes led to a treaty that had a devastating effect on the French film industry. In return for a U.S. loan, France eliminated its prewar import quotas on American movies and agreed to set aside only four weeks in any three-month period for the showing of French films.

These concessions incensed French film producers, intellectuals, and the Communists, all of whom denounced the Blum-Byrnes accord as an attempt by the United States to undermine France's cultural autonomy. For the opponents of the accord, the plight of the French movie industry had come to symbolize France's loss of stature in the world. In 1948, partly as a reaction to the outrage in France, the provisions of the original agreement were slightly altered. The time allotted for the exhibition of French movies during every three months was raised from four to five weeks, and Hollywood consented to a quota on its exports to France of 121 films per year. Nevertheless, the production of French films dropped by 50 percent in 1947, while American movies were playing everywhere.[26] The damage to the French cinema seemed irreversible, though by the early 1960s France again emerged as a center of filmmaking with the appearance of a new generation of directors who, ironically, learned much of their craft by watching and worshiping Hollywood's movies.

Britain had even less leverage than France in bargaining with Washington and especially with Hollywood. Since the 1920s, American studios had regarded Britain—a land filled with English speakers—as their largest and most reliable overseas market. In the decade after World War II, the British box office frequently accounted for more than 60 percent of Hollywood's foreign revenue. This meant that the showing of American movies in Britain was profitable not only for the studios but also for British distributors and theater owners. Consequently, most British exhibitors, not to mention their customers, were hostile to quotas or other restraints on imports from Hollywood.[27]

Still, like their colleagues in France, British filmmakers tried to offer audiences an alternative to the American product. These efforts—particularly on the part of the J. Arthur Rank Organization in the immediate postwar years—were aimed at both the British and American markets.[28] British directors and actors had always been popular in the United States, more so than those from any other country. One could hardly imagine Hollywood in the 1930s and 1940s without the presence of Alfred Hitchcock, Cary Grant, Vivien Leigh, Laurence Olivier, Charles Laughton, Claude Rains, Leslie Howard, or James Mason, just as it would be impossible later on to think of an American film industry that did not include David Lean, Alec Guinness, Richard Burton, Michael Caine, Vanessa Redgrave, Sean Connery, and Anthony Hopkins. The question in the late 1940s was whether British films, either as imitations of or departures from the typical Hollywood epic, could win the affections of British moviegoers.

It did not take long to find out. In 1947, the Labour government sought to bolster the domestic film industry and the postwar economy by levying a 75 percent customs tax on all new films entering Britain. The MPEA replied by halting exports of American movies to Britain, and by cutting back productions at their British facilities. The tax and the resulting boycott succeeded only in angering British audiences and theater owners who were deprived of the latest American movies. Within months, the government rescinded the tax and abolished all import quotas, though it limited the proportion of screen time allowed for the showing of American films to 45 percent. But because British studios could not supply enough of their own movies to local theaters, and because ticket sales for domestic productions remained small, the rules about how often American movies could be exhibited were generally ignored. The government had also declared that the bulk of Hollywood's earnings from the British market were to remain in Britain. American companies, however, used the blocked funds to purchase British studios and invest in British films, thus imperiling the independence and indigenous attributes of the British cinema.[29]

Despite these difficulties, the British film industry did not disappear. While British producers and directors could never compete with Hollywood either internationally or at home, they would nonetheless prosper and become influential within just a few years. In this sense, their fortunes resembled those of their counterparts in France and Italy.

The prospects for Italian filmmaking seemed especially uncertain after the war. Although critics in the United States and in Europe had praised neorealist movies like Roberto Rossellini's *Open City* and Vittorio De Sica's *The Bicycle Thief,* audiences in Italy were unimpressed. During the late 1940s and early 1950s, Italy proved to be the most important market on the Continent for the MPEA, absorbing nearly six hundred American movies a year between 1945 and 1949. Notwithstanding Rome's attempts in 1951 and 1954 to impose quotas on Hollywood's imports, U.S. films earned more money in Italy than in any other European country besides Britain, far outpacing the receipts for local Italian productions.[30]

Italy had a powerful Communist Party, but Soviet films offered no competition for Hollywood either. When the visiting Fulbright scholar Herbert Kubly asked a theater manager in San Gimignano, a Communist stronghold, why local audiences preferred American films, he received an answer that could have summed up the sentiments of moviegoers and exhibitors everywhere in Western Europe. Russian (and by extension European) films were "too sober, not diverting [like] American films," the manager explained. "When Linda Darnell and Jane Russell and Gary Cooper are the stars, then my house is filled and a line waits outside. These Russian films! One hardly hears any laughter during an entire evening."[31]

Kubly's theater manager was more perceptive than most of the government officials in Rome, Paris, and London. No matter what sorts of quotas the European politicians imposed, no matter how vigorously they defended their film industries and the cultural independence of their countries against Hollywood's global ambitions, they still had to deal with the reality of those sold-out movie houses whenever an American picture came to town.

To some extent, the postwar arguments about profits and market shares obscured the basic problems—economic as well as artistic— confronting European filmmakers. The movie industry in Western Europe had neither the financial resources nor the production facilities to turn out as many movies as Hollywood could. Because they were plentiful, American films inevitably dominated the screens in European theaters. By 1951, 61 percent of the movies playing on any given day in Western Europe were American. The figures in individual countries were even more striking: American films occupied 85 percent of the screen time in Ireland; 75 percent in Belgium, Denmark, and Luxembourg; 70 percent in Britain, Finland, Greece, and the Netherlands; 65 percent in Italy and Portugal; 63 percent in Norway; 60 percent in Sweden; and 50 percent in France and Switzerland. By 1958, nearly 50 percent of Hollywood's profits came from abroad (compared to 40 percent in 1937), and European ticket sales accounted for a major portion of these earnings.[32]

Yet Hollywood would not have cared so much about gaining access to markets in Europe, nor would European governments have pursued such protectionist strategies, had European audiences been indifferent to American movies and instead embraced the films made in their own countries. It was obvious, however, that people craved American films, often *only* American films. Hollywood executives and Washington bureaucrats may have worked together to keep the European market open, but they succeeded because they were able to take advantage of a widespread and preexisting demand for American movies. No import quota, customs tax, or subsidy to the local film company was likely to diminish this demand or alter the tastes of the European audience.

What might change the unequal relationship between Hollywood and the European film industry was a new kind of European movie, one that could capture the attention of people on both sides of the Atlantic. Paradoxically, at a moment when European filmmaking seemed increasingly irrelevant, it was on the verge of a renaissance that would influence the content and style of movies throughout the world.

THE REBIRTH OF THE EUROPEAN CINEMA

If one were to focus exclusively on Hollywood's reconquest of the European market in the late 1940s and early 1950s, and on the story of how one European government after another capitulated to the pressures of the State Department and the MPEA, one might conclude— as many film historians have—that America managed yet again to assert its "cultural hegemony" over Europe. The historians' prose is often funereal: The Blum-Byrnes agreement "spelled doom" for the French film industry; the collapse of the Labour government's efforts to levy a tax on Hollywood's imports "sealed the dependence of British film production"; despite the artistry of British movies, the "gradual decline of the British film industry has continued until the present day"; there is "no question that the British cinema has ceased to be a central social institution in the way that it used to be" at some unspecified time before World War II.[33]

Reading these epitaphs, one would never suspect that filmmakers in France and Britain, as well as in Italy and Sweden, were entering a golden age, perhaps the greatest era in the history of the European cinema. The American control of the European film market did not matter, it turned out. What counted, as it ultimately did in all the arts, was talent, originality, and imagination—in this case, the ability of an extraordinary group of European directors and actors to make movies that people not only wanted to see but felt they *had* to see if they cared about movies at all. For a relatively brief period, from the mid-1950s to the late 1960s, American audiences and American directors looked to Europe for examples of what a modern movie could be.

The impetus for the revival of the European film industry in the 1950s was not entirely artistic. Economic factors affecting filmmaking in both Europe and American were also important. In the United States, movie attendance was shrinking as people stayed home to watch television. The studios, forced to cut back production, had fewer films available for export to Europe. In 1966, for example, Hollywood sent 155 of its movies to Italy, a number that seemed substantial until one compared it to the 600 American movies shipped to Italy in 1946. Similarly, of all the films West Germany imported in 1951, 50 percent were American; by 1966, America's share had fallen to 30 percent. The Dutch had received 70 percent of their imports from the United States in 1949; in 1965, only 30 percent. The reduction in American imports created opportunities for filmmakers in Britain, France, and Italy—not just to regain a greater proportion of their home markets, but to export their movies to other countries within Europe and overseas. In fact, by the early 1960s Italy had become the second largest film exporter in the world, behind only the United States, which was why Rome began to be known as Hollywood on the Tiber.[34]

The Europeans were also growing shrewder about the techniques of international marketing. Hollywood staged its Oscar extravaganzas, but Europe countered with film festivals in Cannes and Venice. Particularly at Cannes, where *Open City* won the first award for best picture in 1946, European filmmakers (and aspiring actresses) could display their wares to critics, distributors, financiers, and fans from all over the world who showed up annually to sample the movies and bask in the ballyhoo.[35]

Initially, most Americans remained loyal to Hollywood. Before the mid-1950s, foreign films were rarely popular in the United States. Whether this was due to the overabundance of Hollywood movies or the legendary aversion of American audiences to dubbed and subtitled films, few theaters outside the most cosmopolitan cities and college towns regularly showed pictures from abroad.[36] Appealing mainly to an elite clientele, foreign films were relegated to "art houses," the name itself suggesting an atmosphere of refinement and discrimination despite the often seedy decor. Still, it was in these theaters that some Americans first discovered European movies—Italian neorealist dramas in the late 1940s, British comedies in the 1950s, French psychological thrillers like Henri-Georges Clouzot's *The Wages of Fear* and *Les Diaboliques,* and the early films of Ingmar Bergman and Frederico Fellini.

The majority of Americans continued to ignore European films until 1956. In that year, largely because of one actress and one movie, the art houses started to attract a general audience. The actress was Brigitte Bardot; the movie was *And God Created Woman.* By 1958, its American receipts totaled $4 million, breaking the previous record of $1 million that *Open City* had earned in 1946.[37]

Suddenly, European movies became both fashionable and profitable, and they remained so through the mid-1960s. There were many reasons for the success of these films besides the eroticism of Brigitte Bardot. The decreasing number of Hollywood productions created a vacuum in the United States, as it had in Europe, one that European filmmakers rushed to fill. At the same time, American studios and distributors were investing in European movies, giving the Americans a financial incentive to import films from Britain, France, and Italy.[38] Above all, because of their adult themes, their greater openness about sex, and their unconventional stories and stars, European movies seemed more "contemporary," more realistic, and more emotionally challenging than the family shows on television or the typical Hollywood film, still inhibited by a moralistic production code inherited from the 1930s.

British movies, requiring no dubbing or subtitling, frequently provided Americans with an introduction to the European cinema. For audiences in the United States, British films had a double advantage over those made in France or Italy. On the one hand, they were familiar and accessible, since all the actors spoke English. On the other hand, their style and subject matter seemed sufficiently "foreign" to distinguish them from American movies.

During the 1950s, the British excelled at political satires and sophisticated (often black) comedies, the kinds of movies that had flourished in Hollywood in the 1930s but were now conspicuously absent from the studios' repertoire. If any single actor could take credit for the postwar popularity of British films in the United States, it was Alec Guinness. Beginning with *Kind Hearts and Coronets* in 1949 and extending through *The Man in the White Suit, The Lavender Hill Mob, The Ladykillers,* and *The Horse's Mouth,* Guinness made robbery and

murder seem like thoroughly civilized forms of behavior. His charac-
ters were both ordinary and maniacal, a combination also captured by
Alastair Sim in *The Green Man,* and later (with more frenzy) by Peter
Sellers in *The Mouse That Roared* and *I'm All Right, Jack*.

By the 1960s, comedies gave way to a series of caustic films about the
class divisions in British society: *Room at the Top* (with Lawrence Harvey as a serpentine social climber), *Saturday Night and Sunday Morning,*
*A Taste of Honey, The Loneliness of the Long Distance Runner, This
Sporting Life, Billy Liar,* and *Darling*. These movies were peculiarly
exhilarating in spite of their grim portraits of working-class life, particularly for American audiences unaccustomed to such harsh realism
from Hollywood. Americans were also exposed to the work of a young
group of British directors (like John Schlesinger and Tony Richardson) just beginning their careers, and to the performances of a previously unheralded generation of actors (Albert Finney, Dirk Bogarde,
Richard Harris, Tom Courtenay, Julie Christie) all of whom specialized in characters at once charming and utterly self-absorbed. It was a
sign of Britain's newly acquired preeminence in filmmaking that *Tom
Jones,* directed by Tony Richardson and starring Albert Finney, won
the Oscar for best picture—not best foreign picture but best picture—
in 1963.

Films from other European countries were becoming nearly as
prominent in the United States. If British movies by the 1960s no
longer seemed so exotic to American audiences, they could always
attend an Ingmar Bergman retrospective. For many Americans, *The
Seventh Seal, The Magician, Wild Strawberries,* and *Through a Glass
Darkly* were among the finest, as well as the most enigmatic, imports
from Europe, not least because of Max von Sydow's chilly visage, per-
sonifying the metaphysical agonies at the center of Bergman's dramas.

In France, the "new wave" directors made their debut at Cannes in
1959 with François Truffaut's *The Four Hundred Blows* and Alain
Resnais's *Hiroshima, Mon Amour*. Though they admired Hollywood's
Westerns and gangster tales (Jean-Luc Godard dedicated *Breathless* to
Monogram Pictures), their films—as exemplified by Truffaut's *Shoot
the Piano Player* and *Jules and Jim*—had little in common with
American-style movies. Even a film as commercially successful as
Claude Lelouch's *A Man and a Woman* was popular in America largely
because of its romantic French locales and its quintessentially French
stars, Anouk Aimée and Jean-Louis Trintignant. France was also a
haven for émigré directors, and thus for two of the most provocative
films—one sexual, the other political—of the 1960s: Luis Buñuel's

Belle de Jour and Constantine Costa-Gavras's *Z.* Indeed *Z,* a depiction of honest if powerless individuals struggling to investigate the crimes of the Greek dictatorship, served as the prototype for a number of American films made during the 1970s (notably *Three Days of the Condor* and *All the President's Men*) that were obsessed with the presence of evil in high places.

But it was the Italians who may have had the strongest impact on American audiences and American filmmakers. Since the 1950s, the art houses had featured movies like Frederico Fellini's *La Strada,* Luchino Visconti's *Rocco and His Brothers,* Vittorio de Sica's *Two Women,* and Mario Monicelli's *Big Deal on Madonna Street.* Now, in the 1960s, three films changed the way people in Europe and the United States talked about movies: Michelangelo Antonioni's *L'Avventura* and Fellini's *La Dolce Vita* and *8½.* Along with the work of Bergman, Truffaut, and Godard, the films of Antonioni and Fellini focused attention as never before on the director's personality and pre-occupations. One did not go to see a comedy or a mystery or a romance any longer. One went to see the latest vision of the director as social critic and master of ceremonies. This notion of the director's centrality soon became an article of faith in America as well. The influence of Fellini's charisma and especially his style—eclectic, bizarre, improvisational, autobiographical—could be seen in such films as Robert Altman's *Nashville* and Woody Allen's *Stardust Memories.*

Yet European movies were distinctive in the 1960s not only because of their directors but also because of their stars. In the past, Americans had noticed European actors and actresses only if, like Greta Garbo or Marlene Dietrich, they emigrated to Hollywood. Otherwise, as in the case of Jean Gabin, an actor might achieve fame in his own country while being virtually unknown in the United States. Some of the European performers of the 1960s—Julie Christie, Max von Sydow, Peter Sellers—did follow the example of Garbo and Dietrich. But many others—Brigitte Bardot, Jeanne Moreau, Simone Signoret, Catherine Deneuve, Jean-Paul Belmondo, Yves Montand, Anna Magnani, Sophia Loren, Marcello Mastroianni, Melina Mercouri—remained in Europe, appearing only occasionally, if at all, in American films. Nevertheless, they were international, not merely European, stars. Posters of Bardot and Belmondo were as ubiquitous as those of Marilyn Monroe and James Dean, in the United States as well as in Europe.

The era when European movies seemed superior to those from any-place else in the world did not—perhaps could not—last. For a while, Europe's filmmakers had been able to resist the economic and cultural pressures emanating from Hollywood. But American producers were resilient; American money was still plentiful; American (and European) audiences would be captivated again by the work of American directors. In a way, the Europeans had been almost too influential for their own good. They helped transform the American cinema, so much so that it became a more dominant force by the close of the 1960s than it had been before. As a result, the European film industry found it even harder in the late twentieth century to compete with the world-wide popularity of American movies.

THE AGE OF THE BLOCKBUSTER: AMERICAN FILMS AT THE END OF THE CENTURY

After people see a movie, they may recall the name of the director, but mostly they talk about the actors and how well the story was told. Audiences seldom care about who produced or distributed the film. Nor do they pay attention to the nationality of the bankrollers. For the majority of moviegoers, there is no such thing as a multinational production. A "British" film is one that takes place in Britain (or maybe India), with a British director and a predominantly British cast, regardless of whether it has American financial backing. The same criteria apply to the definition of a "French" or an "Italian" film.

Even in the case of American movies, the identity of the producer is no longer as important as it once was. During the 1930s and 1940s, producers were employees of the Hollywood studios and each studio's style was distinctive; each specialized in a particular kind of movie. One could instantly recognize an MGM musical, a Paramount comedy, a Warner Brothers gangster film or social melodrama. But in the early 1960s, as Hollywood's output continued to decline in the face of the competition from television, the studio system disintegrated. Gone were the long-term contracts that had forced actors, directors, writers, editors, cinematographers, and set designers to work for one studio throughout their careers. The old Hollywood assembly line was replaced by a series of one- or multipicture deals negotiated by stars, directors, agents, and independent producers, with the studios acting as financiers and distributors but not as the creators of the movies that still bore their trademarks.

The collapse of the studios' power led to the rise of new production companies in the United States that were eager to profit from the international enthusiasm for European movies in the 1950s and 1960s. These companies wanted less to export American movies to Europe than to invest in and produce European films that could attract audiences both in the United States and throughout the world.

Hence, American producers and the Hollywood studios themselves began to underwrite a host of European movies. Their financial participation allowed them to benefit from the subsidies offered by various governments, subsidies that were originally intended to aid domestic filmmakers rather than American investors. Although there were fears that the European film industry, like other sectors of the European economy, might be taken over by the United States, the Americans had the capital to keep local studios functioning, and their distribution networks provided access to the U.S. and international markets. So, European filmmakers welcomed American involvement. Between 1961 and 1971, American production companies bankrolled two-thirds of all the movies made in Britain, and they became major players in Italy and France.[39]

American producers, however, were willing to finance only certain types of European movies. They were not interested in supporting films aimed at the art-house crowd. Instead, they preferred movies that seemed "European" in their tone or camera work yet would satisfy the expectations of the ordinary American viewer, movies that were intellectually or esthetically adventurous but sufficiently entertaining to fill the theaters. Their ideal film had a European director and a largely European cast, but also included plenty of action sequences, spectacular scenery and tracking shots, heroes burdened with moral or romantic dilemmas, and often the presence of at least one American star. Most of all, the movie had to be in English in order to reach the American mass audience.[40]

These tenets resulted in films that were exceedingly popular both in Europe and the United States. As early as 1957, the American producer Sam Spiegel and the British director David Lean joined together to make *The Bridge on the River Kwai,* with Alec Guinness and William Holden. In 1960, United Artists financed *Never on Sunday,* a film directed by Jules Dassin (an American who migrated to Europe after having been blacklisted during the McCarthy period) and starring Melina Mercouri. In 1962, Spiegel and Lean collaborated again on *Lawrence of Arabia.* In 1964, Anthony Quinn starred in *Zorba the Greek,* directed by Michael Cacoyannis and produced by 20th Century Fox. In 1965, Lean and the Italian producer Carlo Ponti made *Dr. Zhivago* with funding from MGM. During the mid-1960s, United

Artists became the principal financier of the Italian "spaghetti Westerns," directed by Sergio Leone and starring a young Clint Eastwood. Of all the films that emerged from this marriage of American money and European talent, the most controversial was Bernardo Bertolucci's *Last Tango in Paris,* another United Artists venture, released in 1972, with Marlon Brando as a far more melancholy American in Paris than Gene Kelly had ever been.[41]

It would not have mattered to audiences on either side of the ocean had they known that the survival of the European film industry depended on large transfusions of American cash. Nor did European directors or actors fret about who put up the money as long as they could continue to make movies. If a film was good, the off-screen business details were irrelevant except to accountants and critics of America's "cultural imperialism." But for those government officials and intellectuals in Europe who felt that each country needed an "independent" cinema as a symbol of national pride, the issue of who controlled the purse strings—and therefore who decided which movies were made and how they were marketed—mattered enormously. In their view, movies like *Lawrence of Arabia* and *Never on Sunday* were not European at all, much less British or Greek. These films were so geared to the tastes of the American audience that they might as well have been shot in Hollywood.

The problem for the advocates of a distinctively European cinema was that many of the movies made in Europe after the 1960s seemed increasingly esoteric and impenetrable. The hermetic quality of European movies, their refusal to cater to the needs or tastes of the audience, could be seen not only in the later films of Jean-Luc Godard, but also in the works of such new German directors as Rainer Fassbinder and Wim Wenders. Of course, some European films, particularly those made in Britain, continued to be commercially successful in the United States as well as in Europe. Among the most notable were *Cinema Paradiso, The Postman, The Remains of the Day, In the Name of the Father, The Crying Game,* and *Four Weddings and a Funeral.* But the majority of these movies were either financed or distributed by American companies. From the 1970s on, it was becoming much harder to believe in the proposition that every country in Europe ought to have its own film industry, one that could be economically self-sufficient and artistically competitive with the movies made in America.

The American cinema was itself enjoying a renaissance in the late 1960s and 1970s. Just a few years earlier, Ingmar Bergman, Frederico Fellini, Michelangelo Antonioni, and François Truffaut had been the leading *auteurs,* their work venerated by critics and studied in film schools all over the world, their freedom to write and direct and edit their own movies envied by everyone who wanted to use the camera as a form of personal expression without having to fend off executives screeching about budgets and the bottom line. Now the newest geniuses were American. Liberated from the bonds of the Hollywood studios, seeking both to imitate and surpass their European masters, directors like Sam Peckinpah, Martin Scorsese, Robert Altman, Francis Ford Coppola, Steven Spielberg, and Woody Allen were responsible for the revitalization of American movies. And—though they did not intend it—for the end of Europe's brief reign as the center of imaginative filmmaking.

Beginning in 1967 with Arthur Penn's *Bonnie and Clyde* (to have been directed originally by Truffaut or Jean-Luc Godard), the movies people discussed and remembered, that seemed to speak directly to their social concerns and private predicaments, came once again from the United States. In no other period were American directors so influential or their films so central in shaping the experience and values of audiences everywhere. Over the next thirteen years, the Americans released a succession of remarkable movies, many of them appealing especially to college students and young adults, previously the core audience for European films. These included Mike Nichols's *The Graduate;* Sam Peckinpah's *The Wild Bunch;* Dennis Hopper's *Easy Rider;* George Roy Hill's *Butch Cassidy and the Sundance Kid;* Peter Bogdanovich's *The Last Picture Show;* Bob Rafelson's *Five Easy Pieces;* Francis Ford Coppola's *The Godfather* (*I* and *II*), *The Conversation,* and *Apocalypse Now;* George Lucas's *American Graffiti* and *Star Wars;* Steven Spielberg's *Jaws* and *Close Encounters of the Third Kind;* Robert Altman's *McCabe and Mrs. Miller* and *Nashville;* Martin Scorsese's *Mean Streets* and *Taxi Driver;* Sidney Lumet's *Dog Day Afternoon* and *Serpico;* Woody Allen's *Annie Hall* and *Manhattan;* and the most wrenching film of the 1970s, Michael Cimino's *The Deer Hunter*.

Two of the finest American movies made during this time were directed by émigrés: John Schlesinger's *Midnight Cowboy* and Roman Polanski's *Chinatown*. In fact, critics in Europe frequently argued that the best (which meant their favorite) American directors—Coppola, Altman, Scorsese, Allen—had a "European" sensibility. And it was certainly true that Woody Allen's films sometimes earned more money in France than in the United States.[42]

But by the 1980s and 1990s, an American film did not need to look or sound Bergmanesque to do well in Europe. The age of the intimate and semiautobiographical American movie had given way to the era of the blockbuster. What counted most, at least at the box office, was not the script, the characters, or even the plot but rather the special effects, the ability to transform cartoons into movies and movies into cartoons. The *Batman*s and the *Beverly Hills Cop*s attracted millions of people at home and abroad, making American movies—especially those that were smash hits—more profitable than they had ever been in the years before and after World War II.

In every Western European city (and in Eastern Europe as well after 1989), the theater marquees were crammed with the titles of American movies, a phenomenon abetted by a 25 percent decline in the production of European films during the 1980s. Moreover, the growing popularity in Western Europe of videocassette recorders and videotape rentals, and the proliferation of multiplex theaters, provided new outlets for the exhibition of American movies and new opportunities for U.S. film companies to increase their earnings in the European market. To further enlarge their rentals and ticket sales, American producers regularly introduced their movies (many of which began to win awards) and encouraged their stars to appear at the Venice and Cannes film festivals, thereby "Americanizing" what had once been a showcase for European movies. By the mid-1990s, 81 percent of the films shown in Europe were American made, ranging from a high of 93 percent in Britain to 60 percent in France—the only European country still releasing a substantial number of movies every year.[43]

The receipts from the European market enabled American producers to invest in big-budget movies, which in turn had a greater chance of ringing the cash registers overseas. Yet the films that fascinated European audiences were no different from the ones that captivated Asians, Latin Americans, and people in the United States. The most popular and profitable movies of the 1980s and 1990s, in Europe and everywhere else, were *E.T.,* the Indiana Jones trilogy, *Rambo, Dances with Wolves, The Terminator, Home Alone, Pretty Woman, The Fugitive, The Firm, Jurassic Park,* and *Forrest Gump*.[44]

Whether they were fables, romances, mysteries, revisionist Westerns, or action films, all of these movies were unmistakably American. Only in the United States could filmmakers afford the internationally known superstars, the production costs, and the dozens of technicians required to translate the daydreams of a Steven Spielberg into a coherent and compelling movie. But it was precisely those daydreams, the childhood fantasies brought to the screen, not the money spent on marketing and publicity or the desire to extinguish the cultural traditions of other countries, that made American movies preeminent at the close of the century.

When it came to understanding what moviegoers wanted, the Americans had always been more astute than their rivals. This sensitivity to the audience—to its passions and preoccupations—explained why American television developed into a powerful force as well, at home and abroad.

FROM *BONANZA* TO *BAYWATCH*: AMERICAN TELEVISION IN EUROPE

For nearly forty years, from the 1920s until the 1960s, people overseas learned about America largely through the movies. Thereafter, the impact of America's television programs on audiences throughout the world equaled and sometimes exceeded the influence of American films. The relationship between the Hollywood studios and the television networks was initially adversarial. Yet in achieving its international prominence and popularity, the television industry relied on many of the same strategies, economic and artistic, that American filmmakers had used. In time, the studios and the networks became virtually indistinguishable within the United States and in the global marketplace.

During the late 1940s and 1950s, the years of its infancy and its "golden age," television was mainly an American phenomenon. More television sets were sold in the United States than in any other country. The networks composed their prime-time schedules for and advertisers aimed their messages at a predominantly American audience. Although film was used for some programs from the beginning, almost all the variety shows and dramas were broadcast live, meaning they could not be put into syndication or distributed beyond the borders of the United States.

By the early 1960s, however, the majority of American television programs were either filmed or videotaped, making them easily exportable. The dependence on filmed series, rather than live broadcasts, allowed the Hollywood studios to become major participants in the television business, supplying and producing most of the programs needed by the networks. Soon, everyone—from studio executives to the independent producers and packagers of programs to the heads of the networks—began to view the overseas market as a vehicle to recoup their expenditures and expand their revenues.[45] In effect, they were following the path blazed by the movie industry after 1945.

From the 1960s on, television programs became more expensive to make, and the networks frequently refused to pay for all the costs incurred by the producers. Consequently, foreign sales were increasingly indispensable in erasing losses and ensuring profits. Most decisions about domestic programming were made only after taking the international market into account. Many producers would not continue to finance a show, nor would a network keep it on the air, unless it could be sold overseas. A few shows, notably *Baywatch,* managed to survive and flourish in syndication even after being canceled by a network largely because of the money they were able to earn abroad.[46]

No market was more important than the one in Western Europe. Starting in the 1950s, when the first government-controlled television channels were established, European station managers always required more programs than local producers could provide. The demand intensified in the 1980s and 1990s with the deregulation and privatization of Europe's broadcasting system, the growing use of satellites, and the multiplication of commercial and cable networks in Britain and across the Continent.

Regardless of how it was structured, the European television industry lacked the funds, the production skills, and the artistic talent to create programs comparable in quality to those produced in the United States. In addition, it was usually cheaper for the European television networks, particularly those in the smaller countries, to buy American shows than to make their own. The Danes and the Dutch, for instance, had to spend more money for one minute of an original drama produced in Copenhagen or Amsterdam than for an hour-long episode of *Dallas* or *Miami Vice*. And in any case, their audiences would have preferred Larry Hagman's villainous but vivid J. R. to a pallid Danish or Dutch imitation. Hence, by the 1990s, 75 percent of the airtime in Britain and Western Europe was filled with programs—from ancient reruns of *I Love Lucy* to more recent installments of *Cheers* and *Roseanne*—all made in the United States.[47]

Economic considerations, while important, were not the only or even the principal explanation for the overwhelming presence of American shows on European television stations. America's situation comedies, Westerns, police melodramas, cartoons, and prime-time soap operas were clearly more popular with European audiences than the homegrown, high-toned, heavily informational programming offered by the BBC and other state-subsidized channels in Europe.

Since most U.S. shows were produced in Hollywood, and since the majority of directors and actors had some experience with or wanted eventually to be in the movies, American television programs displayed the same qualities found in American films. And they appealed to European and international audiences for the same reasons. The emphasis on action and adventure (minimizing the need for dubbing or elaborate subtitles), on car chases and special effects, on lavish sets and sumptuous clothes, on panoramic shots of New York skyscrapers or sprawling ranches, on fast-paced stories leading to rapid resolutions in the last fifteen minutes, and on characters exchanging one-liners either for laughs or in moments of crisis, all were familiar from the movies. But they were no less compelling on the small screen.[48]

Thus, the shows people in Europe and elsewhere preferred to watch, if given a choice, were identical to those with the highest ratings in the United States. During the 1960s and 1970s, the programs in greatest demand overseas were *Bonanza, Hawaii Five-O,* and *Kojak.* In the 1980s, *Dallas* could be seen in ninety-nine countries and was, at that point, the most popular program in the history of the medium, although *Dynasty* was not far behind. In the 1990s, *The Cosby Show; The Golden Girls; Columbo; Murder, She Wrote; In the Heat of the Night; Beverly Hills, 90210; Melrose Place;* and *The Simpsons* were staples of programming on Europe's government-run and commercial channels. So too was the National Football League's *Game of the Week.* Yet no show equaled the success of *Baywatch,* on the air in 144 countries, eclipsing the record set by *Dallas* just a few years earlier.[49]

With the introduction of cable, satellite, and commercial broadcasting, European station managers needed not only more American shows but more American money, advice, and participation. When each country had one or two state-licensed channels, advertising was prohibited and ratings did not matter. People watched whatever was on, or they turned their sets off. But in the mid-1990s, Britain alone had 30 channels while France had 22. The entire Continent had 150 channels in operation, with the prospect of another 100 opening up by the end of the century. Now, stations competed feverishly for viewers and advertising revenues under conditions that closely resembled those in the United States. American expertise seemed essential. The Americans knew how to persuade businesses to buy thirty-second or one-minute ads, and how to put together the most effective prime-time schedules that could attract huge audiences. So, at the invitation of European broadcasters and employing the tactics adopted by American corporations and the Hollywood studios in the 1950s and 1960s,

the U.S. television networks, production companies, and media conglomerates began to invest heavily in Europe.[50]

Usually, these investments took the form of joint ventures with European partners to elude governmental restrictions on foreign ownership and to pacify the cultural protectionists offended by the onslaught
of American programs. ABC bought a one-third stake in Hamster, a
French production company, as well as minority shares of similar
companies in Germany, Britain, and Spain. In addition, ABC invested
in RTL-2, one of Germany's leading commercial television stations,
and—through its ESPN subsidiary—purchased a third of Eurosport,
the largest sports network in Europe. In 1993, NBC became the majority shareholder and assumed full control over the Super Channel, a
cable outlet capable of reaching 60 million European viewers, all of
whom could accelerate their "Americanization" by watching Jay
Leno, Tom Brokaw, and Katie Couric. Time Warner invested in
Hungary's new cable system, a pay-television experiment in Scandinavia, local stations in Hamburg and Berlin, and a twenty-four-hour
all-news channel broadcasting throughout Germany. Viacom, the
parent of MTV in the United States and in Europe, launched a separate music video channel in Britain and began to beam its Nickelodeon network to European audiences in conjunction with Rupert
Murdoch's British Sky Broadcasting, Europe's most successful satellite service. In 1994, Disney started to coproduce children's programs
on networks in Spain, Italy, France, and Germany, and created a
family-oriented satellite and cable channel in cooperation with a multimedia company in Luxembourg. Disney also bought a 25 percent
share of GMTV, one of Britain's many commercial stations, and introduced the Disney Channel to British viewers in 1995 through the
facilities of Sky Broadcasting—with the rest of Europe soon to be included. Meanwhile, a group of American investors purchased a 75
percent stake in the Czech Republic's first privately owned television
station.[51]

These investments, purchases, and partnerships enabled the U.S.
television industry to take advantage of the economic and technological revolution occurring in European broadcasting. It also raised the
danger, in the eyes of European intellectuals and government officials, that the United States could control the content and distribution
of, as well as the decision making about, Europe's television programming into the twenty-first century. With America's domination of
the mass media came the power, allegedly, to determine what Europeans thought, how they behaved, and if they would have a national

identity and a set of national traditions they could even recall, much less defend.

The issue, therefore, was whether those on the receiving end of America's mass culture could diminish its magnetism, especially for young audiences who had grown up on American movies, rock music, comic books, and television shows, and who seemed permanently alienated from Europe's older, higher art forms. This then would be a cultural battle not only between Europe and America, but between intellectuals and commoners, parents and children, inside Europe itself.

NINE

Mass Culture:
The European Reception

The controversy within Europe about the effects of America's mass culture was not new. Europeans had been debating the issue among themselves since the 1920s. If anything, in the years after 1945, people in Western Europe were more likely to agree with the goals of American diplomacy than about the content or quality of American culture.

The argument was additionally complicated by a tendency to include some aspects of America's high culture in the discussion of its mass culture. For a number of commentators, like Jean-Paul Sartre, American culture meant primarily American literature. For others, like Jean Baudrillard, America's culture was "space, speed, cinema, technology," a material and "anthropological" culture existing outside and in opposition to the sacred precincts of art.[1]

But however they defined American culture, and whether their attitude was admiring or derisive, the Europeans were really embroiled in a contest over who in their own societies—which generation, which group of artists and intellectuals, which government bureaucrats— would become their leading cultural arbiters in the future. American culture, like America in general, was a weapon to be deployed in an internal dispute, one that had less to do with American movies or literature than with the role of European authority figures—political, intellectual, parental—in a time of class antagonisms and youthful rebellion.

MASS CULTURE AND THE EUROPEAN INTELLIGENTSIA

Despite the Cold War and the fears of Soviet expansion, despite also the "neutralism" of many European intellectuals and their periodic sympathy for the agenda of their local Communist parties, few people expected a socialist uprising in Western Europe or the United States. With the return of prosperity and the rise of the welfare state in America and in Western Europe after World War II, the appeal of orthodox Marxism steadily diminished. No longer was it possible to take seriously the revolutionary potential of the working class, nor could one believe in the eternal villainy of the large landowners and corporate executives.

Yet if capitalism was now unassailable in the West, and if politicians and economists assumed that they at last knew how to eradicate poverty and unemployment, what was left to criticize? How could those who had once yearned to change the world still maintain a sense of alienation or radical fervor when the governments and social institutions in their countries seemed both indestructible and reasonably benevolent?

For American intellectuals, beginning in the 1950s, what remained was the media—the movies, television programs, advertising jingles, best-selling middle-brow books, and incomprehensible lyrics to rock songs that did not so much exploit the poor as manipulate the tastes and values of the bourgeoisie. Mass culture was, from this perspective, the new opiate of the other directed. Similarly, European intellectuals shifted their focus from political and social to cultural criticism.[2] They directed their anger not at the rich but at the rabble, the hypnotized consumers of American entertainment. The Western European intelligentsia found it easier in the postwar era to talk about cultural rather than economic imperialism, to expose America's "hegemony" rather than examine Europe's problems. The palpable impact of American culture served as a convenient target, replacing the less obvious but no less powerful influence of capitalism.

To many European theorists after 1945, echoing the judgments of their predecessors in the nineteenth and early twentieth centuries, America's mass culture seemed brash, superficial, vulgar, infantile, and inane. Worst of all, it was commercial. The Europeans regarded culture as a public service, not as a chance to make money. They were justifiably proud of their governments' sponsorship of the arts. Where American artists and writers had to rely on private patronage because federal support for cultural activities was traditionally minuscule and constantly under assault, most European governments faithfully subsidized ballet and drama companies, orchestras and chamber music groups, book publishers and filmmakers, spending far more per person on culture than the politicians in Washington would ever contemplate. In the United States, Jean Baudrillard pointed out, there was no Ministry of Culture—an observation sufficient in itself to indict the American people for their indifference to the highest forms of artistic expression. Instead, as Theodor Adorno discovered, culture was just another product available for consumption, perpetually for sale, an item to be advertised and merchandised, no different from detergents and washing machines.[3]

Because the American media treated books, music, and movies as commodities, all aimed at the widest possible audience, the lines between high culture, folk culture, and mass culture were continually blurred. This was a complaint frequently voiced by American intellectuals like Dwight Macdonald who detested the spread of kitsch in the United States, particularly the way it corrupted the work of avant-garde artists and diluted the authenticity of regional cultures and class traditions. But in the view of many intellectuals on the other side of the Atlantic, the barriers were crumbling in Europe as well. Already, noted a British critic in the 1950s, the "streamlined, smooth glamour" of America's mass culture had begun to contaminate European classical music. The signs of infection were evident in the "eruption of popular . . . taste into musical aesthetics, a taste incapable of appreciating subtleties of thought or feeling but eager for sensation, rhythms that titillate, and that slick, sweet, warm, and juicy tone quality, melody and harmonization, which we associate with the cinema organ." In the quest for the common denominator, mediocrity would eventually become the hallmark of European culture as it had in America. "A leveling down," warned Herbert von Borch, a disintegration of the distinctions and hierarchies that had previously differentiated Europe from the United States, was "almost unavoidable."[4]

Notwithstanding their occasional laments for the disappearance of folk culture, most European (and American) intellectuals were far more disturbed by the intrusion of the media into their own cultural sanctuaries. Mass culture, having seduced the American people, was now tempting the European citizenry. The result would surely be a lowering of standards and less respect for learning, insisted Bertrand Russell. Not to mention less respect for intellectuals. "The European circulation of your mass-produced magazines," Raymond Aron informed his American audiences in 1951, "the taste acquired by millions of Europeans for your comics, your movies, your capsule-culture journalism and crime stories have . . . frightened the European intelligentsia and been taken by them as a threat to serious thinking and disinterested art."[5] Barbarism was at the gates, and the gatekeepers—the poets and philosophers, artists and academics, who considered themselves the principal defenders of high culture—were being overrun.

The popularity of America's mass culture did seem to undermine the power and prestige of the European intellectual elite. For writers, teachers, and members of the clergy in Britain, West Germany, and Italy, the opposition to "Americanization" was motivated, in large part, by a desire to preserve their position as cultural and moral leaders. Their condemnation of American movies and television shows sprang not only from the fear that Shakespeare, Goethe, and Dante had been forgotten, but also from a profound anxiety about their own loss of status. It reflected as well their increasing inability to influence the attitudes or choices of the less educated who had in the past looked (up) to the intelligentsia for guidance on the latest fashions in art and ideas. This erosion of self-esteem was especially acute among French intellectuals during the 1940s and 1950s. In an effort to remind them of their role as the guardians of French "civilization," Charles de Gaulle made André Malraux, one of France's most famous writers, minister for cultural affairs in 1959, giving him the mission to rescue the ideals of French humanism and rationality from the ravages of American commercial entertainment.[6]

Unfortunately for Malraux, most people in France did not feel imperiled by America's cultural invasion. In France, as elsewhere in Europe, the hostility to mass culture was always greater among intellectuals, government officials, and inhabitants of the upper class.[7] The general public was more likely to welcome American movies and television programs, read American best-sellers, buy American record albums, and adopt American slang. Unable to imagine how the masses could cherish such trash, the European elite blamed Hollywood for cornering the international film market, the American television networks for underselling their foreign competitors, and Madison Avenue for inducing people to purchase what they did not need and otherwise would not want. Regrettably, the common folk had become victims of America's cultural imperialism, their natural instincts momentarily submerged under the weight of the American media. But they might still be susceptible to instruction by those with superior knowledge and better taste.

Behind these beliefs lay the suspicion that mass culture was weakening the democratic ethos by reducing citizens to spectators, no longer capable of participating actively in decisions about political or social policy.[8] Yet mass culture was less a danger to democracy than the notion that governments and intellectuals—in the interest of improving minds and raising standards—ought to control what people could see on television or at the movies. The elites assumed that they alone knew what was good for the people, and that the people should not be allowed to choose for themselves because they would invariably select something bad. But democracy involves free choice, not a paternalistic prescription about which choices are preferable. Essentially, the Western European intellectuals, most of them democrats, had a hard time accepting the idea that the citizens of their own countries were exercising their democratic privilege by opting for America's mass culture. It was even more difficult for the intelligentsia to acknowledge that this culture had not been imposed or inflicted upon the populace, that the people were voluntarily and enthusiastically embracing what their mentors told them to shun.

THE REVOLT OF THE YOUNG

European intellectuals were hardly alone in their discomfort with mass culture. Their unease was shared by many in positions of power who felt threatened by America's cultural influence. Since the early years of the twentieth century, the quarrels about Americanization had taken place in the context of a class and generational struggle, a conflict in Britain and on the Continent over who—the bourgeoisie or the workers, adults or the young—would determine which values and lifestyles were to be championed. The battle lines stiffened after 1945, particularly with the emergence of a prosperous working class and an adolescent subculture, each capable of defying (or ignoring) the established conceptions of refinement and respectability.

The struggle for cultural leadership was often fiercest within families.

However rebellious they themselves might have been in their younger days, members of the prewar generation tended to be more conservative in their tastes and more conventional in their conduct than those who grew up in the postwar era. This was especially the case in families where fathers had been killed in the war, leaving grandparents to pass on to grandchildren the rules for proper behavior, as well as an appreciation of high culture.[9] In West Germany, at least during the late 1940s and 1950s, the authority of the grandparents was visible in the efforts to protect the traditional school structure in the face of America's schemes for educational reform, and in the reign of Konrad Adenauer, the elderly patriarch of the Federal Republic. In France, too, Charles de Gaulle's disdain for American culture mirrored the attitudes of a generation that did not admire mass consumption, the mass media, or rock and roll.

Even in families whose fathers survived the war, parents worried that they were losing control over their children, that the young would be ensnared by American movies, television shows, advertising, and fast food, leading them to renounce the cultural heritage held dear by adults. This apprehension was not unique to the immediate postwar years, of course. In the 1990s, as in the 1920s, European parents expressed dismay at their children's abandonment of the old ways and their eager acceptance of American culture. "How could one not be alarmed," asked a French official in 1989, "if television makes [children] lose all relationship with the culture of their parents and grandparents?" The European young were malleable and most likely to pick up "American" habits, their elders feared, imitating teenagers in the United States, wearing the same clothes, listening to the same music, entranced with the same screen heroes, speaking the same language, thinking the same thoughts.[10]

Parents were not necessarily wrong to fret about their children's rejection of the adult world, a world the parents equated with "European" customs and manners. Each generation after World War II did seem more Americanized than its predecessor. Throughout Western Europe, adolescents learned more about sex, courtship, love, family relationships, fashions, codes of behavior, and the prerequisites for economic and social success from American movies, television soap operas, popular music, and comic strips than from their parents or teachers.[11]

Yet the young did not gravitate to American culture simply because it offered useful lessons in how to dress and act. Many wore T-shirts and blue jeans, chewed gum and drank Coca-Cola, as a gesture of rebellion against both the older generation and all forms of authority. "For most of my teenage friends," recalled one Austrian of his adolescence in the 1950s, "American pop culture became *the* major vehicle of protest against their parents," particularly if the parents had supported the Nazis. To be absorbed with mass culture was also a way for the young to assert their freedom from adult supervision, enjoying a moment of personal liberation before they grew up to become responsible mothers and fathers, burdened with their own obstreperous children, distressed by their inability to communicate with or understand the rituals of the next generation.[12]

One reason for the miscommunication was that the young were more familiar than their elders with the English language, and hence with American colloquialisms. By the 1990s, 70 percent of Western Europeans between the ages of 18 and 24 spoke English, and 83 percent of all teenagers were studying the language in school. In contrast, 40 percent of those over the age of 25, and only 20 percent of those past 55, could read or speak English. A superior knowledge of English, especially of American English, allowed young people to flee from parental prohibitions and enter a universe filled with advertising slogans, movie dialogue, and the lyrics of popular songs, an English-speaking youth culture separate from and in revolt against the linguistic provincialism of the middle aged.[13]

Nevertheless, English was a language one had to work hard to learn, usually from teachers raised on Shakespeare and Dickens. As a subject taught in classrooms, it carried the sanction of parents and educators. For the young, American culture was attractive precisely because its pleasures were unauthorized—because of its vulgarity, its primitivism, its indifference to the pretensions of art and philosophy. From the 1940s on, youthful Europeans identified with those elements in American society that appeared marginal, alienated, and definitely not middle class: juvenile delinquents (as long as they looked like Sal Mineo or James Dean), Beat poets, Black jazz musicians, rock stars (often the same age as their fans and personified by Elvis Presley, who was mobbed when he arrived as a soldier in West Germany in 1958), hippies and new leftists in the 1960s, Native Americans in the 1970s, the urban poor in the 1980s.[14]

Not all of these groups were economically oppressed. But they differed, culturally and stylistically, from the complacent European bourgeoisie, and so they could embody the adolescent spirit of disaffection and impudence even as some of them grew enormously rich. This was best exemplified in the 1990s when the young throughout

Europe began to worship Michael Jordan, Magic Johnson, and Charles Barkley, thanks to the televised broadcasts of NBA basketball games and the triumph of the "dream team" at the 1992 summer Olympics in Barcelona. "You walk down the street, and the kids know exactly who you are," said one player who was touring Britain with the Houston Rockets in 1995. "Anyone over 30, they don't know what team you're playing for, or what sport." Particularly among the children of immigrants, it became fashionable to wear caps and shirts with the logos of the Los Angeles Lakers or the Chicago Bulls, to show off their expensive Nikes or Reeboks, and to imitate the speech patterns and curses of athletes who were overwhelmingly African American and therefore outsiders, no matter how wealthy, both in their own country and in a Europe increasingly inhospitable to people from non-European racial and ethnic backgrounds.[15]

The popularity of the NBA in Europe indicated that American culture appealed not just to the young in general, but specifically to the male offspring of the working class. Since the late 1940s, in Britain and in other countries, observers had noticed the estrangement of blue-collar youths from the European cinema, with its elitist affectations and middle-class moralism, and their affinity for American films full of tough-guy cynicism and physical action rather than high-toned talk. Though some British films in the early 1960s explored the milieu of Manchester and Liverpool, American movies were more effective in capturing—usually through the viewpoint of the outlaw or private eye—the hard-boiled psychology of the working stiff. From Humphrey Bogart to Jack Nicholson, from *The Wild One* to *The Wild Bunch,* Hollywood offered stars playing characters in stories that seemed closer to the experiences of young European workers who had money to spend but no illusions about being admitted to bourgeois society. American movies encouraged a proletarian skepticism toward anyone with authority, whether the police or office-holders or the owner of the mansion on the hill. They also suggested that a certain menacing charm; a sense of personal honor defended, if necessary, with fists or deadlier implements; and an incorruptible loyalty to one's buddies were more important than credentials, status, and a reliance on rational discussion—values associated with the effete middle class.[16] For these reasons, working-class teenagers in Europe often saw their lives and their impulses reflected—indeed mythologized—in American films and in American rock music as well.

Yet just as Elvis was eventually tamed by the army, Las Vegas, and Hollywood, so the working-class young (and their middle-class mim-

ics) were domesticated and converted into buyers of motorcycles, blue
jeans, sneakers, and stereo equipment—the symbols less of insurgency
than of affluence. In Europe and In the United States, the adolescent
revolt against high culture led to an explosion of products aimed at the
teenage market. The young, it turned out, were most influential not
when they wielded their political power but when they demonstrated
their purchasing power.[7] Even in the 1960s, the decade of social
protest and cultural insurrection on both sides of the ocean, left-wing
students seemed committed as much to consumerism as to radicalism.
In Europe especially, they were—in the famous aphorism of Jean-Luc
Godard—the "children of Marx and Coca-Cola." In this paradoxical
sense, they could act—at least for a time—both as the leaders of a revolution and as the agents of "Americanization."

THE USES OF AMERICAN
LITERATURE

Clearly, many European intellectuals and young people were exploiting American mass culture for their own purposes. Intellectuals
denounced its impact in order to defend their traditional role as molders of taste and opinion, while the young adopted its language and
style as a means of challenging the values of the middle class. Both of
these strategies indicated that Europeans did not simply accept American culture, for better or worse. Instead, in each country, people transformed that culture into an instrument which served the needs of different groups in different ways. Whatever the intentions of those in
the United States who exported movies, television shows, music,
sports, food, and clothing to Europe, the Europeans themselves
decided how America's mass culture would be used.

This was also the case with American literature. American novels
became immensely popular in the years after 1945. They attracted a
wide range of readers, not all of them professors and students trained
in American Studies.

The Roosevelt administration was initially responsible for the
spread of American literature throughout Western Europe, in cooperation with the leading U.S. publishers. Just as American troops
landed in Italy and France armed with cases of Coca-Cola and a plentiful supply of Hollywood films, so they also brought with them millions
of American books printed specially by the government for the armed
forces. The State Department soon made inexpensive translations of

American works available in all the liberated countries. For example, 170,000 volumes of these overseas editions flooded into the American zone of western Germany by 1946. By 1955, more than 1,400 American novels, biographies, and histories of literature had been published in German in the Federal Republic, along with thousands of cheap English-language editions under the imprint of paperback houses like Bantam, Mentor, Signet, and Pocket Books. The situation was similar in Austria, Holland (where reviews of American books became commonplace in dozens of magazines and newspapers), Denmark, and Greece. British publishers started to buy the subsidiary rights to American novels; like their counterparts in journalism and the music industry, they acted as transmitters of American literature to the Continent. As a result, Perry Miller noticed in 1949 that "hundreds" of nonacademics were attending his lectures in the Netherlands. They came "not to learn about strange names but to test their insights" about novelists with whom they were already familiar.[18]

But American novels had their greatest impact on the European intelligentsia. Although most intellectuals still believed in the inferiority of America's high culture, some writers were willing to admit that the balance of power in science, the visual arts, fiction, poetry, and drama had shifted decisively to the United States. "Anyone drawing the map of contemporary intellectual geography," Malcolm Bradbury insisted, "would need to put the United States in [a] radiating and central position." In the case of literature, Bradbury pointed out, "American writing has ceased to be . . . marginal" or "provincial." The French critic Henri Peyre acknowledged in 1947 that American literature had surpassed in prestige and influence the novels and plays of Britain, France, and prerevolutionary Russia. Consequently, European writers like Bradbury and Peyre began looking to the United States for literary inspiration.[19]

Several elements of American literature were particularly appealing to European intellectuals in the postwar years. "One of the things we love in the American novel," declared Claude-Edmonde Magny, the French author of a major work on American fiction in 1948, "is its extreme modernity," a trait reflected not only in the subjects American writers chose but in the "rhythm" of their prose. For Malcolm Bradbury, American fiction was modern because it captured the sensation of living in an absurd and amorphous world, a world in which people's anxieties were immeasurably heightened by the Cold War. In such a world, the literature coming from the United States gave voice to one's feelings of "alienation and solitude."[20]

In addition, American novels seemed to have, according to Henri Peyre, a "vitality and a freshness of vision" that European literature—though "expert in technique and subtle in psychological dissection"—conspicuously lacked. "To an exhausted Europe," observed the British critic and editor John Lehmann in 1951, "the air of boyish exuberance about modern American writing" was "invigorating" in spite of the Cold War.[21] But what really attracted intellectuals, particularly in Italy and France, to American fiction was the possibility that it could help liberate them from the esthetic suffocation they felt in their own countries.

In Italy, the "discovery" of American literature actually occurred before World War II. During the 1930s, at a time when Benito Mussolini seemed omnipotent, a number of Italian intellectuals—led by Mario Soldati, Emilio Cecchi, Cesare Pavese, and Elio Vittorini—sought to escape fascist culture by immersing themselves in American books and movies. Unable to oppose the dictatorship explicitly, they became covert critics. Working as translators, journalists, and book reviewers, in some cases traveling to the United States to report their impressions of a land racked by economic collapse but hoping for salvation from the New Deal, they wrote about America as if it were an allegorical alternative to contemporary Italy. With the exception of Cecchi, they were not scholars. On the contrary, they took pride in their subjectivity. Their model was D. H. Lawrence, whose *Studies in Classic American Literature* not only introduced them to the novels of Nathaniel Hawthorne, Herman Melville, and Edgar Allan Poe, but showed them how to use America as a metaphorical device to portray their own personal predicaments and literary ambitions.[22]

Their attitudes toward the United States often differed. Mario Soldati visited America initially as a student in 1929, returning twice in the early 1930s. In 1935 he published *America First Love,* the title conveying his mostly affectionate memories of a country full of energy and romance.

Unlike Soldati, Emilio Cecchi was already a well-known intellectual and the author in 1935 of an influential collection of essays on British and American writers. He was also far more conservative than his younger colleagues. His distaste for modernity and his defense of the Italian literary heritage made him sound quasi-fascist, though his values were closer to those of Dante than Il Duce. Cecchi traveled to the United States in the 1930s, describing the journey in *Bitter America* (1939), a title that revealed his feelings as succinctly as did Soldati's *America First Love.* Cecchi was shocked by America's depression-era poverty, its gangland executions and lynchings of African Americans, and its cultural crudity. He did not much care for its literature either and dismissed the modernist writing of the 1920s as childish. Nevertheless, he conceded that the novels of Melville and William Faulkner had a certain barbaric power.

Cesare Pavese and Elio Vittorini never came to the United States, so their views of the country was based entirely on its literature. Pavese translated *Moby-Dick* in 1932, followed by translations of Sinclair Lewis, Sherwood Anderson, John Dos Passos, and Faulkner. Vittorini also translated Faulkner, as well as John Steinbeck and Erskine Caldwell. In addition, Vittorini edited an anthology of American literature in the early 1940s. Though Mussolini's agents censored the work, Vittorini's prefaces—expunged from the officially approved version but circulated privately—affected many antifascist Italian intellectuals during the war.[23]

Whether they were hostile to the United States, like Cecchi, or sympathetic like Soldati, Pavese, and Vittorini, Italian intellectuals in the 1930s converted America and particularly American literature into an object lesson for fascist Italy. Yet what intrigued them about the United States was not its history, its democratic politics, or the social programs of the Roosevelt administration. Their America—as for so many other European intellectuals in the nineteenth and twentieth centuries—was imaginary, a constellation of traits antithetical to those they associated with their homeland.

Hence, the Italian intellectuals contrasted America's youthfulness and vigor, its openness and informality, with the decadence and pomp of Mussolini's autocratic regime. In their eyes, American culture might be unsophisticated but its works of art were at least credible, not fraudulent and bombastic like the language of fascism. This hunger for honesty and simplicity led the Italians, apart from Cecchi, to cherish the realism of American fiction—the lean prose and attention to social detail in the novels of Lewis, Dos Passos, Caldwell, Steinbeck, and especially Ernest Hemingway. In American literature, the Italians detected the sounds of their own everyday lives, the echoes (in Elio Vittorini's words) of the "jazz they heard playing in the streets"; of the "movies they went to on Sundays"; of the "trolleys and trains on which they rode" and the "cars in which they bummed a ride"; of the "shop, the office, and the newspaper where they worked." The feeling that their personal experiences were being captured in American fiction inspired them to think that they too could be novelists, perhaps when circumstances changed. Meanwhile, the very act of reading

American books, usually in secret, constituted a protest against the entrenched literary genres in Italy, as well as a way of symbolically defying Mussolini.[24]

After the collapse of fascism and the end of the war, Italian authors and neorealist filmmakers copied for a time the documentary style of American literature in the 1930s. But the prewar generation of intellectuals no longer needed or welcomed American novels as an antidote to fascist regimentation. Moreover, America now seemed to them an adversary that supported conservative governments in Rome. The United States had ceased to be a mythic land. With its soldiers, products, and advertising slogans, it became for the intellectuals a daily and discomforting presence in Italian life.[25]

By the late 1940s, writers like Cesare Pavese acknowledged their discouragement with American policies and their indifference to American fiction. "More books come to us from America than ever before," Pavese declared, "but today we open them and read them without excitement." Similarly, the novelist Alberto Moravia—an early admirer of Hemingway—proclaimed that the most famous American writers of the 1920s and 1930s had grown "tired." A later generation would discover American literature once again, beginning with the Beat novelists and poets of the 1950s. But for the moment, in Italy, the fascination with American writing passed from the amateurs to the academics. With the rise of American Studies programs in the universities, literature entered the domain of the scholars and teachers. It was therefore appropriate that with the translation of F. O. Matthiessen's *American Renaissance* in 1954, Matthiessen—a respectable if politically engaged academic—supplanted D. H. Lawrence in the minds of Italian professors as the authoritative interpreter of American literature.[26]

The disillusion felt by Italian intellectuals in the postwar years was not shared in France. Indeed, the reaction of French writers to America's literature and to American culture generally was often startling and paradoxical. French intellectuals were Europe's fiercest critics of "Americanization"—constantly on guard against the spread of American words, ideas, policies, products, or anything else connected with the United States that threatened to subvert the political and cultural independence of France and Western Europe. Yet they also became Europe's most ardent advocates of American novels and films, frequently more appreciative of modern American fiction and Hollywood movies than were intellectuals in the United States. Like other Europeans, the French were contemptuous of America's high culture. But they made a special exception for American literature. In addition, they analyzed certain forms of America's mass culture with a solemnity that others in Europe reserved exclusively for the classics.

No one was more contradictory in his attitudes toward the United States than Jean-Paul Sartre. During the late 1940s and 1950s, at the height of McCarthyism and the Cold War, Sartre's denunciations of America's political and economic institutions and its foreign policy sounded increasingly vitriolic. Yet he did not repudiate his early infatuation with American culture and, above all, with American literature. In 1946, he described how exciting it had been a decade before to encounter the work of a new generation of American writers. "The greatest literary development in France between 1929 and 1939," Sartre recalled, "was the discovery of Faulkner, Dos Passos, Hemingway, Caldwell, Steinbeck." Novels like *Light in August* and *A Farewell to Arms* seemed as revolutionary to Sartre as James Joyce's *Ulysses*. "For thousands of young [French] intellectuals," he exclaimed, "the American novel took its place, together with jazz and the movies, among the best of the importations from the United States," presenting an image of America that was "tragic, cruel, and sublime."[27] The most passionate partisan of the United States could not have composed a more eloquent tribute to the importance of American fiction.

But Sartre's encomium did not end with the 1930s. Like their Italian colleagues, he pointed out, French intellectuals during World War II read American novels surreptitiously as a "symbol of resistance" to the Nazi occupation. Other French writers remembered how the portrait of irrationality in the novels of Hemingway and Faulkner, the depiction of desperate human beings caught in extreme situations, captured the "incomprehensible violence" of the war years.[28]

Most of all, Sartre and his contemporaries praised American fiction as a way of ridiculing and rejecting what was, to them, the calcified literary tradition in France and the stuffy bourgeois culture of Europe.[29] They delighted in their role as patrons of American vulgarity, scandalizing the highbrow critics and middle-brow readers on both sides of the Atlantic. They were also calling attention to the innovative qualities in their own work. When Sartre and André Malraux acted as publicists for John Dos Passos and William Faulkner, when André Gide proclaimed his enthusiasm for Dashiell Hammett, when Albert Camus tried in his novels to mimic Ernest Hemingway, they were identifying with modern American fiction in order to challenge the European intellectual establishment and to assert their credentials as the leading writers and critics in France.

Just as European adolescents turned to American mass culture as an escape from the prudishness of their elders, so the postwar French intellectuals liked to contrast the exotic backgrounds and earthy preoccupations of America's novelists with the elitism and gentility of the European literati. "American writers come from more diversified social classes than do French writers," observed Claude-Edmonde Magny. The interwar generation of American novelists were not "recruited from among the intellectuals, civil servants, or professors, or from among those whose wealth [allowed] them to dispense with a profession." Instead, the Americans had been "newsboys, elevator operators, private detectives." Nor were the characters in their books restricted to the "ranks of the upper bourgeoisie," as was the case in French fiction. American novels, according to Magny, were populated with "vagabonds, inveterate drunkards, the unemployed; tough guys stripped of all romanticism—simple victims of economic misfortune," together with "black people separated from white people by barriers even more insuperable than those of poverty." Yet it was the studied indifference of America's novelists to "preestablished literary conventions," Magny argued, their willingness to write about what they felt and saw and experienced in the mean streets and back alleys of American life, that enabled them to blow a "fresh wind into the Republic of Letters."[30]

Magny was herself romanticizing the tough guys. But she was not alone. From the 1920s on, European readers and critics confined their admiration to a particular group of American writers—social realists like Theodore Dreiser, Sinclair Lewis, John Steinbeck, and Richard Wright, or those whom Edmund Wilson called the "boys in the back room," the unsentimental authors of hard-bitten Hollywood-style thrillers like Raymond Chandler, Horace McCoy, and James M. Cain.

The Europeans appeared to revel in the bitterness they thought these writers displayed toward the United States. "The best American novelists," Bertrand Russell announced in 1951, were "savage, cynical, and pessimistic." With good reason, he might have added. John Lehmann was equally struck by the American writers' "hatred for, [and] revulsion against, their own civilization." No wonder they specialized in murder and mayhem, mused Henri Peyre; their predilection for bloody scenes and crazed heroes was a "healthy if brutal reaction" to the "monotony and standardization" rampant in American society.[31] European critics therefore lauded those novelists who allegedly told the truth about America. Or who at least confirmed what Europeans wanted to believe was the truth.

Intellectuals in the United States and American professors teaching in Britain or on the Continent were often dismayed by what they regarded as the second-rate writers the Europeans admitted to their literary pantheon. Or, even worse, into their beds, as when Simone de Beauvoir had a love affair with Nelson Algren, author of the relentlessly proletarian *Somebody in Boots,* during her 1947 trip through the United States. Meanwhile, William Phillips reported, de Beauvoir had never heard of *Partisan Review*'s more cerebral superstars: Robert Frost, Wallace Stevens, William Carlos Williams, Robert Lowell, Robert Penn Warren, Lionel Trilling, and Mary McCarthy, all of whom "might just as well have been Eskimos for all [de Beauvoir] knew about them." Other Americans complained that Europe's students and commentators ignored Henry James, F. Scott Fitzgerald, Edith Wharton, and Willa Cather, novelists who seemed to the Europeans disinterested in the plight of the poor or the existential agonies of the private eye.[32]

The Americans were also annoyed by the Europeans' presumption that only by reading the chroniclers of southern depravity, urban decay, and working-class misery could they obtain an authentic description of life in the United States. Leslie Fiedler found that in Italy, his students treated American novels as "anthropological documents." In the Netherlands, the people who came to Perry Miller's lectures supposed that John Dos Passos did "no more than reproduce a panorama of horrors, or that in the Mississippi of Faulkner, rape, incest, and lynching [were] daily occurrences." No one made a "rudimentary effort at evaluation," Miller grumbled; "as long as a book flaunted the stigmata of American violence, it was accepted uncritically as the real thing."[33]

In reply, a number of European critics argued that the writers esteemed by American intellectuals lacked the raw "power" expected from the new American literature. Henry James, for example, reminded Jean-Paul Sartre of the excessively "analytical" novelists who were all too prevalent in France. Sartre and his cohorts had grown "weary" of psychological intricacies, elaborate ironies, and endless philosophizing.[34] In effect, James and Wharton, Fitzgerald and Cather, Lowell and Frost, were too rarefied, too abstract, too "European" for those writers in Europe who loved the sordidness and specificity of a Faulkner or Hemingway novel.

Still, European intellectuals were electrified not so much by the subjects as by the style of American fiction. "We have not sought with morose delight stories of murder and rape," Sartre insisted, "but lessons in a renewal of the art of writing." For many writers in France and in the rest of postwar Europe, the strength of the American novel lay in its esthetic inventiveness, rather than in its sociological insights.[35]

The Europeans were extremely impressed with the new narrative methods of America's novelists, and their original ways of presenting characters. They particularly admired the Americans' reticence toward their material, a trait very different from the inclination of European writers to tell their readers everything, including what to think. "The heroes of Hemingway and Caldwell," Sartre pointed out, "never explain themselves—do not allow themselves to be dissected. They act only." Their "feelings and intentions" were rarely "expressed in words," nor did their creators intrude with "commentaries" or "moral judgments." Hemingway's characters (and Faulkner's as well) were always described "from the outside," Sartre wrote with approval; their motives were buried "somewhere below the level of clear consciousness." The reader was left to "witness" their conduct, and try to divine its significance. Sartre found this approach emancipating. The Americans had brought about a *technical* revolution" in his own work and in the novels of his contemporaries in France.[36]

Claude-Edmonde Magny was similarly spellbound by the stylistic virtuosity of America's writers. But their impact on her was more cinematic than literary. In *The Age of the American Novel* (1948), Magny set out to demonstrate the intimate relationship between fiction and films. What made the American novel distinctive, she asserted, was its resemblance to a screenplay. The author functioned much like a director, looking at every character and episode through the objective eye of the camera. A Faulkner or Dos Passos anticipated Orson Welles in the way they used close-ups and long shots, "juxtaposing ... the foreground and the background in a single image" but always "keeping both in sharp focus," constantly changing the scenes and editing the action rather than relying on a traditional linear narrative, shifting back and forth between the past and the present. In addition, Magny's writers had learned from Hollywood to show, not interpret, behavior, to be discreet and elliptical. In her account, however, the typical protagonist of the American novel seemed closer to John Wayne than to Charles Foster Kane. Like Sartre, Magny believed that American writers had created a new type of hero, borrowed from the movies: strong, taciturn, with no evident "inner life," a man (it was invariably a man) fond of his guns and his horses who knew how "to keep his own counsel" and had no patience for self-examination or extended "interior monologues."[37]

There was a certain condescension in the European intellectuals' applause for America's novelists. In complimenting the "realists" for their stylistic restraint, their focus on physical action, and their refusal to scrutinize or speculate, critics like Sartre and Magny seemed to be hinting that American writers would do well to leave the deep thoughts and avant-garde experiments to the French or the Germans. The Americans, apparently, should stick to what they were good at: detective stories, pseudo-journalistic exposés of crime and corruption, novels with fast-paced plots and monosyllabic dialogue featuring characters who were not introspective and spent little time contemplating the meaning of their lives. Besides, the Europeans implied, a country as pragmatic and anti-intellectual as the United States would, of course, produce a literature better known for its techniques than its ideas.

The patronizing tone in the books and essays of the French critics, the tendency to glorify the collected works of Dashiell Hammett and Erskine Caldwell while snubbing Henry James, was precisely what irritated many American intellectuals. But the French were not really intent on revising the American literary canon. Their preoccupation with "technical problems," as Claude-Edmonde Magny admitted, and their affection for the unadorned prose and concrete concerns of modern American fiction, reflected their "discontent with the [current] state of the French novel." Jean-Paul Sartre hoped that his colleagues would continue to absorb and digest the methods of America's writers, though carefully adapting these devices to French needs and tastes.[38]

To a considerable extent, the adaptation had already occurred. Initially, the Europeans were awed by the new and astonishing voices from across the ocean. Yet during the 1940s, intellectuals in France reinvented the American novel, endowing it with a vision of the world that was peculiarly French. In their reading, the Hemingway or Faulknerian hero emerged as a jaded idealist, besieged by chaos and absurdity, at times alienated and disengaged, burdened with the sins of others, in search (as Magny put it) of "a salvation that must still be worked out and will always have to be rewon."[39] Hemingway's Jake Barnes might be reconciled to failure, but he retained a sense of existential possibility, displaying an ambivalence toward his fate that seemed more French than American.

Thus, in their passage from the United States to Europe, America's writers began to sound less unique and more like the familiar figures of the wartime Resistance, a product of the European rather than the American imagination. American filmmakers would soon make the same symbolic journey and undergo a similar metamorphosis.

FROM HOLLYWOOD TO THE NEW WAVE: FRENCH CRITICS AND AMERICAN MOVIES

Claude-Edmonde Magny could easily have written a sequel to *The Age of the American Novel* entitled *The Age of the American Movie.* Throughout her book, she made it clear that she considered film directors to be the artistic equals of her favorite novelists. At one point, she predicted that the time would soon come when "the movie, like the novel, will unambiguously and unreservedly be attributable to one author." Then critics could talk about the *oeuvre* of Orson Welles or Preston Sturges with the same seriousness that they discussed the achievements of William Faulkner.[40]

The moment arrived, in France, beginning in the late 1940s. For decades, film reviewers on both sides of the Atlantic had dismissed American movies as mere entertainment, or (when they were feeling less charitable) as an exemplification of the commercialism and tastelessness that was characteristic of America's mass culture. In either case, there appeared to be no point in analyzing the work of the hacks who labored on the Hollywood assembly line. Now, however, a new generation of French film critics (many of them aspiring filmmakers) "discovered" American movies, much as other writers in Italy and France had discovered American literature. Suddenly, in the pages of film magazines and in the special exhibitions of Hollywood movies at cinema clubs, French intellectuals detected the directorial signature of John Ford and William Wyler; the veiled messages in the camera work of Alfred Hitchcock and Howard Hawks; the lonely heroism of Nicholas Ray; and, ultimately, the "subversive" talents—unrecognized by American audiences—of Jerry Lewis.

Nowhere else in Western Europe was there as extensive or as favorable a reassessment of American movies as in France during the 1950s. And in no other country did the intelligentsia marshal so many theories and so much knowledge about the esthetics, if not the prosaic details, of filmmaking to defend such a previously maligned industry. The major accomplishment of the young French critics was to invest American movies—often quite ordinary movies—with meanings and metaphors normally discerned only in the greatest works of fiction, poetry, the theater, and philosophy.[41] But then, if movies were raised to the level of art, the film critics could hope some day to become artists themselves.

Their guide and father figure was André Bazin. In the 1940s, Bazin wrote a series of essays championing the sound film and praising directors like William Wyler and Orson Welles who abandoned the montage techniques of the silent cinema, relying instead on camera movement, deep focus, and long continuous takes, all as a way of enhancing the realism and narrative power of the movies. Armed with these concepts, Bazin reexamined the Hollywood films of the 1930s and 1940s, arguing that American directors had turned out a body of work which was comparable in quality to the best of the prewar European movies.[42]

In 1951, Bazin became coeditor of a new journal, *Cahiers du Cinéma*. Among the other editors and frequent contributors were François Truffaut, Jean-Luc Godard, Claude Chabrol, Jacques Rivette, and Eric Rohmer. *Cahiers* quickly developed into the most influential film journal in all Western Europe and acquired a number of disciples in the United States. By the end of the 1950s, the magazine and its writers had revolutionized the way movies, especially American movies, were seen and evaluated.

The distinctive feature of the *Cahiers* essay was its emphasis on the role of the director as *auteur*. As applied to the European cinema, this was not a novel idea. For a long time, critics in Europe had referred to Jean Renoir, Carl Dreyer, and F. W. Murnau as the "authors" of their respective films. What made the *Cahiers* writers unusual as well as controversial was their insistence that directors in Hollywood were also the creators of their own movies. Whereas other critics customarily described the American director as a hired hand, assigned to a picture by the studio moguls, with no control over the script or the cast, the *Cahiers* critics searched through the reels of Hollywood's movies for the director's idiosyncratic personality and point of view.

Indeed the Hollywood movie seemed to them the perfect place to look for the director's vision, precisely because of the pressures to conform to whatever the studio wanted. American directors emerged, in the estimation of *Cahiers,* as alienated artists, struggling against the obstructions of witless producers and the ignorance of the bourgeois audience, injecting into their films an array of clues to their private preoccupations and convictions that only those who were most attuned to the hidden symbols and images could uncover. The lowly Hollywood director was transformed into a master of indirection, a secret poet and subtle moralist, a "craftsman" in the "kingdom of mechanization" (as François Truffaut called Nicholas Ray), an abused and neglected genius whom only the French intellectuals could comprehend.[43]

Yet how did one identify an authentic *auteur*? Certainly not by bothering with the subject matter of the director's film. Like those literary critics who focused on the technical proficiency of America's novelists, the *Cahiers* essayists were primarily interested in the style, rather than the content, of American movies. Studio heads often interfered with the story and the acting, they knew, but this left directors free to concentrate on camera angles, lighting, pace, the orchestration of the actors' performances, and the relationship of one shot to another. Plots and dialogue might be important in novels, but they were irrelevant to films. What mattered to the *Cahiers* critics was the specifically cinematic component of movies, the mystical core of film-making they labeled the *mise-en-scène*. Here, the director converted ("as if by magic" in the words of a regular contributor) material concocted and imposed by somebody else into an instrument of personal expression, enlivening and transfiguring the most "trivial" or "idiotic" scenarios. Only in the formal structure of a movie could one locate the director's true individuality, intentions, and values. The "meaning" of a film was embedded not in its screenplay but in the *mise-en-scène*.[44]

This stress on visual style enabled *Cahiers* to launch or rescue the reputation of dozens of Hollywood directors. Since many of the writers for the journal were not fluent in English, they could readily disregard the banality of a film's script and its hackneyed plot. Instead, they paid attention to the majestic landscapes looming over the doomed cavalry in a John Ford Western, the accelerated rhythms of a gangster movie, the glances between a man and a woman in a Howard Hawks action picture, the haze of cigarette smoke and the gloom of a rain-drenched street in those late-1940s psychodramas reborn in the lexicon of *Cahiers* as *film noir*. No doubt, the French idolized Jerry Lewis—declaring him a comedian equivalent to Charlie Chaplin—not because of Lewis's clever repartee, but because of his physical contortions and skills as a mime. The esthetic concerns of the *Cahiers* reviewers were especially beneficial to directors whose abilities might not otherwise have been noticed or appreciated in the 1950s and 1960s: Otto Preminger, Joseph Mankiewicz, Billy Wilder, Vincente Minnelli, Robert Rossen, Arthur Penn.

Nevertheless, just as some French writers exaggerated the talents of a Dashiell Hammett or Erskine Caldwell, so *Cahiers* inflated the significance of minor directors and B movies, often by obliterating the distinctions between high and mass culture that most European intellectuals were struggling so hard to maintain. It was easy enough for *Cahiers* to celebrate the artistic brilliance of Orson Welles or Alfred

Hitchcock. It was more audacious to talk about Raoul Walsh as if he were a reincarnation of Nietzsche, or to assert (as did one reviewer) that Joseph Losey was "immeasurably superior to Stendhal." Eric Rohmer managed to describe Hollywood in the 1950s as a "haven" for filmmakers much like Florence had been "for painters of the Quattrocento or Vienna for musicians in the nineteenth century." At times, Rohmer argued, even mediocre American movies dealt with the Aristotelian issues of "power and the law, will and destiny," freedom and necessity, "Good and Evil."[45]

On other occasions, the *Cahiers* critics suggested that the typical Hollywood movie should be viewed as a "parable" exposing the repressiveness of modern capitalism. If a film did not explicitly challenge the political and social system, it still raised questions about the "fetishization of money"; the "demands of success"; the bourgeois obsession with "profit, social climbing, and the need to defend the advantage acquired."[46] In this interpretation, Hollywood directors were potentially more radical than the Communists, a hypothesis unfortunately shared by the members of the House Un-American Activities Committee in the 1950s.

Yet despite these tributes to the intellectual or political sophistication of the American cinema, *Cahiers* did not imagine that Hollywood directors actually resembled European-style theorists. On the contrary, when the journal's writers glorified the technical agility of a given director, they frequently sounded as patronizing as Jean-Paul Sartre extolling the American novelist's aversion to ideas or analysis. American filmmakers were "real and natural," proclaimed Jean-Luc Godard. They operated "instinctively" and spontaneously, with a "gift for . . . simplicity." It was their "know-how," not their "intellect," that François Truffaut most admired.[47] Once again, the French were commending American culture for its lack of artifice and its flair for improvisation—traits that did not to pose any threat to the artistic preeminence of France.

In fact, many *Cahiers* critics defended American movies for reasons that had less to do with the excellence of filmmaking in the United States than with their contempt for the present state of filmmaking in France. They hailed the realism and the uniquely cinematic quality of Hollywood movies because they believed that postwar French films were too prim, too didactic, and too content simply to illustrate novels and plays. And they stressed the role of the *auteur* because, as Godard admitted, "all of us at *Cahiers* thought of ourselves as future directors."[48] Like the French literary critics, they enlisted American culture—in this case, the movies—in a crusade against the people they regarded as their enemies in France. Using the Hollywood film as their model, Truffaut, Godard, Chabrol, Rohmer, and Rivette set out to transform the French cinema and, not incidentally, to establish themselves as the chief creators of an entirely new kind of movie in Europe.

By the early 1960s, the *auteur* theory and the concept of the *mise-en-scène* had entered the vocabulary of film critics throughout the world, in large part because some of the writers identified with *Cahiers* were now successful directors and leaders of the New Wave. Yet at the moment of its greatest influence, *Cahiers* began to question the centrality of the *auteur,* along with what one writer called the "ill-conceived sanctification of the whole of American cinema." Many contributors to *Cahiers* now acknowledged that their earlier worship of the Hollywood director had led them to minimize the constraints of the studio system, particularly the power of producers with their preference for worn-out genres at the expense of truly seminal works. Moreover, *Cahiers* conceded that it had often confused technical competence with artistic originality. Most American directors, the journal submitted, were neither rebels nor *auteurs* but merely diligent professionals who depended on the collaborative efforts of their editors and cinematographers, and who were willing to bow whenever necessary to commercial demands. The genuine *auteur* was rare, so the term should not have been bestowed on every "jobber" with a long list of screen credits.[49]

This reappraisal coincided with the experience of the New Wave directors who discovered that, in actually making movies, they too had to cope with financiers, distributors, publicists, unprepared actors, and disgruntled technicians toiling in obscurity behind the cameras. But *Cahiers* was also losing interest in American movies, whether good or bad, as the 1960s wore on. With the rebirth of the French and the European cinema, the journal's editors no longer needed to look to Hollywood for films that exemplified their ideas. Besides, the golden age of American movies seemed to be over. The directors *Cahiers* had exalted—Ford, Hawks, Welles, Hitchcock, and Ray—were now in decline or approaching the end of their careers. No one, Jean-Luc Godard complained, was "taking their place." The American cinema, he concluded, was "only a poor shadow" of what it had once been. The young new directors and their experimental—often politically radical—films could be found elsewhere: in Brazil, Poland, Italy, and of course France.[50]

Godard's pronouncements reflected his (and the journal's) growing disgust with America's economic institutions and foreign policy in the 1960s, as well as the difficulties he had personally encountered in combating Hollywood's "domination" of the international film market.[51] But Godard's disparagement of Hollywood and his salute to the revolutionary spirit of the foreign *auteurs* was more than a little self-serving. Both *Cahiers* and Godard found it more convenient to flirt with Maoism and denounce America's imperialistic adventures in Vietnam than to notice the emergence in the late 1960s of a revitalized and highly personal cinema in the United States.

Godard and many of his colleagues also forgot in the 1960s what they had learned from Hollywood in the 1950s. Increasingly, they turned out movies the average person could not understand and would not watch, a display of arrogance toward the mass audience that neither the studios nor the most visionary American directors would have tolerated.

Still, the French fascination with American movies, like their passion for American novelists, served as an endorsement of America's culture. Most American writers and filmmakers, despite their resentment at being praised for their stylistic dexterity rather than their intelligence, cared deeply about what the Europeans thought. In the 1940s and 1950s, a number of European intellectuals seemed to be confirming the presence in the United States of a literary and cinematic tradition worthy of respect, and even one that was capable occasionally of reaching the summit of art.

DALLAS IN HOLLAND

The Europeans' arguments about American culture were always affected by the differing agendas of those who interpreted its sounds, images, and meanings for the mass audience. Depending on the motives of whomever was speaking, the impact of America's culture could be insidious or invigorating, an assault upon the hierarchies of education and intellect or a protest against elitism in the arts, a menace to parental authority and bourgeois decorum or an inspiration for the next generation to create for itself a new music, new fashions, a new literature, and a new cinema.

Yet for all the efforts of the intellectuals and the young to make American culture serve their own aims, few analysts tried to find out how ordinary Europeans responded to the records, books, movies, and television shows imported from the United States. It was possible that audiences paid no attention to what they were supposed to think or feel, that intellectuals, government officials, media theorists, literary and film critics, the adolescents who imagined rock and roll to be the anthem of the revolution—in short, all the groups that appointed themselves the people's counselors—had little influence on how American culture was actually received.

The chasm between the opinions of the intelligentsia and the behavior of the common folk was never more evident than in their antithetical reactions to *Dallas*. For members of the European elite, *Dallas* epitomized the dangers and the decadence of American mass culture. In 1983, at the height of its popularity in Europe and in the United States, *Dallas* was denounced by no less an eminence than the French minister of culture, Jack Lang, as the latest and most troubling instance of America's cultural imperialism, a threat to the national identity of France and to all the other countries in Western Europe.[52]

Underlying this proclamation was the fear, shared by many intellectuals and political leaders, that European audiences would be enticed by the power and wealth of the Ewing family, the elegant clothes and automobiles, the palatial ranch, the ubiquitous oil wells, and the cheerful rapacity of J. R.[53] Some Europeans, too easily impressionable, might even want to live and act like that themselves. What then would happen to the European sense of communal responsibility, the concern for the less fortunate, the humane and compassionate foundations on which the postwar social democracies rested? The altruism of the welfare state could be a bit oppressive, after all. In the eyes of their European critics, the Ewings personified American greed and ruthlessness, but they did have a certain exuberance compared to the dullness of Europe's middle class. Might *Dallas* lure audiences overseas into becoming even more "Americanized" than they already were?

It was, of course, difficult to know exactly what effect *Dallas* had on people in Europe. But at least one writer in Holland decided to ask some regular viewers. As in other countries during the early 1980s, more than 50 percent of the population in the Netherlands watched *Dallas* every week. Seeking to explain the program's enormous appeal, Ien Ang "placed a small advertisement in a Dutch women's magazine," inviting readers to describe their attitudes toward *Dallas*. She received forty-two letters, most of them from women, which was hardly surprising given who normally read the magazine. The sample was small, unscientific, and heavily weighted in favor of feminine (if not feminist) reactions to the story line and the characters. Nonetheless, Ang set out to evaluate the replies in the context of the larger debate about American mass culture. More important, she hoped to show how her respondents incorporated *Dallas* into their personal lives. Like those writers in Italy and France who had taken American novels and films seriously, Ang approached *Dallas* not as an object of scorn but as an opportunity to ponder the methods and the consequences of popular entertainment. In 1982, she published her initial conclusions in Holland, followed in 1985 by a revised English-language version called, appropriately, *Watching Dallas*.[54]

Ang discovered that the majority of the letter writers had internalized the assumptions of the critics of mass culture. Whether they liked *Dallas* or not, most viewers accepted the premise that shows like this were "bad" for them. The respondents who frowned on *Dallas* had a set of "ready-made conceptions," borrowed from the proponents of European high culture, with which to express their disapproval. In the opinion of one viewer, *Dallas* was "a typical American program, simple and commercial," obsessed solely with "money and sensation." To another, *Dallas* was filled with preposterous clichés about how people lived in the United States. Several seemed to be influenced by the feminist attacks on *Dallas,* complaining that the program portrayed women as passive and fatalistic victims, prone to comply with, rather than resist, the "patriarchal status quo."[55]

Even the partisans of *Dallas* apparently felt guilty about enjoying the show. Perhaps because they were answering an advertisement that asked them to justify their preferences, many either apologized for their poor taste or tried to differentiate themselves from the average viewer who was presumably bewitched by the glamour of life at Southfork. The latter group posed as elitists, temporarily slumming. They regarded *Dallas* as "a comedy to be laughed at," a stance that enabled them to indulge their pleasure each week without suffering any "pangs of conscience" about wasting their time on such trivia. Still, they sounded defensive. They could not, Ang believed, reject the paternalism or the adverse judgments of the intelligentsia and freely admit their fondness for *Dallas*. They had to demonstrate that they too thought the program was inane and escapist.[56]

Yet Ang was not all that interested in the verdicts of her respondents. She was fascinated instead by the "emotional energy" they invested in *Dallas* and by the way they interacted with the show. Ang insisted that audiences in the Netherlands were not sedentary consumers, accepting whatever American programs Dutch television executives chose to purchase and broadcast. Rather, the viewers started "playing" with *Dallas,* redefining its message and imagery to fit their own experiences.[47] In the process, they domesticated *Dallas*, converting it from a glossy American import to a drama that illuminated their private lives.

Ang based her contention not only on the lengthy comments of the letter writers, but on an analysis of the program's formal structure and style. Like the French literary and film critics, she did not care much about content. For Ang, the popularity of *Dallas* sprang from its adherence to the conventions of the soap opera—with one important exception.

Since *Dallas* was broadcast at night, in prime time, it had to appeal to the entire family, not just to women, as was the case with daytime serials. This requirement accounted for the program's inclusion of strong male characters and its focus on "masculine" activities, notably the corporate intrigues of J. R. Ewing. But otherwise, in its rhythms and preoccupations, *Dallas* remained a classic soap opera. The episodic format of *Dallas,* Ang pointed out, the sense that things were happening to the characters during the days when the program was off the air, made it appear that the lives of the Ewings—like those of their viewers—continued to unfold between broadcasts. Hence, each episode allowed the audience to renew its acquaintance with the characters and their numerous tribulations, in much the same way that members of a family reunited for a weekly dinner.[58] After a while, the Ewings seemed like close, if eccentric, relatives whose outrageous behavior in the dining room was predictable and thus oddly comforting.

The impression of intimacy was reinforced, Ang suggested, by a concentration on problems that were ultimately personal. Even when the plot turned to the Ewings' complicated business affairs, the story was told from a psychological rather than an economic perspective, as if public events were important only as they affected the emotional conflicts within the family. The obligatory "cliffhanger" at the end of each episode invariably focused on the inner struggles of a particular character, with anger or frustration revealed through a close-up of his or her face. This emphasis on the "private sphere"—on how parents and siblings, husbands and wives, related to and felt about one another—were for Ang the hallmarks of the soap opera, a set of rules that *Dallas* honored and faithfully followed.[59]

Although few people in Holland were as rich or as domineering as the Ewings, the problems of the various characters did not seem extraordinary to Ang's viewers. Repeatedly, her letter writers reported that the Ewings resembled "real" human beings with "recognizable" personalities, wrestling with everyday predicaments (illnesses, sibling rivalries, marital disputes) that viewers themselves had encountered in their own families.[60] It was therefore easy for audiences in the Netherlands to identify with the Ewings, no matter how often intellectuals and socialist politicians ridiculed *Dallas* as a fantasy about a foreign lifestyle that only the most gullible Europeans would wish to imitate.

In Ang's estimation, the elitist disdain for American mass culture overlooked the extent to which a soap opera like *Dallas* was "emotionally" realistic, especially for women who were among its most loyal viewers in Holland. The show appealed to women not because it made them want to emulate Sue Ellen, much less J. R., but because they were "accustomed to facing situations psychologically." *Dallas* presented what many women considered to be an accurate picture of marriage and family life—an "endless fluctuation" of highs and lows, affection and rage, happiness and misery, constant crises and temporary resolutions, all of these reflecting their own experiences and deepest anxieties. Far from encouraging viewers (either female or male) to forget their troubles or flee in their imaginations from the "drabness" of their circumstances, *Dallas* implied that the problems they confronted each day were special, significant, and deserving of attention.[61]

Ang admired *Dallas* because it raised the same issues—about love and hate, sex and power, success and tragedy—that one found in works of high culture. She acknowledged that on one level, *Dallas* was merely an entertaining melodrama created by the American television industry. But on another level, the program dealt with universal themes and feelings, which explained its popularity in Europe and throughout the world.

Ang may have exaggerated the profundity of *Dallas,* much as Jean-Paul Sartre or the contributors to *Cahiers* overestimated the insights lodged in Erskine Caldwell's narrative style or in the *mise-en-scène* of a gangster movie. Nevertheless, her investigation of the techniques and meanings of *Dallas,* like their explorations of American novels and films, indicated that some European intellectuals and many in the European audience were actively engaged in reshaping America's mass culture in accordance with their own professional aspirations and personal concerns. Along the way, *Dallas*—together with Hollywood and Hemingway, Elvis Presley and Michael Jordan, Coca-Cola and McDonald's—became as characteristically European as they had once been uniquely American.

TEN

From Gaullism to GATT

Resisting America in the 1980s and 1990s

Although a variety of Western Europeans, for their own reasons, were drawn to American novels, movies, and television programs, government officials and the majority of intellectuals remained unimpressed. During the last three decades of the twentieth century, European leaders continued to look for ways to combat America's cultural ascendancy. Indeed, their efforts intensified as the development of cable and satellite broadcasting, and the increasing use of videocassette recorders, enabled the American media to enter European homes directly, without having first to obtain the blessings of someone in the ministry of culture or trade.

From the late 1960s to the early 1990s, a growing number of European politicians and social critics referred almost automatically to America's cultural and linguistic "imperialism" whenever they wanted to describe the effects of Europe's subservience to the American entertainment industry. They worried more than ever about the disappearance of European cultural traditions and the diminished sense of national "identity." And in their most far-reaching attempt yet to impose continent-wide restrictions on America's cultural exports, they succeeded in excluding audiovisual products from the antiprotection-ist provisions of the 1993 General Agreement on Tariffs and Trade, known colloquially as GATT.

Many people in the United States, including the GATT negotiators for the State and Commerce Departments, were mystified by the Europeans' qualms about America's mass culture. Usually, they dismissed Europe's opposition to American movies or TV shows as a ploy by French or German filmmakers and television producers to wring more subsidies from their respective governments and from U.S. media companies.

The American bewilderment was not surprising. Not since the early nineteenth century, when the United States was still searching for its own national identity outside the British orbit, had Americans felt threatened by the culture of another country. The era when writers like Ralph Waldo Emerson called for "American" poets, "American" scholars, and a distinctively "American" literature had long since passed. Now, Americans could not imagine what it might be like if most of their movie theaters showed only French films, or if the bulk of the programs on their television screens came from Germany, or if nearly all the songs they heard on the radio were sung in Italian.[1] Nor could they conceive of having to learn Danish or Dutch to survive economically in the modern world.

Many Americans had no contact with foreign cultures, and they were equally oblivious to the impact of their own culture on other nations. As a result, they could not understand what Europeans meant by cultural imperialism or why the concepts of free trade and open markets sounded so dangerous to intellectuals, movie and television directors, and cultural ministers on the other side of the Atlantic. In the 1980s and 1990s, the Europeans and the Americans recapitulated the cultural arguments of the 1920s and 1940s, but with even less comprehension of how their experiences and perspectives radically differed in the century's final years.

THE CONSEQUENCES
OF CULTURAL IMPERIALISM

The tendency among radical intellectuals, academics, and university students to emphasize cultural rather than political or economic issues coincided with the birth in the 1960s of a "new" Left in both Europe and the United States. Inspired by the ideas of Antonio Gramsci, Herbert Marcuse, Max Horkheimer, and Theodor Adorno, people on the Left began to talk about a form of Western imperialism that, in addition to exploiting the economies of "Third World" countries, also manipulated the values and tastes of the native populations.

According to this theory, those who owned the media in the West were intimately involved in making sure that Europe and the United States maintained their mastery over their former colonies and current client states. Films, radio and television broadcasts, newspapers and magazines, advertising, all these had become the primary instruments of political and social control. Mass culture was what the stronger nations used to impose their social systems on weaker, dependent countries. It was also the means by which less powerful groups within the West itself—especially the working class—were seduced into accepting the economic and political outlook and policies of the governing elite. In sum, the cultural imperialists acted purposefully to subjugate everyone else. They turned the masses all over the globe into robotic consumers of superfluous products and vacuous entertainment, unable to decide for themselves what was in their best economic interest or how to satisfy on their own their personal or cultural needs.[2]

Such ideas minimized the possibility that audiences in other parts of the world might find Western culture, particularly Western mass culture, inherently attractive. The critics of the Western media often romanticized local cultures. So they were astonished and horrified when people in the provinces chose—freely and intentionally—to watch Hollywood movies or MTV.

Moreover, the image of one country seeking to unload its culture on another conveyed the impression that nations, whether dominant or subordinate, were culturally homogeneous and impervious to change unless they came under pressure from "foreign" influences. Yet this notion overlooked the ways in which cultures were affected by regional, ethnic, racial, and class antagonisms, conflicts that existed within the borders of every country, large or small, rich or impoverished. It underestimated as well the extent to which a society and its culture were constantly in flux, responding to internal realignments as much as to outside forces.[3] The idea of a purely "national" culture, one that could be easily identified and defined, was a handy polemical weapon in the struggle against the "imperialism" of the media moguls. But as an explanation of what happened when different and diversified cultures collided, it was mostly a myth.

Still, the sense of living in a country inundated with movies and situation comedies manufactured beyond one's national boundaries was not entirely imaginary. Neither was the feeling that one's own culture, however conceptualized, was under siege. For people residing far away from the centers of power but bombarded with the messages of those supposedly in charge of the machinery of mass communications, it did seem as if Western (and, above all, American) culture was a single, unified entity bent on global supremacy. Never mind social or cultural complexities. The "West" meant science and technology. "America" meant blue jeans and McDonald's.[4]

By the 1970s and 1980s, the conviction that there was such a thing as cultural imperialism became widespread among members of the left-wing intelligentsia in Latin America, Africa, and Asia, as well as in the West. For many in Europe, however, the principal imperialists no longer operated out of London and Paris. Their home office was in New York or Los Angeles. Though the idea of cultural imperialism had been employed initially to portray the unequal relationship between the West and the Third World, it was now used by Europeans to bewail their own impotence in the face of America's massive export of news and entertainment.[5] The European Left grew less interested in protecting the indigenous cultures of the ex-colonies. It seemed more urgent at present to defend the culture of Europe against the media invasion from the United States.

This was a more formidable task in the 1980s and 1990s than it had been in the years after World War II. Most commentators in Europe, and not only those on the Left, had complained for decades that culture and information flowed in only one direction—that in the international communications market, Europeans and other outlanders were merely customers for what the Americans created and sold abroad. But in the late twentieth century, Europeans found it even harder to break out of their role as the leading consumers of a mass culture produced primarily in the United States.

European bookstores, for example, were now flooded not only with the works of America's literary heavyweights, but also with innumerable American best-sellers. Beginning in the 1980s, U.S. publishing houses paid increasing attention to the overseas market, following the example of the movie studios and the television networks. No doubt, a number of publishers adopted a global perspective because they were being taken over by media giants like Viacom, Rupert Murdoch, and Time Warner, each accustomed to operating all over the world. Yet even without pressure from the conglomerates, American publishers recognized that they could earn back a portion of the multi-million-dollar advances they were giving to celebrity authors and add substantially to their revenues by selling foreign (and especially European) rights to their books. As with films, videocassettes, and television shows, this overseas income frequently determined whether a book would ultimately make money.[6]

At the same time, European publishers—while eager to buy books by well-known American writers—usually had trouble selling the works of their authors to U.S. houses. Americans apparently disliked books translated from foreign languages almost as much as they loathed dubbed or subtitled movies. Editors were therefore unwilling in most instances to purchase the rights of a European novel that had little chance of appealing to American readers.[7]

The aggressiveness with which American houses sold their titles in Europe and their reluctance to reciprocate by publishing many French or German, much less Belgian or Austrian, books in the United States seemed yet another form of cultural imperialism to many European writers. They believed that America's domination of the European book trade would make it more difficult for them to attract a large audience either in their own countries or abroad.

Europeans were at an even greater disadvantage when it came to movies and television programs. In 1969, at a time when American audiences were more attentive than ever before to the films of French, Italian, and Japanese directors, foreign-language movies (the majority made in Europe) captured just 4 percent of all box-office receipts in the United States. From this hardly majestic peak, the European share of the American film market fell to 2 percent by the 1980s. The decline was hastened by the closing of many locally run art houses where foreign movies had once flourished, and by a relentless increase in the number of theater chains and multiplexes specializing exclusively in domestic blockbusters. Foreigners had no better luck infiltrating America's television market. Only 1 percent of the prime-time shows on American television in the early 1990s came from abroad, and most of these appeared on cable stations or PBS rather than on the major commercial networks.[8] Meanwhile, 80 percent of the movies and 75 percent of the television programs shown in Europe were imported from the United States.

This imbalance was accentuated by the tendency of U.S. film companies and TV networks to remake European movies and television shows, using American stars and changing the settings and story lines to accommodate the expectations of American audiences, thereby reducing the chances that the original versions would ever be seen in the United States. *All in the Family,* for instance, was modeled on the

British situation comedy *Till Death Us Do Part. Three Men and a Baby, Sommersby, Point of No Return,* and *The Birdcage* were adapted from French films (the prototypes were *Trois Hommes et un Couffin, Le Retour de Martin Guerre, La Femme Nikita,* and *La Cage Aux Folles*), while *Scent of a Woman* was based on an Italian movie.[9]

In addition, Hollywood continued to bring European film directors to the United States, offering them larger budgets, higher salaries, more publicity, and greater international exposure for their movies than they could expect to obtain at home. Among the more notable migrants in the 1980s and 1990s were Paul Verhoeven from Holland, Barbet Schroeder from France, and Neil Jordan from Ireland.[10]

The recruitment of European directors, and the remolding of their movies and TV shows for American consumption, weakened the already fragile film and television industries in Britain and on the Continent. It was no wonder, then, that moviemakers, television producers, and government ministers throughout Western Europe objected, with mounting anger by the 1980s, to the one-sided cultural relationship between their countries and the United States.

Underlying the ire was the century-long fear that Europe's folkways were crumbling under the weight of America's influence. Any moment now, it would all be gone—the ancient neighborhoods, the traditional family relationships, the older patterns of courtship and child rearing, the ways in which people had once entertained themselves at nights and on the weekends, even the national language; everything familiar and cherished might soon recede into memory unless the impact of the American media could somehow be blunted.

In almost every country in Western Europe, the sense of impending loss grew more acute from the 1960s on. Where British intellectuals like George Orwell and Richard Hoggart had lamented in the 1940s and 1950s the disintegration of a distinctive working-class culture before the onslaught of consumerism and American television programs, Francis Williams in 1962 was disturbed by the threat to "Englishness" itself, a threat that transcended region or class. The British, Williams complained, were accepting "more of [American culture] than it is possible for our society to assimilate and still remain true to its own virtues." If this trend continued, he warned, "we may kill much that gives to English life its color and zest and character," much of "what is specifically English in our civilization." In the same vein, an Italian commentator spoke for many of his intellectual colleagues when he suggested in the early 1990s that "the more we import and absorb American cultural models, the more we should be scared of them, since . . . we risk losing our own cultural identity."[11]

The French, as always, were more hyperbolic than anyone else in describing the disastrous effects of American culture on their national heritage. In *The American Challenge* (1967), Jean-Jacques Servan-Schreiber had been distressed not only by America's economic superiority but by the implications of its cultural dominance. If the French allowed their movie and television studios, as well as their magazines and publishing houses, to be taken over by American companies, he argued, "our system of education—in the large sense of channels of communication by which customs are transmitted and ways of life and thought [are] formulated—would be controlled from the outside." Twenty-six years later, when Steven Spielberg's *Jurassic Park* opened in Paris in 1993, Servan-Schreiber's admonitions about an alien conquest of French institutions seemed to have taken place. Spielberg's movie dinosaurs were denounced by the press and the government alike as monsters devouring the remnants of French culture. In the wake of Euro Disney, along with the flood of immigrants from North Africa, the dinosaurs represented one more assault upon French uniqueness. As one foreign policy expert put it, "there is less and less of France abroad, and more and more that is foreign in France."[12]

Satellites, cable and commercial television, computers and VCRs, all heightened the danger of Europe's "cultural suicide" (in the melodramatic phrase of a bureaucrat in Brussels). But the spread of the new technology did not, by itself, signal the death of a "European" consciousness. The end would come when Italians and Germans, Greeks and Norwegians, the Poles and the Portuguese, each decided that their private fantasies and favorite folktales were not as compelling as the intricate plots of a John Grisham novel or the larger-than-life heroes in *The Terminator* and on *Baywatch*.[13] No longer willing or able to invent their own stories, people in Europe would rely in the future, far more than they had in the past, on the American media for the emotional sustenance that their local cultures once provided but now could not.

To most Europeans, this was potentially the grimmest consequence of America's cultural imperialism. Still, the obliteration of European culture was not inevitable. It was up to the governments of Western Europe, led by France, to devise yet another strategy to resist America, one that might be more effective than those that had failed in the 1920s and 1940s. And for the French, the chief targets were not just the imported images in movie theaters and on television screens. The counterattack had to begin with the words people used.

LANGUAGE AND NATIONAL IDENTITY

In 1994 France's minister of culture, Jacques Toubon, wrote an article in *Le Monde* explaining what the French language meant to the French people. "It is their primary capital," he proclaimed, "the symbol of their dignity, the passageway to integration, . . . a common heritage, part of the French dream."[14] This glorious and once-global language, this key to French history and culture, was being sabotaged by English, Toubon warned. Not just by ordinary English words, too many of which had already invaded the French vocabulary, but even worse by American slang.

Cultural ministers in other countries, equally bothered by the Americanisms polluting German, Italian, Spanish, or the Queen's English for that matter, could have delivered a similar jeremiad. Throughout Europe, American idioms were becoming impossible to ignore. One saw and heard them everywhere: in American movies, on American television programs (especially those that broadcast basketball and football games to European audiences), in advertising jingles, on MTV, in fashion magazines, on the menus at fast-food restaurants, and from the mouths of American tourists.

The United States came to represent modernity because many of the trends associated with the Western world in the twentieth century occurred first in America. In the same way, certain expressions that were considered typically "American" had been coined in the United States to describe new but eventually universal developments like consumerism and suburbanization. Once these phenomena crossed the Atlantic, so too did the words, particularly when no comparable term existed in the local language. Why make up a word when it was easier to use the American original? Hence *commuter, weekend, motel, blues, gangster, cocktail, cheeseburger, ketchup, chewing gum, aspirin, Kleenex, supermarket, drive-in, software, talk show, prime time,* and thousands of other Americanisms entered the European lexicon.[15] The French may have objected to "Franglais," but everyone starting speaking a sort of patois, combining native and American phrases, creating a hybrid language that was ultimately more intercontinental than uniquely American.

In some instances, Europeans adopted an American word even when it was not needed, when the Germans or the Italians or the Swedes had an expression in their own language that would have done just as well. This was precisely what irritated French politicians and intellectuals. Anglo-American phrases were replacing perfectly suitable French terms, they grumbled. Although only 2 percent of the words in the contemporary French vocabulary came from Britain or the United States, these unwelcome imports inspired charges of linguistic colonization, as if France's cultural independence was now in serious jeopardy. In no other country in Europe did the elite seem so perturbed by the use of English, despite the fact that 80 percent of the students in French secondary schools and universities were studying the language by the 1990s.[16] It was still necessary to defend the special character of France by banishing as many Anglo-American words as possible from the national discourse.

From Charles de Gaulle in the 1960s to Jacques Toubon in the 1990s, French officials tried to restrict the number of English and American phases that could appear in government documents, scientific journals, and the media. The *Commission Supérieure de L'Audiovisuel,* for example, monitored every film to make sure that foreign members of the cast spoke impeccable French. The commission also had the power to block producers from receiving government subsidies if they allowed extraneous Americanisms to creep into their scripts. In 1992, the Academy of Cinematic Arts and Technology declared that only French-language movies would be eligible to win a *César* (the French equivalent of Hollywood's Oscar) for best picture of the year. This edict meant that the films of directors like Louis Malle, who had often employed English-speaking actors in movies intended for worldwide distribution, were now to be excluded from the competition for the highest award, though they could contend in other, lesser categories.[17]

It was ironic that the academy should issue such a decree at a time when French directors and producers were complaining about the omnipresence of American movies in theaters all over France while their own films could barely penetrate the U.S. market. Movies featuring bilingual actors or two versions of the same movie—one in French, the other in English—might have enabled French filmmakers to honor French culture and simultaneously attract American audiences. Nevertheless, the overseers of the French film industry resembled the executives at Ford, Chrysler, and General Motors who blamed Tokyo's protectionist policies for their failure to sell cars in

Japan, but who refused for a long time to manufacture automobiles with steering wheels on the right to accommodate the needs of Japanese drivers.

The most draconian effort to regulate the use of Anglo-American words occurred in 1994. In that year, Jacques Toubon urged the National Assembly to pass a law banning three thousand English phrases from all commercial and governmental publications, radio and television broadcasts, and advertisements, whenever a French term—any French term, however cumbersome and infelicitous—was available. The government provided a dictionary to help with the transition from English to French. Under its guidelines, *popcorn* was to be called *maïs soufflé, fast food* would become *restauration rapide, best-seller* turned into *succès de librairie,* prime time became *heures de grande écoute,* and the approved term for *airbag* was now *coussin gonflable de protection*. In addition, the National Assembly ordered all radio programs featuring popular music to set aside at least 40 percent of their airtime for French-language songs.[18]

In an op-ed piece published in the *New York Times,* Toubon attempted to justify his opposition to English on the grounds of practicality, an approach he assumed would appeal to American readers. The French government was simply requiring "the use of the French language in France," he submitted, "so that employees can understand their work contracts and product instructions," and consumers could decipher the "safety warnings" on the labels of the merchandise they brought home from the store. Besides, he pointed out, many federal agencies and state governments in the United States insisted on the use of English for the same reasons. In effect, Toubon's ministry was behaving no differently from the guardians of public health at the U.S. Food and Drug Administration.[19]

Toubon's rationale was ingenious, but it probably did not convince most Americans. It certainly failed to persuade France's Constitutional Council, which ruled that the government's language policies violated the principle of freedom of expression, guaranteed by the French Revolution and its Declaration of the Rights of Man. The government, the council argued, had no authority to prohibit business executives, scientists, advertisers, radio and television broadcasters, and ordinary citizens from using whatever words they wished.[20]

Still, American phrases were not always more convenient than their French equivalents. Nor were they even comprehensible, particularly when they were shrouded in jargon. At a United Nations conference on women and the problems of population growth held in Cairo in

1994, a meeting whose predominant language was Americanese, many participants had no idea what some of the trendier idioms were supposed to mean. "We have no term for 'female empowerment,'" a French translator confessed. Her Chinese counterpart wondered "who is empowering whom?" An Arabic speaker thought "family leave" indicated that spouses should separate after a child was born, while a Russian translation implied that the entire family had left on vacation. Similarly, "reproductive health" reappeared in Russian as "health that reproduces itself again and again." The chief Russian translator did not know what to do with "coping mechanisms," though the Russian people, no doubt, had developed quite a lot of these over the course of their history.[21] Given the befuddlement of foreigners confronted with the argot of the U.S. delegates, perhaps the French need not have worried about America's linguistic preeminence.

Yet the desire to prevent one's native language from being corrupted by a host of alien Anglo-Americanisms was not all that bizarre, especially when the skirmish over words was seen as part of a larger battle to preserve and strengthen one's national culture. Charles de Gaulle and his successors repeatedly emphasized this connection. They also denied that they were chauvinists. Instead, the French asserted—never more vigorously than in the GATT negotiations during the 1980s and early 1990s—that they were defending not just the culture of France but the culture of all the countries in Europe.

PROTECTIONISM, FREE TRADE, AND THE MASS MEDIA

For nearly a century, European governments had been trying, in a variety of ways, to protect their cultural industries from American domination. Repeatedly, the Europeans claimed that first their films and then their television programs were artistically ambitious and socially uplifting whereas American moviemakers and TV producers—compelled to maximize profits—catered to, rather than challenged, their audiences. However familiar these arguments were, at no point did European politicians or intellectuals sound as antagonistic to the American media or as apprehensive about the survival of their own cultural institutions as in the last two decades of the twentieth century. Although their rhetoric during the GATT discussions was often overheated, European (and especially French) officials were wrestling with an issue that none of their predecessors had been able to

resolve. Could the countries of Europe retain their national idiosyncrasies or must they surrender to a standardized and homogeneous
culture allegedly imposed by America on every nation in the world?

The opening salvo in this latest campaign to combat the influence of
America's media was delivered by Jack Lang, France's minister of culture through most of the 1980s. At a conference in Mexico City in 1982,
Lang castigated the cultural imperialists (presumably headquartered
in the United States) who interfered "in the interior affairs of other
countries, and more seriously, in the consciousness of the citizens of
those countries," taking over their "trains of thought" and "ways of
life." Lang's tocsin reverberated in the speeches of other leaders over
the next eleven years. During the climax of the GATT negotiations in
1993, French President François Mitterrand insisted that no single
country "should be allowed to control the images of the whole world,"
that each nation had a right to its own culture, including the right to its
own movies and television programs, free from outside (which meant
American) intrusion.[22]

Unfortunately for the French, the purpose of GATT was to encourage free trade by eliminating quotas and subsidies in the realm of
commerce, as well in culture. But the pronouncements of Lang and
Mitterrand indicated why France, and ultimately the rest of Western
Europe, were intent on exempting the cinema, television, and any new
audiovisual ventures from the terms of the pact. As in the past, the
Europeans wanted to limit the number of American films and TV
shows that could be shown in movie theaters and on television stations,
whether state controlled or privately owned. The French government,
in particular, was adamant about maintaining its generous subsidies to
the arts, and to its movie and television industries, in order to shield
the country from any further Anglo-American incursions.[23]

The GATT talks took place at a time when the European cinema
was in its worst shape since the end of World War II. In fact, only
France still had an independent and vigorous film industry, capable
(with financial help from the government) of turning out 150 movies a
year. But even in France, filmmakers could not compete with their
American counterparts either internationally or at home. Faced with
high labor costs and declining box-office receipts, French producers
normally preferred low-budget movies that lacked the American-style
special effects so popular with foreign audiences. As a consequence,
where American film companies could expect to receive half their income from overseas ticket sales, French studios had to depend almost

entirely on domestic revenues, a heavy burden for an industry whose home market was one-fifth the size of the market in the United States.[24]

French audiences, however, were not rushing to French movies. Despite the image of France as a country devoted to "serious" films, attendance at French movies plummeted from 93 million in 1983 to 40 million in 1992. If the French public was losing interest in the French cinema, some *auteurs* were equally indifferent to their customers. According to an organizer of a film festival in Deauville, a number of French directors seemed "completely content" to make movies that were "seen by nobody."[25]

Nonetheless, the French government set out to safeguard its film industry in the GATT negotiations by demanding that quotas and subsidies be incorporated into any agreement. Several prominent European directors endorsed the French position, stating that these policies should be applied across the Continent. In an "open letter" addressed to Steven Spielberg and Martin Scorsese and signed by Bernardo Bertolucci of Italy, Wim Wenders of Germany, and Pedro Almodóvar of Spain, the Europeans explained that they were "desperately" seeking to save their national cinemas from "annihilation" by Hollywood. Should American movies continue to overwhelm local productions, they warned, "there will be no . . . European film industry left by the year 2000." In an interview with an Italian journalist, Bertolucci envisioned a greater calamity. "The world hegemony of American films," he predicted, would lead to "a dreadful monoculture, a kind of cultural totalitarianism."[26]

When it came to television, the Europeans were no less gloomy. "What will remain of our cultural identity," a French official wanted to know, "if audiovisual Europe consists of European consumers sitting in front of Japanese TV sets showing American programs?" As in the case of the movies, Europe's television industry could apparently be rescued only by quotas. To reduce the import of American shows and motivate local television producers to increase their output, the European Community in 1989 directed its member-states to reserve at least 51 percent of their airtime for programs manufactured in Europe.[27] The governments hoped that this regulation too would become part of the GATT treaty.

Yet the reaction among the diverse constituencies in the European television industry was mixed. On the one hand, directors, actors, and scriptwriters applauded the ruling; they believed it would preserve jobs and stimulate the production of homemade programs. On the other hand, broadcasters—especially those who ran the new cable and satellite services—were less enthusiastic because they wanted to buy as many American shows as possible to fill up their schedules and sell more ads.[28]

The U.S. negotiators displayed no such ambivalence about Europe's efforts to restrict America's cultural exports. In every international forum since 1945, American diplomats and media executives had opposed all barriers to the free flow of movies, television programs, and music across national borders. In 1948, for example, Washington persuaded the United Nations General Assembly to include in its Universal Declaration on Human Rights the principle that "everyone has the right to . . . impart information and ideas through any media and regardless of frontiers." In addition, the Americans consistently argued that the market, not governments, should determine whose culture was most in demand. From the U.S. perspective, any attempt to meddle with the mass media was both a form of censorship and economically unwise because it deprived consumers of the power to decide for themselves what they thought, how they wished to be entertained, and which communications products they wanted to buy.[29]

American officials reiterated all of these points during the debate over GATT. But their European interlocutors were not convinced. The Europeans feared that an open market for culture and ideas would not result in greater freedom and more choices for audiences. Rather, the market would simply be dominated by the largest and most technologically sophisticated media companies, most of which were American. Furthermore, the prospect of America's movie studios and television networks transmitting their messages and images unimpeded by quotas of any kind meant that European governments might no longer be able to influence the social values and cultural pursuits of their own citizens.[30]

Frustrated by Europe's refusal to let audiovisual merchandise be treated like any other commodity in the marketplace, the Americans became increasingly cynical about what was really at stake in the GATT discussions. To Mickey Kantor, the Clinton administration's trade representative, and Jack Valenti, president of the Motion Picture Association of America, the Europeans were less concerned about the potential loss of their cultural sovereignty than about how to protect their inept film and television industries from having to compete with America's superior movies and TV shows. Kantor and Valenti were especially incensed by a tax levied by France on all foreign movies, television films, and videocassettes as a means of subsidizing the French cinema. Since American movies accounted for nearly 60 percent of the box-office receipts in French theaters and an even higher percentage for video rentals, the U.S. negotiators charged that France was taking advantage of Hollywood's talent and creativity to pay for mediocre French films.[31]

With the Europeans accusing the Americans of wanting to monopolize the world's media, and the Americans accusing the Europeans of being driven only by greed, it was inevitable that there would be no agreement on how to handle mass culture. In December 1993, the impasse over audiovisual products was resolved by leaving them out of the GATT treaty. Each country could thus set its own rules about cultural imports without regard for the ideals of free trade. This arrangement enabled France and other Western European countries to preserve for a while their system of quotas, taxes, and subsidies.[32] But Europe's victory did not diminish the popularity of America's movies and television programs in Britain, Scandinavia, or on the Continent. Nor would it inhibit the expansion of satellite and cable networks, slow down the sale of VCRs and computers, or counteract the appeal of the Internet, each an instrument for the spread of American culture.

Yet perhaps Europe was not in as much danger of abandoning its cultural heritage and becoming increasingly Americanized as the quarrel over GATT and the allegations of linguistic imperialism might have suggested. Despite the anxieties of the Europeans and the insensitivity of the Americans, a more complicated interchange between the two continents was taking place, an encounter that in the late twentieth century helped to transform the cultural "identity" both of Europe and the United States.

ELEVEN

The Europeanization of American Culture

Over the decades, the words changed. *Americanization, homogenization, coca-colonization, media imperialism, global hegemony*—at one time or another, critics overseas and in the United States employed all these terms to describe America's domination of the planet through the export of its products, its culture, and its way of life. By the end of the twentieth century, it seemed as if the world had indeed become "Americanized," confirming William Stead's glum prediction in 1901.

Or had it? America's imprint was certainly noticeable, particularly in Western Europe after 1945 and in Eastern Europe after the end of the Cold War. The blue jeans and sneakers, the use of American slang, the pervasiveness of rock and roll, the popularity of American movies and television shows, the ubiquitous advertisements for Coca-Cola and Kentucky Fried Chicken, the debut of Euro Disney, each might well move a European to complain (as did a character in a Wim Wenders film) that "the Yanks have colonized our subconscious." Yet how widespread was America's influence, and how deeply did it affect the psyches of people in Europe?

Probably more than many Europeans would have liked but less

than they feared. The "Americanization" of Europe, if not also the world, was mainly symbolic—a phenomenon too easily associated with a set of highly visible brand names, icons, and trademarks, from CNN to Mickey Mouse and the Marlboro Man to the golden arches of McDonald's. Nevertheless, European lifestyles and attitudes were only partially altered by the presence of America's mass culture and merchandise. The American impact, reputedly destructive of local and national traditions, was always restrained by Europe's disparate institutions and customs, and by its ethnic and linguistic diversity. To a considerable extent, Europeans resisted the standardization and homogeneity allegedly inflicted on them by their American masters. Instead, they adapted America's products and culture to their own needs, "Europeanizing" and domesticating most of the items and images they received from the United States.

Europeans also exported their culture and their consumer goods to America, especially from the 1970s on. In fact, the postwar relationship between the United States and Europe was never as unequal as European writers and political leaders claimed. It was marked more by a process of cross-fertilization, a reciprocal exchange of ideas about filmmaking and fashion, architecture and literary criticism, furnishings and food. In this sense, too, American culture was partly "Europeanized." In the end, there was no such thing as a completely Americanized society—not in Europe and not even, as it turned out, in the United States.

THE LIMITS OF AMERICA'S INFLUENCE

To understand how Europeans actually coped with and deflected the pressures of Americanization, one has to dispense with a notion dear to the critics of mass culture and consumerism on both sides of the Atlantic. Implicit in almost all the attacks on America's "cultural imperialism" was the assumption that people in Europe and elsewhere were little more than receptacles, mindlessly ingesting and internalizing the messages of the American media. According to its opponents, mass culture converted audiences into a collection of zombies, docile and passive, too drugged to discriminate between art and trash, too hypnotized to switch off the television set or get off the information highway.[1] The shrines in which these poor souls congregated—and whose attractions they could neither question nor reject—were the supermarket, the shopping mall, the fast-food restaurant, and the theme park. The American media supposedly made people not only acquiescent but helpless, incapable of eluding or moderating its influences, or of having any thoughts and feelings of their own.

Yet this account of how mass culture functions in people's lives is much too simplistic. Audiences are not merely containers into which the media pours its instructions and images. Nor are they compliant consumers, tempted or coerced by advertisers into buying worthless products or watching movies and television shows that give them only fleeting pleasure but no real satisfaction.

On the contrary, audiences both in the United States and in Europe have been active participants in determining the effects of mass culture, constantly reinterpreting its messages to fit their own social or personal circumstances. Whether it was Jean-Paul Sartre and François Truffaut using America's novels and films to overthrow the literary and cinematic old guard in postwar France, or European adolescents in the 1950s defying their parents by identifying with rock musicians, or Dutch viewers in the 1980s relating the plot twists of *Dallas* to the problems in their private lives, each has reflected the ability of people to take from American culture whatever they wanted and needed at any particular moment.[2]

Also underlying the criticisms of mass culture was a nostalgia for the vanished era when families sat around dining-room tables sharing the events of the day, and then read books in the evening rather than retreating (as they did in the later years of the century) to their separate rooms to watch television or listen to compact discs. This lament first surfaced in the 1920s with the arrival of radio. From that moment on, the critics complained that the media severed social bonds and encouraged solitude at the expense of companionship.

But reading a book can be one of the most solitary experiences imaginable. Meanwhile a radio broadcast, a movie, a television program, or a rock concert could become an occasion for members of the audience to exchange impressions with one another about what they had seen and heard, as well as a chance to talk back or even to stop listening altogether. The mass communications industry in the United States did not so much manipulate or isolate its domestic and foreign audiences as offer them opportunities to interact in ways that were often unexpected and unintended.

At bottom, the European intellectuals and government officials who detested the American media overestimated its power to sway the citizens of their respective countries. People in Europe (and in America too) are not permanently plugged in—not to their computers, their television sets, their Walkmans, or their VCRs. They spend much of their time doing other things. They walk, read, converse with their spouses and neighbors, and play with their children. In all these activities, they are influenced less by the media than by the events of their childhoods, by how their parents raised them, by the opinions of their peers, by their experiences at work, and by the environment in which they live.

Furthermore, people have been selective in their reactions to mass culture. Residents of the modern world, continually exposed to the modern media, they are accustomed to its endless chatter. But they do not silently submit. They tend to be skeptical, accepting some information while distrusting most of what comes over the airwaves. They filter out the political and cultural messages that sound jarring or implausible, discarding whatever has no relevance to their daily concerns. As a consequence, audiences may have been more sophisticated about and more unaffected by mass culture than the media critics and politicians in Europe or the United States gave them credit for.

In addition, the messages themselves are frequently contradictory and ambiguous. The European foes of America's "cultural imperialism" seemed to believe that the executives who controlled the movie studios, the television networks, the record companies, and the publishing houses were engaged in a cabal to transmit a unified and distinctively "American" set of values to their customers abroad. The Europeans went on to presume that unwary foreigners, regardless of their dissimilar social backgrounds and life histories, would absorb these values in the same way. But the notion that the media barons wanted to convey some specifically American message ignored how hard it is for anyone in the entertainment or book business to predict what will sell. The success of a movie, a TV show, or a novel usually depends on luck or a chain of happy accidents, not on someone's grand design. Given the volatility of the market and the shifting preferences of the audience, the American media could hardly afford to be ideological in its themes or uniform in its structure. Instead, it has prospered by remaining competitive and eclectic, offering a multiplicity of icons and viewpoints that had different meanings for different audiences at different times in different countries.[3] The result was not a homogenous or a monocultural world, but a reinforcement of cultural diversity.

And sometimes political diversity as well. American movies and television programs have no doubt promoted conservative ideas and strengthened the status quo. But the media also helped to inspire rebellions, as in the 1960s when it focused on issues like racism and the war in Vietnam. In this instance, the news stories and television pictures created a community of dissenters, both in the United States and in Western Europe, transforming many people from spectators to political activists. In Eastern Europe and the Soviet Union, where Communist propaganda put people to sleep, America's mass culture—its rock music and blue jeans—appeared "subversive" and liberating, providing a symbolic alternative to the hackneyed slogans of the existing regimes. The circumstances in a particular country, then, determined whether the American media would be an instrument of pacification or insurgency.[4]

Often, however, the impact of America's culture and consumer goods has been negligible. At least more so than a lot of European intellectuals, politicians, and parents were willing to admit. Drinking a Coke, eating a Big Mac, buying a pair of Nikes, watching a Steven Spielberg movie, or going to Euro Disney did not mean that one had become "Americanized." Sometimes a movie is just a movie and a cheeseburger is just a cheeseburger. Americans never supposed that driving a Toyota or a Volvo implied a surrender to Japanese or Swedish values. Neither did the purchase of American-made sneakers by a Danish adolescent or the decision of a Belgian family to have dinner at the nearby Pizza Hut signify an embrace of the American way of life.

The presence and popularity of American products in Europe did not necessarily lead to a change in the European psyche. Europeans adopted American customs only if these were compatible with their own experiences and expectations. Hard work, after all, is as much a German or a Norwegian as an American ideal. Individualism is a trait as honored in France as in the United States. And the American addiction to fast food like burgers and fries is not so different from the British enthusiasm for fish and chips. American habits were most likely to be copied when they corresponded to local traditions and tastes.[5]

Even when Europeans did borrow American ideas or imitate American patterns of behavior, the ideas and the behavior were modified to suit the special requirements of France or Britain, Italy or Sweden. America's culture did not cross the Atlantic intact, any more than European culture retained its original shape after it was brought to the New World. In *The American Democracy,* Harold Laski reminded his European readers that whatever was "taken or received from the Old World [became] different as it . . . adapted to its new home" in the United States. Americans revised the languages, religions, architecture, music, and political institutions inherited from Britain and other countries in Europe, mixing up the ingredients to create a civilization that was unique and exotic, but not entirely unfamiliar to European immigrants and travelers. Similarly, Europeans appropriated certain elements of the American lifestyle, intertwining them with native attitudes and mores. What emerged was a hybrid culture, part American and part European.[6]

Thus, American products and attitudes were not directly imposed upon Europe. The influence of America's exports depended instead on how easily they could be integrated with the social and cultural folkways that existed in each of the countries on the other side of the ocean.

THE TRANSATLANTIC COUNTERCULTURE

At no point in the late twentieth century was the fusion of American and European ideas and experiences more evident than during the 1960s. It is customary to describe America in this decade as the epicenter of a series of political and cultural earthquakes, whose aftershocks radiated outward to other countries, causing convulsions similar to those that ripped the United States apart. But the upheavals of the 1960s did not originate in America alone. Although young Americans unquestionably influenced the tone, the style, the vocabulary, the tactics, and the aims of the counterculture and the New Left, the generational conflicts and the radical movements of the 1960s were a transatlantic phenomenon. They were affected as much by conditions in London, Amsterdam, Paris, Berlin, and Prague as by the freedom summers in Mississippi, the hippie subculture in Haight-Ashbury, the antiwar demonstrations in Berkeley and Boston, the riots at the Democratic Party's convention in Chicago, and the killings of four college students at Kent State. The turmoil in America coincided with unrest in Europe, and with postwar developments in all the industrialized nations, provoking a rebellion that failed to achieve its most utopian aspirations but that did succeed in challenging the conventional wisdom and changing some of the institutions in every Western society.[7]

It is, of course, an oversimplification to conceive of the "1960s" as a unified whole. When people speak of the 1960s, they are usually referring to the later years of the decade. And they are recalling its most vivid images: apolitical adolescents engulfed in long hair and attired in costumes from every historical era, stoned on pot or tripping on acid, living in collectives and repudiating the parental path of upward mobility and professional advancement, working at odd jobs and communing at rock festivals. Or alternatively, radicalized students attending mass rallies, occupying administration buildings at elite universities, being teargassed and clubbed by infuriated cops dispatched by the authorities to restore order on campuses and city streets.

Yet there was another 1960s, the decade's opening years, before the class and generational explosions, before the assassinations and the bloodshed in distant jungles, before the days of rage. A time "full of hope," the British historian J. H. Plumb called it, remembering his optimism following the election of John F. Kennedy in 1960. The "dawn of a new age," or so it seemed to a Dutch historian looking back on this period from the less confident and certainly less innocent vantage point of the early 1980s.[8]

Such sentiments reflected the still-favorable impressions of the United States among many Europeans at the beginning of the 1960s, despite the anti-Americanism of some intellectuals in France and elsewhere. America's prestige in Western Europe was at its height during these years, not only because of Kennedy's diplomatic skills, but also because of his wit, his urbanity, and his ironic sensibility, traits that made him sound more "European" than conventionally American. In Holland and Norway, newspapers praised the dynamism of the Kennedy presidency, contrasting it to the lethargy of the Eisenhower administration. In West Germany, and especially in West Berlin, students and professors applauded Kennedy as ardently as did ordinary Germans during his triumphal visit in the summer of 1963. Even in France, the spectacle of the American people electing a president who appeared comfortable in the presence of writers, and who had himself "authored" several books, moved journalists and intellectuals to concede that maybe America was not a cultural wasteland after all.[9]

The euphoria ended in November 1963. After the murder of Kennedy in Dallas, European suspicions about America's leadership reemerged. More ominously, the racial divisions, the spread of urban violence and decay, and the growing unpopularity of the Johnson administration raised doubts abroad about whether the United States could continue to pose as an exemplar either of social progress or political stability.

Nothing damaged America's reputation overseas or undermined

its image as the savior of postwar Europe more than the war in Vietnam. Europeans no longer saw the Americans as benevolent liberators. Now television newscasts showed American soldiers napalming Vietnamese children, burning peasant huts, bringing the Cold War to the Mekong Delta. Throughout Western Europe, people began to question the "Atlantic Alliance," the identification with and reliance on American power. Even those who had previously sympathized with America's ideals and objectives were disillusioned. "My former enthusiasm," wrote Sigmund Skard, "was replaced by a deep perplexity, often a despondency," and finally a decision to organize his fellow Norwegian Americanists in a "public protest" against the saturation bombing of North Vietnam. By the late 1960s, a French intellectual observed, many in Europe ceased to believe in the "myth of American infallibility." The United States "had rejoined the ranks of the mortal nations." The "guardian of the ideals of the free world" turned out to be just "like the rest of us—sinful [and] corrupt," concluded J. H. Plumb.[10] America—morally and structurally flawed—was a country whose policies seemed no different from and no better than those of the British in India, the Dutch in Indonesia, or the French in Algeria.

Vietnam, however, did not so much cause as contribute to the pandemonium of the 1960s. There were other, more significant factors underlying the decade's political and cultural strife. America's postwar prosperity and Western Europe's economic recovery in the 1950s camouflaged a growing sense of dissatisfaction, particularly among young people, with the emphasis on making money, pursuing careers, and postponing immediate pleasures in the interest of future comfort and security. These frustrations were exacerbated by a feeling of powerlessness in an age of large corporations and remote government officials determining in their inner sanctums whether to wage war or peace without consulting the citizens whose lives depended on such decisions.

In the 1950s, the disaffection of American and European adolescents was reflected in their admiration for Jack Kerouac and J. D. Salinger, Miles Davis and Elvis Presley, James Dean and Marlon Brando—in short, anyone who seemed like a nonconformist. But by the 1960s, as they began to enter college, the idea that the baby boomers belonged to a distinctive generation, one that transcended geographic boundaries, with its own language and styles of dress, and its greater tolerance for sexual experimentation, led to the emergence of a counterculture and a passion for radical politics both in Europe and the United States.

The specific motives for rebellion differed from country to country. In America, the civil rights movement and the war in Vietnam destroyed the prevailing consensus on domestic and foreign policy, and precipitated a widespread revolt by young people, as well as by many of their parents. In Britain, the Netherlands, West Germany, and France, children were growing up without sharp memories of World War II or the poverty and rationing of the late 1940s. Nor did they recollect the tensions of the early Cold War years. Instead, in an era of affluence, they felt free to challenge what they considered to be the conservatism and complacency of the postwar social order.[11]

Whatever the differences between the United States and Europe, mass communications—the wealth of information, images, and sounds conveyed through newspapers and magazines, television, movies, and record albums—made it possible for the counterculture to leap over national borders, and move back and forth across the Atlantic. Initially, European youths—lacking native political or cultural heroes—were drawn to the highly publicized representatives of an insurgent America, a cluster of dissidents who inhabited a country antithetical to the one that worshipped capitalism, segregated African Americans, and slaughtered the Vietnamese. America might be racist and repressive, but it also supplied the leaders and the troubadours of the revolution: Malcolm X and Bob Dylan, Angela Davis and Joan Baez, the Students for a Democratic Society and the Jefferson Airplane. A young person living in Austria, Holland, or Italy could denounce the imperialists in the White House and the Pentagon while at the same time learning from the media how to emulate the adversarial style of the American counterculture and the tactics of the civil rights and antiwar movements in the United States. Yet eventually, Europe produced its own legendary agitators (like Rudi Dutschke in Berlin and Daniel Cohn-Bendit—better known as "Danny the Red"—in Paris) and its own anthems composed by the Beatles and the Rolling Stones. Soon, Amsterdam—where drug-drenched flower children camped out in Vondelpark or sought sanctuary in an abandoned church, now a youth club renamed "Paradiso"—could claim to be as much the home of the counterculture as San Francisco.[12]

In cities on both continents, universities became the focal points and the staging areas for radical demonstrations. Universities were where young people gathered in ever greater numbers, encountering similar problems and demanding similar reforms, regardless of which country they lived in. Just as college enrollments soared during the 1960s in the United States, so attendance at universities in Western Europe rose too. Higher education, particularly in Europe, came to be regarded less as a privilege reserved for the children of the elite and more as an opportunity open to the offspring of the middle class.[13] But as universities sought to democratize their admissions procedures, they grew larger and more impersonal, developing into "multiversities" not only in America but also in Germany and France.

Efforts by officials in Bonn to make higher education more accessible for young West Germans, for example, put an inordinate strain on university faculties, classrooms, and libraries. The pressures were especially noticeable at the Free University in West Berlin. During the late 1940s and 1950s, when the university served as a symbol of Western values in an enclave surrounded by Communist tyranny, students, professors, and administrators believed that they had a common purpose. In the 1960s, the Free University found itself burdened with overcrowded facilities and an increasingly bureaucratic structure, and the sense of community disintegrated. Alienated and radicalized students started to treat professors and administrators as enemies, rather than allies. Adopting the slogans and strategies of the Free Speech Movement at Berkeley, they began in 1965 to call for fundamental changes in the way their own university was run. For the rest of the decade and into the 1970s, students, assistant instructors, and university employees engaged in a fierce struggle that involved class and generational, as well as academic, issues. The rebels borrowed methods from their American counterparts, holding teach-ins, occupying buildings, and disrupting classes. Yet their objectives—equal participation in decision making and governance, the creation of Marxist institutes, the end of professorial control over courses and reading lists—were shaped by the situation in Berlin. Still, by the late 1960s, the student uprising at the Free University spread to other West German universities in Frankfurt, Bremen, and Hamburg, and to other countries in Western Europe.[14]

The French government tried to cope with expanding enrollments by establishing new universities, with American-style "campuses" and dormitories, on the outskirts of the major cities. But students consigned to these installations complained that were being cut off from urban cafés, bookstores, movie theaters, and street life. It was not surprising, then, that the upheavals in France in 1968 originated at the University of Nanterre, a campus located outside Paris. In addition to those who felt isolated in the suburbs, the majority of French students—like their colleagues in Germany and the United States—were angered by large classes, aloof professors, and what they regarded as an "irrelevant" curriculum.[15] But unlike American or West German undergraduates and teaching assistants, who concentrated mainly on problems within their own universities, French students joined French workers in a series of violent battles with the police, nearly bringing down the government.

However much they were swayed by local circumstances, the counterculture and the student movements of the 1960s blended elements from the American and the Western European experience. The same mixture of influences could be seen in the emergence of an intercontinental New Left.

In fact, the concept of a "New Left" first appeared in Britain, not in the United States. During the late 1950s and early 1960s, young British radicals, most of them from middle-class families, became the leaders of a worldwide campaign for nuclear disarmament. The "ban the bomb" movement featured extemporaneous, rather than rigidly organized, rallies and marches. It had few formal rules or membership lists, and it rejected the hierarchical structure of the old Left political parties. This improvisational spirit would soon be adopted by the American New Left. The movement also spawned a number of scholarly Marxist magazines, based at universities like Oxford, London, Leeds, and Hull. The most influential of these journals was the *New Left Review,* which made its debut in 1960. Although British youths, flocking to "swinging London" later in the decade, gained more notoriety for their tastes in clothes and music than for their commitment to "serious" politics, the ideas expounded in the left-wing journals impressed American intellectuals like C. Wright Mills, as well as the founders of the Students for a Democratic Society.[16]

Other Europeans contributed to the revival of radicalism in the 1960s. Some of the writers associated with the Frankfurt School—Max Horkheimer, Theodor Adorno, and especially Herbert Marcuse—had a significant impact on the West German and American New Left. Horkheimer, Adorno, and Marcuse all emigrated to the United States in the 1930s. After World War II, Horkheimer and Adorno returned to Frankfurt where, as professors and authors, they renewed their relationships with German students and intellectuals. Marcuse remained in America but frequently lectured at West German universities. In both countries, therefore, many young radicals accepted as gospel the Frankfurt School's criticisms of mass culture, "bourgeois liberalism," the passivity of the middle class, and the surrender of the American and European labor movements to capitalism and consumerism. Similarly, by the late 1960s, Antonio Gramsci in

Italy and a brigade of neo-Marxist, postmodernist theoreticians in France (Louis Althusser, Claude Lévi-Strauss, Jacques Lacan, Michel Foucault, Jacques Derrida, and Roland Barthes) helped to transform the language and the ideology of aspiring revolutionaries on each side of the Atlantic.[17]

Across the ocean, American liberal and leftist intellectuals sounded less abstract than their European comrades. The Americans were more likely to offer concrete arguments and to trust their own experiences. Nonetheless, social critics like C. Wright Mills, Vance Packard, Paul Goodman, Michael Harrington, and John Kenneth Galbraith—in their attacks on centralized power, the manipulations of the advertising industry, the bourgeois rat race, and the persistence of poverty in the "affluent society"—gave empirical support to the speculations of German and French intellectuals. The works of these American writers were widely translated and read in Western Europe during the 1960s.[18]

As one might have expected, the insights of American activists were more welcome in France than were the analyses of American intellectuals. French radicals, particularly those who were hostile to the Communist Party, revered America's underground newspapers, its "guerrilla" theater groups, its experimental filmmakers, and its feminist movement. The Americans—in contrast to the old-fashioned Stalinists and trade union functionaries in France—seemed spontaneous and antiauthoritarian.[19]

No band of American revolutionaries received a warmer embrace from French writers and students than the Black Panthers. Having already translated the memoirs and speeches of Malcolm X and Stokely Carmichael, French journals and left-wing publishing houses now offered their readers Eldridge Cleaver's *Soul on Ice,* along with the pronouncements of Huey Newton and Bobby Seale. Meetings and concerts were held at the Sorbonne and other French universities to raise funds for the Panthers' legal expenses, the result of their continuing confrontations with the FBI and the Oakland police (the "pigs" in the Panther vernacular, "les porcs" in the manifestoes of the French New Left). For a brief moment in the late 1960s and early 1970s, French radicals persuaded themselves that the Panthers had a coherent ideology which could mobilize the majority of whites and African Americans in the United States, and that the Panthers' jargon and tactics were also applicable to France. The Panthers thus became visionary mentors for their French disciples, even though conditions in the ghettos of America in no way resembled life on the Left Bank of the Seine.[20]

The transatlantic exchange of slogans and strategies depended not just on book translations and published interviews with movement leaders but also on personal contacts. Cheap airfares and charter flights in the 1960s allowed young people to travel easily between Europe and the United States. Dutch, German, and French students visited the centers of left-wing activity in New York, Boston, Madison, and San Francisco. American students spent summers in Paris or West Berlin. These journeys enabled radicals to compare experiences, form friendships and political alliances, find out what was going on in each other's countries. The encounters reinforced the notion that the New Left was a genuinely international crusade. And that direct action, not a reliance on parliamentary procedures, would overthrow the elites, give more power to women and minorities, and stop the war in Vietnam.[21]

The shared concerns of the American and European New Left did not mean that radicals were everywhere the same. New Leftists in the United States could transport their methods and goals to Western Europe only when these were suited to the political and cultural situation in a particular city or country.[22] Even then, each student movement had its own distinctive attributes.

Local variations were discernible in 1968, the most tumultuous year of the decade in many parts of the world—a year of riots, political rebellions, and "cultural revolutions" in America, France, West Germany, the Netherlands, and Czechoslovakia (as well as in Mexico, Brazil, and China). In the United States, the New Left's main enemy was Lyndon Johnson, whose announcement in March that he would not run for reelection led radicals and liberals alike to fantasize about the coming presidency of Robert Kennedy or Eugene McCarthy. In Prague, students, workers, and reform-minded politicians indulged in a springtime of hope that, with Soviet permission, socialism might be humanized. In West Berlin, the presence of U.S. troops intensified the rage of Marxist students and instructors at the Free University, who saw the soldiers not as protectors but as potential war criminals if they were sent to Vietnam. Once a repository for American culture, the America House—located near the Kurfürstendamm in the center of West Berlin—now became a symbol of America's imperialism and a convenient target for young German demonstrators. In France, the struggles in May summoned up memories of the Paris Commune, complete with huge rallies, general strikes, sit-ins at factories, the shutdown of the Sorbonne, street fighting, and calls for an end to the autocratic Gaullist regime.[23]

Despite these national dissimilarities, the New Left in Europe and in the United States faced a common disaster at the close of the 1960s. Charles de Gaulle remained in power, at least for a while. Soviet tanks crushed the dissidents in Prague. Martin Luther King and Robert Kennedy were assassinated, and Richard Nixon was elected. In West Berlin, tensions persisted until the 1970s before they gradually dissipated.

Still, the movements of the 1960s left a legacy among people on both continents. Before he himself was shot and disabled in Berlin during the Easter holidays in 1968, the student leader Rudi Dutschke urged his followers to embark on a "long march through the institutions."[24] The phrase, and the idea behind it, spread within and beyond the Federal Republic. Over the next three decades, the graduates of the 1960s evolved into squatters in Holland; members of the Green Party in Germany; antinuclear protesters in Britain; post-Communist Western-style democrats in Eastern Europe; and feminists, environmentalists, lawyers, journalists, filmmakers, and academics throughout Europe and the United States. Along the way, they may have jettisoned their revolutionary impulses and become more conservative, politically and culturally. But as Dutschke foresaw, they infiltrated—and sometimes took over—the major institutions in their countries. More important, they helped to alter the values of the very different societies in which they all lived.

GOING NATIVE: THE ADAPTATION OF AMERICAN PRODUCTS TO EUROPEAN TASTES

While there was a great deal of symmetry between the experiences of young radicals in Western Europe and in the United States during the 1960s, the transatlantic resemblances were less perceptible when it came to other facets of life on the two continents. If anything, the disparities were much more striking. For all the anxieties about "Americanization," the work habits and vacation customs of ordinary Europeans, their forms of evening and weekend recreation, their shopping patterns, their choice of cars, their tastes in food and entertainment, and their attitudes toward high technology and the role of government continued to diverge in significant ways from those of Americans throughout the last half of the twentieth century.

Urban life was one area where the differences were dramatic—

though this was not always acknowledged by visiting Americans or even by Europeans themselves. American tourists, trying to feel at home in Europe, loved to describe a particular city—Milan, Frankfurt, West Berlin—as being indistinguishable from an American metropolis. Milan, devoted to commerce and industry, seemed to Herbert Kubly in the early 1950s a "nondescript modern city with an American personality." Another American writer called Milan the "Chicago of Italy." In 1994 Stephen Kinzer, the Berlin bureau chief for the *New York Times,* characterized West Berlin as "the most Americanized of European cities," largely because of the longtime presence of American troops. He was not alone in this opinion. A sixteen-year-old Berliner told Kinzer that had it not been for the U.S. soldiers, "we wouldn't have baseball caps. We wouldn't have malls or fast-food shops or skateboards. Life just wouldn't be as good."[25]

One reason why Frankfurt or Rotterdam seemed as if they belonged in the United States was that in rebuilding their cities after World War II, European architects and urban planners copied American construction methods and materials (which were themselves partly based on the ideas of the prewar Bauhaus movement). Hotels and office buildings were mass-produced, and they often looked like the glass-and-steel skyscrapers that towered over the business districts of American cities. Sometimes the new structures seemed incongruous, given the surrounding devastation. Alfred Kazin compared the "American-style" buildings rising above the ruins in "shiny, neon-lighted" postwar Cologne with the "pink skin grafted into the faces of so many wounded soldiers."[26]

Yet despite its occasionally derivative architecture, no European city could be mistaken for New York or Los Angeles. Legal, financial, and geographic constraints in Britain and on the Continent prevented Europe's architects and engineers from reproducing Manhattan's skyline. In addition, the traditional European preference for medium-sized buildings that did not convert the streets into murky canyons, making people feel as if they were ants, survived the war. Hence, most of the tallest edifices constructed in the 1950s were neither urban nor commercial. Instead, they were concrete housing projects erected on the outskirts of the cities, notably in Eastern Europe where they reflected the esthetics of Stalinism, rather than some inflexible American commitment to the modernist glass box. In the cities themselves, "old towns" were faithfully restored, and many postwar buildings were designed to harmonize with prewar structures.[27]

Europeans also "used" their cities differently than did Americans.

Although a growing number of families moved to the suburbs from the 1950s on, the majority of Europeans still lived in, rather than commuted to, the city centers. Whereas middle-class Americans distrusted cities and longed to flee to exclusively residential sanctuaries that were rigidly zoned to prohibit the outside world from encroaching on all the well-tended lawns, most Europeans remained attached to urban neighborhoods, with their blend of communal and commercial activities. Because European cities were not normally gang infested, urban street life offered people a variety of amusements, rather than a good chance of being mugged, as in the United States. Given the dangers of being downtown at night, Americans tended to retreat to the shelter of their relatively spacious homes, where they could socialize in safety with friends. Europeans—regarding their small flats as havens to be reserved for private family gatherings—frequently spent their leisure time in public places like cafés and pubs, or strolling on the boulevards after the stores had closed. Even when suburban malls began to spring up in the European countryside, these complexes did not obliterate the urban arcades and pedestrian shopping streets in the way that American malls destroyed downtown businesses, leaving only banks, insurance buildings, and trendy restaurants.[28]

If most Europeans did not live like people in the United States, neither did they agree with Americans about the responsibility of the state to guarantee its citizens a sense of economic and social security. The suspicion of the federal government is deeply rooted in American history. The U.S. Constitution was designed to restrain the exercise of power through an elaborate apparatus of checks and balances. And America was populated by immigrants who preferred to flee their homelands, rather than wait an eternity for government-sponsored social reforms. Thus, Americans have rarely looked upon the state as a savior. The notion that success or failure was up to the individual encouraged the middle class in the United States to believe that taxes were an unbearable burden and should be reduced, that private entrepreneurs could solve social problems and promote economic growth more effectively than politicians or bureaucrats, and that public spending benefited only the poor. These convictions ignored the vast array of services the government actually provided to the middle class—from farm price supports and insured bank deposits to funds for highways and airports and the regulation of the stock exchange. Nevertheless, Americans have been less tolerant of governmental activism and more willing to entrust their fate to the free market than were the majority of Europeans.

In a Europe haunted by two world wars and the messianic rhetoric of Hitler and Stalin, there was a greater demand for the political, social, and economic tranquillity that the welfare state supplied. "Europeans want to be sure that there is no adventure in the future," remarked the governor of Belgium's National Bank in 1996. "They have had too much of that. They want stability and orthodoxy," not risk and uncertainty. Accordingly, they were readier to pay higher income and sales taxes than Americans would ever put up with. But in return for their money, Western Europeans got free education and medical care, subsidized nursing homes and childcare facilities, generous pensions and unemployment compensation, a superb mass transit and national railroad system, and cleaner streets with lower crime rates than in the United States.[29]

The benefits of living in a country where the government was expected to furnish all essential social services were obvious in France. In 1995, French mothers—whether married or single, rich or poor—received the equivalent of $150 a month from the government for each of their children under age eighteen. Apartment owners could not evict tenants who were behind on their rent during the winter months. Office workers had the right to a desk by a window where they could see the sunrise or sunset. Employers in Paris were required to pay for half the commuting costs of their employees. Everyone was entitled to a vacation, usually lasting five weeks. In the case of poorer families, the government subsidized the holiday, including the costs of transportation to the mountains or the Mediterranean.[30]

These policies, in France and elsewhere in Western Europe, resulted in an egalitarianism unknown in the United States. Ordinary people had access to many of the pleasures and advantages enjoyed by those in the upper class. Workers could spend a night at the theater or August at a resort. And they could go through life free of worries about monstrous hospital bills, children barred from elite schools because of their family's modest bank account, aging parents unable to afford a housekeeper or a nurse, or the loss of one's house after the loss of a job.[31]

Yet equality came at a high price, one that inevitably strained the resources of governments across Western Europe. By the 1990s, prime ministers found themselves in combat with their electorates over the need to cut spending and balance budgets by diminishing the costs (and the indulgences) of the welfare state. In 1995, French workers and students demonstrated against the government's efforts to economize, nearly shutting down Paris and other cities with strikes and mass marches reminiscent of 1968. An identical battle raged in the United States, though with less opposition from a middle class that was far more conservative, ideologically, than the Western European bourgeoisie.

American ideas and techniques, even when imitated, were often transformed in the European context. This was certainly true of factory work. During the late 1940s and 1950s, management experts from the United States, under the auspices of the Marshall Plan, tried to persuade European executives to raise productivity by organizing their plants along American lines. Many industrialists in Western Europe adopted America's mass production methods, just as Jean-Jacques Servan-Schreiber said they should. But with the return of prosperity, they also began to pay more attention to what workers did and how they felt on the job.

In the 1970s and 1980s, some manufacturers—especially in the automobile industry—came to believe that Europe's productivity would exceed America's if workers were given more responsibility, letting them decide how best to use their skills. In Sweden, Volvo abolished the assembly line, a heretical act in the eyes of the dinosaurs who still ran General Motors and Ford. Volvo's president explained that his company thought it both "humiliating" and inefficient to have workers chasing after "a product that moves constantly and continuously on a conveyor belt." Volvo redesigned its plants so that people could "work in groups, instead of as isolated individuals," performing "many different functions" on a car that remained "stationary." This new way of organizing the workplace might minimize the monotony and encourage "a higher involvement" on the part of the labor force. Other European automobile firms followed Volvo's path. Moreover, the finished products—whether a Volvo, a Fiat, a Peugeot, or a BMW—tended to be smaller than the typical American car, in accordance with the needs of European drivers faced with the higher price of petrol in Europe and the narrowness of European streets.[32] The changes at Volvo were a classic example of the way Western European corporations modified, rather than simply embraced, American industrial practices.

In view of the differences between the United States and Europe, American companies had to make adjustments in the items they sold and in how these were advertised on the other side of the Atlantic. The American corporation, after all, was still in the business of satisfying its customers, whether they lived in Chicago or Copenhagen. Accommodating their products and messages to the European market, however,

was sometimes harder than executives in the United States anticipated.

Europeans, for instance, seemed ambivalent about American food.
They were occasionally impressed with its nutritional value, particularly after World War II when America's victorious soldiers looked
heftier and healthier than Europe's civilians. Later on, it was the convenience of American food—canned, frozen, or ready to be mi-
crowaved—that appealed to European shoppers. With the rise in the
number of families headed by a single parent or ones in which both
spouses worked, lavish gourmet meals gave way to dishes that were
easy to prepare. Even in France, the home of haute cuisine, American-style food—Aunt Jemima pancake mix, Skippy peanut butter,
Kraft macaroni and cheese, potato chips and instant mashed potatoes,
quick-cooking rice, packaged croutons, dried pasta, frozen pizza,
chili con carne, Hershey's chocolate syrup—became increasingly popular.[33]

Many of these products could be found not just in specialty stores
but in supermarkets, where many Europeans preferred to shop because the prices were generally lower and they could load their gro-
ceries into a cart rather than lugging around bags full of everything
from celery to Coke bottles. European supermarkets, though, like
European refrigerators, were tiny compared to those in the United
States. And they were rarely surrounded by parking lots. An Irma in
Copenhagen or an Albert Hein in Amsterdam—unlike a gigantic suburban Safeway—was essentially a neighborhood store, to which nearby
residents walked. When it was open. The stores normally closed after
7 P.M. on weeknights, in the afternoons on Saturdays, and all day
Sunday—hours that would have stunned an American shopper accustomed to supermarkets that never shut their doors, except maybe
on Christmas morning.

No matter what the attractions of American food on the shelves
of European supermarkets, national eating habits did not entirely
change. Nor were traditional shopping patterns abandoned. People
still patronized their local bakeries and butcher shops, as well as the
outdoor markets brimming with fresh produce and unfrozen chick-
ens. On any day in Amsterdam, the food and clothing stalls stretching
for blocks on Albert Cuypstraat were jammed with customers. The
scene was the same at the open-air markets in Paris and in other European cities.

In addition, some American foods either failed to please the European palate or clashed with regional predilections. Europeans every-

where scorned American coffee and beer. In Britain and Ireland, breakfast cereals like Kellogg's corn flakes were enormously popular. But in France, Spain, Italy, and Greece, breakfast continued to mean a cup of hot espresso or café au lait (not slivers of dried wheat or rice floating in cold milk) and perhaps a croissant, often consumed standing up at a bar rather than seated at the kitchen table. A box of cereal was also more expensive in Western and Eastern Europe because the costs of the ingredients, labor, and television advertising were higher than in the United States. In Latvia, even after the demise of Communism, the price of corn flakes was so exorbitant that people bought them not to eat but to present as gifts.[34]

At times, American companies could flood the European market with an item that was genuinely novel, as in the case of Coca-Cola. But they most often succeeded in Europe when their products conformed to existing tastes. Europeans accepted Heinz ketchup, for example, because they frequently made their own tomato sauce and so were familiar with its texture and uses. Buying bottled ketchup, then, was just simpler than whipping up a sauce from scratch. U.S. firms also profited when they filled a need unmet by local industries. Thus, Polaroid's instant cameras did extremely well in post-Communist Russia because there were as yet few places where one could go to get film developed.[35]

When products in their original American version did not jibe with European expectations, companies had no qualms about altering the ingredients. Kellogg substituted golden unsugared raisins in the Raisin Bran it sold in Europe for the brown frosted raisins favored by American cereal eaters, and the Froot Loops it shipped across the Atlantic contained no green "loops" because Europeans thought these looked artificial. Similarly, Kraft added lemons, eggs, or mustard to its mayonnaise, depending on the preferences of consumers in a particular European country.[36]

This readiness to give the Europeans what they wanted was evident in the way the American computer industry sought to adapt to European conditions during the 1990s. The potential market for personal computers, printers, software, modems, and on-line services was greater in Europe than in the United States because many Europeans had not yet purchased any of the new technology. While computers could be found in 37 percent of U.S. households by 1995, the figures per household in Europe were much lower: 19 percent in Germany and Britain, 15 percent in France, and 14 percent in Italy.

The statistics reflected again the underlying dissimilarities between

Europe and the United States. Fewer European children were exposed to computers in their classrooms, and fewer adults used computers at work or at home. An estimated 12 million Americans operated businesses out of their homes by the mid-1990s, and many others brought work home in the evenings or on weekends. These Americans needed computers in their residences. Europeans, in contrast, were more tenacious about preserving the barriers between their jobs and their family lives. Besides, European flats were usually too cramped to allow room for a full-fledged home office, complete with a fax machine and other peripheral equipment.

Furthermore, computers cost more in Europe than in the United States, a result of the value-added tax (which increased the total price by as much as 20 percent) and the relative absence of high-volume discount outlets, which meant that Europeans had to purchase their computers at smaller, more expensive retail stores. Access to the Internet was also costlier in Europe because government telephone monopolies charged users more to log on, especially if they lived far from large cities and had to pay high rates for long-distance calls. Consequently, those Europeans who did own computers were more often wealthy than middle class, as in America.[37]

American companies, such as CompuServe and America Online, that offered links to the Internet and wished to penetrate the British and continental markets faced some additional obstacles: competition from European firms like Deutsche Telekom, and the suspicion (particularly in France) that the Internet was yet another instrument of America's cultural imperialism. These problems could be partially overcome by joining with local partners, just as the American television networks had done. Hence, America Online entered into an arrangement in 1995 with Bertelsmann A.G. to begin operating in Germany.

But transatlantic partnerships were less important than the ability of U.S. companies to provide whichever Internet services their European customers craved. "Our strategy," declared an America Online executive, "is to make local services for each country that reflect that country rather than exporting the U.S. service there." Americans might depend on the Internet primarily for E-mail, but many Germans utilized it more for electronic banking; in France, for information directories; and in Britain, for international news. Far from functioning in Europe as cultural imperialists, American computer and telecommunications companies would prosper only if they showed (in the words of one industry analyst) "a real sensitivity to the needs of European users."[38]

Here, advertising could help—not only with computers but with other items too. Yet a sensitivity to local concerns was not always the hallmark of American advertising in Europe or anywhere else.

Often, U.S. advertisers assumed that everyone in the global village wanted the same products as did American consumers, and that they could be reached with the same slogans and imagery. "We've found," said a publicist for Procter & Gamble in 1992, that "the desire for a more attractive complexion or a drier baby" did not "vary much from geography to geography." More to the point, it cost American companies less to invest in a single commercial for international distribution—using upbeat English-language jingles and quick cuts reminiscent of MTV's music videos—than to develop diversified advertising strategies that took into account the different tastes and aspirations of consumers in each country.[39]

Advertising agencies from the 1920s on also believed, not without justification, that the most effective way to sell American products abroad was to sell "America" itself. Marketing campaigns set out to persuade the foreign purchaser that he or she was buying not just an American-made car or a carton of cigarettes but a piece of America's opulence, its streamlined efficiency, its power, its modernity. Goodyear, for instance, advertised its tires in Germany with references to the Indianapolis 500-mile automobile race. Alternatively, companies identified their products with the rugged traditions of the pioneer West. The Marlboro Man or a cowboy in Levi's jeans conjured up romantic images of personal freedom, open space, John Wayne riding off into the sunset. In Britain, Jeeps appeared in advertisements parked in front of a log cabin. Lands' End and Budweiser promoted their products with scenes of male models in rustic Wisconsin, or fishing in a Montana lake, or resting at a truck stop in Nevada. European advertisers recognized the benefits of Western symbolism as well, picturing French or German cars perched on the edge of the Grand Canyon or speeding along a Los Angeles freeway.[40] This effort to associate American and European merchandise with American values was precisely why many parents in Europe worried that their Pepsi-drinking, Marlboro-smoking, Nike-clad children were becoming "Americanized."

But messages originally designed for a continent-wide American market unified by a common culture were not necessarily suitable in a region like Europe that was fragmented by language, history, and intense national prejudices. Europeans might have hungered for American clothes and cosmetics, but they could not all be counted on to respond in the same way to American-style appeals. Different countries required different approaches. Especially in Eastern Europe. After the end of the Cold War, advertisers discovered that Poles, Czechs, and East Germans were swayed less by commercials displaying affluent Americans than by those that provided factual information about a particular product.[41]

So U.S. companies began to tailor their messages to specific audiences. Nike and Reebok captured 50 percent of the European market by 1993, partly by advertising their sneakers as appropriate for everyday wear, not just for sports—a selling point effective in countries like France, where sedentary adults were likelier to look simply for comfortable shoes than to fantasize about becoming the next Michael Jordan.[42]

American newspapers, magazines, and television networks made similar concessions to their European clientele. As with advertisements, not all news stories and TV programs aimed at the American audience traveled or translated well overseas. The inside jokes on a situation comedy or the manic behavior of contestants on a quiz show could baffle viewers in Britain and Germany.[43] Reports on train wrecks in Georgia or the fate of the Boston Red Sox did not fascinate readers in Italy. The question for American publishers and media executives was how far should they go in modifying their products for European consumption.

For *Time, Newsweek,* and the *Wall Street Journal,* the answer in the 1970s and 1980s was to create special European editions meant for readers who were interested primarily in European news, business, culture, and sports. Previously, each publication presumed that its domestic coverage and its ability to communicate the "American" point of view about world affairs, combined with foreign advertisements, would appeal to an elite international audience. When readers in London, Brussels, Paris, or Zürich found this approach too parochial, the publishers decided to put out a version that retained the American format and some American material, but that employed a largely European staff who contributed editorials and commentaries on European events, and who presented a "European" perspective even on news stories dealing with the United States. The results in all three cases were publications that appealed to a multinational audience and that differed substantially in tone and emphasis from their domestic prototypes.[44]

CNN underwent a comparable transformation. To attract a worldwide audience, Ted Turner launched CNN International in 1985.

But by the 1990s, Turner's new venture faced competition from the BBC's World Service Television, a twenty-four-hour news station with equally global aspirations, and from regional networks like Rupert Murdoch's Sky News, located in Britain, which could reach most of the European continent by satellite. Worse, foreigners attacked CNN International for being essentially an insular, Atlanta-based, English-language news service that merely recycled U.S. stories for Americans living or traveling abroad. To counter these criticisms, CNN's programs in Europe and in other parts of the world began to feature local news, sports, and weather forecasts delivered by non-American anchors and reporters. Its most popular talk show, *Larry King Live*, made a point of taking telephone calls from viewers outside the United States.[45]

Other U.S. television networks with cable or satellite outlets in Europe imitated CNN in catering to the interests of their European viewers. On its Super Channel, NBC broadcast a mixture of American and European programs in English, German, and Dutch. Viewers could watch the *Today* and *Tonight* shows and the *NBC Nightly News,* as well as programs that focused on European business, politics, and entertainment.[46]

MTV, which made its debut in America in 1981, went further than NBC or CNN when it expanded its operations to Europe in 1987. Rather than showcasing American pop stars almost exclusively, MTV Europe devoted most of its programming to the videos of European singers and rock bands. Even rap videos, which originally reflected the pressures of life in the African American urban ghetto, became in MTV's transatlantic incarnation the music of Europe's immigrant communities, especially those from the Caribbean and Africa. MTV also added shows on European fashion and public affairs. In effect, MTV reinvented itself for its young European viewers, concentrating on their tastes and preoccupations instead of simply exporting the formulas that had worked in the United States.[47]

America's television networks did not ignore Europe's children. Given the large amounts of money to be made in this particular overseas market, the Disney Channel, the Cartoon Network (owned, like CNN, by Turner Broadcasting), and Nickelodeon (a unit, like MTV, of Viacom), along with the Fox Children's Network (an American subsidiary of Rupert Murdoch's News Corporation) vied with one another in the 1990s to capture as many preadolescent European viewers as possible. But the heads of all the networks agreed that the way to increase their ratings and revenues in Europe was to balance American and local programming. Joint ventures, coproductions, the dubbing of Bugs Bunny or the Flintstones into French, Spanish, Swedish, Finnish, and Dutch—all were important. The key, however, as a Nickelodeon executive put it, was "to make British [and other] kids feel like it was *their* Nickelodeon" by offering programs based on the fairy tales and favorite cartoon figures of children in each country.[48]

Clearly, the purpose of these strategies—whether pursued by food and computer manufacturers, advertising agencies, newspapers and mass circulation magazines, or television networks—was to boost a company's profits, not to broaden the cultural horizons of its executive officers and stockholders. Still, corporate America did acknowledge, however reluctantly, that the world was not homogeneous and that the inclinations, however peculiar, of Europeans and other foreigners had to be respected. Hence, American companies and the American media were willing to tinker with their products and fine-tune their messages, to go native if necessary, in order to thrive in cultures that might never be fully Americanized.

Big Macs on the Spanish Steps

Apart from Coca-Cola, no product seemed more quintessentially American than fast food. Nor was any American export more popular or more controversial, especially in Europe. Fast food came to represent for many Europeans one of the more menacing forms of Americanization. It exemplified as well the frenzied pace of modern life, along with the erosion of family rituals and the emergence of a youth culture that cared little about fine dining or anything else connected with civilized (meaning parental) norms of good taste and behavior.

In response, the Americans who supervised the fast-food business in Europe tried—like other U.S. entrepreneurs overseas—to placate their critics by conforming, architecturally and gastronomically, to the local scene. In the process, they spawned European imitators who created equally eclectic cuisines for what were increasingly heterogeneous societies.

From the 1960s on, the restaurant chains most identified with the United States—starting with McDonald's, Burger King, Pizza Hut, and Kentucky Fried Chicken, followed later by more upscale emporiums like Chili's, Planet Hollywood, and TGI Friday's—became ubiquitous in Western Europe. By 1995, there were fifty American-type restaurants, from Chicago Pizza Pie Factory to Cactus Charlie's Tex-Mex, operating in Paris alone.[49]

After the end of the Cold War, fast-food restaurants also swept through Eastern Europe. The cleanliness and speedy service of a Burger King or a Pizza Hut appealed to Polish and Hungarian diners, who now had more disposable income but less time under capitalism for the heavy sleep-inducing lunches that, in the old days, could close down a socialist factory or office for hours. The most successful fast-food restaurant behind the former Iron Curtain, however, was the McDonald's in the heart of Moscow, in Pushkin Square. Featuring the "Beeg Mek," Moscow's McDonald's drew 80 million customers between 1990 when it opened and 1995, attracting more people than the Kremlin or Lenin's Tomb, and making it the busiest McDonald's in the world.[50]

The proliferation of fast-food restaurants overseas was no accident, as the Communists once would have said. Having saturated the fiercely competitive American market, the chains—emulating the movie studios and book publishers—began to look abroad for additional revenues. By the 1990s, McDonald's was receiving more than 50 percent of its profits from overseas.[51] It was no wonder, then, that when McDonald's announced plans in 1996 to open over three thousand new restaurants, almost all of them were to be located outside the United States.

To those in Europe who cringed at the prospect of yet more golden arches desecrating their ancient cities, McDonald's epitomized America's tawdry values and its disrespect for history. When the first McDonald's appeared in Rome in 1986, just off the Piazza di Spagna, local journalists and environmentalists were indignant at the sight of Italian adolescents and ignorant tourists munching cheeseburgers on the Spanish Steps. In Cracow, McDonald's intention in 1994 to open a restaurant in the old market square aroused opposition from historians, ecologists, and architects. McDonald's symbolized, for one professor of architecture, the vulgarity of mass culture intruding upon the pristine landscape and artistic traditions of central Europe. "You don't put a jukebox in a salon," he snorted.[52]

Among French food critics and restaurateurs, the reaction to McDonald's was marked both by disdain for its standardized fare and a fear that young people would never learn the art of authentic French cooking. Or the pleasures of drinking French wine. According to a poll taken in 1995, only 5 percent of twenty-five year olds reported that they regularly drank wine with their meals, compared with 25 percent who said they did in 1980. To combat the American fast-food invasion, French elementary schools in the 1990s added to their regular curricula courses designed to teach students how to be more discriminating about what they ate. After receiving the proper instruction, it was hoped, the students would henceforth prefer escargots and a good Bordeaux to a quarter-pounder with fries and a Coke. These efforts seemed unavailing; the four hundred-seat McDonald's on the Champs-Elysées was almost as packed as the McDonald's in Moscow.[53]

One of the most common complaints about McDonald's and other fast-food restaurants was that—like the media—they undermined social and family relationships. Fast food got its name for a reason. It was cheap, mass-produced, and meant for customers in a hurry. No one went to a fast-food restaurant for its communal ambience. People ate quickly, often at small tables in an antiseptic setting that inhibited the lengthy conversations and general conviviality to be found, presumably, in neighborhood bistros or at home surrounded by family and friends. In this sense, McDonald's embodied modernity in all its unpleasantness.

Yet fast-food restaurants were profitable in Europe, as they had been in America, precisely because they filled a niche in the modern world. As the workday in Europe grew more demanding in the 1980s and 1990s, many people no longer had enough time to go home or to fancy restaurants for elaborate and leisurely lunches. The stores, the banks, and the stock markets stayed open; there were goods to be sold and deals to be made. Even in Mediterranean countries, the siesta was becoming increasingly obsolete.[54] Lunch now meant a snack, or takeout, or a slice of pizza rapidly devoured before dashing back to the office.

Fast food, however, did not contribute to the destruction of European family life. Nor were McDonald's, Burger King, Pizza Hut, and Kentucky Fried Chicken popular only with the young. On the contrary, these establishments advertised themselves in France and elsewhere as family restaurants. Unlike the temples of haute cuisine, with their pretentious waiters, slow service, and outrageous prices, McDonald's was inexpensive, informal, noisy, and therefore a perfect place for parents to take their unruly children.[55] In any case, a meal at a fast-food restaurant hardly precluded large family dinners at home. People could and did enjoy both at different times.

Fast-food restaurants also had to contend with the allegation that they were instruments of America's culinary, if not its cultural, imperialism. In a European McDonald's, its detractors noted, customers encountered the same menu, the same shiny decor, and the same smil-ing uniformed employees as in the United States. McDonald's, appar-ently, was exporting not only American-style food but America's fake geniality and obsession with efficiency.

To defuse these arguments, McDonald's sought to minimize its ties to the United States, at least in Europe. "We do not want people to see us as American imperialists," declared the marketing manager for McDonald's in Belgium in 1994. "Our objective is to be a local com-pany," insisted the chief executive of McDonald's International, notwithstanding the name of the division over which he presided.[56]

Accordingly, McDonald's in Germany publicized the fact that it hired only German managers and German employees, and depended exclusively on German suppliers for its German-produced ingredi-ents. McDonald's also departed from its American practice of in-stalling its newest outlets on highways or in suburbs and shopping malls, choosing instead to locate in the centers of Europe's largest cities. But the chain did not want to inflame local politicians by call-ing undue attention to its presence. In the face of the opposition in Cracow, McDonald's promised that its golden arches would be dis-crete, almost invisible, and that its building would blend in with the fourteenth- and fifteenth-century facades in the market square.[57]

Above all, McDonald's, like Kellogg, was willing to tamper with its previously sacrosanct recipes in order to meet the expectations of its European clientele. In France, McDonald's put less sugar and more mustard in its salad dressings, and added beer and Evian mineral water to the menu. In Italy, a customer could order insalata caprese, rather than french fries. In a Norwegian McDonald's, it was possible to spurn a Big Mac and to dine instead on a salmon burger.[58] These modifications did not obscure McDonald's American origins, but they allowed the chain's European managers more flexibility in responding to local tastes.

Impressed with the success of America's fast-food restaurants in Britain and on the Continent, a number of European entrepreneurs set out to mimic the methods of McDonald's and Pizza Hut. Sometimes the European chains simply posed as American creations. In Norway, advertisements for "American" Chicken & Burger featured skyscrap-ers and the American flag, even though the restaurants were owned and operated by native Norwegians. At other times, European restau-rateurs offered their customers local versions of American fast food. Beginning in the 1980s, two French hamburger chains with Ameri-can-sounding names, Quick and Freetime, became McDonald's strongest competitors throughout France. Freetime's specialty was a "longburger," a rectangular hamburger enclosed in a minibaguette. Meanwhile, another chain—the Croissanterie—served its sandwiches in croissants.[59]

The post-Communist Russians were also eager to apply American techniques to traditional dishes. In 1995, the Russkoye Bistro—the first in a series of Russian-style fast-food restaurants—opened opposite McDonald's in Moscow. Here, one could order (and receive promptly) borscht, blini, pirogi, or mushroom soup, accompanied—of course—by vodka. "They sell hamburgers," conceded the Bistro's manager, referring to his American rival, "but [our] food is in the Russian blood."[60]

In truth, the notion of a distinctive "national" cuisine was itself outdated by the 1990s. With the ability of people to travel more than ever before, and with waves of immigrants moving from one region of the world to another, eating habits everywhere were becoming less provincial.[61] Certainly, this was true in America. In Europe too, there were "Mexican" cantinas in Copenhagen, "Italian" trattorias in Amsterdam, "Greek" tavernas and "Spanish" tapas bars in Berlin, "Parisian" bistros in London, and "English" tearooms (not to mention a multitude of "Chinese," "Japanese," "Vietnamese," and "North African" restaurants) in Paris.

The dishes in most of these ethnic establishments were hardly authentic. Rather, restaurant owners and chefs combined domestic and foreign ingredients in a mixture that was essentially new. Fast food was only another, peculiarly American, addition to the European smorgasbord. And in the end, fast food became less an American invention than a hybrid cuisine for a Europe that was now more diversified, culturally and demographically—even if those who considered themselves native-born Europeans were still suspicious of the strangers in their midst.

DISNEYLAND IN PARIS

The readiness of Kellogg and McDonald's, Nike and Reebok, *Time* and *Newsweek*, CNN and MTV, to adapt their products and their advertising to a culture different from the United States was pivotal to their success in the European market. Any American company that ignored this lesson could invite disaster, as the people running Walt Disney's enterprises found out. The initial problems of Euro Disneyland illustrated not only the difficulties of exporting a commodity inextricably associated with American culture to Europe, but also the sorts of changes Disney officials had to make to survive in an unfamiliar and occasionally hostile environment.

That Disneyland had such trouble establishing itself in Europe was ironic, since amusement parks were as much a European as an American invention. Indeed, they exemplified the cultural cross-breeding that had always marked the relationship between the two continents. Amusement parks, both in Europe and the United States, emerged in the nineteenth century often in conjunction with world's fairs and national expositions. The fairs promoted a vision of the future in which human beings (at least in the Western world) would enjoy a better life thanks to science, technology, industry, and commerce, while the parks provided the masses with new forms of public entertainment.[62]

The parks themselves could be either tranquil and genteel like Copenhagen's Tivoli Gardens, or raucous and vulgar like New York's Coney Island. In either case, they offered rides, games, plenty of food, garden paths or boardwalks where people could stroll, and a pleasurable respite from the daily pressures of moneymaking and hard work. What they did not possess was an overarching principle binding together all the sights and sounds.

When Walt Disney decided to build his first park in the 1950s, his model was Tivoli, not Coney Island. In Disney's judgment, the early twentieth-century American amusement parks were too disorderly and too disturbing to the morals of the middle class. Disney wanted to reproduce Tivoli's Danish sense of decorum and safety, its cleanliness and meticulously planned use of space. His park would be a place where families could feel comfortable, where they could flee temporarily from the chaos and violence of urban America, where they could have a carefully controlled adventure in a sanitized setting, rather like a Saturday outing at the mall.[63]

But unlike the disparate amusements at Tivoli or Coney Island, the thrills at Disney's park would have a unifying theme. They would be tied to a series of mostly American images as distilled by Disney himself from his cartoons, full-length movies, and television shows: Main Street, Frontierland, Fantasyland, Adventureland, Tomorrowland, and Sleeping Beauty's Castle, with the ever-present Mickey Mouse as chief greeter and master of ceremonies.

The original Disneyland opened in Anaheim, California, in 1955. It was followed in 1971 by Disney World, located near Orlando in Lake

Buena Vista, Florida, a complex that eventually included the Magic Kingdom, Epcot Center, the Disney-MGM Studios theme park, and a variety of resorts.

If Walt Disney imported some of his ideas from Europe, his successors believed they could reexport those ideas, now thoroughly transformed, to Europe and to other parts of the world. Their optimism was reinforced by the staggering success of Tokyo Disneyland, which opened for business in 1983 and consistently attracted more visitors than Disneyland in Anaheim.

There may, however, have been special reasons for Disneyland's popularity in Japan. Just as Heinz ketchup was accepted in Europe because its ingredients were familiar, so the structure of Disney's theme park coincided with certain qualities the Japanese admired. Its order and coherence, its immaculate grounds and peaceful atmosphere, even its obvious artificiality evidently reminded the natives of a Japanese garden, a precise and flawless but miniature rendition of nature that was more enchanting and less threatening than anything they encountered in the real world. Moreover, neither Main Street nor the Old West seemed fake because these did not exist in Japan— except as fantasies which, after all, was what Disney excelled at. The Japanese were able to domesticate Disneyland because they already felt at home in its embrace. "We took the foreignness out of it and digested it," observed a Japanese professor who wrote extensively on Tokyo Disneyland. People in Japan were "enjoying not the American Dream, but their own Japanese Dream."[64]

The ability of Disneyland to harmonize with Japanese culture might not be easily duplicated elsewhere. Nevertheless, Disney executives were convinced that they could repeat their Tokyo triumph in Western Europe. The only question to be decided was where to locate their European theme park. They considered Barcelona because of its warm weather, but Spain was too far away from the center of European and international tourism. So in 1987 Michael Eisner, the chairman of Disney, entered into an agreement with French Prime Minister Jacques Chirac to build a European Disneyland in Marne-la-Vallée, twenty miles east of Paris.

Chirac and his colleagues were eager to win the contest for Euro Disney because they thought it would create jobs for French workers and strengthen Paris's claim to be the leader of high technology and mass entertainment in Western Europe. Consequently, the French government, through its right of eminent domain, made 4,700 acres of prime real estate available at below-market prices to Disney for construction of the park as well as hotels, office buildings, shops, and campgrounds. The government also arranged for low-interest loans from state-owned banks, helped recruit private investors, and consented to extend the RER (the commuter rail lines connecting Paris to its suburbs) and the new high-speed train network to the site of the park.[65]

For his part, Michael Eisner seemed to assume at the outset that conditions in France were the same as those in Anaheim and Orlando. Therefore, the formulas that worked so well in America could be transferred without much modification to Europe. Given these beliefs, Disney's planners made few concessions to their Parisian locale or to French culture and history. They created a park that was identical in its layout and landmarks to Disneyland and Disney World. In addition, they erected six hotels with a total of 5,200 rooms. Apart from the Disneyland Hotel, a quasi-Victorian structure, the others—the Newport Bay Club, the Hotel New York, the Hotel Sequoia, the Santa Fe Hotel, and the Cheyenne Hotel—were each supposed to reflect an American (not a European or a French) architectural style and to represent some facet of America's geography and social life, past and present. But Disney's blueprints included more than a theme park. The French countryside surrounding the park was to be converted into a grander version of Disney World, even if this meant reproducing Orlando's suburban sprawl. Here, the visitor would find an entertainment complex with stores and restaurants, a golf course, an artificial lake, apartments and vacation homes, and soon a second theme park.[66]

The notion that the joys of Disneyland in California and Disney World in Florida could be transplanted to France led to a series of spectacular miscalculations. Some of these were the result of not knowing much about France itself. Disney officials believed, for example, that the support they received from the French government would encourage the French intelligentsia to be similarly enthusiastic. Yet the hostility of French intellectuals and journalists to Euro Disneyland was implacable, if also predictable.

When the park opened in April 1992, writers competed with one another to see whose denunciations were the most hyperbolic. A "cultural Chernobyl" exclaimed the theater director Ariane Mnouchkine. "A terrifying giant's step toward world homogenization," the philosopher Alain Finkielkraut declared. To another commentator, Euro Disney was "a horror made of cardboard, plastic and appalling colors, a construction of hardened chewing gum and idiotic folklore taken straight out of comic books written for obese Americans." According to the French intellectuals, Disney commercialized the fairy tales of children everywhere, thereby stifling their dreams and preparing them to become mere spectators and consumers. Disney's latest theme park was "the very symbol of the process by which people's cultural standards are lowered and money becomes all-conquering," argued Jean-Marie Rouart, a novelist and literary critic for *Le Figaro,* adding that she "would be ashamed to go there." Worst of all, Disneyland was no longer over *there,* across the ocean, in America, the home of mass culture. Now it was right *here,* in the heart of French civilization, practically within the boundaries of Paris itself. Like McDonald's, Euro Disney was for Jack Lang, the French minister of culture, "an enclave of the American leisure industry in France." And like McDonald's as well, the park's connection with art and philosophy, noted a socialist politician, was equivalent to the relation between fast food and gastronomy.[67]

Yet perhaps Euro Disney was not quite as alien to French or to European culture as the intellectuals liked to insist. Among their favorite observations about Disneyland in Anaheim, a recurring idea in the works of Jean Baudrillard and Umberto Eco, was that it offered tourists a simulation of reality, a fraudulent sense of living in another time in a foreign land. This might be fine for America's rubes, but why would Europeans chose an imitation of the Matterhorn or a German castle when they could go see the original just down the road? Such a question ignored the fact that many Europeans, no matter how cosmopolitan, were as enamored with replicas as the Americans who flocked to Disneyland. Eco himself pointed out that wax museums, enormously popular in Europe, served the same purpose as an American theme park.[68] Furthermore, European families had been traveling to Disneyland and Disney World for several decades, while Mickey Mouse was a treasured icon in the comic books of French children since the 1930s. Thus, Euro Disney was not so much another instance of "Americanization" as a more sophisticated set of amusements perfected in the United States but nonetheless rooted in the European experience.

Still, battered by the criticisms, Eisner and the other executives in charge of Euro Disney tried to respond—albeit speciously—to the sensitivities of their European clientele. Disney publicists asserted that their movies and theme parks had always depended on European novels and folktales. Cinderella, they emphasized, was fundamentally French; Pinocchio was Italian; Snow White was German; Peter Pan was British. On the theory that Europeans—unlike Americans—were less interested in the future than in the heroes of the past, the park's managers quickly changed the name of Tomorrowland to Discoveryland, replacing the Star Wars imagery with tributes to Leonardo da Vinci, H. G. Wells, and Jules Verne. Then there was the founding father, Walt Disney, or "D'Isgny" as one company official imagined, who it appeared was an authentic descendant of France.[69]

Cosmetic alterations, however, could not solve the deeper problems the park confronted in Europe. Here again, Euro Disney's difficulties sprang from the mistaken—and arrogant—belief that European tourists would behave like their American counterparts. For a variety of reasons, most Europeans did not follow Disney's script.

To begin with, the sunny climate in southern California and Florida induced people to come to Disneyland and Disney World at all times of the year. But the weather in France could be freezing in winter, a season when northern Europeans normally migrated to the Mediterranean for their holidays (if they went anywhere at all). What they were not willing to do, at least not in huge numbers, was to spend January or February slogging through the snow at an outdoor theme park, which was why Tivoli always closed for the winter.

Secondly, where American families might fly to Anaheim or Orlando for a hectic four-day splurge, many Europeans preferred, particularly in the summertime, a month-long holiday during which they could relax at a relatively inexpensive inn. If they did stop off at Euro Disney, European customers acted in ways that the park's American sponsors had not anticipated. "Everyone arrives at 9:30, leaves at 5:30, and they want lunch at 12:30," Michael Eisner remarked with astonishment. This European inflexibility, this refusal to be whimsical about schedules or to snack during the day as Americans did, led to long lines of cranky people waiting for admission to the park's attractions and to its restaurants all at the same time. Nor was the mood of the patrons visibly improved when they discovered that Euro Disney, in keeping with its policies in the United States, prohibited the sale of wine and beer, a policy the park rescinded in 1993.[70]

A third problem for Euro Disney, one beyond its control, was the general state of the European economy. In the early 1990s, just as Euro Disney opened, Western Europe was enduring its worst recession in a decade. The recession, coupled with a devaluation of the British, French, and Italian currencies, made the prices at Euro Disney seem unreasonably high. Consequently, though 19 million people visited the park by the beginning of 1994, they spent less on food, rides, and souvenirs than Disney's executives had confidently projected.[71]

The discrepancy between the company's expectations and the conduct of Europe's tourists was evident at the park's hotels. The six hotels were built on the assumption that Europeans would fill up the rooms as Americans did at Disney World. But while there was little incentive for American tourists to stay in Orlando and commute to Disney World, Paris was a different matter. The city offered cheaper lodgings than Euro Disney, fast trains to the park during the day, and more intriguing diversions at night. Hence, the occupancy rates at Euro Disney's hotels hovered around 55 percent. Those who did stay at the hotels tended not to use the minibars or the golf course, and they walked to the park rather than paying to take the tram.[71]

The failure of Disney's executives to understand the culture in which they were operating was costly. During its first three years, Euro Disney lost $1.5 billion.[73] The business sections of newspapers in France and the United States were filled with rumors that the park was on the brink of bankruptcy and would soon close.

But the Disney corporation was resourceful. Its officers restructured the park's finances and persuaded French bankers to allow the company to temporarily suspend or delay interest payments on its loans. More important, Euro Disney started adjusting to its surroundings and to the pocketbooks of European consumers. It reduced the price of admission by 20 percent, on tickets to the various rides by 2 percent, on food at the restaurants by 18 to 20 percent, and on hotel rooms by 13 percent. A new popular roller-coaster ride called "space mountain" became yet another celebration of Jules Verne and his novel *From the Earth to the Moon*. The results were striking. Attendance at the park substantially increased in 1995. More people began to stay overnight at the hotels, raising the average occupancy rate to 68 percent. Finally, Euro Disney announced that in the fiscal year from September 1994 to September 1995, the park had made money for the first time since it opened in 1992—earning a profit of $23 million.[74]

Whether or not Euro Disney will remain profitable in the future, it served as a model for Europe's own theme parks, just as McDonald's inspired some European restaurateurs to emulate America's fast-food techniques. "Thanks to Disney," acknowledged the manager of a park in Belgium, "people expect better service, better-quality attractions, bigger sensations and bigger thrills."[75]

Yet if McDonald's and Disneyland were not thoroughly "Europeanized" once they crossed the Atlantic, neither did the European parks seem "Americanized." Instead, they retained their national characteristics even as they competed with Euro Disney for the same customers. The directors of Legoland, the theme park in Denmark launched in 1968 by the manufacturer of miniature plastic building blocks for children, opened a similar park outside London in 1996. But the British Legoland devoted itself to a display of Danish artisanship, rather than surrendering to Disney's mass production of trinkets and images. Parc Astérix, near Paris, in business since 1989, remained distinctively Gallic. The park was named after France's most popular comic-strip character, and it focused self-consciously on French history and fiction, as if to suggest that Disney's famous mouse was hardly a match for the Three Musketeers.[76]

Actually, the esthetics of the theme parks, American and European, were interchangeable. All of them blurred the lines between reality and myth, art and popular culture. They reflected an amalgamation of styles, from Tivoli to Disneyland to Legoland. In this sense, Europe influenced America as much as America influenced Europe. And not only in the realm of theme parks, but in other arenas of social and cultural life as well.

THE EUROPEAN IMPACT ON AMERICA IN THE LATE TWENTIETH CENTURY

The concept of Americanization presupposed that America had a unified culture which it systematically imposed upon the world. But from the mid-1960s on, as millions of Hispanic and Asian immigrants poured into the United States, and as African Americans attained greater prominence in the nation's political and cultural life, America appeared to be a much more heterogeneous society than it was in the 1940s and 1950s. This diversity was reflected in America's movies, television shows, music, food, dress, and language. In addition, certain sectors of American culture—universities, the Broadway stage, publishing houses, and magazines—were deeply affected by European intellectuals, artists, and entrepreneurs. It was increasingly difficult, therefore, to know what foreigners meant when they complained about being Americanized since America, having grown more cosmopolitan, no longer stood for a single set of ideals (if it ever did).

In the 1970s, following the Vietnam War and the Watergate scandal, many people in Europe doubted whether the United States had any ideals at all. During the reign of Gerald Ford and Jimmy Carter, America's power and prestige declined, particularly in the eyes of those who remembered the omnipotence of the United States in the early postwar years. "Nobody, either in Europe, or the United States," mused a Dutch historian, "would have believed in the late forties that the position of the United States in the world would crumble so rapidly." J. H. Plumb was struck in the mid-1970s by the "diminution of America to human size, after the extraordinary inflation of her image through World War II, the atomic bombs and the Marshall Plan." Americans now lacked "self-assurance," Sigmund Skard observed. The United States was "losing its magnetism" for Europeans, wrote Rob Kroes at the close of the decade. The era when America could serve as a "touchstone for other societies," a laboratory for the future, was passé in the judgment of Michel Crozier.[77]

If the United States had ceased to be a model for the rest of the world, Europeans were happy to claim that role. Even America was influenced by Europe's commercial and cultural vitality as it had not been since the end of World War II.

The shift in the economic relationship between the two continents was especially dramatic. From 1945 until the late 1960s, European intellectuals and policymakers worried that they could not overcome the "American challenge," that the United States would remain both more productive and more advanced technologically than the countries of Western Europe. Yet by the 1970s, the fear of America's economic domination and the resentment of its wealth subsided. The U.S. economy—hit hard by the oil crisis—stagnated, losing its aura of superiority. Meanwhile, Europeans were buying cars, television sets, refrigerators, washing machines, and packaged tours to distant lands, raising their standard of living to the level Americans alone had once enjoyed. Measured by income and consumer spending, Western Europe was now as affluent as the United States.[78]

At the same time, America found itself confronting the "challenge" of Europe and Japan in the competition for global supremacy in trade, technology, investment, and productivity. Japan threatened to surpass the United States in the field of electronics and automobiles; Germany, in chemicals and engineering; France, in aeronautics, space research, and the production of weapons and nuclear power. Phillips in Holland, Siemens in Germany, Sony in Japan—these names became as respected internationally as IBM or General Motors. And as intimidating, especially when European and Japanese corporations began investing heavily in the United States, penetrating the American market in the same way that U.S. multinationals had previously invaded markets overseas.[79]

American consumers, however, were the beneficiaries of Europe's and Japan's new economic strength. Disenchanted with the quality of domestically manufactured merchandise, Americans turned to European and Japanese products for excellence in workmanship and design. Italian leather goods, British raincoats and sweaters, Scandinavian furnishings and glassware, Japanese television sets, and German or Japanese cars could be seen in any middle-class home and garage.

The U.S. economy rebounded in the 1980s while Western Europe plunged into a recession with high rates of unemployment in the 1990s. Nevertheless, America was unlikely to seem as masterful economically or as imperious politically as it had during its postwar preeminence.

Just as America's power contributed to its cultural supremacy after World War II, so Europe's prosperity in the 1970s and 1980s helped reestablish its reputation as a center of intellectual activity. The revival of interest in European writers was discernible in the United States. Americans had not paid much attention to the culture of the Old World since the 1930s and 1940s—a period when European émigrés exerted an enormous impact on American science, psychology and anthropology, classical music, painting and architecture, and the film industry. But in the 1970s, American academics started looking again to France and Germany for the latest ideas, methods, and terminologies. The fascination with linguistics and structural anthropology, and the notion that literary criticism could be revolutionized through a "deconstruction" of "texts," had their origins not in the works of refugees who resettled permanently in the United States, but in Europe's own universities and scholarly publications.

The luminaries of the European intellectual renaissance included linguists and literary theorists like Jacques Derrida, Ferdinand de Saussure, Paul de Man, and Roman Jacobson; neo-Freudians like Jacques Lacan; anthropologists like Claude Lévi-Strauss; cultural critics like Michel Foucault, Roland Barthes, and Jean Baudrillard; and philosophers like Jürgen Habermas. The European intellectuals shared a belief that the rationalism of the Enlightenment and the rituals of parliamentary politics obscured the real forces shaping human behavior. Thus, they dedicated themselves to exposing the impersonal structures and unconscious assumptions underlying the emergence of modern capitalism and consumerism, and the ways—often hidden—that words and symbols reinforced the existing social order and the power of the ruling elites while simultaneously oppressing the underclass.[80]

In their insistence on the connections between culture and political power, one could hear the echoes of the generational uprisings in the 1960s, especially the slogans used by students in the battles of Paris and West Berlin. Not for nothing were Derrida and Foucault, Barthes and Baudrillard, called the "philosophers of '68." But given the Europeans' emphasis on theory, on decoding texts, on the subtle implications of language, and given as well their abstract and often inaccessible prose, it made sense that they might concentrate in the 1970s on transforming academia, rather than joining a political movement to change the larger society.

Their most fervent disciples, it turned out, were not in Europe but in the United States. Where American scholars had crossed the Atlantic after World War II to teach Europeans about the history and literature of the United States, now European intellectuals traveled to America to lecture professors and graduate students. As the works of the Europeans were translated, their fame and their entourage of admirers steadily increased. Soon, at prestigious American universities, the departments of English, Linguistics, Comparative Literature, and Anthropology were dominated by postmodernists, poststructuralists, deconstructionists, and the practitioners of "cultural studies." Academic journals were swamped with articles reflecting the preoccupations and techniques of the European masters. University presses published and promoted much of the new scholarship, but so too did many commercial houses.

Like consumers and audiences in Europe who adapted America's products and culture to their own needs, American professors seized on the ideas of the European theorists for reasons that had less to do with the philosophical and ideological debates in France or Germany than with the politics and career pressures of academic life in the United States. The Europeans armed their American colleagues, at least those on the Left, with a vocabulary that could be used on behalf of feminism and multiculturalism or to empower blue-collar workers, ethnic groups, African Americans, and homosexuals.[81] The works of what were, after all, a bunch of not-yet-dead white European males could even be deployed in an assault on the bastions of "Eurocentrism" itself. On a more practical level, the efforts in the 1980s and 1990s to revise the literary canon, to include in history textbooks and classrooms the tales of people previously ignored, to alter the composition of a department by hiring more scholars who were considered to be on the "cutting edge" of their disciplines, and to draw up politically correct speech codes for faculty and students, all promised to create more jobs for and enhance the stature of America's professors—on campus, if not in the outside world.

Yet at the very moment that many young American academics were converting themselves into European-style theoreticians and ideologues, the European intelligentsia was abandoning the political radicalism of the 1960s. This was especially the case with French intellectuals in the 1970s and 1980s. A series of events shattered their lingering attachment to Marxism, the Soviet Union, and revolutionary movements in the Third World. Their disillusion began with the publication in 1974 of Aleksandr Solzhenitsyn's *The Gulag Archipelago*. But there more shocks to come: the metamorphosis of Cambodia into a killing field under Pol Pot and the Khmer Rouge; the flight of the boat people from Vietnam; the Soviet invasion of Afghanistan; the suppression of Solidarity in Poland in 1981; the recognition, by the mid-1980s, that China and Cuba were totalitarian states, rather than exemplars of socialism and anti-imperialism; and, finally, the collapse of the Communist regimes in Eastern Europe in 1989.[82]

As a result, a new generation of writers in France—typified by Alain Finkielkraut, André Glucksmann, Philippe Sollers, and Julia Kristeva—turned against the "philosophers of '68." Although some had been on the Parisian barricades a few years earlier, they were now less skeptical than their postmodernist predecessors about the objectivity of language or the virtues of rationality. They were also more centrist politically, more enthusiastic about democratic institutions and individual freedom, and more tolerant of bourgeois society.[83] At times, they endorsed America's domestic and foreign policies, though they continued to denounce the export of American mass culture. And they were often appalled by the obsession with multiculturalism and political correctness in America's universities.

Academics in the United States were generally unaware that the majority of France's intellectuals had moved on. In the same way that European audiences remained enthralled by old reruns of *Dallas* and *Cheers* long after these shows had disappeared from America's television screens, American professors continued to embrace the theories and methodologies of their European mentors even after the Europeans themselves no longer paid homage to the utopian visions of 1968.

The majority of Americans, however, were less affected by Europe's high culture than by its popular art forms. Outside the universities, "European" culture meant mostly British television programs, rock bands, and musical comedies, not the arcane meditations of French or German philosophers. Indeed, the influence in America of Britain's mass culture during the closing years of the twentieth century was a significant exception to the global dominance of the American entertainment industry.

Since the major commercial networks almost never broadcast foreign-made television shows, PBS became the primary American outlet for programs produced by the BBC and other British TV companies. Much as the art houses of the 1950s had introduced American movie audiences to foreign films, PBS exposed television viewers to stylish British programs like *Masterpiece Theater* and the mystery miniseries *Prime Suspect.* In the case of both foreign movies and British television shows, the American cognoscenti regarded the overseas products as infinitely superior to the pap churned out by Hollywood. But PBS did not have enough money or viewers to satisfy the BBC's financial needs and its hunger to reach a wider American audience. By the 1990s, faced with rising production costs and searching for new revenues, the BBC began to sell its programs increasingly to the cable networks, especially the Arts and Entertainment and the Discovery channels, thereby becoming a more visible presence on American television.[84]

Starting in the 1960s, Britain's impact on the American record industry, radio disk jockeys, concert promoters, and musical theater was far greater than its success with the minority of viewers who were attracted to highbrow television programs. That British composers and performers should have been so influential in the United States was itself a reversal of America's traditional preeminence in popular music.

From the 1920s through the 1950s, the giants of modern pop music were overwhelmingly American. Their fame was due, in part, to America's control over the mechanisms of mass entertainment—movies, records, radio, jukeboxes—all of which had either been developed or perfected in the United States. But America's musicians were also enormously talented. In no other country did songwriters have as much of an effect on the theater and films as did George Gershwin, Cole Porter, Irving Berlin, or Richard Rodgers and Oscar Hammerstein. Nor were performers elsewhere as idolized or as imitated as Frank Sinatra, Elvis Presley, Miles Davis, and John Coltrane.

American music of all kinds—pop, country, rock and roll, folk, blues, and jazz—dominated record sales and radio programming in Europe until the mid-1960s. In the 1950s, 68 percent of the recorded music broadcast by the BBC came from the United States. The percentage of American recordings was even higher on the off-shore "pirate" radio stations that beamed their "top 40" shows to Britain and the Continent. Singers, bands, and composers in Britain and Western Europe copied the vocal styles (including, if necessary, a rural twang or an urban African American accent), the chord progressions, and the rhyming patterns of U.S. performers and songwriters. In their lyrics, the Europeans often referred to American fads and locales, rather than drawing on topics and idioms native to their own countries. As a result, the popularity of recordings and concerts by American performers accelerated the decline of indigenous cultural institutions like the British music hall.[85]

All this changed in the 1960s. Suddenly, the most imaginative musicians were British, not American. With the arrival of the Beatles and the Rolling Stones, British bands and singers stopped mimicking whatever they heard on American records. Now they created music that expressed their own experiences, but that resonated with young audiences on both sides of the ocean. As the successors to Gershwin and Porter, Sinatra and Coltrane, the British rock groups took over the task of translating popular music into works of art.

No group more skillfully synthesized the older American styles with a newer, more British and a more "European" sensibility than the Beatles. Theirs was a hybrid music that mingled African American gospel and blues, bluegrass ballads, 1950s rock and roll, the complex poetic lyrics of Bob Dylan, the vaudevillian traditions of the British music hall (resurrected in albums like *Sergeant Pepper's Lonely Hearts Club Band*), and the sophisticated wit of the continental cabaret.[86]

The Beatles managed to be avant-garde and commercial at the same time. After their spectacular tour of the United States in 1964, the directors of America's record companies realized that Britain was not merely a market in which to sell albums but a hotbed of musical innovation. Producers signed any British group they could find to a recording contract. American radio programs featured the latest British music. American singer-composers like Simon and Garfunkel tried to emulate the artistry of the Beatles. Soon, American and British groups sounded indistinguishable. By the 1970s, a transatlantic style had emerged, combining elements of British and American popular music, embodied best in the albums and concert performances of Elton John.[87]

An identical transformation occurred on Broadway. Once the exclusive preserve of American songwriters, the Broadway musical theater grew increasingly dependent in the 1980s and 1990s on imports from Britain. Andrew Lloyd Webber may not have been as experimental or as daring as Stephen Sondheim. But as the dependable author of long-running and immensely profitable blockbusters like *Cats, Evita,* and *Phantom of the Opera,* Webber was certainly the equal, at least commercially, of Rodgers and Hammerstein.

The cultural rejuvenation of Britain and Western Europe was reflected even more strongly in mass communications. The emergence of a new generation of media tycoons based in Britain, France, Germany, and Italy, as well as in Australia and Japan, was another sign that while Americans for the most part still determined the content of mass culture, they no longer controlled all by themselves the economics of the worldwide information and entertainment industries.

During the 1980s and 1990s, at the very moment when American companies were entering into partnerships with European television networks, foreigners began to buy a substantial number of American movie studios, record companies, book publishers, newspapers, and magazines. Among these overseas entrepreneurs, none was more aggressive in acquiring cultural properties in the United States than Rupert Murdoch. Having made his fortune initially as a newspaper owner in his native Australia, Murdoch moved his operations to Britain where as chairman, chief executive officer, and principal shareholder of the News Corporation, he became a multimedia mogul on a global scale. While earlier press titans like William Randolph Hearst, Henry Luce, and Lord Beaverbrook had specialized in newspapers or magazines in the United States or Britain, Murdoch by the 1990s built a media empire with outposts on six continents that embraced print journalism, books, television, movies, videos, and the Internet. As of 1994, in the United States alone, Murdoch owned or had a majority interest in the 20th Century Fox film studio, the Fox Television Network, Harper-Collins Publishers (one of whose divisions was Basic Books, the publisher of this book), *TV Guide, Mirabella,* the *New York Post,* and the *San Antonio Express-News.*[88]

Hollywood was especially attractive to other foreign investors because its studios continued to produce the most popular and profitable movies and television programs in the world. So, following Murdoch's purchase of 20th Century Fox in 1985, Sony bought Columbia Pictures in 1989. Matsushita, the parent of Panasonic, bought the Music Corporation of America and its subsidiary, Universal Pictures, in 1990 (later selling both after losing millions of dollars in the movie business). Both the venerable MGM studio and United Artists found themselves under the temporary stewardship of a French bank, *Crédit Lyonnais,* in the mid-1990s. In addition, a growing percentage of American movies were being financed abroad. Films like Oliver Stone's *J.F.K., Terminator 2,* and *Leaving Las Vegas* were all made with French money.[89]

Foreigners also gobbled up American record companies. Sony bought CBS Records in 1988. As part of its purchase of MCA, Matsushita—which knew far more about the Japanese electronics industry than about American pop music—became the proud, if not permanent, owner of MCA Records, Geffen Records, and Motown. The British record company EMI bought Capitol, while Bertelsmann—one of the largest German publishing houses and media companies—bought RCA and Arista.[90]

Rupert Murdoch was not the only foreigner interested in establishing himself as a major publisher of books and magazines in the United States. If he could acquire Harper & Row, then Bertelsmann could take over Bantam, Doubleday, and Dell, as well as the Literary Guild.[91] In 1995, Murdoch bankrolled a new conservative journal of opinion, the *Weekly Standard,* whose publisher was the Republican Party's guru William Kristol. The same year, Hachette—France's leading book and magazine publisher—helped launch *George,* the brainchild of John F. Kennedy Jr. Not every American magazine, new or old, required a prominent American at the helm. In the mid-1990s, the editors of the *New Yorker* and the *New Republic,* two of America's most influential weeklies, were both British. So too was the head of the adult trade books division of Random House, the largest book publisher in the United States.

As early as the 1980s, many Americans began to worry that all these foreign acquisitions were endangering the economic independence and the cultural identity of the United States. How could they not be uneasy when in 1989, the Japanese purchased an 80 percent stake in Rockefeller Center, one of America's premier cultural institutions whose very name recalled the golden age of American capitalism?[92] The fears of politicians and ordinary citizens in the United States seemed identical to those of European intellectuals and government officials who spent most of the twentieth century denouncing the impact of American movies, television shows, and consumer goods on their own countries. At times, the American reaction—nationalist and protectionist—sounded as if it could have been orchestrated by Charles de Gaulle.

Yet the spectacle of foreign corporations buying some of America's media outlets hardly implied that American culture would be fundamentally altered. Sony and Matsushita did not change American music or filmmaking, nor (with the possible exception of the *New York*

Post) did Rupert Murdoch affect what was actually said in his American publications. European and Japanese entrepreneurs entered the U.S. entertainment market to make money, not to trigger a cultural revolution. Much as McDonald's or MTV in Europe tailored their products to the demands of European consumers and audiences, so Murdoch, Bertelsmann, and Hachette accommodated themselves to the values and tastes of their American customers.

In fact, the European conglomerates may have had less of a cultural impact on the United States than they did on Europe itself. They had the resources to accomplish, at least potentially, what decades of subsidies and import quotas failed to do. to lay the foundations for a vibrant "European" culture that would cross national boundaries and offer the people of Britain and the Continent an alternative to America's media exports.

Until the 1980s, the idea of a common European culture was largely a fantasy. Western and Eastern Europe were still divided, politically and geographically, by the Cold War. Despite the Common Market, Western Europe remained a collection of nation-states that jealously guarded their borders, their separate economic and monetary systems, their languages, and their national identities. Britain continued to pursue its "special relationship" with the United States and refused to think of itself as a part of Europe.

Culturally, most governments enacted protectionist policies designed to salvage their national film and television industries. Although movie companies in various countries entered into coproduction arrangements, these were usually undertaken for financial, not artistic, reasons. Consequently, there was no such thing as an authentic European cinema. The prospects for a transcontinental journalism were equally bleak. Apart from London's *Financial Times* and the *International Herald Tribune* (primarily an American product, drawing on material supplied by the *New York Times* and the *Washington Post*), no newspaper consistently attracted readers throughout Western Europe. As for television, the government-run stations relied on American imports, together with locally produced news and entertainment programs geared to an audience that seemed to prefer hearing about events in its own country (and perhaps in the United States) but not about what was going on in the country next door, much less in another corner of the Continent.[93]

Nevertheless, as Europe became more politically and economically unified in the 1980s and after the end of the Cold War, and as Britain began to act more like a European than a transatlantic power, the possibilities of Europe's cultural integration were enhanced. Certainly, the privatization of television broadcasting and the growing popularity of cable and satellite channels opened up opportunities both for joint government ventures and for Europe's media magnates.

When European governments cooperated with one another, they normally stressed the virtues of high culture and supported programming designed for elite audiences. In 1992, for example, the French and German governments introduced Arte, a cable and satellite television network featuring European documentaries, films, plays, and concerts. The purpose of the network was to present programs that were different from the usual diet of American movies and situation comedies found on other stations. The network's directors also hoped to give Europe's viewers a feeling that they belonged to a distinctive cultural community. Similarly, in 1993 a coalition of European public service broadcasters inaugurated Euronews. Its intention was to compete with CNN and the BBC by providing audiences interested in global affairs with news shows (broadcast in English, French, German, Italian, and Spanish) covering international events but analyzed from a "European" point of view. Not to be outmaneuvered, the BBC announced in 1994 that it too would start a news and entertainment channel beamed at the European continent.[94]

But the individuals and corporations who owned Europe's commercial outlets were far more adept at reaching a continent-wide mass audience. Rupert Murdoch's British Sky Broadcasting enveloped Europe with sports, movies, and entertainment, the sort of programming that did not have to confine itself to purely national concerns. Luxembourg's CLT, a media consortium, forged partnerships with local broadcasters across the Continent. Like CLT, Fininvest—Italy's first private TV network, founded in the mid-1980s by Silvio Berlusconi (later prime minister)—had, as its name implied, a number of investments in television stations in other countries. The leaders of Germany's communications industry included not only the Bertelsmann organization and Axel Springer Verlag—the country's largest and most politically influential newspaper publisher—but also Leo Kirch, an entrepreneur who wanted to create an alliance of European television networks that would be strong enough to protect the Continent from America's cultural domination. By 1995, Kirch and his family controlled 30 percent of the German television market. The rest was mostly in the hands of Murdoch, Springer, Bertelsmann, CLT, Fininvest, and France's Canal Plus, with a small stake held by Disney and ABC.[95]

The most ambitious plans for uniting Europe, at least in terms of television, were yet to come. Hoping to exploit the potentially huge pay-TV market in Europe, Rupert Murdoch announced in 1996 that he was teaming up with Bertelsmann and Canal Plus to offer a digital satellite channel aimed at viewers throughout the Continent. The channel would show programs similar to those on America's Home Box Office network.[96] No doubt other European television executives would soon follow Murdoch's lead.

The combined effects of Western Europe's economic power, the unification of Germany, the efforts of the post-Communist countries in the East to reenter the capitalist world, the growth of continental exchange programs enabling students to stay in and travel around Europe, and the rise of a transnational media all appeared to inspire in the 1990s a greater awareness—especially among the young—of being "European." American journalists commented on this phenomenon as if it were a new and startling trend. According to the Americans, national origins now mattered less to the European young than did a shared generational outlook. Youthful viewers of Europe's MTV "tend to think of themselves . . . as Europeans, rather than as Spaniards or Italians," observed a *Newsweek* reporter in 1995. According to William Schmidt, a correspondent for the *New York Times*, the young did not dream, as did their elders, of seeing America. "When young people were asked [in a marketing survey] to name the place they would most like to visit someday, they were likely to say Barcelona or Berlin before New York or Los Angeles." They were looking "to the countries around [them], rather than to the United States, for [their] cultural signals," Schmidt concluded.[97] If true, this was surely a change from the early postwar years when America dominated Europe's consciousness.

American reporters probably exaggerated Europe's emerging cultural unity, particularly at a time when "Europe" was being inundated with refugees from Bosnia to Asia. Moreover, America's movies and television shows, its fashions and fads, its packaged and fast food, its theme parks and slang, would remain a crucial component of any pan-European culture.[98] Europe's increasingly influential mass media might have contributed not so much to a sense of continental solidarity as to a global Western culture made up both of American and Western European elements. It was precisely the internationalization of Western culture that provoked a nationalist reaction in the rest of the world, and ultimately within Europe and the United States too.

————TWELVE————

The Globalization of Western Culture

I n the last two decades of the twentieth century, more than ever before, people in countries all over the world began to worry about the emergence of a global economy and a global culture. Rapid technological change, the impact of mass communications, rampant consumerism, and the decline of national languages and identities—all previously seen as the products of America's cultural imperialism— were now regarded less as the fault of the United States than as the result of international trends beyond the control of governments everywhere, including the one in Washington.

Globalization was a vague and, to some, a terrifying concept. In its most benign construction, it meant free-trade agreements and the opening of borders for the unfettered movement of goods, services, people, and ideas. In its more ominous construction, it referred to the worldwide computer-linked interdependence of banks, financial markets, and stock exchanges, along with the wave of mergers and acquisitions that led in the 1980s and 1990s to a growing concentration of economic power, especially in the United States.

Alarmed by the new globalism, many writers and politicians on both sides of the Atlantic warned that the multinational corporations—though nominally based in America, Western Europe, and Japan—were chiefly concerned with expanding their worldwide investments and remaining internationally competitive by drawing on an abundant supply of cheap labor in the Third World. Consequently, it was said, the multinationals cared little about a particular country's economic priorities, ignoring the need to preserve jobs and domestic industries.

In addition, the critics of globalization argued that the widespread appeal of mass entertainment was a threat to the nation-state. The international popularity of movies, television, pop music, theme parks, shopping malls, and the Internet made it difficult for democratic governments to shore up their local cultural industries or influence what their citizens saw and did. Worse, a global culture threatened to obliterate regional and local eccentricities, promoting instead a set of universal values and images that made the world more homogeneous and much less interesting.

These complaints were not new. In one form or another, they had been voiced since the 1920s. But now it was globalization, rather than "Americanization," that became the main enemy for those in Europe and the United States who loathed the century-long trend toward economic and cultural conformity. And as in the 1920s and 1930s, the discomfort with modernity produced a political and cultural backlash that swept through the Western world, as well as through the Middle East, Africa, Asia, and Latin America—a mixture of nationalism, populism, and ethnic assertiveness, erupting at times into street violence and civil war.

Yet the menace of globalism, like the dangers of Americanization, may have been overestimated. Just as the countries of Western Europe maintained their social and economic idiosyncrasies despite the pervasiveness of America's products and its mass media, so regional and local cultures were not really on the verge of extinction despite the pressures of globalization. The national and the international continued to coexist, however uneasily, at the end of the twentieth century much as they had at its dawn.

MERGERS AND MULTINATIONALS

In 1996, Coca-Cola—a company whose name had become almost a synonym for America—announced that administratively it was eliminating the traditional separation between its "domestic" and "international" operations. Henceforth, the American unit was no longer to be regarded as special. Instead, it would be treated as just another part of the company's overall structure, equal to but no more important than the divisions in charge of Europe, Canada and the Pacific, Latin America, the Middle East, and Africa. There was a good reason for this decision. By the mid-1990s, the American market accounted for only 21 percent of all the Cokes sold in the world.[1]

Exports and overseas markets, of course, had always been vital to American companies. But this was even more the case in the 1990s. In the previous two decades, European and Japanese investments in the United States exceeded American investments abroad. Now U.S. companies were again building factories and opening branch offices in other countries, buying subsidiaries, cooperating with local partners, and setting up multinational enterprises, as they did in the 1920s and in the years following World War II. Between 1993 and 1995, American corporations invested $150 billion abroad, tripling what they had spent outside the United States in the late 1980s.[2]

These developments were unquestionably tied to the rise of a global economy. They represented as well the compulsion of American companies to merge with one another and to more tightly integrate their activities in order to compete in the international arena.

In no sphere was the corporate mania for acquisitions and takeovers more prevalent, and to many observers more unsettling, than in the U.S. communications industry. For all the talk overseas of a conspiracy on the part of "Hollywood" or the television networks to monopolize information and entertainment, America's media companies had operated in an economic environment that was relatively decentralized for most of the twentieth century. But in the 1980s, the idea that companies should concentrate on their own specialties, and respect the differences between one type of entertainment and another, seemed increasingly quaint. The pristine distinctions between movie studios and book publishers, newspaper owners and cable or satellite broadcasters, computer manufacturers and software developers vanished. It became clear that companies controlling both the creation and the distribution of news and entertainment, the content of a TV program as well as the means of delivering it into millions of homes, would have an incomparable advantage in the international marketplace.[3] Corporations and individual entrepreneurs rushed to invest in every facet of the communications business, buying up anything that could conceivably enhance their own position in the race for global profits and influence.

As usual, Rupert Murdoch showed the way. In the 1980s and 1990s, he purchased movie studios, television networks, publishing houses, newspapers, magazines, and satellite broadcasting systems in Europe and Asia. Yet he had his counterparts in America. In 1989, Time, Inc., and Warner Communications joined forces. The result was an international media giant that could compete on equal terms with Murdoch. During the early 1990s, the holdings of Time Warner included the Warner Brothers film and television studios, Home Box Office and Cinemax, the former Luce magazine empire (whose leading publications were *Time, Fortune, People,* and *Sports Illustrated*), book publishers (Time-Life, Warner Books, and Little, Brown), the Book-of-the-Month Club, fifty record labels (among them Warner, Elektra, and Atlantic), and the Six Flags theme parks. In 1996, Time Warner bought Turner Broadcasting for $7.5 billion, forming an even larger communications cartel that embraced Ted Turner's own movie studios (Castle Rock Entertainment and New Line Cinema), as well as his ownership of the MGM and United Artists film libraries, CNN, WTBS (an Atlanta TV station carried nationwide on cable), TNT (another cable outlet specializing in films and entertainment programs), and two sports franchises—the Atlanta Braves in baseball and the Atlanta Hawks in basketball.[4]

Other companies, while not operating on as huge a scale as Rupert Murdoch or Time Warner, still managed to follow their example. In 1986, General Electric bought NBC; a decade later, Westinghouse bought CBS. In 1994, Viacom (the parent of MTV and the Nickelodeon network) purchased the Paramount film studio which, in turn, owned the Simon & Schuster and Macmillan publishing houses. Viacom also took over the Blockbuster video chain. Meanwhile, Disney absorbed ABC in 1996, creating a media combine diversified enough to make money from movies, network and cable television shows, videocassettes, theme parks, soundtrack albums, books, and related merchandise, both in America and throughout the world.[5]

Perhaps this penchant for consolidation was best symbolized by the announcement in 1995 that Steven Spielberg, Jeffrey Katzenberg (formerly at Disney), and David Geffen (of Geffen Records) would join with Bill Gates (chairman of Microsoft) to launch a venture called "DreamWorks SKG." Their aim was to produce a variety of multimedia and interactive entertainments for a global audience bound together by the Internet.[6]

In the fluid world of media mergers, all of these alliances were subject to change. But it was not the details of any particular partnership that bothered the critics of globalism. Rather, the highly publicized passion for "synergy" on the part of the media titans suggested to the critics a lack of appreciation for cultural differences, for national quirks, for the vagaries of personal taste, for privacy itself. The opponents of a global mass culture did not want to live in a world dominated by Rupert Murdoch and Bill Gates, Time Warner and Disney. So they tried to challenge the internationalization of the American and European media as the century drew to a close.

THE DECLINE OF DIVERSITY

What exactly was wrong with a global culture? Why shouldn't people all over the world have access to the same information and the same forms of entertainment available to Americans and Western Europeans? Was it not preferable to live on a planet with a common culture, rather than one in which ethnic and national "identities" were often preserved through civil wars or religious crusades?

To those who disliked the globalization of commerce and culture, these were not the right questions. The critics had no sympathy for extreme nationalists, Islamic fundamentalists, or proponents of ethnic cleansing. But neither did they believe that the global village offered people a shared set of political and moral ideals. Instead, they insisted, people were linked together only by their familiarity with the celebrities and products publicized by the Western mass media.

Moreover, in the eyes of the critics, globalism led inexorably to a world where everything looked identical—from cities, to airports and hotels, to the items sold in department stores and supermarkets, to movies and television programs. When the purveyors of mass culture had to attract an international audience to earn back their production costs and guarantee that their films, TV shows, or CDs would be profitable, they could not afford to immerse themselves in local customs or idioms. Entertainment became generic and nondescript, the critics charged, without any effort to reflect the experience of a particular country or social group. As one British writer put it, globalism sought to abolish a sense of "cultural and psychological differentiation" between nations and peoples. Or, in the words of an American observer, "global economic and technological forces [demanded] integration and uniformity."[7]

Yet the disappearance of diversity was not the most serious problem posed by the new globalism. "Nations on all continents," declared an analyst of America's mass media, "feel that their sovereignty is threatened, that their destinies are ever more influenced by outsiders, and that within their own borders they are losing control." He and others meant by this that the economies of individual countries were increasingly vulnerable to decisions made by international banks and trade associations, currency speculators, Middle Eastern oil cartels, and megacorporations acting independently of any government and willing to relocate their plants or shift their assets whenever conditions seemed more favorable elsewhere. For the multinationals, what mattered were markets, not the policies of elected officials; the tastes of the customer, not the needs of the citizen. And there seemed to be no way of compelling the global capitalists to accept the supervision of parliaments or the courts.[8]

This situation was especially frustrating in the realm of culture. The lords of the American and Western European media, asserted their critics, were able to operate as if national frontiers did not exist. The new forms of global communication—cable, satellites, computers, faxes, E-mail, VCRs—overrode any attempt by a government to protect its country's cultural heritage. The National Assembly in France might force radio disk jockeys to devote 40 percent of their airtime to songs performed in French, but audiences could simply buy CDs in order to hear whatever music they wished. Nor did quotas on the importation of films prevent people from renting videocassettes. Meanwhile, satellite dishes picked up television programs from everywhere.[9] When culture no longer corresponded to old-fashioned political boundaries, then those in charge of the nation-state could never hope to erect barriers impervious enough to halt the invasion of alien languages, values, and ideas.

What the American and European critics of globalism wanted was a revival of cultural pluralism. They yearned as well for democracies sufficiently vigorous to regulate the multinational corporations. In the post–Cold War years, however, the West found itself confronting a resurgence of tribalism and ethnic bigotry. Clearly, this was not the sort of diversity the critics had in mind. But their pessimism led them to misjudge the ability of national cultures—democratic as well as authoritarian—to survive and even flourish in the age of globalization.

International Culture and Cultural Nationalism

One of the great paradoxes of the late twentieth century was the reinvigoration of nationalism in Europe and, to a degree, in the United

States at precisely the moment when the economies and communications systems of the advanced industrial nations had become more intertwined. Two trends collided in the 1990s. On the one hand, most government leaders, corporate officials, and media executives in the West and in the Pacific Rim nations eagerly adopted a global perspective. On the other hand, many people in these same countries joined movements promising a restoration of traditional religious beliefs, a renewed appreciation of local languages and dialects, and a heightened sense of ethnic or national pride.

The nationalist impulse was stimulated, in part, by the end of the Cold War. In a world no longer so attentive to policies formulated in Washington or Moscow, it was easier for nations everywhere to reassert their independence. Furthermore, the collapse of the Soviet empire unleashed in Eastern Europe all the ethnic and religious hatreds, as well as the feelings of national humiliation, that the Communist regimes had managed for forty years to suppress.

Yet there were deeper reasons for the appeal of nationalism in the 1990s. In America and in Europe, nationalist and protectionist ideas were attractive to those who resented everything associated with globalization. Millions of people felt victimized by the forces of modernity: by international markets and bankers, by America's mass culture, by Western Europe's economic unification, by immigrants with strange customs who refused to assimilate, by free-trade treaties that destroyed local industries. But no aspect of globalism frightened them more than the loss of blue-collar jobs to low-paid but productive workers in other lands, or the "downsizing" of corporations—a euphemism for the abrupt dismissal of thousands of white-collar employees who had once thought they were indispensable.[10]

At its worst, this hostility to the changes taking place in the world inflamed the neo-Nazi skinheads in Germany and the right-wing militias in the United States. A similar anger inspired a new generation of "populist" demagogues—Vladimir Zhirinovsky in Russia, Slobodan Milosevic in Serbia, Franjo Tudjman in Croatia, Jean-Marie Le Pen in France, and Pat Buchanan in America. Sometimes a distrust of foreigners and a desire to live in an ethnically homogeneous society persuaded nationalities to separate peacefully, as in the case of the Czechs and the Slovaks. But the more venomous forms of tribal and religious sectarianism could lead to the slaughter of innocent people, as they did in Northern Ireland and Bosnia.

At its best, however, nationalism coupled with a respect for regional and local values might create a society that was both diverse and relatively tolerant. The willingness of a government to grant a measure of autonomy to the various ethnic and linguistic groups within its borders could result in a reduction of tension and a sharing of power. Such an arrangement strengthened the bonds among German, French, and Italian speakers in Switzerland, and among Flemish and French speakers in Belgium.

But no matter whether its effects were sinister or benign, nationalism represented a rejection of the new world order. Still, despite the bellicose rhetoric of xenophobic politicians or the more sober objections of the media critics, globalism was unlikely to demolish the nation-state or eradicate the culture of a particular locale.

In fact, the globalization of mass communications often led not to cultural uniformity but to cultural fragmentation. English, for example, may have spread throughout the world, but it did not thereby become a universal language, understood in the same way by everyone everywhere. Instead, millions of non-native speakers added their own words and meanings, creating a hybrid language that was less a reflection of British or American culture than one rooted in local needs. Similarly, although English was the preeminent language of the Internet, computer companies by 1995 were developing software that would automatically translate messages into French, German, Spanish, Chinese, or Japanese. Thus, if cyberspace became genuinely multilingual, it would cease to be an instrument of American or Western domination. Rather, it could become a device for the wider diffusion of many different languages and cultures.[11]

The already-strong interest in multiculturalism among American academics—the emphasis on the unique experiences of workers, women, Hispanics, and African Americans—was another means of resisting the drift toward global conformity. A comparable reaction occurred in Europe, where the presence of a global culture stimulated a greater commitment in some countries to the preservation of regional dialects like Gaelic, Welsh, Frisian, Provençal, and Catalan.[12]

The trend toward diversity could be seen even in the Western mass media, presumably the command center of the global culture. While the cinema remained a predominantly American medium, several European movies in the 1990s were surprisingly successful in the United States though they focused on cultural or social situations very different from what American audiences were accustomed to. Among the more notable of these films were *Sense and Sensibility*, with its evocation of Jane Austen's England; *Hate*, a raw semidocumentary portrait of life in the ethnic slums on the outskirts of Paris; and *Il Postino*

(The Postman), an Italian romance that in 1996 became the first foreign-language film since Ingmar Bergman's *Cries and Whispers* in 1973 to be nominated for an Oscar for best picture.

In the meantime, the proliferation of cable and satellite television networks in Europe and the United States meant that people would have a far greater range of programs to chose from (at least in theory), while the popularity of VCRs offered them more freedom to decide not only what they wanted to watch but when. Under these circumstances, mass culture could no longer be the unifying influence that it had been in the era when people saw movies only in theaters, and when they relied for their home entertainment on the three commercial networks in America or the state-run television channels in Europe.

None of these tendencies pointed to globalism's imminent demise. Instead, people in the future might have to maintain a dual set of allegiances—one, to their local or national traditions and institutions and the other, to an international culture and a global economy. "I'm European," a student in Bonn told an American journalist in 1993, echoing her generation's attachment to the Continent and its culture, "but I'm also German."[13] This double identity, a sort of cultural schizophrenia, was a way for Europeans as well as Americans to acknowledge, finally, that they live in a pluralistic world.

An acceptance of pluralism carries with it the need for a new approach to the familiar cultural conflicts between the United States and Western Europe. After the Cold War, and fifty years of transatlantic political arguments and intellectual rivalries, it no longer makes sense for Americans to think of themselves as cultural leaders or for Europeans to think of Americans as cultural imperialists. Their societies have become too complex and too interdependent to go on waging indefinitely the old battle for cultural supremacy.

To recognize the obsolescence of these conflicts means that it is necessary to adopt a more relaxed attitude toward one's own culture and toward the culture of one's competitors. It would be hard, of course, for Americans in particular to give up the notion that theirs is an ideal society worthy of emulation. To some extent, people in all countries believe that others want to, or should want to, live like they do. But the history of America's relations with Europe in the twentieth century suggests that the United States could not easily export its culture across the Atlantic. Europeans in each country were (and are) selective in what they accept from America. And they have been successful in preserving their distinctive cultural characteristics despite the efforts of Washington to persuade them to embrace the American model.

It is possible, moreover, that "models" based on a single national experience are outmoded. We are now exposed to the cultures of many countries. And within each country, there are regional, class, ethnic, and racial variations—further complicating the transmission of a unified "culture" from one land to another. That is what it means to live in a global culture while simultaneously retaining one's affection for a specific town or neighborhood.

Given these multiple influences, it was inevitable that the Marshall Planners, along with other American missionaries, should have failed to "Americanize" Europe. The Europeans did not then and do not today wish to be just like us. Nor have we ever wished to be exactly like them. People in Europe and in America have different cultures, different styles of living, and different expectations. But we can all thrive on the differences.

Notes

The page numbers of all the *New York Times* articles, except for those published in the Magazine and the Book Review sections, are taken from the newspaper's national edition.

CHAPTER ONE
CULTURAL RELATIONS BEFORE 1945

1. For an extended discussion of these claims, see Melvin Lasky, "Literature and the Arts: Transatlantic Letters—Restoration but Not Renaissance," in Lewis Galantière, ed., *America and the Mind of Europe* (London: Hamilton, 1951), p. 89; Marcus Cunliffe, "New World, Old World: The Historical Antithesis," in Richard Rose, ed., *Lessons from America: An Exploration* (London: Macmillan, 1974), pp. 28–30; and Marcus Cunliffe, "The Anatomy of Anti-Americanism," in Rob Kroes and Maarten van Rossem, eds., *Anti-Americanism in Europe* (Amsterdam: Free University Press, 1986), p. 30.

2. There are many treatments of European attitudes toward America. For examples, see Harold Laski, *The American Democracy: A Commentary and an Interpretation* (New York: Viking, 1948), p. 62; Edward Chester, *Europe Views America: A Critical Evaluation* (Washington, D.C.: Public Affairs Press, 1962), p. 36; Allen Davis, "Introduction: The American Impact on the World," in Davis, ed., *For Better or Worse: The American Influence in the World* (Westport, Conn.: Greenwood Press, 1981), p. 7; Laurence Wylie and Sarella Henriquez, "French Images of American Life," *Tocqueville Review* 4 (1982), pp. 244–47; Peter Duignan and L. H. Gann, *The Rebirth of the West: The Americanization of the Democratic World, 1945–1958* (Cambridge, Mass.: Blackwell, 1992), p. 411; and Guy Sorman, "United States: Model or Bête Noire?" in Denis Lacorne, Jacques Rupnik, and Marie-France Toinet, eds., *The Rise and Fall of Anti-Americanism: A Century of French Perception*, trans. Gerry Turner (New York: St. Martin's Press, 1990,

c. Paris 1986), p. 214. Hereafter, a publication date given in this fashion means that the copyright was, in this case, 1986, but that the pagination is from the 1990 edition.

3. For Europe's ambivalence about America, see Malcolm Bradbury, "How I Invented America," *Journal of American Studies* 14 (April 1980), p. 116; Davis, "The American Impact on the World," p. 4; Reinhold Wagnleitner, "Propagating the American Dream: Cultural Policies as Means of Integration," *American Studies International* 24 (April 1986), p. 64; Maurizio Vaudagna, "The American Historian in Continental Europe: An Italian Perspective," *Journal of American History* 79 (September 1992), p. 536; and Tony Judt, *Past Imperfect: French Intellectuals, 1944–1956* (Berkeley: University of California Press, 1992), pp. 187–88.

4. See Sigmund Skard, *American Studies in Europe: Their History and Present Organization*, vol. 1 (Philadelphia: University of Pennsylvania Press, 1958), pp. 27, 29, 236; and Kaspar Maase, "'Halbstarke' and Hegemony: Meanings of American Mass Culture in the Federal Republic of Germany During the 1950s," in Rob Kroes, Robert Rydell, and Doeko F. J. Bosscher, eds., *Cultural Transmissions and Receptions: American Mass Culture in Europe* (Amsterdam: VU University Press, 1993), p. 157.

5. André Visson, *As Others See Us* (Garden City, N.Y.: Doubleday, 1948), p. 230; Skard, *American Studies in Europe,* vol. 1, pp. 25–26, 210–11, 236; Sigmund Skard, *American Studies in Europe,* vol. 2 (Philadelphia: University of Pennsylvania Press, 1958), p. 405; Donald Heiney, *America in Modern Italian Literature* (New Brunswick, N.J.: Rutgers University Press, 1964), p. 9; A. N. J. den Hollander, "On 'Dissent' and 'Influence' as Agents of Change," in den Hollander, ed., *Contagious Conflict: The Impact of American Dissent on European Life* (Leiden: Brill, 1973), p. 6.

6. Skard, *American Studies in Europe*, vol. 1, pp. 232–33, 253; Maase, "'Halbstarke' and Hegemony," pp. 157–58.

7. For Europe's view of America's cultural inferiority complex, see Laski, *The American Democracy*, pp. 63–64; Skard, *American Studies in Europe*, vol. 1, pp. 28, 47; and Serge Guilbaut, *How New York Stole the Idea of Modern Art: Abstract Expressionism, Freedom, and the Cold War*, trans. Arthur Goldhammer (Chicago: University of Chicago Press, 1984, c. 1983), p. 43.

8. See Davis, "The American Impact on the World," p. 11; Richard Rose, "America: Inevitable or Inimitable?" in Rose, ed., *Lessons from America*, p. 10; Marcus Cunliffe, "European Images of America," in Arthur Schlesinger and Morton White, eds., *Paths of American Thought* (Boston: Houghton Mifflin, 1963), p. 506; and Chester, *Europe Views America*, p. 129.

9. Sigmund Skard, *Trans-Atlantica: Memoirs of a Norwegian Americanist* (Oslo: Universitetsforlaget, 1978), p. 17; Skard, *American Studies in Europe*, vol. 1, pp. 34, 134, 156; Skard, *American Studies in Europe*, vol. 2, p. 478.

10. The aims and misfortunes of the Creel Committee are fully discussed in Thomas Sorensen, *The Word War: The Story of American Propaganda* (New York: Harper & Row, 1968), pp. 5–7; John Henderson, *The United States*

Information Agency (New York: Praeger, 1969), pp. 24–26, 28–29; Allan Winkler, *The Politics of Propaganda: The Office of War Information, 1942–1945* (New Haven, Conn.: Yale University Press, 1978), pp. 2–3; and Emily Rosenberg, *Spreading the American Dream: American Economic and Cultural Expansion, 1890–1945* (New York: Hill & Wang, 1982), pp. 79–81.

11. For Europe's reaction to America's wartime power, see Frank Costigliola, *Awkward Dominion: American Political, Economic, and Cultural Relations with Europe, 1919–1933* (Ithaca, N.Y.: Cornell University Press, 1987, c. 1984), pp. 21, 167–71; Michael Harrison, "French Anti-Americanism Under the Fourth Republic and the Gaullist Solution," in Lacorne et al., eds., *The Rise and Fall of Anti-Americanism*, pp. 170–71; and Judt, *Past Imperfect*, pp. 189, 193.

12. Rosenberg, *Spreading the American Dream*, pp. 19–21.

13. Ibid., pp. 23–26; Costigliola, *Awkward Dimension*, p. 149.

14. Costigliola, *Awkward Dimension*, pp. 139, 149–50, 154–55; Rosenberg, *Spreading the American Dream*, pp. 122–25; David Strauss, *Menace in the West: The Rise of French Anti-Americanism in Modern Times* (Westport, Conn.: Greenwood Press, 1978), pp. 100, 139–40, 145; Peter Masson and Andrew Thorburn, "Advertising: The American Influence in Europe," in C. W. E. Bigsby, ed., *Superculture: American Popular Culture and Europe* (Bowling Green, Ohio: Bowling Green University Popular Press, 1975), p. 97; Nico Wilterdink, "The Netherlands Between the Greater Powers," in Rob Kroes, ed., *Within the U.S. Orbit: Small National Cultures vis-à-vis the United States* (Amsterdam: VU University Press, 1991), p. 23.

15. For a discussion of American tourism in the late nineteenth century and the 1920s, see Arnold Rose, "Anti-Americanism in France," *Antioch Review* 12 (December 1952), p. 473; Foster Rhea Dulles, *Americans Abroad: Two Centuries of European Travel* (Ann Arbor: University of Michigan Press, 1964), pp. 1–3, 169; and Costigliola, *Awkward Dominion*, pp. 172–73.

16. Skard, *Trans-Atlantica*, p. 25; Skard, *American Studies in Europe*, vol. 1, p. 31; Judt, *Past Imperfect*, p. 188; Costigliola, *Awkward Dominion*, pp. 19–20, 141, 167–68, 178, 183; Victoria de Grazia, "Americanism for Export," *Wedge* 7–8 (Winter–Spring 1985), p. 74; Wilterdink, "The Netherlands Between the Greater Powers," pp. 21–22; Ralph Willett, *The Americanization of Germany, 1945–1949* (London: Routledge, 1989), p. 108; Michael Kimmelman, "The Lure of Fordism, Jazz and 'Americanismus,'" *New York Times* (February 11, 1990), sec. 2, p. 37; D. W. Brogan, "From England," and Peter von Zahn, "From Germany," in Franz Joseph, ed., *As Others See Us: The United States Through Foreign Eyes* (Princeton, N.J.: Princeton University Press, 1959), pp. 3–4, 95–96.

17. Heiney, *America in Modern Italian Literature*, p. 9; John Sears, "Bierstadt, Buffalo Bill, and the Wild West in Europe," and Robert Bieder, "Marketing the American Indian in Europe: Context, Commodification, and Reception," in Kroes et al., eds., *Cultural Transmissions and Receptions*, pp. 4–6, 21.

18. Sears, "Bierstadt, Buffalo Bill, and the Wild West in Europe," pp. 5–6, 9, 12, 14; Bieder, "Marketing the American Indian in Europe," p. 15.

19. For a more detailed description of America's early efforts to compete in the field of global mass communications, see Rosenberg, *Spreading the American Dream*, 88–92, 94–95; and Costigliola, *Awkward Dominion*, p. 151.

20. See Paul Oliver, "Jazz Is Where You Find It: The European Experience of Jazz," in Bigsby, ed., *Superculture*, pp. 140–43; Davis, "The American Impact on the World," p. 12; Kimmelman, "The Lure of Fordism, Jazz and 'Americanismus,'" p. 37; and Reinhold Wagnleitner, "The Irony of American Culture Abroad: Austria and the Cold War" in Lary May, ed., *Recasting America: Culture and Politics in the Age of the Cold War* (Chicago: University of Chicago Press, 1989), p. 294.

21. Victoria de Grazia, "Mass Culture and Sovereignty: The American Challenge to European Cinemas, 1920–1960," *Journal of Modern History* 61 (March 1989), p. 57; Peter Lev, *The Euro-American Cinema* (Austin: University of Texas Press, 1993), p. 17. In 1912, nearly 90 percent of all film exports came from France. See Reinhold Wagnleitner, *Coca-Colonization and the Cold War: The Cultural Mission of the United States in Austria After the Second World War*, trans. Diana Wolf (Chapel Hill: University of North Carolina Press, 1994), p. 230.

22. For a discussion of the war's direct effect on European filmmaking, see William Read, *America's Mass Media Merchants* (Baltimore: Johns Hopkins University Press, 1976), p. 42; Thomas Guback, "Hollywood's International Market," in Tino Balio, ed., *The American Film Industry* (Madison: University of Wisconsin Press, 1985), p. 465; Strauss, *Menace in the West*, p. 146; and Lev, *The Euro-American Cinema*, p. 17.

23. Guback, "Hollywood's International Market," pp. 465–66; de Grazia, "Mass Culture and Sovereignty," pp. 57–58, 61; Strauss, *Menace in the West*, p. 147; Rosenberg, *Spreading the American Dream*, p. 101. Often, American distributors controlled centrally located theaters in such major European cities as Paris, Brussels, and Berlin, where they could premier Hollywood's new movies. See Ian Jarvie, "The Postwar Economic Foreign Policy of the American Film Industry: Europe 1945–1950," in David Ellwood and Rob Kroes, eds., *Hollywood in Europe: Experiences of a Cultural Hegemony* (Amsterdam: VU University Press, 1994), pp. 158–59. Block booking refers to Hollywood's practice of forcing theater owners to exhibit several films released by a studio in order to receive the studio's most popular movies, which meant the ones that would sell the most tickets. In 1948, the Supreme Court ruled that this practice violated the antitrust laws.

24. De Grazia, "Mass Culture and Sovereignty," pp. 59–60; Costigliola, *Awkward Dominion*, p. 176; Wagnleitner, *Coca-Colonization and the Cold War*, p. 232. Many other commentators have offered similar figures to demonstrate the preponderance of American films on European screens.

25. Guback, "Hollywood's International Market," p. 468.

26. On Europe's fears about Hollywood's cultural influence in the 1920s,

see Rosenberg, *Spreading the American Dream*, pp. 101–2; Costigliola, *Awkward Dominion*, pp. 22, 168, 177; Strauss, *Menace in the West*, pp. 147–48; and de Grazia, "Mass Culture and Sovereignty," p. 53.

27. Guback, "Hollywood's International Market," p. 469; Costigliola, *Awkward Dominion*, p. 177.

28. De Grazia, "Mass Culture and Sovereignty," p. 62; Rosenberg, *Spreading the American Dream*, p. 102; Strauss, *Menace in the West*, pp. 146–47.

29. Thomas Guback, *The International Film Industry: Western Europe and America Since 1945* (Bloomington: Indiana University Press, 1969), p. 9; Costigliola, *Awkward Dominion*, p. 177. *The Blue Angel*, for example, was released in both English and German in 1930, thanks to a coproduction arrangement between Paramount and the leading German studio, UFA. See Wagnleitner, *Coca-Colonization and the Cold War*, p. 234.

30. David Reynolds, "Whitehall, Washington and the Promotion of American Studies in Britain During World War Two," *Journal of American Studies* 16 (August 1982), p. 166; Heiney, *America in Modern Italian Literature*, pp. 22–24; Roger Asselineau, "A Complex Fate," *Journal of American Studies* 14 (April 1980), p. 70.

31. David Ellwood, "Hollywood's Star Wars," *History Today* (April 1994), p. 2; de Grazia, "Mass Culture and Sovereignty," p. 62; Jeremy Tunstall, *The Media Are American* (New York: Columbia University Press, 1977), p. 49; Rosenberg, *Spreading the American Dream*, p. 204.

32. See Brogan, "From England," pp. 4–5; and Strauss, *Menace in the West*, pp. 187–93.

33. Skard, *Trans-Atlantica*, p. 19; Wilterdink, "The Netherlands Between the Greater Powers," p. 22; Brogan, "From England," p. 5.

34. The European descriptions of America in the 1920s as a mass society are fully discussed in Richard Kuisel, *Seducing the French: The Dilemma of Americanization* (Berkeley: University of California Press, 1993), pp. 2, 12; Strauss, *Menace in the West*, pp. 175–76, 181; and Cunliffe, "European Images of America," p. 506.

35. Rob Kroes, "Americanization: What Are We Talking About?" in Kroes et al., eds., *Cultural Transmissions and Receptions*, p. 303; Strauss, *Menace in the West*, pp. 82, 209; de Grazia, "Americanism for Export," p. 79; Judt, *Past Imperfect*, p. 189.

36. For an account of how different countries in Europe defined *Europeanism,* see Rob Kroes, "Among the Receivers: American Culture Transmitted Abroad," and Rob Kroes, "American Films in the Netherlands," in Kroes, ed., *Within the U.S. Orbit*, pp. 7, 76; Wilterdink, "The Netherlands Between the Greater Powers," p. 23; and Judt, *Past Imperfect*, p. 193.

37. For a more detailed description of the Rockefeller Foundation's activities, see Merle Curti, *American Philanthropy Abroad: A History* (New Brunswick, N.J.: Rutgers University Press, 1963), pp. 316–17, 336; and Claus-Dieter Krohn, *Intellectuals in Exile: Refugee Scholars and the New School for Social Research*, trans. Rita and Robert Kimber (Amherst: Univer-

sity of Massachusetts Press, 1993, c. 1987), p. 33. The Rockefeller Foundation played a crucial role in helping to develop theoretical physics in the United States through its grants to American universities (especially the California Institute of Technology, Berkeley, Chicago, Princeton, and Harvard). The foundation gave money not only for scholarly exchanges but also for the construction of laboratories and expensive scientific instruments like particle accelerators and telescopes. On the foundation's support for physics in America, see Gerald Holton, "The Migration of Physicists to the United States," in Jarrell Jackman and Carla Borden, eds., *The Muses Flee Hitler: Cultural Transfer and Adaptation, 1930–1945* (Washington, D.C.: Smithsonian Institution Press, 1983), pp. 176–77.

38. Marie Jahoda, "The Migration of Psychoanalysis: Its Impact on American Psychology," and Colin Eisler, "*Kunstgeschichte* American Style: A Study in Migration," in Donald Fleming and Bernard Bailyn, eds., *The Intellectual Migration: Europe and America, 1930–1960* (Cambridge, Mass.: Charles Warren Center for Studies in American History, 1968), pp. 420, 565–66; Krohn, *Intellectuals in Exile*, pp. 11–12, 15.

39. See Herbert Strauss, "The Movement of People in a Time of Crisis," in Jackman and Borden, eds., *The Muses Flee Hitler*, p. 51; and Charles Weiner, "A New Site for the Seminar: The Refugees and American Physics in the Thirties," in Fleming and Bailyn, eds., *The Intellectual Migration*, pp. 218–19.

40. Donald Fleming and Bernard Bailyn, "Introduction," in Fleming and Bailyn, eds., *The Intellectual Migration*, p, 7; Jahoda, "The Migration of Psychoanalysis," p. 429; Krohn, *Intellectuals in Exile*, pp. 14–17.

41. For the internationalization of intellectual life, especially in physics and psychoanalysis, and the readiness of American institutions to accept European refugees, see Fleming and Bailyn, "Introduction," pp. 3, 8; Weiner, "A New Site for the Seminar," pp. 191–97, 200–2, 215, 221, 227; Holton, "The Migration of Physicists to the United States," pp. 171, 175, 177–79, 183–84; Jean and George Mandler, "The Diaspora of Experimental Psychology: The Gestaltists and Others," in Fleming and Bailyn, eds., *The Intellectual Migration*, p. 373; Jahoda, "The Migration of Psychoanalysis," pp. 421–24, 429; and H. Stuart Hughes, *The Sea Change: The Migration of Social Thought, 1930–1965* (New York: McGraw-Hill, 1977, c. 1975), p. 4. In addition to Enrico Fermi and Niels Bohr, other famous European physicists visited or lectured in America during the 1920s and early 1930s. Among these were Albert Einstein, Arnold Sommerfeld, Ernest Rutherford, Paul Ehrenfest, Max Born, Erwin Schrödinger, Wolfgang Pauli, and Werner Heisenberg.

42. Strauss, "The Movement of People in a Time of Crisis," p. 54; Hughes, *The Sea Change*, p. 2.

43. Weiner, "A New Site for the Seminar," pp. 217, 225–26.

44. See Peter Rutkoff and William Scott, *New School: A History of the New School for Social Research* (New York: Free Press, 1986), p. 93; Krohn, *Intellectuals in Exile*, pp. 27–28; and A. M. Sperber, *Murrow: His Life and Times* (New York: Bantam Books, 1987, c. 1986), p. 52. The young Edward R. Mur-

row served for a time as assistant secretary of the Emergency Committee, coordinating its activities, raising money, interviewing refugees, and trying to find jobs for them in the United States.

45. Krohn, *Intellectuals in Exile*, pp. 6, 23, 28–29, 32, 34.

46. Ibid., pp. 22–24, 28; Weiner, "A New Site for the Seminar," p. 214.

47. Rutkoff and Scott, *New School*, p. 96; Weiner, "A New Site for the Seminar," p. 207; Krohn, *Intellectuals in Exile*, pp. 5, 158, 191; Eisler, "*Kunstgeschichte* American Style," pp. 546, 552, 568–69, 572, 582–83, 625.

48. Rutkoff and Scott, *New School*, pp. xii, 33, 84–86, 101, 106; Arthur Vidich, "Foreword" to Krohn, *Intellectuals in Exile*, pp. viii–ix; Krohn, *Intellectuals in Exile*, pp. 32, 59–61, 68, 181.

49. Vidich, "Foreword," p. ix; Krohn, *Intellectuals in Exile*, pp. 29, 86–88; Rutkoff and Scott, *New School*, p. 134.

50. See Krohn, *Intellectuals in Exile*, pp. 80, 86. From August 1940 until September 1941, some of Europe's most important artists and intellectuals escaped from Vichy France to the United States. They were aided by a young Harvard-trained classicist, Varian Fry, who operated out of Marseilles as the representative of the newly formed Emergency Rescue Committee. Among those whose flight Fry arranged were Hannah Arendt, Marc Chagall, Marcel Duchamp, Jacques Lipchitz, Max Ernst, and André Breton. For a description of Fry's activities, see Cynthia Jaffee McCabe, " 'Wanted by the Gestapo: Saved by America'—Varian Fry and the Emergency Rescue Committee," in Jackman and Borden, eds., *The Muses Flee Hitler*, pp. 79–91.

51. On the French exiles in wartime America, see Fleming and Bailyn, "Introduction," p. 6; Rutkoff and Scott, *New School*, pp. 153, 156, 159, 170; and Krohn, *Intellectuals in Exile*, pp. 84–85.

52. Vidich, "Foreword," p. xii; Krohn, *Intellectuals in Exile*, pp. 140, 161, 176; Hughes, *The Sea Change*, pp. 103, 174–75; Eisler, "*Kunstgeschichte* American Style," p. 584; Holly Shulman, *The Voice of America: Propaganda and Democracy, 1941–1945* (Madison: University of Wisconsin Press, 1990), p. 29.

53. Duignan and Gann, *The Rebirth of the West*, p. 420; J. M. Mitchell, *International Cultural Relations* (London: Allen & Unwin, 1986), pp. 23, 47.

54. Mitchell, *International Cultural Relations*, p. 427; Duignan and Gann, *The Rebirth of the West*, p. 420; Philip Coombs, *The Fourth Dimension of Foreign Policy: Educational and Cultural Affairs* (New York: Harper & Row, 1964), p. 84.

55. See Charles Thompson and Walter Laves, *Cultural Relations and U.S. Foreign Policy* (Bloomington: Indiana University Press, 1963), p. 32.

56. See Henderson, *The United States Information Agency*, pp. 28–29; Sorensen, *The Word War*, p. 8; and Shulman, *The Voice of America*, p. 4.

57. Coombs, *The Fourth Dimension of Foreign Policy*, p. 85; Rosenberg, *Spreading the American Dream*, p. 204.

58. Mitchell, *International Cultural Relations*, pp. 19, 45; Tunstall, *The Media Are American*, p. 34.

59. Thompson and Laves, *Cultural Relations and U.S. Foreign Policy*, p. 35.

60. Ibid., pp. 27–28, 38, 45; Rosenberg, *Spreading the American Dream*, pp. 205, 208; Mitchell, *International Cultural Relations*, p. 53.

61. On the centrality of the Voice of America, see Rosenberg, *Spreading the American Dream*, p. 211.

62. Ibid., p. 52; Thompson and Laves, *Cultural Relations and U.S. Foreign Policy*, pp. 52–53; Edward Barrett, *Truth Is Our Weapon* (New York: Funk & Wagnalls, 1953), pp. 25–26.

63. Winkler, *The Politics of Propaganda*, pp. 112, 115, 118–21, 125–28; Barrett, *Truth Is Our Weapon*, pp. 26–28; Sorensen, *The Word War*, pp. 19–20.

64. Winkler, *The Politics of Propaganda*, pp. 154, 156; Shulman, *The Voice of America*, pp. 130–31, 141, 151.

65. Shulman, *The Voice of America*, pp. 180, 184–85, 187; Sorensen, *The Word War*, p. 21.

CHAPTER TWO
AMERICAN CULTURE AND THE COLD WAR: THE RESHAPING OF WESTERN EUROPE

1. For the European image of the American soldier, see André Visson, *As Others See Us* (Garden City, N.Y.: Doubleday, 1948), p. 224; and Dick Hebdige, "Towards a Cartography of Taste, 1935–1962," in Hebdige, *Hiding in the Light: On Images and Things* (London: Routledge, 1988), p. 53.

2. See Vittorio Zincone, "Moral America," in James Burnham, ed., *What Europe Thinks of America* (New York: John Day, 1953), p. 54; Kaspar Maase, "'Halbstarke' and Hegemony: Meanings of American Mass Culture in the Federal Republic of Germany During the 1950s," in Rob Kroes, Robert Rydell, and Doeko F. J. Bosscher, eds., *Cultural Transmissions and Receptions: American Mass Culture in Europe* (Amsterdam: VU University Press, 1993), p. 153; and Peter von Zahn, "From Germany," in Franz Joseph, ed., *As Others See Us: The United States Through Foreign Eyes* (Princeton, N.J.: Princeton University Press, 1959), p. 97.

3. Charles Thompson and Walter Laves, *Cultural Relations and U.S. Foreign Policy* (Bloomington: Indiana University Press, 1963), p. 93; Ralph Willett, *The Americanization of Germany, 1945–1949* (London: Routledge, 1989), pp. 90, 92; Michael Watts, "The Call and Response of Popular Music: The Impact of American Pop Music in Europe," in C. W. E. Bigsby, ed., *Superculture: American Popular Culture and Europe* (Bowling Green, Ohio: Bowling Green University Popular Press, 1975), p. 128; Stephen Kinzer, "The G.I.s' Legacy: Basketball and Sweet Memories," *New York Times* (September 27, 1994), p. A8; Sigmund Skard, *American Studies in Europe: Their History and Present Organization*, vol. 1 (Philadelphia: University of Pennsylvania Press, 1958), p. 295.

4. Henry Kellerman, *Cultural Relations as an Instrument of U.S. Foreign Policy* (Washington, D.C.: U.S. Government Printing Office, 1978), pp. 17–18; James Tent, *Mission on the Rhine: "Reeducation" and Denazification in American-Occupied Germany* (Chicago: University of Chicago Press, 1982), pp. 39, 53, 65–66.

5. See James Tent, *The Free University of Berlin: A Political History* (Bloomington: Indiana University Press, 1988), p. 374; and Tent, *Mission on the Rhine*, pp. 36, 54, 83, 107, 159.

6. Tent, *The Free University of Berlin*, p. 236; Tent, *Mission on the Rhine*, p. 107.

7. For a description of Germany at "ground zero," see Skard, *American Studies in Europe*, vol. 1, p. 291; Kellerman, *Cultural Relations as an Instrument of U.S. Foreign Policy*, p. 26; and Tent, *Mission on the Rhine*, pp. 42, 57–58, 69, 122.

8. The U.S. government also attempted to impose American-style reforms on its zone in Austria during its ten-year military occupation between 1945 and 1955. For a comprehensive discussion of these efforts, see Reinhold Wagnleitner, *Coca-Colonization and the Cold War: The Cultural Mission of the United States in Austria After the Second World War*, trans. Diana Wolf (Chapel Hill: University of North Carolina Press, 1994), pp. 66–120.

9. Tent, *Mission on the Rhine*, pp. 10–11, 13; Leonard Sussman, *The Culture of Freedom: The Small World of Fulbright Scholars* (Savage, Md.: Rowman & Littlefield, 1992), p. 19.

10. Kellerman, *Cultural Relations as an Instrument of U.S. Foreign Policy*, pp. 24, 100.

11. Ibid., p. 59; Tent, *Mission on the Rhine*, pp. 8, 161, 318. The quotation is from von Zahn, "From Germany," p. 98.

12. Tent, *Mission on the Rhine*, pp. 3, 8, 116–17; Kellerman, *Cultural Relations as an Instrument of U.S. Foreign Policy*, pp. 21, 23, 30, 59, 115–16; Skard, *American Studies in Europe*, vol. 1, p. 303. Americans were also eager to transform the Austrian educational system and proposed many of the same ideas. See Reinhold Wagnleitner, "The Irony of American Culture Abroad: Austria and the Cold War" in Lary May, ed., *Recasting America: Culture and Politics in the Age of the Cold War*, (Chicago: University of Chicago Press, 1989), pp. 291–92; and Wagnleitner, *Coca-Colonization and the Cold War*, pp. 150–53.

13. Skard, *American Studies in Europe*, vol. 1, p. 303; Willett, *The Americanization of Germany*, p. 18; Tent, *Mission on the Rhine*, pp. 124, 145, 162, 167–68, 198–99, 207, 228, 238, 251, 310, 312; Kellerman, *Cultural Relations as an Instrument of U.S. Foreign Policy*, pp. 22, 29–30; Thompson and Laves, *Cultural Relations and U.S. Foreign Policy*, p. 78. The Austrians were equally recalcitrant, and Americans abandoned their educational experiments in 1948. See Wagnleitner, "The Irony of American Culture Abroad," p. 291; and Wagnleitner, *Coca-Colonization and the Cold War*, p.154. The French and the British were no more successful than the Americans in reforming the

German educational structures in their zones. See Tent, *Mission on the Rhine*, pp. 211, 309, 313–14.

14. Tent, *Mission on the Rhine*, pp. 2, 200; Willett, *The Americanization of Germany*, p. 27; Hans-Peter Wagner, "Stepping Out of Hitler's Shadow to Embrace Uncle Sam? Notes Toward a History of American Literary Studies in West Germany," in Huck Gutman, ed., *As Others Read Us: International Perspectives on American Literature* (Amherst: University of Massachusetts Press, 1991), p. 101; Thompson and Laves, *Cultural Relations and U.S. Foreign Policy*, p. 73.

15. Sigmund Skard, *American Studies in Europe: Their History and Present Organization*, vol. 2 (Philadelphia: University of Pennsylvania Press, 1958), p. 503, Tent, *The Free University of Berlin*, pp. 60, 89; Tent, *Mission on the Rhine*, pp. 240–41, 314–15.

16. Tent, *The Free University of Berlin*, pp. 68–69; 84–85; Skard, *American Studies in Europe*, vol. 2, pp. 588–89.

17. Tent, *Mission on the Rhine*, pp. 288, 290; Tent, *The Free University of Berlin*, pp. 41, 43, 64, 66, 85–86, 88, 90–91, 125–27, 131, 174.

18. For the American interest in and contributions to the creation of the Free University, see Skard, *American Studies in Europe*, vol. 1, p. 332; Tent, *The Free University of Berlin*, pp. 54, 74, 76, 78, 90, 93–94, 100–101, 147, 157, 173; and Tent, *Mission on the Rhine*, p. 317.

19. Tent, *The Free University of Berlin*, pp. 2, 93, 161–63, 166.

20. Ibid., pp. 96, 104, 174–75; Tent, *Mission on the Rhine*, p. 299.

21. Tent, *The Free University of Berlin*, pp. 98, 141, 209, 212, 227, 231, 267, 274; Francis Sutton, "The Ford Foundation: The Early Years," *Daedalus* 116 (Winter 1987), p. 69. One of the key intermediaries between the U.S. government and the Ford Foundation was Shepard Stone. A former *New York Times* reporter and editor, and a specialist on German affairs, Stone was director of public affairs under John J. McCloy, the U.S. High Commissioner for Germany in the early 1950s, before he became head of the Ford Foundation's International Affairs Program. In his dual role as government official and foundation executive, Stone urged support for the Free University, describing it to his superiors as a bastion of democracy and anti-Communism in a politically suspect Europe. His arguments were extremely effective in obtaining funds for the university. Years later, as director of the Aspen Institute in West Berlin, Stone would lament the radicalization of the Free University during the late 1960s and early 1970s. For Stone's background and activities, see Peter Coleman, *The Liberal Conspiracy: The Congress for Cultural Freedom and the Struggle for the Mind of Postwar Europe* (New York: Free Press, 1989), p. 233; and Tent, *The Free University of Berlin*, pp. 209, 228–29.

22. Thompson and Laves, *Cultural Relations and U.S. Foreign Policy*, p. 205; Kellerman, *Cultural Relations as an Instrument of U.S. Foreign Policy*, pp. 75, 153–54.

23. See Tent, *Mission on the Rhine*, pp. 167, 251, 253; and Kellerman, *Cultural Relations as an Instrument of U.S. Foreign Policy*, pp. 35–36, 77.

24. Hans Tuch, *Communicating with the World: U.S. Public Diplomacy Overseas* (New York: St. Martin's Press, 1990), pp. 23, 65; Willett, *The Americanization of Germany*, pp. 20–21; Skard, *American Studies in Europe,* vol. 1, p. 331;Thompson and Laves, *Cultural Relations and U.S. Foreign Policy*, p. 122; Kellerman, *Cultural Relations as an Instrument of U.S. Foreign Policy*, p. 127. In the early 1950s, there were also twelve America Houses in Austria, engaged in the same sorts of activities as their counterparts in West Germany. See Reinhold Wagnleitner, "Propagating the American Dream: Cultural Policies as Means of Integration," *American Studies International* 24 (April 1986), p. 67; Wagnleitner, "The Irony of American Culture Abroad," p. 289; and Wagnleitner, *Coca-Colonization and the Cold War*, pp. 129–35, 198, 276. *Porgy and Bess* was a hit not only in Germany and Austria, but throughout Western Europe.

25. Jeremy Tunstall, *The Media Are American* (New York: Columbia University Press, 1977), p. 154; Kellerman, *Cultural Relations as an Instrument of U.S. Foreign Policy*, p. 58; Willett, *The Americanization of Germany*, pp. 12, 81, 85.

26. Thompson and Laves, *Cultural Relations and U.S. Foreign Policy*, p. 75; Tent, *Mission on the Rhine*, p. 284; Kellerman, *Cultural Relations as an Instrument of U.S. Foreign Policy*, pp. 27, 98–99, 103, 107, 109, 159, 211, 236–37, 240–41.

27. For an extended discussion of the results of the State Department's surveys of West German visitors to the United States in the 1950s, see Kellerman, *Cultural Relations as an Instrument of U.S. Foreign Policy*, pp. 215, 218, 220, 235. For more general descriptions of the West German response to America, see Maase, "'Halbstarke' and Hegemony," p. 158; Tyler Marshall, "American Culture Is Europe's Common Bond," *Austin American-Statesman* (June 5, 1994), p. C5; and Tuch, *Communicating with the World*, p. 152.

28. On the reactions of West German students to America, see Kellerman, *Cultural Relations as an Instrument of U.S. Foreign Policy*, p. 214.

29. For an analysis of George Marshall's address, see Frank Costigliola, *France and the United States: The Cold Alliance Since World War II* (New York: Twayne, 1992), p. 61; and David Ellwood, *Rebuilding Europe: Western Europe, America and Postwar Reconstruction* (London: Longman, 1992), pp. 85–86.

30. Michael Hogan, *The Marshall Plan: America, Britain, and the Reconstruction of Western Europe, 1947–1952* (New York: Cambridge University Press, 1989, c. 1987), pp. 103, 414.

31. Ibid., 89; Costigliola, *France and the United States*, p. 45; David Ellwood, "From 'Re-Education' to the Selling of the Marshall Plan in Italy," in Nicholas Pronay and Keith Wilson, eds., *The Political Re-Education of Germany and Her Allies After World War II* (Totowa, N.J.: Barnes & Noble Books, 1985), p. 227; Serge Guilbaut, *How New York Stole the Idea of Modern Art: Abstract Expressionism, Freedom, and the Cold War*, trans. Arthur Goldhammer (Chicago: University of Chicago Press, 1984, c. 1983), pp. 144–45.

32. For descriptions of America's efforts to influence postwar politics in

Western Europe, see Cor de Feyter, "The Selling of an Ideology; The Long Term Economic Expectations of the Marshall Aid and Their Impact in the Netherlands," in Rob Kroes, ed., *Image and Impact: American Influences in the Netherlands Since 1945* (Amsterdam: Amerika Instituut, 1981), p. 58; Richard Kuisel, *Seducing the French: The Dilemma of Americanization* (Berkeley: University of California Press, 1993), p. 21; David Ellwood, "The Impact of the Marshall Plan on Italy; The Impact of Italy on the Marshall Plan," in Kroes et al., eds., *Cultural Transmissions and Receptions*, p. 103; Ellwood, "From 'Re-Education' to the Selling of the Marshall Plan in Italy," pp. 219, 225; Frances Pohl, *Ben Shahn: New Deal Artist in a Cold War Climate, 1947–1954* (Austin: University of Texas Press, 1989), p. 151; Costigliola, *France and the United States*, pp. 65–66, 78; and Visson, *As Others See Us*, p. 128.

33. Thompson and Laves, *Cultural Relations and U.S. Foreign Policy*, p. 91; Guilbaut, *How New York Stole the Idea of Modern Art*, p. 136; Rob Kroes, "The Nearness of America," in Kroes, ed., *Image and Impact*, p. 9; Costigliola, *France and the United States*, p. 45; Ellwood, "From 'Re-Education' to the Selling of the Marshall Plan in Italy," pp. 228–33; Ellwood, "The Impact of the Marshall Plan on Italy," pp. 100, 106–7; David Ellwood, "Introduction: Historical Methods and Approaches," in Ellwood and Kroes, eds., *Hollywood in Europe: Experiences of a Cultural Hegemony* (Amsterdam: VU University Press, 1994), pp. 7–8; Hogan, *The Marshall Plan*, p. 89.

34. Kuisel, *Seducing the French*, p. 71; Amaury de Riencourt, *The Coming Caesars* (New York: Coward-McCann, 1957), p. 322; Thompson and Laves, *Cultural Relations and U.S. Foreign Policy*, p. 92; Kroes, "The Nearness of America," p. 11. The quotation is from Michel Crozier, *The Trouble with America*, trans. Peter Heineggn (Berkeley: University of California Press, 1984), p. 24.

35. For a discussion of the French "technical missions," see Kuisel, *Seducing the French*, pp. 70–72, 81, 91–93, 95; and Arnold Rose, "Anti-Americanism in France," *Antioch Review* 12 (December 1952), p. 481.

36. Luigi Barzini, *Americans Are Alone in the World* (New York: Random House, 1953), pp. 109, 173; Visson, *As Others See Us*, pp. 20, 124, 128. See also Costigliola, *France and the United States*, p. 43. Barzini, a longtime resident of the United States, was widely admired and read by Americans because they believed he understood and sympathized with their national mood.

37. For descriptions of how the Europeans felt about the Marshall Plan, see Barzini, *Americans Are Alone in the World*, p. 109; Visson, *As Others See Us*, pp. 12, 131, 231; Guido Piovene, "Ungrateful Europe," and Raymond Aron, "The United States as the Dominant Economy," in James Burnham, ed., *What Europe Thinks of America* (New York: John Day, 1953), pp. 119, 121, 192–93; Rose, "Anti-Americanism in France," p. 480; Kuisel, *Seducing the French*, pp. 31, 76; Ellwood, "From 'Re-Education' to the Selling of the Marshall Plan in Italy," pp. 234–35; and "Questions of Cultural Exchange: The NIAS Statement on the European Reception of American Mass Culture," in Kroes et al., eds., *Cultural Transmissions and Receptions*, p. 328.

38. Visson, *As Others See Us*, pp. 125, 128; Barzini, *Americans Are Alone in the World*, p. 131; Julian Amery, "The American Choice," in Burnham, ed., *What Europe Thinks of America*, p. 138.

39. See Hogan, *The Marshall Plan*, pp. 443–44; and de Feyter, "The Selling of an Ideology," pp. 59–60.

40. Aron, "The United States as the Dominant Economy," p. 197.

41. Gary Kraske, *Missionaries of the Book: The American Library Association and the Origins of United States Cultural Diplomacy* (Westport, Conn.: Greenwood Press, 1985), p. 231; Robert Summers, "Psychological Warfare: American Background," in Summers, ed., *America's Weapons of Psychological Warfare* (New York: Wilson, 1951), p. 12; Thompson and Laves, *Cultural Relations and U.S. Foreign Policy*, p. 63.

42. See Frank Ninkovich, *The Diplomacy of Ideas: U.S. Foreign Policy and Cultural Relations, 1938–1950* (New York: Cambridge University Press, 1981), pp. 110, 140, 145.

43. For Senator Fulbright's own descriptions of what he intended, and for examples of the wording contained in the various laws from 1946 to 1961 that authorized and justified the programs, see J. William Fulbright, "Foreword," in Walter Johnson and Francis Colligan, *The Fulbright Program: A History* (Chicago: University of Chicago Press, 1965), p. viii; Dudden and Dynes, "Introduction," in Dudden and Dynes, eds., *The Fulbright Experience, 1946–1986: Encounters and Transformations* (New Brunswick, N.J.: Transaction Books, 1987), p. 1; Sussman, *The Culture of Freedom*, p. 23; and Beverly Watkins, "Scholars Push for Revitalization of the Fulbright Program," *Chronicle of Higher Education* 34 (April 14, 1993), p. A42.

44. For details on the official roles and responsibilities of the agencies administering the Fulbright program, see Sussman, *The Culture of Freedom*, pp. 2, 20, 43; Thompson and Laves, *Cultural Relations and U.S. Foreign Policy*, pp. 60–61, 68; Philip Coombs, *The Fourth Dimension of Foreign Policy: Educational and Cultural Affairs* (New York: Harper & Row, 1964), p. 30; Dudden and Dynes, "Introduction," pp. 3, 5; and Watkins, "Scholars Push for Revitalization of the Fulbright Program," p. A42.

45. Robert Spiller, "The Fulbright Program in American Studies Abroad: Retrospect and Prospect," in Robert Walker, ed., *American Studies Abroad* (Westport, Conn.: Greenwood Press, 1975), p. 5; Johnson and Colligan, *The Fulbright Program*, pp. 23, 114–16; Tuch, *Communicating with the World*, p. 76. The binational commissions in each country were normally chaired by the public affairs officer or the cultural attaché but sometimes by the deputy chief of mission. The funding for the Fulbright program remained heavily American until the 1960s, when certain countries whose economies had recovered from the war began to share more equally in the financial arrangements. Bonn agreed to underwrite 50 percent of the Fulbright program's budget in West Germany in 1962; by the 1970s and 1980s, it was paying for two-thirds to 80 percent of the costs. In 1963, the Austrian government also

started to assume two-thirds of the costs of the program. See Kellerman, *Cultural Relations as an Instrument of U.S. Foreign Policy*, pp. 176, 254; and Wagnleitner, *Coca-Colonization and the Cold War*, p. 157.

46. On the initial Fulbright agreements and their orientation toward Western Europe, see Watkins, "Scholars Push for Revitalization of the Fulbright Program," p. A42; Richard Arndt and David Rubin, "The Forties: Creating the Myth" and "The Fifties: Growing and Flowering," in Arndt and Rubin, eds., *The Fulbright Difference, 1948–1992* (New Brunswick, N.J.: Transaction Books, 1993), pp. 13, 53; Dudden and Dynes, "Introduction," p. 3; Sussman, *The Culture of Freedom*, p. 20; and Johnson and Colligan, *The Fulbright Program*, pp. 25, 111, 209, 242, 250, 318. The program in China ended abruptly when the Communists seized power in 1949. Between 1948 and 1958, 22,000 Europeans came to the United States under the auspices of the Fulbright program, and nearly 10,000 Americans went to Europe. See Wagnleitner, *Coca-Colonization and the Cold War*, p. 157.

47. For summaries of the congressional trips and quotations from the various reports the representatives and senators wrote on their return to the United States, see Ninkovich, *The Diplomacy of Ideas*, pp. 131–32; Thompson and Laves, *Cultural Relations and U.S. Foreign Policy*, p. 66; Edward Barrett, *Truth Is Our Weapon* (New York: Funk & Wagnalls, 1953), p. 61; Coombs, *The Fourth Dimension of Foreign Policy*, p. 31; Kraske, *Missionaries of the Book*, pp. 230–31; and Guilbaut, *How New York Stole the Idea of Modern Art*, p. 193.

48. The official title of Smith-Mundt was the United States Information and Educational Exchange Act of 1948, cosponsored by two conservative Republicans: Senator H. Alexander Smith of New Jersey and Representative Karl Mundt of North Dakota. On the purposes of the legislation, see Lois Roth, "Public Diplomacy and the Past: The Search for an American Style of Propaganda, 1952–1977," *Fletcher Forum* 8 (Summer 1984), p. 356; Thompson and Laves, *Cultural Relations and U.S. Foreign Policy*, pp. 64, 67, 70–71; Ninkovich, *The Diplomacy of Ideas*, pp. 128–29, 133; Holly Shulman, *The Voice of America: Propaganda and Democracy, 1941–1945* (Madison: University of Wisconsin Press, 1990), p. 189; Kraske, *Missionaries of the Book*, p. 232; Tuch, *Communicating with the World*, p. 17; John Henderson, *The United States Information Agency* (New York: Praeger, 1969), pp. 40, 64–65; and Visson, *As Others See Us*, p. 119.

49. The quotations are from Tiziano Bonazzi, "The Beginnings of American History in Italy," and Harvey Feigenbaum, "Exchanges and Excursions in France," in Arndt and Rubin, eds., *The Fulbright Difference*, pp. 152, 361.

50. See Johnson and Colligan, *The Fulbright Program*, pp. 9, 27, 206, 241, 249, 254. Senator Fulbright's admission that his program had political implications can be found in Sussman, *The Culture of Freedom*, p. 57; the British comment is from Rhodri Jeffreys-Jones, "The Teaching of United States History in British Institutions of Higher Learning," in Lewis Hanke, ed.,

Guide to the Study of United States History Outside the U.S., 1945–1980, vol. 2 (White Plains, N.Y.: Kraus International Publications, 1985), p. 329.

51. Officially called the Mutual Educational and Cultural Exchange Act of 1961, Fulbright-Hays consolidated all the American government's cultural activities under one law. It sanctioned new exchanges and strengthened the legal basis for those that already existed. In addition, it authorized the translation of American books and periodicals, the operation of cultural centers attached to U.S. embassies, American participation in international festivals and exhibitions, the government's financing and sponsorship of international scholarly conferences, and support for American Studies programs abroad. See Coombs, *The Fourth Dimension of Foreign Policy*, p. 50; Roth, "Public Diplomacy and the Past," p. 370; Tuch, *Communicating with the World*, p. 28; and Johnson and Colligan, *The Fulbright Program*, p. 312.

CHAPTER THREE
TRUTH, PROPAGANDA, AND CULTURAL COMBAT: THE CONTEST WITH THE SOVIET UNION

1. On the success of the Stockholm appeal in France, see Richard Kuisel, *Seducing the French: The Dilemma of Americanization* (Berkeley: University of California Press, 1993), p. 38.

2. The quotations from Truman's speech are reproduced in Robert Summers, ed., *America's Weapons of Psychological Warfare* (New York: Wilson, 1951), pp. 28–29, 31, 156. Edward Barrett, who had been in the Office of War Information during the war, returned to the government from *Newsweek* in 1950 to serve as assistant secretary of state for public affairs. He suggested that Truman call for a "campaign of truth" and directed its operations until 1952. For his ideas about what the campaign meant, see Edward Barrett, *Truth Is Our Weapon* (New York: Funk & Wagnalls, 1953), pp. ix–x, 72–73.

3. Holly Shulman, *The Voice of America: Propaganda and Democracy, 1941–1945* (Madison: University of Wisconsin Press, 1990), p. 189; Barrett, *Truth Is Our Weapon*, pp. 79, 92–93, 214; Kuisel, *Seducing the French*, p. 25; Frank Costigliola, *France and the United States: The Cold Alliance Since World War II* (New York: Twayne, 1992), p. 88; Charles Thompson and Walter Laves, *Cultural Relations and U.S. Foreign Policy* (Bloomington: Indiana University Press, 1963), pp. 81, 84–85, 204; Philip Coombs, *The Fourth Dimension of Foreign Policy: Educational and Cultural Affairs* (New York: Harper & Row, 1964), p. 33; Hans Tuch, *Communicating with the World: U.S. Public Diplomacy Overseas* (New York: St. Martin's Press, 1990), p. 22; Thomas Sorensen, *The Word War: The Story of American Propaganda* (New York: Harper & Row, 1968), p. 43.

4. Frank Ninkovich, *The Diplomacy of Ideas: U.S. Foreign Policy and Cultural Relations, 1938–1950* (New York: Cambridge University Press, 1981),

p. 167; Thompson and Laves, *Cultural Relations and U.S. Foreign Policy*, pp. 82, 87; Costigliola, *France and the United States*, p. 87. For the language and intentions of the Board of Foreign Scholarship's statement in 1951, see Walter Johnson and Francis Colligan, *The Fulbright Program: A History* (Chicago: University of Chicago Press, 1965), pp. 69, 71, 73.

5. Bertrand Russell, "The Political and Cultural Influence," in Russell et al., *The Impact of America on European Culture* (Boston: Beacon Press, 1951), p. 18; Denis de Rougemont, "Minds and Morals: The Conquest of Anarchy," in Lewis Galantière, ed., *America and the Mind of Europe* (London: Hamilton, 1951), pp. 30–31; Malcolm Bradbury, "How I Invented America," *Journal of American Studies* 14 (April 1980), p. 118; Wyndham Lewis, *America and Cosmic Man* (London: Nicholson & Watson, 1948), p. 14.

6. See Edward Chester, *Europe Views America: A Critical Evaluation* (Washington, D.C.: Public Affairs Press, 1962), p. 75; and André Visson, *As Others See Us* (Garden City, N.Y.: Doubleday, 1948), pp. 115–16.

7. For analyses of French neutralism in the 1950s, see Jean-Philippe Mathy, *Extrême Occident: French Intellectuals and America* (Chicago: University of Chicago Press, 1993), p. 138; Denis Lacorne and Jacques Rupnik, "Introduction: France Bewitched by America," Michael Harrison, "French Anti-Americanism Under the Fourth Republic and the Gaullist Solution," and Marie-France Toinet, "Does Anti-Americanism Exist?" in Lacorne, Rupnik, and Toinet, eds., *The Rise and Fall of Anti-Americanism: A Century of French Perception*, trans. Gerry Turner (New York: St. Martin's Press, 1990, c. Paris 1986), pp. 14–15, 172–73, 224; Tony Judt, *Past Imperfect: French Intellectuals, 1944–1956* (Berkeley: University of California Press, 1992), p. 256; and Costigliola, *France and the United States*, pp. 42, 50.

8. Kuisel, *Seducing the French*, p. 32; Costigliola, *France and the United States*, p. 83; Judt, *Past Imperfect*, p. 259.

9. Barrett, *Truth Is Our Weapon*, pp. 193–94, 196.

10. Lewis Galantière, "Introduction," in Galantière ed., *America and the Mind of Europe*, p. 15. See also Frances Pohl, *Ben Shahn: New Deal Artist in a Cold War Climate, 1947–1954* (Austin: University of Texas Press, 1989), pp. 138–40.

11. Raymond Aron, "Transatlantic Relations: Does Europe Welcome American Leadership?" in Galantière, ed., *America and the Mind of Europe*, pp. 21–22; Russell, "The Political and Cultural Influence," p. 19. Russell vehemently rejected this position in the 1960s, emerging as one of America's most outspoken European critics during the Vietnam War.

12. On the Communist "peace" conferences and the response of American intellectuals and government officials, see S. A. Longstaff, "The New York Intellectuals and the Cultural Cold War: 1945–1950," *New Politics* 2 (Winter 1989), pp. 159–60, 164; Peter Coleman, *The Liberal Conspiracy: The Congress for Cultural Freedom and the Struggle for the Mind of Postwar Europe* (New York: Free Press, 1989), p. 5; William Phillips, *A Partisan View: Five Decades of the Literary Life* (New York: Stein & Day, 1983), pp. 147–48; and

Ninkovich, *The Diplomacy of Ideas*, pp. 163–64. I discussed the reaction of American writers to the Waldorf Conference and the Soviet propaganda offensive at greater length in Richard Pells, *The Liberal Mind in a Conservative Age: American Intellectuals in the 1940s and 1950s* (New York: Harper & Row, 1985), pp. 121–28.

13. For the background and intentions of those who attended or supported the first meeting of the Congress for Cultural Freedom, see Coleman, *The Liberal Conspiracy*, pp. 10–12, 20–22, 27, 31, 48; Longstaff, "The New York Intellectuals and the Cultural Cold War," p. 166; Christopher Lasch, "The Cultural Cold War: A Short History of the Congress for Cultural Freedom," in Lasch, *The Agony of the American Left* (New York: Knopf, 1969), p. 64; and Costigliola, *France and the United States*, p. 88. In 1951, an American branch of the congress was established, filled with equally luminous names. But the American Committee for Cultural Freedom suffered from internal conflicts and periodic defections over issues like McCarthyism, the investigation of J. Robert Oppenheimer as a national security risk, and the course of the Cold War. It had fallen apart by 1957 and finally disbanded in 1963. I analyzed both the congress and the American committee in *The Liberal Mind in a Conservative Age*, pp. 128–30, 340–41, 344.

14. On the careers and personalities of Melvin Lasky and Michael Josselson, see Coleman, *The Liberal Conspiracy*, pp. 15–16, 19, 40–41; Longstaff, "The New York Intellectuals and the Cultural Cold War," p. 165; and Phillips, *A Partisan View*, pp. 190, 212.

15. Coleman, *The Liberal Conspiracy*, p. 220; Charles Frankel, *High on Foggy Bottom: An Outsider's Inside View of the Government* (New York: Harper & Row, 1969), p. 161; Kathleen McCarthy, "From Cold War to Cultural Development: The International Cultural Activities of the Ford Foundation, 1950–1980," *Daedalus* 116 (Winter 1987), pp. 99, 105.

16. Thomas Braden, "I'm Glad the CIA Is 'Immoral,' " *Saturday Evening Post* (May 20, 1967), pp. 10, 14. See also Coleman, *The Liberal Conspiracy*, pp. 47–48, 220, 228; Longstaff, "The New York Intellectuals and the Cultural Cold War," p. 168; Lasch, "The Cultural Cold War," p. 99; Eva Cockcroft, "Abstract Expressionism, Weapon of the Cold War," in Francis Frascina, ed., *Pollock and After: The Critical Debate* (New York: Harper & Row, 1985), pp. 128, 132; Phillips, *A Partisan View*, p. 152; and Ninkovich, *The Diplomacy of Ideas*, p. 177.

17. Coleman, *The Liberal Conspiracy*, pp. 9, 140.

18. On the congress's Paris festival, see Kuisel, *Seducing the French*, p. 28; Costigliola, *France and the United States*, p. 89; Cockcroft, "Abstract Expressionism," p. 128; and Coleman, *The Liberal Conspiracy*, p. 56.

19. Coleman, *The Liberal Conspiracy*, pp. 60–61, 65, 77; Lasch, "The Cultural Cold War," p. 106.

20. Coleman, *The Liberal Conspiracy*, pp. 53–54, 83, 88–91, 134; Kuisel, *Seducing the French*, pp. 46–47; Phillips, *A Partisan View*, p. 158; Reinhold Wagnleitner, *Coca-Colonization and the Cold War: The Cultural Mission of the*

United States in Austria After the Second World War, trans. Diana Wolf (Chapel Hill: University of North Carolina Press, 1994), p. 190.

21. For a discussion of the congress in the 1960s and the attempts to keep some version of it alive in the 1970s, see Coleman, *The Liberal Conspiracy*, pp. xi, 10, 171–72, 174, 183, 212–14, 225–26, 236, 240, 244–45; Phillips, *A Partisan View*, p. 162; and McCarthy, "From Cold War to Cultural Development," p. 105. In response to the worldwide commotion about the congress's hidden financial arrangements with the CIA, the Johnson administration decided in 1967 to end all covert support for America's overseas cultural activities.

22. For a description of painting in the 1930s and the ways abstract expressionism differed, see Jane Matthews, "Art and Politics in Cold War America," *American Historical Review* 81 (October 1976), p. 782; and Serge Guilbaut, *How New York Stole the Idea of Modern Art: Abstract Expressionism, Freedom, and the Cold War*, trans. Arthur Goldhammer (Chicago: University of Chicago Press, 1984, c. 1983), pp. 46–47, 68, 70.

23. One of the problems with Guilbaut's accusation that New York "stole" the idea of modern art from Paris is its tendency to minimize the role of the European expatriates—artists, dealers, and gallery owners—in teaching their American counterparts and promoting abstract expressionism. For a higher estimation of the expatriates' significance, see William Jordy, "The Aftermath of the Bauhaus in America: Gropius, Mies, and Breuer," and Colin Eisler, "*Kunstgeschichte* American Style: A Study in Migration," in Donald Fleming and Bernard Bailyn, eds., *The Intellectual Migration: Europe and America, 1930–1960* (Cambridge, Mass.: Charles Warren Center for Studies in American History, 1968), pp. 486, 597–99, 602; Matthews, "Art and Politics in Cold War America," p. 774; and William Drozdiak, "Hitler's Artistic Gift to the United States," *Washington Post National Weekly Edition* (September 11–17, 1989), p. 25. Hans Hofmann, for example, gave a series of lectures in New York on modernist painting in 1938 and 1939. Among those who attended the lectures were Willem de Kooning, Jackson Pollock, Arshile Gorky, Clement Greenberg, and Harold Rosenberg. See Jarrell Jackman, "Introduction," in Jackman and Carla Borden, eds., *The Muses Flee Hitler: Cultural Transfer and Adaptation, 1930–1945* (Washington, D.C.: Smithsonian Institution Press, 1983), pp. 21–22. Peggy Guggenheim's Art of This Century gallery, which opened in 1942, was especially important in bringing together the ideas and works of Europeans and Americans. The gallery served as a meeting place and an exhibition space for the new transatlantic (albeit increasingly American) art. Guilbaut does emphasize the role of this gallery, as well as the centrality of the New York art market in converting abstract expressionism into a consumer item for the affluent. See *How New York Stole the Idea of Modern Art*, pp. 65, 67, 76, 91–92, 95.

24. Guilbaut, *How New York Stole the Idea of Modern Art*, pp. 1, 5, 98, 115, 168, 172, 194; Costigliola, *France and the United States*, p. 75; Deborah Solomon, "The Cologne Challenge: Is New York's Art Monopoly Kaput?"

New York Times Magazine (September 6, 1992), p. 30; Tom Wolfe, *The Painted Word* (New York: Bantam Books, 1976, c. 1975), p. 52. Clement Greenberg reprinted his analyses of modern artists in *Art and Culture: Critical Essays* (Boston: Beacon Press, 1965, c. 1961), pp. 37–171, 189–231.

25. A number of historians have made much of the connection between the techniques and temperaments of the abstract expressionists and the "ideology" of the Cold War, as if the painters themselves were either co-opted by or were active collaborators in America's contest with the Soviet Union. For examples, see Cockcroft, "Abstract Expressionism," p. 129; Guilbaut, *How New York Stole the Idea of Modern Art*, pp. 85, 143, 193, 200–201, 205; Matthews, "Art and Politics in Cold War America," p. 780; and Thomas Bender, *New York Intellect: A History of Intellectual Life in New York City, from 1750 to the Beginnings of Our Own Time* (New York: Knopf, 1987), pp. 345–46. But given the hostility to modernism on the part of some in the U.S. Congress (and, on occasion, President Truman), this argument is suggestive but ultimately unconvincing.

26. Matthews, "Art and Politics in Cold War America," p. 763, 774, 783–85.

27. Ibid., pp. 762–63, 772, 775–76; Pohl, *Ben Shahn*, pp. 37, 73.

28. For the specific effects of McCarthyism on the government's use of modern art, see Emily Rosenberg, *Spreading the American Dream: American Economic and Cultural Expansion, 1890–1945* (New York: Hill & Wang, 1982), p. 216; John Henderson, *The United States Information Agency* (New York: Praeger, 1969), pp. 234–35; Gary Kraske, *Missionaries of the Book: The American Library Association and the Origins of United States Cultural Diplomacy* (Westport, Conn.: Greenwood Press, 1985), pp. 229; Matthews, "Art and Politics in Cold War America," pp. 771, 777–79; Cockcroft, "Abstract Expressionism," p. 130; Thompson and Laves, *Cultural Relations and U.S. Foreign Policy*, p. 122; and Barbara Gamarekian, "The Art of Putting America's Culture on Its Embassy Walls," *New York Times* (February 19, 1990), p. B4.

29. On the role of the Museum of Modern Art, see Pohl, *Ben Shahn*, pp. 134, 140–41, 152–53; and Cockcroft, "Abstract Expressionism," pp. 129, 131. The Ford Foundation played a smaller role. Beginning in 1953, it subsidized for three years the publication of *Perspectives, U.S.A.*, a magazine devoted to American fiction, poetry, literary criticism, philosophy, and the arts. The magazine's aim was to persuade European intellectuals that the United States had a high culture that deserved their respect. See Pohl, *Ben Shahn*, pp. 144–45; and Bradbury, "How I Invented America," pp. 126–27.

30. Barrett, *Truth Is Our Weapon*, p. 101. See also Sorensen, *The Word War*, p. 33.

31. Thompson and Laves, *Cultural Relations and U.S. Foreign Policy*, p. 100; Kraske, *Missionaries of the Book*, pp. 248–49; Pohl, *Ben Shahn*, p. 138.

32. Kraske, *Missionaries of the Book*, p. 249; Sorensen, *The Word War*, p. 35; Reinhold Wagnleitner, "The Irony of American Culture Abroad: Austria

and the Cold War" in Lary May, ed., *Recasting America: Culture and Politics in the Age of the Cold War*, (Chicago: University of Chicago Press, 1989), p. 290; Pohl, *Ben Shahn*, p. 149.

33. For the language of the State Department directives, see Henderson, *The United States Information Agency*, pp. 236–37. See also Thompson and Laves, *Cultural Relations and U.S. Foreign Policy*, p. 102; and Wagnleitner, *Coca-Colonization and the Cold War*, pp. 136–37.

34. For the numbers and names of the banned authors and artists, see Kraske, *Missionaries of the Book*, p. 250; and Wagnleitner, *Coca-Colonization and the Cold War*, pp. 137–38.

35. For the language of the modified State Department policy, see Thompson and Laves, *Cultural Relations and U.S. Foreign Policy*, pp. 103–4. See also Kraske, *Missionaries of the Book*, pp. 250, 263.

36. On the criticisms of the "campaign of truth," see Thompson and Laves, *Cultural Relations and U.S. Foreign Policy*, p. 96; and Kraske, *Missionaries of the Book*, p. 251.

37. J. M. Mitchell, *International Cultural Relations* (London: Allen & Unwin, 1986), pp. 16, 19, 60, 168; Allen Hansen, *USIA: Public Diplomacy in the Computer Age* (New York: Praeger, 1984), pp. 161, 164, 167; Coombs, *The Fourth Dimension of Foreign Policy*, pp. 80, 82, 85; Leonard Sussman, *The Culture of Freedom: The Small World of Fulbright Scholars* (Savage, Md.: Rowman & Littlefield, 1992), p. 16; Peter Duignan and L. H. Gann, *The Rebirth of the West: The Americanization of the Democratic World, 1945–1958* (Cambridge, Mass.: Blackwell, 1992), pp. 422–25.

38. For the precise language of President Eisenhower's statement on USIA's mission, see Lois Roth, "Public Diplomacy and the Past: The Search for an American Style of Propaganda, 1952–1977," *Fletcher Forum* 8 (Summer 1984), p. 383. See also Thompson and Laves, *Cultural Relations and U.S. Foreign Policy*, pp. 98, 106–7; Sorensen, *The Word War*, pp. 46, 50, 71–72; and Coombs, *The Fourth Dimension of Foreign Policy*, p. 33. In 1978, all the State Department's remaining cultural activities were transferred to USIA.

39. Thompson and Laves, *Cultural Relations and U.S. Foreign Policy*, pp. 123–25; Tuch, *Communicating with the World*, pp., 81–82.

40. Wagnleitner, *Coca-Colonization and the Cold War*, pp. xi, 199–200, 210–13. See also Thompson and Laves, *Cultural Relations and U.S. Foreign Policy*, p. 123.

41. Thompson and Laves, *Cultural Relations and U.S. Foreign Policy*, p. 127; Sorensen, *The Word War*, p. 87; Tuch, *Communicating with the World*, pp. 127, 134.

42. At the time of the "kitchen debate," Hans Tuch was USIA's cultural and press attaché in Moscow. For his description of the exhibit and his memories of escorting Khrushchev through the displays, see *Communicating with the World*, pp. 62–64. See also Sorensen, *The Word War*, p. 110.

43. For the results of the 1960 poll, see Chester, *Europe Views America*, pp. 159–61; and Sorensen, *The Word War*, p. 179.

44. Sorensen, *The Word War*, pp. 82–83; Henderson, *The United States Information Agency*, p. 55.

45. On Murrow's importance to USIA, see Sorensen, *The Word War*, pp. 123–24, 134, 219; and A. M. Sperber, *Murrow: His Life and Times* (New York: Bantam Books, 1987, c. 1986), p. 632.

46. Sperber, *Murrow*, pp. 614, 620, 624, 635–36; Henderson, *The United States Information Agency*, p. 86; Sorensen, *The Word War*, pp. 126–27, 129, 142; Tuch, *Communicating with the World*, p. 26. In 1963, President Kennedy incorporated these promises to Murrow in a mandate outlining USIA's responsibilities. For the language of the mandate, see Roth, "Public Diplomacy and the Past," p. 385.

47. On Murrow's lack of knowledge about the impending Bay of Pigs operation, see Sorensen, *The Word War*, pp. 139–40.

48. Ibid., pp. 130 32, 250, **255**; Shulman, *The Voice of America*, p. 191; Sperber, *Murrow*, pp. 624, 676–78.

49. These passages are quoted in Sorensen, *The Word War*, p. 145.

50. Tuch, *Communicating with the World*, pp. 88, 90–91; Mitchell, *International Cultural Relations*, pp. 219, 222; Hansen, *USIA*, p. 165.

51. For Murrow's contradictory attitudes toward and John Chancellor's uneasy tenure at the Voice of America, see Henderson, *The United States Information Agency*, pp. 164–65, 170, 191; Sorensen, *The Word War*, pp. 231–32, 234, 239, 244, 248; and Sperber, *Murrow*, pp. 634, 643–44, 665.

52. Sorensen, *The Word War*, p. 134; Sperber, *Murrow*, pp. 629, 631.

53. Frankel, *High on Foggy Bottom*, pp. 11, 16. This book was Frankel's memoir of his experiences from 1965 to 1967 as assistant secretary of state for educational and cultural affairs.

54. Ibid., pp. 26, 28, 193.

55. Charles Frankel, *The Neglected Aspect of Foreign Affairs: American Educational and Cultural Policy Abroad* (Washington, D.C.: Brookings Institution, 1966), pp. 100, 104–5.

56. Ibid., pp. 138–40.

57. Ibid., pp. 142–44; Frankel, *High on Foggy Bottom*, pp. 36, 65, 164. See also Sorensen, *The Word War*, p. 74; and Roth, "Public Diplomacy and the Past," p. 372.

58. Frankel, *High on Foggy Bottom*, pp. 127, 130, 198, 205, 221, 228.

CHAPTER FOUR
AMERICAN STUDIES IN EUROPE

1. Harold Laski, *The American Democracy: A Commentary and an Interpretation* (New York: Viking, 1948), pp. ix, 722.

2. Peter von Zahn, "From Germany," in Franz Joseph, ed., *As Others See Us: The United States Through Foreign Eyes* (Princeton, N.J.: Princeton

University Press, 1959), p. 95; Sigmund Skard, *Trans-Atlantica: Memoirs of a Norwegian Americanist* (Oslo: Universitetsforlaget, 1978), pp. 12, 15, 21, 23.

3. For descriptions of the indifference displayed by European academics toward America in the nineteenth and early twentieth centuries, see Sigmund Skard, *American Studies in Europe: Their History and Present Organization*, vols. 1 and 2 (Philadelphia: University of Pennsylvania Press, 1958), pp. 51–52, 60, 65, 153, 253, 366, 370, 404, 406, 423–24, 440–41, 443, 468, 515, 517, 528, 534; Sigmund Skard, "Fulbrighters in Norway," in Arthur Dudden and Russell Dynes, eds., *The Fulbright Experience, 1946–1986: Encounters and Transformations* (New Brunswick, N.J.: Transaction Books, 1987), p. 245; Siegfried Beer, "The Development of Teaching and Research on United States History in Austria," in Lewis Hanke, ed., *Guide to the Study of United States History Outside the U.S., 1945–1980*, vol. 1 (White Plains, N.Y.: Kraus International Publications, 1985), p. 178; Inga Floto, "The Development of United States History in Denmark," and Rhodri Jeffreys-Jones, "The Teaching of United States History in British Institutions of Higher Learning," in Lewis Hanke, ed., *Guide to the Study of United States History Outside the U.S., 1945–1980*, vol. 2 (White Plains, N.Y.: Kraus International Publications, 1985), pp. 14, 309; Herbert Nicholas, "The Education of an Americanist," *Journal of American Studies* 14 (April 1980), p. 14; Rob Kroes, "Among the Receivers: American Culture Transmitted Abroad," in Kroes, ed., *Within the U.S. Orbit: Small National Cultures vis-à-vis the United States* (Amsterdam: VU University Press, 1991), p. 4; Tiziano Bonazzi, "American History: The View from Italy," *Reviews in American History* 14 (December 1986), p. 523; and Elzbieta Foeller-Pituch, "Catching Up: The Polish Critical Response to American Literature," and Rolf Lundén, "The Dual Cannon: A Swedish Example," in Huck Gutman, ed., *As Others Read Us: International Perspectives on American Literature* (Amherst: University of Massachusetts Press, 1991), pp. 205, 236.

4. Skard, *American Studies in Europe*, vol. 1, p. 27; A. N. J. den Hollander, "Cultural Diversity and the Mind of the Scholar: Some Thoughts on American and European Thinking," in den Hollander, ed., *Diverging Parallels: A Comparison of American and European Thought and Action*, (Leiden: Brill, 1971), p. 219; Guy Sorman, "United States: Model or Bête Noire?" in Denis Lacorne, Jacques Rupnik, and Marie-France Toinet, eds., *The Rise and Fall of Anti-Americanism: A Century of French Perception*, trans. Gerry Turner (New York: St. Martin's Press, 1990, c. Paris 1986), p. 215; Laski, *The American Democracy*, p. 722.

5. Skard, *American Studies in Europe*, vols. 1 and 2, pp. 29, 136, 215, 518; Maurizio Vaudagna, "The American Historian in Continental Europe: An Italian Perspective," *Journal of American History* 79 (September 1992), p. 535.

6. On Huizinga's complaints about America, see Maarten van Rossem, "Le Defi Europeen," in Rob Kroes, ed., *Image and Impact: American Influences in the Netherlands Since 1945* (Amsterdam: Amerika Instituut, 1981), pp. 22–23.

7. Skard, *Trans-Atlantica*, pp. 28–29; Skard, *American Studies in Europe*, vol. 2, p. 432; Geir Lundestad, "Research Trends and Accomplishments in Norway on United States History," in Lewis Hanke, ed., *Guide to the Study of United States History Outside the U.S., 1945–1980*, vol. 3 (White Plains, N.Y.: Kraus International Publications, 1985), pp. 250, 252.

8. Stanley Williams, "Who Reads an American Book?" *Virginia Quarterly Review*, 28 (Autumn 1952), p. 527; Skard, vol. 1, pp. 157, 163; Jeanine Brun-Rovet, "Teaching and Research on United States History in France," in Hanke, ed., *Guide to the Study of United States History Outside the U.S.*, vol. 2, pp. 172, 174.

9. Skard, *American Studies Abroad*, vol. 1, pp. 235, 260, 280, 283, 290; Skard, *Trans-Atlantica*, p. 139; Wolfgang Helbich, "United States History in the Federal Republic of Germany: Teaching and Research," in Hanke, ed., *Guide to the Study of United States History Outside the U.S.*, vol. 2, p. 43.

10. John Hope Franklin, "A Modest Imperialism: United States History Abroad," and Harry Allen, "United States History in Great Britain and the European Association for American Studies: A Personal Memoir," in Hanke, ed., *Guide to the Study of United States History Outside the U.S.*, vol. 1, pp. 32, 37, 49; Jeffreys-Jones, "The Teaching of United States History in British Institutions of Higher Learning," pp. 311, 313; David Thelen, "Of Audiences, Borderlands, and Comparisons: Toward the Internationalization of American History," *Journal of American History* 79 (September 1992), p. 435.

11. For developments in Britain between the wars, see David Reynolds, "Whitehall, Washington and the Promotion of American Studies in Britain During World War Two," *Journal of American Studies* 16 (August 1982), p. 169; Jeffreys-Jones, "The Teaching of United States History in British Institutions of Higher Learning," p. 311; and Nicholas, "The Education of an Americanist," pp. 9–10, 12.

12. Skard, *American Studies in Europe*, vol. 1, p. 70; Jeffreys-Jones, "The Teaching of United States History in British Institutions of Higher Learning," pp. 314; Nicholas, "The Education of an Americanist," pp. 13–14; Reynolds, "Whitehall, Washington and the Promotion of American Studies in Britain During World War Two," pp. 167–68.

13. Detailed accounts of the promotion of American Studies in wartime Britain can be found in Jeffreys-Jones, "The Teaching of United States History in British Institutions of Higher Learning," pp. 315–16, 320, 333; Reynolds, "Whitehall, Washington and the Promotion of American Studies in Britain During World War Two," pp. 165, 172–76, 183; and Skard, *American Studies in Europe*, vol. 1, p. 73. Alfred Kazin recalled his experiences as a lecturer in "Carrying the Word Abroad," *American Studies International* 26 (April 1988), p. 62, as did J. Frank Dobie in *A Texan in England* (Boston: Little, Brown, 1945).

14. Reynolds, "Whitehall, Washington and the Promotion of American Studies in Britain During World War Two," pp. 184–86.

15. Norman Podhoretz, *Making It* (New York: Bantam Books, 1969, c. 1967), p. 67; italics his.

16. Harry Allen, "American Studies and the Study of America: The Future of American Studies in Europe," *American Studies International* 17 (Spring 1979), pp. 13–14; Michael Heale, "American History: The View from Britain," *Reviews in American History* 14 (December 1986), p. 501; Michael Heale, "Writings in Great Britain on United States History, 1945–1980: Some Reflections on a Liberal Moment," in Hanke, ed., *Guide to the Study of United States History Outside the U.S.*, vol. 2, p. 372; Skard, *American Studies in Europe*, vol. 2, pp. 634, 641.

17. Jeffreys-Jones, "The Teaching of United States History in British Institutions of Higher Learning," p. 317; Heale, "American History: The View from Britain," p. 501; Heale, "Writings in Great Britain on United States History," p. 372; Floto, "The Development of United States History in Denmark," p. 14; Savas Patsalidis, "(Mis)Understanding America's Literary Canon: The Greek Paradigm," and Theo D'haen, "Cutting Loose: American Literary Studies in the Netherlands," in Gutman, ed., *As Others Read Us*, pp. 114, 193.

18. Henry Kellerman, *Cultural Relations as an Instrument of U.S. Foreign Policy* (Washington, D.C.: U.S. Government Printing Office, 1978), p. 180; Skard, *American Studies in Europe*, vol. 1, p. 293; Wolfgang Helbich, "Interview with Maurizio Vaudagna," in Maurizio Vaudagna, ed., "Forum: American Studies in Europe," *Storia Nordamericana* 7 (1990), p. 130; Alfred Kazin, *New York Jew* (New York: Knopf, 1978), pp. 215, 218.

19. Denis Donoghue, *Reading America: Essays on American Literature* (New York: Knopf, 1987), p. 4; Stephen Spender, "We Can Win the Battle for the Mind of Europe," *New York Times Magazine* (April 25, 1948), p. 33; Max Beloff, "The Projection of America Abroad," *American Quarterly* 1 (Spring 1949), pp. 27–28.

20. For descriptions of the role of the U.S. government and the private foundations in promoting American Studies in various European countries during the postwar years, see Thomas Sorensen, *The Word War: The Story of American Propaganda* (New York: Harper & Row, 1968), p. 108; Robert Spiller, "The Fulbright Program in American Studies Abroad: Retrospect and Prospect," and Marcus Cunliffe, "American Studies in Europe," in Robert Walker, ed., *American Studies Abroad* (Westport, Conn.: Greenwood Press, 1975), pp. 5, 47; Robert Spiller, "American Studies Abroad: Culture and Foreign Policy," in Spiller, *Late Harvest: Essays and Addresses in American Literature and Culture* (Westport, Conn.: Greenwood Press, 1981), p. 243; Carl Bode, "Narrowing the Ocean: A Memoir," *American Studies International* 26 (April 1988), p. 39; Kellerman, *Cultural Relations as an Instrument of U.S. Foreign Policy*, p.182; Skard, *American Studies in Europe*, vols. 1 and 2, pp. 169, 413, 490; Skard, *Trans-Atlantica*, pp. 117, 157, 160; Franklin, "A Modest Imperialism," pp. 33–34; Beer, "The Development of Teaching and Research on United States History in Austria," pp. 180–81; Helbich, "United

States History in the Federal Republic of Germany," p. 112; Brun-Rovet, "Teaching and Research on United States History in France," p. 181; Jeffreys-Jones, "The Teaching of United States History in British Institutions of Higher Learning," p. 320; and Walter Johnson and Francis Colligan, *The Fulbright Program: A History* (Chicago: University of Chicago Press, 1965), pp. 122–23, 125, 135.

21. The quotations from Perry Miller in this and the preceding paragraph appeared in his preface to *Errand Into the Wilderness* (New York: Harper & Row, 1964, c. 1956), pp. vii, ix.

22. On the origins of the Salzburg Seminar, see Timothy Ryback, "Encounters at the Schloss," *Harvard Magazine* 90 (November–December 1987), p. 68; Henry Nash Smith, "The Salzburg Seminar," *American Quarterly* 1 (Spring 1949), pp. 30–32, 36; Skard, *American Studies in Europe*, vol. 2, pp. 634–35; F. O. Matthiessen, *From the Heart of Europe* (New York: Oxford University Press, 1948), pp. 10–11; Kazin, *New York Jew*, p. 111; and Kirsten Gallagher, "A Center for Intellectual Exchange," *Chronicle of Higher Education* 40 (January 19, 1994), p. A40.

23. Ryback, "Encounters at the Schloss," p. 70; Johnson and Colligan, *The Fulbright Program*, p. 122; Smith, "The Salzburg Seminar," pp. 32–33; Matthiessen, *From the Heart of Europe*, p. 11; Kazin, *New York Jew*, p. 168.

24. Matthiessen, *From the Heart of Europe*, pp. 6, 14; Kazin, "Carrying the Word Abroad," p. 63; Kazin, *New York Jew*, pp. 170–71; italics Kazin's.

25. See Skard, *American Studies in Europe*, vol. 2, pp. 636–37; Kazin, "Carrying the Word Abroad," p. 64; Ryback, "Encounters at the Schloss," p. 70; and Gallagher, "A Center for Intellectual Exchange," p. A40.

26. For a discussion of the Fulbright program's preference for lecturers over researchers and graduate students, see Johnson and Colligan, *The Fulbright Program*, p. 220; Leonard Sussman, *The Culture of Freedom: The Small World of Fulbright Scholars* (Savage, Md.: Rowman & Littlefield, 1992), p. 99; and Frank Freidel, "The Fulbright Program in American Studies Abroad: A Continuing Challenge," in Walker, ed., *American Studies Abroad*, p. 11.

27. Matthiessen, *From the Heart of Europe*, pp. 1, 107; Kazin, "Carrying the Word Abroad," p. 64; Leslie Fiedler, "Fulbright I: Italy 1952," in Richard Arndt and David Rubin, eds., *The Fulbright Difference, 1948–1992* (New Brunswick, N.J.: Transaction Books, 1993), pp. 88, 91. For information about other guest professors, see Nicholas, "The Education of an Americanist," p. 11; Jeffreys-Jones, "The Teaching of United States History in British Institutions of Higher Learning," p. 305; Perry Miller, "What Drove Me Crazy in Europe," in Miller, *The Responsibility of Mind in a Civilization of Machines* (Amherst: University of Massachusetts Press, 1979), p. 89; Sussman, *The Culture of Freedom*, pp. 68, 71; Brun-Rovet, "Teaching and Research on United States History in France," p. 178; Edmund Wilson, *A Piece of My Mind: Reflections at Sixty* (New York: Farrar, Straus & Cudahy, 1956), p. 53; "Selected American Alumni of the Fulbright Program," *United States Information Agency* (July 1986), p. 2; and J. H. Plumb, "Introduction: 'O My

America, My Newfoundland,' " in Plumb, *The American Experience*, vol. 2 of *The Collected Essays* (Athens: University of Georgia Press, 1989), p. 9.

28. Skard, *American Studies in Europe*, vol. 2, p. 650; John Garraty and Walter Adams, *From Main Street to the Left Bank: Students and Scholars Abroad* (East Lansing: Michigan State University Press, 1959), p. 155; James Lacey, "Institutional Structures and American Studies at Universities in the Federal Republic of Germany," in Richard Horwitz, ed., *Exporting America: Essays on American Studies Abroad* (New York: Garland Publishing, 1993), pp. 241–42.

29. Allen, "American Studies and the Study of America," p. 23; Skard, *American Studies in Europe*, vol. 2, p. 642.

30. Harry Allen, "Foreword," *Journal of American Studies* 14 (April 1980), p. 6; Skard, *Trans-Atlantica*, pp. 34–35, 38, 40, 64.

31. Skard, *Trans-Atlantica*, pp. 36, 41–46, 48, 51, 55–56.

32. Ibid., pp. 52–54, 58–59, 94.

33. Ibid., 58, 61, 67, 69–70, 78, 105. See also Lundestad, "Research Trends and Accomplishments in Norway on United States History," p. 249.

34. Skard, "Fulbrighters in Norway," p. 246; Skard, *Trans-Atlantica*, pp. 67, 82–84, 88, 107, 110–11, 147.

35. Skard, *American Studies in Europe*, vol. 2, p. 653; Skard, *Trans-Atlantica*, pp. 77, 89, 95–99. See also Lundestad, "Research Trends and Accomplishments in Norway on United States History," pp. 253–54, 285.

36. Skard, *Trans-Atlantica*, pp. 70–71, 87, 124–25, 128, 149, 182; Lundestad, "Research Trends and Accomplishments in Norway on United States History," p. 258.

37. For information about the careers of Mario Praz and A. N. J. den Hollander, see Donald Heiney, *America in Modern Italian Literature* (New Brunswick, N.J.: Rutgers University Press, 1964), p. 96; Agostino Lombardo, "Introduction to Italian Criticism of American Literature," *Sewanee Review* 68 (Summer 1960), pp. 359, 361; Jan Willem Schulte Nordholt, "Developments in the Netherlands Concerning United States History," in Hanke, ed., *Guide to the Study of United States History Outside the U.S.*, vol. 3, p. 188; Rob Kroes, "Americanistics in the Netherlands," *American Studies International* 25 (October 1987), pp. 56, 60; and Skard, *American Studies in Europe*, vol. 2, p. 375.

38. Roger Asselineau, "A Complex Fate," *Journal of American Studies* 14 (April 1980), pp. 67, 73–75, 81.

39. Nicholas, "The Education of an Americanist," pp. 16, 18; Marcus Cunliffe, "Backward Glances," *Journal of American Studies* 14 (April 1980), p. 86.

40. Skard, *American Studies in Europe*, vol. 1, p. 102. Other European Americanists were equally envious of the British. See Willi Paul Adams, "American History Abroad: Personal Reflections on the Conditions of Scholarship in West Germany," *Reviews in American History* 14 (December 1986), p. 563. For a discussion of the "Atlanticist" perspective of the first generation of British Americanists, and their emphasis on colonial and diplomatic history, see Jeffreys-Jones, "The Teaching of United States History in British

Institutions of Higher Learning," p. 337; Heale, "Writings in Great Britain on United States History," pp. 369, 382–83, 388; and Heale, "American History: The View from Britain," pp. 502, 504, 506–8. A number of British Americanists published books in the United States between 1945 and the early 1960s, including D. W. Brogan, Marcus Cunliffe, Henry Pelling, Maldwyn Jones, and Esmond Wright. See Tony Badger, "Confessions of a British Americanist," *Journal of American History* 79 (September 1992), p. 521.

41. Cunliffe, "Backward Glances," p. 90. Cunliffe continually described himself in this essay as a missionary, though "in no danger of martyrdom"; see p. 88. See also Jeffreys-Jones, "The Teaching of United States History in British Institutions of Higher Learning," p. 328; and Heale, "Writings in Great Britain on United States History," pp. 366, 369.

42. Malcolm Bradbury, "How I Invented America," *Journal of American Studies* 14 (April 1980), pp. 119–20; Cunliffe, "Backward Glances," p. 88. *Hoggartian* refers to Richard Hoggart, the British sociologist and communications specialist who studied the culture of the English working class in the 1950s. See his classic book, *The Uses of Literacy: Aspects of Working Class Life with Special Reference to Publications and Entertainments* (London: Chatto & Windus, 1957). For a lengthier discussion of the British Americanists as "outsiders," see Jeffreys-Jones, "The Teaching of United States History in British Institutions of Higher Learning," pp. 329–30.

43. Allen, "United States History in Great Britain and the European Association for American Studies," p. 64; Jeffreys-Jones, "The Teaching of United States History in British Institutions of Higher Learning," p. 329; Heale, "Writings in Great Britain on United States History," pp. 379, 398.

44. D. W. Brogan, *The American Character* (New York: Knopf, 1956, c. 1944), pp. x, 4–5; Cunliffe, "Backward Glances," p. 87.

45. Cunliffe, "Backward Glances," p. 90; Jeffreys-Jones, "The Teaching of United States History in British Institutions of Higher Learning," pp. 321, 323; Reynolds, "Whitehall, Washington and the Promotion of American Studies in Britain During World War Two," p. 187; Nicholas, "The Education of an Americanist," p. 23; Allen, "United States History in Great Britain and the European Association for American Studies," p. 67.

46. For information on the European Association for American Studies and other organizations in Western Europe, see Lacey, "Institutional Structures and American Studies at Universities in the Federal Republic of Germany," p. 261; Skard, *American Studies in Europe*, vol. 2, pp. 637–38; Max Silberschmidt, "My Life Experience with the United States and Its History," in Hanke, ed., *Guide to the Study of United States History Outside the U.S.*, vol. 1, p. 96; Skard, *Trans-Atlantica*, p. 147; Marc Chénetier, "American Literature in France: Pleasures in Perspective," in Gutman, ed., *As Others Read Us*, p. 90; Laurence Wylie and Sarella Henriquez, "French Images of American Life," *Tocqueville Review* 4 (1982), p. 189; Reginald de Schryver, "The Development of Teaching and Research in Belgium on United States History," in Hanke, ed., *Guide to the Study of United States History Outside the U.S.*, vol. 1,

p. 199; Sergio Perosa, "American Studies in Italy," and Tyrus Hillway, "American Studies in Austria," in Walker, ed., *American Studies Abroad*, pp. 81, 89; and Kroes, "Americanistics in the Netherlands," p. 64.

47. For a description of the professionalization of British Americanists, see Heale, "Writings in Great Britain on United States History," p. 370.

48. Willi Paul Adams, "Interview with Maurizio Vaudagna," in Vaudagna, ed., "Forum: American Studies in Europe," p. 129; Adams, "American History Abroad," p. 557.

49. Adams, "Interview with Maurizio Vaudagna," p. 131; Adams, "American History Abroad," pp. 557–60; Willi Paul Adams, "On the Significance of Frontiers in Writing American History in Germany," *Journal of American History* 79 (September 1992), pp. 466, 470.

50. For a discussion of the indifference displayed by postwar French historians to the United States, see Marianne Debouzy, "American History in France," *Reviews in American History* 14 (December 1986), pp. 542–44; and Brun-Rovet, "Teaching and Research on United States History in France," pp. 191–93.

51. For examples of how difficult European scholars thought it was to study U.S. history without access to primary sources, see Vaudagna, "The American Historian in Continental Europe," p. 534; Floto, "The Development of United States History in Denmark," p. 21; Robert Lawson-Peebles, "Dean Acheson and the Potato Head Blues or, British Academic Attitudes to America and Its Literature," in Gutman, ed., *As Others Read Us*, p. 32; Helbich, "United States History in the Federal Republic of Germany," pp. 84, 87; Adams, "On the Significance of Frontiers in Writing American History in Germany," p. 470; Heale, "Writings in Great Britain on United States History," pp. 404–5; and Heale, "American History: The View from Britain," p. 513.

52. For descriptions of how interdisciplinary programs fared in specific countries in Western Europe, see A. N. J. den Hollander, "Headaches, Harvests and Hopes: Fulbright Americanists in Europe," in Walker, ed., *American Studies Abroad*, p. 22; Robin Winks, "At Home Abroad/Abroad At Home," *American Studies International* 26 (April 1988), p. 76; Adams, "American History Abroad," p. 563; Lacey, "Institutional Structures and American Studies at Universities in the Federal Republic of Germany," pp. 242–43; Rob Kroes, "The Netherlands: A Contribution by Rob Kroes," in Vaudagna, ed., "Forum: American Studies in Europe," p. 174; and Bonazzi, "American History: The View from Italy," p. 525.

53. Skard, *American Studies in Europe*, vol. 1, pp. 39, 100; Kellerman, *Cultural Relations as an Instrument of U.S. Foreign Policy*, p. 182; Reinhold Wagnleitner, *Coca-Colonization and the Cold War: The Cultural Mission of the United States in Austria After the Second World War*, trans. Diana Wolf (Chapel Hill: University of North Carolina Press, 1994), pp. 154, 159; Franco Minganti, "Rock'N'Roll in Italy: Was It True Americanization?" in Rob Kroes, Robert Rydell, and Doeko F. J. Bosscher, eds., *Cultural Transmissions*

and Receptions: American Mass Culture in Europe (Amsterdam: VU University Press, 1993), p. 142; James Tent, *The Free University of Berlin: A Political History* (Bloomington: Indiana University Press, 1988), p. 414; Michele Bottalico, "A Place for All: Old and New Myths in the Italian Appreciation of American Literature," in Gutman, ed., *As Others Read Us*, p. 155; D'haen, "Cutting Loose: American Literary Studies in the Netherlands," p. 193; Lundén, "The Dual Cannon," p. 246; Johnson and Colligan, *The Fulbright Program*, p. 158; Hans Tuch, *Communicating with the World: U.S. Public Diplomacy Overseas* (New York: St. Martin's Press, 1990), p. 71.

54. Many Americanists commented, sometimes ruefully, on the dominance of literature over history in the American Studies programs of their own countries and throughout Western Europe. For examples, see Allen, "United States History in Great Britain and the European Association for American Studies," pp. 58, 70, 62; den Hollander, "Headaches, Harvests and Hopes," p. 23; Roger Asselineau and Simon Copans, "American Studies in France: The New Face of a Tradition," in Walker, ed., *American Studies Abroad*, p. 64; Schulte Nordholt, "Developments in the Netherlands Concerning United States History," p. 188; de Schryver, "The Development of Teaching and Research in Belgium on United States History," p. 199; Hans-Peter Wagner, "Stepping Out of Hitler's Shadow to Embrace Uncle Sam? Notes Toward a History of American Literary Studies in West Germany," in Gutman, ed., *As Others Read Us*, p. 106; Helbich, "United States History in the Federal Republic of Germany," p. 56; Adams, "American History Abroad," p. 562; Adams, "Interview with Maurizio Vaudagna," p. 122; Vaudagna, "Forum: American Studies in Europe," p. 143; Hillway, "American Studies in Austria," p. 93; Perosa, "American Studies in Italy," pp. 77–79; Sylvia Hilton, "American Studies in Spain: Recent Trends," *American Studies International* 32 (April 1994), p. 43; and Skard, *American Studies in Europe*, vol. 2, p. 497. See also Thelen, "Of Audiences, Borderlands, and Comparisons," p. 451; and Heiney, *America in Modern Italian Literature*, pp. 95, 97–98.

55. On conditions in Eastern Europe during the 1950s and early 1960s, see Skard, *American Studies in Europe*, vol. 2, pp. 581, 584–85, 593, 604–7, 616, 621, 623, 625; Janez Stanonik, "American Studies in Yugoslavia," in Walker, ed., *American Studies Abroad*, pp. 95–96; Marija Vilfan, "From Yugoslavia," in Joseph, ed., *As Others See Us*, p. 126; Foeller-Pituch, "Catching Up: The Polish Critical Response to American Literature," p. 206; Allen, "United States History in Great Britain and the European Association for American Studies," p. 71; and Cunliffe, "American Studies in Europe," p. 52.

56. Cunliffe, "Backward Glances," p. 95; Skard, *American Studies in Europe*, vol. 1, p. 42. When he lectured in Western Europe during the 1950s, Alfred Kazin was "aware of being both needed and resented." See Kazin, "Carrying the Word Abroad," p. 64.

57. Burton Bollag, "Enrollment Soars in Europe," *Chronicle of Higher Education* 41 (September 7, 1994), pp. A59–A60. In Britain, Greece, and Portugal,

the enrollment rate for those of college age in the early 1990s was 30 percent; in Denmark and France, it was 50 percent. In the United States, by comparison, 44 percent of twenty- and twenty-one year olds were enrolled in college in 1992.

58. Rob Kroes, "The Nearness of America," in Kroes, ed., *Image and Impact*, pp. 12–13. For the number of Americanists in Europe, see John Blair, "Directionality in Fulbright Transformations," in Dudden and Dynes, eds., *The Fulbright Experience*, p. 164.

59. Jeffreys-Jones, "The Teaching of United States History in British Institutions of Higher Learning," pp. 332, 337–38, 342; Helbich, "Interview with Maurizio Vaudagna," p. 123. Tony Badger exemplified the British Americanists in the 1970s and 1980s who sought to make their books indistinguishable from those written in the United States. See his "Confessions of a British Americanist," p. 516.

60. D'haen, "Cutting Loose: American Literary Studies in the Netherlands," pp. 194, 197; Brun-Rovet, "Teaching and Research on United States History in France," pp. 181, 183; Bonazzi, "American History: The View from Italy," pp. 528–29; Skard, *Trans-Atlantica*, pp. 123, 196; Helge Pharo, "The Teaching of United States History in Norwegian Universities," in Hanke, ed., *Guide to the Study of United States History Outside the U.S.*, vol. 3, p. 241; Lundestad, "Research Trends and Accomplishments in Norway on United States History," pp. 270, 286.

61. For developments in West Germany, especially at the Free University of Berlin, see Helbich, "United States History in the Federal Republic of Germany," p, 44; Lacey, "Institutional Structures and American Studies at Universities in the Federal Republic of Germany," pp. 250–51; Adams, "American History Abroad," p. 560; and Tent, *The Free University of Berlin*, p. 336.

62. Tent, *The Free University of Berlin*, pp. 409–13, 427, 433; Brun-Rovet, "Teaching and Research on United States History in France," p. 184; Marianne Debouzy, "The Influence of American Political Dissent on the French New Left," in A. N. J. den Hollander, ed., *Contagious Conflict: The Impact of American Dissent on European Life* (Leiden: Brill, 1973), p. 57; Jeffreys-Jones, "The Teaching of United States History in British Institutions of Higher Learning," p. 331.

63. For descriptions of the new trends in literary criticism in Europe, see Chénetier, "American Literature in France," p. 84; Wagner, "Stepping Out of Hitler's Shadow to Embrace Uncle Sam?" pp. 104, 109; Bottalico, "A Place for All," pp. 152–53; D'haen, "Cutting Loose: American Literary Studies in the Netherlands," p. 202; and Patsalidis, "(Mis)Understanding America's Literary Canon," pp. 128–29.

64. Marianne Debouzy, "From American Studies to American History: A French Point of View," *Journal of American History* 79 (September 1992), pp. 491–93, 498. See also Heale, "Writings in Great Britain on United States History," pp. 375, 386, 393; Heale, "American History: The View from Britain,"

pp. 512, 518; Badger, "Confessions of a British Americanist," p. 523; Hans-Jürgen Puhle, "Comparative Approaches from Germany: The 'New Nation' in Advanced Industrial Capitalism, 1860–1940—Integration, Stabilization and Reform," and Ferdinando Fasce, "American Labor History, 1973–1983: Italian Perspectives," *Reviews in American History* 14 (December 1986), pp. 601, 606–8, 615; and Bonazzi, "American History: The View from Italy," pp. 530–31, 535.

65. On the contraction of American Studies in Britain during the 1980s, see Allen, "United States History in Great Britain and the European Association for American Studies," p. 65; Jeffreys-Jones, "The Teaching of United States History in British Institutions of Higher Learning," p. 343; Heale, "Writings in Great Britain on United States History," p. 365; and Heale, "American History: The View from Britain," p. 516.

66. D'haen, "Cutting Loose: American Literary Studies in the Netherlands," p. 200; Debouzy, "American History in France," p. 549; Adams, "American History Abroad," p. 558; Bottalico, "A Place for All," p. 156.

67. For developments in Britain in the 1990s, see Alina Tugend, "A British Boom in American Studies," *Chronicle of Higher Education* 41 (April 14, 1995), p. A40; and John Darnton, "New Oxford Fashion: United States Studies," *New York Times* (September 6, 1995), p. A6. For analyses of the growth of American Studies in Poland and Eastern Europe from the 1970s to the 1990s, see "Poland: Maurizio Vaudagna Interviews Michal Rozbicki," in Vaudagna, ed., "Forum: American Studies in Europe," pp. 137, 144–45; Foeller-Pituch, "Catching Up: The Polish Critical Response to American Literature," p. 217; and Gallagher, "A Center for Intellectual Exchange," p. A39.

68. On the problems of the language barrier for scholars on the European continent, in contrast to their American and British counterparts who could write in English and expect to be read throughout the world, see Vaudagna, "The American Historian in Continental Europe," p. 534; and Adams, "On the Significance of Frontiers in Writing American History in Germany," pp. 469, 471. Adams's first book, published in German, got no attention in the United States. Only when it was translated with the assistance of a 1976 Bicentennial Award from the American Historical Association and was published in 1980 by the University of North Carolina Press (as *The First American Constitutions: Republican Ideology and the Making of the State Constitutions in the Revolutionary Era*) did it receive, according to Adams, "full and expert reviews" in the United States "and [find] its way into American bibliographies and footnotes. Had there not been the translation . . . the book for all practical purposes would not exist for American Americanists." See Adams, "American History Abroad," pp. 564, 568. Similarly, Reinhold Wagnleitner's *Coca-Colonization and the Cold War* originated as an Austrian dissertation, published in German in 1991. It was translated with support from foundations in the United States and Austria and was published in America in 1994, again by the University of North Carolina Press. By the early 1990s, the *Journal of American History* was making a concerted

effort to print articles by European Americanists. Meanwhile, all the relevant academic organizations in the United States—the American Historical Association, the Organization of American Historians, and the American Studies Association—were regularly inviting European Americanists to present papers at their annual meetings.

69. Adams, "American History Abroad," p. 563; Vaudagna, "The American Historian in Continental Europe," p. 539. For a discussion of the same sort of dilemma that Polish Americanists faced after 1989, see Foeller-Pituch, "Catching Up: The Polish Critical Response to American Literature," p. 204.

70. Cunliffe, "American Studies in Europe," pp. 50–51; Badger, "Confessions of a British Americanist," p. 523. For more examples of this lament, see Heale, "Writings in Great Britain on United States History," p. 371; Bonazzi, "American History: The View from Italy," p. 537; and Debouzy, "American History in France," p. 551.

71. Badger, "Confessions of a British Americanist," p. 519; Skard, *American Studies in Europe*, vol. 2, p. 654; Bradbury, "How I Invented America," p. 134.

72. In reviewing a series of volumes on American culture and social life, published in Amsterdam, whose editors and contributors were largely European, Allen Davis pointed out the advantages of writing about America from the "outside." See his "American Studies: The View from Europe," *American Quarterly* 40 (September 1983), p. 413.

73. Vaudagna, "Forum: American Studies in Europe," p. 118. Rob Kroes was equally sensitive to the transformation of American Studies in its journey across the Atlantic. See his essay, "The Nearness of America," p. 13.

74. Tiziano Bonazzi, "The Beginnings of American History in Italy," in Arndt and Rubin, eds., *The Fulbright Difference*, p. 160; Debouzy, "American History in France," pp. 547–48; Heale, "Writings in Great Britain on United States History," p. 402; Adams, "Interview with Maurizio Vaudagna," p. 132.

75. Kroes, "Americanistics in the Netherlands," p. 59; Vaudagna, "Forum: American Studies in Europe," p. 147.

CHAPTER FIVE
TRANSATLANTIC MISUNDERSTANDINGS:
AMERICAN VIEWS OF EUROPE

1. Herbert Kubly, *American in Italy* (New York: Simon & Schuster, 1955), p. 16.

2. Edward McCreary, *The Americanization of Europe: The Impact of Americans and American Business on the Uncommon Market* (Garden City, N.Y.: Doubleday, 1964), pp. 238, 242. For other descriptions of how visiting Americans behaved in postwar Europe, see Francis Williams, *The American*

Invasion (New York: Crown, 1962), p. 14; John Garraty and Walter Adams, *From Main Street to the Left Bank: Students and Scholars Abroad* (East Lansing: Michigan State University Press, 1959), pp. 175–77; Joseph Wechsberg, "The American Abroad," *Atlantic Monthly* 200 (November 1957), p. 266; and Foster Rhea Dulles, *Americans Abroad: Two Centuries of European Travel* (Ann Arbor: University of Michigan Press, 1964), p. 170.

3. André Visson, *As Others See Us* (Garden City, N.Y.: Doubleday, 1948), p. 29; Kubly, *American in Italy*, p. 27.

4. For analyses of postwar tourism, see Dulles, *Americans Abroad*, pp. 4, 169–70, 173–74, 176, 180; Daniel Boorstin, *The Image: A Guide to Pseudo-Events in America* (New York: Atheneum, 1972, c. 1962), pp. 79–80, 83–86, 90–92, 97, 99, 102; Horace Sutton, "Transatlantic Travel: 400,000 'Diplomats' on the Loose," in Lewis Galantière, ed., *America and the Mind of Europe* (London: Hamilton, 1951), p. 117; C. W. E. Bigsby, "Europe, America and the Cultural Debate," in Bigsby, ed., *Superculture: American Popular Culture and Europe* (Bowling Green, Ohio: Bowling Green University Popular Press, 1975), p. 2; Garraty and Adams, *From Main Street to the Left Bank*, pp. 174–75; and Kubly, *American In Italy*, p. 199.

5. See Dulles, *Americans Abroad*, pp. 170–71; Bigsby, "Europe, America and the Cultural Debate," p. 3; and Wechsberg, "The American Abroad," pp. 265–66.

6. Edmund Wilson, *A Piece of My Mind: Reflections at Sixty* (New York: Farrar, Straus & Cudahy, 1956), pp. 61–62.

7. William Phillips, *A Partisan View: Five Decades of the Literary Life* (New York: Stein & Day, 1983), pp. 202, 221; Leslie Fiedler, "Italian Pilgrimage: The Discovery of America," in Fiedler, *An End to Innocence: Essays on Culture and Politics* (Boston: Beacon Press, 1955), p. 91; James Baldwin, "The Discovery of What It Means to Be an American," in Baldwin, *Nobody Knows My Name* (New York: Dell, 1963, c. 1961), p. 23.

8. Wilson, *A Piece of My Mind*, p. 54; Edmund Wilson, *The Fifties: From Notebooks and Diaries of the Period*, ed. Leon Edel (New York: Farrar, Straus & Giroux, 1986), p. 139; Saul Bellow, "The French as Dostoyevsky Saw Them," "Writers, Intellectuals, Politics: Mainly Reminiscences," and "My Paris," in Bellow, *It All Adds Up: From the Dim Past to the Uncertain Future* (New York: Viking, 1994), pp. 39, 106–7, 232–33, 239.

9. Wilson, *The Fifties*, p. 378. For a general description of the attitudes of American intellectuals toward postwar Europe, see Harold Laski, *The American Democracy: A Commentary and an Interpretation* (New York: Viking, 1948), p. 61; and Guido Piovene, "Ungrateful Europe," in James Burnham, ed., *What Europe Thinks of America* (New York: John Day, 1953), p. 113.

10. Wilson, *The Fifties*, p. 392; Phillips, *A Partisan View*, pp. 202–3; Bellow, "My Paris," pp. 235, 237–38.

11. Mary McCarthy, *The Stones of Florence* (New York: Harcourt Brace Jovanovich, 1963, c. 1959), pp. 3–5, 37, 108, 110–11, 119, 130, 155, 181–82.

12. Ibid., pp. 39, 54, 87, 89, 107–8, 118, 126, 189.

13. Ibid., pp. 75, 166–67, 191.

14. Ibid., pp. 28, 32, 71, 86, 120, 129, 142, 225.

15. Ibid., pp. 7, 10, 14, 16–17, 53, 128, 219, 221.

16. Mary McCarthy, *Venice Observed* (New York: Harcourt Brace Jovanovich, 1963, c. 1956), p. 12.

17. Ibid., pp. 1, 3, 6–10, 14–15, 17, 82, 105–6, 144; McCarthy, *The Stones of Florence*, p. 107.

18. McCarthy, *Venice Observed*, pp. 27, 36, 46, 48–49, 50–52, 55–57, 64, 69, 115, 121.

19. Ibid., pp. 34–35.

20. Ibid., p. 35; Mary McCarthy, "America the Beautiful: The Humanist in the Bathtub," in McCarthy, *On the Contrary: Articles of Belief, 1946–1961* (New York: Noonday Press, 1962, c. 1961), pp. 9, 13. This essay was originally published in *Commentary* 4 (September 1947), pp. 201–7.

21. Much of the preceding discussion about what American academics were likely to encounter in Europe is based on my experience as a Fulbright lecturer. Other authors, both American and European, have offered similar descriptions. See Garraty and Adams, *From Main Street to the Left Bank*, pp. 14–15, 17–18, 24, 32, 98, 110–12, 125, 161, 166, 182; Perry Miller, "What Drove Me Crazy in Europe," in Miller, *The Responsibility of Mind in a Civilization of Machines* (Amherst: University of Massachusetts Press, 1979), p. 100–102; A. N. J. den Hollander, "Headaches, Harvests and Hopes: Fulbright Americanists in Europe," in Robert Walker, ed., *American Studies Abroad* (Westport, Conn.: Greenwood Press, 1975), pp. 19–20; Henry Kellerman, *Cultural Relations as an Instrument of U.S. Foreign Policy* (Washington, D.C.: U.S. Government Printing Office, 1978), p. 184; and McCreary, *The Americanization of Europe*, p. 231.

22. Leslie Fiedler, "The 'Good American,'" in Fiedler, *An End to Innocence*, p. 111; James Baldwin, "Encounter on the Seine: Black Meets Brown," in Baldwin, *Notes of a Native Son* (Boston: Beacon Press, 1957, c. 1955), p. 121.

23. Fiedler, "The 'Good American,'" pp. 109, 112; Norman Podhoretz, *Making It* (New York: Bantam Books, 1969, c. 1967), p. 65. For similar reactions, see Otto Larsen, "The Evolution of an Ethnic Identity," in Arthur Dudden and Russell Dynes, eds., *The Fulbright Experience, 1946–1986: Encounters and Transformations* (New Brunswick, N.J.: Transaction Books, 1987), p. 111; and Richard Horwitz, "Coming to Terms with International American Studies," in Richard Arndt and David Rubin, eds., *The Fulbright Difference, 1948–1992* (New Brunswick, N.J.: Transaction Books, 1993), p. 466.

24. Podhoretz, *Making It*, p. 64.

25. James Baldwin, "A Question of Identity," in Baldwin, *Notes of a Native Son*, pp. 126, 128, 130–31; italics his. For more sympathetic descriptions of the Americans' homesickness, see Garraty and Adams, *From Main Street to the Left Bank*, p. 145; and Abby Johnson, "Circle of Light: A Year in Arctic Norway," in Arndt and David Rubin, eds., *The Fulbright Difference*, p. 337.

26. Baldwin, "The Discovery of What It Means to Be an American," pp. 17–18, 21; Baldwin, "A Question of Identity," 134; Podhoretz, *Making It*, p. 63; Johnson, "Circle of Light," pp. 338–39; Ray Marshall, "Reminiscences About Finland," Albert Wilhelm, "The Shortest Way Home," and Mary Lee Field, " 'That Thing,' " in Dudden and Dynes, eds., *The Fulbright Experience*, pp. 117, 119, 131.

CHAPTER SIX
TRANSATLANTIC MISUNDERSTANDINGS:
EUROPEAN VIEWS OF AMERICA

1. See Rob Kroes, "Among the Receivers: American Culture Transmitted Abroad," in Kroes, ed., *Within the U.S. Orbit: Small National Cultures vis-à-vis the United States* (Amsterdam: VU University Press, 1991), p. 3; and André Visson, *As Others See Us* (Garden City, N.Y.: Doubleday, 1948), p. 230.

2. S. Gorley Putt, ed., *Cousins and Strangers: Comments on America by Commonwealth Fund Fellows from Britain, 1946–1952* (Cambridge, Mass.: Harvard University Press, 1956), pp. 2–3. See also Rob Kroes, "Americanization: What Are We Talking About?" in Kroes, Robert Rydell, and Doeko F. J. Bosscher, eds., *Cultural Transmissions and Receptions: American Mass Culture in Europe* (Amsterdam: VU University Press, 1993), p. 310; D. W. Brogan, *The American Character* (New York: Knopf, 1956, c. 1944), pp. ix–x; and Julian Marias, "From Spain," in Franz Joseph, ed., *As Others See Us: The United States Through Foreign Eyes* (Princeton, N.J.: Princeton University Press, 1959), p. 26. Some European intellectuals did view America as different and unique. See Raymond Aron, "From France," in Joseph, ed., *As Others See Us*, pp. 58, 60; and Guido Piovene, "Ungrateful Europe," in James Burnham, ed., *What Europe Thinks of America* (New York: John Day, 1953), pp. 112–13.

3. Kroes, "Among the Receivers," p. 2; Richard Kuisel, *Seducing the French: The Dilemma of Americanization* (Berkeley: University of California Press, 1993), p. 6, 47, 159–60; Theodore Zeldin, "Foreword," in Denis Lacorne, Jacques Rupnik, and Marie-France Toinet, eds., *The Rise and Fall of Anti-Americanism: A Century of French Perception*, trans. Gerry Turner (New York: St. Martin's Press, 1990, c. Paris 1986), p. x.

4. On the close ties between Italy and America, see Donald Heiney, *America in Modern Italian Literature* (New Brunswick, N.J.: Rutgers University Press, 1964), pp. 5, 15–16.

5. Arnold Rose, "Anti-Americanism in France," *Antioch Review* 12 (December 1952), p. 472; Sigmund Skard, *American Studies in Europe: Their History and Present Organization*, vol. 1 (Philadelphia: University of Pennsylvania Press, 1958), p.133; Raymond Aron and August Heckscher, *Diversity*

of Worlds: France and the United States Look at Their Common Problems (New York: Reynal, 1957), p. 6; Frank Costigliola, *France and the United States: The Cold Alliance Since World War II* (New York: Twayne, 1992), pp. 41, 86.

6. See Annie Kriegel, "Consistent Misapprehension: European Views of America and Their Logic," *Daedalus* 101 (Fall 1972), pp. 88, 92; and Ezra Suleiman, "Anti-Americanism and the Elite," in Lacorne et al., eds., *The Rise and Fall of Anti-Americanism*, p. 109.

7. Aron and Heckscher, *Diversity of Worlds*, p. xii; Kuisel, *Seducing the French*, p. 22; Costigliola, *France and the United States*, pp. 81, 83.

8. Herbert Kubly, *American In Italy* (New York: Simon & Schuster, 1955), pp. 34, 43–44, 49; Perry Miller, "What Drove Me Crazy in Europe," in Miller, *The Responsibility of Mind in a Civilization of Machines* (Amherst: University of Massachusetts Press, 1979), p. 99.

9. Luigi Barzini, *Americans Are Alone in the World* (New York: Random House, 1953), pp. 84–85, 205.

10. William Phillips, *A Partisan View: Five Decades of the Literary Life* (New York: Stein & Day, 1983), p. 189. For further information on Raymond Aron, see Marie-Christine Granjon, "Sartre, Beauvoir, Aron: An Ambiguous Affair," in Lacorne et al., eds., *The Rise and Fall of Anti-Americanism*, pp. 116, 121, 125, 130–31; Jeanine Brun-Rovet, "Teaching and Research on United States History in France," in Lewis Hanke, ed., *Guide to the Study of United States History Outside the U.S., 1945–1980*, vol. 2 (White Plains, N.Y.: Kraus International Publications, 1985), p. 176; and Peter Coleman, *The Liberal Conspiracy: The Congress for Cultural Freedom and the Struggle for the Mind of Postwar Europe* (New York: Free Press, 1989), p. 40.

11. For a general discussion of Western Europe's ambivalence toward America, see Raymond Aron, "Transatlantic Relations: Does Europe Welcome American Leadership?" in Lewis Galantière, ed., *America and the Mind of Europe* (London: Hamilton 1951), p. 26; Aron, "From France," p. 60; Putt, ed., *Cousins and Strangers*, p. 2; Costigliola, *France and the United States*, pp. 68, 70; Visson, *As Others See Us*, pp. 47, 159–60; Nico Wilterdink, "The Netherlands Between the Greater Powers," and Rolf Lundén, "America in Sweden: Visible and Invisible Influence," in Kroes, ed., *Within the U.S. Orbit*, p. 26, 139–40; Jean-Philippe Mathy, *Extrême Occident: French Intellectuals and America* (Chicago: University of Chicago Press, 1993), p. 35; Edward McCreary, *The Americanization of Europe: The Impact of Americans and American Business on the Uncommon Market* (Garden City, N.Y.: Doubleday, 1964), p. 257; Vittorio Zincone, "Moral America," in Burnham, ed., *What Europe Thinks of America*, p. 47; Yves-Henri Nouailhat, "Franco-American Relations: French Perspectives," *Reviews in American History* 14 (December 1986), p. 665; Marianne Debouzy, "From American Studies to American History: A French Point of View," *Journal of American History* 79 (September 1992), p. 496; Steinar Bryn, "Norway and America: Looking at Each Other," *Scandinavian Review* 76 (Summer 1988), p. 159; Jan Gretlund, "The

American Within: Danes and American Literature," and Michele Bottalico, "A Place for All: Old and New Myths in the Italian Appreciation of American Literature," in Huck Gutman, ed., *As Others Read Us: International Perspectives on American Literature* (Amherst: University of Massachusetts Press, 1991), pp. 65, 148; and Leslie Fiedler, "Italian Pilgrimage: The Discovery of America," in Fiedler, *An End to Innocence: Essays on Culture and Politics* (Boston: Beacon Press, 1955), p. 94.

12. J. H. Plumb, "Introduction: 'O My America, My Newfoundland,'" "The Wider Issues," "British Attitudes to the American Revolution," "The Burgeoning of American History," and "Introduction: At Large in America," in Plumb, *The American Experience*, vol. 2 of *The Collected Essays* (Athens: University of Georgia Press, 1989), pp. 7–8, 10, 12, 46, 129, 171, 173; Jean Baudrillard, *America*, trans. Chris Turner (New York: Verso, 1988, c. Paris 1986), p. 88.

13. D. W. Brogan, "From England," in Joseph, ed., *As Others See Us*, p. 15; Barzini, *Americans Are Alone in the World*, p. 130. See also Paul Hollander, *Anti-Americanism: Critiques at Home and Abroad, 1965–1990* (New York: Oxford University Press, 1992), p. 390.

14. On Britain's reduced role and self-image, see Visson, *As Others See Us*, pp. 21–22, 46; Malcolm Bradbury, "How I Invented America," *Journal of American Studies* 14 (April 1980), p. 117; Duncan Webster, *Looka Yonder! The Imaginary America of Populist Culture* (London: Routledge, 1988), pp. 184, 209, 239, 243; Dick Hebdige, "Towards a Cartography of Taste, 1935–1962," in Hebdige, *Hiding in the Light: On Images and Things* (London: Routledge, 1988), p. 53; and Daniel Snowman, *Britain and America: An Interpretation of Their Culture, 1945–1975* (New York: New York University Press, 1977), pp. 30–31, 263.

15. On France, see Rose, "Anti-Americanism in France," p. 479; Visson, *As Others See Us*, p. 130; Tony Judt, *Past Imperfect: French Intellectuals, 1944–1956* (Berkeley: University of California Press, 1992), pp. 195, 200; Kuisel, *Seducing the French*, pp. 20, 24; Denis Lacorne and Jacques Rupnik, "Introduction: France Bewitched by America," Jacques Rupnik and Muriel Humbertjean, "Images of the United States in Public Opinion," and Michael Harrison, "French Anti-Americanism Under the Fourth Republic and the Gaullist Solution," in Lacorne et al., eds., *The Rise and Fall of Anti-Americanism*, pp. 15, 81, 169; Costigliola, *France and the United States*, pp. 45, 76; and Zeldin, "Foreword," p. xi.

16. Hollander, *Anti-Americanism*, p. 378.

17. Barzini, *Americans Are Alone in the World,* p. 131; Bradbury, "How I Invented America," p. 118.

18. Amaury de Riencourt, *The Coming Caesars* (New York: Coward-McCann, 1957), pp. 311–12; Visson, *As Others See Us*, pp. 48, 96. For similar views, see Cyril Connolly, "Introduction to Art on the American Horizon," *Horizon* 16 (October 1947), p. 11; Harry Allen, "American Studies and the Study of America: The Future of American Studies in Europe," *American*

Studies International 17 (Spring 1979), p. 13; and Marcus Cunliffe, "The Anatomy of Anti-Americanism," in Rob Kroes and Maarten van Rossem, eds., *Anti-Americanism in Europe* (Amsterdam: Free University Press, 1986), p. 31.

19. Visson, *As Others See Us*, pp. 25 27, 30, 34, 47; Aron, "Transatlantic Relations," p. 24. For an extended discussion of these ideas, see Pierre Nora, "America and the French Intellectuals," *Daedalus* 107 (Winter 1978), p. 325; Kroes, "Among the Receivers," p. 3; Judt, *Past Imperfect*, pp. 261–62; and Kuisel, *Seducing the French*, pp. 119, 235–36.

20. Cunliffe, "The Anatomy of Anti-Americanism," p. 26; R. H. Pear, "Students and the Establishment in Europe and the U.S.A.," in A. N. J. den Hollander, ed., *Diverging Parallels: A Comparison of American and European Thought and Action* (Leiden: Brill, 1971), p. 99; Aron, "From France," p. 66; Michel Winock, "The Cold War," in Lacorne et al., eds., *The Rise and Fall of Anti-Americanism*, p. 74; Judt, *Past Imperfect*, pp. 201–2; Peter Duignan and L. H. Gann, *The Rebirth of the West: The Americanization of the Democratic World, 1945–1958* (Cambridge, Mass: Blackwell, 1992), p. 415; Hollander, *Anti-Americanism*, pp. 369, 383; Mathy, *Extrême Occident*, p. 153; Kuisel, *Seducing the French*, pp. 34–35.

21. Jacques Rupnik, "Anti-Americanism and the Modern: The Image of the United States in French Public Opinion," in John Gaffney, ed., *France and Modernization* (Aldershot, England: Avebury, 1988), pp. 194, 200; Aron, "Transatlantic Relations," pp. 22–23, Visson, *As Others See Us*, pp. 65, 206; Rose, "Anti-Americanism in France," pp. 474–75; Norman Kogan, "Italian Intellect and Foreign Influences," in Richard Arndt and David Rubin, eds., *The Fulbright Difference, 1948–1992* (New Brunswick, N.J.: Transaction Books, 1993), p. 173; Heiney, *America in Modern Italian Literature*, p. 85; Fabrice Montebello, "Hollywood Films in a French Working Class Milieu: Longwy 1945–1960," in David Ellwood and Rob Kroes, eds., *Hollywood in Europe: Experiences of a Cultural Hegemony* (Amsterdam: VU University Press, 1994), p. 213; Serge Guilbaut, *How New York Stole the Idea of Modern Art: Abstract Expressionism, Freedom, and the Cold War*, trans. Arthur Goldhammer (Chicago: University of Chicago Press, 1984, c. 1983), pp. 150–51; Webster, *Looka Yonder!* pp. 192–93; Hollander, *Anti-Americanism*, pp. 339, 384, 402; Kuisel, *Seducing the French*, pp. 16, 24; Costigliola, *France and the United States*, pp. 155, 190–91; Mathy, *Extrême Occident*, pp. 158–59; Granjon, "Sartre, Beauvoir, Aron," pp. 122–23.

22. See Theodore Stanger, "The Devil Across the Sea," *Newsweek* European edition (November 14, 1994), p. 24.

23. Leslie Fiedler, "The 'Good American,'" in Fiedler, *An End to Innocence*, p. 110.

24. See Marcus Cunliffe, "European Images of America," in Arthur Schlesinger and Morton White, eds., *Paths of American Thought* (Boston: Houghton Mifflin, 1963), p. 510; and Harold Laski, *The American Democracy: A Commentary and an Interpretation* (New York: Viking, 1948), p. 61.

25. On America as a scapegoat for Western Europeans, while the Soviet

Union was not, see Hollander, *Anti-Americanism*, pp. 343, 381; and Gerry Waller, "The American Film: The Impact and Image of Images," in Rob Kroes, ed., *Image and Impact: American Influences in the Netherlands Since 1945* (Amsterdam: Amerika Instituut, 1981), p. 102.

26. For examples of the thesis that anti-Americanism was similar to anti-Semitism, see Cunliffe, "The Anatomy of Anti-Americanism," pp. 20, 33; John Vinocur, "Europe's Intellectuals and American Power," *New York Times Magazine* (April 29, 1984), p. 74; Duignan and Gann, *The Rebirth of the West*, p. 411; and Hollander, *Anti-Americanism*, p. 380. On Europe's anti-Americanism as a form of self-criticism, see Fiedler, "The 'Good American,'" p. 113; and Jean-François Revel, *Without Marx or Jesus: The New American Revolution Has Begun*, trans. J. F. Bernard (Garden City, N.Y.: Doubleday, 1971, c. Paris 1970), p. 259.

27. For the reactions of the Americans to de Beauvoir's visit, see William Barrett, *The Truants: Adventures Among the Intellectuals* (Garden City, N.Y.: Doubleday, 1982), pp. 115–16; Phillips, *A Partisan View*, pp. 124–29; and Mary McCarthy, "Mlle. Gulliver en Amérique," in McCarthy, *On the Contrary: Articles of Belief, 1946–1961* (New York: Noonday Press, 1962, c. 1961), p. 27. For de Beauvoir's attitudes toward her American counterparts, see Simone de Beauvoir, *America Day by Day*, trans. Patrick Dudley (London: G. Duckworth, 1952, c. Paris 1948), pp. 36–37, 263.

28. De Beauvoir, *America Day by Day*, p. 60; Barzini, *Americans Are Alone in the World*, p. 79; Bradbury, "How I Invented America," p. 130; J. H. Plumb, "Brooklyn Through English Eyes," in Plumb, *The American Experience*, p. 228; Rom Landau, *Among the Americans* (London: Hale, 1953), p. 50.

29. Plumb, "'O My America, My Newfoundland,'" p. 4; Plumb, "Brooklyn Through English Eyes," p. 226; J. H. Plumb, "New York Vindicated," in Plumb, *The American Experience*, pp. 231, 234; de Beauvoir, *America Day by Day*, pp. 9, 12; Connolly, "Introduction to Art on the American Horizon," p. 3. For similar views of New York, see Landau, *Among the Americans*, p. 197; and Putt, ed., *Cousins and Strangers*, p. 66.

30. De Beauvoir, *America Day by Day*, p. 88; Barzini, *Americans Are Alone in the World*, p. 36. The quotation from Marcus Cunliffe is in Putt, ed., *Cousins and Strangers*, pp. 79–80.

31. De Beauvoir, *America Day by Day*, p. 89; Putt, ed., *Cousins and Strangers*, p. 83; Chistopher Isherwood, "Los Angeles," *Horizon* 16 (October 1947), p. 145; Barzini, *Americans Are Alone in the World*, p. 38.

32. Jean-Paul Sartre, "American Cities," and "New York, the Colonial City," in Jean-Paul Sartre, *Literary and Philosophical Essays*, trans. Annette Michelson (London: Rider, 1955), pp. 115–20, 122; italics his; Baudrillard, *America*, pp. 53, 58, 66, 125; de Beauvoir, *America Day by Day*, pp. 65, 89–90. On the absolute necessity of owning a car in America, see also Isherwood, "Los Angeles," p. 143; and Herbert von Borch, *The Unfinished Society*, trans. Mary Ilford (New York: Hawthorn Books, 1962, c. Germany 1960), p. 83.

33. The quotation from Cunliffe is in Putt, ed., *Cousins and Strangers*, p. 45; Barzini, *Americans Are Alone in the World*, p. 79; Brogan, *The American Character*, pp. 43–46. See also Rob Kroes, "The Netherlands: A Contribution by Rob Kroes," in Maurizio Vaudagna, ed., "Forum: American Studies in Europe," *Storia Nordamericana* 7 (1990), pp. 175–76; and J. Martin Evans, *America: The View from Europe* (Stanford, Calif.: Stanford University Press, 1976), p. 65.

34. Jacques Freymond, "From Switzerland," in Joseph, ed., *As Others See Us*, pp. 85–86.

35. De Beauvoir, *America Day by Day*, p. 291; Baudrillard, *America*, pp. 5, 8, 16, 86, 95; italics his.

36. Baudrillard, *America*, pp. 28, 32, 70, 101, 104; de Beauvoir, *America Day by Day*, p. 131.

37. Freymond, "From Switzerland," pp. 91–92; Alessandro Portelli, "The Transatlantic Jeremiad: American Mass Culture and Counterculture and Opposition Culture in Italy," in Kroes et al., eds., *Cultural Transmissions and Receptions*, p. 132; Laski, *The American Democracy*, pp. 5, 34, 40, 400–401. See also Evans, *America: The View from Europe*, p. 66.

38. For the European recognition of the different meanings associated with the word *frontier,* see Brogan, *The American Character*, p. 5; and Kroes, "The Netherlands," p. 167.

39. Jacqueline Paskow, "Germany Remembered and Reconsidered," in Arndt and Rubin, eds., *The Fulbright Difference*, pp. 377, 379; Baudrillard, *America*, pp. 93–94.

40. For examples of these ideas, see Landau, *Among the Americans*, p. 66; Geoffrey Gorer, *The American People: A Study in National Character* (New York: Norton, 1948), pp. 95–96, 141, 182–83; Jacques Maritain, *Reflections on America*, (New York: Scribner's, 1958), p. 93; Laski, *The American Democracy*, pp. 6, 486, 716; Brogan, *The American Character*, p. xxvi; Sartre, "American Cities," pp. 110–11; and Isherwood, "Los Angeles," pp. 143–44.

41. Laski, *The American Democracy*, pp. 23–24; de Riencourt, *The Coming Caesars*, p. 282; Landau, *Among the Americans*, p. 33; Plumb, "New York Vindicated," p. 234; de Beauvoir, *America Day by Day*, pp. 26, 225; Michel Crozier, *The Trouble with America*, trans. Peter Heineggn (Berkeley: University of California Press, 1984), pp. 28, 106.

42. Gorer, *The American People*, pp. 27, 31, 40, 46.

43. Laski, *The American Democracy*, pp. 56–57; Landau, *Among the Americans*, p. 63; Gorer, *The American People*, p. 183; Baudrillard, *America*, p. 124. See also Crozier, *The Trouble with America*, pp. 7, 133; Evans, *America: The View from Europe*, pp. 47, 49, 58–59; and Henri Mendras, "On Being French in Chicago, 1950–1951," in Arndt and Rubin, eds., *The Fulbright Difference*, p. 61.

44. De Riencourt, *The Coming Caesars*, p. 280; Baudrillard, *America*, p. 76; de Beauvoir, *America Day by Day*, p. 293; Laski, *The American Democracy*, pp. 5, 342, 729. See also Maritain, *Reflections on America*, p. 25; Crozier, *The Trouble*

with America, p. 58; Edward Chester, *Europe Views America: A Critical Evaluation* (Washington, D.C.: Public Affairs Press, 1962), pp. 11, 125.

45. De Beauvoir, *America Day by Day*, pp. 291, 293; italics hers; Bertrand Russell, "The Political and Cultural Influence," in Russell et al., *The Impact of America on European Culture* (Boston: Beacon Press, 1951), pp. 14–15; Gorer, *The American People*, p. 178; Barzini, *Americans Are Alone in the World*, p. 87. Many other European visitors and intellectuals expressed the belief that Americans were ignorant of history. For examples, see Putt, ed., *Cousins and Strangers*, pp. 3, 14, 24, 109, 247; de Riencourt, *The Coming Caesars*, p. 275; Laski, *The American Democracy*, pp. 6–8, 716; Crozier, *The Trouble with America*, p. xvii; André Maurois, *From My Journal*, trans. Joan Charles (New York: Harper, 1948), pp. 174, 176; Maritain, *Reflections on America*, p. 37; Brogan, *The American Character*, p. 178; Connolly, "Introduction to Art on the American Horizon," p. 5; Aron, "From France," p. 62; and A. N. J. den Hollander, "Cultural Diversity and the Mind of the Scholar: Some Thoughts on American and European Thinking," in den Hollander, ed., *Diverging Parallels*, p. 210.

46. Marias, "From Spain," p. 47; Cunliffe, "European Images of America," p. 511. For other expressions of surprise at the Americans' propensity to disclose and criticize the defects of their country, see Maritain, *Reflections on America*, p. 38; von Borch, *The Unfinished Society*, p. 33; Plumb, "Brooklyn Through English Eyes," p. 228; Baudrillard, *America*, p. 91; and Barzini, *Americans Are Alone in the World*, p. 82.

47. De Beauvoir, *America Day by Day*, p. 165.

48. For my analysis of the ideas of postwar American social critics, see Richard Pells, *The Liberal Mind in a Conservative Age: American Intellectuals in the 1940s and 1950s* (New York: Harper & Row, 1985), especially chaps. 3–4. For a discussion of the influence of American intellectuals in Europe, see Cunliffe, "The Anatomy of Anti-Americanism," pp. 26–27; and Hollander, *Anti-Americanism*, pp. 400, 408. During the 1960s, the works of David Riesman, John Kenneth Galbraith, and William Whyte were translated into French. In the 1980s, Michel Crozier called Riesman "the best analyst of American society." See Kuisel, *Seducing the French*, p. 203; and Crozier, *The Trouble with America*, p. 134.

49. Von Borch, *The Unfinished Society*, pp. 18, 25–26, 43, 67, 71, 84; Francis Williams, *The American Invasion* (New York: Crown, 1962), pp. 90, 94, 101. Even before the critiques of American intellectuals in the 1950s, Simone de Beauvoir insisted that Americans were becoming more trapped in the social hierarchy. See *America Day by Day*, pp. 226, 238.

50. Brogan, *The American Character*, pp. xii, 118; de Beauvoir, *America Day by Day*, p. 77; Gorer, *The American People*, p. 184; Landau, *Among the Americans*, p. 70. The quotation from Marcus Cunliffe is in Putt, ed., *Cousins and Strangers*, p. 49. For other examples of the complaints about standardization, see Maurois, *From My Journal*, p. 171; Visson, *As Others See Us*, pp. 31, 160; and Chester, *Europe Views America*, p. 10.

51. De Beauvoir, *America Day by Day*, p. 292; de Riencourt, *The Coming Caesars*, p. 279; J. E. Morpurgo, "Hollywood: America's Voice," in Russell et al., *The Impact of America on European Culture*, p. 56; Williams, *The American Invasion*, p. 107. See also Landau, *Among the Americans*, pp. 70, 72; and Maritain, *Reflections on America*, p. 164.

52. Morpurgo, "Hollywood," p. 56; de Riencourt, *The Coming Caesars*, pp. 276, 279, 284. For similar views about the American distrust of eccentricity, see Russell, "The Political and Cultural Influence," p. 17; Wyndham Lewis, *America and Cosmic Man* (London: Nicholson & Watson, 1948), p. 20; Putt, ed., *Cousins and Strangers*, pp. 14–16; and Chester, *Europe Views America*, p. 27.

53. Gorer, *The American People*, pp. 106–8, 110, 133, 174; Jean-Paul Sartre, "Individualism and Conformism in the United States," in Sartre, *Literary and Philosophical Essays*, pp. 100–102; Baudrillard, *America*, pp. 92–93; Isherwood, "Los Angeles," p. 147. See also Mathy, *Extrême Occident*, p. 117.

54. De Beauvoir, *America Day by Day*, p. 294; Aron, "From France," p. 59; Landau, *Among the Americans*, p. 64; Baudrillard, *America*, pp. 33–34.

55. Gorer, *The American People*, pp. 38, 142, 174; Baudrillard, *America*, pp. 39, 50, 60, 95; Brogan, *The American Character*, p. 7; Maritain, *Reflections on America,* pp. 46, 156; von Borch, *The Unfinished Society*, pp. 21, 203; Connolly, "Introduction to Art on the American Horizon," p. 7; de Riencourt, *The Coming Caesars*, p. 284; Laski, *The American Democracy*, p. 16. On the penchant for random, individualistic mayhem in America and its contrast with Europe's state-supported violence, see also Harry Allen, "The Impact of American Violence on Britain," in A. N. J. den Hollander, ed., *Contagious Conflict: The Impact of American Dissent on European Life* (Leiden: Brill, 1973), p. 77; Evans, *America: The View from Europe*, p. 70; and John Dean, "Deliberate Differences: Using Cross-Cultural Studies to Understand the European-American Relationship," in Kroes et al., eds., *Cultural Transmissions and Receptions*, p. 223.

56. Sartre, "Individualism and Conformism in the United States," p. 101; de Beauvoir, *America Day by Day*, p. 66; Aron, "From France," p. 64; Crozier, *The Trouble with America*, pp. 58, 120, 122, 136–37; Baudrillard, *America*, pp. 35–36, 85; Gorer, *The American People*, p. 61; Barzini, *Americans Are Alone in the World*, p. 24. See also Chester, *Europe Views America*, p. 35; and Kuisel, *Seducing the French*, p. 124. The most famous and influential European portraits of the American denial of death, as displayed in its funeral practices, were Evelyn Waugh's *The Loved One: An Anglo-American Tragedy* (London: Chapman & Hall, 1948); and Jessica Mitford's *The American Way of Death* (London: Hutchinson, 1963).

57. Laski, *The American Democracy*, pp. 165–66, 170; de Beauvoir, *America Day by Day*, p. 294; Sartre, "Individualism and Conformism in the United States," p. 103; Gorer, *The American People*, pp. 180–81. For other expressions of these ideas, see Morpurgo, "Hollywood," pp. 56–57; and Snowman, *Britain and America*, pp. 68–69.

58. See, for example, Laski, *The American Democracy*, p. 725; Russell, "The Political and Cultural Influence," p. 16; Maritain, *Reflections on America*, pp. 30, 33–34; and de Riencourt, *The Coming Caesars*, p. 282.

59. Cunliffe's remarks are in Putt, ed., *Cousins and Strangers*, pp. 167–68; Laski, *The American Democracy*, p. 165, 170.

60. Barzini, *Americans Are Alone in the World*, p. 163; Baudrillard, *America*, p. 87. See also Maritain, *Reflections on America*, p. 97; and Laski, *The American Democracy*, pp. 365, 724, 727.

61. Laski, *The American Democracy*, pp. 12, 166. See also Reyner Banham, "Europe and American Design," in Richard Rose, ed., *Lessons from America: An Exploration* (London: Macmillan, 1974), p. 90.

62. See Theodor Adorno, "Scientific Experiences of a European Scholar in America," and Colin Eisler, "*Kunstgeschichte* American Style: A Study in Migration," in Donald Fleming and Bernard Bailyn, eds., *The Intellectual Migration: Europe and America, 1930–1960* (Cambridge, Mass.: Charles Warren Center for Studies in American History, 1968), pp. 350, 613; and Mendras, "On Being French in Chicago," pp. 63–64.

63. Adorno, "Scientific Experiences of a European Scholar in America," pp. 338–41, 355, 365–66; italics his. See also H. Stuart Hughes, *The Sea Change: The Migration of Social Thought, 1930–1965* (New York: McGraw-Hill, 1977, c. 1975), p. 151; and Claus-Dieter Krohn, *Intellectuals in Exile: Refugee Scholars and the New School for Social Research*, trans. Rita and Robert Kimber (Amherst: University of Massachusetts Press, 1993, c. 1987), p. 192.

64. Von Borch, *The Unfinished Society*, p. 137. Other critiques of American education can be found in Laski, *The American Democracy*, pp. 340–41, 363, 366; Williams, *The American Invasion*, p. 81; de Riencourt, *The Coming Caesars*, p. 286; Gorer, *The American People*, p. 99; de Beauvoir, *America Day by Day*, p. 216; and Putt, ed., *Cousins and Strangers*, pp. 24, 88–91, 194–95. See also John Garraty and Walter Adams, *From Main Street to the Left Bank: Students and Scholars Abroad* (East Lansing: Michigan State University Press, 1959), pp. 24–26, 199.

65. Lewis, *America and Cosmic Man*, p. 216; Marais, "From Spain," p. 26; de Beauvoir, *America Day by Day*, pp. 23, 38, 85, 203.

66. Connolly, "Introduction to Art on the American Horizon," p. 4; Morpurgo, "Hollywood," pp. 60–61; von Borch, *The Unfinished Society*, pp. 118–19; de Beauvoir, *America Day by Day,* p. 264; Maritain, *Reflections on America*, p. 76.

67. For examples of this argument, see Marais, "From Spain," p. 26; Visson, *As Others See Us*, p. 24; Gorer, *The American People*, p. 140; de Riencourt, *The Coming Caesars*, p. 278; and Laurence Wylie and Sarella Henriquez, "French Images of American Life," *Tocqueville Review* 4 (1982), pp. 209, 223. See also Chester, *Europe Views America*, p. 127.

68. A typical instance of this disdain for American music can be found in Martin Cooper, "Revolution in Musical Taste," in Russell et al., *The Impact of America on European Culture*, pp. 68–69, 77. See also Reinhold Wagnleitner,

Coca-Colonization and the Cold War: The Cultural Mission of the United States in Austria After the Second World War, trans. Diana Wolf (Chapel Hill: University of North Carolina Press, 1994), p. 196.

69. To his credit, Harold Laski insisted that culturally, America was not a "minor outpost" of Europe. He also understood that the Europeans' disparagement of American culture was a reflection of their own loss of self-esteem in artistic and intellectuals matters. See *The American Democracy*, pp. 398, 727–28. For a similar insight, see Claude-Jean Bertrand, "American Cultural Imperialism—A Myth?" *American Studies International* 25 (April 1987), p. 51.

70. De Beauvoir, *America Day by Day*, p. 77; Crozier, *The Trouble with America*, p. 61. For other examples of how Europeans described and often misinterpreted American politics, see Visson, *As Others See Us*, p. 234; den Hollander, "Cultural Diversity and the Mind of the Scholar," p. 208; Gorer, *The American People*, pp. 148, 164; Laski, *The American Democracy*, p. 13; Wylie and Henriquez, "French Images of American Life," p. 224; Putt, ed., *Cousins and Strangers*, p. 173; and Marais, "From Spain," p. 28. See also Kuisel, *Seducing the French*, p. 126.

71. Barzini, *Americans Are Alone in the World*, pp. 104, 106; Williams, *The American Invasion*, p. 45; Putt, ed., *Cousins and Strangers*, pp. 8, 11–12; Gorer, *The American People*, pp. 193–94, 221.

72. Gorer, *The American People*, p. 225.

73. Aron, "Transatlantic Relations," p. 27. For similar arguments about the nonapplicability of America's historical experience, see Barzini, *Americans Are Alone in the World*, p. 62; and von Borch, *The Unfinished Society*, pp. 17–18. See also Chester, *Europe Views America*, p. 32.

74. See Rose, "Anti-Americanism in France," p. 469; Lacorne and Rupnik, "France Bewitched by America," p. 27; Guy Sorman, "United States: Model or Bête Noire?" and Marie-France Toinet, "Does Anti-Americanism Exist?" in Lacorne et al., eds., *The Rise and Fall of Anti-Americanism*, pp. 213, 233; and Kuisel, *Seducing the French*, pp. 127, 236.

75. For examples of the contradictory ways in which Europeans criticized American foreign policy, see Barzini, *Americans Are Alone in the World,* pp. 104, 107, 114, 121, 124, 199; Aron, "From France," p. 62; Zincone, "Moral America," pp. 42, 49, 51; Piovene, "Ungrateful Europe," p. 117; Rupnik and Humbertjean, "Images of the United States in Public Opinion," p. 85; den Hollander, "Cultural Diversity and the Mind of the Scholar," p. 213; Putt, ed., *Cousins and Strangers*, p. 8; and Visson, *As Others See Us*, p. 12.

76. Brogan, "From England," p. 21. For other views of America's immaturity in foreign affairs and its need for a healthy dose of European realism, see Visson, *As Others See Us*, pp. 14, 80, 233; Wylie and Henriquez, "French Images of American Life," p. 250; Webster, *Looka Yonder!* p. 240; Hollander, *Anti-Americanism*, p. 390; Piovene, "Ungrateful Europe," pp. 122, 129; Zincone, "Moral America," pp. 41–42, 49, 56; Kriegel, "Consistent Misapprehension," p. 87; and Barzini, *Americans Are Alone in the World*, pp. 8, 124.

77. I discussed the debate about Graham Greene's novel among intellectuals in the United States, particularly between Diana Trilling and Philip Rahv, in *The Liberal Mind in a Conservative Age*, p. 352.

78. Graham Greene, *The Quiet American* (London: Penguin Books, 1977, c. 1955), pp. 28, 96, 129.

79. Ibid., pp. 32, 90. See also Evans, *America: The View from Europe*, p. 101.

80. Greene, *The Quiet American*, pp. 20, 37, 60, 174, 183.

CHAPTER SEVEN
THE AMERICANIZATION OF
EUROPE'S ECONOMIC AND SOCIAL LIFE

1. David Ellwood, "The Impact of the Marshall Plan on Italy; The Impact of Italy on the Marshall Plan," in Rob Kroes, Robert Rydell, and Doeko F. J. Bosscher, eds., *Cultural Transmissions and Receptions: American Mass Culture in Europe* (Amsterdam: VU University Press, 1993), p. 121; David Ellwood, *Rebuilding Europe: Western Europe, America and Postwar Reconstruction* (London: Longman, 1992), pp. 205, 222; Richard Kuisel, *Seducing the French: The Dilemma of Americanization* (Berkeley: University of California Press, 1993), p. 95; Edward McCreary, *The Americanization of Europe: The Impact of Americans and American Business on the Uncommon Market* (Garden City, N.Y.: Doubleday, 1964), p. 13.

2. For the general aims of American corporations in Europe during the 1950s and 1960s and statistics on the transfer of American capital, see Thomas Guback, "Film and Cultural Pluralism," *Journal of Aesthetic Education* 5 (April 1971), p. 39; Thomas Guback, "Cultural Identity and Film in the European Economic Community," *Cinema Journal* 14 (Fall 1974), p. 8; Kuisel, *Seducing the French*, p. 182; Francis Williams, *The American Invasion* (New York: Crown, 1962), p. 16; and McCreary, *The Americanization of Europe*, p. 4.

3. Jean-Jacques Servan-Schreiber, *The American Challenge*, trans. Ronald Steel (New York: Atheneum, 1968, c. Paris 1967), pp. 12–13; Williams, *The American Invasion*, pp. 17, 19–21, 25, 28–29; Kuisel, *Seducing the French*, pp. 160, 168. In France by 1965, General Motors had sales nineteen times larger than Renault's, while Goodyear's sales were four times larger than Michelin's.

4. Servan-Schreiber, *The American Challenge*, pp. 14–15; Dick Hebdige, "Towards a Cartography of Taste, 1935–1962," in Hebdige, *Hiding in the Light: On Images and Things* (London: Routledge, 1988), p. 73; Williams, *The American Invasion*, pp. 16, 29; Pehr Gyllenhammar, "The Impact of American Culture on Management Organization and the Transportation Industry," in Allen Davis, ed., *For Better or Worse: The American Influence in the World* (Westport, Conn.: Greenwood Press, 1981), pp. 106–7.

5. Servan-Schreiber, *The American Challenge*, pp. 11, 13, 26, 28, 39, 43, 45, 102, 156; italics his. See also Kuisel, *Seducing the French*, p. 179.

6. Servan-Schreiber, *The American Challenge*, pp. 27, 83, 260; Raymond Aron and August Heckscher, *Diversity of Worlds: France and the United States Look at Their Common Problems* (New York: Reynal, 1957), pp. 103, 105, 110. See also McCreary, *The Americanization of Europe*, pp. 35, 40, 173, 193, 195; Ezra Suleiman, "Anti-Americans and the Elite," and Christian Stoffaës, "The Limits of the American Model," in Denis Lacorne, Jacques Rupnik, and Marie-France Toinet, eds., *The Rise and Fall of Anti-Americanism: A Century of French Perception*, trans. Gerry Turner (New York: St. Martin's Press, 1990, c. Paris 1986), pp. 112–13, 162; and Kuisel, *Seducing the French*, pp. 84–85, 87–88, 99, 114.

7. Aron and Heckscher, *Diversity of Worlds*, p. 112; Kuisel, *Seducing the French*, p. 162.

8. For examples of how the Europeans framed this dilemma, see Raymond Aron, "The United States as the Dominant Economy," in James Burnham, ed., *What Europe Thinks of America* (New York: John Day, 1953), p. 210; Aron and Heckscher, *Diversity of Worlds*, pp. 116, 154; and Steinar Bryn, "Norway and America: Looking at Each Other," *Scandinavian Review* 76 (Summer 1988), p. 159. See also Kuisel, *Seducing the French*, p. 3.

9. On Charles de Gaulle's economic and military policies, see Michael Harrison, "French Anti-Americanism Under the Fourth Republic and the Gaullist Solution," in Lacorne et. al., eds., *The Rise and Fall of Anti-Americanism*, pp. 171, 175–77; David Strauss, *Menace in the West: The Rise of French Anti-Americanism in Modern Times* (Westport, Conn.: Greenwood Press, 1978), p. 268; and Kuisel, *Seducing the French*, pp. 134–36, 139, 145–46, 157, 159–60, 167, 182.

10. On the domestic popularity of and the problems with de Gaulle's economic nationalism, see Kuisel, *Seducing the French*, pp. 141–42; Servan-Schreiber, *The American Challenge*, pp. 19, 21; and Frank Costigliola, *France and the United States: The Cold Alliance Since World War II* (New York: Twayne, 1992), p. 152.

11. Servan-Schreiber, *The American Challenge*, pp. 111, 153–55; Strauss, *Menace in the West*, p. 275; Guback, "Cultural Identity and Film in the European Economic Community," p. 15.

12. James Baldwin, "The Northern Protestant," in Baldwin, *Nobody Knows My Name* (New York: Dell, 1963, c. 1961), p. 139.

13. See Tom Hooson, "Exporting the Pursuit of Happiness," in Richard Rose, ed., *Lessons from America: An Exploration* (London: Macmillan, 1974), pp. 162–66, 191; D. W. Brogan, "From England," in Franz Joseph, ed., *As Others See Us: The United States Through Foreign Eyes* (Princeton, N.J.: Princeton University Press, 1959), pp. 16, 23; Norman Kogan, "Italian Intellect and Foreign Influences," in Richard Arndt and David Rubin, eds., *The Fulbright Difference, 1948–1992* (New Brunswick, N.J.: Transaction Books, 1993), p. 172; Daniel Snowman, *Britain and America: An Interpretation of*

Their Culture, 1945–1975 (New York: New York University Press, 1977), p. 263; and McCreary, *The Americanization of Europe*, pp. 2, 252.

14. Kuisel, *Seducing the French*, pp. 104–5, 150–51; Snowman, *Britain and America*, p. 174; David Ellwood, "From 'Re-Education' to the Selling of the Marshall Plan in Italy," in Nicholas Pronay and Keith Wilson, eds., *The Political Re-Education of Germany and Her Allies After World War II* (Totowa, N.J.: Barnes & Noble Books, 1985), p. 235; Ralph Willett, *The Americanization of Germany, 1945–1949* (London: Routledge, 1989), p. 120.

15. Joseph Wechsberg, "The American Abroad," *Atlantic Monthly* 200 (November 1957), p. 265; McCreary, *The Americanization of Europe*, pp. 14–15. By the early 1960s, two out of five cars in Britain were manufactured in American-owned plants. In France between 1960 and 1973, the percentage of households with an automobile doubled from 30 to 60 percent. See Williams, *The American Invasion*, p. 21; and Kuisel, *Seducing the French*, p. 150.

16. Snowman, *Britain and America*, pp. 183, 200; Arnold Sywottek, "The Americanization of Everyday Life? Early Trends in Consumer and Leisure-Time Behavior," in Michael Ermarth, ed., *America and the Shaping of German Society, 1945–1955* (Providence, R.I.: Berg, 1993), p. 147.

17. For descriptions of and statistics on the changes in French society, see David Bell, "Bye-Bye Mitterrand," *New Republic* 212 (March 20, 1995), p. 27; Costigliola, *France and the United States*, p. 189; and Stanley Hoffmann, "France: Keeping the Demons at Bay," *New York Review of Books* 41 (March 3, 1994), p. 10. On the existence and consequences of urban poverty elsewhere in Europe, see Harry Allen, "The Impact of American Violence on Britain," in A. N. J. den Hollander, ed., *Contagious Conflict: The Impact of American Dissent on European Life* (Leiden: Brill, 1973), pp. 73–74, 83; and J. H. Plumb, "New York Vindicated" and "Crime Against the Person," in Plumb, *The American Experience*, vol. 2 of *The Collected Essays* (Athens: University of Georgia Press, 1989), pp. 229, 249.

18. See Kenneth Jackson, *The Crabgrass Frontier: The Suburbanization of the United States* (New York: Oxford University Press, 1987, c. 1985), pp. 288, 290–91, 293, 295–96.

19. Reyner Banham, "Mediated Environments Or: You Can't Build That Here," in C. W. E. Bigsby, ed., *Superculture: American Popular Culture and Europe* (Bowling Green, Ohio: Bowling Green University Popular Press, 1975), pp. 74–75; Jackson, *The Crabgrass Frontier*, pp. 303–4; Bell, "Bye-Bye Mitterrand," p. 27.

20. A number of commentators remarked on the European fascination with American kitchens, and the way European women anticipated a change in their roles as a result of copying their American counterparts. See Reinhold Wagnleitner, "Propagating the American Dream: Cultural Policies as Means of Integration," *American Studies International* 24 (April 1986), p. 76; Williams, *The American Invasion*, p. 140; Ellwood, *Rebuilding Europe*, pp. 234–35; and McCreary, *The Americanization of Europe*, p. 101.

21. For a more detailed discussion of Coke's expansion into the international, and especially the European, market from the 1930s through the early 1950s, see Kuisel, *Seducing the French*, pp. 52–53; Costigliola, *France and the United States*, p. 77; and Willett, *The Americanization of Germany*, pp. 100, 102–3, 105.

22. F. O. Matthiessen, *From the Heart of Europe* (New York: Oxford University Press, 1948), p. 60.

23. Kuisel, *Seducing the French*, pp. 54, 56, 68; Costigliola, *France and the United States*, p. 77.

24. Kuisel, *Seducing the French*, p. 68.

25. On developments in Eastern Europe during the 1990s, see Nathaniel Nash, "Coke's Great Romanian Adventure," *New York Times* (February 26, 1995), sec. 3, pp. 1, 10; and Allesandra Stanley, "Clinton Chooses Coke in Russia's Cola War," *New York Times* (May 11, 1995), p. C6.

26. Wyndham Lewis, *America and Cosmic Man* (London: Nicholson & Watson, 1948), p. 17; Raymond Aron, "From France," in Joseph, ed., *As Others See Us*, p. 71. The equation of America with the future is also discussed in Richard Rose, "America: Inevitable or Inimitable?" in Rose, ed., *Lessons from America*, p. 1; Snowman, *Britain and America*, p. 259; Duncan Webster, *Looka Yonder! The Imaginary America of Populist Culture* (London: Routledge, 1988), pp. 180, 217; and Strauss, *Menace in the West*, p. 253.

27. A number of writers, both European and American, have commented on the connections between Americanization and modernization. For examples, see Rob Kroes, "Americanization: What Are We Talking About?" in Kroes et. al., eds., *Cultural Transmissions and Receptions*, p. 303; Rob Kroes, "Among the Receivers: American Culture Transmitted Abroad," in Kroes, ed., *Within the U.S. Orbit: Small National Cultures vis-à-vis the United States* (Amsterdam: VU University Press, 1991), p. 6; Rose, "America: Inevitable or Inimitable?" p. 10; Snowman, *Britain and America*, pp. 230, 264; and Luigi Barzini, *Americans Are Alone in the World* (New York: Random House, 1953), p. 11.

28. See Snowman, *Britain and America*, p. 265; Hoffmann, "France: Keeping the Demons at Bay," pp. 12, 16; Paul Hollander, *Anti-Americanism: Critiques at Home and Abroad, 1965–1990* (New York: Oxford University Press, 1992), p. 404; Reinhold Wagnleitner, *Coca-Colonization and the Cold War: The Cultural Mission of the United States in Austria After the Second World War*, trans. Diana Wolf (Chapel Hill: University of North Carolina Press, 1994), p. 292; and Kuisel, *Seducing the French*, p. 186.

29. Sigmund Skard, *Trans-Atlantica: Memoirs of a Norwegian Americanist* (Oslo: Universitetsforlaget, 1978), p. 153. For similar sentiments see Webster, *Looka Yonder!* p. 193; Michel Winock, "The Cold War," in Lacorne et. al., eds., *The Rise and Fall of Anti-Americanism*, p. 75; and Kuisel, *Seducing the French*, p. ix.

CHAPTER EIGHT
MASS CULTURE: THE AMERICAN TRANSMISSION

1. Michele Bottalico, "A Place for All: Old and New Myths in the Italian Appreciation of American Literature," and Jan Gretlund, "The American Within: Danes and American Literature," in Huck Gutman, ed., *As Others Read Us: International Perspectives on American Literature* (Amherst: University of Massachusetts Press, 1991), pp. 66, 156; Alessandro Portelli, "The Transatlantic Jeremiad: American Mass Culture and Counterculture and Opposition Culture in Italy," in Rob Kroes, Robert Rydell, and Doeko F. J. Bosscher, eds., *Cultural Transmissions and Receptions: American Mass Culture in Europe* (Amsterdam: VU University Press, 1993), p. 130. For descriptions of how ubiquitous American mass culture was in other Western European countries, see Daniel Snowman, *Britain and America: An Interpretation of Their Culture, 1945–1975* (New York: New York University Press, 1977), pp. 262–63; Malcolm Bradbury, "How I Invented America," *Journal of American Studies* 14 (April 1980), p. 120; Richard Kuisel, *Seducing the French: The Dilemma of Americanization* (Berkeley: University of California Press, 1993), p. 151; Theo D'haen, "Cutting Loose: American Literary Studies in the Netherlands," in Gutman, ed., *As Others Read Us*, p. 192; and Nico Wilterdink, "The Netherlands Between the Greater Powers," in Rob Kroes, ed., *Within the U.S. Orbit: Small National Cultures vis-à-vis the United States* (Amsterdam: VU University Press, 1991), pp. 28–29. By the 1960s and 1970s, America's culture was infiltrating Eastern Europe, particularly Poland. See "Poland: Maurizio Vaudagna Interviews Michal Rozbicki," in Maurizio Vaudagna, ed., "Forum: American Studies in Europe," *Storia Nordamericana* 7 (1990), p. 147.

2. Barry Newman, "Global Chatter," *Wall Street Journal* (March 22, 1995), p. A1; Peter Lev, *The Euro-American Cinema* (Austin: University of Texas Press, 1993), p. 67; William Read, *America's Mass Media Merchants* (Baltimore: Johns Hopkins University Press, 1976), p. 14.

3. Lev, *The Euro-American Cinema*, p. 67; Jeremy Tunstall, *The Media Are American* (New York: Columbia University Press, 1977), pp. 126–28.

4. For discussions of the role of Britain and West Germany as conveyor belts for American culture in Europe, see Tunstall, *The Media Are American*, pp. 95, 130, 133; Mel van Elteren, "Reflections on Cultural Identity and 'Americanization' in Relation to the Cultural Dimensions of the Recent GATT Agreement," unpublished paper, Tilburg, the Netherlands, 1994, pp. 12–13; Franco Minganti, "Rock 'N' Roll in Italy: Was It True Americanization?" and Mel van Elteren, "Sounds from America in Holland: The Counter-Culture of the Sixties," in Kroes et al., eds., *Cultural Transmissions and Receptions*, pp. 144, 172; Tiziano Bonazzi, "The Beginnings of American History in Italy," in Richard Arndt and David Rubin, eds., *The Fulbright Difference, 1948–1992* (New Brunswick, N.J.: Transaction Books, 1993), p. 152; and Reinhold Wagnleitner, *Coca-Colonization and the Cold*

War: The Cultural Mission of the United States in Austria After the Second World War, trans. Diana Wolf (Chapel Hill: University of North Carolina Press, 1994), p. 293.

5. Read, *America's Mass Media Merchants*, pp. 11, 63, 70; Tunstall, *The Media Are American*, pp. 17–18, 75–77.

6. For a general discussion of the influence of American journalism on Europe, see Read, *America's Mass Media Merchants*, pp. 3, 118–19; Tunstall, *The Media Are American*, pp. 28–29, 31, 33–35, 45, 49; Snowman, *Britain and America*, pp. 206–7; and Claude-Jean Bertrand and Miguel Urabayen, "European Mass Media in the 1980s," in Everett Rogers and Francis Balle, eds., *The Media Revolution in America and in Western Europe* (Norwood, N.J.: Ablex, 1985), p. 41.

7. See Richard Stevenson, "Hollywood Takes to the Global Stage," *New York Times* (April 16, 1989), sec. 3, p. 8.

8. A number of analysts have commented on the heterogeneity of the American audience as a factor in the globalization of American culture. For examples, see Emily Rosenberg, *Spreading the American Dream: American Economic and Cultural Expansion, 1890–1945* (New York: Hill & Wang, 1982), p. 100; Read, *America's Mass Media Merchants*, pp. 40, 188; and Todd Gitlin, "World Leaders: Mickey, et al.," *New York Times* (May 3, 1992), sec. 2, p. 30.

9. Fabrice Montebello, "Hollywood Films in a French Working Class Milieu: Longwy 1945–1960," in David Ellwood and Rob Kroes, eds., *Hollywood in Europe: Experiences of a Cultural Hegemony* (Amsterdam: VU University Press, 1994), pp. 227, 229.

10. The quotation from Woody Allen can be found in Annette Wernblad, *Brooklyn Is Not Expanding: Woody Allen's Comic Universe*, (Cranbury, N.J.: Associated University Presses, 1992), p. 9. For Sydney Pollack's quotation, see his speech, "The Way We Are," reprinted in "The Controversy About Popular Culture," *American Enterprise* 3 (May–June 1992), p. 94. See also Gitlin, "World Leaders: Mickey, et al.," p. 30.

11. Charles Goldsmith and Charles Fleming, "Film Industry in Europe Seeks Wider Audience," *Wall Street Journal* (December 6, 1993), p. B1; Roger Cohen, "U.S.–French Cultural Trade Rift Now Snags a World Agreement," *New York Times* (December 8, 1993), p. C2.

12. On the wartime plight of European filmmaking and the consequent opportunities for Hollywood, see Thomas Guback, "Hollywood's International Market," in Tino Balio, ed., *The American Film Industry* (Madison: University of Wisconsin Press, 1985), p. 470; and Thomas Guback, *The International Film Industry: Western Europe and America Since 1945* (Bloomington: Indiana University Press, 1969), p. 16.

13. Guback, *The International Film Industry*, p. 3; Lev, *The Euro-American Cinema*, p. 17.

14. Guback, *The International Film Industry*, pp. 9–10, 164; Guback, "Hollywood's International Market," p. 465; Paul Swann, *The Hollywood Feature*

Film in Postwar Britain (New York: St. Martin's Press, 1987), pp. 117–18. For a definition of block booking, see chap. 1, note 23. The fate of Kevin Costner's 1995 blockbuster, *Waterworld*, exemplifies the importance of the international market. *Waterworld* cost $175 million to make, but earned only $88 million in the United States. The movie was a commercial failure at home, but by 1996 it had grossed $166 million overseas, thereby becoming a profitable film despite the predictions when it was released that it would lose a huge amount of money. See Louis Menand, "Hollywood's Trap," *New York Review of Books* 43 (September 19, 1996), p. 5.

15. David Ellwood, "Introduction: Historical Methods and Approaches," in Ellwood and Kroes, eds., *Hollywood in Europe*, p. 9; Tunstall, *The Media Are American*, pp. 223–24; Swann, *The Hollywood Feature Film in Postwar Britain*, pp. 114, 119.

16. Guback, *The International Film Industry*, p. 124; Rosenberg, *Spreading the American Dream*, p. 210; Reinhold Wagnleitner, "Propagating the American Dream: Cultural Policies as Means of Integration," *American Studies International* 24 (April 1986), p. 71.

17. Guback, *The International Film Industry*, p. 23; Ian Jarvie, "The Postwar Economic Foreign Policy of the American Film Industry: Europe 1945–1950," in Ellwood and Kroes, eds., *Hollywood in Europe*, p. 157.

18. On the activities of the Motion Picture Export Association, see Guback, "Hollywood's International Market," pp. 471, 474; and Guback, *The International Film Industry*, pp. 5, 94–95. The original members of the MPEA were MGM, Paramount, 20th Century Fox, Warner Brothers, Columbia, Universal, RKO, United Artists, and Allied Artists. See Reinhold Wagnleitner, "American Cultural Diplomacy, the Cinema, and the Cold War in Central Europe," in Ellwood and Kroes, eds., *Hollywood in Europe*, p. 200–201.

19. For the purposes and results of the Informational Media Guarantee Program, see Guback, *The International Film Industry*, pp. 17, 120, 132; Paul Swann, "The Little State Department: Washington and Hollywood's Rhetoric of the Postwar Audience," in Ellwood and Kroes, eds., *Hollywood in Europe*, p. 182; Charles Thompson and Walter Laves, *Cultural Relations and U.S. Foreign Policy* (Bloomington: Indiana University Press, 1963), p. 117; and C. W. E. Bigsby, "Europe, America and the Cultural Debate," in Bigsby, ed., *Superculture: American Popular Culture and Europe* (Bowling Green, Ohio: Bowling Green University Popular Press, 1975), p. 4.

20. Guback, *The International Film Industry*, p. 132; Swann, "The Little State Department," pp. 180, 195.

21. Swann, *The Hollywood Feature Film in Postwar Britain*, p. 131; Guback, *The International Film Industry*, p. 17.

22. Guback, *The International Film Industry*, pp. 20–21.

23. On Hollywood's ambitions in the West German film market, see Tunstall, *The Media Are American*, pp. 137–38; Guback, *The International Film Industry*, pp. 104–6, 131, 134; and Wagnleitner, *Coca-Colonization and the Cold War*, pp. 244, 256. Hollywood's success in Germany led to its domination of

the Austrian film market as well. See Wagnleitner, "American Cultural Diplomacy, the Cinema, and the Cold War in Central Europe," pp. 205–6.

24. For the statistics on French film production before and immediately after World War II, and the state of the industry during the Vichy regime, see Guback, *The International Film Industry*, p. 21; and Tony Judt, *Past Imperfect: French Intellectuals, 1944–1956* (Berkeley: University of California Press, 1992), p. 201.

25. Wagnleitner, *Coca-Colonization and the Cold War*, p. 240; Wagnleitner, "American Cultural Diplomacy, the Cinema, and the Cold War in Central Europe," p. 201; Guback, *The International Film Industry*, p. 23.

26. For the terms of the Blum-Byrnes agreement, its subsequent revision, and its impact on the French film industry, see Kuisel, *Seducing the French*, p. 19; Guback, "Hollywood's International Market," p. 475; Guback, *The International Film Industry*, p. 22; Serge Guilbaut, *How New York Stole the Idea of Modern Art: Abstract Expressionism, Freedom, and the Cold War*, trans. Arthur Goldhammer (Chicago: University of Chicago Press, 1984, c. 1983), p. 133; Michel Winock, "The Cold War," in Denis Lacorne, Jacques Rupnik, and Marie-France Toinet, eds., *The Rise and Fall of Anti-Americanism: A Century of French Perception*, trans. Gerry Turner (New York: St. Martin's Press, 1990, c. Paris 1986), p. 69; Jean-Philippe Mathy, *Extrême Occident: French Intellectuals and America* (Chicago: University of Chicago Press, 1993), p. 153; Frank Costigliola, *France and the United States: The Cold Alliance Since World War II* (New York: Twayne, 1992), pp. 55–56; Wagnleitner, *Coca-Colonization and the Cold War*, p. 241; and Victoria de Grazia, "Mass Culture and Sovereignty: The American Challenge to European Cinemas, 1920–1960," *Journal of Modern History* 61 (March 1989), p. 82.

27. Guback, *The International Film Industry*, p. 55; Swann, *The Hollywood Feature Film in Postwar Britain*, p. 115; Jarvie, "The Postwar Economic Foreign Policy of the American Film Industry," p. 171. French theater owners and audiences were opposed to quotas for the same reasons. See Costigliola, *France and the United States*, p. 56.

28. Jarvie, "The Postwar Economic Foreign Policy of the American Film Industry," p. 165; Swann, *The Hollywood Feature Film in Postwar Britain*, pp. 82, 147.

29. On Hollywood's dealings with Britain in the late 1940s, see Swann, *The Hollywood Feature Film in Postwar Britain*, pp. 92, 100; Wagnleitner, *Coca-Colonization and the Cold War*, pp. 241–42; Guback, *The International Film Industry*, pp. 19, 32–34; and Guback, "Hollywood's International Market," p. 474.

30. Guback, "Hollywood's International Market," p. 475; Guback, *The International Film Industry*, pp. 26, 52; de Grazia, "Mass Culture and Sovereignty," p. 82.

31. Herbert Kubly, *American In Italy* (New York: Simon & Schuster, 1955), p. 109.

32. Jarvie, "The Postwar Economic Foreign Policy of the American Film

Industry," p. 171; Wagnleitner, *Coca-Colonization and the Cold War*, pp. 249–50. There is considerable debate over exactly when Hollywood's international sales equaled its domestic box-office receipts. In 1995, *Variety* reported that for the first time, foreign grosses were roughly comparable to Hollywood's earnings in the North American market (which included Canada). But other sources give much earlier dates for this accomplishment. Given the mysterious bookkeeping practices of the major studios, it is difficult to get precise information about overseas profits. See Terry Pristin, "How to Do Boffo Abroad," *New York Times* (May 12, 1996), sec. 4, p. 14.

33. These quotations can be found, respectively, in Guilbaut, *How New York Stole the Idea of Modern Art*, p. 136; Wagnleitner, *Coca-Colonization and the Cold War*, p. 242; and Swann, *The Hollywood Feature Film in Postwar Britain*, p. 139.

34. Read, *America's Mass Media Merchants*, pp. 49, 53; Guback, *The International Film Industry*, pp. 38, 40, 43, 45–46; de Grazia, "Mass Culture and Sovereignty," p. 83.

35. Lev, *The Euro-American Cinema*, p. 9.

36. On the lowly status of foreign films in America before the 1950s, see Guback, *The International Film Industry*, p. 68, Guback, "Hollywood's International Market," pp. 467, 477; Lev, *The Euro-American Cinema*, pp. 4, 9; and Swann, *The Hollywood Feature Film in Postwar Britain*, p. 96.

37. Lev, *The Euro-American Cinema*, pp. 8, 13.

38. For the factors underlying the popularity of European films in the United States in the late 1950s and early 1960s, see Guback, *The International Film Industry*, pp. 70, 73–74, 87; and Lev, *The Euro-American Cinema*, pp. 9, 11.

39. On the nature and potential consequences of American investments in the European film industry, see Guback, *The International Film Industry*, pp. 35, 72, 166, 171, 200; Guback, "Hollywood's International Market," pp. 478–79; Thomas Guback, "Film and Cultural Pluralism," *Journal of Aesthetic Education* 5 (April 1971), p. 45; Read, *America's Mass Media Merchants*, p. 56; and Lev, *The Euro-American Cinema*, pp. 24–25.

40. Lev, *The Euro-American Cinema*, pp. xii, 31, 68.

41. Aljean Harmetz, "Hollywood Sets Up Shop in Europe," *New York Times* (January 11, 1990), p. 17; Lev, *The Euro-American Cinema*, pp. 43, 46–47, 52.

42. See John Rockwell, "Woody Allen: France's Monsieur Right," *New York Times* (April 5, 1992), sec. 2, p. 26; and Roger Cohen "Aux Armes! France Rallies to Battle Sly and T. Rex," *New York Times* (January 2, 1994), sec. 2, p. 22.

43. For a general description of, as well as statistics on, the unequal relationship between the American and European film industries in the 1980s and 1990s, see Philip Schlesinger, "Europe's Contradictory Communicative Space," *Daedalus* 123 (Spring 1994), p. 40; Lev, *The Euro-American Cinema*, p. 26; Joseph Garncarz, "Hollywood in Germany: The Role of American Films in Germany, 1925–1990," in Ellwood and Kroes, eds., *Hollywood in Europe*, p.

95; Harmetz, "Hollywood Sets Up Shop in Europe," p. 17; Richard Hudson, "Uncommon Market," *Wall Street Journal* (March 26, 1993), p. R15; Benjamin Barber, *Jihad vs. McWorld* (New York: Times Books, 1995), pp. 91–92; John Tagliabue, "The Americanization of the Venice Film Festival," *New York Times* (September 6, 1995), pp. B1–B2; Jolie Solomon, "Here Comes a New Golden Age— Literally," *Newsweek* **122** (August 23, 1993), p. 51; Alina Tugend, "A British Boom in American Studies," *Chronicle of Higher Education* 41 (April 14, 1995), p. A40; and Dick Polman, "American Culture: It's Awesome Overseas," *Austin American-Statesman* (April 2, 1995), p. J4.

44. Costigliola, *France and the United States*, p. 195; Lev, *The Euro-American Cinema*, p. 26; "Global Smarming: America's Pop Influence," *New York Times* (January 20, 1994), sec. 2, p. 31; Polman, "American Culture: It's Awesome Overseas," p. J4.

45. Read, *America's Mass Media Merchants*, pp. 71, 75.

46. Stevenson, "Hollywood Takes to the Global Stage," pp. 1, 8; Steven Greenhouse, "For Europe, U.S. May Spell TV," *New York Times* (July 31, 1989), p. 26; "Foreign Appeal Affects U.S. Networks," Show World, *Austin American-Statesman* (July 25, 1993), p. 14.

47. On the economic reasons for America's domination of the European television market from the 1960s to the 1990s, see Tunstall, *The Media Are American*, p. 144; Stevenson, "Hollywood Takes to the Global Stage," p. 8; Greenhouse, "For Europe, U.S. May Spell TV," pp. 19, 26; Steven Greenhouse, "Europe Reaches TV Compromise; U.S. Officials Fear Protectionism," *New York Times* (October 4, 1989), p. 41; Read, *America's Mass Media Merchants*, pp. 90–91, 152; Martin Esslin, "The Television Series as Folk Epic," in Bigsby, ed., *Superculture*, p. 196; Gitlin, "World Leaders: Mickey, et al.," p. 1; Ien Ang, *Watching Dallas: Soap Opera and the Melodramatic Imagination*, trans. Della Couling (London: Methuen, 1985), p. 3; and David Thelen, "Of Audiences, Borderlands, and Comparisons: Toward the Internationalization of American History," *Journal of American History* 79 (September 1992), p. 442.

48. For a discussion of the stylistic elements in American television programs that appealed to international audiences, see Ken Auletta, "TV's New Gold Rush," *New Yorker* 69 (December 13, 1993), p. 86; Read, *America's Mass Media Merchants*, p. 91; John Dean, "Deliberate Differences: Using Cross-Cultural Studies to Understand the European-American Relationship," in Kroes et al., eds., *Cultural Transmissions and Receptions*, pp. 222–23; and Ang, *Watching Dallas*, p. 5.

49. Read, *America's Mass Media Merchants*, pp. 24, 92; Paul Farhi, "Stars and Hypes Forever," *Washington Post National Weekly Edition* (November 13–19, 1989), p. 9; "Global Smarming," p. 31; Barber, *Jihad vs. McWorld*, p. 101; Bill Carter, "Stand Aside CNN. America's No. 1 TV Export Is—No Scoffing, Please—'Baywatch,' " *New York Times* (July 3, 1995), p. C27. Locally produced television shows did become increasingly popular in Britain, France, Germany, and Italy by the mid-1990s. There were two reasons for

this development. First, the price of American TV programs began to soar, permitting European producers to undersell their American competitors. Second, European audiences seemed to prefer shows offering home-grown stars as well as plots and settings that had a national or local flavor, as long as these programs also displayed some of the sophistication for which American TV shows were known. Still, the most successful European-made programs usually imitated the style and format of American shows. Moreover, where America's TV programs continued to attract audiences throughout the world, the shows produced in France, Germany, and Italy rarely attracted viewers in other countries, nor were they able to penetrate the American market. For a discussion of the strengths and weakness of European television shows in the 1990s, see John Tagliabue, "Local Flavor Rules European TV," *New York Times* (October 14, 1996), pp. C1, C3.

50. Richard Stevenson, "Lights! Camera! Europe!" *New York Times* (February 6, 1994), sec. 3, p. 1; Auletta, "TV's New Gold Rush," pp. 84, 88.

51. For more detailed descriptions of the joint ventures between American and European television networks and companies, see Auletta, "TV's New Gold Rush," pp. 85–86; Stevenson, "Lights! Camera! Europe!" pp. 1, 6; Richard Stevenson, "Foreign Horizons Lure U.S. Broadcast Networks," *New York Times* (November 15, 1993), p. C5; Richard Covington, "American TV Invades the World," *International Herald Tribune* (October 19, 1994), p. 11; and "Disney Debut on British TV," *New York Times* (October 4, 1995), p. C3. In 1996, Viacom entered into a partnerships with the Kirsch Group, the operators of pay- and free television stations in Germany. Kirsch agreed to broadcast Viacom's Nickelodeon and MTV programs in exchange for access to the films and television shows produced by Paramount, which Viacom owned. See Geraldine Fabrikant, "TV Agreement Gives Viacom Greater Access to Germany," *New York Times* (April 9, 1996), p. C1. In the Czech Republic, Ronald Lauder (the heir of the Estée Lauder cosmetic company and a former American ambassador to Austria) operated Nova TV, the country's highest-rated television network. By blending American shows like *E.R.* with locally produced news, entertainment, and sports programs, Nova TV gained a 70 percent share of the Czech television audience by 1996. See Mark Landler, "In Europe, an Ex-Ambassador's New Empires," *New York Times* (April 1, 1996), p. C3.

CHAPTER NINE
MASS CULTURE: THE EUROPEAN RECEPTION

1. Jean Baudrillard, *America*, trans. Chris Turner (New York: Verso, 1988, c. Paris 1986), p. 100.

2. For my analysis of the postwar critiques of mass culture by American intellectuals, see Richard Pells, *The Liberal Mind in a Conservative Age: American*

Intellectuals in the 1940s and 1950s (New York: Harper & Row, 1985), pp. 216–32. For a general description of the European intellectuals' shift from political to cultural criticism, see Duncan Webster, *Look a Yonder! The Imaginary America of Populist Culture* (London: Routledge, 1988), p. 240.

3. Baudrillard, *America*, p. 100; Theodor Adorno, "Scientific Experiences of a European Scholar in America," in Donald Fleming and Bernard Bailyn, eds., *The Intellectual Migration: Europe and America, 1930–1960* (Cambridge, Mass.: Charles Warren Center for Studies in American History, 1968), p. 346. For more examples of how Europeans viewed America's mass culture, and how they judged the differences between European and American support for the arts, see Francis Williams, *The American Invasion* (New York: Crown, 1962), pp. 12, 39; Raymond Aron, "From France," in Franz Joseph, ed., *As Others See Us: The United States Through Foreign Eyes* (Princeton, N.J.: Princeton University Press, 1959), p. 68; Richard Kuisel, *Seducing the French: The Dilemma of Americanization* (Berkeley: University of California Press, 1993), p. 117; Deborah Solomon, "The Cologne Challenge: Is New York's Art Monopoly Kaput?" *New York Times Magazine* (September 6, 1992), p. 45; and Alan Riding, "Europe Still Gives Big Doses of Money to Help the Arts," *New York Times* (May 4, 1995), pp. B1, B4. France alone spent the equivalent of $3 billion a year on the arts in the 1990s. See Alan Riding, "Where Is the Glory That Was France?" *New York Times* (January 14, 1996), sec. 2, p. 1.

4. Martin Cooper, "Revolution in Musical Taste," in Bertrand Russell et al., *The Impact of America on European Culture* (Boston: Beacon Press, 1951), p. 75; Herbert von Borch, *The Unfinished Society*, trans. Mary Ilford (New York: Hawthorn Books, 1962, c. Germany 1960), p. 197. See also Paul Swann, *The Hollywood Feature Film in Postwar Britain* (New York: St. Martin's Press, 1987), p. 15; Kuisel, *Seducing the French*, p. 119; and Dick Hebdige, "Towards a Cartography of Taste, 1935–1962," in Hebdige, *Hiding in the Light: On Images and Things* (London: Routledge, 1988), pp. 47, 52.

5. Bertrand Russell, "The Political and Cultural Influence," in Russell et al., *The Impact of America on European Culture*, p. 18; Raymond Aron, "Transatlantic Relations: Does Europe Welcome American Leadership?" in Lewis Galantière, ed., *America and the Mind of Europe* (London: Hamilton, 1951), pp. 24–25. See also Rob Kroes, "Among the Receivers: American Culture Transmitted Abroad," in Kroes, ed., *Within the U.S. Orbit: Small National Cultures vis-à-vis the United States* (Amsterdam: VU University Press, 1991), p. 8.

6. Edward McCreary, *The Americanization of Europe: The Impact of Americans and American Business on the Uncommon Market* (Garden City, N.Y.: Doubleday, 1964), p. 264; Nicolas Nabokov, "Performers and Composers: Festivals and the Twelve-Tone Row," in Galantière, ed., *America and the Mind of Europe*, p. 98; André Visson, *As Others See Us* (New York, 1948), p. 39; Hebdige, "Towards a Cartography of Taste," p. 51; Alessandro Portelli, "The Transatlantic Jeremiad: American Mass Culture and Coun-

terculture and Opposition Culture in Italy," and Kaspar Maase, "'Halb-starke' and Hegemony: Meanings of American Mass Culture in the Federal Republic of Germany During the 1950s," in Rob Kroes, Robert Rydell, and Doeko F. J. Bosscher, eds., *Cultural Transmissions and Receptions: American Mass Culture in Europe* (Amsterdam: VU University Press, 1993), pp. 129, 167, 169; Donald Heiney, *America in Modern Italian Literature* (New Brunswick, N.J.: Rutgers University Press, 1964), p. 26; Jacques Rupnik, "Anti-Americanism and the Modern: The Image of the United States in French Public Opinion," in John Gaffney, ed., *France and Modernization* (Aldershot, England: Avebury, 1988), p. 199; Michel Winock, "The Cold War," in Denis Lacorne, Jacques Rupnik, and Marie-France Toinet, eds., *The Rise and Fall of Anti-Americanism: A Century of French Perception*, trans. Gerry Turner (New York: St. Martin's Press, 1990, c. Paris 1986), p. 74; Kuisel, *Seducing the French*, pp. 127, 191.

7. Jacques Rupnik and Muriel Humbertjean, "Images of the United States in Public Opinion," in Lacorne et al., eds., *The Rise and Fall of Anti-Americanism*, pp. 93–94; Kuisel, *Seducing the French*, p. 33.

8. This is one of the main arguments in Benjamin Barber's *Jihad vs. Mc-World* (New York: Times Books, 1995). Some European intellectuals did not accept the idea that American mass culture was imposed on a passive European population. Instead, they recognized that democracy meant voluntary choice, and that audiences could therefore choose to patronize American movies and television shows, even if most intellectuals disapproved of the choices the audiences made. For examples of this position, see Marcus Cunliffe, "European Images of America," in Arthur Schlesinger and Morton White, eds., *Paths of American Thought* (Boston: Houghton Mifflin, 1963), p. 510; and D. W. Brogan, *The American Character* (New York: Knopf, 1956, c. 1944), p. 216. See also John Tomlinson, *Cultural Imperialism: A Critical Introduction* (Baltimore: Johns Hopkins University Press, 1991), pp. 95–95.

9. Reinhold Wagnleitner, "American Cultural Diplomacy, the Cinema, and the Cold War in Central Europe," in David Ellwood and Rob Kroes, eds., *Hollywood in Europe: Experiences of a Cultural Hegemony* (Amsterdam: VU University Press, 1994), p. 197.

10. The quotation from the French official can be found in Steven Greenhouse, "The Television Europeans Love, and Love to Hate," *New York Times* (August 13, 1989), sec. 2, p. 24. See also Swann, *The Hollywood Feature Film in Postwar Britain*, pp. 25, 42; and Herbert Gans, "Hollywood Films on British Screens: An Analysis of the Functions of American Popular Culture Abroad," *Social Problems* 9 (Spring 1962), p. 327.

11. See David Ellwood, *Rebuilding Europe: Western Europe, America and Postwar Reconstruction* (London: Longman, 1992), pp. 234–35; Ralph Willett, *The Americanization of Germany, 1945–1949* (London: Routledge, 1989), p. 122; Williams, *The American Invasion*, p. 35; and Kuisel, *Seducing the French*, p. 218.

12. Reinhold Wagnleitner, *Coca-Colonization and the Cold War: The Cultural Mission of the United States in Austria After the Second World War*, trans. Diana Wolf (Chapel Hill: University of North Carolina Press, 1994), p. x; italics his. Wagnleitner offered a similar appraisal in "Propagating the American Dream: Cultural Policies as Means of Integration," *American Studies International* 24 (April 1986), p. 76, and in his contribution to the symposium on "The Controversy About Popular Culture," *American Enterprise* 3 (May–June 1992), p. 74. See also David Thelen, "Of Audiences, Borderlands, and Comparisons: Toward the Internationalization of American History," *Journal of American History* 79 (September 1992), p. 442; Nico Wilterdink, "The Netherlands Between the Greater Powers," in Kroes, ed., *Within the U.S. Orbit*, pp. 23–24; Ellwood, *Rebuilding Europe*, p. 235; and Portelli, "The Transatlantic Jeremiad," p. 128.

13. William Schmidt, "In Europe, America's Grip on Popular Culture Is Fading," *New York Times* (March 28, 1993), sec. 1, p. 3; Barry Newman, "Global Chatter," *Wall Street Journal* (March 22, 1995), p. A15; J. M. Mitchell, *International Cultural Relations* (London: Allen & Unwin, 1986), p. 164; Mel van Elteren, "Sounds from America in Holland: The Counter-Culture of the Sixties," in Kroes et al., eds., *Cultural Transmissions and Receptions*, p. 188.

14. Mel van Elteren, "Reflections on Cultural Identity and 'Americanization' in Relation to the Cultural Dimensions of the Recent GATT Agreement," unpublished paper, Tilburg, the Netherlands, 1994, p. 13; van Elteren, "Sounds from America in Holland," p. 175; Williams, *The American Invasion*, p. 139; Wagnleitner, *Coca-Colonization and the Cold War*, pp. 214–15; Maase, "'Halbstarke' and Hegemony," p. 167.

15. The player's quote appears in Harvey Araton, "N.B.A. Circus Comes to London," *New York Times* (October 22, 1995), sec. 1, p. 25. See also Christopher Clarey, "France's Newest Passion: The N.B.A," *New York Times* (June 16, 1993), pp. B9–B10. The popularity of American-style professional basketball in Europe was even more remarkable since Italy, Spain, and many countries in Eastern Europe had been international basketball powers for a long time, with leagues that in some instances preceded the formation of the NBA.

16. Swann, *The Hollywood Feature Film in Postwar Britain*, pp. 27–28, 51, 63; Webster, *Looka Yonder!* p. 186; Maase, "'Halbstarke' and Hegemony," p. 169; Fabrice Montebello, "Hollywood Films in a French Working Class Milieu: Longwy 1945–1960," in Ellwood and Kroes, eds., *Hollywood in Europe*, p. 233; Peter Lev, *The Euro-American Cinema* (Austin: University of Texas Press, 1993), p. 69; Gans, "Hollywood Films on British Screens," p. 325.

17. Hebdige, "Towards a Cartography of Taste," p. 69; Maase, "'Halbstarke' and Hegemony," pp. 168–69.

18. Wagnleitner, *Coca-Colonization and the Cold War*, p. 140; Wagnleitner, "Propagating the American Dream," pp. 73–74; Willett, *The Americanization of Germany*, p. 55; John Frey, "Postwar Germany: Enter American Literature," *American-German Review* 21 (October–November 1954),

p. 11; Reinhold Wagnleitner, "The Irony of American Culture Abroad: Austria and the Cold War," in Lary May, ed., *Recasting America: Culture and Politics in the Age of the Cold War* (Chicago: University of Chicago Press, 1989), p. 291; Jan Bakker, "The Dutch Response to Modern American Literature," in Rob Kroes, ed., *Image und Impact: American Influences in the Netherlands Since 1945* (Amsterdam: Amerika Instituut, 1981), pp. 119–20; Sigmund Skard, *American Studies in Europe: Their History and Present Organization*, vol. 2 (Philadelphia: University of Pennsylvania Press, 1958), p. 426; Savas Patsalidis, "(Mis)Understanding America's Literary Canon: The Greek Paradigm," in Huck Gutman, ed., *As Others Read Us: International Perspectives on American Literature* (Amherst: University of Massachusetts Press, 1991), p. 116; Malcolm Bradbury, "How I Invented America," *Journal of American Studies* 14 (April 1980), p. 124; Perry Miller, "Europe's Faith in American Fiction," in Miller, *The Responsibility of Mind in a Civilization of Machines* (Amherst: University of Massachusetts Press, 1979), p. 123.

19. Bradbury, "How I Invented America," p. 115; Malcolm Bradbury, "The Art of Novel Writing, 1945–1970," in A. N. J. den Hollander, ed., *Diverging Parallels: A Comparison of American and European Thought and Action*, (Leiden, Netherlands: Brill, 1971), pp. 111–12; Henri Peyre, "American Literature Through French Eyes," *Virginia Quarterly Review* 23 (Summer 1947), p. 421.

20. Claude-Edmonde Magny, *The Age of the American Novel: The Film Aesthetic of Fiction Between the Two Wars*, trans. Eleanor Hochman (New York: Ungar, 1972, c. Paris 1948), p. 38; Bradbury, "How I Invented America," p. 123; Bradbury, "The Art of Novel Writing," p. 117.

21. Peyre, "American Literature Through French Eyes," pp. 423, 432; John Lehmann, "The Lesson of the Pupil," in Russell et al., *The Impact of America on European Culture*, p. 29.

22. Heiney, *America in Modern Italian Literature*, pp. 60–61, 93, 95; Agostino Lombardo, "Introduction to Italian Criticism of American Literature," *Sewanee Review* 68 (Summer 1960), p. 366; Portelli, "The Transatlantic Jeremiad," p. 126; Leslie Fiedler, "Italian Pilgrimage: The Discovery of America," in Fiedler, *An End to Innocence: Essays on Culture and Politics* (Boston: Beacon Press, 1955), p. 102.

23. For a more extended discussion of the works and attitudes of Soldati, Cecchi, Pavese, and Vittorini, see Heiney, *America in Modern Italian Literature*, pp. 14, 30, 34–38, 59, 61, 64–65; and Fiedler, "Italian Pilgrimage," p. 99.

24. Elio Vittorini, "American Influences on Contemporary Italian Literature," *American Quarterly* 1 (Spring 1949), pp. 6–7. See also Portelli, "The Transatlantic Jeremiad," p. 127; Heiney, *America in Modern Italian Literature*, pp. 58–60; Maurizio Vaudagna, "The American Historian in Continental Europe: An Italian Perspective," *Journal of American History* 79 (September 1992), p. 535; Michele Bottalico, "A Place for All: Old and New Myths in the Italian Appreciation of American Literature," in Gutman, ed., *As Others*

Read Us, pp. 150–51; Skard, *American Studies in Europe*, vol. 2, pp. 482–83; and Fiedler, "Italian Pilgrimage," p. 104.

25. Fiedler, "Italian Pilgrimage," pp. 100–101; Lombardo, "Introduction to Italian Criticism of American Literature," pp. 368–69; Heiney, *America in Modern Italian Literature*, pp. 58, 85; Bottalico, "A Place for All," p. 151; Portelli, "The Transatlantic Jeremiad," p. 129.

26. The quotation from Cesare Pavese originally appeared in Turin's *L'Unità* on August 3, 1947. It was reprinted in Heiney, *America in Modern Italian Literature*, p. 247. Alberto Moravia offered his opinion in Rome's *Il Mondo* in 1949; it was reprinted in Moravia, "Two American Writers," *Sewanee Review* 68 (Summer 1960), p. 477. On the popularity of the Beat writers and F. O. Matthiessen in Italy, see Bottalico, "A Place for All," p. 151; Portelli, "The Transatlantic Jeremiad," pp. 128–29, Heiney, *America in Modern Italian Literature*, p. 93; and Lombardo, "Introduction to Italian Criticism of American Literature," pp. 370, 374.

27. Jean-Paul Sartre, "American Novelists in French Eyes," *Atlantic Monthly* 178 (August 1946), p. 114.

28. Ibid., p. 115; Peyre, "American Literature Through French Eyes," p. 435.

29. See Peyre, "American Literature Through French Eyes," p. 433; Jeanine Brun-Rovet, "Teaching and Research on United States History in France," in Lewis Hanke, ed., *Guide to the Study of United States History Outside the U.S., 1945–1980*, vol. 2 (White Plains, N.Y.: Kraus International Publications, 1985), p. 176; and Jean-Philippe Mathy, *Extrême Occident: French Intellectuals and America* (Chicago: University of Chicago Press, 1993), p. 156.

30. Magny, *The Age of the American Novel*, pp. 38, 44–45.

31. Russell, "The Political and Cultural Influence," p. 13; Lehmann, "The Lesson of the Pupil," p. 31; Peyre, "American Literature Through French Eyes," p. 431.

32. William Phillips, *A Partisan View: Five Decades of the Literary Life* (New York: Stein & Day, 1983), p. 125. See also Peyre, "American Literature Through French Eyes," p. 424.

33. Leslie Fiedler, "The 'Good American,'" in Fiedler, *An End to Innocence*, p. 110; Miller, "Europe's Faith in American Fiction," pp. 124, 126. For a similar lament, see Joseph Baker, "How the French See America," *Yale Review* 47 (Winter 1958), p. 245.

34. Peyre, "American Literature Through French Eyes," pp. 426, 432; Sartre, "American Novelists in French Eyes," p. 116. See also Lehmann, "The Lesson of the Pupil," p. 25; and F. O. Matthiessen, *From the Heart of Europe* (New York: Oxford University Press, 1948), p. 45.

35. Sartre, "American Novelists in French Eyes," p. 118. For other European views of the stylistic originality of American fiction, see Bradbury, "The Art of Novel Writing," p. 127; Baker, "How the French See America," p. 246; Marc Chénetier, "American Literature in France: Pleasures in Perspective," in Gutman, ed., *As Others Read Us*, pp. 81, 83; and Jens Peter Becker, "The Mean Streets of Europe: The Influence of the American

'Hard-Boiled School' on European Detective Fiction," in C. W. E. Bigsby, ed., *Superculture: American Popular Culture and Europe* (Bowling Green, Ohio: Bowling Green University Popular Press, 1975), p. 153.

36. Sartre, "American Novelists in French Eyes," p. 117; italics his. See also Marie-Christine Granjon, "Sartre, Beauvoir, Aron: An Ambiguous Affair," in Lacorne et al., eds., *The Rise and Fall of Anti-Americanism*, p. 117.

37. Magny, *The Age of the American Novel*, pp. 3, 29, 38–41, 43, 48–49, 55–56, 66, 72, 218.

38. Ibid., pp. 36–37; Sartre, "American Novelists in French Eyes," p. 118. For a similar description of the utility of American literary techniques, see Peyre, "American Literature Through French Eyes," p. 436.

39. Magny, *The Age of the American Novel*, p. 232. See also Thomas Elsasser, "Two Decades in Another Country: Hollywood and the Cinéphiles," in Bigsby, ed., *Superculture*, p. 208.

40. Magny, *The Age of the American Novel*, pp. 32–33.

41. For a general discussion of the assumptions and intentions of the French film critics, see Elsasser, "Two Decades in Another Country," pp. 199–200, 207, 210–11.

42. Ibid., pp. 202–4. For a collection of André Bazin's most important essays, see André Bazin, *What Is Cinema?*, vols. 1 and 2, trans. Hugh Gray (Berkeley: University of California Press, 1967 and 1971).

43. François Truffaut, "A Wonderful Certainty," in Jim Hillier, ed., *Cahiers du Cinéma: The 1950s—Neo-Realism, Hollywood, New Wave* (Cambridge, Mass.: Harvard University Press, 1985), p. 108. For interpretations of the *auteur* theory, see Hillier's "Introduction," in *Cahiers du Cinéma: The 1950s*, p. 5; Jim Hillier, "Introduction: *Cahiers du Cinéma* in the 1960s," in Hillier, ed., *Cahiers du Cinéma: The 1960s—New Wave, New Cinema, Re-Evaluating Hollywood* (Cambridge, Mass.: Harvard University Press, 1992), p. 3; Andrew Sarris, *The American Cinema: Directors and Directions, 1929–1968* (New York: E. P. Dutton, 1968), p. 31; and Elsasser, "Two Decades in Another Country," p. 205. For examples of how the theory was applied to American movies, see Jacques Rivette, "Notes on a Revolution," Eric Rohmer, "Ajax or the Cid?" Jacques Rivette, "The Genius of Howard Hawks," Pierre Kast, "Flattering the Fuzz: Some Remarks on Dandyism and the Practice of Cinema," and André Bazin, "On the *Politique des Auteurs*," in Hillier, ed., *Cahiers du Cinéma: The 1950s*, pp. 96, 111, 128, 228, 257.

44. Fereydoun Hoveyda, "Nicholas Ray's Reply: *Party Girl,*" and Fereydoun Hoveyda, "Sunspots," in Hillier, ed., *Cahiers du Cinéma: The 1960s*, pp. 123, 127, 138–39, 142. See also Hillier's "Introductions" in *Cahiers du Cinéma: The 1950s*, pp. 78, 225; Hillier, "Introduction: *Cahiers du Cinéma* in the 1960s," pp. 5–6; Sarris, *The American Cinema*, p. 31; and Elsasser, "Two Decades in Another Country," pp. 211–12.

45. Michel Mourlet, "In Defense of Violence," in Hillier, ed., *Cahiers du Cinéma: The 1960s*, pp. 132, 134; Eric Rohmer, "Rediscovering America," in Hillier, ed., *Cahiers du Cinéma: The 1950s*, pp. 89–91.

46. Kast, "Flattering the Fuzz," p. 230; Jean Domarchi, "Knife in the Wound," in Hillier, ed., *Cahiers du Cinéma: The 1950s*, p. 243.

47. The quotations from Godard and Truffaut can be found in Jean-Luc Godard, "From Critic to Film-Maker: Godard in Interview," and Claude Chabrol et al., "Questions About American Cinema: A Discussion," in Hillier, ed., *Cahiers du Cinéma: The 1960s*, pp. 64, 174, 177.

48. Godard, "From Critic to Film-Maker," p. 59. See also Elsasser, "Two Decades in Another Country," p. 212; and Sarris, *The American Cinema*, p. 29.

49. The quotation and some of these criticisms can be found in Jean-André Fieschi's contribution to Jean-Louis Comolli et al., "Twenty Years On: A Discussion About American Cinema and the *Politique des Auteurs*," in Hillier, ed., *Cahiers du Cinéma: The 1960s*, pp. 197–98, 203. For additional examples of the journal's reevaluation of the *auteur* theory, see Bazin, "On the *Politique des Auteurs*," p. 257; Jean-Louis Comolli, "Notes on the New Spectator," in Hillier, ed., *Cahiers du Cinéma: The 1960s*, p. 213; and Comolli's contribution to "Twenty Years On," pp. 204–5.

50. Jean-Luc Godard, "Struggling on Two Fronts: Godard in Interview with Jacques Bontemps et al.," in Hillier, ed., *Cahiers du Cinéma: The 1960s*, p. 295. See also Eric Rohmer, "The Old and the New: Rohmer in Interview with Jean-Claude Biette et al.," in Hillier, ed., *Cahiers du Cinéma: The 1960s*, p. 88; Fieschi's statement in "Twenty Years On," p. 197; and Hillier, "Introduction: *Cahiers du Cinéma* in the 1960s," pp. 6,8, 13.

51. See Jean-Luc Godard's contribution in Chabrol et al., "Questions About American Cinema," p. 176; Hillier, "Introduction: *Cahiers du Cinéma* in the 1960s," pp. 9, 15; Jim Hillier, "Introduction: Re-Thinking the Function of Cinema and Criticism," in Hillier, ed., *Cahiers du Cinéma: The 1960s*, p. 228; and Elsasser, "Two Decades in Another Country," p. 215.

52. Ien Ang, *Watching Dallas: Soap Opera and the Melodramatic Imagination*, trans. Della Couling (London: Methuen, 1985), p. 2.

53. See Tomlinson, *Cultural Imperialism*, p. 46.

54. Ang, *Watching Dallas*, pp. vii, 1, 10. Ang was not alone in trying to analyze seriously the effects of *Dallas* on local populations. In Israel during the 1980s, Tamar Liebes and Elihu Katz organized several focus groups to gain a better understanding of how different audiences responded to the program. Comparing the reactions of a group of Israeli Arabs, new émigrés from Russia to Israel, second-generation immigrants from Morocco, members of a Kibbutz, and Americans in Los Angeles, Liebes and Katz concluded that all these viewers were active participants in reinterpreting the "meaning" of *Dallas*, usually in terms of their own cultural backgrounds, personal expectations, and family lives. For Liebes and Katz, people were not passive receptacles for the messages of the mass media; instead, audiences revised and re-created a particular program to suit their own needs and purposes. For the results of their work, see Elihu Katz and Tamar Liebes, "Mutual Aid in the Decoding of *Dallas*: Preliminary Notes from a Cross-Cultural Study," in Phillip Drummond and Richard Paterson, eds., *Televi-*

sion in Transition: Papers from the First International Television Studies Conference (London: British Film Institute, 1985), pp. 187–98; and Tamar Liebes and Elihu Katz, *The Export of Meaning: Cross-Cultural Readings of Dallas* (New York: Oxford University Press, 1990).

55. Ang, *Watching Dallas*, pp. 35, 91, 95, 114, 119, 123.

56. Ibid., pp. 96–101, 107, 109–10, 115.

57. Ibid., pp. 23–24.

58. Ibid., pp. 52–53, 56–57, 117.

59. Ibid., pp. 53, 60, 68.

60. Ibid., pp. 30–31, 34, 36, 42–44.

61. Ibid., pp. 45–47, 54, 58, 79–80, 82–83, 122–23. The Israeli analysts reached a similar conclusion. See Katz and Liebes, "Mutual Aid in the Decoding of *Dallas*, pp. 190, 197.

CHAPTER TEN
FROM GAULLISM TO GATT: RESISTING AMERICA IN THE 1980S AND 1990S

1. An Austrian historian and student of American culture, Reinhold Wagnleitner, asked his American readers to consider issues such as these in *Coca-Colonization and the Cold War: The Cultural Mission of the United States in Austria After the Second World War*, trans. Diana Wolf (Chapel Hill: University of North Carolina Press, 1994), p. xii.

2. For a more extensive discussion of these theories, see John Tomlinson, *Cultural Imperialism: A Critical Introduction* (Baltimore: Johns Hopkins University Press, 1991), pp. 2–3, 7, 20, 126, 128, 175–76. See also Dick Hebdige, "Towards a Cartography of Taste, 1935–1962," in Hebdige, *Hiding in the Light: On Images and Things* (London: Routledge, 1988), pp. 67, 72.

3. Tomlinson, *Cultural Imperialism*, pp. 70, 73–74, 90; Mel van Elteren, "Reflections on Cultural Identity and 'Americanization' in Relation to the Cultural Dimensions of the Recent GATT Agreement," unpublished paper, Tilburg, the Netherlands, 1994, p. 3.

4. Tomlinson, *Cultural Imperialism*, p. 75.

5. Rob Kroes, "The Great Satan Versus the Evil Empire: Anti-Americanism in the Netherlands," in Kroes and Maarten van Rossem, eds., *Anti-Americanism in Europe* (Amsterdam: Free University Press, 1986), p. 48; Philip Schlesinger, "Europe's Contradictory Communicative Space," *Daedalus* 123 (Spring 1994), p. 38.

6. Mary Tabor, "Book Deals: Losing Nothing in Translation," *New York Times* (October 16, 1995), p. C8.

7. "A Shorter Attention Span?" *New York Times* (October 13, 1993), p. B4; Katherine Knorr, "German Publisher Makes a Run at the U.S.," *International Herald Tribune* (November 7, 1994), p. 18.

398—Notes to Pages 267–271

8. For statistics on the importation of foreign movies and television programs to the United States, see Richard Turner, "English, Please," *Wall Street Journal* (March 26, 1993), p. R10; Roger Cohen "Aux Armes! France Rallies to Battle Sly and T. Rex," *New York Times* (January 2, 1994), sec. 2, p. 22; and Todd Gitlin, "World Leaders: Mickey, et al.," *New York Times* (May 3, 1992), sec. 2, p. 30.

9. Michael Malloy, "America, Go Home," *Wall Street Journal* (March 26, 1993), p. R7; Cohen "Aux Armes!" p. 23; William Read, *America's Mass Media Merchants* (Baltimore: Johns Hopkins University Press, 1976), p. 89; Turner, "English, Please," p. R12.

10. Peter Lev, *The Euro-American Cinema* (Austin: University of Texas Press, 1993), p. 76; Turner, "English, Please," p. R12.

11. Francis Williams, *The American Invasion* (New York. Crown, 1962), pp. 11, 147, 150; Michele Bottalico, "A Place for All: Old and New Myths in the Italian Appreciation of American Literature," in Huck Gutman, ed., *As Others Read Us: International Perspectives on American Literature* (Amherst: University of Massachusetts Press, 1991), p. 148. See also Hebdige, "Towards a Cartography of Taste," p. 51; and Duncan Webster, *Looka Yonder! The Imaginary America of Populist Culture* (London: Routledge, 1988), pp. 195–96.

12. Jean-Jacques Servan-Schreiber, *The American Challenge*, trans. Ronald Steel (New York: Atheneum, 1968, c. Paris 1967), p. 192. For the French response to *Jurassic Park* and the quote about foreign influences in France, see Roger Cohen, "The French, Disneyed and Jurassick, Fear Erosion," *New York Times* (November 21, 1993), sec. 4, p. 2.

13. For the predictions of Europe's cultural suicide, see Steve Lohr, "European TV's Vast Growth: Cultural Effect Stirs Concern," *New York Times* (March 16, 1989), p. 39. On the insinuation of the American media into the fantasy lives of Europeans, see Jeremy Tunstall, *The Media Are American* (New York: Columbia University Press, 1977), p. 39; and Martin Esslin, "The Television Series as Folk Epic," in C. W. E. Bigsby, ed., *Superculture: American Popular Culture and Europe* (Bowling Green, Ohio: Bowling Green University Popular Press, 1975), p. 197.

14. The quotation from Jacques Toubon can be found in Alan Riding, "France's 'Mr. All-Good' Is Defeated by English," *New York Times* (August 7, 1994), sec. 1, p. 4.

15. Daniel Snowman, *Britain and America: An Interpretation of Their Culture, 1945–1975* (New York: New York University Press, 1977), pp. 266–67; David Crystal, "American English in Europe," in Bigsby, ed., *Superculture*, pp. 62–63, 65; Benjamin Barber, *Jihad vs. McWorld* (New York: Times Books, 1995), p. 171.

16. Crystal, "American English in Europe," p. 65; Denis Lacorne and Jacques Rupnik, "Introduction: France Bewitched by America," in Lacorne, Rupnik, and Marie-France Toinet, eds., *The Rise and Fall of Anti-Americanism: A Century of French Perception*, trans. Gerry Turner (New York: St. Martin's Press, 1990, c. Paris 1986), pp. 22–23; Richard Kuisel, *Seducing the French: The*

Dilemma of Americanization (Berkeley: University of California Press, 1993), p. 191; Marlise Simons, "Bar English? French Bicker on Barricades," *New York Times* (March 15, 1994), p. A6

17. Michael Harrison, "French Anti-Americanism Under the Fourth Republic and the Gaullist Solution," in Lacorne et al., eds., *The Rise and Fall of Anti-Americanism*, p. 175; Kuisel, *Seducing the French*, p. 193; Joseph Hanania, "Fleeing a Fallow France for Greener U.S. Pastures," *New York Times* (October 22, 1995), sec. 2, p. 14; John Rockwell, "French Strike a Blow for la Gloire in Their Film Industry's Oscars," *New York Times* (January 18, 1993), pp. B1, B4; Barber, *Jihad vs. McWorld,* p. 92.

18. Riding, "France's 'Mr. All-Good' Is Defeated by English," p. 4; Simons, "Bar English?" pp. A1, A6; Theodore Stanger and Marcus Mabry, "Liberté, Egalité, Médiocrité," *Newsweek* 123 (June 20, 1994), p. 50.

19. Jacques Toubon, "Tempest in a Demitasse," *New York Times* (April 4, 1994), p. A15.

20. Riding, "France's 'Mr. All-Good' Is Defeated by English," p. 4.

21. For a description of the United Nations conference and the quotations used in this paragraph, see Peter Waldman, "Lost in Translation: How to 'Empower Women' in Chinese," *Wall Street Journal* (September 13, 1994), pp. A1, A4.

22. Jack Lang's critique is reproduced in Chantal Cinquin, "President Mitterrand Also Watches *Dallas*: American Mass Media and French National Policy," in Roger Rollin, ed., *The Americanization of the Global Village: Essays in Comparative Popular Culture* (Bowling Green, Ohio: Bowling Green State University Popular Press, 1989), p. 12. For Mitterrand's statement, see David Ellwood, "Introduction: Historical Methods and Approaches," in Ellwood and Rob Kroes, eds., *Hollywood in Europe: Experiences of a Cultural Hegemony* (Amsterdam: VU University Press, 1994), p. 9.

23. Roger Cohen, "Europeans Back French Curbs on U.S. Movies," *New York Times* (December 12, 1993), sec. 1, p. 14; Stanley Hoffmann, "France: Keeping the Demons at Bay," *New York Review of Books* 41 (March 3, 1994), p. 13; Alan Riding, "Europe Still Gives Big Doses of Money to Help the Arts, *New York Times* (May 4, 1995), p. B1.

24. Roger Cohen, "U.S.–French Cultural Trade Rift Now Snags a World Agreement," *New York Times* (December 8, 1993), p. C2; Hanania, "Fleeing a Fallow France for Greener U.S. Pastures," p. 14.

25. The statistics on declining attendance and the quote from the festival official can be found in John Rockwell, "Hollywood for the French Who Don't Scorn It," *New York Times* (September 9, 1993), p. B2.

26. For the statements of the European directors, see Bernard Weinraub, "Directors Fight for GATT's Final Cut and Print," *New York Times* (December 12, 1993), sec. 1, p. 14; and Dick Polman, "American Culture: It's Awesome Overseas," *Austin American-Statesman* (April 2, 1995), p. J4. See also Cohen, "Aux Armes!" p. 23.

27. The French official's question can be found in Daniel Pedersen, "A

'Grenade' aimed at Hollywood," *Newsweek* 114 (October 16, 1989), p. 58. For the rationale behind and details of the European Community's directive, see Steven Greenhouse, "Europe Reaches TV Compromise; U.S. Officials Fear Protectionism," *New York Times* (October 4, 1989), p. 41; Cohen, "U.S.–French Cultural Trade Rift Now Snags a World Agreement," p. C2; and Ken Auletta, "TV's New Gold Rush," *New Yorker* 69 (December 13, 1993), p. 87.

28. Steven Greenhouse, "For Europe, U.S. May Spell TV," *New York Times* (July 31, 1989), pp. 19, 26; Steven Greenhouse, "The Television Europeans Love, and Love to Hate," *New York Times* (August 13, 1989), sec. 2, p. 24.

29. For the freedom-of-information clause in the UN's Declaration on Human Rights, see Read, *America's Mass Media Merchants*, pp. 20, 144. For other U.S. arguments on behalf of free trade in cultural products, see Cinquin, "President Mitterrand Also Watches *Dallas*," p. 19; Greenhouse, "Europe Reaches TV Compromise," p. 41; and Schlesinger, "Europe's Contradictory Communicative Space," p. 39.

30. For discussions of how the free flow of culture and ideas would invariably benefit American media giants, see Emily Rosenberg, *Spreading the American Dream: American Economic and Cultural Expansion, 1890–1945* (New York: Hill & Wang, 1982), p. 219; Tunstall, *The Media Are American*, p. 208; and Paul Swann, "The Little State Department: Washington and Hollywood's Rhetoric of the Postwar Audience," in Ellwood and Kroes, eds., *Hollywood in Europe*, pp. 178–79.

31. For examples of the way American negotiators and media executives reduced the European position on GATT to a protectionist defense of inferior cultural products, see Malloy, "America, Go Home," p. R7; Auletta, "TV's New Gold Rush," p. 88; and Cohen, "Aux Armes!" p. 22. On the American response to the French tax on foreign films, see Cohen, "U.S.-French Cultural Trade Rift Now Snags a World Agreement," p. C2; and Cohen, "Europeans Back French Curbs on U.S. Movies," p. 14.

32. Cohen, "Aux Armes!" p. 22; Barber, *Jihad vs. McWorld*, pp. 92–93.

CHAPTER ELEVEN
THE EUROPEANIZATION OF
AMERICAN CULTURE

1. For a satirical portrait of these ideas, see Duncan Webster, *Looka Yonder! The Imaginary America of Populist Culture* (London: Routledge, 1988); p. 199; Jean-François Revel, *Without Marx or Jesus: The New American Revolution Has Begun*, trans. J. F. Bernard (Garden City, N.Y.: Doubleday, 1971, c. Paris 1970), p. 153; and Robert Hughes, "The Patron Saint of Neo-Pop," *New York Review of Books* 36 (June 1, 1989), p. 30. In the 1990s, Benjamin

Barber offered one of the most serious and sustained critiques of American mass culture in *Jihad vs. McWorld* (New York: Times Books, 1995).

2. The idea of the audience as an active participant in a cultural process that is basically social, rather than private, owes much to the arguments advanced by contemporary media theorists. Their influence on analysts of America's cultural impact abroad has been extensive. For examples of this influence, see Ien Ang, *Watching Dallas: Soap Opera and the Melodramatic Imagination*, trans. Della Couling (London: Methuen, 1985), pp. 26, 116; Webster, *Looka Yonder!* p. 185; Claude-Jean Bertrand, "American Cultural Imperialism—A Myth?" *American Studies International* 25 (April 1987), pp. 52–53; Rob Kroes, "Among the Receivers: American Culture Transmitted Abroad," in Kroes, ed., *Within the U.S. Orbit: Small National Cultures vis-à-vis the United States* (Amsterdam: VU University Press, 1991), p. 9; Elihu Katz and Tamar Liebes, "Mutual Aid in the Decoding of *Dallas*: Preliminary Notes from a Cross-Cultural Study," in Phillip Drummond and Richard Paterson, eds., *Television in Transition: Papers from the First International Television Studies Conference* (London: British Film Institute, 1985), pp. 187–88; and John Tomlinson, *Cultural Imperialism: A Critical Introduction* (Baltimore: Johns Hopkins University Press, 1991), pp. 47–50, 56.

3. Katz and Liebes, "Mutual Aid in the Decoding of *Dallas*," p. 187; Tomlinson, *Cultural Imperialism*, p. 3; Mel van Elteren, "Reflections on Cultural Identity and 'Americanization' in Relation to the Cultural Dimensions of the Recent GATT Agreement," unpublished paper, Tilburg, the Netherlands, 1994, p. 11; Webster, *Looka Yonder!* p. 179; Dick Hebdige, "Towards a Cartography of Taste, 1935–1962," in Hebdige, *Hiding in the Light: On Images and Things* (London: Routledge, 1988), p. 74.

4. A number of writers on both sides of the Atlantic have recognized the conservative and radicalizing potential of the mass media. See Webster, *Looka Yonder!* pp. 179, 211; Revel, *Without Marx or Jesus*, pp. 163, 180–81; Steve Fox, "'My Bitter Love for America': The Role of Mass Culture in New Identities for East Germans Before and After the Wall," in Rob Kroes, Robert Rydell, and Doeko F. J. Bosscher, eds., *Cultural Transmissions and Receptions: American Mass Culture in Europe* (Amsterdam: VU University Press, 1993), p. 200; Charles Krauthammer's contribution to the symposium on "The Controversy About Popular Culture," *American Enterprise* 3 (May–June 1992), p. 88; and David Thelen, "Of Audiences, Borderlands, and Comparisons: Toward the Internationalization of American History," *Journal of American History* 79 (September 1992), p. 442.

5. For arguments similar to these, see Edward McCreary, *The Americanization of Europe: The Impact of Americans and American Business on the Uncommon Market* (Garden City, N.Y.: Doubleday, 1964), p. 3; Webster, *Looka Yonder!* p. 211; William Read, *America's Mass Media Merchants* (Baltimore: Johns Hopkins University Press, 1976), p. 181; Roger Rollin, "Introduction: On Comparative Popular Culture, American Style," in Rollin, ed., *The Americanization of the Global Village: Essays in Comparative Popular*

Culture (Bowling Green, Ohio: Bowling Green State University Popular Press, 1989), p. 6; and Rolf Lundén, "America in Sweden: Visible and Invisible Influence," in Kroes, ed., *Within the U.S. Orbit*, pp. 141–42.

6. Harold Laski, *The American Democracy: A Commentary and an Interpretation* (New York: Viking, 1948), p. 397. For other analyses of how the elements in American and European culture were combined and transformed, see Tomlinson, *Cultural Imperialism*, p. 48; and John Dean, "Deliberate Differences: Using Cross-Cultural Studies to Understand the European-American Relationship," and Rob Kroes, "Americanization: What Are We Talking About?" in Kroes et al., eds., *Cultural Transmissions and Receptions*, pp. 225, 307–8, 312.

7. For a theoretical description of the "convergence" of American and European radicalism in the 1960s, see Rob Kroes, "The Influence of the American New Left on Dutch Political Life," in A. N. J. den Hollander, ed., *Contagious Conflict: The Impact of American Dissent on European Life* (Leiden, Netherlands: Brill, 1973), p. 10.

8. J. H. Plumb, "President Kennedy and After," in Plumb, *The American Experience*, vol. 2 of *The Collected Essays* (Athens: University of Georgia Press, 1989), p. 180; Maarten van Rossem, "Le Defi Europeen," in Rob Kroes, ed., *Image and Impact: American Influences in the Netherlands Since 1945* (Amsterdam: Amerika Instituut, 1981), p. 23.

9. Nico Wilterdink, "The Netherlands Between the Greater Powers," in Kroes, ed., *Within the U.S. Orbit*, p. 26; van Rossem, "Le Defi Europeen," pp. 25–26; Geir Lundestad, "Research Trends and Accomplishments in Norway on United States History," in Lewis Hanke, ed., *Guide to the Study of United States History Outside the U.S., 1945–1980*, vol. 3 (White Plains, N.Y.: Kraus International Publications, 1985), pp. 263; James Tent, *The Free University of Berlin: A Political History* (Bloomington: Indiana University Press, 1988), p. 281; Kurt Shell, "The American Impact on the German New Left," in den Hollander, ed., *Contagious Conflict*, p. 45; Jacques Rupnik, "Anti-Americanism and the Modern: The Image of the United States in French Public Opinion," in John Gaffney, ed., *France and Modernization* (Aldershot, England: Avebury, 1988), p. 198.

10. Sigmund Skard, *Trans-Atlantica: Memoirs of a Norwegian Americanist* (Oslo: Universitetsforlaget, 1978), pp. 184–85; Pierre Nora, "America and the French Intellectuals," *Daedalus* 107 (Winter 1978), p. 328; J. H. Plumb, "The Fatal Flaw," in Plumb, *The American Experience*, p. 220. For descriptions of other European reactions to the war in Vietnam, see van Rossem, "Le Defi Europeen," p. 25; Frans Alting von Geusau, "The Broken Image: America as Seen by Westeuropeans," in Kroes, ed., *Image and Impact*, p. 78; Frank Costigliola, *France and the United States: The Cold Alliance Since World War II* (New York: Twayne, 1992), pp. 154–55; Tent, *The Free University of Berlin*, pp. 286, 288–89, 307; Lundestad, "Research Trends and Accomplishments in Norway on United States History," p. 264; and Rob Kroes, "The Great Satan Versus the Evil Empire: Anti-Americanism in the Nether-

lands," in Kroes and Maarten van Rossem, eds., *Anti-Americanism in Europe* (Amsterdam: Free University Press, 1986), p. 44.

11. For a general discussion of the factors leading to the emergence of a youth culture in Western Europe during the 1950s and early 1960s, see Marianne Debouzy, "The Influence of American Political Dissent on the French New Left," in den Hollander, ed., *Contagious Conflict*, p. 54; Daniel Snowman, *Britain and America: An Interpretation of Their Culture, 1945–1975* (New York: New York University Press, 1977), pp. 207, 215; R. H. Pear, "Students and the Establishment in Europe and the U.S.A.," in A. N. J. den Hollander, ed., *Diverging Parallels: A Comparison of American and European Thought and Action* (Leiden, Netherlands: Brill, 1971), p. 94; Michael Watts, "The Call and Response of Popular Music: The Impact of American Pop Music in Europe," in C. W. E. Bigsby, ed., *Superculture: American Popular Culture and Europe* (Bowling Green, Ohio: Bowling Green University Popular Press, 1975), p. 133; and Tent, *The Free University of Berlin*, pp. 288, 319.

12. J. H. Plumb, "Secular Heretics," in Plumb, *The American Experience*, pp. 242–43; Tyler Marshall, "American Culture Is Europe's Common Bond," *Austin American-Statesman* (June 5, 1994), p. C5; Revel, *Without Marx or Jesus*, p. 261; Reinhold Wagnleitner, *Coca-Colonization and the Cold War: The Cultural Mission of the United States in Austria After the Second World War*, trans. Diana Wolf (Chapel Hill: University of North Carolina Press, 1994), p. xi; Wilterdink, "The Netherlands Between the Greater Powers," p. 27; van Elteren, "Reflections on Cultural Identity and 'Americanization' in Relation to the Cultural Dimensions of the Recent GATT Agreement," pp. 11–12; Alessandro Portelli, "The Transatlantic Jeremiad: American Mass Culture and Counterculture and Opposition Culture in Italy," and Mel van Elteren, "Sounds from America in Holland: The Counter-Culture of the Sixties," in Kroes et al., eds., *Cultural Transmissions and Receptions*, pp. 129–30, 183, 194.

13. Kroes, "The Influence of the American New Left on Dutch Political Life," p. 20; Burton Bollag, "Enrollment Soars in Europe," *Chronicle of Higher Education* 41 (September 7, 1994), pp. A59–A60.

14. Tent, *The Free University of Berlin*, pp. 292, 306, 334–35, 338–39, 343–45, 357, 425, 443. The turbulence in Berlin and in Paris affected students at universities in the Netherlands who copied not only the Free Speech Movement at Berkeley, but also the tactics of their fellow activists in West Germany and France. See Kroes, "The Influence of the American New Left on Dutch Political Life," pp. 12, 22–23.

15. Marianne Debouzy, "The Americanization of the French University and the Response of the Student Movement, 1966–1986," *American Studies International* 28 (October 1990), pp. 27–28; Costigliola, *France and the United States*, p. 155.

16. On the British New Left, see Pear, "Students and the Establishment in Europe and the U.S.A.," pp. 96–97; and Watts, "The Call and Response of Popular Music," p. 137.

17. Shell, "The American Impact on the German New Left," pp. 35, 37–40; Costigliola, *France and the United States*, pp. 156, 192.

18. For the effect of these ideas on German radicals, see Shell, "The American Impact on the German New Left," pp. 40–44.

19. Marianne Debouzy, "From American Studies to American History: A French Point of View," *Journal of American History* 79 (September 1992), pp. 496–97; Debouzy, "The Influence of American Political Dissent on the French New Left," pp. 55–56, 58–59, 61, 65–66. The activities of the American New Left also affected Italian radicals. See Tiziano Bonazzi, "American History: The View from Italy," *Reviews in American History* 14 (December 1986), p. 534.

20. On the impact of the Black Panthers in France, see Marie-Christine Granjon, "Sartre, Beauvoir, Aron: An Ambiguous Affair," in Denis Lacorne, Jacques Rupnik, and Marie-France Toinet, eds., *The Rise and Fall of Anti-Americanism: A Century of French Perception*, trans. Gerry Turner (New York: St. Martin's Press, 1990, c. Paris 1986), p. 124; and Debouzy, "The Influence of American Political Dissent on the French New Left," pp. 55, 58–59.

21. Debouzy, "The Influence of American Political Dissent on the French New Left," pp. 57; van Elteren, "Sounds from America in Holland," pp. 183, 188; Shell, "The American Impact on the German New Left," pp. 31, 39; Kroes, "The Influence of the American New Left on Dutch Political Life," pp. 12–14.

22. For a general statement of this principle, and the way it applied to conditions in the Netherlands, see Kroes, "The Influence of the American New Left on Dutch Political Life," pp. 11, 15–17, 20, 23–24.

23. The incendiary presence of American soldiers in West Berlin, and the role of the America House as a target of protest, is discussed in Shell, "The American Impact on the German New Left," p. 45; and Tent, *The Free University of Berlin*, pp. 308, 335. On events in France in May 1968, see Costigliola, *France and the United States*, pp. 155, 157.

24. Tent, *The Free University of Berlin*, p. 372.

25. Herbert Kubly, *American in Italy* (New York: Simon & Schuster, 1955), p. 34; Donald Heiney, *America in Modern Italian Literature* (New Brunswick, N.J.: Rutgers University Press, 1964), p. 34; Stephen Kinzer, "The G.I.s' Legacy: Basketball and Sweet Memories," *New York Times* (September 27, 1994), p. A8.

26. Alfred Kazin, *New York Jew* (New York: Knopf, 1978), p. 215. For an account of how postwar architects in other German cities imitated the techniques of their American colleagues, see Ralph Willett, *The Americanization of Germany, 1945–1949* (London: Routledge, 1989), pp. 50–51, 118.

27. Reyner Banham, "Mediated Environments Or: You Can't Build That Here," in Bigsby, ed., *Superculture*, p. 76; and Willett, *The Americanization of Germany*, p. 51.

28. On the differences between the American and European attitudes

toward their homes and their contrasting views of public space, see Marshall McLuhan, "The Implications of Cultural Uniformity," in Bigsby, ed., *Super-culture*, p. 44. Suburban shopping malls and huge discount outlets modeled on Wal-Mart promised the same benefits to Europeans as they did to Americans: lower prices for consumers and new white-collar jobs for displaced blue-collar workers. Nevertheless, mall developers in Europe encountered considerable resistance from local and national governments bent on preserving historic city centers, as well as from small shop-owners and environmentalists. Thus the malls—while increasingly popular in Europe—had not become at the end of the twentieth century as omnipresent as they were in America. For an example of how people in British towns outside London hated the arrival of American-style shopping malls in the 1990s, see William Schmidt, "This Blessed Plot, This Glitzy Mall, This England," *New York Times* (May 9, 1993), sec. 4, p. 16. For a general discussion of the opposition to suburban shopping centers throughout Europe, see John Tagliabue, "Europeans Agonize Over the Mall," *New York Times* (September 10, 1996), pp. C1, C5.

29. The quotation from the Belgian banker can be found in Nathaniel Nash, "The Welfare State Is Alive and Welcome in Western Europe," *New York Times* (January 2, 1996), p. C8. See also Nathaniel Nash, "Europeans Shrug as Taxes Go Up," *New York Times* (February 16, 1995), p. A4. According to a poll taken in 1992, only 38 percent of Americans believed that the government should reduce the differential between the rich and the poor, compared with 65 percent in Britain, 66 percent in West Germany, and 80 percent in Italy. See James Pinkerton, "Not Just Another Country," Book Review, *New York Times* (February 11, 1996), p. 7. In *American Exceptionalism: A Double-Edged Sword* (New York: Norton, 1996), Seymour Lipset compared American and European attitudes on a variety of subjects, arriving at many of the same conclusions as had European visitors to the United States. Lipset argued that Americans were more hostile to taxes, the welfare state, and government intervention in economic affairs than were Europeans. Americans were also, according to Lipset, less politically obedient and deferential to authority figures; less interested in the virtues of an egalitarian society; and more wedded to the values of individualism, personal achievement, and social mobility. Yet their skepticism toward the state led Americans to participate more often in voluntary organizations and to give more money to charity than did ordinary Europeans. See especially pp. 19–22, 26–28, 67–68, 70–71, 73–74, 82–83.

30. Youssef Ibrahim, "To French, Solidarity Outweighs Balanced Budget," *New York Times* (December 20, 1995), pp. A1, A7. Germans enjoyed similar benefits, including a $135-per-month subsidy from the government for each child, full pay for the first six weeks of sick leave, and six-week vacations every year. When Helmut Kohl—faced with soaring deficits, high unemployment rates, a stagnant economy, and the huge costs of German unification—announced plans in 1996 to cut some of these previously sacrosanct services, he

encountered fierce opposition from labor unions and the Social Democrats. Throughout Western Europe, governments trying to reduce deficits and inflation levels in order to qualify by 1999 for a common currency under the guidelines of the Economic and Monetary Union sought—despite popular resistance—to convert the European welfare state into a structure resembling the British and American models. This meant more deregulation of the communication industries, fewer medical benefits with their costs controlled by profit-oriented health maintenance organizations, a shrinking role for the state in providing social services, and a greater emphasis on privatization—policies which Western European politicians hoped would meet the demands of global competition and stem the flight of companies and jobs to countries in Eastern Europe and in Asia. Yet even if all these reforms were enacted, Europe was not in danger of becoming just like America. The European welfare state would still provide more benefits and offer people more protection from the hazards of capitalism than even the most liberal American politician could ever endorse. See Alan Cowell, "Germany's Leader Calls for Big Cuts in Welfare State," *New York Times* (April 27, 1996), pp. 1, 4; Thomas Kamm and Cecile Rohwedder, "Continental Divide: Many Europeans Fear Cuts in Social Benefits in One-Currency Plan," *Wall Street Journal* (July 30, 1996), pp. A1, A8; Craig Whitney, "Rising Health Costs Threaten Generous Benefits in Europe," *New York Times* (August 6, 1996), pp. A1, A5; and Edmund Andrews, "New Hard Line by Big Companies Threatens German Work Benefits," *New York Times* (October 1, 1996), p. C3.

31. Ibrahim, "To French, Solidarity Outweighs Balanced Budget," pp. A1, A7.

32. Pehr Gyllenhammar, "The Impact of American Culture on Management Organization and the Transportation Industry," in Allen Davis, ed., *For Better or Worse: The American Influence in the World* (Westport, Conn.: Greenwood Press, 1981), pp. 107–8. See also David Ellwood, "The Impact of the Marshall Plan on Italy; The Impact of Italy on the Marshall Plan," in Kroes et al., eds., *Cultural Transmissions and Receptions*, p. 123.

33. Magnus Pyke, "The Influence of American Foods and Food Technology in Europe," in Bigsby, ed., *Superculture*, p. 89; Gabriella Stern, "French Add Convenience to Customary Cuisine," *Wall Street Journal* (October 11, 1995), p. B1; Craig Whitney, "France and Watercress Sandwiches," *New York Times* (May 19, 1995), p. A4; "American Restaurants All the Rage in Paris," *Austin American-Statesman* (March 18, 1995), p. A20.

34. Pyke, "The Influence of American Foods and Food Technology in Europe," p. 87; John Tagliabue, "Spoon-to-Spoon Combat Overseas," *New York Times* (January 7, 1995), p. 29; Joseph Treaster, "Kellogg Seeks to Reset Latvia's Breakfast Table," *New York Times* (May 19, 1994), p. C20.

35. Pyke, "The Influence of American Foods and Food Technology in Europe," p. 85, 87–88; Marshall Goldman, "Do Business in Russia? For Now, No," *New York Times* (August 7, 1994), sec. 3, p. 9.

36. Sara Franks, "Overseas, It's What's Inside That Sells," *Washington Post*

National Weekly Edition (December 5–11, 1994), p. 21. The willingness to adjust to European conditions was also reflected in the policies of American clothing chains. Beginning in 1987, when it opened its first store in Britain, The Gap tried to apply the formulas that worked in the United States. It changed its inventory more quickly and held more frequent sales than did European retailers. Nevertheless, The Gap tended to stock smaller sizes in France to conform to the average French physique, while in Germany it featured clothes in darker colors in accordance with the preferences of German customers. See John Tagliabue, "Enticing Europe's Shoppers," *New York Times* (April 24, 1996), pp. C1, C18.

37. On the conditions that limited computer usage in Europe, and the differences in usage between Europe and the United States, see John Tagliabue, "Europeans Buy Home PC's at Record Pace," *New York Times* (December 11, 1995), pp. C1, C8. For statistics on the number of Americans who operated home businesses, see R. Michelle Breyer, "Home Sweet Office," *Austin American-Statesman* (January 14, 1996), p. G1. The European state-run telephone monopolies were scheduled for deregulation in 1998.

38. A description of the strategies used by American Internet access companies to overcome European competition and resistance, and the quotations from the America Online executive and the industry analyst, can be found in Kara Swisher, "American Internet Services Go Overseas," *Austin American-Statesman* (December 15, 1995), p. D5.

39. For the statement from Procter & Gamble, as well as a discussion of the global advertising campaigns of American companies, see Paul Farhi, "I'd Like to Sell the World a Coke," *Washington Post National Weekly Edition* (June 22–28, 1992), p. 20. See also McCreary, *The Americanization of Europe*, pp. 90, 130.

40. Webster, *Looka Yonder!* pp. 223, 226, 228; Barber, *Jihad vs. McWorld*, p. 60; John Dorst, "Miniaturizing Monumentality: Theme Park Images of the American West and Confusions of Cultural Influence," in Kroes et al., eds., *Cultural Transmissions and Receptions*, pp. 256–57; Dana Milbank, "Made in America Becomes a Boast in Europe," *Wall Street Journal* (January 19, 1994), pp. B1, B5; Mark Nelson, "Peacetime Invasion," *Wall Street Journal* (April 24, 1995), p. R11.

41. Peter Masson and Andrew Thorburn, "Advertising: The American Influence in Europe," in Bigsby, ed., *Superculture*, p. 103; McCreary, *The Americanization of Europe*, pp. 97, 143, 153; Fox, "'My Bitter Love for America,'" p. 203.

42. Joseph Pereira, "Off and Running," *Wall Street Journal* (July 22, 1993), pp. A1, A8.

43. For accounts of the difficulties that American situation comedies and quiz shows faced in Europe, see Steven Greenhouse, "For Europe, U.S. May Spell TV," *New York Times* (July 31, 1989), p. 26; and Monica Houston-Waesch, "Try to Imagine: A Subdued 'Family Feud,'" *Wall Street Journal* (March 26, 1993), p. R4.

44. On the emergence of the European editions of *Time* and *Newsweek*, and their contrast with the American version, see Read, *America's Mass Media Merchants*, pp. 15, 123–25, 129, 131–35, 155. For the appearance of the *Wall Street Journal* in Europe, see Claude-Jean Bertrand and Miguel Urabayen, "European Mass Media in the 1980s," in Everett Rogers and Francis Balle, eds., *The Media Revolution in America and in Western Europe* (Norwood, N.J.: Ablex, 1985), pp. 41 42.

45. Ken Auletta, "Raiding the Global Village," *New Yorker* 69 (August 2, 1993), pp. 25–26, 28–29; Mark Robichaux, "Cable-Ready," *Wall Street Journal* (March 26, 1993), p. R14.

46. On NBC's Super Channel, see Richard Stevenson, "Foreign Horizons Lure U.S. Broadcast Networks," *New York Times* (November 15, 1993), pp. C1, C5.

47. On MTV in Europe, see Robichaux, "Cable-Ready," p. R14; William Schmidt, "In Europe, America's Grip on Popular Culture Is Fading," *New York Times* (March 28, 1993), sec. 1, p. 3; and "MTV Europe Is Rocking to a Local Beat," *New York Times* (February 6, 1994), sec. 3, p. 6.

48. For the quotation from the Nickelodeon executive (italics his) and a general discussion of the strategies pursued by American children's television networks overseas, see Lawrie Mifflin, "Can the Flintstones Fly in Fiji?" *New York Times* (November 27, 1995), pp. C1, C4. See also Richard Stevenson, "Lights! Camera! Europe!" *New York Times* (February 6, 1994), sec. 3, p. 6.

49. "American Restaurants All the Rage in Paris," p. A20.

50. Jane Perlez, "Poles a Quick Study with Fast Food," *New York Times* (October 6, 1993), p. C3; Roger Cohen, "Pizza and Persistence Win in Hungary," *New York Times* (May 5, 1992), pp. C1, C7; Michael Specter, "Borscht and Blini to Go," *New York Times* (August 9, 1995), p. C1.

51. Steven Greenhouse, "McDonald's Tries Paris, Again," *New York Times* (June 12, 1988), sec. 3, p. 14; Eben Shapiro, "Overseas Sizzle for McDonald's," *New York Times* (April 17, 1992), p. C1; Allen Myerson, "Investments Abroad Reach Record Pace," *New York Times* (November 24, 1995), p. C4.

52. For the reaction to McDonald's in Rome, see Paul Hofmann, "Agrippa and the Hamburger," *New York Times* (January 24, 1988), sec. 10, p. 41. For the reaction in Cracow, including the quote from the Polish professor, see Jane Perlez, "A McDonald's? Not in Their Square; The City Clings to Its Medieval Past," *New York Times* (May 23, 1994), p. A4.

53. Greenhouse, "McDonald's Tries Paris, Again," pp. 1, 14; Craig Whitney, "At Dinner Table, More Than Beef Falls from Grace," *New York Times* (May 3, 1996), p. A4; Judith Valente, "The Land of Cuisine Sees Taste Besieged By 'Le Big Mac,'" *Wall Street Journal* (May 25, 1994), pp. A1, A5; Shapiro, "Overseas Sizzle for McDonald's," p. C1.

54. On the decline of the siesta in Italy, see Hofmann, "Agrippa and the Hamburger," p. 41.

55. Greenhouse, "McDonald's Tries Paris, Again," p. 15; "American Restaurants All the Rage in Paris," p. A20; Fareed Zakaria, "Paris Is Burning," *New Republic*, 214 (January 22, 1996), p. 30.

56. The two quotations can be found, respectively, in Franks, "Overseas, It's What's Inside That Sells," p. 21; and Shapiro, "Overseas Sizzle for McDonald's," p. C3.

57. Paul Hollander, *Anti-Americanism: Critiques at Home and Abroad, 1965–1990* (New York: Oxford University Press, 1992), p. 382; Shapiro, "Overseas Sizzle for McDonald's," p. C3; Perlez, "A McDonald's? Not in Their Square," p. A4.

58. Greenhouse, "McDonald's Tries Paris, Again," p. 15; Hofmann, "Agrippa and the Hamburger," p. 41; Franks, "Overseas, It's What's Inside That Sells," p. 21.

59. Steinar Bryn, "Norway and America: Looking at Each Other," *Scandinavian Review* 76 (Summer 1988), p. 158; Costigliola, *France and the United States*, p. 194; Greenhouse, "McDonald's Tries Paris, Again," p. 15.

60. For a description of the Russkoye Bistro and the quote from its manager, see Specter, "Borscht and Blini to Go," pp. C1, C3.

61. Dana Thomas, "Sushi Cordon Bleu?" *Newsweek* 127 (January 15, 1996), p. 41; Whitney, "France and Watercress Sandwiches," p. A4.

62. For a brief description of the purposes of the world's fairs, see Barber, *Jihad vs. McWorld*, p. 129.

63. Dorst, "Miniaturizing Monumentality," pp. 260–61, 265; Miles Orvell, "Understanding Disneyland: American Mass Culture and the European Gaze," in Kroes et al., eds., *Cultural Transmissions and Receptions*, pp. 249–51.

64. For an analysis of the popularity of Tokyo Disneyland and the quote from the Japanese professor, see James Sterngold, "Tokyo's Magic Kingdom Outshines Its Role Model," *New York Times* (March 7, 1994), p. C7. See also Mary Yoko Brannen, "'Bwana Mickey': Constructing Cultural Consumption at Tokyo Disneyland," in Amy Kaplan and Donald Pease, eds., *Cultures of United States Imperialism* (Durham, N.C.: Duke University Press, 1993), pp. 617–34.

65. Jolie Solomon, "Mickey's Trip to Trouble," *Newsweek* 123 (February 14, 1994), p. 36; Alan Riding, "Only the French Elite Scorn Mickey's Debut," *New York Times* (April 13, 1992), p. A6; Costigliola, *France and the United States*, pp. 196, 198.

66. Roger Cohen, "When You Wish Upon a Deficit," *New York Times* (July 18, 1993), sec. 2, p. 19; William Schmidt, "Visiting Disney's French Kingdom," *New York Times* (May 24, 1992), sec. 5, pp. 8–9; Paul Goldberger, "A Curious Mix of Versailles and Mickey Mouse," *New York Times* (June 14, 1992), sec. 2, p. 28; Solomon, "Mickey's Trip to Trouble," p. 36; Peter Gumbel and Richard Turner, "Mouse Trap," *Wall Street Journal* (March 10, 1994), p. A12.

67. For Ariane Mnouchkine's statement, see Todd Gitlin, "World Leaders: Mickey, et al.," *New York Times* (May 3, 1992), sec. 2, p. 1. For Jean-Marie

Rouart's quote, see Cohen, "When You Wish Upon a Deficit," p. 18. The other quotations can be found in Riding, "Only the French Elite Scorn Mickey's Debut," pp. A1, A6. See also Orvell, "Understanding Disneyland," p. 241.

68. Banham, "Mediated Environments," p. 82; Orvell, "Understanding Disneyland," pp. 243–44, 252.

69. Gitlin, "World Leaders: Mickey, et al.," p. 1; Orvell, "Understanding Disneyland," p. 250; Riding, "Only the French Elite Scorn Mickey's Debut," p. A6; Mark Frankel, Christopher Dickey, William Underhill, and Dorinda Elliott, "Welcome to Euro-World!" *Newsweek* 125 (June 12, 1995), p. 59; Costigliola, *France and the United States*, p. 198.

70. For Michael Eisner's observation, see David Jefferson, "Cheap Thrills," *Wall Street Journal* (March 26, 1993), R11. On the different vacation habits of Europeans and their behavior at Euro Disney, see Solomon, "Mickey's Trip to Trouble," p. 36; Gumbel and Turner, "Mouse Trap," p. A12; and Cohen, "When You Wish Upon a Deficit," p. 19.

71. Cohen, "When You Wish Upon a Deficit," pp. 18–19; Solomon, "Mickey's Trip to Trouble," p. 34.

72. Solomon, "Mickey's Trip to Trouble," pp. 36–37; Cohen, "When You Wish Upon a Deficit," p. 1; Gumbel and Turner, "Mouse Trap," p. A12.

73. Nathaniel Nash, "Euro Disney Turns Profitable, But Analysts Remain Cautious," *New York Times*, (July 26, 1995), p. C1.

74. Ibid.; "Euro Disney Reports Loss Narrowed During First Half," *New York Times* (April 22, 1995), p. 31; "Disney Tries Harder in France," *New York Times* (June 18, 1995), sec. 5, p. 3; "Euro Disney Has a '95 Profit, but Its Future Remains Cloudy," *New York Times* (November 16, 1995), p. C2.

75. The statement from the manager of the Belgian theme park can be found in Frankel et al., "Welcome to Euro-World!" p. 59.

76. Ibid.; Dorst, "Miniaturizing Monumentality," pp. 264–65; John Tagliabue, "A Comic-Strip Gaul Battles Disney," *New York Times* (August 15, 1995), p. A6.

77. Van Rossem, "Le Defi Europeen," p. 19; Plumb, "The Fatal Flaw," p. 220; Skard, *Trans-Atlantica*, p. 196; Rob Kroes, "The Nearness of America," in Kroes, ed., *Image and Impact*, p. 14; Michel Crozier, *The Trouble with America*, trans. Peter Heineggn (Berkeley: University of California Press, 1984), pp. 119, 145.

78. For examples of how Europeans reacted to America's economic decline and their own prosperity in the 1970s and 1980s, see Wilterdink, "The Netherlands Between the Greater Powers," p. 28; van Rossem, "Le Defi Europeen," p. 28; Crozier, *The Trouble with America*, pp. xix, 141; and Plumb, "The Fatal Flaw," p. 220. By the 1990s, after the fall of Communism, the signs of Western-style consumerism were increasingly noticeable in Eastern Europe, particularly in Poland, Hungary, and the Czech Republic. As more people entered the middle class, they started to buy (often on credit) larger cars and refrigerators, color television sets, washing machines, VCRs, and cosmetics. They also began to take annual vacations to ski resorts in Aus-

tria or to the beaches in France and Italy. See Jane Perlez, "A Bourgeoisie Blooms and Goes Shopping," *New York Times* (May 14, 1996), pp. C1, C8.

79. European commentators were impressed with the emergence of their own countries, as well as Japan, as economic rivals of the United States. See van Rossem, "Le Defi Europeen," pp. 18, 28; and Christian Stoffaës, "The Limits of the American Model," in Lacorne et al., eds., *The Rise and Fall of Anti-Americanism*, p. 161.

80. The ideas of the new generation of European intellectuals are effectively summarized by Paul Berman, "The Fog of Political Correctness," *Tikkun* 7 (January–February 1992), p. 53; and Costigliola, *France and the United States*, pp. 189, 193.

81. Berman, "The Fog of Political Correctness," pp. 56, 96. For the view of a French scholar on the uses of European theory in American universities, see Marc Chénetier, "American Literature in France: Pleasures in Perspective," in Huck Gutman, ed., *As Others Read Us: International Perspectives on American Literature* (Amherst: University of Massachusetts Press, 1991), p. 85.

82. John Vinocur, "Europe's Intellectuals and American Power," *New York Times Magazine*, (April 29, 1984), p. 76; Costigliola, *France and the United States*, pp. 191–92; Diana Pinto, "The French Intelligentsia Rediscovers America," in Lacorne et al., eds., *The Rise and Fall of Anti-Americanism*, p. 99; Liz McMillen, "A New Wave of French Thinkers," *Chronicle of Higher Education* 41 (November 23, 1994), p. A7.

83. For a more extended discussion of the positions of younger French intellectuals in the 1970s and 1980s, see Costigliola, *France and the United States*, p. 192; Stanley Hoffmann, "France: Keeping the Demons at Bay," *New York Review of Books* 41 (March 3, 1994), pp. 10, 12; McMillen, "A New Wave of French Thinkers," p. A7; Berman, "The Fog of Political Correctness," pp. 54–55; and Richard Kuisel, *Seducing the French: The Dilemma of Americanization* (Berkeley: University of California Press, 1993), p. 221. A similar embrace of democratic political and economic ideas was occurring among Italian intellectuals. See Norman Kogan, "Italian Intellect and Foreign Influences," in Richard Arndt and David Rubin, eds., *The Fulbright Difference, 1948–1992* (New Brunswick, N.J.: Transaction Books, 1993), p. 174.

84. Read, *America's Mass Media Merchants*, p. 89; David Thomson, "The British Invasion," *New Republic* 210 (April 25, 1994), p. 40; Bill Carter, "BBC Finds America Is a Cable-Ready Market," *New York Times* (September 18, 1989), p. 30. In 1996, the BBC and the Discovery Channel announced a joint venture to produce programs and launch new cable and satellite stations in the United States and throughout the world. Their plans included the creation of an American television channel that would broadcast the BBC's dramatic and performing arts programs, and a news channel that would carry reports from the BBC's World Service. For the details of this project, see Lawrie Mifflin, "Discovery and BBC Plan Joint Programming Venture," *New York Times* (September 28, 1996), p. 22.

85. For a more detailed analysis of the influence of American music on radio

programming, performance styles, and local cultural institutions in Britain and Western Europe, see Jeremy Tunstall, *The Media Are American* (New York: Columbia University Press, 1977), pp. 91–92, 132; Francis Williams, *The American Invasion* (New York: Crown, 1962), p. 37; Read, *America's Mass Media Merchants*, p. 148; Charlie Gillett, "Big Noise from Across the Water: The American Influence on British Popular Music," in Davis, ed., *For Better or Worse*, pp. 62–63, 72–73; van Elteren, "Sounds from America in Holland," pp. 178–79; Wagnleitner, *Coca-Colonization and the Cold War*, p. 287; and Watts, "The Call and Response of Popular Music," p. 128.

86. Gillett, "Big Noise from Across the Water," pp. 75, 79; Watts, "The Call and Response of Popular Music," pp. 131–34.

87. Gillett, "Big Noise from Across the Water," pp. 74, 76, 78–79, 83; van Elteren, "Sounds from America in Holland," p. 173.

88. Ken Auletta, "The Pirate," *New Yorker* 71 (November 13, 1995), p. 80; "Murdoch Assembles a World Network," *New York Times* (May 29, 1994), sec. 4, p. 3. Murdoch ultimately became a naturalized American citizen and moved his News Corporation to the United States, partly because of laws prohibiting foreign ownership of newspapers and television stations in the United States. These laws, however, did not prevent British Telecommunications from announcing plans in 1996 to acquire America's second largest telephone company, MCI Communications.

89. Richard Stevenson, "Hollywood Takes to the Global Stage," *New York Times* (April 16, 1989), sec. 3, p. 8; Barber, *Jihad vs. McWorld*, pp. 141–42; Roger Cohen "Aux Armes! France Rallies to Battle Sly and T. Rex," *New York Times* (January 2, 1994), sec. 2, p. 23; David Ansen, "If Pigs Could Fly," *Newsweek* 127 (January 22, 1996), p. 58. *Crédit Lyonnais* had to sell MGM by 1997, but among the potential buyers were media companies in Britain, France, and the Netherlands. Ultimately, MGM was bought by a consortium of American and foreign investors headed by Kirk Kerkorian who had owned the studio once before, in the 1980s. See Bernard Weinraub, "After Being Given Up for Dead, the MGM Movie Studio Has Come Roaring Back to Life," *New York Times* (April 1, 1996), p. C5; and David Lieberman, "Old Guard Tactic Is Old Brand Names," *USA Today* (July 18, 1996), p. 2B.

90. Barber, *Jihad vs. McWorld*, p. 141; Paul Farhi, "Stars and Hypes Forever," *Washington Post National Weekly Edition* (November 13–19, 1989), p. 9.

91. Barber, *Jihad vs. McWorld*, p. 126.

92. See Rollin, "On Comparative Popular Culture, American Style," p. 4; Allen Myerson, "American Money Makes the Whole World Sing," *New York Times* (December 17, 1995), sec. 4, p. 14; and Claudia Deutsch, "NBC Will Buy Rockefeller Center Space," *New York Times* (May 4, 1996), p. 30. In the face of mounting losses, Mitsubishi (the Japanese company that bought Rockefeller Center) gave up its investment in 1993. Apparently, the Japanese found American real estate as risky an investment as American movie studios.

93. On the paucity of European-wide newspapers and the tendency of

European audiences to prefer news about local or national, rather than continental, events, see Bertrand and Urabayen, "European Mass Media in the 1980s," pp. 38, 40; and Philip Schlesinger, "Europe's Contradictory Communicative Space," *Daedalus* 123 (Spring 1994), pp. 33–35, 42.

94. John Rockwell, "Europe's Television Borders Start to Fall," *New York Times* (June 15, 1992), p. C7; Schlesinger, "Europe's Contradictory Communicative Space," pp. 41–42; Richard Stevenson, "Mondo Murdoch: Networking, Globally and Relentlessly," *New York Times* (May 29, 1994), sec. 4, p. 3.

95. For more details on the interlocking holdings and partnerships of the European media barons, see Schlesinger, "Europe's Contradictory Communicative Space," pp. 33, 35; Stevenson, "Foreign Horizons Lure U.S. Broadcast Networks," p. C5; Nathaniel Nash, "A Dominant Force in European TV," *New York Times* (August 28, 1995), pp. C1, C8; Nathaniel Nash, "New Rules on Ownership for German TV," *New York Times* (October 30, 1995), p. C7; and "Who Owns German Television," *New York Times* (October 30, 1995), p. C7.

96. Nathaniel Nash, "Murdoch Joins Europe Venture for Digital TV," *New York Times* (March 7, 1996), pp. C1, C5. In 1996 as well, Bertelsmann and Luxembourg's CLT announced plans to merge their digital television operations. See Martin du Bois, "European TV Switches Over to New Show," *Wall Street Journal* (April 3, 1996), pp. A3, A12. In a world of shifting media alliances, Rupert Murdoch later defected from his agreement with Bertelsmann and Canal Plus in order to join up with Leo Kirch. But all the European media entrepreneurs were seeking partnerships with one another to improve their respective positions in the continental television market.

97. Marc Levinson, "Rock Around the World," *Newsweek* 125 (April 24, 1995), p. 65; Schmidt, "In Europe, America's Grip on Popular Culture Is Fading," p. 3. See also Alan Riding, "In a Time of Shared Hardship, The Young Embrace Europe," *New York Times* (August 12, 1993), pp. A1, A7.

98. Europeans themselves recognized how important the American elements in Europe's culture still were at the end of the century. See Schlesinger, "Europe's Contradictory Communicative Space," pp. 34, 46; and the observation of Christine Ockrent, a French television commentator, that "the only true pan-European culture is the American culture," quoted in Mark Nelson, "Peacetime Invasion," *Wall Street Journal* (April 24, 1995), p. R11.

Chapter Twelve
The Globalization of Western Culture

1. Glenn Collins, "Coke Drops 'Domestic' and Goes One World," *New York Times* (January 13, 1996), pp. A17, A19.

2. Allen Myerson, "Investments Abroad Reach Record Pace," *New York*

Times (November 24, 1995), p. C1; David Sanger, "Model Forecasts for U.S. Shift Focus Overseas," *New York Times* (January 2, 1996), p. C3.

3. Benjamin Barber, *Jihad vs. McWorld* (New York: Times Books, 1995), pp. 114, 140; Steve Lohr, "To Divide or Combine?" *New York Times* (September 25, 1995), p. C6.

4. "Big and Bigger," *New York Times* (August 31, 1995), p. C4; Doreen Carvajal, "Triumph of the Bottom Line," *New York Times* (April 1, 1996), p. C1; Barber, *Jihad vs. McWorld*, p. 126.

5. Barber, *Jihad vs. McWorld*, pp. 125–26, 141, 143; Neal Gabler, "Revenge of the Studio System." *New York Times* (August 22, 1995), p. A11. In 1996, Disney and McDonald's announced a cross-promotional agreement to last for at least ten years. McDonald's restaurants will help advertise Disney's movies (drawing attention to the new releases in the increasingly competitive summer and Christmas seasons), videocassettes, and theme parks, and will sell Disney merchandise related to these entertainments. In return, McDonald's will sponsor an attraction at Disney's Animal Kingdom, to open at Disney World in 1998, and benefit from the "family" aura that both enterprises seek to profit from. See Stuart Elliott, "Disney and McDonald's Become Double Feature," *New York Times* (May 24, 1996), pp. C1, C6.

6. Barber, *Jihad vs. McWorld*, p. 125.

7. Martin Esslin, "The Television Series as Folk Epic," in C. W. E. Bigsby, ed., *Superculture: American Popular Culture and Europe* (Bowling Green, Ohio: Bowling Green University Popular Press, 1975), p. 197; Benjamin Barber, "From Disney World to Disney's World," *New York Times* (August 1, 1995), p. A11. For other expressions and discussions of these sentiments, see Barber, *Jihad vs. McWorld*, p. 17; Paul Farhi, "I'd Like to Sell the World a Coke," *Washington Post National Weekly Edition* (June 22–28, 1992), p. 20; John Tomlinson, *Cultural Imperialism: A Critical Introduction* (Baltimore: Johns Hopkins University Press, 1991), p. 26; Richard Turner, "Hollyworld," and Meg Cox, "We Are the World," *Wall Street Journal* (March 26, 1993), pp. R6, R17; Thomas Guback, *The International Film Industry: Western Europe and America Since 1945* (Bloomington: Indiana University Press, 1969), pp. 176, 198–99; and Thomas Guback, "Film and Cultural Pluralism," *Journal of Aesthetic Education* 5 (April 1971), p. 49.

8. William Read, *America's Mass Media Merchants* (Baltimore: Johns Hopkins University Press, 1976), p. 178. See also Barber, *Jihad vs. McWorld*, p. 13, 23; Edward McCreary, *The Americanization of Europe: The Impact of Americans and American Business on the Uncommon Market* (Garden City, N.Y.: Doubleday, 1964), pp. 270, 272, 278; and Tomlinson, *Cultural Imperialism*, p. 176.

9. Read, *America's Mass Media Merchants*, p. 19; Barber, *Jihad vs. McWorld*, p. 114; "French Government Forces Radio to Play Homegrown Music," *National Public Radio Morning Edition* (January 24, 1996), pp. 22–23; Richard Stevenson, "Mondo Murdoch: Networking, Globally and Relentlessly," *New York Times* (May 29, 1994), sec. 4, p. 1; Richard Stevenson, "Lights! Camera! Europe!" *New York Times* (February 6, 1994), sec. 3, p. 6.

10. See Barber, *Jihad vs. McWorld*, p. 4; Thomas Friedman, "Revolt of the Wannabes," *New York Times* (February 7, 1996), p. A15; and John Judis, "White Squall," *New Republic* 214 (March 11, 1996), p. 30. Downsizing was not a uniquely American phenomenon. By the mid-1990s, companies throughout Europe—trying to stay competitive in the global economy—were also firing white-collar employees despite the promise, in effect since World War II, that European workers would have jobs for life. See John Tagliabue, "In Europe, a Wave of Layoffs Stuns White-Collar Workers," *New York Times* (June 20, 1996), pp. A1, C17.

11. On the tendency of non-native speakers to adapt English to their own needs, see Barry Newman, "Global Chatter," *Wall Street Journal* (March 22, 1995), pp. A1, A15; and Peter Lev, *The Euro-American Cinema* (Austin: University of Texas Press, 1993), p. 75. On the efforts to make the Internet multilingual, see Andrew Pollack, "A Cyberspace Front in a Multicultural War," *New York Times* (August 7, 1995), pp. C1, C4; and Michael Specter, "World, Wide, Web: 3 English Words," *New York Times* (April 14, 1996), sec. 4, pp. 1, 5.

12. Barber, *Jihad vs. McWorld*, pp. 172, 174.

13. The quotation from the student can be found in Alan Riding, "In a Time of Shared Hardship, The Young Embrace Europe," *New York Times* (August 12, 1993), p. A7. For a more detailed elaboration of the idea of dual loyalties, see Read, *America's Mass Media Merchants*, pp. 186–88; and Mel van Elteren, "Reflections on Cultural Identity and 'Americanization' in Relation to the Cultural Dimensions of the Recent GATT Agreement," unpublished paper, Tilburg, the Netherlands, 1994, pp. 5–6.

Bibliography

What follows is a review of some of the primary and secondary sources that were enormously useful to me in writing this book. Most of these works deal with specific countries, topics, or time periods. But they can all help the reader gain a greater understanding of America's cultural relationship with Europe in the twentieth century.

Although no single work covers the entire subject, several collections of essays provide a general introduction to the differing ways that American culture affected Europeans. The best of these articles, by writers on both sides of the Atlantic, can be found in Lewis Galantière, ed., *America and the Mind of Europe* (London: Hamilton, 1951); Bertrand Russell et al., *The Impact of America on European Culture* (Boston: Beacon Press, 1951); A. N. J. den Hollander, ed., *Diverging Parallels: A Comparison of American and European Thought and Action*, (Leiden: Brill, 1971); A. N. J. den Hollander, ed., *Contagious Conflict: The Impact of American Dissent on European Life* (Leiden, Netherlands: Brill, 1973), which is particularly good on the 1960s; Richard Rose, ed., *Lessons from America: An Exploration* (London: Macmillan, 1974); and Allen Davis, ed., *For Better or Worse: The American Influence in the World* (Westport, Conn.: Greenwood Press, 1981).

There have been some extremely valuable studies of the American impact on particular countries. In the 1950s, Richard Hoggart wrote what became a classic (and highly critical) analysis of America's contribution to the transformation of British culture and social life: *The Uses of Literacy: Aspects of Working Class Life with Special Reference to Publications and Entertainments* (London: Chatto & Windus, 1957). Later, but equally interesting, discussions of the British experience include Daniel Snowman's *Britain and America: An Interpretation of Their Culture, 1945–1975* (New York: New York University Press, 1977); Duncan Webster's *Looka Yonder! The Imaginary America of Pop-*

ulist Culture (London: Routledge, 1988); and Dick Hebdige's essay, "Towards a Cartography of Taste, 1935–1962," in Hebdige, *Hiding in the Light: On Images and Things* (London: Routledge, 1988), pp. 45–76.

Two of the most thoughtful books on the West German response to American policies are by James Tent: *Mission on the Rhine: "Reeducation" and Denazification in American-Occupied Germany* (Chicago: University of Chicago Press, 1982), which focuses on events in the late 1940s; and *The Free University of Berlin: A Political History* (Bloomington: Indiana University Press, 1988), which traces the evolution of one of Europe's most interesting educational experiments, one that was heavily but always uneasily dependent on American support. These books should be supplemented by Henry Kellerman's *Cultural Relations as an Instrument of U.S. Foreign Policy* (Washington, D.C.: U.S. Government Printing Office, 1978) which, despite its broad title, concentrates exclusively on West Germany in the 1940s and 1950s; and Ralph Willett's *The Americanization of Germany, 1945–1949* (London: Routledge, 1989), which, despite its more limited title, raises issues that continued to affect German-American relations beyond the immediate postwar years. Much of what the U.S. government tried to do in Germany, it also attempted in Austria, often with similar results. Reinhold Wagnleitner's *Coca-Colonization and the Cold War: The Cultural Mission of the United States in Austria After the Second World War*, trans. Diana Wolf (Chapel Hill: University of North Carolina Press, 1994), offers an important assessment of America's cultural diplomacy in both Austria and West Germany during the height of the conflict with the Soviet Union.

Rob Kroes has edited two books of insightful essays on the Dutch reaction to American culture: *Image and Impact: American Influences in the Netherlands Since 1945* (Amsterdam: Amerika Instituut, 1981); and *Within the U.S. Orbit: Small National Cultures vis-à-vis the United States* (Amsterdam: VU University Press, 1991). Donald Heiney's *America in Modern Italian Literature* (New Brunswick, N.J.: Rutgers University Press, 1964) deals primarily with the changing images of America in the minds of Italy's prewar and postwar intellectuals.

It is not surprising that the most extensive work has been done on the conflicts between America and France. The Franco-American competition for cultural preeminence is explored in Raymond Aron and August Heckscher, *Diversity of Worlds: France and the United States Look at Their Common Problems* (New York: Reynal, 1957); David Strauss, *Menace in the West: The Rise of French Anti-Americanism in Modern Times* (Westport, Conn.: Greenwood Press, 1978); Denis Lacorne, Jacques Rupnik, and Marie-France Toinet, eds., *The Rise and Fall of Anti-Americanism: A Century of French Perception*, trans. Gerry Turner (New York: St. Martin's Press, 1990, c. Paris 1986); Frank Costigliola, *France and the United States: The Cold Alliance Since World War II* (New York: Twayne, 1992); Jean-Philippe Mathy, *Extrême Occident: French Intellectuals and America* (Chicago: University of Chicago Press, 1993); and Richard Kuisel, *Seducing the French: The Dilemma of Americanization* (Berkeley: University of California Press, 1993), which is the most illuminating study of America's actual impact on French society.

A number of articles deal with the contest between France and the United States as well: Arnold Rose, "Anti-Americanism in France," *Antioch Review* 12 (December 1952), pp. 468–84; Joseph Baker, "How the French See America," *Yale Review* 47 (Winter 1958), pp. 239–53; Pierre Nora, "America and the French Intellectuals," *Daedalus* 107 (Winter 1978), pp. 325–37; Laurence Wylie and Sarella Henriquez, "French Images of American Life," *Tocqueville Review* 4 (1982), pp. 176–274; and Jacques Rupnik, "Anti-Americanism and the Modern: The Image of the United States in French Public Opinion," in John Gaffney, ed., *France and Modernization* (Aldershot, England: Avebury, 1988), pp. 189–205. Although Tony Judt's *Past Imperfect: French Intellectuals, 1944–1956* (Berkeley: University of California Press, 1992) is principally concerned with cultural and political developments within France itself, it too discusses the attitudes of French writers toward the United States. The titles of most of these works reveal the intensity of the French preoccupation and discomfort with America's postwar power.

The most informative books on America's emerging cultural influence in the early twentieth century are Emily Rosenberg's *Spreading the American Dream: American Economic and Cultural Expansion, 1890–1945* (New York: Hill & Wang, 1982); and Frank Costigliola's *Awkward Dominion: American Political, Economic, and Cultural Relations with Europe, 1919–1933* (Ithaca, N.Y. Cornell University Press, 1987, c. 1984). On the role of American foundations between the world wars, see Merle Curti, *American Philanthropy Abroad: A History* (New Brunswick, N.J.: Rutgers University Press, 1963). The flight of Europe's intellectuals to the United States in the 1930s, and their effects on American cultural and academic life, are analyzed in Donald Fleming and Bernard Bailyn, eds., *The Intellectual Migration: Europe and America, 1930–1960* (Cambridge, Mass.: Charles Warren Center for Studies in American History, 1968), a volume that contains incisive essays by the refugees themselves. In addition, one should consult the essays in Jarrell Jackman and Carla Borden, eds., *The Muses Flee Hitler: Cultural Transfer and Adaptation, 1930–1945* (Washington, D.C.: Smithsonian Institution Press, 1983). Peter Rutkoff and William Scott, *New School: A History of the New School for Social Research* (New York: Free Press, 1986), and Claus-Dieter Krohn, *Intellectuals in Exile: Refugee Scholars and the New School for Social Research*, trans. Rita and Robert Kimber (Amherst: University of Massachusetts Press, 1993, c. 1987) both discuss the institution that, more than any other, sheltered the émigrés after they arrived in the United States.

There are numerous studies of Washington's role in exporting American culture during and after World War II. Allan Winkler's *The Politics of Propaganda: The Office of War Information, 1942–1945* (New Haven, Conn.: Yale University Press, 1978), and Holly Shulman's *The Voice of America: Propaganda and Democracy, 1941–1945* (Madison: University of Wisconsin Press, 1990) both evaluate the government's propaganda efforts following the attack on Pearl Harbor. For more general treatments of America's cultural diplomacy, especially in the early years of the Cold War, see Charles Thompson and Walter Laves, *Cultural Relations and U.S. Foreign Policy* (Bloomington: Indiana University Press, 1963), which is a detailed and extremely useful narrative; and Frank Ninkovich, *The Diplomacy of Ideas: U.S. Foreign Policy and Cultural Relations, 1938–1950* (New York: Cambridge University Press, 1981), a more critical interpretation of Washington's intentions. The speeches and position papers of government officials during the "campaign of truth" are excerpted in Robert Summers, ed., *America's Weapons of Psychological Warfare* (New York: Wilson, 1951). Two books by policymakers who served in the State Department in the 1950s and early 1960s are particularly helpful: Edward Barrett, *Truth Is Our Weapon* (New York: Funk & Wagnalls, 1953); and Philip Coombs, *The Fourth Dimension of Foreign Policy: Educational and Cultural Affairs* (New York: Harper & Row, 1964).

The government always tried to enlist private organizations in its cultural programs. For examples of this frequently tense collaboration, see Gary Kraske, *Missionaries of the Book: The American Library Association and the Origins of United States Cultural Diplomacy* (Westport, Conn.: Greenwood Press, 1985); and Kathleen McCarthy, "From Cold War to Cultural Development: The International Cultural Activities of the Ford Foundation, 1950–1980," *Daedalus* 116 (Winter 1987), pp. 93–117.

J. M. Mitchell compares Washington's policies, sometimes unfavorably, with the strategies of other Western governments in *International Cultural Relations* (London: Allen & Unwin, 1986). But Charles Frankel offered the most persuasive critique of America's cultural diplomacy, one that is still relevant today, in *The Neglected Aspect of Foreign Affairs: American Educational and Cultural Policy Abroad* (Washington, D.C.: Brookings Institution, 1966); and *High on Foggy Bottom: An Outsider's Inside View of the Government* (New York: Harper & Row, 1969).

Several authors have concentrated on specific government programs and agencies. For histories of USIA, see John Henderson, *The United States Information Agency* (New York: Praeger, 1969); Lois Roth, "Public Diplomacy and the Past: The Search for an American Style of Propaganda, 1952–1977," *Fletcher Forum* 8 (Summer 1984), pp. 353–96, which includes the official language of much of the enabling legislation; and Allen Hansen, *USIA: Public Diplomacy in the Computer Age* (New York: Praeger, 1984). The first two decades of USIA's existence, from the early 1950s to the late 1960s, were the most interesting years for many of those who worked in the agency. The turbulence of this era is described by Thomas Sorensen in his memoir, *The Word War: The Story of American Propaganda* (New York: Harper & Row, 1968). The last two chapters of A. M. Sperber's *Murrow: His Life and Times* (New York: Bantam Books, 1987, c. 1986) portray Murrow's unhappy tenure at USIA in the early 1960s. Hans Tuch served with the agency from the late 1950s through the 1980s, and recorded his often-candid observations in *Communicating with the World: U.S. Public Diplomacy Overseas* (New York: St. Martin's Press, 1990).

The Marshall Plan, predictably, has attracted widespread interest among scholars in Europe and the United Sates. America's assumptions and objectives are cogently examined in Michael Hogan, *The Marshall Plan: America, Britain, and the Reconstruction of Western Europe, 1947–1952* (New York: Cambridge University Press, 1989, c. 1987). David Ellwood presents the European response to the plan in his essay "From 'Re-Education' to the Selling of the Marshall Plan in Italy," in Nicholas Pronay and Keith Wilson, eds., *The Political Re-Education of Germany and Her Allies After World War II* (Totowa, N.J.: Barnes & Noble Books, 1985), pp. 219–39; and in his book *Rebuilding Europe: Western Europe, America and Postwar Reconstruction* (London: Longman, 1992).

Two studies of the Fulbright program are filled with information: Walter Johnson and Francis Colligan, *The Fulbright Program: A History* (Chicago: University of Chicago Press, 1965); and Leonard Sussman, *The Culture of Freedom: The Small World of Fulbright Scholars* (Savage, Md.: Rowman & Littlefield, 1992). Individual Fulbright grantees, American as well as European, commented on what they learned about themselves and the "foreign" culture in which they temporarily lived in Arthur Dudden and Russell Dynes, eds., *The Fulbright Experience, 1946–1986: Encounters and Transformations* (New Brunswick, N.J.: Transaction Books, 1987); and Richard Arndt and David Rubin, eds., *The Fulbright Difference, 1948–1992* (New Brunswick, N.J.: Transaction Books, 1993).

The most controversial activity undertaken by the American government was the CIA's involvement with the Congress for Cultural Freedom. After the exposure of the CIA's financial support for the congress in the late 1960s, Christopher Lasch attacked the entire operation in a famous essay, "The Cultural Cold War: A Short History of the Congress for Cultural Freedom," in Lasch, *The Agony of the American Left* (New York: Knopf, 1969), pp. 63–114. But a more sympathetic account of the congress's adventures can be found in Peter Coleman, *The Liberal Conspiracy: The Congress for Cultural Freedom and the Struggle for the Mind of Postwar Europe* (New York: Free Press, 1989).

Among the forms of American culture that the State Department and the Congress for Cultural Freedom were most eager to publicize was abstract expressionism. Two works argue that America's postwar artists were conscripted, often without their knowledge or assent, into the crusade against Communism: Serge Guilbaut, *How New York Stole the Idea of Modern Art: Abstract Expressionism, Freedom, and the Cold War*, trans. Arthur Goldhammer (Chicago: University of Chicago Press, 1984, c. 1983); and Eva Cockcroft, "Abstract Expressionism, Weapon of the Cold War," in Francis Frascina, ed., *Pollock and After: The Critical Debate* (New York: Harper & Row, 1985), pp. 125–33. For a less polemical discussion of the role of American artists, see Frances Pohl, *Ben Shahn: New Deal Artist in a Cold War Cli-*

mate, 1947–1954 (Austin: University of Texas Press, 1989). As it happened, conservatives in Congress were not necessarily enamored of modern art, either on esthetic or political grounds. Jane Matthews depicts the McCarthyite opposition to modernism in "Art and Politics in Cold War America," *American Historical Review* 81 (October 1976), pp. 762–87.

Despite Washington's underwriting of exchange programs with Europe after World War II, much of the contact between Americans and Europeans took place without government sponsorship. This was especially the case with tourism, a subject comprehensively treated in Foster Rhea Dulles, *Americans Abroad: Two Centuries of European Travel* (Ann Arbor: University of Michigan Press, 1964). Daniel Boorstin's chapter, "From Traveler to Tourist: The Lost Art of Travel," in *The Image: A Guide to Pseudo-Events in America* (New York: Atheneum, 1972, c. 1962), pp. 77–117, is still a seminal discussion of the ways in which mass tourism has made it nearly impossible for people to get to know a foreign country. The experience of Americans participating in educational exchanges during the 1950s is recounted in John Garraty and Walter Adams, *From Main Street to the Left Bank: Students and Scholars Abroad* (East Lansing: Michigan State University Press, 1959).

The judgments of American intellectuals traveling through postwar Europe were often ambivalent. For examples, see Edmund Wilson's *Europe without Baedeker: Sketches Among the Ruins of Italy, Greece, and England* (Garden City, N.Y.: Doubleday, 1947), as well as his essays on Europe in *A Piece of My Mind: Reflections at Sixty* (New York: Farrar, Straus & Cudahy, 1956), and *The Fifties: From Notebooks and Diaries of the Period*, ed. Leon Edel (New York: Farrar, Straus & Giroux, 1986); F. O. Matthiessen's *From the Heart of Europe* (New York: Oxford University Press, 1948); Perry Miller's two articles written after he returned from Holland in 1950: "What Drove Me Crazy in Europe," and "Europe's Faith in American Fiction," in Miller, *The Responsibility of Mind in a Civilization of Machines* (Amherst: University of Massachusetts Press, 1979), pp. 98–109, 122–33; and Herbert Kubly's *American In Italy* (New York: Simon & Schuster, 1955). Other writers included their impressions of Europe in their autobiographies or collections of essays. See the relevant sections or chapters in Leslie Fiedler, *An End to Innocence: Essays on Culture and Politics* (Boston: Beacon Press, 1955); James Baldwin, *Notes of a Native Son* (Boston: Beacon Press, 1957, c. 1955), and *Nobody Knows My Name* (New York: Dell, 1963, c. 1961); Norman Podhoretz, *Making It* (New York: Bantam Books, 1969, c. 1967); Alfred Kazin, *New York Jew* (New York: Knopf, 1978); William Phillips, *A Partisan View: Five Decades of the Literary Life* (New York: Stein & Day, 1983); and Saul Bellow, *It All Adds Up: From the Dim Past to the Uncertain Future* (New York: Viking, 1994). No American intellectual wrote with greater sensitivity about Europe than did Mary McCarthy in her two "travel" books, *Venice Observed* (New York: Harcourt Brace Jovanovich, 1963, c. 1956), and *The Stones of Florence* (New York: Harcourt Brace Jovanovich, 1963, c. 1959).

European visitors to the United States were just as ambivalent as their

American counterparts in Europe. Several secondary accounts discuss these mixed feelings: André Visson, *As Others See Us* (Garden City, N.Y.: Doubleday, 1948); Edward Chester, *Europe Views America: A Critical Evaluation* (Washington, D.C.: Public Affairs Press, 1962); Marcus Cunliffe, "European Images of America," in Arthur Schlesinger and Morton White, eds., *Paths of American Thought* (Boston: Houghton Mifflin, 1963), pp. 492–514; and J. Martin Evans, *America: The View from Europe* (Stanford, Calif.: Stanford University Press, 1976). Three books present essays or observations by a sampling of European writers, scholars, and students: James Burnham, ed., *What Europe Thinks of America* (New York: John Day, 1953); S. Gorley Putt, ed., *Cousins and Strangers: Comments on America by Commonwealth Fund Fellows from Britain, 1946–1952* (Cambridge, Mass.: Harvard University Press, 1956); and Franz Joseph, ed., *As Others See Us: The United States Through Foreign Eyes* (Princeton, N.J.: Princeton University Press, 1959). Europe's chronic hostility to what America represented is examined in Rob Kroes and Maarten van Rossem, eds., *Anti-Americanism in Europe* (Amsterdam: Free University Press, 1986); and Paul Hollander, *Anti-Americanism: Critiques at Home and Abroad, 1965–1990* (New York: Oxford University Press, 1992), which argues that much of the animosity toward the United States originated in America, among radical writers and activists, and was then copied overseas.

British intellectuals and scholars tended to be more knowledgeable and more dispassionate about the United States than did their colleagues on the Continent. The shrewdest interpretations of America's politics and social life are D. W. Brogan's *The American Character* (New York: Knopf, 1956, c. 1944); Harold Laski's *The American Democracy: A Commentary and an Interpretation* (New York: Viking, 1948); Geoffrey Gorer's *The American People: A Study in National Character* (New York: Norton, 1948); and J. H. Plumb's *The American Experience*, vol. 2 of *The Collected Essays* (Athens: University of Georgia Press, 1989). The Italian journalist Luigi Barzini wrote an equally perceptive book, *Americans Are Alone in the World* (New York: Random House, 1953).

French visitors were usually more opinionated. Perhaps the two books that caused the most irritation among American readers were Simone de Beauvoir's *America Day by Day*, trans. Patrick Dudley (London: G. Duckworth, 1952, c. Paris 1948); and Jean Baudrillard's *America*, trans. Chris Turner (New York: Verso, 1988, c. Paris 1986). For examples of other French views, not all of them antagonistic, see André Maurois, *From My Journal*, trans. Joan Charles (New York: Harper, 1948); Jean-Paul Sartre's three essays from the mid-1940s: "Individualism and Conformism in the United States," "American Cities," and "New York, the Colonial City," in Sartre, *Literary and Philosophical Essays*, trans. Annette Michelson (London: Rider, 1955), pp. 97–124; Amaury de Riencourt, *The Coming Caesars* (New York: Coward-McCann, 1957); Jacques Maritain, *Reflections on America* (New York: Scribner's, 1958); Jean-François Revel, *Without Marx or Jesus: The New American*

Revolution Has Begun, trans. J. F. Bernard (Garden City, N.Y.: Doubleday, 1971, c. Paris 1970); and Michel Crozier, *The Trouble with America*, trans. Peter Heineggn (Berkeley: University of California Press, 1984).

Some writers were unsure what to make of postwar America. In October 1947, the British literary magazine *Horizon* devoted an entire issue (vol. 16) to the United States. The two most interesting essays were Cyril Connolly's "Introduction to Art on the American Horizon," pp. 1–11; and Chistopher Isherwood's "Los Angeles," pp. 142–147. Additional instances of this uncertainty can be detected in Wyndham Lewis, *America and Cosmic Man* (London: Nicholson & Watson, 1948); Rom Landau, *Among the Americans* (London: Hale, 1953); and Herbert von Borch, *The Unfinished Society*, trans. Mary Ilford (New York: Hawthorn Books, 1962, c. Germany 1960).

One way that the United States could be better understood was through the American Studies movement in Europe, a movement Washington encouraged. Many European Americanists have written about their "discovery" of the field, and its impact on their attitudes and careers. Sigmund Skard's two-volume *American Studies in Europe: Their History and Present Organization* (Philadelphia: University of Pennsylvania Press, 1958) remains a majestic survey of American Studies programs through the 1950s; its exploration of the origins of the movement in the nineteenth and early twentieth centuries is especially valuable. Skard described his own conversion to American Studies, as well as his shifting feelings about the United States, in *Trans-Atlantica: Memoirs of a Norwegian Americanist* (Oslo: Universitetsforlaget, 1978). The essays in the first three volumes of Lewis Hanke, ed., *Guide to the Study of United States History Outside the U.S., 1945–1980* (White Plains, N.Y.: Kraus International Publications, 1985) are essential because they cover developments in every European country since Skard conducted his initial investigation. For additional details and personal reminiscences, see Robert Walker, ed., *American Studies Abroad* (Westport, Conn.: Greenwood Press, 1975), as well as the special issues of *Reviews in American History* 14 (December 1986), Maurizio Vaudagna, ed., "Forum: American Studies in Europe," *Storia Nordamericana* 7 (1990), and the *Journal of American History* 79 (September 1992).

Numerous Americanists on both sides of the ocean have written articles about their involvement in the movement, along with evaluations of its strengths and weaknesses in various European countries. For the best of these accounts, see Harry Allen, "American Studies and the Study of America: The Future of American Studies in Europe," *American Studies International* 17 (Spring 1979), pp. 10–26; vol. 14 of the *Journal of American Studies* (April 1980), which contains Herbert Nicholas's "The Education of an Americanist," pp. 9–26, Roger Asselineau's "A Complex Fate," pp. 67–81, Marcus Cunliffe's "Backward Glances," pp. 83–102, and Malcolm Bradbury's "How I Invented America," pp. 115–35; Robert Spiller, "American Studies Abroad: Culture and Foreign Policy," in Spiller, *Late Harvest: Essays and Addresses in American Literature and Culture* (Westport, Conn.: Greenwood Press, 1981), pp. 228–49;

David Reynolds, "Whitehall, Washington and the Promotion of American Studies in Britain During World War Two," *Journal of American Studies* 16 (August 1982), pp. 165–88; Rob Kroes, "Americanistics in the Netherlands," *American Studies International* 25 (October 1987), pp. 56–65; vol. 26 of *American Studies International* (April 1988), which contains Carl Bode's "Narrowing the Ocean: A Memoir," pp. 36–41, and Alfred Kazin's "Carrying the Word Abroad," pp. 62–66; and Sylvia Hilton, "American Studies in Spain: Recent Trends," *American Studies International* 32 (April 1994), pp. 41–69. Two of the most revealing essays on the early Salzburg Seminar are by Henry Nash Smith, "The Salzburg Seminar," *American Quarterly* 1 (Spring 1949), pp. 30–37; and Timothy Ryback, "Encounters at the Schloss," *Harvard Magazine* 90 (November–December 1987), pp. 67–72.

America's literature was the principal means by which many Europeans learned about the United States. Malcolm Bradbury has provided an overview of how novelists on both continents constructed an imaginary America as well as an imaginary Europe in *Dangerous Pilgrimages: Transatlantic Mythologies and the Novel* (London: Secker & Warburg, 1995). On the Italian interest in American fiction during the 1930s and 1940s, see Elio Vittorini, "American Influences on Contemporary Italian Literature," *American Quarterly* 1 (Spring 1949), pp. 3–8; and vol. 68 of the *Sewanee Review* (Summer 1960), particularly the essays by Agostino Lombardo, "Introduction to Italian Criticism of American Literature," pp. 353–74, and by Alberto Moravia, "Two American Writers," pp. 473–81. The postwar French attraction to American literature is best represented by Jean-Paul Sartre's "American Novelists in French Eyes," *Atlantic Monthly* 178 (August 1946), pp. 114–18; Henri Peyre's "American Literature Through French Eyes," *Virginia Quarterly Review* 23 (Summer 1947), pp. 421–38; and Claude-Edmonde Magny's *The Age of the American Novel: The Film Aesthetic of Fiction Between the Two Wars*, trans. Eleanor Hochman (New York: Ungar, 1972, c. Paris 1948). For the influence of American fiction and poetry later in the century and in the rest of Europe, see Denis Donoghue, *Reading America: Essays on American Literature* (New York: Knopf, 1987); and Huck Gutman, ed., *As Others Read Us: International Perspectives on American Literature* (Amherst: University of Massachusetts Press, 1991).

Clearly, the issue that most concerned Europeans, whether or not they traveled to or studied the United States, was the "Americanization" of their own societies. Two significant books published in the 1960s address the economic dimensions of this problem: Francis Williams, *The American Invasion* (New York: Crown, 1962); and Jean-Jacques Servan-Schreiber, *The American Challenge*, trans. Ronald Steel (New York: Atheneum, 1968, c. Paris 1967). So too does a work by an American writer, Edward McCreary, in *The Americanization of Europe: The Impact of Americans and American Business on the Uncommon Market* (Garden City, N.Y.: Doubleday, 1964).

Yet "Americanization" was seen as a cultural, even more than an economic, issue. Consequently, there are a number of important works that deal with the impact of America's mass culture on Europe and on the world: C. W. E. Bigsby, ed., *Superculture: American Popular Culture and Europe* (Bowling Green, Ohio: Bowling Green University Popular Press, 1975); William Read, *America's Mass Media Merchants* (Baltimore: Johns Hopkins University Press, 1976); Jeremy Tunstall, *The Media Are American* (New York: Columbia University Press, 1977); Everett Rogers and Francis Balle, eds., *The Media Revolution in America and in Western Europe* (Norwood, N.J.: Ablex, 1985); Rob Kroes, Robert Rydell, and Doeko F. J. Bosscher, eds., *Cultural Transmissions and Receptions: American Mass Culture in Europe* (Amsterdam: VU University Press, 1993); and Rob Kroes, *If You've See One, You've Seen the Mall: Europeans and American Mass Culture* (Urbana: University of Illinois Press, 1996). On should also read the contributions by American and European media critics to a symposium conducted by the American Enterprise Institute, published as "The Controversy About Popular Culture," *American Enterprise* 3 (May–June 1992), pp. 72–96, as well as Philip Schlesinger's essay, "Europe's Contradictory Communicative Space," *Daedalus* 123 (Spring 1994), pp. 25–52.

No form of American mass culture has received more attention than the movies. Several works concentrate on the structural elements that enabled Hollywood to control film markets overseas, and the economic and political implications of this domination. See especially Thomas Guback, *The International Film Industry: Western Europe and America Since 1945* (Bloomington: Indiana University Press, 1969), which is a detailed investigation of Hollywood's postwar policies; Victoria de Grazia, "Mass Culture and Sovereignty: The American Challenge to European Cinemas, 1920–1960," *Journal of Modern History* 61 (March 1989), pp. 53–87; and David Ellwood and Rob Kroes, eds., *Hollywood in Europe: Experiences of a Cultural Hegemony* (Amsterdam: VU University Press, 1994). Herbert Gans, "Hollywood Films on British Screens: An Analysis of the Functions of American Popular Culture Abroad," *Social Problems* 9 (Spring 1962), pp. 324–28, and Paul Swann, *The Hollywood Feature Film in Postwar Britain* (New York: St. Martin's Press, 1987), both analyze the influence of American movies on British life during the 1940s and 1950s. To understand why a young generation of French film critics in the 1950s were so fascinated with American movies, and why they eventually became disillusioned with their own analyses, see the essays in André Bazin, *What Is Cinema?*, vols. 1 and 2, trans. Hugh Gray (Berkeley: University of California Press, 1967 and 1971); Jim Hillier, ed., *Cahiers du Cinéma: The 1950s—Neo-Realism, Hollywood, New Wave* (Cambridge, Mass.: Harvard University Press, 1985); Jim Hillier, ed., *Cahiers du Cinéma: The 1960s—New Wave, New Cinema, Re-Evaluating Hollywood* (Cambridge, Mass.: Harvard University Press, 1992); and Andrew Sarris's "Toward a Theory of Film History," the introductory essay to his *The American Cinema: Directors and Directions, 1929–1968* (New York: E. P. Dutton, 1968), pp. 19–37. Peter Lev's *The Euro-American Cinema* (Austin: University of Texas Press, 1993) shows how the esthetics of American and European filmmaking converged from the 1960s on.

The notion that America's mass culture has become an unstoppable global force, an idea that bothers Europeans and many Americans, appears in Roger Rollin, ed., *The Americanization of the Global Village: Essays in Comparative Popular Culture* (Bowling Green, Ohio: Bowling Green State University Popular Press, 1989). The argument is presented more directly and provocatively in Benjamin Barber, *Jihad vs. McWorld* (New York: Times Books, 1995), which also evaluates the nationalist reactions to the global culture and economy.

Other writers, however, have emphasized the capacity of national and local cultures to resist America's global influence. See, for example, Claude-Jean Bertrand's "American Cultural Imperialism—A Myth?" *American Studies International* 25 (April 1987), pp. 46–60; and especially John Tomlinson's *Cultural Imperialism: A Critical Introduction* (Baltimore: Johns Hopkins University Press, 1991). Two books, both studying the effects of one of America's most popular television shows on audiences overseas, also demonstrate the ability of foreigners to reshape American mass culture to suit their own needs: Ien Ang, *Watching Dallas: Soap Opera and the Melodramatic Imagination*, trans. Della Couling (London: Methuen, 1985); and Tamar Liebes and Elihu Katz, *The Export of Meaning: Cross-Cultural Readings of Dallas* (New York: Oxford University Press, 1990).

Finally, the *Wall Street Journal* and the business and entertainment sections of the *New York Times* are indispensable for anyone wishing to know about the contemporary export and reception of American culture throughout the world.

Index